SchNEWS

PEACE de RESISTANCE
ANNUAL 2003
Issues 351-401

C000279528

PEACE de RESISTANCE
SchNEWS Annual 2003

published by SchNEWS, June 2003

ISBN: 09529748 7 8

Printed by Calverts Press, London

British Library Cataloguing in Publication Data: a catalogue record for this book is available from the British Library.

Cover by Joe Plant www.joeplant.com

SchNEWS is a free weekly news sheet published by volunteers in Brighton. It is obtainable by sending first class stamps (ten for nine issues) or donations (in UK pounds, payable to "Justice?") to SchNEWS, c/o On The Fiddle, P.O. Box 2600, Brighton, East Sussex, BN2 0EF, UK
Phone +44 (0)1273 685 913

SchNEWS is also online www.schnews.org.uk. The website is updated each week with the latest issue of SchNEWS as well as new Party & Protest listings: our guide to parties, festivals, demos and actions happening in Britain and elsewhere. (If you would like to put an event in this then contact us...)

You can also receive SchNEWS each week for free in either PDF or text file version by email - see 'Subscribe' on the website.

Also available on the banana yellow website:
* back issues of SchNEWS from issue 1 (Nov 94) onwards.
* DIY guide - direct action how-to guides
* Yellow Pages - regularly updated contacts list featuring around 800 direct action, community, alternative media, etc etc groups, campaigns & centres in Britain and abroad (a shortened version updated to June 2003 is in the back of this book).
* The articles featured in our previous book 'SchNEWS Of The World'.
* Prisoner support page
* search facility

Your turn now: As Indymedia say - 'don't hate the media, become the media' - keep SchNEWS (and all other alternative media) up to date with the news of actions and events - big & small - global & local - to help inspire others and keep us all in touch. And we are already open to submissions for - cor blimley - next years book - so send in yer articles and photos of events & actions, UK & abroad, or any satirical images, cartoons, subverts, subverted billboards and the like. (Send pics preferrably as email tifs/jpg files - the higher the res the better.)

CONTENTS

FOREWORD

Welcome to the eighth SchNEWS annual. As per usual with our books, this is a compilation of another 50 issues (actually, 51 this time) of the free weekly direct action newsletter produced in Brighton, plus loads of additional articles, photos, satire and more. This book covers issues 351-401, the period of April 2002 to April 2003.

SchNEWS has been producing weekly newsletters (as well as maintaining a website, producing annual books, touring festivals and doing countless info-stalls) since November 1994. It is funded by donations and run by a group of volunteers, people otherwise involved in a range of activities in Brighton: community organisation, direct action and culture (ie not career journalists). We cram each issue with frontline stories from the fight against the forces of global environmental and social havoc, and about those working to build sustainable alternatives to consumer capitalism and ecological meltdown.

In eight odd years this has seen us go from focussing on the big road protests and resistance to the Criminal Justice Act in the mid nineties, through to the mass anti-capitalist events like June 18th and Genoa in latter years, and all stops in between: genetically modified food, climate change, Neo Labour privatisation, and the rest. Which brings us to the past twelve months.

This year something unique happened for SchNEWS – we covered the same story every week for over six months. That story, of course, was the war in Iraq. But it wasn't just the deceitful manoeuvrings of the gangsters who led the war that got covered: we were more interested in the myriad of actions being taken to stop it, and doing all we could as an alternative media outlet to let people know how to get involved. When we came to put this annual together we decided to build on the SchNEWS anti-war coverage by adding further articles to them - making this an 'anti-war special'. There were two reasons for this. First, we wanted to get a sense of the scale of what happened in the global protests, to look at the range of tactics that were used and give people a chance to think about what was effective and

what wasn't. Second, we wanted to give the coverage SchNEWS gave week in week out a bit more of the background it hasn't got the space for - so there's extra stuff here about the history of Iraq, the question of oil, the uprisings and the sanctions, as well as loads about the direct actions and protests against the war that happened across the globe.

In our coverage of the global anti-war protests we capture just part of the incredible force that reared it's head against the war machine. What we saw was what a much-quoted New York Times editorial called 'the second superpower: public opinion'. Military bases around the world are now under the glare of attention from those ready to sabotage the war effort. The throngs of schoolkids who came out across the world for their own mass actions showed that the brutal reality of this system is reaching kids younger these days – and they're also finding out earlier that it's healthy to do something about it. People came out on the streets all over the world for this one, in numbers never seen before. US Embassies from Jakarta to Athens have never had so many visitors. And for every organised event, there must have been countless unreported and autonomous efforts, like kids smashing the windows of US military vehicles in Turkey.

But of course this book isn't just about the war on Iraq. Outside the war coverage it's business as usual for SchNEWS, with a spectrum of articles from the counter-culture and direct action frontlines. There's reports on the International Solidarity Movement in Palestine; the spectacular Pink Castle GM crop action in Dorset; the Castlemorton free festival and the rise of the Criminal Justice Act; the riots against privatisation across South America and more. But it's not all heavy going - there's also bags of laughs including Kenneth Williams starring as Tony Blair in 'Carry On Bombing' and pages of choice cartoons and subverts.

About this book...

You may notice that the SchNEWS issues reprinted in this book are spread out over extra pages, with other text and pictures inserted in and around them. This is because in previous books there was criticism about the microscopic size of the print in the SchNEWS issues, particularly the back pages. So this time we are bringing the actual SchNEWS articles to the fore by making sure you can actually read them. If this is sacrilege then get the 'proper' layouts in pdf format off our website.

Thanks to everyone who contributed to this book (knowingly or otherwise) including Squall, Bristle, all the activists who sent us stuff, and everyone who posted stuff on Indymedia and Ainfos that's been reproduced here.

Disclaimer: Everything in this book is for education and entertainment purposes only. SchNEWS wouldn't encourage anyone to get off the arses and do anything at all. Honest.

EN ATTENDANT LA FIN DES DINOSAURES

'Waiting for the end of the dinosaurs'

PINK CASTLE

Weeding out every single GM plant from the field.

Down in the dungeon of the Pink Castle.

Hardcore GM crop-trashing or Historical Re-enactment Society - you decide...

Once upon a time, in a field not far away, a pink castle appeared by the light of the moon, on one of the two GM sites that besiege Littlemoor in Dorset.

From the 25th April the pink fortification stood guard over the field in which the mutant remains of the previous year's GM maize crop could still be found. The castle residents hoped to obstruct the farmer and prevent further GM contamination.

On the 16th May, three weeks into the occupation, farmer Charles Foot entered the field with seven tractors and a massive police presence. People d-locked onto his digger, and a further thirty local Littlemoor residents risked arrest for aggrevated trespass to join the protest. The several tractors which were immobilised with d-locks went on to plant the field with Aventis GM maize – albeit having to work around the Pink Castle and the other stranded vehicles. Four people were arrested.

After the police and media had left, at least 20 locals - entire families - were seen digging the freshly sown seeds from the ground. It is worth pointing out that picking up the seeds and sending them back to Bayer/Aventis would constitute neither Criminal Damage or Theft, and Aggravated Trespass can only apply when there is a worker present whose current work you are interfering with. In other words, there is no sensible charge that would stick, so if you wanted to get involved ...

Only two thirds of the field was planted so the pink castle remained to defend the rest. Of course there was plenty to do after the maize went in and loads of people visited to ensure that the job was done.

Last year, Littlemoor residents decontaminated a massive 70% of the maize planted in the field and all five Dorset GM trials were destroyed or damaged. Within hours of the seeds being sown, at least 20 locals were seen digging them from the ground.

Within a few weeks of this years planting, it became obvious that both Aventis and the farmer had written off the 'trial'. The 'scientists' never came to put down the insect traps, the field was never marked out and the farmer never returned to spray. Further more, by early June, the entire crop of GM maize had been pulled up by visitors to the pink castle.

On Saturday 15th June there was a celebration at the pink castle - a silly sports day with activities such as welly wanging, three legged chicken race, crazy golf, seed and spoon race and pin the law suit on the farmer.

The pink castle was dismantled on Sunday and by the following evening the residents and their camp had gone. Update: On 7th March 2003 an English judge found that activists in Littlemoor who built a big pink castle on a field about to be sown with GM seeds were acting reasonably in order to try and prevent damage to neighbouring crops. They were acquitted of all charges against them. The magistrate noted that the activists, "acted reasonably by locking themselves onto tractors because simply standing in front of them would not have prevented the crop being sown". http://www.sayhi.to/thecastle

Modifying The Crops

It has been another busy year for people opposing the introduction of genetically modified (GM) crops, as both covert nighttime raids and open daytime actions continue to hold back the development of GM crops in the UK, whilst decontaminating local environments where test sites are planted.

Last July there was a national celebration of GM crop trashing - an open show of defiance against Neo Labour's blatant backing of GM companies. A convoy of about 200 people carried bags of genetically modified produce that had been torn up from seventeen different fields across Britain and dumped them on the steps of DEFRA (Department of Food and Rural Affairs). The poor minion sent out to talk to the crowd never really stood a chance. Outraged grandmothers and stroppy fairies queued up to have firm words with him over a megaphone whilst dumping bags of oilseed rape and maize at his feet. "We don't want your GM crops, and we'll take them out if you plant them there again" pronounced a Scottish mum as she deposited her offering.

Such actions are not popular with the government. Blair had said about anti-GM protesters "It is wrong to make heroes of people who are preventing basic scientific research taking place... Those people who want to protest should do it lawfully..." Well Tony, the GM field trials have about as much to do with "basic scientific research" as bombing Iraq had to do with "freedom and democracy". And considering that juries nearly always acquit people who have trashed GM crops – then maybe their actions are legal! And what happens when a GM crop has been planted illegally? Do the police arrest those responsible and have the crop pulled up and destroyed? Yeah, right...

On 16th August 2002 the government announced that at least 25 farmscale trials of GM oilseed rape (planted over a four year period) had been accidentally contaminated with an unlawful variety of rapeseeds which contained genes for antibiotic resistance. The government admitted that a clear-up would be necessary, so the good folk of Dorset hastily rallied round to help. Three days later around 50 people attended a Sunday afternoon protest at their neighbouring field in Hilton. Around 20 people in white paper suits entered the site to start the cleanup job, but were interrupted by some 40 police who, not to be outdone on the short-notice accessories front, brought dogs, several vans and a helicopter. Four months later they were told no prosecutions would be pressed.

The news was reported in the national media, but as a 'protesters make blunder story', based on a police press release which claimed that the wrong crop had been damaged and no GM plants removed.

Hilton, Dorset 18th August 2002

This was despite everyone on the ground, including the (now) disgruntled farmer running the trial, being very clear that the right plants were targeted. After the story had been covered the police issued a second press release admitting their first statement was wrong, but issued no apology or explanation for the discrepancy.

Bags of GM crops dumped at DEFRA, July 2002   Pic: Bill Poster

When news of the contamination broke, the DEFRA Minister issued a statement that the biotech company responsible, Bayer, could be prosecuted for "possible breach of contract". In addition to the embarrassment of a highly regulated 'trial' being part of an unlawful mix up, later negligence had made matters worse. Bayer were told about the problem in June when decisive action could have removed the threat before other crops were pollinated, but they kept the contamination from the government until August. The Hilton field (with the exception of the

'Anarchy & Organic Vegetables'

bit that was trashed by protesters) was not harvested until many of the seedpods had shattered. To date no legal action has been taken against them.

Most people facing trial in England and Wales for GM actions have their cases dropped before trial, get acquitted by a jury or receive light fines for their actions. (Protesters in Scotland have suffered more heavily). But it had to happen that eventually a jury would find someone guilty. In April 2002 two women, Yvonne Davies and Rowan Tilly, were arrested during an anti-GM protest against the last remaining GM trial site in Wales. The two women defended themselves, saying that they pulled up GM crops to protect the crops of other farmers, public health and the environment. They were fined £400 and £750 for their efforts. Yvonne Davies, of Carmarthen, said: "I am disappointed with the verdict but nevertheless I took my action with the support of the people of Wales. With the threat of commercialisation around the corner we must keep giving a clear message that Wales will not accept GM crops."

While it's good to pull up crops as they're planted, it's surely a better tactic to stop the crop being planted in the first place. In Tinkleton, Devon everyone in the village signed a petition asking the farmer not to plant, and he respected their wishes. Activists in Devon and Dorset went on an outreach exercise talking to farmers. They cycled around the area, stopping at random as they passed farms and seeing if they could find anyone up for a chat. About 40 farmers were visited in all; awareness of GM among those they met varied, but most were eager to explain the problems they were facing, and they only encountered one "get orf my land" type comment. Leaflets were left to counter the promises made about GM in the farming press, and a GM-free-zone pledge collected a respectable number of signatures. One of the riders concluded, "Pressurising producers and consumers is probably a more effective tactic with GM, as the stranglehold of the supermarkets has left dairy producers in crisis. But we learnt a lot from talking to farmers, and they got

a glimpse of a new threat on the horizon which they may now try and avoid."

The most spectacular GM action this year was the Pink Castle in Dorset in May 2002 (see previous article).

For more information on decontaminating fields of genetically modified crops contact Genetic Engineering Network: 0845 456 9329 www.genetic saction.org.uk

Munlochy Monster

The anti-GM movement against the farmscale trials in Munlochy in the north of Scotland has been so successful that the Scottish Executive has cancelled further crop trials in the Highlands, thus creating a GM-free zone. Nice One!

Last September, a Scottish farmer growing GM crops, Shirley Harrison was presented with a cake and a bottle of whiskey by anti-GM protesters! Er, why? Well the cake was made with genetically modified ingredients and the whisky contained 2.7% methanol, which is an acceptable level of contamination according to Shirley Harrison and Aventis, whose crop she was growing. We doubt she ate the cake or drank the whisky, but she did carry on with the crop trial until...

On 6th October a free decontamination of Mrs. Harrison's farm took place, with nearly all the crop destroyed, "Silently we came, silently we left, to strike a blow for a GM-free Scotland" said the crop pullers. The Police are appealing for anyone with any information concerning the incident to contact Crimestoppers on 0800 55111. In a concurrent investigation, campaigners are appealing to anyone with information regarding the farming of Genetically Modified Crops to contact Crimestoppers on 0800 55111.

For info on keeping Scotland GM free contact "pro-Natural Food Scotland", 35 Hamilton Drive, Glasgow, G12 8DW. www.gmfreescotland.net

The successes in Scotland have come at a price, notably fines (usually between £100 and £300) for all involved in destroying GM crops. The fact that more Scottish activists have been found guilty is down to slight differences in their legal system, notably the lack of a jury trial. In England and Wales nearly all GM activists to go before a jury have been acquitted.

Hilton, Dorset 18th August 2002

8

GET PREPARED

Mayday falls slap-bang in the middle of the week, so make sure you have the day off work, school, college or university. Call a strike (you know it makes sense), phone in sick (or well!), bunk off - do whatever it takes to be on the streets of Mayfair on Wednesday 1st May.

For Mayday in Mayfair to be a huge success we all need to prepare. Make costumes, banners, flags, placards, whistles, claxons and musical instruments. Get hold of inflatables, balls, nets and other props. Make food and bring it to share. Look at a map of Mayfair and consider the possibilities.

Contact us for leaflets and stickers or produce your own. Spread the word. Get together with your friends and form an affinity group - a group of people you know and trust who will look out for each other on the day. Above all get planning as Mayday is fast approaching!

weekly SchNEWS

www.schnews.org.uk

Friday 26th April 2002   Free/Donation   Issue 351

MAYBE MAYFAIR MAYHEM

Two weeks ago the Radical Dairy, a squatted social centre in Stoke Newington, was raided by the cops on the pretext that drugs and electricity were being used illegally. No arrests were made but two computers were taken as 'evidence' that electricity was being smoked, and just for good measure the leccy board then dug up the road and removed the centre from the National Grid! This sort of over-the-top activity can only mean one thing - May Day will soon be upon us. It's that time of year again - when anarchists climb out of their winter gutters and threaten the very fabric of our society.

The raid on the London centre follows increased activity from the cops, which has been steadily building over the past few months. The Met Police threatened to raid any internet servers who dared host the website for this year's 'Mayday Festival of Alternatives' while at MayDay meetings and fundraisers cops hang around outside like a bad smell snapping pictures and putting pressure on landlords of any venues that are being used. Meanwhile the corporate media have talked about the most violent May Day for decades and running battles with the cops.

Throwing a Wombly

Seven WOMBLES (whose dress sense makes the police break out into hot sweats and reach for their truncheons) are up in court at the beginning of next week after being nicked on Hallowe'en. They were arrested while walking down Oxford Street on their way to a party, many wearing white overalls to symbolise ghosts (the original context of the white overall movement in Italy) and Halloween

masks. The cops involved were part of "Operation Calm", an anti-terrorist response to September 11th who calmly started pushing people up against shop windows, arresting them for complaining then holding them for up to 19 hours. By some amazing co-incidence the trial will be going on during May Day and it looks like the judge will be Roger Davies who was in charge of all last years Mayday trials. This is the man who sent down someone for three months for throwing a crumpled up piece of paper at a cop and told a Romanian woman that he'd put their children into care if they were caught begging again.

Last summer the Legal Defence and Monitoring Group (LDMG) uncovered secret Mayday Sentencing Guidelines that instruct Judges to hand down heavy sentences to those arrested during May Day actions. The document titled "Mayhem" first came to the attention of the LDMG at Middlesex Guildhall Crown Court. The defence barrister asked to look at the document, but the court refused this on the grounds that it was secret! As for the Radical Dairy – well the centre is still running thanks to generators, candles and a lot of local goodwill.

The centre has proved very popular with local residents who have seen Hackney Council shut down and sell off community assets in order to try to pay off its debts. One local resident said, "The people here have been nothing but good for the local community. This place was empty for three years, that's bad for everybody: it was unsafe and it was unhealthy. It is now clean, occupied, safe. It's used for socially constructive purposes." One local 15-year-old girl added "I

think the Radical Dairy is a good place for the community. It's a better place for us kids to go because we can play on the decks and also learn new things like yoga and shiatsu which are fun …the police should not be bothering the people in The Radical Dairy when there is so much criminal activity happening on the streets of Hackney. We can use the computers here to do school work and use the Internet free for research."

So, while the police are no doubt scanning the computers for links between the anti-capitalist movement and Al-Qaeda, a few local pissed off kids are wondering when they will get their homework back.

* The Wombles Trial is from 29 April - 3 May at Horseferry Road Magistrates Court, SW1. Demo outside everyday wear a white overall/white armband in solidarity. Details: 07960 973847 sevensupport@temporary.org.uk www.wombles.org.uk

* The Radical Dairy is at 47 Kynaston Road, Stoke

London Calling

Full list of the 'Mayday Festival of Alternatives' from 26th April till May 6th and "attempting to provide constructive ideas and alternatives to commercial and corporate Britain" check out www.ourmayday.org.uk or call 07786 716335.

* 7.30am Critical Mass – from the south (Camberwell Green) and north (Camden Town Tube), to meet up at 10am outside US Embassy, Grosvenor Square.

* 9am Breakfast Against Routine Fit-ups. - Vegan breakfast outside WOMBLES trial at Horseferry Road, SW1.

1pm Mass Action: "Mayday in Mayfair" - Multiple Meet-up Points with four themes - Travelling Circus, Wake for Capitalism, Carniball! (old fashioned footie) and Critical Mass bike ride.

"Now one of the most opulent and cloistered areas in the capital, full of luxury pads, exclusive shops, fancy hotels and national embassies, (Mayfair) takes its name from the fair which was held every year from 1 May for 15 days until its suppression in the mid-18th century. Mayday in Mayfair will be a fluid, spontaneous and exciting return to the Mayfayre, happening everywhere at once, without a fixed starting point or finish..! We all need to take the initiative in Mayfair... keep moving and don't let the cops trap and surround you! This way our festivities will not be crushed."

* 5pm "Nobody is illegal" Sexual Freedom Coalition event in Soho, with sex workers union & samba band - meet Cambridge Circus.

* 8pm - 1am Comedy and magic night at Chats Palace, 42 Brooksby's Walk, Homerton, E8. Nearest train station: Homerton.

May Procession

Brighton April 30th Sainsbury's go to court to evict the Locomotive Works Community Project. Demo against Sainsbury's meet Sat 27th 1pm at the Loco Works (1 New England St). Mayday - events at the Loco Works, with Beltane Bonfire show at 9pm. 01273-622727.

Liverpool Noon from St Lukes (bombed out church) on Bury St. Nightime. Play about Tolpuddle Martyrs at Casa, Hope Street followed by bands and entertainment. www.peoplenotprofit.co.uk

Bradford 12.30pm Infirmary Fields, Westgate (adj Beehive pub) march through town to Centenary Square. www.1in12.com

Edinburgh Noon onwards in Princes Street Gardens (West) 0131 557 6242 www.ourmayday.org/edinburgh/

Glasgow Noon outside Buchanan tube in the city centre. www.ourmayday.org/glasgow

Haringey - 10 days of Mayday activities & a spoof newspaper Tel. 0208 374 5027

Mayday Mayhem against the Fur Trade 10am outside Fairheads, 60-64 Cranbrook Rd., Ilford. Call day before to check event is still happening 12pm Philip Hockley's, 20 Conduit St., W1 - biggest fur shop left in London. London Animal Action 0845 4584775 laa@londonaa.demon.co.uk

Noon Sat 4th Nottingham Carnival from Forest Recreation Ground to The Old Market Square, live music stage and speakers till 4.30 pm maydayuk@yahoo.co.uk

Caterpillars of Society

On April 11th pro-Palestinian activists occupied the Caterpillar HQ in Desford, Leicestershire in protest at the bulldozer-building company profiteering from the murderous Israeli activity in Palestine. Activists gained access to all parts of the site, occupied the managing director's office, and leafleted the 1,500 workforce some of who helped by handing some out to their colleagues. Israel uses Caterpillar bulldozers to wreak enormous destruction in the Occupied Territories - bulldozing Palestinians' homes, creating roadblocks, and digging mass graves.

* Check out what's really going on in Palestine www.electronicintifada.com/diaries/index.html ** Peace activists who've recently returned from Palestine are holding a meeting on Monday (29th) Quaker Meeting House, 10 St James St, Sheffield ** The Sussex University Students who took part in international solidarity actions in Palestine are giving a talk next Saturday (4) 2 pm. at the Friends Meeting House, Ship Street, Brighton ** From 24th June- 7th July the International Solidarity Movement are organising non-violent direct actions in Palestine alongside the Palestinians. As they say "We do not know what the situation will be like this summer. If the Occupation continues, we will resist. If it ends, we will joyfully reconstruct". To prepare for this there will be a UK training weekend. uksolidarity@yahoo.co.uk, www.palsolidarity.org

April 20 Washington DC
Over 100,000 people from a diverse range of groups including anti-war activists, muslim communities and Latin American solidarity groups marched on Washington DC in the largest pro-Palestinian rally in U.S. history. Another 35,000 turned out in San Francisco.
www.internationalanswer.org

Close Chavez

> *"There isn't a single political person in Latin America who does not believe that the CIA was involved in some form, and in the same way, as it was in Chile. Those responsible for Latin America in the state department are the most extremist, off-the-wall team - 7 out of the top 12 officials in the Latin American department are Cuban-Americans"* - Larry Birns Director of the Council of Hemispheric Affairs.

The Venezuelan people stuck two fingers up at the US this month and reinstated President Hugo Chavez, less than 48 hours after a US backed coup had overthrown him. Chavez, who led his own failed coup in 1992, was overthrown by a military junta following violence at an anti-Chávez demonstration. The coup had all the hallmarks of a classic CIA-backed plot with misinformation, black propaganda and agent provocateurs casually shooting demonstrators, creating a situation of fear and panic which would allow the military to step in, overthrow the president and bring calm back to the country. Unconvinced? A cable sent from the CIA to its station chief in Chile during the overthrow of Salvador Allende read: "Re: Coup. Activities to include propaganda, black operations, disinformation, or anything else your imagination can conjure..."

The coup began with an Anti-Chavez demonstration with over 150,000 people gathered in E Caracas; the wealthy homeland of his opponents, in support of striking oil workers. When the protestors decided to march on the presidential palace word got out to Chavez supporters who mobilised to stop the march. Violent clashes broke out during which gunmen casually fired from rooftops and bridges into the crowd killing at least 14 people and wounding over 100 more.

Anti-Chavez supporters claim it was the Chavez supporters who started firing at them yet eyewitnesses have said the shooting began from a roadway overpass controlled by the anti-Chavez Metropolitan Police, and the first to be killed were pro-Chavez demonstrators. Confirmation of the eyewitness reports came from the secretary of health for metropolitan Caracas, who reported that of those who died 'the most serious wounds were in the cranium and cheek... they appeared to be shots from above'. According to the military they intervened to stop further bloodshed.

When confronted over the shootings Chavez resigned and handed the presidency over to the junta. No resignation note has been produced. With the Junta in command the presidency went to Pedro Carmona, head of Venezuela's Federation of Chambers of Commerce & Industry and organiser of the oil strike. He immediately operated like a dictator dismissing the entire Congress and Supreme Court, abolishing the constitution and the right to fire any elected state or municipal leader.

With the newly imposed president sipping champagne in the presidential palace the US Ambassador visited to give the coup the US's blessing. At the same time neighbouring Latin American countries condemned the coup and refused to recognise the illegitimate, un-elected president. Worse still Venezuela was not going to sit there and allow a govt to be imposed on them by the US and so set about getting their real and democratically elected president back. Protests broke out through Venezuela. The middle-ranking members of the military influenced by the demos and the international response changed their mind about the coup, had the 5 senior members of the junta arrested, forced Carmona to resign and handed the presidency over to Chavez's vice president who then handed it back to Chavez- the 3rd president in 3 days!

www.narconews.com

Kissing Ass

Demonstrators turned out on Wednesday to greet Henry Kissinger who was in London to give a talk at the Institute of Directors' conference. Kissinger served as US National Security Adviser from 1969-73 and as Secretary of State between 1973-77 and has been described as the world's biggest war criminal. A Spanish judge unsuccessfully sought to have Britain send Kissinger to Madrid to testify about his alleged involvement in "Operation Condor," a concerted plot by former military dictatorships in Brazil, Argentina, Chile, Paraguay and Uruguay to persecute and eliminate their opponents during the 1970s and 1980s. Outside London's Royal Albert Hall demonstrators held a mock trial with a huge effigy of Kissinger. The road outside was blocked for a while before heavy handed police moved in, two people were arrested. As one protester said "Despite a huge policing operation, Kissinger was not arrested".
www.indymedia.org.uk

Lodgers Wanted

The Forest Lodge Collective squatted housing project in Nottingham has been renovating its grade 2 listed building since 1998. The lodge has been housing homeless people, providing them with a stepping-stone to save money for more secure accommodation. The lodge is now facing eviction by the council, who own the building, and who have refused to say what they are doing with the property. The Collective are desperately trying to gain an order of consent that will allow them to stay until there are definite plans for the building. They'd greatly appreciate any help/advice. theforestlodge@hotmail.com, www.forestlodge.150m.com

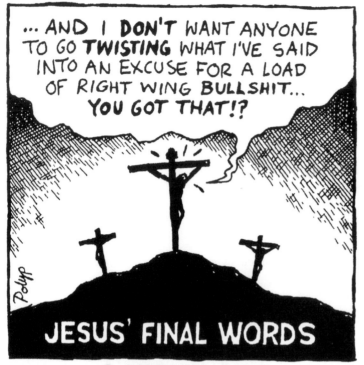

... AND I **DON'T** WANT ANYONE TO GO **TWISTING** WHAT I'VE SAID INTO AN EXCUSE FOR A LOAD OF **RIGHT WING BULLSHIT**... YOU GOT THAT!?

JESUS' FINAL WORDS

SchNEWS in brief

12 towns and cities took part in Wednesday's day of action against casualisation organised by the **Simon Jones Memorial Campaign**. In Brighton 80 people including a band, lots of balloons and an old dragon demonstrated outside Personnel Selection, the temp agency that sent Simon to his death. The company decided to shut down for the afternoon as a mark of respect. www.simonjones.org.uk ** **75,000 marched in Washington DC last Saturday**. Originally planned as a mobilisation against the World Bank and IMF, people also marched against the wars on drugs and terror and for **Israel to withdraw from Palestine.** http://dc.indymedia.org **Choke on It** demo outside **Downing Street** where the Queen, Tony Blair and ex-Prime Ministers will be having a tea party. Meet 6pm, Monday 29th www.fuckthejubilee.com Tel: 07931 301901 ** **Cold Bath Times** is a new alternative monthly newsletter currently being set up in Southampton. If you'd like to get involved coldbathinfo@yahoo.co.uk

** **Stourbridge ABC** are campaigning against a bypass that will destroy 37m of green belt land. They would really appreciate any help/advice kari@cauldron90.free serve.co.uk ** April 16 saw **the first general strike in Italy for 20 yrs** with the country brought to a halt by over 80% of union workers stopping work for 8 hrs, and over 2m people took part in street protests against govt labour policies. ** **Five acres of GM crops in the Highlands have been mysteriously destroyed**. The incident comes only days after a Scottish parliamentary committee called for the crop trial, which had just started to flower, to be ploughed up www.genetixactionscotland.org.uk ** **A pink castle** has appeared on a field near Littlemoor estate, Weymouth, which is due to be planted with GM maize soon. Castle residents are vowing to stay to prevent the crop being planted. Support is urgently needed Tel: 07815 925214 www.sayhi.to/thecastle ** **Sheffield Toxic Avengers** were stopped by police from building a 13' model of an incinerator in the

front garden of Councillor Peter Moore. A spokesperson for the group said "Peter Moore wants to build an incinerator in our front yard, so we thought we'd build one in his." ** **Manchester's 2nd radical bookfair** is happening on the 5th May, 1-5pm, at Merci, Bridge Mill, 22A Beswick St, Ancoats. www.radicalbookfair.org.uk ** **Two ex-Black Panthers**, one who spent years in American prisons are on a tour of N England over May Day week, inc. a date at the Manchester Bookfair. *See SchNEWS party and protest site for details*

RIP

* **Pablo**, who died in his sleep two weeks ago. Well known around the old protest camps, living life in the fast lane. * 22 year old **Beth O'Brien** died after falling 150 ft from a tree at Eagle Creek tree protest site in the Mt. Hood National Forest Oregon, USA. Beth's death came as protestors were packing up camp after winning their battle to save the woodland from road developers. www.cascadiaforestalliance.org

...and finally...

On Thursday residents of Faslane Peace Camp were told by police they were in danger thanks to an unexploded bomb. The road was closed for a couple of hours while a controlled explosion took place. But wait a minute….what is that on the other side of the fence? Yes, it's a huge unexploded nuclear bomb ferried around by Trident submarines. But don't worry peace campers and the rest of the world. Those bombs are in the safe hands of the British government.
* In June the Camp will be celebrating 20 years of existence. Fun and frolics planned 01436 820901 www.faslanepeacecamp.com

Disclaimer

SchNEWS warns all readers now Commander Paddick's seen the anarchist light he's gonna be May Queen with Druids dancin' round his pole. Honest!

Congo:
The Lost World War

The war on Iraq is not the only war in the world and it is not the only war being fought for our material benefit. Western consumers' seemingly insatiable demand for mobile phones, laptops, games consoles and other luxury electronic goods has been fuelling violent conflict and killing millions in the Democratic Republic of Congo (formerly Zaire).

by Erik Vilwar (from www.corporatewatch.org.uk)

Either side of an 1800 mile front-line, a country the size of western Europe with a population no larger than England's has been carved up by warring factions and foreign armies from nine different countries, leaving millions dead or homeless. What little infrastructure dictator Mobutu Sese Seko did not wreck during his three decades of misrule has mostly been destroyed by fighting, or has finally succumbed to neglect.

The Democratic Republic of Congo (DRC) is possibly the most mineral rich place on earth – though this has proved a curse to the people of the Congo. The Congo holds millions of tons of diamonds, copper, cobalt, zinc, manganese, uranium (the atomic bombs dropped on Hiroshima and Nagasaki were built using Congolese uranium), and coltan. Coltan, a substance made up of columbium and tantalum, is a particularly valuable resource – used to make mobile phones, night vision goggles, fiber optics, and micro-capacitors.

What Is Coltan?

Coltan looks like black mud, but is three times heavier than iron and only slightly lighter than gold. It is found in abundance in eastern Congo and can be mined with minimal equipment. Coltan is vital to the high tech economy. Wireless electronic communication would not exist without it. The 'mud' is refined into tantalum – a metallic element that is both a superb conductor of electricity and extremely heat-resistant. Tantalum powder is a vital component in capacitors, for the control of the flow of current in miniature circuit boards. Capacitors made of tantalum are found inside every laptop, pager, personal digital assistant, and mobile phone. Tantalum is also used in the aviation and atomic energy industries. A very small group of companies in the world process coltan. These include H.C.Starck (Germany, a subsidiary ot Bayer), Cabott Inc. (US), Ningxia (China), and Ulba (Kazakhstan). The world's biggest coltan mines are in Australia and they account for about 60% of world production. It is generally believed, however, that 80% of the world's reserves are in Africa, with DRC accounting for 80% of the African reserves.

At the end of 2000, there was an unprecedented 'gold rush for coltan'. Over a few months the price rose tenfold. In January 2000, an international trader would have paid between US$30 and US$40 for a pound (lb) of unprocessed coltan. By December 2000 the price has risen to US$380/lb. This dramatic price increase was driven by a sudden and steep rise in the demand for tantalum powder, caused by an overvaluation of the technology market triggered by a new generation of mobile phones and the consumer rush following the launch of the Sony Playstation 2.

At the height of the demand for coltan, it is known that Rwandan soldiers and other affiliated criminal groups were making roughly US$20 million a month solely from the trade in coltan. However, the coltan boom was short-lived and prices rapidly fell as more and more coltan came on to the market. By October 2001, coltan prices were back to where they started. In the meantime, thousands of destitute Congolese people had gone digging for the precious ore, a few international traders had made a fortune and millions of dollars had flowed to the parties waging war. Prices have fallen from the late 2000 peak, but the trade in coltan is still fuelling the war.

The human costs of this conflict have been horrific. According to the UN, up until last September, in the five Eastern provinces of DRC alone, between 3 and 3.5 million people had died directly because of the war. Many were killed and tortured but most died of starvation and disease. The destruction of farms has resulted in malnutrition and starvation. Millions of people have been forced from their homes. Years of war have led to a social environment in which men abuse women on a staggering scale and children become instruments of war, forced to work in mines and conscripted into armed forces. Surveys in Butembo found that 90% of people were living on less than 20 cents a day and only one meal.

Most people in Britain appear ignorant of this war. The underlying causes of the war and the role of the British government and British companies are obfuscated by the media presentation of the war as a confusing ethnic conflict, involving seven African states and many rebel groups. In fact, the war is quite simple to understand. It is about money.

The 'second Congolese war' supposedly began in August 1998, with an attempt by Tutsi rebels backed by Uganda and Rwanda to depose former Congolese president Laurent Kabila, whom they accused of sheltering the Hutu Interahamwe militias responsible for the 1994 slaughter of some 800,000 Tutsis in Rwanda. Soldiers from Angola, Zimbabwe, Namibia and Chad were sent in, ostensibly to save Kabila's regime. It is clear that the primary motivation for the intervention of these armies was to loot Congo's rich resources and sell them.

The looting of the Congo's natural resources is carried out by elite networks consisting of a small core of political and military elites and business persons and, in the case of occupied areas, selected rebel leaders. These networks ensure the viability and profitability of their economic activities through control over the military and other security forces that they use to intimidate, threaten, torture and kill. Actual commercial activities are carried out through front companies, supported by organised transnational criminal groups. 'The role of the private sector in the exploitation of natural resources and the continuation of the war has been vital.'

UN Panel of Experts

Last October, an independent panel of experts reported to the United Nations Security Council that 85 multinational companies based in Europe, the US and South Africa had facilitated the plunder of the Congo and illegally profited from the war. Twelve of the companies named in the report are based in Britain.

Mahmoud Kassen, chairperson of the UN Panel of Experts, said 'The role of these companies is really important. Corporations have a direct and indirect role. Without them this kind of commerce would not be possible'.

The Panel's investigations had previously led them to conclude that the war in the Congo 'has become mainly about access, control and trade' of minerals, the most important being coltan. The one thing that unites the warring parties is the desire for money. 'Because of its lucrative nature,' the Panel said, the war 'has created a win-win situation for belligerents. Adversaries and enemies are at the same time partners in business, get weapons from the same dealers and use the same intermediaries. Business has superseded security.'

Britain is not only involved in the exploitation of the Congo's natural resources; it also armed all the sides involved in the DRC conflict. UK arms manufacturers have been granted export licenses to sell weapons to Zimbabwe, Uganda, Angola, Namibia and Burundi.

In a speech to the Labour Party Conference last year, Tony Blair said that, with UK help, the world community could 'sort out the blight that is the continuing conflict in the Democratic Republic of Congo, where three million people have died through war or famine in the last decade'. What Blair refers to as 'the blight' within the DRC was exacerbated by his own government's sanctioning of military exports and training into the region. Since the Labour Party came to power, Britain has more than quadrupled arms sales to Africa.

Congo History in a Nutshell

The Congo has been relentlessly pillaged for more than a century. To begin with, it was taken over as a personal possession by Belgian King Leopold II following a series of fraudulent treaties with African kings. Leopold thought a good name would be the Congo Free State, perhaps because he got it for nothing. Private companies were brought in to do the dirty work, extracting as much rubber and ivory as possible, and making money hand over fist. Leopold's rule was tyrannical and vicious and killed more than half the population in less than 20 years.

In 1909, Belgium took the country over and renamed it the Belgian Congo. They eased up on the killing but kept the forced labour. Fierce rioting in 1959 resulted in Belgium abruptly granting independence in 1960. The country was renamed the Democratic Republic of Congo. Shortly after independence, the US took over in a bloody coup. The CIA arranged the murder of Patrice Lumumba, the country's first elected leader. In his place they installed their paid agent Colonel Mobutu Sese Seko.

In Mobutu's 37 years as ruler of the Congo (which he renamed Zaire) he managed to amass a huge personal fortune and continued to oppress the general population. Nevertheless, he remained popular with Western governments and companies. From 1965 to 1991, Zaire received more than $1.5 billion in US economic and military aid. According to the World Bank (a long-time supporter of Mobutu), 64.7% of Zaire's budget was reserved for Mobutu's discretionary spending. Mobutu's greed was ultimately his downfall. When he tried to stop sharing the Congo's wealth with his Western backers, the US prepared for him to be overthrown. In October 1996, the Rwandan army along with Ugandan troops invaded Zaire and by May 1997 had forced Mobutu to flee to Morocco. The invasion was disguised as a local rebellion. The Tutsi Rwandan forces called themselves the Alliance of Democratic Forces for the Liberation of Congo-Zaire (ADFL) and recruited Laurent Kabila, an exiled Congolese Marxist, as a figurehead leader. Kabila was installed as President and changed the country's name back to the Democratic Republic of Congo. In July 1998, Kabila expelled Rwandan and Ugandan forces from the Congo. On 2nd August, Rwanda and Uganda invaded the eastern region of the Congo and set up surrogate 'rebel' armies. Angola, Zimbabwe and Namibia sent their armies to support Kabila and Burundi joined the Rwandans and the Angolans. This was the start of the second Congo war. The US backed the Rwandan and Ugandan invasion and pressured Kabila into signing the Lusaka Accord which treated the conflict as a civil war. The result is a partitioned Congo with Rwanda and Uganda still occupying the eastern half and ignoring all deadlines for leaving. On 17th January 2001, on the fortieth anniversary of the assassination of Lumumba, Laurent Kabila was assassinated. Joseph Kabila, Laurent's son, took over as President.

For the full article see www.corporatewatch.org.uk

"COR BLIMEY! RUN - IT'S THE ANARCHIST SECRET WEAPON"

weekly SchNEWS

www.schnews.org.uk

Friday 3rd May 2002   Free/Donation   Issue 352/353

MAYWATCH

"Mayday has been a celebration of life, renewal and pleasure since ancient times. More recently it was declared International Workers' Day to commemorate the execution of four anarchists in Chicago for their part in the struggle for an eight-hour working day. Both these aspects of Mayday were intertwined - a festival against work, want and denial, and a vision of freedom and plenty throughout the world."

From 'Our May Day' website What does May Day mean to you? Well, if you're a Pagan maybe you were out on the lash drinking flagons of mead and dancing naked around a fire to welcome Beltane – the coming of Spring and the rebirth of life. If you're part of the corporate media then it's always a time to relax, dust off some of those old clichés and talk about the end of civilisation, as we know it. If you're a copper then it's a time to get physical and talk about a hardcore of violent protestors bent on changing the status quo. If you're an anti-capitalist then there are a number of choices. It could be the opportunity you were looking for to try out that outrageous new outfit – chances are the media will love it and want to chat you up (but try to think of something good to say beforehand). Or you could dress in black and look all moody at that McDonalds window. If you're a trade unionist, then what better way of using one of your days off work than to march around with a placard and listen to some riveting speeches from some Old Labour politicians.

Wherever you're coming from there's no doubt that over the past few years May Day has been put firmly back onto the political map with millions across the world taking to the streets. The biggest demos were in France with an estimated one million protesting against the fascist Le Pen. In Australia thousands turned out in Melbourne beginning the day by blockading the entrance of the company that runs the country's immigration detention centres. In Indonesia thousands took to the streets calling for the day to be made a national holiday, higher minimum wages and a halt to subsidy cuts on fuel and electricity demanded by the International Monetary Fund. In Athens four separate demonstrations marched to the United States and Israeli embassies to protest Israeli attacks against Palestinians. In Seoul more than 10,000 people called on the government to swiftly introduce a five-day work week and to withdraw its plans to privatise state-run industries.

Hardcore

Across the UK the demonstrations were smaller, but on the whole thought to be more successful than the last few years especially in London where six thousand cops patrolled the streets with four helicopters buzzin' over head. The idea in Mayfair was for people to adopt a theme and be 'fluid and spontaneous…without a fixed starting point or finish.'

This meant crowds kept moving and the police couldn't use their trusty old Section 60 so easily (that's when they pen a crowd in for hours because they 'fear violence might happen') So it was a 'Travelling Cir-

cus' with a thousand sparkle-faced anarchists wheeling round a huge red and yellow shiny plastic Big-Top flanked by pixies, lusty crusty wenches, clowns and screaming queens. Then there was Carniball – old fashioned footie – kicking off down Oxford Street with inflatable beach balls, and two five foot wide red footballs that got the crowds through police lines and provided a new sense of team-crowd spirit, as they bounced off the heads of the plod quite gloriously amid cries of 'GOAL!!'. Or what about a critical mass of bike rides heading for the American Embassy; or a carnival of colour as part of the sex workers parade in Soho (which later got Section 60'd and turned violent as the police hemmed everyone in to take down peoples particulars [pardon]).

Some complained about walking around aimlessly, but on such a do-it-yourself day this just shows the importance of people organising be-

Maywatch cont...

forehand and forming affinity groups. This needn't be rocket science, just a bunch of mates getting together to plan actions, anything from bringing along props to targeting specific companies. A dozen anarchists from Worthing took the initiative by protesting in Berkeley Square, Mayfair, outside the HQ of the Carlyle Group, an American finance firm closely linked to the US government and the arms trade. Other smartly dressed English gentlemen and women showed those ghastly American coffee chains a thing or two about etiquette, setting up stalls outside their stores and dishing out some good old fashioned tea & cucumber sandwiches to the protesting masses.

Last year the press reckoned it was one nil to the cops after they penned everyone in Oxford Street for eight hours. Not this year. As one anarchist 'ringleader' told Schnews "Any suggestion of the cops winning the game are shallow - the cops were on the hop constantly. People broke away spontaneously into groups and reclaimed the streets of central London at the action's height. Hopefully next year we can learn to generate more autonomous actions, bring along more musical instruments, rinky-dink sound systems, balls etc and build on this, because it's definitely a better way to structure mass actions." Or as one reveller told SchNEWS "This year I think we won on away goals."

May the first last

This years events in London weren't just focused on May Day but ten days of activities under the banner of May Day Festival of Alternatives. "We want to show our goals of creating a society based on solidarity, autonomy and co-operation – in practice. We want to show that there is a future beyond capitalism, wage-labour and the state; that we can create our own alternatives and that our land, time, resources, entertainment, and ultimately, our lives, can be reclaimed from a system that has disempowered us from realising our individual and collective potential for centuries."

* Just over 50 were nicked, mainly for minor charges. However if previous May Day court cases are anything to go by, then sentences for even minor offences could be harsh. If you saw any arrests contact the Legal, Defence and Monitoring Group ldmgmail@yahoo.co.uk
* Find out what happened around the world www.indymedia.org
* For the incomplete history of Mayday www.midnightnotes.org/mayday
* For in-depth history of the Haymarket martyrs http://dwardmac.pitzer.edu/Anarchist_Archives/haymarket/Haymarket.html
* Get clued up on section 60 www.urban75.org/mayday02/s60

Inside SchNEWS

Satpal Ram was sentenced to life imprisonment after defending himself against a violent racist attack, he has been moved 72 times in the 13 years he has been inside and SchNEWS reckons this is some sort of Guinness Book of Records. Satpal is now back in open prison. He'd like to thank all those who faxed and wrote over the last period. Though he is back in open conditions, he is grounded for a month for risk assessment. write direct to him: Satpal Ram, HMP Blantyre House, Horden, Goudhurst, Kent, TN17 2NH. Or email the campaign SatpalRam@satpalram.connectfree.uk.com

* Long-term US anarchist prisoner **Harold H. Thompson** is challenging a decision that will decide whether inmates across the States are able to receive mail containing so called 'political content'. Currently up to 25,000 prisoners receive anarchist, environmental or animal rights literature. SchNEWS itself has had newsletters returned because apparently the content was 'unsuitable.' One supporter told SchNEWS "This is a seriously heavyweight legal contest with far-reaching implications for every prisoner held in US jails nationwide, particularly those prepared to stand and fight the system from behind cell bars." Harold desperately needs more money to fight the case. Donations can be sent to (payable to Friends of Harold H.Thomson') PO Box 375, Knaphill, Woking, Surrey, GU21 2XL

Crooks

This month the International Criminal Court was finally ratified by enough countries to be established (SchNEWS 326). It's aim is to "investigate and bring to justice individuals who commit war crimes, crimes against humanity and genocide." Shame it can't try crimes committed before 1 July 2002, the date it officially comes into force otherwise you'd have a few ex-US presidents and advisors running for cover. As it is George W is doing all he can to make sure he won't be appearing in the Hague, by refusing to ratify the treaty. China, Israel and Iraq are also refusing to sign up, no prizes for guessing why! www.iccnow.org www.hrw.org

"You can search me I haven't got your fucking maypole" Mayday, London Pic: Alec Smart

Group 4 Profit

It's still unclear what happened to the asylum seekers still missing after the Yarl's Wood Detention Centre fire in February (SchNEWS 348). After the fire, detainees were described as 'being at large', but a former detention officer recently contacted a Bedfordshire paper to say that she believes a group of 10 detainees who were in the prayer room were killed in the fire.

Campaigners calling for an independent enquiry into the incident have so far been ignored. In what appears to be a massive cover up, witnesses to the event are being deported and 10 of the detainees have now been charged with "violent disorder". An Early Day Motion calling for an independent enquiry and the halt of deportations, has so far only been signed by 48 MP's. You can fax your MP free through www.ncadc.org.uk and ask them to sign EDM1048.

Meanwhile Group 4 who run Yarl's Wood and Campsfield Detention Centre in Oxfordshire, are making big bucks out of making asylum seekers lives a misery. They've recently bought up Wakenhut the company that runs all of Australia's detention centres and other centres around the world with a total of 40,000 units. With the planned expansion of asylum detention in the UK under Labour's new immigration law Group 4 must be glad they've got involved in the 'immigration industry'.

Charlatans

In Rio de Janiero in 1992 World leaders met to discuss what they were going to do about our polluted planet. The decade since Rio has seen rampant destruction of our environment. This September 10 years later - leaders are meeting again in Johannesburg, South Africa, to pat each other on the back and vow to carry on as normal. Campaigners going to Johannesburg are demanding that an international court for crimes against the earth be set up, and are asking people for their nominations. Post yours at www.res istenceisfertile.org.earthcrimes

SchNEWS in brief

Cops in **Montreal, Canada** are carrying out mass arrests on people who are having the cheek to get out and demonstrate. In March 371 people were held for five hours before being arrested on a demo in support of International day against police brutality. And last Friday hundreds of people demonstrating against G8 labour ministers (the G8 is made up of the eight most industrialised nations of the world) being in town were surrounded and 170 arrested, the majority charged with "unlawful assembly." http://montreal.indymedia.org ** The controversial **Itoiz dam in Spain has been declared illegal** by the Spanish Supreme Court. The Court upheld its opinion that filling the dam is illegal, due to the fact that it would destroy three nature reserves. Previous rulings have however so far failed to stop the building of the dam. ** **Last weekend activists managed to storm the stage at the Annual get together of Bayer** in Germany to let the company know that their new venture into **Genetically Modified (GM) crops** isn't going to go unopposed. All the activists were removed by security, but not before they were given the chance to vote on a number of shareholder issues, as they all had share certificates. **Bayer, at the end of last year bought up biotech baddies Aventis Crop Science,** this acquisition will make them the leading company pushing for the commercialisation of GM crops in Europe. www.Bayerhazard.com ** Wales now has it's own bi-lingual Indymedia site at www.indycymru.org.uk ** **OneWorld** have set up a video website showing documentaries about global issues www.oneworld.net. Contributions welcome contact tv@oneworld.net ** **A-spire, the Leeds squatted social centre** is facing eviction next Wednesday. Events are running till then, including : Talks and Videos on International Resistance on Monday (6th) from 5pm, followed by a benefit gig, and an anti fascist speaker on Tuesday (7th) 07796 343 085 www.a-spire.org.uk ** **The Locomotive Works squat** (ex-Harvest Foresty shop, 1 New England Street) in Brighton, set up to oppose the Sainsbury's development is facing eviction on Tuesday (7th), see it before it's gone and lend a hand.

OH COME ON... I'M NOT PAYING *TOURIST* PRICES!

FINE. SO WORK OUT THE MINIMUM WAGE FOR TWELVE HOURS WORK IN *YOUR* COUNTRY AND PAY ME THAT.

Polyp

IT'S YER SCHNEWS SUMMER PARTY AND PROTEST GUIDE

MAY

5 Bass-heavy punky reggae bash with Restarts, Nomadix Roots, One Style + DJ Dave (Zion Train) 8pm-2am, Arsenal Tavern, 175 Blackstock Road, London N4. **5 Manchester Radical Bookfair** 1pm-5pm Merci, Bridge 5 Mill, 22A Beswick Street, Manchester. www.radicalbookfair.org.uk for latest updates! **6 Film: Incitement to riot** - packed with footage from all the best riots of the past, and a hard hitting soundtrack at 6pm; followed by **Film: New Kids on the Black Block**. London Action Resource Centre, 62 Fieldgate Street, London. **6 Radical Bookfair,** 11am-5pm, Exchange Community Centre, Sebbon Street, Islington, N1. **8 CITY meeting** CWU Building Edinburgh 7.30pm Edinburgh direct action groups get together www.EdinburghCITY.org.uk **8 Benefit gig for Kurdish Human Rights Group** . Wild Angels - live music plus comedy from Mark Thomas, Mark Steel, and others. The 100 Club, Oxford Street, London. 7.30pm **8 A Police Service for Northern Ireland?** Meeting on the 5th anniversary of Robert Hamill's death. Committee Room 10, The House of Commons, 7:30pm. www.hamillcampaign. freeserve.co.uk **9 'War against Hedonism' Party** in aid of Stop the War and CND DJs from London's best free parties playing house, funk and drum n bass.8pm-1am The Black Horse, 168 Mile End Road, London, free Indian buffet. £3/£2 waragainsthedonism@hotmail.com **9 Rock for Cuba at Night and Day,** 7:30pm, Oldham St., Manchester. £3. 1**0 No Sweat Comedy Cabaret** fundraiser for no sweat 'Indonesian workers' solidarity campaign. Starring Rob Newman and Attilla the Stockbroker, 7pm-late, The Bread and Roses 68A Clapham Manor Street, London. Tickets £15/£10/£5 07904 431 959 **10 Black Panther speaking tour and benefit gig** with Ashram plus DJ's, The Cumberland Arms, Byker Buildings, Byker 7pm £3/2. **10-12 Wind Generators and Solar Electrical Systems** - learn to run household appliances with wind and solar power. Redfield Community, Buckinghamshire. £150/100 all meals and accommodation included. Contact LILI, Redfield Community, Buckingham Road, Winslow, Bucks, MK18 3L. 01296 714184 www.greendragonenergy.co.uk www.lowimpact.org **11 Plan Colombia and its impact on human rights and the environment.** Two women speakers from the Colombia Solidarity Campaign talk about US military intervention in Latin America. News From Nowhere Club, The Epicentre, West St, (Leton Station) Free 020 8555 5248 **11 Sources of Radicalism** - the history of popular protest and radical social, political and cultural movements, Manchester. £7/£3, including lunch. Early booking advised. anne.morrow@man.ac.uk www.leftdirect.co.uk/sources.htm **11 Was your granny a Suffragette?** The Women's Library, Old Castle St., London. 020 8858 5545 **11 Fanclub, the anticonsumerist group**, at the Dundee Centre for Contemporary Art. www.fanclubbers.org **12 How can we save the countryside?** talk and discussion on the proposals of the Curry Report on the Future of Farming. £15 ncluding lunch, tea and coffee. 9.30am-6.00pm at Braziers Park, Ipsden, Nr Wallingford, Oxon. 01702 556600 agkipps@hotmail.com **12 Poole Skate Fest**, Baiter Park, trick competitions in Skateboarding, Inline and BMX with new music talent from Hip Hop to Punk 11am-8pm www.temptfate.co.uk **12 Speak Out Against Racism: Don't let the extreme right set the agenda**. Rally in Trafalgar Square, followed by march and human chain around Parliament. 1pm Trafalgar Square AA_R@compuserve.com **14 Invest in caring not killing!** Arab & Jewish women speak out against the holocaust in Palestine. Conway Hall, 25 Red Lion Square, London. 7pm £3/£1 020 7482 2496 http://women strike8m.server101.com **15 Prison activist and former Black Panther Robert King Wilkerson**, one of the prisoners known as "the Angola 3" will be speaking in Easton Community Centre, Bristol 8pm. www.marsbard.com/kebele **15 Benefit for Faslane Peace Camp/ Ploughshares** 8.30pm, Nice N Sleazy, Sauchiehall St, Glasgow. 0131 664 3231 **15 What's wrong with the war** - 'Not in my Name' and 'Greetings from Missile Street' Part of Tyneside Radical Film Festival at The Side Cinema, Newcastle Quayside 5.30 pm and 8pm 0191 2724635 radical.filmfest@tesco.n et **15 International Concientious Objectors' Day Ceremony,** Tavistock Square, London. 020 7424 9444. Temple of Peace, Cardiff, 12.30-2.30 pm 01446 774452 **16 'Zero de Conduite'** a film by Jean Vigo. Followed by discussion. Organised by Nought for Conduct Film Club 7.30pm Marchmont Community Centre Marchmont Street, London. £2/£1 07946 214590 **17 Anarchy's big problem.** Talk and discussion, London Anarchist Forum, 8pm, Conway Hall, Red Lion Square, London. £2 donation appreciated LAF@anarchic.co.uk**17-19 Knockengorroch festival** in the remote Galloway glen of the Water of Deugh, Scotland. Featuring Zion Train, Croft Number 5, Burach, Nusa, Trudge Euphoria and the Wallace Clan with DJ's from Eden, Tonque n Groove and Flying Rhino plus many more folk, roots and world musicians Also open stage, session tents, stalls, story-telling, sculpture park, a multitude of workshops and demonstrations of country crafts, fine food, real ale. Tickets £28.50 £25. Young children free. Free camping. 01644 460662 www.knockengorroch.org.u k **17-19 Wheaton Aston Festival** , near Telford, Shropshire. "We're a small, warm and friendly Festival and have great music - an eclectic line-up of music, song and dance, some familiar, some less so, but all of the very best. The Festival occurs within the village and as well as concerts, there'll be sessions, workshops, street activities and dancing, a French ball, craft fair, food available and a campsite near the village centre." Weekend ticket £27. (camping £3 per person) www.wheatonastonfestival.supanet.com **18 National rally and demonstration for Palestine** Noon Hyde Park for march to Trafalgar Square. www.palestinecampaign.org Coaches from Brighton 01273 329925 **18 HAG Cabaret benefit for the Cowley Club** 8pm, Ray Tindle Centre, Brighton £5 in advance from Peace Centre/£6 on the nite. **18 Stop ESSO Day II** The aim is to boycott every Esso garage in the UK. 0870 0109510 www.stopesso.com **18 Magpie 10th anniversary festival**, Saunders Park, Brighton. FREE **19 McLibel Anniversary of the 1997 High Court Victory!!** Leaflets from Veggies: 0845 4589595 **20 Join Christian CND in visiting Embassies of the nuclear weapons states** to ask how they are progressing in their "undertaking..to...accomplish...nuclea r disarmament." 020 7700 4200 **22 An introduction to the Trade Justice Movement**, led by Elened Jones of Christian Aid. 7 30pm Trinity Church Hall, Woodland Place, Penarth. 02920 711943, philipt@kingstonp.fsnet.co.uk **22-24 Temporary Autonomous Art 5** "Explosion of art and culture from the underground. Gallery space and cafe throughout with all contributions welcome. Thursday night is open access film night and Friday night host live music and performance." mid-day to midnight. Free. 07050 614804 http://randomartists.org **24 10th Anniversary of the legendary Castlemorton Free Festival** "Diverse meeting of all soundsystems and all walks of life - sometime around then but expect date to change, don't expect a venue unitil the last moment, if at all." www.guilfin.net/database/showevent.php3?ev_id=evINET1140 **25 Maidstone Green Fair**, Mote Park, Maidstone, Kent FREE. Two or three music stages and various incidental entertainments. Blues, folk, jazz rock and world, with markets, arts and crafts, kids activities, street theatre and workshops. Midday until about 9pm. **25 Campaigning For Peace**. A series of events looking at women's roles as campaigners, including Vera Brittain's pacifism, Greenham Common protests and women's role in Afghanistan. 12 noon The Women's Library, Old Castle St., London. 020 8858 5545 sam@chamerlain mcauley.co.uk **25 Samba Festival** hosted by Brightons Carnival Collective. All the UK's samba bands coming together in one place...arghhhhh **25 Sixth Global Boycott Procter & Gamble Day**. Last year activists in over 25 countries took 130 separate actions to highlight Procter & Gamble's cruel and unnecessary animal testing policies, conveying the message "If you buy Procter & Gamble products, you are actively supporting and sustaining animal testing." www.uncaged.co.uk 0114-2722220 **25 James Connolly/Bobby Sands commemoration**. March and rally starting at Seven Sisters Tube at 1pm and marching to Haringey Irish Centre, Pretoria Road, London. Wolfe Tone Society 020-8442 8778 www.wolfetone.org.uk **25/26 Permaculture Introductory Weekend**, Bowlers Community Nursery, 81 Crouch Hill, London. Full cost £80, but negotiable. 0845 4584697 naturewise1@hotmail.com **26 Save Titnore Woods**. Protest against threat to destroy ancient woodland. 2pm Titnore Lane entrance to Northbrook College, Durrington, Worthing (Goring-by-Sea railway station). Bring banners, music and food. www.worthinga 27.freeserve.co.uk **28 Annual Levellers Day**, Warwick Hall Garden, Burford, Oxon. "Space, Peace or War" speakers include Bruce Kent (CND), Lindis Percy (peace campaigner and base invader) £8. **29 Questioning Development** - 'Work in Progress' and 'Ancient Futures: Learning from Ladakh' Part of the Tyneside Radical Film Festival at The Side Cinema, Newcastle Quayside (near Crown Posada Pub, Dean St.) 5.30 pm and 8pm 0191 2724635 radical.fi lmfest@tesco.net The Bell Centre, Blaenllechau, Wales 11am- 11pm ffaldau2000@hotmail.com **31-2 June Feeling Of Life Festival** - 'somewhere' "A Celabration of 14 years of the scene representing music from the past and the present in a happy - safe environment inc systems from all over the U.K . A Party With True Free Party Spirit. www.dubbit-up.com **31-2 June Off The Tracks Festival**, Donnington Park, Isley Walton. The Levellers, Nagus, Prego, Andy Boles, Diego Brown and the Good Fairy Jerry Carnhill ~ Spokane. "The organisers of this intimate gathering are old festival heads steering clear of the money-motivated corporate trend. They aim to create an honest, friendly event for up to 1,500 people." Weekend tickets with camping £25 advance 01332 384518 www.offthetracks.co.uk

Up the Rector

An Essex Vicar who was under investigation by the police for an article about the September 11th attacks has had his case dropped. Rev. Nigel Cooper in his monthly letter to parishioners expressed his opinion that the 3000 people that died in the Twin Towers weren't entirely innocent. Both towers were full of people working for the banks that fund the IMF, who in turn cause 30,000 deaths a day in the southern hemisphere. He also thought Bush was a greater threat to peace than terrorism, and that the US response was more to do with fighting for an empire than for civilisation. One reader took offence to the article and contacted the thought police who obviously couldn't find anything wrong with the comments, and have discontinued their investigations.

Positive SchNEWS

Poolsbrook in Derbyshire is set to become the first village in Europe to set up a power station fuelled by methane piped from their rubbish tip to heat homes and generate electricity. The villagers set up a limited company and are raising the £2million they need for the project. The prices will be set by the villagers themselves at a meeting and the profit the company makes will be put back into community activities. It will cut the heating bills in half and drastically reduce CO_2 emissions. Brian Cave-from Poolsbrook heating development said "We have a high ratio of unemployed, single parent families and pensioners so affordable heat is vital to them."

Can-Can't

The Can Masdeu squatted social centre in Barcelona, which played a major part in March's massive protests against the EU summit, was surrounded by police on Tuesday. As SchNEWS went to press the centre was being blockaded by 14 vans and police are refusing protesters inside access to food, water and blankets. They have so far failed to evict the squatters because a judge has said doing so would endanger the lives of 10 people who are hanging from ropes in various parts of the building. Attempts have been made to get food and blankets to them, including one by a group of 15 women who tried to break the police line and a mass action involving 200 people that was violently dealt with by the police. Just to be nice they also prevented the people who were injured in the actions from getting any medical attention. People are arriving continually to Can Masdeu to show support. 120 people stopped the traffic in both directions on the Rhonda de Dalt (a major ring-road) for an hour in solidarity. Police are threatening to move the ropes that the people inside are suspended from if there are more attempts to get them food http://barcelona.indymedia.org

...and finally...

Steven Boffey has just landed himself one of the most environmentally destructive jobs in the West Midlands. Employed by Midland Expressway, the corporate crooks behind the new Birmingham Northern Relief Road (BNRR) (Britains first toll road); his job is to encourage 100,000 drivers a day to use their brand new spanking road. The catch is that they have to pay a toll for the privilege. The road will be built with private investment, and Boffey's job will be to ensure that his new bosses line their pockets whilst the local people continue to suffer from shit air quality.

SchNEWS tried to contact Mr Boffey to discuss the benefits of his road over say the spaghetti junction, but he was unavailable, undoubtedly having a laugh at our expense. Cos' with £400million of tax payers money being spent on widening the M42 near the toll road, to cope with increased traffic, rather than on public transport, the locals aren't going to have any alternative other than to jump in their cars. The BNRR 'M6 Toll experience' is due to open in 2004. Contact Mr Boffey to discuss his job on 0845 6013611. More info on opposition to the road at www.ds.dial.pipex.com/beep/bnrr

*AMEC the nasty construction company who are involved in the BNRR also are playing their part in the Yusefeli Dam project in Turkey. They are having their AGM next Wednesday (8th) and would love to see you. Protests are planned. Meet 10am Speaker's Corner at the Marble Arch End of Hyde Park. Contact 0207566 1681 kathb@foe.co.uk www.ilisu.org.uk

Disclaimer

SchNEWS warns all readers this Summer don't be a dope or let the grass grow under yer feet. For the latest blow against capitalism check out our stash of info for action. Honest.

SchNEWS

www.schnews.org.uk

New Age PEACE CONVOY

Neo Labour POLICE CONVOY

Friday 10th May 2002   Free/Donation   Issue 354

FESTIVAL PIED

"Society needs to condemn a little more and understand a little less. New age travellers? Not in this age! Not in any age!"
- John Major, 1992.

It was ten years ago this month when Castlemorton Common became home to the largest free festival this country had seen since the Stonehenge celebrations in the early eighties.

Travellers heading for the Avon Free Festival found themselves up against Avon and Somerset Police's all-new fun-stopping information-gathering 'Operation Nomad' with "dedicated resources…to gather intelligence in respect of the movement of itinerants and travellers and deal with minor acts of trespass." So people found themselves across the border heading for the picturesque Malvern valley where a truly amazing free festival sprung up with around forty thousand people partying for seven days and nights.

The Free Festival scene had been happening up and down the country since the early 70's, and this new explosion was a fusion of old style traveller culture and weekend ravers attracted to the soundsystems of DIY, Spiral Tribe, Bedlam and a host of others. One leaflet at the time explained "To be at one of these gatherings is to feel a surge of energy; to feel a people free from the restrictions of rip-off clubs, crap pubs, dumb shit security, money-mad promoters." Of course the authorities didn't exactly share this view and with the press whipping itself up into a frenzy ("Hordes of Marauding Locusts" and "These

Foul Pests must be Controlled" being a couple of classic headlines) - new laws we were warned, were just around the corner.

The authorities in particular seemed to be going gung-ho for a group of people who had pushed the free party boundaries for the past two years - Spiral Tribe. 13 people were nicked and put on trial for 'conspiracy to cause a public nuisance' with the judge promising two years in prison if they were found guilty. Thankfully they weren't despite a trial that lasted four and a half months and cost the taxpayer £4 million.

As a result of the free festival scene, mixing with the first stirrings of the road protest movement at Twyford Down and the M11, the Tory Home Secretary ranted about getting "Tough on rapists, tough on armed robbers and tough on squatters" a hotch-potch of a Bill was introduced into parliament - the most draconian ever to be aimed at alternative British culture. It's name - the Criminal Justice and Public Order Act 1994 (which SchNEWS was a part response to, but that's another story).

Pig Posse Payout

Fast forward 10 years. This year's Welsh Green Gathering has been cancelled for the second year running - thanks to objections once again from the cops. Last year Dyfed Powys police objected on the grounds that festival land would be contaminated with "human waste, diesel and cannabis." This year the

gathering, in the planning since June last year, was to take place in Margam Country Park, South Wales and all seemed to be going well. Until the Detective Inspector of Port Talbot police stuck his oar in and said he feared serious public disorder so £60,000 to police the crowd of just four thousand had to be coughed up. The Council, fearing a riot, cancelled the booking.

Er, public disorder at a Green Gathering? Maybe if you count people overdosing on lentil flapjacks or being trapped in dozens of deadly dream catchers or perhaps a pack of pedal-powered powder peddlers pelting police with a barrage of crystals. In fact, the event was going to be so riotous members of the Welsh National Assembly were planning to take part in green forums and the Centre For Alternative Technology along with other such axe-wielding maniacs were to busy themselves at the event promoting sustainable living. Not to mention the festival helping to restore the park and converting to solar power the presently disused road-train.

The Welsh Green Gathering is now seriously out of pocket and threatening to sue the Council. Organisers reckon the decision was linked to a yearlong direct action campaign against an incinerator in Swansea. Yesterday the incinerator was given the green light. Green Party spokesman Martin Shrewsbury commented "Port Talbot council are supporting an incinerator to poison us all and cancelling a festival about alternative sustainable energy."

Barricading for eviction at the entrance to the old Harvest Forestry building, on the corner of the site of the proposed development

SQUATTERS -
MAKING LIFE TASTE BETTER

The day SchNEWS hits the street the squatted community centre at the old Harvest Forestry organic shop in Brighton is due to be evicted. The centre, which has been open for two months and used as an info shop, occasional café, art space and for children's activities, was occupied in protest against the proposed Sainsbury's led New England Consortium's development due to be built there. The proposal includes a car park, two posh hotels, yuppie flats, inadequate key-worker bedsit style accommodation and, a massive new Sainsbury's.

There has been massive local opposition to this plan and residents have vowed to resist the eviction by barricading themselves inside and are willing to risk arrest. They have put out a call for Brightonians to come down to show their support for community centres not corporate developments - as early as you can get down to the ex-Harvest Forestry building on New England St (near Hobgoblin pub).

Party On

Glastonbury has now gone to the Mean Fiddler dogs, with licensing regulations stating that the same sort of surveillance techniques ironically first used against travellers ten years ago now will now be used at this year's event. So it's watch towers and CCTV and infra-red cameras for gatecrashers and ticket holders alike.

So what are we gonna do about it? Isn't it time to rediscover the free festival spirit? Perhaps keeping our shit together and looking after each other at Stonehenge again this year can be a start to build on. As Tash, a free festival veteran, told SchNEWS "People nowadays expect to pay their money and for everything to be provided. In the old festival days, people had to do things for themselves such as sorting out the infrastructure such as toilets and welfare."

Of course, the state has now all the laws it wants to deal with any unregulated fun, so we've got to be cunning and we've got to be organised. But if we are to once again break away from the bureaucrats, cops and corporate leeches then what other alternative is there?

* For more on Castlemorton and the history of free festivals http://tash.gn.apc.org/
* Party and protest throughout the summer www.schnews.org.uk/pap/guide
* Festival Eye out soon. Send £3 to BCM 2002, London WC1N 3XX (out end of May). www.festivaleye.com

Inside SchNEWS

Last Friday five of the seven WOMBLES had their charges thrown out of court. On Halloween last year the seven were walking to a party dressed in white overalls and Halloween masks when they were set upon by the cops and then nicked. Two were found guilty of threatening behaviour and were fined £100 each but both are planning to appeal.

The two who were found guilty answered police questions in custody, this was the only evidence that convicted them. Remember if arrested answer "No Comment" to all police questions.

Marchers at the Free Palestine March, London May 18th   Pic: Guy Smallman

U'WA, U'WOT?

The U'wa tribe of Colombia were celebrating last Friday, after it was announced at Occidental Petroleum's AGM that the company were giving up drilling oil on their ancestral land. According to Occidental, after spending $16 billion on exploration drilling they have decided there is no oil at that particular site. When Occidental's plans became clear in the early 90's, the U'wa became a symbol of resistance to oil exploration. Using tactics ranging from blockades at the drill site, lawsuits, shareholder resolutions and non-violent civil disobedience, the U'wa along with activists in over twenty countries have confronted Occidental and its major shareholders.

The U'wa at one point threatened a mass suicide if and when Oxy moved in to their mountains. The tribal leaders said that many would throw themselves off a high cliff in an act of mass ritual suicide. In a statement they said "the U'wa way of life is not negotiable" - an alien concept to corporations who believe that everything ultimately has a price. Unsurprisingly Occidental responded with the might of the US backed Colombian military who have violently repressed them and their supporters, killing activists and U'wa children in the evictions. Perez, President of the U'wa Traditional Authority said about the struggle, "the blood spilled will not go unpunished… It will be a bittersweet memory that will remain in the minds of those who participated in the most difficult moments of this process."

Occidental also finds itself centre stage in the growing scandal around the Bush administration's military aid proposal to hand over $98 million of U.S. taxpayers' money to defend the companies Caño Limon oil pipeline in Colombia, which runs through traditional U'wa land. Operations have been suspended since February because of intensive guerrilla attacks. This pipeline shows how oil drilling destroys an area - an estimated 1.7 million barrels of crude oil has been spilled since 1986, deforestation has occurred with forests cleared for oil exploration, production and roads, opening the forest to outsiders. The oil brought violence, with the Colombian military, leftist FARC guerrillas, right-wing paramilitaries and drug traffickers battling over resources.

The U'wa are still threatened by another oil company, Repsol. As Kevin Koenig, from Amazon Watch. said "this is an important victory and a real milestone in the larger struggle to win recognition and respect for indigenous peoples rights around the world. Unfortunately, until we address our society's addiction to fossil fuels by transitioning to renewable energy sources, the world's remaining pristine ecosystems and traditional cultures will continue to be threatened by unscrupulous oil corporations."

More about the connection between the oil industry, threats to indigenous populations and global climate change at www.moles.org/ ProjectUnderground/motherlode/ drilling/intro.html

SchNEWS in brief

Police last night declined to comment on whether **the 300-400 hardcore anarchist troublemakers** they warned of on May Day, had got on the wrong train and ended up at Millwall ** **DAAWN (Direct Action Against War Now)** have called for an anti-capitalist bloc at the Palestine Solidarity demo on Saturday 18th May. Meet 12pm at Speakers Corner. http://DAAWN.cjb.net ** There have been protests throughout Europe at the inclusion of the **Kurdistan Workers Party (PKK)** being added to the EU list of banned terrorist organisations. Yet they have given up armed struggle over the past years, and are changing its name! SchNEWS waits with baited breath to see if Turkey are added to the list for it's continuing military terrorism against the Kurdish people. www.khrp.org ** This Sat (11th) there will be **a mass trespass at Hatfield Moor** to protest against the commercial peat extraction. Only last week power lines mysteriously 'fell' down causing havoc in the peat mine. Meet 12pm, Tyrham Hall Hotel A614 south of Hatfield Woodhouse. 0778 778 2259 www.peatalert.org.uk ** On Sat 18th May there will be a demo against those **baby killers Nestle** at their UK HQ in Croydon 11am – 12 noon more info www.babymilkaction.org/press/ press6may02.html ** The **hotbed of anti-capitalism and socialism which is Surrey** is now publishing a monthly newsletter 'Black Star'. Offers of help call 07810 595392 or black_star_news@hotmail.com.** **The Subversive Sussex Walk** takes in rebellions, sabotage, squatting, etc. starts 2pm on the seafront outside the Old Ship Hotel, Sat 11th and 18th.

'You are free'   'I am free'

23

Positive SchNEWS

On Wednesday AMEC, the company that wants to build the Yusufeli dam in Turkey (SchNEWS 346) held its AGM at the Portland Hotel, London. This time though the activist shareholders outnumbered the non-activist shareholders, so armed with a share each, whistles and red cards they messed up the proceedings.

The plan was to have 3 different noise demos throughout the morning - so that everyone wouldn't be thrown out at once- and to ask some quality questions from the floor. The first noise demo started after about 20 minutes leading to a dozen people being thrown out. Another happened about half an hour later and led to more being forcibly evicted by the now pissed off security. Each resolution was easily voted down by the activists which meant the company would have to conduct a poll after the meeting.

Questions were raised about not only the Yusufeli Dam, but also the Chalillo Dam in Belize and the Bingley and Birmingham bypasses. One shareholder who had nothing to do with the protest stood up to berate the board for dragging the company into this sort of situation. These sort of demos serve as a warning to other companies that grassroots movements won't take environmental destruction lying down.

THE DRINKS ARE ON US

Veterans for Peace was started in 1985 by ex-soldiers and peace activists who dedicated themselves to setting up non-profit educational and humanitarian projects in countries torn apart by war. As they put it "We know the consequences of American foreign policy because once, so many of us carried it out. We find it sad that war seems so delightful, so often, to those that have no knowledge of it. We will proudly, and patriotically, continue to denounce war despite whatever misguided sense of euphoria supports it." Their latest project is to rebuild Iraqi water treatment plants that were bombed during Desert Storm. They are trying to raise more than $60,000 so that many Iraqi people can access safe drinking water. www.veteransforpeace.org

THUGS-IN-BLUE™

On May Bank holiday Irish activists held the biggest yet Reclaim the Streets party in Dublin, turning much of the city centre into a traffic-free party zone. That is until the thugs-in-blue™ put 24 people in hospital and arrested another 20, after repeated baton charges on a peaceful crowd. The protest started with a Critical Mass, which after causing chaos for 2 hours, met up with the mass of party people at the pre-arranged point. Here crowd barriers were d-locked together across the street to prevent the cops from following the now 1000+ carnival to the final destination. Two sound systems quickly set up and were joined by a samba band. At 4.30pm RTS activists pushed a broken down car, which they had bought and stashed nearby, into the party.

This was the cue for the pigs to steam in, batons drawn, but as they pushed people back someone threw a flare into the car, filling it with pink smoke and sending the pigs into a right tizzy. Lashing out with their batons they repeatedly beat one man while he was on the floor, attacked another who was on crutches and arrested people from Ireland Indymedia who were filming what was going on. Even a photographer from the Irish Independent was nicked after he refused to hand over his camera, while others from the corporate press had the batteries taken out of their cameras rendering them useless.

After a tense stand off, the crowd and a sound system moved off with the cops baton charging them and making more arrests, including on one occasion a man who had nothing to do with the protest and was just walking past. Further up the road riot vans drove at high speed at the front of the demo and tooled up cops charged into the crowd smashing skulls and beating people while they were on the floor. One youngster, who eyewitnesses put at about 14, was attacked by five thugs-in-blue™ leaving him with a cracked skull. At 9pm more people gathered at Pearce St. police station to protest at the brutality and in solidarity with those inside.

For more info check out www.indymedia.ie

JOLLY ROGERS

This Sunday (12th) at 1pm, A-Spire the Leeds squatted social centre will be leaving the Concord Street squat in a giant pirate ship setting sail for the city centre. Once there they will be giving out free coffee outside Starbucks, free info outside Borders and free clothes outside Harvey Nicks. As they say "They gentrify our areas, we will downgrade theirs."

www.a-spire.org.uk

...and finally...

With the American war on terrorism in full swing and busy checking out anyone who dare question the status quo, then it's reassuring to know that the Denver Police Dept. have been playing their bit to crackdown on dissent for years. They've been busy gathering 'evidence' on their local 'criminal extremists.' Dodgy characters like Sister Antonia Anthony, a 73-year-old Franciscan nun and the American Friends Service Committee, a pacifist Quaker group that has won the Nobel Peace Prize for its advocacy of non-violent social change! These 'criminal extremists' as the police like to call them, now have extensive files with lists of members, information about being seen at demos, physical descriptions, home addresses, places these do-gooders frequent... you get the picture. The American Civil Liberties Union are now suing the police for all this unconstitutional spying, and trying to get a court order prohibiting the Denver cops from making any more nosey-parky files. Info: www.aclu.org.

Disclaimer

SchNEWS warns all festival goers not to let the pigs treat ya like sheep. Honest boyo!

Subscribe! Keep SchNEWS FREE! Send 1st Class stamps (e.g. 10 for next 9 issues) or donations (payable to Justice?) Ask for "Originals" if you can make copies. Post *free* to all prisoners. SchNEWS, c/o on-the-fiddle, P.O. Box 2600, Brighton, East Sussex, BN2 0EF.
Tel/Autofax +44 (0)1273 685913 *Email* schnews@brighton.co.uk *Download a PDF of this issue or subscribe at* www.schnews.org.uk

Common Ground

The spring of 2002 saw the 10th anniversary of the now legendary Castlemorton Free Festival, the biggest and most notorious free party ever to take place in the UK. The anniversary was celebrated on Jubilee weekend with a massive teknival on Steart beach in Somerset. At least 50 rigs and 10,000 party people gathered on the beach for a 5-day party to commemorate the creativity and determination of the original sound systems, and to celebrate 10-years of underground rave culture. At a time when most of the country was being bored shitless with television specials about the anniversary of the coronation, the Castlemorton anniversary was a powerful reminder that real culture grows from the ground up, and that to stay alive it has to constantly mutate.

It's important to remember Castlemorton because that was where the battle lines were drawn up for many of the struggles of the last decade. The government clampdown that followed the festival, which began with the arrest and prosecution of members of Spiral Tribe for their involvement in the event and culminated in the 1994 Criminal Justice Act, made it clear that the authorities saw the emerging free party community not as just a nuisance but as a political threat. In the following article, one of the defendants in the Castlemorton trial explains the history, and the connection of the free party movement to other struggles to reclaim public space for public use.

Rightly or wrongly, the names Castlemorton Common and Spiral Tribe have become synonymous with the biggest illegal free party in Britain to date. But behind the outrage and glamour of the front-page headlines of the time, there was another, more important story unfolding. To understand what actually happened we must go back and look at events leading up to that weekend in May 1992.

Spiral Tribe were a ragtag collective of musicians, artists, rappers, DJs and cyber-punk types who bounced about the country in a convoy of black, jelly-moulded trucks, putting on free parties. They identified with the primordial, all-connecting symbol of the Spiral - a representation of the asymmetric shape of nature and the turbulence in its fractal flow. With no door policy (and

Tas

often, no door), the parties set out to create, and maximise, free social space. Bringing into being a place of contact for all people - all tribes. Actively resisting the rightwing regime built upon violence, private ownership of land and profiteering, the Spirals aligned their artistic and musical spirit with a relentless campaign of events that for brief (yet intense) moments took back the land into the realms of common shared experience [1].

In the decade immediately preceding the Spiral's whirlwind tour of the British Isles, it was business as usual with UK plc violently oppressing free gatherings, protests and nomadic life styles:

1981, 5th Sept: Peace Camp at the US base at Greenham Common starts, and survives several violent eviction attempts and serious abuses from troops.

1982: The meandering convoy of free festival types is named "The Peace Convoy" after travelling from the Stonehenge Free Festival to join the peace camp at Greenham Common.

1984: The Last Stonehenge free festival before the English Heritage ban.

1984: Nostle Priory near Leeds. The violence against the Peace Convoy steps up.

1984-85: The Miner's strike. Police use unprecedented violence and make 11,000 arrests.

1985 Feb: Rainbow Fields Village protest camp, Molesworth US base. Violent eviction involving over 2,000 troops and police.

1985, 1st June: Battle of the Beanfield. 140 vehicles smashed and the men, women (including pregnant women) and children are viciously attacked by 1,000 police officers following "Operation Daybreak".

1986: New Public Order Act gives police more control over public gatherings and greater powers to evict trespassers from land.

1986, June: Stoney Cross, authorities launch massive attack against travellers, impound all vehicles and attempt (unsuccessfully) to snatch 47 children from their parents [2].

1989: Chief Superintendent Ken Tappenden, of Miner's Strike fame, starts national database on illegal parties and organisers.

Tash

1990, March 31st: The Poll Tax Riot.

1990: The introduction of the Bright Bill, which increased fines for throwing an unlicensed party from £2,000 to £20,000 and 6 months in prison.

The Spirals staged their first party in October 1990. By June 1991 they had a mobile rig and had pulled off events at some of the most sensitive areas in the country - namely the displaced Stonehenge Solstice Free Festival at Longstock and another at Stoney Cross. A flyer from the Tribe at the time read, "We are here to re-connect the Earth."

From then on the Spirals held an event every weekend (weekends that often overlapped into weeks) and by February of 1992 they'd taken a string of cheeky, high profile venues. This helped to boost morale on the festival scene, despite the jack-booted oppression it had suffered.

To the Spirals, building a creative culture independent and out of reach of the parasitic commercial cartels was of the utmost importance. "The real energy in the rave scene comes from the illegal parties, the pirate radio stations and from white label 12 inch singles that bypass the music industry altogether."[3] But the police and their paymasters where already well aware of this, "...cracking down on illegal raves while allowing nightclubs to stay open longer – was intended to undermine the basis of the scene"[4].

Undaunted, the Spirals beat the shamanic drums, liquefying air with gurgling techno and skipping breakbeats. New life germinated in decaying urban voids. Inner city kids were teleported into the deep and mystic green of the British countryside. "The Spirals understood [the countryside] as a politically charged environment. A historic arena for a clash between rebels and oppressors ...that free parties were shamanic rites which could reconnect urban youth to the Earth with which it had lost contact, thus averting imminent ecological crisis."[5]

But the contempt they displayed for authority and consumer culture was making a mockery of the bureaucrat's clampdown on unlicensed events. And, as is always the way when corrupt politicians run out of plausible argument, they resorted to violence. The Territorial Support Group were sent in - an anonymous paramilitary squad, their faces masked and ID numbers removed.

The TSG surrounded the Spirals' crowded warehouse in Acton Lane, London, on Easter Monday. They beat everyone who tried to enter or leave. Panicked partygoers barricaded themselves into the building, but after a bloody two and a half hour siege the police breached the concrete wall and beat everyone inside to the ground, including a pregnant woman. One boy who had tried to escape onto the roof was thrown off by officers breaking both his arms and legs. Outside victims were frog marched past three gloating fat-hats. Two were British; the third wore a US police chief's uniform. He was heard to say "In the States we would have cleared the building in twenty minutes"[6] To this day there has been no explanation as to who this man was and why he was there.

The next day the Spiral's convoy was escorted out of London by a low flying police helicopter. There were no charges brought against them – it had been a terror attack, pure and simple.

Shaken and bruised, with most of their equipment smashed, the attack had left the Spirals with a strengthened resolve. The following weekends they staged huge gatherings on Chobham Common, Surrey (another Digger stronghold), Stroud Common and then the Cotswolds where, for Beltane, they teamed up with Bedlam to stage a 10,000-strong outdoor event at Lechlade. Then on again to a party in Wales. But as the Spirals played in a honeycomb of ancient mines, another trap was being devised for them in the bowels of Whitehall.

After regaining some of their former strength, they decided to go and take it easy at someone else's party for a change. So the next morning they set off to the Avon Free Festival.

On route there was a phone call. Avon had been quashed and JCBs had dug ditches around the site. Hundreds of vehicles were being moved off by police but all was not lost: the caller was a Bedlam scout just ahead of the evicted convoy (according to one of Avon

Free's organisers, it was, "more like a 35 mile traffic jam" [7]), and the Bedlam crew had managed to get on to the Common at Castlemorton.

The Spirals cut across country and by the afternoon they were approaching the Common. Smiling Policemen waved them on to a track that ran under the strangely abrupt slopes of the Malvern Hills, to a deep blue lake in a flooded quarry. On either side were beautiful expanses of flat springy turf – too perfect.

The Spirals swung their vehicles into a wide circle and joined the other systems and circuses that were already rigging up. Great heaps of speakers were dumped out of the trucks. The infamous instrument of G-force exhilaration, the Gyrocycle, was set up centre stage. Black flags and banners with silver designs of crop-circle circuitry were hoisted high. Terror-strobes strategically positioned. And still the convoy of travellers rumbled onto site.

Soon the music was on (from all directions) and the crew could relax in a summer haze of bassline vibrations. But for some there was an uncomfortable feeling about the place. It's difficult to say whether it was just a delayed reaction to the hammering they'd taken at Acton Lane, or a sense of impending doom triggered by the eerie sight of smiling policemen. But there was no turning back, the convoy was still pouring onto site – in fact it continued throughout the weekend, swelling numbers to 50,000 plus.

The festival was cool - untold systems all putting on a great show, ravers, travellers, tourists, TV crews, a shed-load of liberated battery hens, skinny dippers, daredevil divers, and even a few police (but they were too busy enjoying the sunshine and playing rounders to bother anyone). Military jets buzzed the site (why do they do that?) and a police helicopter filmed, in minute detail, every scrap of rubbish being picked up by the people below – evidence that was used later in the court case to prove how clean the site was kept. At the time a Spiral-type commented to the press: "Since we've been here there's been more taken out of the ozone layer by jets and helicopters than any damage that we've done" [8].

By the end of the weekend everyone was exhausted, the rig was blown, the back drops in tatters, the vehicles' batteries flat. Time to go chill. No such luck. As the Spirals drove off site they were ambushed by police and arrested for conspiracy [9].

Everyone was locked up, along with some innocent bystanders who got caught in the swoop. Vehicles, equipment, money, personal effects - all were confiscated as evidence. After being formally charged and sent before a magistrate they were released awaiting trial. They walked out of the police station with nothing - so they camped on the station steps for almost two weeks.

In that time a man drove up to them in a large white Rover and handed them a piece of paper. On it was a pencil sketch

of riot police kicking a pregnant woman who was lying on the ground, underneath was written "Oh my god what have we done?"[10]. Later, on the steps of the court of the committal proceedings, Superintendent Clift (the chap who's jurisdiction the Common was under) came up to the accused and said, "I just want you to know that I don't agree with what is happening to you here, this is a political stitch up"[11]. Evidence he later gave (from his hospital bed) was of great help to the defence. But the case would take two years to get to crown court.

In that time the Spirals wangled a small record deal to buy a recording studio, which they installed as a community resource in a converted showman's trailer. They got a rig and vehicles together and disappeared into Europe to start the Teknival movement and numerous independent record labels. When the case finally got to Crown Court it became one of the longest running and most expensive cases in legal history, lasting four months and costing the country £4 million. Before the end of the trial, the judge told the defendants that if they were found guilty, he would be giving them each two years in jail. But the jury (bless 'em) found everyone "not guilty!"

Despite the vindication of the Spirals, the huge police investigation and court case finding nothing criminal about the Castlemorton gathering, UK plc, hell bent on protecting it's interests, went on to install the monstrous Criminal Justice Bill. An act that has not delivered the intended deathblow to the dissenting masses, but has instead catalysed a generation into action and inspired a blossoming of creative resistance.

Footnotes: [1] At that time 87% of land in the UK was in private ownership. Marion Shoard, This Land Is Our Land, '87, Paladin, p.120 **[2]** From conversations between the author and Spider from Circus Normal. **[3]** A Spiral in Melody Maker, 06/06/92 **[4]** Mathew Collin on Chief Superintendent Ken Tappenden's role in setting up the police data base on illegal parties, in Altered State, '98, Serpent's Tail, p120 **[5]** Ibid.p.203-4 **[6]** Witnessed by author. **[7]** John quoted in George Mckay's Senseless Acts of Beauty, '96, Verso, p.120 **[8]** The Guardian 28/05/92 **[9]** Later modified by the CPS to causing a public nuisance, "We prefer to call it causing a public new sense." said a Spiral quoted in Lowe and Shaw's Travellers, '93, Fourth Estate, p.169 **[10]** Witnessed by author. **[11]** Witnessed by author.

'These Boots Are
Made For Walkin''
- Nancy Sinatra

www.schnews.org.uk

Friday 17th May 2002   **Free/Donation**   **Issue 355**

AMERICAN WET DREAM

On Tuesday the UN Security Council unanimously voted to overhaul the economic sanctions against Iraq – a move so radical it was immediately condemned by the sanctions-busting group Voices in the Wilderness, four of whom are currently in Iraq distributing medical supplies. They called the resolution "a deadly fraud that will do little to alleviate the on-going humanitarian crisis."

Forget the cruel tyrant Saddam Hussein (once supported by the West when he towed their line), what about the ordinary people of Iraq? Who, thanks to these economic sanctions imposed on them by the West for nearly 12 years have seen 500,000 of their children die. Denis Halliday and Hans Von Sponeck, who were both at one time responsible for the UN's humanitarian programme in Iraq, both resigned in protest at what the sanctions were doing. Last year they wrote, "The death of 5-6,000 children a month is mostly due to contaminated water, lack of medicines and malnutrition."

And it will be the ordinary Iraqi people who wil again be suffering if President Bush and his cronies use their so-called war on terrorism to start bombing a country, that has already been bombed back to the dark ages. The Pentagon's 'medium case scenario' is that a war on Iraq could condemn to death more than 10,000 civilians. But this could be even worse if, as journalist John Pilger puts it, the Americans "implement their current strategy of 'total war' and target Iraq's electricity and water."

Not that we should forget that American and British aircraft have, in a largely forgotten war, been bombing Iraq week-in week-out, for more than four years. The Wall Street Journal reported that the US and Britain faced a "dilemma" because "few targets remain." "We're down to the last out-house" bemoaned a Pentagon official.

Still, the US insists that action is necessary because Iraq has been defying United Nations resolutions and represents an imminent threat to the world, and to the U.S. in particular. Excuse us, but defying UN resolutions and ignoring international treaties is what the Bush administration does best, with Bush making it clear that he will not honour any treaty if he reckons it might harm U.S. interests. In fact just last week Bush pulled out of the International Criminal Court – you know that radical idea to create the world's first permanent tribunal to prosecute people for war crimes, genocide, and other crimes against humanity (see SchNEWS 326).

Bush and his militaristic government argue that they have to bomb Iraq because Saddam won't comply with United Nations weapons inspectors. So best forget that the Bush administration denied international inspectors access to U.S. chemical and biological weapons-related facilities because it might violate "commercial interests".

Still the truth slipped out earlier this month when US Secretary of State Colin Powell said "regardless of what the inspectors do, the people of Iraq and the people of the region would be better off with a different regime in Baghdad." Not that

SchNEWS could disagree with that – a lot of countries would be better off without dictators and corrupt governments - it's just the US wants another Saddam Hussein, but this time one who'll do what they say.

Meanwhile Cuba is now being added to the US hit list, because hey the US right has always hated Cuba. In a speech entitled 'Beyond the Axis of Evil', Under Secretary of State John Bolton pointed the finger at Cuba because of the country's advanced biomedical industry. Forget that Cuba's advance biomedics has more do with their better-than-the-US Health Service and their policy of sending doctors to help third world countries (so hey, let's add them to the list). Plus Castro's visits last year to three "rogue states" accused by the US state department of sponsoring terrorism: Iraq, Syria and Libya. "States that renounce terror and abandon WMD [weapons of mass destruction] can become part of our effort," Mr Bolton said. "But those that do not can expect to become our targets."

So it's back to that old "you are either with us or against us" mantra. Each new stage of the war against terrorism makes it clearer that the real aim has little to do with what happened on September 11th and

TAKING THE PEACE

Israeli Human rights organisation B'Tselem has just published a report showing that Israel has illegally taken over 42% of the West Bank since they first occupied the area in 1967. Although built-up Jewish settlements occupy only 1.7% of the land, various excuses, including seizure for 'military needs', for being 'Abandoned assets' and even an obscure 19th century Law about 'state Land' - has been used to take over the rest. Although the Land Grabbing is a violation of international law and of the Palestinians' human rights it is upheld by the Israeli high court. The settlers are not only more privileged than the Palestinians, they are treated better than other Israelis. In 2000, settlement councils received 165% more land than councils in other territories.

American Wet Dream cont...

more to do with what the American military describes as "full spectrum dominance". A document from the US Space Command spells it out "The United States will remain a global power and exert global leadership...Widespread communications will highlight disparities in resources and quality of life – contributing to unrest in developing countries.." So while everyone else must abandon those weapons of mass destruction the US this week got the green light from Russia this week to go ahead with its plan for the National Missile Defence Project or Star Wars II to keep us all in check (SchNEWS 307).

Rotten Apple Pie

When it comes to Israel of course then it's a different tune. Israel has been defying U.N. resolutions for more than 30 years. No action has been taken against their bloody and illegal rampage through Palestine. Hey, they were after terrorists. They face no sanctions for blocking a United Nations fact-finding mission into military action at the Jenin refugee camp. In fact their two fingers to the world earned them a serious reprimand in the US Senate who er… voted for an increase in military aid to Israel.

Is this because the Palestinian civilians, just like the Iraqis and the five thousand Afghani civilians killed in the last holy war against terror, are what John Pilger calls the Unpeople. "The killing of Iraqi infants, like the killing of Chechens, like the killing of Afghan civilians, is rated less morally abhorrent than the killing of Americans."

America's war on terrorism is just another word for imperialism – and Iraq is currently head of its wish list of countries where a new head of state needs to be put in place, one that will be a lot more open to Uncle Sam's way of doing things.

* John Pilger's new book The New Rulers of the World will be published by Verso soon. Read more of his articles at www.johnpilger.com

* The sanction busters will be giving a report on their visit next Friday (24) at Conway Hall, Red Lion Square, London (nearest tube Holborn) 7.30pm. Contact: Voices in the Wilderness 08454560282 www.viwuk.freeserve.co.uk

* Bypass the corporate media: www.znet.org www.alternet.org

PALESTINE

March for Palestine this Saturday Assemble 12 noon Speakers' Corner (Marble Arch tube) Why not join the Anti Capitalist Bloc, not hard to spot, look for the only part of the march surrounded by Cops.

More than 1000 activists from around the world have been in Israel on solidarity actions since the army began its latest series of attacks against Palestinians. There'll be another group of peace observers going from the UK this summer and there'll be training weekends in Manchester, London and possibly Scotland and Newcastle for people intending to go, or planning to be part of support teams organising actions in this country or doing press work. The weekends will include non-violent direct action training, information on the area and opportunities to talk with former volunteers.

Marcia Tubbs, a British citizen recently in Palestine said "In the prison we were in, 3 Palestinian medical workers were also detained. You could hear people screaming as they were beaten. We can make such a difference by just being there as international observers, doing what the UN and governments are unwilling to do, protecting the basic human rights of the Palestinian people." More info: uksolidarity@yahoo.co.uk, or write to ISM, box 29, 22a Beswick Street, Manchester M4 7HR. www.palsolidarity.org

* On Monday, about 15 activists did a solidarity action against the Israeli embassy in London. They were beaten back by Israeli military police using golf umbrellas! On the same day another group did an action against the Israeli Tourism Information office and the office of El-Al, the Israeli airline which has been deporting international activists.

* "Dispatches: State of Terror" is being repeated on Channel 4, Sunday 19th 2.45am Dispatches reporter Deborah Davies was one of the first journalists to enter the Jenin refugee camp after the Israeli Army's brutal offensive. The programme looks at the real victims of this 'anti terrorist action.'

* Yigal Rosenberg and Yair Hilu, who signed an open letter along with more than 120 other high school seniors and refused to do military service in the Occupied Territories, are back in prison. Each of them has been imprisoned four times, 21 other objectors are currently in prison. They are asking for people to write to them and show support. c/o The Forum in Support of Conscientious Objectors, POB 41199, Jaffa 61411, Israel. matzpoon@yahoo.com www.indymedia.org.il/imc/israel/

SchNEWS in brief

Park Nook Protest Camp is back. After a campaign to give the woodland in central Liverpool 'town green' status was lost, trees are now being cut and the camp needs people, tat, rope etc. Picnics on Sun 19th & 26th May. 0780 3609271. ** **London action resource centre** have an open evening with protest singer David Rovics, table-tennis and refreshments. 18th May, 4.30-10pm. LARC, 62 Fieldgate St. 020-7377-9088 www.londonarc.org ** Debate **The Problems of Anarchy** tonight (17th) at the London Anarchist Forum, Conway Hall, Red Lion Square, Holborn 8pm ** **Not this Time- The Story of the Simon Jones Campaign.** The revamped film has its premier showing introduced by Mark Thomas, Tues 21st 7pm Ritzy Cinema, Brixton. £5/£3. If you are interested in organising a showing of the film email action@simonjones.org.uk ** A protester against the **Newchurch Guinea Pig Farm** in Staffordshire had to go to hospital after being punched by a neighbour of one of the farm's workers. The police, despite kn owing who was responsible for the attack, have made no arrests. Now there's a surprise! www.guineapigs.org.uk

PINK CASTLE

The Pink Castle occupied on the site of a proposed GM maize crop near Weymouth was surrounded by 30 cops on Thursday morning. The farmer brought some tractors in and some protestors managed to lock themselves onto them (four were arrested for aggravated trespass), however it seems that the farmer had borrowed some more as he had six tractors and managed to plant the crop. Last week the local TV crew had been down looking for Swampy (of road protest fame). Despite the castle denying he had been there the TV said that protestors had refused to confirm or deny if he had been there! More people are urgently needed and occupiers of the castle say they intend to decontaminate the field. More info: 07773 640159 www.sayhi.to/thecastle

* Earth Crimes - a newspaper giving the low-down on the biotech baddies produced for April's Convention on Biological Diversity (See SchNEWS 346) is available now, send SAE to GEN 1 Archway Resource Centre, 1a Waterlow Road, Archway London N19. 020 7272 1586.

Inside SchNEWS

An international day of action is taking place on 5th June in solidarity with the 41 people who have so far been sent to prison after the protests during last summer's EU Summit in Gothenberg.(see SchNEWS 310). Many of the convictions have been based on very dodgy evidence and sentences are extremely harsh. Organisers of the day of action are calling for people to protest outside Swedish embassies, consulates or to do other similar actions in solidarity with the prisoners, and to call for the halt of the criminalisation of summit protesters. www.manifest.se/upprop

* **Evgeni Novozhilov,** a human rights activist and anarchist sympathiser has been sent to a mental hospital in Krasnodar, on the false charge of practising a "hoax about an act of terror". Two years ago he wrote an article in the local paper about the atrociites the Russian army committed in the 1994 Chechen civil war, since then he has been harassed by the FSB (former KGB). He has been imprisoned since last October, for an indefinite period, after the FSB tapped one of his phonecalls where he made a vague reference to skyscrapers and planes. This repression of free speech is akin to the soviet era where forced treatment in mental hospitals was a notorious anti-dissident tool. Evgeni feels very isolated and desperately wants to make contact with other people. Contact him through his mother, by writing to:

Evgeni Novozhilov, ul. Ignatova 51, kv. 105, 350061 Krasnodar, Russia. Evgeni speaks English, German and Swedish. Read more about the case at www.anarchistblackcross.org

* A release fund has been set up for **Mark Barnsley**, the framed anarchist prisoner from Sheffield. Mark will have served 8 years this summer, and is expected to be released but will be homeless. His case has only just gone before the Criminal Cases Review Commission so he'll need money to continue his case from the outside, travel expenses etc. Send cheques/Postal Orders (made out to "Mark Barnsley Release Fund") /train vouchers (and anything else useful you can think of!) to Mark Barnsley Release Fund, Sumac Centre, Box CC, 73 Beech Avenue, Nottingham, NG7 7LR.

* This weekend **Emma Murphy-Ellis** who was sentenced to four months imprisonment in Portland, Oregon for blocking a road in front of a forest that was being destroyed is celebrating her 19th Birthday. Send letters of support and birthday cards to:Emma Murphy-Ellis Clackamas County Jail 9000 SE McBrod Milwaukie, OR 97222, USA.

* **Haven Distribution** who supply books to prisoners have a new catalogue, available to prisoners for a second class stamp. They are also very skint and need donations. Haven Distribution, 27 Old Gloucester Street, London WC1N 3XX.

DON'T BUY THE WAR TALK

Brighton Briefs

The **Harvest Forestry** squat saw off Bailiffs on Monday, and expect eviction soon, keep up to date at the links page of http://deltatraffic.co.uk/off ** **Magpie** have their 10th Birthday Bash at Saunders Park, noon-8pm 18th May ** For the **StopEsso** day of action (18th) every Esso station in Brighton will be targeted - start noon - and a mass gathering at Hollingdean Road Esso 3pm. Info on demos nationwide 020 7354 5708, www.stopesso.com** **Ex-Black Panther Robert King Wilkerson** speaks about the case of the Angola 3 who were framed for organising the local chapter of the Black Panther Party for Self Defence in Angola (Louisiana state penitentiary). Robert talks about 29 years behind bars, and the two men still imprisoned for a crime they did not commit! The Queens Head (opposite Brighton train station), 21st May, 7pm ** **Brighton Animal Rights Campaign** have a demo against Proctor and Gamble outside Sainsbury's on London Road, 1pm 25th May.

...and finally...

Cops doing it doggy style

Because of continued stop and searches by police with sniffer dogs on trains in Australia, activists have come up with a novel way of confounding the canine cops. Jokers (or is that tokers) have been spraying carriages with bong water and making the dogs, who have been trained to sniff out pot, go mental every time they board a train thus leading to commuters being frisked by over zealous cops. The railway companies have denied that the late arrivals have been due to grass on the line. More info: www.nswccl.org.au

Disclaimer

SchNEWS warns all readers not to attend any illegal gatherings or take part in criminal activities. Just stay at home, watch TV and go on endless shopping sprees, filling your lives with pointless consumer crap, then you'll feel happy. Honest.

CHECHNYA

This week saw one of the most senior Russian officers facing trial for the murder two years ago of Kheda Kungayev, an 18-year-old Chechen girl. This is the first trial of a Russian soldier over any atrocity that has occured in Chechnya since Russia invaded in 1999.(See Schnews 334) After getting drunk the general and his men seized Kheda Kungayev. She was taken from her home, bound in a blanket, to the colonel's sleeping quarters. What is clear from the initial post mortem is that Kheda was then stripped and beaten, before being raped and finally strangled.

Although the colonel does not deny the killing, he claims that he strangled Kheda in a moment of rage during a night-time interrogation, which is being fully supported by the State's psychiatrists. He is claiming temporary insanity and if the court accepts this then he can walk free.

While large-scale fighting in Chechnya nominally ended in 2000, Russian forces continue to detain hundreds of people without charges. Pressure from the UN and human rights organisations have forced the Russian authorities to introduce some improvements, including the formal opening of investigations of war crimes although they have refused to allow designated UN human rights investigators into Chechnya. Unsurprisingly most abuses remain uninvestigated which could expain why only one soldier has been brought to trial when thousands of civilians have been killed by Russian forces.

For more info see Human Rights Watch www.hrw.org/europe/russia.php

Subscribe!

Keep SchNEWS FREE! Send 1st Class stamps (e.g. 10 for next 9 issues) or donations (payable to Justice?) Ask for "Originals" if you can make copies. Post *free* to all prisoners. SchNEWS, c/o on-the-fiddle, P.O. Box 2600, Brighton, East Sussex, BN2 0EF. *Tel/Autofax* +44 (0)1273 685913 *Email* schnews@brighton.co.uk *Download a* **PDF** *of this issue or subscribe at* www.schnews.org.uk

weekly SchNEWS
www.schnews.org.uk

Friday 24th May 2002   Free/Donation   Issue 356

BLOOD ON THE TRACKS

"The money he was getting was danger money. As far as I am concerned my son was murdered." - *Mrs Mungovan.*

Michael Mungovan had only been working on the railways for three days when he was sent to work unsupervised near Vauxhall station in south London. He was securing a section of track when he stepped into the path of a train travelling at 50 mph. The 22 year old student died instantly.

During a two week inquest that ended on Monday, the jury was told that Mr Mungovan did not have a valid track safety card, his colleague on the day of the accident did not have the relevant supervision skills and the experienced worker who Michael had been assigned to work with was suspended at the time. The jury at the inquest decided that Michael was "unlawfully killed" and the police will now be reopening a criminal investigation.

The death of Michael mirrors that of Simon Jones, who was sent to work as a docker with no training and killed within two hours. Michael had been in a classroom for only one and a half days' training and given just half a day on a rural single line before being sent to work on one of the busiest junctions in the country. His death once again highlights the hazards of untrained casual workers being given dangerous jobs with little training. Jobs that not so long ago would have been done by a highly skilled railway union workforce.

In a submission to the House of Commons Transport Select Committee last year, the RMT rail union said that the number of permanent staff employed on the tracks had fallen from 31,000 before privatisation to between 15,000 and 19,000. The union's former general secretary, Jimmy Knapp, told MPs that many of them were being replaced by casual workers recruited in pubs and clubs. "There are now 100,000 individuals that have got personal track safety certificates. Who these people are I would not know, and who looks after them and sees that they are doing the right things I would not know, but that is a staggering figure."

Michael was employed by temp agency McGinley Recruitment Services, who in turn were being used as subcontractors by Balfour Beatty Rail Maintenance Ltd, who were in turn paid to maintain the line for Railtrack - an illustration of the long chain of command now operating on the railways. As for the devastated family, they said in a statement that privatisation of the railways had led to a "low regard for human life".

MAKING A KILLING

The Transport Select Committee attacked Railtrack's recruitment practices because it doesn't actually employ the gangs of engineers who keep the railways running, nor does it train them. No, that's left to companies like Balfour Beatty and Jarvis who at the weekend blamed saboteurs for the recent Potters Bar rail crash

CRAP ARRESTS OF THE WEEK
For having the wrong views...
New York animal rights activist Andrew Stepanian was recently sentenced to 6 months in prison after he asked one too many questions on a routine traffic stop. Watching a friend being beaten and arrested, he dared to speak up, an act which, unsurprisingly, ended with his arrest and beating. For his trouble, Andy received prison time for resisting arrest and obstructing government authority, "obstructing" being defined as getting in the way of a police officer's fist, apparently. This type of harassment is not new to Andy, a dedicated and well-known local activist in the fight against Huntington Life Sciences.

Andy has lived with a video surveillance camera pointed at his driveway since January 2000 and was told by a judge during his sentencing that he participates in "a level of activism not welcome in our society." ! Maybe that explains why another six months has been tacked onto his sentence for speaking at a demo back in March. Write to Andy at: Andrew Stepanian, NCC 0200 1777, c/o Nassau County Corrections, 100 Carman Avenue, East Meadow, NY 11554-1160, USA.

where seven people died.

Just six days before Potters Bar, Jarvis were successfully prosecuted by the Health and Safety Executive (HSE) for "unsafe practice during railway maintenance work." They were fined £7,000 for nearly running over several track workers, with the HSE railway inspector commenting, "The company's failure...led to people who were not competent being expected to do jobs they were not able to properly discharge." Not

Making A Killing cont...

that this is the first time Jarvis has been in the dock.

In July 1999 they were fined £7,000 after a worker lost an eye because they had failed to carry out a proper risk assessment and had too few staff working on the track. A year later they were fined £500,000 after two separate train derailments because it "failed to check the track before trains were allowed to run, exposing employees and passengers to risk of injury." In October 2000, 41 year old Mark Meadowcroft was killed by a train while working for Jarvis. Still, forgetting about all that, Railtrack's replacement, Network Rail, has appointed Jarvis as a "technical adviser" on safety issues!

As for Balfour Beatty, not only have they been found guilty by the HSE on numerous occasions for causing the death and serious injury of its workers, but they are also the proud winners of a record £1.2 million fine

after part of the tunnel they were building on the rail link to Heathrow airport 'collapsed'. And we're sure readers will be pleased to know that both Jarvis and Balfour Beatty are part of the consortiums wanting to take over the London Underground.

So what will happen now? Yesterday the Crown Prosecution Service announced a new investigation into the Paddington rail crash with a view to bringing corporate manslaughter charges. And hours before Monday's verdict, Transport Secretary Stephen Byers promised to examine the role of contractors and sub-contractors who work on railway maintenance. "A new relationship is needed…one based on best value, not lowest cost, providing a quality maintenance and renewal programme for railway track that puts the interests of the travelling public first."

Nice words - but surely private companies are always going to be in it for the money and cut costs to make

a few extra bucks. As Colin Chalmers from the Simon Jones campaign told SchNEWS "Profits are all these companies and their directors think about. If getting untrained students to do dangerous jobs makes more money than employing skilled workers, they'll do it. Casualisation kills – but it's good for dodgy companies' profits. These companies will only stop when we kick up enough fuss and make sure that directors start going to jail."

* 'Not this time – the Story of the Simon Jones Memorial Campaign (2002 update)' is out now. They are hoping to organise showings of this 25-minute film, with speakers, across the country in July. If you're interested in arranging a showing, email: action@simonjones.org.uk. For copies of the film send a cheque for £5 to Simon Jones Memorial Campaign, PO Box 2600, Brighton BN2 0EF. www.simonjones.org.uk

SchNEWS in brief

The **Harvest Forestry** squat opposing the Sainsbury's development in Brighton are still waiting for the baliffs to show-up. Support needed call 01273-680499 ** Next Monday (27th) the **Bhopal Medical Appeal** hold a talk on how to make corporations liable for the environmental and social disasters they cause. In particular Dow Chemicals, the company that caused the chemical disaster at Bhopal. Function room, Queens Head (near Brighton station). 07762265427 ** **Hereford now has its very own anarchist group -** herefordanarchists@hotmail.com ** Training weekend for people going on **International Solidarity Movement Direct Action** programmes in Palestine 1-2 June in Manchester, uksolidarity@yahoo.co.uk ** **Womanzone** - discussions, self defence films, socialising and creche. Sat 25th noon-10pm, The London Action Resource Centre, 62 Fieldgate Street, E1. 020 7377 9088, fieldgate@gn.apc.org ** May 29th is **International Day of Action Against Depleted Uranium**. Action planned in the Manchester area. 0161-273-8293 www.cadu.org.uk ** Biotech giants **Monsanto** are taking action to shut down the spoof

website www.monsanto.org, check it out now to get the low down on their dirty dealings. ** The field in Dorset that is being squatted by the **Pink Castle** has now unfortunately been two thirds planted with Aventis GM maize. But, the castle remains and actions are taking place to dig up the seeds. Brave knights are still urgently needed to help defend the castle. 07733 640159 www.sayhi.to/thecastle ** A group has recently formed to support asylum seekers arriving at the planned **Bicester Accommodation Centre.** They have their first meeting at the Rainbow Room, Bicester Methodist Church Sheep Street, Sunday 26 May, 4pm - 6pm. BicesterRefugeeSupport@btopenworld.com

'Are you sure this is the only possible route?'

Going Bananas

More than a thousand Ecuadorian banana workers have been on strike at the plantation complex Los Alamos since May 6. On May 16, armed men broke through the picket line of non-violent, unarmed workers, taking 25 hostage. The hostages were eventually freed by their colleagues, though two workers were wounded by shotgun fire. The gun-toting thugs were apparently employed by presidential candidate Alvaro Noboa, whose company exports Bonita brand bananas and is violently opposed to the fledgling union organizing. FENACLE, the national union federation seeking to organise the workers, is saying that solidarity action from trade union and human rights organisations is urgently needed.

Positive SchNEWS

Sustainability Works is a new website for anybody interested in sustainable housing. It's packed full of references and ideas on what sustainable housing is all about, and provides support for organisations wanting to develop their own sustainable housing policy. www.sustainabilityworks.org.uk

The Culture of Capital

NO CON 2008

2002 2008 EEK

I CANNOT BEAR THIS DEMAND AFTER TWENTY FIVE YEARS OF Punk

London by the sea the BANE of ENGLAND

Censpiracy Chief Culprit

Peter Poole

Royal Briefs

Celebrating 25 years of punk (oh and the Queen's Jubilee) 1 June **Jambouree against the Jubilee** Bristol Centre (Fountains/St Augustines Parade) Contact: black_cat_collective@yahoo.co.uk ** Also on the 1st **Never Mind the Jubilee** The Zion Housing Co-op in association with Hebden Bridge Cricket Club. Third Annual Cricket Festival with live music, fun, frolics, stalls, food and drink. Salem Fields, Hebden Bridge. £2 Tel: 07960 055846 ** And the **Anti-Jubilee Street** Festival. At the Radical Dairy 47 Kynaston Rd., Stoke Newington, London. 020 7249 6996 1pm onwards theradicaldairy@hotmail.com ** 2-4 June **Up the republic! Stuff the Monarchy!** A long weekend of music, debate, videos, talks, practical sessions and direct action at Clwb y Bont, Pontypridd, Wales. For more details of events, accommodation, crêche and tickets, contact PO Box 661, Wrecsam, LL11 1QU Tel 02920 830 029 stuffthemonarchy@yahoo.co.uk

Lethal Lessons

Welsh schools in Newport and Llandudno are being sold off for a profit and the schools are then being rebuilt on toxic landfill sites.

Ysgol John Bright School in Llandudno is being rebuilt on a former gasworks, which, among other things, is contaminated with arsenic, cadmium, lead, mercury and asbestos. And then there's the gas itself—apparently there are "explosive levels" of methane still on the site, which have not yet been removed. And just to brighten things up a bit, the site is also on a floodplain, which adds to the danger of chemicals escaping. And what, you may ask, will become of the original school buildings? Why they'll be replaced by a shiny new Asda superstore, of course.

Durham Rd School and Nursery in Newport will be rebuilt on the site of an old municipal dump once used by GM giant Monsanto. It's a load of rubbish, but not just any old rubbish - this is rubbish with added ingredient "X" - a mystery gift from Monsanto. Nobody seems to know exactly what was dumped there, and there is no official record of it, but when soil samples were taken there were "some small explosions".

Locals have been assured everything will be peachy once a "protective membrane" is put over the site, sealing in the toxins, but as John Martin of Glebelands Action Group says, these membranes are notoriously ineffective. "This is just window dressing," says Martin. "I don't think they can make it safe." An alternative, relatively uncontaminated site had been proposed for the new school, but after soil testing, Newport council decided to sell the clean site to housing developers and put the school and accompanying nursery on the toxic waste dump.

Both Newport and Llandudno councils have avoided debate, fudged information and ignored local opinion. In the words of the Corporatewatch website, they are "As transparent as mud and as accountable as God."

So why have schools been shoved onto land considered unfit for housing? Who gains from this cavalier treatment of children's futures? Local campaigner Lesley McCarthy has claimed there are "Three levels of Exploitation"- first, the companies that made the mess (Monsanto), second, the companies profiting from building the new schools (McAlpine), and third, the companies that buy up the old school sites (Newport housing developers and Asda) for more information, go to: www.corporatewatch.org/news/private_sector_may_15.htm

Kernow of Knowledge

It's hard to believe that last month 20,000 people took to the streets of **Penzance** and there's not even been a whisper of news about it beyond Plymouth. The protest, the largest in Cornish history, was in opposition to the proposed closure of the Accident and Emergency department of West Cornwall Hospital, which according to officials is no longer economic. Closure of the A+E would mean patients would have to travel 35 plus miles to Truro for emergency treatment. A week after the march, a dozen protesters stripped down and blocked the front of the hospital in another attempt to get their message out, but were again ignored apparently because there weren't enough 'fit birds'. A decision has yet to be made on the future of the hospital, but campaigners have vowed they will do whatever it takes to make sure they keep their A+E unit open.

*SchNEWS VocabWatch Kernow=Cornwall

Embargo Farrago

The US embargo on Cuba, which has been in effect for more than 40 years, is set to continue after a speech made by George 'Dumbya' Bush just before he jetted off for a fund raising tour of Florida. Incidentally, Miami has a large population of anti-Castro Cuban-Americans who are big supporters of the Republican Party. Bush said that there's no way the embargo would be lifted until elections are held there, which is pretty ironic on two counts. Firstly, the U.S. treats Saudi Arabia, Kuwait, China and Pakistan as their good buddies but in all of these countries elections are as rare as Accrington Stanley FC winning the Champions League. Secondly, cast your mind back to the US elections in 2000, where in Florida, 26,000 votes for the Democrats were not counted leading to Bush becoming president. Double helpings of hypocrisy anybody?

Subscribe!

"I've come to meet the head of the family" Alternative Jubilee Street Party London 3rd June

UN-Independence Day

After an independence struggle that lasted for 24 years and claimed 200,000 lives, East Timor became an independent state on Monday. Just how independent it is though is pretty hard to figure out, considering that their currency is the US dollar, and that most donor countries won't fund the new state unless the money goes through the World Bank. They've also been forced to sign away their oil and gas reserves, the most valuable national resource, to Australia. Australia negotiated a deal with Timor over the oil in which Timor stands to get 90% of the profits on resources taken from a joint Australian/Timor area. Sound good? Take a closer look at the fine print and you find that the richest oil and gas reserves are outside this area and so will be taken over by Australia. So Timor is getting 90% profits of bugger all while Australia gets to take resources from within what should be Timor's maritime boundaries.

This may have had something to do with the fact that it was the UN and not the East Timorese Government negotiated the deal. All that Mari Alkatiri, the Timorese prime minister, got to do was sign. Most Timorese don't even know their new nation's resources have already been signed away. More info visit www.etan.org, or www.melbourne.indymedia.org

...and finally...

SchNEWS has heard some corkers in its time, but **Councillor Woolsey Smith of the Democratic Unionist Party** (Ian Paisley's party) in N. Ireland has got to win a prize for the biggest dumb arse of the year. In the six counties, cycle paths are outlined in green, the road junctions, as ever, are painted white, while the double yellow lines are unsurprisingly painted yellow – which all together make the colours of the Irish flag, green white and gold. According to Councillor Smith, this stunning fact shows bias to the Nationalist community. When the Department of the Environment heard of this 'complaint', they thought it was a belated April Fool's prank until they were assured that Woolsey was being quite serious. Now, some members of SchNEWS have at least one time after a mash up party/festival been a tad worse for the wear, but never have they been paranoid about road markings. So Woolsey Smith, if you're reading this, for your own sake start taking some chill pills before the men in white coats come to take you away and lock you up in a padded cell with the leprechauns.

Disclaimer

SchNEWS warns all old buffers with one track minds if ya get side-tracked on the wrong side of the tracks start making tracks before you lose track then you'll be right on track. Honest.

Keep SchNEWS FREE! Send 1st Class stamps (e.g. 10 for next 9 issues) or donations (payable to Justice?) Ask for "Originals" if you can make copies. Post *free* to all prisoners. SchNEWS, c/o on-the-fiddle, P.O. Box 2600, Brighton, East Sussex, BN2 0EF.
Tel/Autofax +44 (0)1273 685913 *Email* **schnews@brighton.co.uk** *Download a* **PDF** *of this issue or subscribe at* **www.schnews.org.uk**

WAKE UP! WAKE UP! IT'S YER BIT OF NUKIE

weekly SchNEWS
www.schnews.org.uk

Friday 31st May 2002   Free/Donation   Issue 357/358

There are two sides to the Kashmir conflict...

...And both of them need weapons

KASHMIR SWEATER

"24,000 people, mostly children, die from poverty every day. This is the true terrorism and it is aided and abetted by politicians from rich, privileged and powerful countries who, in the cause of profit and reigning respectability, are salesman of death." - *John Pilger.*

We're sorry dear SchNEWS readers to interrupt your enjoyment of the World Cup and the right royal knees-up, and we know that for most of us it's a very long way away, but it looks like, a nuclear war could be just around the corner.

With a million battle-ready soldiers facing off against each other on the India-Pakistan border and nuclear warheads at the ready; India is talking of a "decisive victory" whilst Pakistan rattles its nuclear sabre by carrying out missile tests as the rest of the world looks on, strangely powerless. Neither Pakistan or India seems to care that a nuclear war could see 12 million dead and 7 million wounded in the space of a single hour – an instant slaughter unprecedented in the history of mankind.

Still, we in England can be proud of the role we have played. No, not by the last minute diplomatic visits by the Foreign Secretary but by our generous arms dealings. In 2000 the Government approved nearly 700 export licenses to India and Pakistan, showing how we haven't lost our sense of fair play by flogging weapons and military equipment to both countries. Is this what Neo-Labour meant when they talked about an 'ethical foreign policy' when they first came to power?

Hawking Jets

In January, as the two countries prepared for war, a 'Presidential' Blair arrived in the subcontinent on what was called a "peace mission" – which coincided with the UK flogging 60 Hawk jets to India for a billion pounds – some peace there. Three weeks later, the British High Commission in New Delhi threw a party at an arms fair for a group of arms salesman licking their lips at the Afghanistan and Kashmir crisis.   In fact so keen has the Blair government been to exploit this opportunity of war that a British official has the full time assignment in New Delhi of "defence supply."

As for our Foreign Secretary calling on the two countries for restraint, Defence Minister Geoff Hoon showed good old British reserve (or hypocrisy) when he recently told the Defence Select Committee "There are clearly some states who would be deterred by the fact that the United Kingdom possesses nuclear weapons and has the willingness and ability to use them in appropriate circumstances... They can be absolutely confident that in the right conditions we would be willing to use our nuclear weapons". Which makes all of us at SchNEWS Towers sleep a lot more soundly at night.

So even if our boys don't bring back the World Cup, we can at least all be proud of the fact that this country is still up with the best in the world (second behind the good old US of A) when it comes to selling weapons to anyone who wants them, especially if they are on the brink of war.

CRAP ARRESTS OF THE WEEK

For naming children…
Nine families in the Turkish town of Izmar have been charged with being "a tool of propaganda" for the Kurdistan Workers Party (PKK) for the treacherous act of giving their children traditional Kurdish names. In its tyrannical fight against the PKK, the Turkish government has drawn up a list of banned Kurdish names, even though some of the names, such as Helin and Baran, are common in Turkey and are used by Turks as well as Kurds. And while another case, held just one day earlier in the town of Dicle, saw similar charges against seven parents dropped, the Izmar families are not so lucky - it's likely they'll be forced by the courts to rename their children!

20th Century Kashmir

"The leaders of India and Pakistan have now appropriated to themselves, as others had done before, the power that was God's alone to kill mountains, make the earth quake, bring the sea to boil, and destroy humanity." - *Eqbal Ahmad, political activist and writer.*

As the British Empire crumbled British forces withdrew from the Indian subcontinent, leaving a country divided, primarily on religious grounds, into India and Pakistan. At that time Kashmir was said to be part of India, but this has been contested ever since. The major stumbling block has been religious, as Kashmir's population is predominantly Muslim, which sets it apart from the Indian population which is predominantly Hindi.

In 1947 a United Nations resolution called for a referendum in Kashmir, but it was never carried out, the probable reason being that the Indian government feared the population would support Kashmir's unification with Pakistan.

This lack of any decision over Kashmir's sovereignty has made it the obvious place for Pakistan and India to play out their differences, with Kashmir becoming a part religious part political football cum time bomb.

Over the last 11 years around 30,000 people have died in the Kashmir conflict and what happens there is at the heart of the continuing tension between the two nations. Since the attack on the Indian Parliament building in December 2001, this tension has grown considerably with India accusing Pakistan of supporting terrorist groups; while Pakistan, in turn, pledges its support for Kashmiri freedom fighters, proving that one state's terrorist is another's freedom fighter. There have been three India/Pakistan wars since 1947, the difference this time round is that both sides have nuclear weapons.

1 in 10

It has been 25 years since the Peace Tax Campaign was established, encouraging people to withhold 10% of their taxes from the government, roughly the estimated amount that is spent on the military in the UK. One man who is refusing wrote in an open letter to the Inland Revenue "withdrawing financial support for the war seems to be the only means of objecting to the bombing... Every week, civilians including children are maimed or killed by unexploded cluster ordinance left in Kosovo by American and British forces more than two years ago. Their use in Afghanistan is unforgivable and I won't pay for it." Peace Tax Campaign 0870-7773223 info@conscienceonline.org.uk

Positive SchNEWS

Grants are now available towards installation costs of solar panels. By applying you could save yourself between 40 and 65% on total installation costs. For more information see www.solargrants.org.uk or call the Application Helpline 0800-2983978

According to the Campaign Against Arms Trade, the price of one Hawk bomber is roughly the amount needed to provide 1.5 million people with fresh water for life.
* Stop the Arms Trade Week: 8-16 June organised by Campaign Against Arms Trade. This year the focus is on the public funding of the arms trade - both the £760m of government subsidies per annum as well as the estimated £1 billion of local authority investments in arms trade companies. For an info pack email: chris.cole@caat.demon.co.uk or call 020-7281-0297 To check out your favourite arms companies operating in the UK see www.caat.org.uk.

* 13-18 June Trident Ploughshares Disarmament Camp, outside Aldermaston Atomic Weapons Establishment near Reading, Berkshire. Aldermaston was recently involved in nuclear weapon tests in America and they want to carry out more tests in Britain to refine and develop the current bombs ensuring they will have the biggest bang! 0845-4582544 www.gn.apc.org/tp2000

* Bypass the Corporate Media: http://india.indymedia.org

* Recommended reading: John Pilger 'The New Rulers of the World' (Verso 2002). Salman Rushie 'Midnight Children'.

Inside SchNEWS

Tomek Wilkoszewski, a Polish student, is currently serving 15 years in a Polish jail after been framed for murder. Tomek, who was studying in Radomsko, was subject to regular attacks from local Nazis who started fights with people that didn't come from the town. During one of these fights, those being attacked decided to defend themselves and one of the Nazis died after bleeding to death whilst waiting for an ambulance. Tomek was accused of the murder after a flawed trial. He was sentenced to 15 years whilst the Nazi's involved in the incident received only 8 years each. Tomek has been refused parole.

His supporters now want the president to look at his case. In the meantime, they would like to raise funds for a lawyer who may be able to help make conditions in jail better for him. Write to (in English preferably) Tomek Wilkoszewski, Zaklad Karny, Ul. Orzechowa 5, 98-200 Sieradz, Poland. The 25th June is a day of action for Tomek Wilkoszewski and the campaign is asking people to protest outside Polish Embassies on the day. www.tomek.most.org.pl

*A protester at this years May Day who was arrested for allegedly throwing a bottle at police urgently needs witnesses, otherwise he could be facing 6 months in prison. The alleged offending plastic bottle was in fact a harmless punctured football. If you saw the incident please contact the SchNEWS office or email kubla.khan@ntlworld.com

www.cleansurface.org

PROTEST CAMPS

For those of you who love nothing more than a dirty weekend... in-between partying at all the lovely festivals, get yerselves down to one of these camps set up to protect beautiful areas, even if it's just for a day or two:

Friarton Rd, Perth, Scotland

URGENT HELP NEEDED - Police are due on Monday 3rd June.

A protest camp - with a treehouse in a willow - has started, fighting to stop a small woodland on Friarton Rd, Perth from getting turned into a roundabout for a new tescos store. Police are due on Monday - so get up there NOW. Contact 07753808709 crusty_bob@hotmail.com

Park Nook, Liverpool

Planning permission to build luxury flats on Park Nook in Liverpool has been granted following a 3 year legal battle. Chainsaw men started to cut down trees earlier this month until the site was re-occupied by people opposed to the destruction. The site is now squatted with a camp and 24hour presence. There are still a couple of treehouses left and plenty of trees to build other treehouses. Eviction is imminent and people are needed now www.parknook.da.ru 0780 3609271

Nine Ladies, Derbyshire

For the last two years the nine ladies anti-quarry campaign has prevented the destruction of Stanton Moor hillside in the Peak District National Park.

There are also natural springs that supply water to the local village. If the proposed quarry is allowed to go ahead, this would have a disasterous impact on the area. Tel: 07974 049369 web: www.nineladies.uklinux.net

Peaceful Camps

If you want to help fight the war machine, there are some camps in Britain that are a thorn in the side of the military:

Faslane Peace Camp, Clyde, Scotland

The Camp celebrates its 20th birthday in June this year! This permanent camp has over 20 residents from Scotland, England, Wales, Finland, Belgium, Canada and the Netherlands with visitors from around the world stopping by to stay for a few days or weeks at a time. There are 11 Caravans, a Bus, a Tepee, a Bender, a Tree House and various sheds and self-built structures. The purpose of the camp is to oppose nuclear weapons and to live an alternative lifestyle to that of the mass of British society. Britain's nuclear weapons system is 'Trident' four submarines with nuclear warhead missiles based at Faslane Naval Base. The Peace Camp is on the east verge of the A814 road, which leads to HMNB Clyde and beyond. FPC is therefore visible to all traffic coming towards the base from the direction of Helensburgh. The camp is about 30 miles west of Glasgow, by the Gareloch, a river Clyde estuary sea loch. Faslane Naval base is on the Gareloch. Contact: 01436-820901 www.faslanepeacecamp.com

Nine Ladies camp

Menwith Hill, Yorkshire

The Women's camp at Menwith Hill spy base, near Harrogate North Yorkshire, a US base spy base is still going despite an injunction against anyone camping there. More women are urgently needed to camp or visit. WoMenwith Hill Women's Peace Camp, P.O. Box 105, Harrogate. HG3 2FE. Yorkshire CND 01274-730795 or cndyorks@gn.apc.org

Fylingdales' Star Peace Camp

The Star Peace Camp is a new permanent peace camp outside Fylingdales spy base, in the North York Moors. If the US have their way the base have their way will soon play an important part in the their National Missile Defence policy also known as 'Star Wars'. The camp is based at Ellerbeck to the east of the main entrance. People are welcome to visit or stay, but must come self-sufficient. There's also a Party on the Moor (14-15 June), public meeting on 14 June followed by a walk to Fylingsdale for a rally there on Saturday 15 June. 0845-4588366 www.tridentploughshares.org

Modified Camps

Not only are there camps to save the countryside and fight the war machine but also camps opposing GM crops:

Pink Castle, Weymouth

Protestors, who put up a pink castle on the site of a GM maize crop near Weymouth are still there despite a farmer recently turning up with the police in order to plant GM crops,. Within hours of the seeds being sown, at least twenty locals were seen digging the freshly sown seeds from the ground. This has continued with daily visits by people of all ages. Knights urgently needed. www.sayhi.to/thecastle 07773640159

Munlochy GM Vigil, Scotland

Camp next to a field growing genetically modified oil seed rape. It was set up soon after the GM seeds were planted and now has planning permission to remain until August 2002!. The camp has been the focus for the campaign for a GM free Scotland. A substantial amount of the GM crops has now been damaged. Contact Munlochy GM Vigil, The Layby, By Roskill Farm, Munlochy, Ross-Shire, IV8 8PAl. 0781-330-7337 jacko@roskill.fsnet.co.uk or munlochyvigil@tiscali.co.uk. www.munlochygmvigil.org.uk

It's yer SchNEWS Summer

June

The Nestlé sponsored Hay-on-Wye Literary Festival (31 May - 9 June) is in trouble as writers like Germaine Greer and Will Self have pulled out in protest over the involvement of Nestle. The World Health Organisation estimates that 1.5 million infants die each year because they are not breastfed. Nestle's baby milk marketing campaigns in Third World countries are a major cause of women choosing powered milk over breast. www.babymilkaction.org/pages/hayonwye.html **1 Halifax Green Fair**, Piece Hall, Halifax Check out the Generator X Wonky Weather Tour and find out all about climate change **5 International day of action for Gothenberg Prisoners**. In Solidarity with the 41 people who have so far been sent to prison after the protests against the EU Summit in Gothenberg last year. www.manifest.se/upprop **7 Benefit meal for Mark Barnsley and the Anarchist Black Cross**. 3 courses - pay what you can 7.30pm at Bradford's 1in 12 Club. 01274-734160 **7-11 Earth Spirit Festival Spring Awakening Camp**, near Tunbridge Wells, Kent. Music, dance, kids stuff, crafts, healing, camping, eco forum, workshops. £75 01273-685553 **7 So Lost In Music**, Sherwood Forest, Nottinghamshire. Dance fest. 1pm-6am £43.25 www.wayahead.com **7-15 Faslane Peace Camp 20th Birthday celebrations** outside the Trident nuclear submarine base. 01436-820901 www.faslanepeacecamp.com **8 Strawberry Fair**, Midsummer Common, Cambridge. FREE. SchNEWS favourite one day festie, where you'll find us sitting by the river drinking pims and eating strawberries. 01223-560160 www.strawberry-fair.org.uk **8 Hackney Stop the War film Screening** of "Not in My Name" followed by a public discussion at the Rio Cinema. 4.00pm, 107 Kingsland High Street, London E8. £2.50/£1.50 07979-066447 hstwc@hotmail.com **8-9 World Development Movement Conference**, Institute of Education, London with John Pilger, our mates the World Trade Organisation and others. 020-7737-6215 www.wdm.org.uk **8-9 International Solidarity Movement Training for Summer Campaign in Palestine** "ISM participants will visit Palestine this summer in solidarity with the Palestinian people. We will carry out peaceful protests and non-violent actions against the military occupation, and we will live and work with families in the refugee camps." uksolidarity@yahoo.co.uk **8-16 Stop the Arms Trade Week** www.caat.org.uk **10-13 World Food Summit**, Italy www.italy.indymedia.org **12 Direct from Palestine 'Frontiers of Dreams and Fears.'** at The Side Cinema, Newcastle Quayside (near Crown Posada Pub, Dean St.) 5.30pm and 8pm. 0191-2724635 radical.filmfest@tesco.net **12-14 Sustainability in Education** The fifth International COPERNICUS Conference in Sweden will examine how we can further incorporate sustainability into higher education. Goteborg, Sweden. www.mls.miljo.gu.se/COPERNICUS/ **13 March and Rally for Palestine**. 1pm Speakers Corner, Hyde Park, then march to Trafalgar Square. Organised by Muslim Association of Britain www.islamevents.com **15 Albion Community Arts Trust benefit night,** Norwich Arts Centre to help fund the Earlham Park Festival. 7.30pm-midnight, £5/£4 www.albionarts.org **15 Heavyfest II** with Sloth, Evil Kneivel and The Sex Maniacs. 2pm-late. The 1 in 12 club, Bradford £7/£6 01274-7344160 **15 Justice for Palestine** - No war in the Middle East. 10.30am Whitworth Park, Wilmslow Road, Manchester. 07760-224580 / 0161-2738283 **15-16 Leamington Peace Festival** FREE! www.peacefestival.org.uk The Midlands premier free festival with stalls, bands and workshops. Held in the Pump Room Gardens, Leamington Spa. **15 National Protest at Harmondsworth Detention Centre**. Protest to kick off the Refugee Week of Action 12-2pm. Outside the Detention Centre, near Heathrow. Bring banners, whistles, drums and ballons. 07960-309457 info@defend-asylum.org **1522 Week of Action in Support of Migrants, Refugees and Asylum Seekers** info@barbedwirebritain.org.uk/info@defend-asylum.org/ info@ncrm.org.uk/ncadc@ncadc.org.uk **14 Electronic Civil Disobedience Action.** A virtual sit-in as part of the campaign to close down Huntingdon Life Sciences www.huntingdonsucks.com/ecd.html **14-16 Middlewich Folk and Boat Festival**, Cheshire. Two dedicated stages with stuff like Fairport Convention, Lindisfarne and Isla St Clair! £55. www.middlewichfolkandboatfestival.com **15 SK8+** Springfield Park, Hackney - hip-hop, skate-metal and graffiti art. Free. www.stokenewingtonfestival.co.uk **16-22 Stoned 2002** "Environmental arts and healing festival." Only £145! www.stoned2002.co.uk **17-18 People and Planet Summer Festival**. A student festival for action to end world poverty, defend human rights and protect the environment. Braziers Park, Oxfordshire £10/£12 01865-245678 www.peopleandplanet.org/summerfestival **17-20 Eurosatory Arms Fair** at Villepinte, Paris France. www.caat.org.uk **17-23 Refugee Week**. www.refugeecouncil.org.uk **19 McLibel Anniversary of the 1997 High Court Victory!!** Leaflets from Veggies: 0845-4589595 **20-21 Dartford Festival**, Central Park. FREE Very diverse festival including music, dog shows and the Dartford half marathon ! Tel 01322-343961 www.dartfordfestival.co.uk

Stonehenge Solstice

The stones can be accessed from 8pm 20th June, last entry at 4.30am on 21st for sunrise at 4.53am, stones close at 7am and car park at 1pm. English Heritage Solstice Hotline 0 870 3331186. Peace Stewards are urgently needed to help out on the night (see website for details). A site for a park up after the solstice has been sought but this has been hampered by police. The police have promised to shut down and confiscate equipment of anybody who tries to have a free party. Talks are underway for their to be a legal free party after the Solstice next year. www.summersolsticecelebration.org

21 'Woomera 2002' a video from Australia receives its UK premiere. 7pm Tower Room, Conway Hall, 25 Red Lion Square, London. Followed by a discussion. www.chilout.org.uk/events.htm **21-22 EU Summit Seville, Spain** www.nodo50.org www.antiue.net **22 Cambridge Anti-Capitalist Street Party** 2pm Castle Hill for critical mass bike ride and Midsummer Common at same time for people on foot. Wear anti-capitalist colours (red/black/green/pink n silver), bring music, food to share, footballs, games etc. **22 Privatisation and war - what next in Colombia?** 6.30pm Conway Hall, Red Lion Square, London.. Speakers include Alexander Lopez, former President of SINTRAEMCALI Plus Music and Colombian food. £10/£5 07950-923448 colombia_sc@hotmail.com **22 Gatecrasher,**

Party and Protest Guide

Turweston Aerodrome, Brackley, Northamptonshire. 15 hours for £50. 0870-1210121 www.gatecrasher.co.uk **22 Porton Down. Rally against animal experimentation**. 01980-629692 **23 Camden Green Fair,** St James Gardens, Camden. London. 12-6pm **24-26 World Bank Annual Conference**, Oslo, Norway www.indymedia.no www.oslo2002.no **26-28 G8 Meeting, Kanannaskis, Alberta, Canada**. Protests planned http://g8.activist.ca www.alberta.indymedia.org

28-30 Glastonbury Festival SOLD OUT www.glastonbury-festival.co.uk News from Guilfin: "Mean Fiddler, who organise Reading in such a methodical and efficient manner ARE involved ... the local council insisted on them being in charge of site infrastructure. Reports suggest they get 20% of the net profit now, rising to 40%. They are not in charge of the actual festy. Yet. The Traveller's Field is apparently a big no-no ... they were more complaints about that than anything else last time. If a big party goes off outside the fence this time, the council are threatening to imprison Eavis." Open letter from Michael Eavis on why people shouldn't jump the fence. www.glastonburyfestivals.co.uk/michaelsletter.html Stuff about the Mean Fiddler security www.guilfin.net/reports/?id=rwINET941 This will make you puke - VIP's helicoptering into the festival. www.flyglastonbury.com Latest is that Guilfins Ambient Lounge, Squall and the Greenpeace stage have been refused tickets. Rumours of free festies gathering pace...we will keep you posted. (SchNEWS 340).

28 Terrorism - mapping the new legal framework. A one-day conference organised by Justice at The Hatton, Hatton Garden, London. 020-77626437 rallen@justice.org.uk **29-30 Diaspora free festival**, Kew Gardens, London. Noon-9 pm 020-7456-0404 www.culturalco-operation.org **29-30 South West Permaculture Convergence** at Plants For A Future in Blagdon, Devon. 01208-872963/07813-067250 www.pfaf.org

---

WOT?

On Tuesday, May 21st at a conference for Australian accountants, a representative of the World Trade Organisation (WTO) announced that his organisation was going to dissolve and reform, and begin to assist the world's poor. The Australian accountants, after the initial shock had worn off, soon came around to the idea of "giving something back to the countries we've been doing so well from." Hearing of the announcement, the Canadian government discussed it in Parliament, but couldn't decide how they'd cope without the WTO to tell them who they could trade with. The Canadians were therefore pleased to hear that the whole thing was a hoax. Although the Australians thought they were listening to somebody from the WTO, it was in fact an impostor from the now infamous 'Yes Men' whose parody website http://gatt.org has managed to fool unsuspecting capitalists to book them to represent the WTO delegates at conferences.

Despite being discovered, the Yes Men believe the joke's on the WTO. "We've already demonstrated that audiences of experts will accept anything whatsoever so long as it comes from the mouth of the WTO."

NO BORDERS

A European Union report has blasted all the myths governments are using to justify their racist immigration policies. The report concludes that refugees far from coming to Europe 'to live a life of luxury on benefits', are largely fleeing war and persecution in their own countries. The report also goes on to say that Europe's 'flood' of refugees is more like a trickle compared to other much poorer countries. This year the UK is expected to get 78,000 asylum application. Rather insignificant compared to the 2 million refugees in Pakistan and 680,000 in Tanzania.

The European No Border network was set up to bring together campaign groups across Europe to protest against the harmonising of brutal immigration policies in 'Fortress Europe' while countries put up barricades to asylum seekers they are pulling down barriers to trade so we can be swamped by sweatshop consumer crap. This summer a chain of border camps is taking place across Europe. The camps aim to create a space for people to gather, discuss and take action against militarised borders and racist immigration policies. Seven camps are so far planned for this year in Germany, Poland, Finland, Slovenia and France.

The No Borders camp in Strasbourg, France (19-28 July) is described as 'a ten-day laboratory of creative resistance and civil disobedience to reinforce demands for freedom of movement and settlement'. Strasbourg was chosen as the location of the camp because it is home to the central database o-f the Schengen Information System (SchNEWS 312). A European wide computer system that can be consulted to determine whether a person is wanted for deportation or arrest, as well as providing other information used to monitor an individual's movements and activities. www.noborders.org

---

GRAIN OF TRUTH

Malawi the sixth poorest country in the world is on the verge of famine, and if nothing is done, it is expected that at least 2 million of it's 11 million population will die. But the Malawian government are trying to keep their problem under wraps so it "doesn't put off tourists".

The famine has been blamed on excessive rains and prolonged drought. But this is only part of the picture. Just three months before the crisis began the International Monetary Fund (IMF) ordered Malawi to sell off the grain it had in storage the money they made then undoubtedly went straight back to line the pockets of the IMF. Now Malawi are facing a severe grain shortage and are being forced to import grain at three times the cost of that they sold a few months ago. Doh! 70% of the population can no longer feed themselves and are starving. A small minority of the population though are doing very well out of the IMF's screwed up economic policies and the country now has the second highest disparity between rich and poor in the world. The IMF have refused to help the Malawi government anymore, so they've been forced to plunge themselves further into debt with another bunch of dodgy loan sharks. www.wsws.org/articles/2002/mar2002/mala-m14.shtml

PENALTY LABOUR

Nike, Reebok and friends are all expecting to net fat profits from the World Cup, but they have yet to clean up their act on child labour and working conditions. Although FIFA and UNICEF are joining forces to dedicate the World Cup to the children (bless 'em). "Child labour is still common and other labour standards are still grossly violated despite the fact that the contracts between FIFA and sporting goods companies promise the opposite," so says Kailash Satyarthi, from the Global March Against Child Labour. "We hope that FIFA and the sporting goods industry will take the leadership to make football truly a fair game for all", declared Satyarthi.

If Nike were to reduce its publicity and promotion budget by just 3.4%, it could double the pay of all employees working for Nike contractors in China and Indonesia. In Indonesia, production line workers earn an average of 80p per day. David Beckham earns £110,000 a week, more than enough to keep Posh in dresses. Nike has spent $73 million to buy the right to use an Elvis song in its World Cup marketing campaign. But in the dodgy, subcontracted factories Nike uses around the world, starvation wages are paid to the thousands of workers who produce their goods. Instead of paying their workers a living wage, Nike's profits (over $400 million a year) are helping their chairman Phil Knight increase his $6 billion personal fortune, and paying for flash advertising campaigns to keep the cash rolling in.

So, NoSweat is bringing the struggle to NIKETOWN, the flagship UK store. Forget Nike's 3-a-side tournament and come to Oxford Circus to shut down NIKETOWN. Bring your mates and a football for the 3-a-side No Sweat Match of the Day. Let's turn Nike's advertising blitz into an own goal. On Saturday June 15th 2pm, Oxford Circus, Central London. There's also a 5-a-side tournament the weekend after the World Cup (7th July) to raise funds for Indonesian trade unions. Rob Newman and Billy Bragg will be there and it is rumoured that the winners will have to face comedian Mark Thomas in a croquet match. More info: No Sweat 07904-431959 www.nosweat.org.uk

BUNCH OF TITS

The Police's attempts to stop protesters taking part in last weekends protest at Titnore Woods near Worthing in Sussex were unsuccessful as hundreds of people still turned out and managed to block Titnore Lane for a couple of hours. In the run up to the protest, police had spurred on the local rag to run a story entitled "Don't walk into trees trouble" with warnings that militant eco-activists were going to take over the protest, and then tramp across fields, damage crops, and disturbs wildlife. Which of course is going to cause a lot more damage than the bulldozing of the woodland to build 895 homes. www.worthinga27.freeserve.co.uk

...and finally...

Attention walkers, ramblers, and lovers of the great outdoors! Are you bored, restless, looking for something NEW to spice up your treks? Do your countryside hikes lack a pervading sense of danger, aggression, and militaristic threat?

If so, SchNEWS has found the book for you - the newly published fourth edition of "Walks on MOD Lands." Always helpful, the Ministry of Defence assures hikers that walks through "danger areas" are only open on "non-firing days," and has even developed a sunny grading system for its walks, including such categories as "Walk on the Wildside," "Sunday Stroll" and "A Taste of the Sea." Top tip for your MOD lands experience: "Do not approach, touch or pick up any metal objects lying on the ground." Otherwise you could be doing a bit of flying. For more info on this exciting new outdoor opportunity, visit www.defence-estates.mod.uk/access/walks_index.htm or write to Wendy Molyneux, Agency Secretariat, Defence Estates, St. Georges House, Blakemore Drive, Sutton Coldfield, West Midlands, B75 7RL and tell her just where she can put her disused metal objects!!

Disclaimer

SchNEWS warns all readers there's nothing like a big bang at the end of a garden party. Honest.

No SchNEWS next week – too busy flag waving for the Jubilee and watching the World Cup in our nuclear bunkers.

SchNEWS in brief

REBEL ALLIANCE: Brighton's get together of Direct Action groups and individuals, 7.30pm 11th July at Harvest Forestry squat, New England Street. ** **Free Alternative Jubilee Alldayer** 4th June noon-dusk, Concorde2, Brighton - Jamaican & Ital food, DJ's, Bands, fire jugglers, steel drumming, stalls and fun 4 kidz. ** Any holiday plans? Get hold of **The Good Alternative Travel Guide** with info on ethical tourist projects. Tourism Concern, 020-7753-3330 www.tourismconcern.org.uk ** The government in a momentary fit of sanity has refused permission for the expansion of an **incinerator in Edmonton,** North London which would have turned it into one of the largest in the world. www.greenpeace.org.uk ** A **Hungarian Radical Bookshop** is facing closure unless they can raise over 1000 Euros to pay their rent (that's about £600). They'd really appreciate any donations. Postal address is Goldolko Auntonom Antikvarium, Budapest 1066 O u40, Hungary. www.geocities.com/subesipu/ ** **Envision** is trying to recruit at least 30 people to help schools in London develop their own eco-projects. More info check out www.envision.org.uk ** **A new Social Centre** has just been opened at 227 Deptford High St, London. ** In a report published this week, **Amnesty International** have accused the British Government of using the attack on the Twin Towers to rush through legislation "unparalleled in Europe" which seriously erodes our human rights – all in the name of national security. Amnesty rated the UK's civil liberties-robbing reaction to the Twin Towers alongside those of India and South Korea, who knows what further steps are being dreamt up in the Home Office, all in the name of the 'war against terrorism.'

weekly SchNEWS

www.schnews.org.uk

Here's looking at you kid

Friday 14th June 2002   **Free/Donation**   **Issue 359**

F. B. LIED

After decades of harassing, framing, imprisoning, or "eliminating" anyone seen as a threat to the American status quo of big business, big brother, and big shopping malls, the FBI is finally getting a taste of long-overdue justice. In a landmark ruling reached on Tuesday (11th), a US jury found three FBI agents and three police officers guilty of violating the rights of Earth First! activists Judi Bari and Darryl Cherney.

This tale of FBI lies and repression began on May 24th 1990, when Judi Bari, a Californian environmental activist, was nearly killed by a motion-triggered pipe bomb wrapped with nails that exploded directly under the driver's seat of her car. Judi was maimed and disabled and Darryl Cherney, the passenger, was also injured. Upon arriving at the scene, the FBI and local police decided to help Bari and Cherney through this traumatic event by blatantly ignoring evidence of their victimisation, and deciding instead to arrest them for the bombing, telling the media that Bari and Cherney were violent Earth First! activists who had accidentally blown themselves up on the way to carry out some evil terrorist plot.

And just why did the FBI and local authorities want to ignore this attempt on Bari's life and instead use the incidence as an opportunity to slag her off in the media? Because Bari and Cherney were fighting against commercial logging in an area where the timber industry has friends in high places. On the day of the bombing, Bari and Cherney had been driving through California on a speaking tour aimed at recruiting college students for Redwood Summer - a campaign of non-violent mass protests against intensive logging. She and Cherney were seen as such a massive threat to the corporate logging industry that in the two months prior to the bombing, both had received numerous death threats from timber industry supporters. They reported these threats to police, who told Bari "If you turn up dead, then we'll investigate."

But instead of investigating the bombing as attempted murder, the FBI and Oakland Police, tried to frame Judi and Darryl for the bombing, accusing them of knowingly transporting the bomb that nearly killed them. These sensational false charges made national headlines, and the FBI and their accomplices kept a two-month media smear campaign going with a series of false claims about physical evidence linking Judi to building the bomb. But after delaying formal charges for seven weeks, when it was finally time for the State to present evidence in court, surprise, surprise, the FBI and Oakland Police didn't actually have any. The State announced it would not file charges, citing the lack of evidence. The Oakland Police closed their "investigation," but the FBI continued theirs, using the pretext of "investigating" the bombing as a cover for spying on Earth First! activists, sending agents to create files on over 500 people who had nothing to do with the bombing.

A year after the bombing, when it was clear that the authorities were making no genuine effort to solve the case, Judi and Darryl filed a federal civil rights suit against the FBI and Oakland Police Department. The lawsuit was delayed from coming to trial for nearly 11 years by legal shenanigans aimed at wearing down Bari and Cherney. The FBI gained an immense advantage when Judi died of breast cancer in 1997, but Judi's estate, Darryl Cherney, their legal team and supporters have kept the suit alive and have cleared every hurdle and won every appeal.

The trial that had taken 11 long years to come to court finally ended with a stunning vindication of Judi and Darryl, and a $4.4 million award of damages. A full 80% of the damages were for free speech violations, showing that the jury understood that the motivation for the false arrest and illegal searches was to interfere with Judi and Darryl's political activism. "This case is not just about me or Darryl or Earth First!," Judi once said. "This case is about the rights of all political activists to engage in dissent without having to fear the government's secret police." More details: www.judibari.org or www.sf.indymedia.org

BUG EYED

Pic: Tash

This week England became Champions of the World. Not on the football pitch, but in the Nosey Parker Premier League thanks to plans to give a whole host of bureaucrats the power to spy on us. From NHS executives to your local council, the Department of Work and Pensions to the Department for Transport; from the Home Office to the Post Office all could be getting the same powers of surveillance as the police. This brilliant idea comes thanks to a proposed amendment to the Regulation of Investigator Powers (RIP) Act. If the order is approved by MPs next Tuesday and the Lords a week later, these organisations will be able to make telephone companies and internet service providers hand over detailed personal information on any of us - without a court order.

The RIP Act was passed two years ago and authorises the targeting of groups or individuals in order, as the Home Office puts it, "to obtain a picture of his life, activities and his associates". It also authorises the bugging of homes and cars and the use of undercover agents. It covers the interception of pagers, mobile and satellite phones and e-mail, as well as private networks, including office switchboards.

Victims of surveillance cannot even appeal under the Human Rights Act, which supposedly enshrines the right to privacy because the RIP Act explicitly prevents such appeals. Your only chance to complain is to a tribunal - which of course meets in secret.

Not to be outdone and no doubt cheered-on by the British government, the European Parliament recently gave further powers to all EU governments to retain all communications data, monitor internet, phone and email traffic. European governments are now also able to force Internet service providers and phone companies to keep logs of their users' communications for an as yet unspecified length of time. These records will allow investigators to build up a detailed picture of an individual's movements online, including which websites they have visited, the nature of internet searches they have made, who they have e-mailed and when.

Since September 11th governments across the world have used the threat of terrorism to pass new laws to listen in on our every move. As Tony Bunyan, editor of Statewatch, says, "This is the latest casualty in the war against terrorism as far as civil liberties are concerned. The problem with wanting to monitor a few people is that you end up having to keep data on everybody." Ian Brown, Director of the Foundation for Information Policy Research added "which websites we visit or where we travel with a mobile phone in our pocket reveals a great deal of personal information. Accessing this information needs to be made more difficult, not opened up to this huge range of new enquirers. I look at this list and wonder not at who they've added, but if I can possibly think of anyone they've left out."

* Statewatch: 020 8802 1882 www.statewatch.org
* For more on surveillance: http://tash.gn.apc.org/watched1.htm
* www.stand.org.uk, the campaigning group that fought against the original RIP Act, has been resurrected to fight the new powers.

SchNEWS in brief

McDonalds has agreed to pay $10 million to vegetarian and Hindu groups who'd taken them to court after they had failed to tell customers that they used beef based flavouring in their french fries (sorry excuse for a chip). ** **Aldermaston International Disarmament Camp** will take place 13th-18th June, at the Atomic Weapons Establishment near Reading, Berkshire. On Saturday (15th) there will be a carnival and march in Reading, and on Monday an action day against AWE Burghfield, Info: 07905-917532 or www.gn.apc.org/tp2000 ** **Trade Justice March** against international trade rules and practices, taking place in London next Wednesday (19th) 020-7404-0530 www.tradejusticemovement.org.uk ** **56a Infoshop** are running a month of freeschool events throughout June, from vegan baking to sex toy making, from haircutting to clay oven construction. Visit them at 56a Crampton Street, London SE17 www.eroding.org.uk/freeschool ** 15th-22nd is the **week of action in support of asylum seekers**. Begins on the 15th with protest outside Harmondsworth Detention Centre near Heathrow 12-2pm. Info: 07960 309457. And ends on 22nd with a National Demonstration Against Attacks on Asylum Seekers 12 noon at Malet St, London W1. Transport from Brighton. Tickets £6 from The Peace Centre, Gardner St, Brighton www.barbedwirebritain.org.uk ** Work has started on a 100 meter wide roundabout which is part of the **A701 Edingburgh City bypass** in Midlothian, Scotland. Campaigners would really appreciate any help. www.spokes.org.uk/naag

Inside SchNEWS

Wayne Heaton, an anti-fascist activist, has been sentenced to 18 months for violent disorder during the Burnley riots last summer. Wayne, who grew up in Burnley, was none too happy seeing the growth of support for the BNP in his home town. So when the police defended the BNP, Wayne like many locals stood up and fought. He'd love letters of support. Wayne Heaton - GK 7292, Wing G1 8, H.M. Prison, 2 Ribblestone Lane, Preston PR1 5AB.

A MOX ON YOU

On Tuesday, a British Nuclear Fuels (BNFL) train transporting a nuclear flask collided with a lorry at a level crossing in Kent. The flask was on its way to Dungeness, where it was due to be filled with up to five tonnes of radioactive spent uranium flue rods before heading to Sellafield for reprocessing. The collision came in the same week as two BNFL boats arrived in Japan to pick up enough useable plutonium to create 50 nuclear bombs.

The plutonium is supposedly on its way back to Britain after BNFL were forced by Japanese anti-nuclear groups to admit falsifying data. Although Greenpeace is attempting to stop the plutonium shipment with a legal challenge in the UK. One of the ships will be acting as an armed escort and the other will be carrying plutonium mixed oxide fuel (MOX) that had originally been reprocessed at Sellafield nuclear plant in Cumbria by BNFL and transported to Japan in 1999 for use in their power plants. The return of this material will be in defiance of both international and UK law.

There is fear that they could be sitting ducks for 'rogue states' and 'terrorists' that could capture the plutonium and use it for weapons.

Former government nuclear physicists, ex-MoD senior staff and authorities on international terrorism warn that the journey is too risky but there is too much money involved for BNFL and Blair to heed these warnings. Refusal to take back the plutonium would sabotage around £4bn of investment between Japan and BFNL. The new MOX plant at Sellafield cost $500 million to build and therefore needs this trade with its biggest potential customer Japan to justify its existence.

As journalist George Monbiot points out "this programme can sustain itself only until the public grasps the two unavoidable facts of nuclear power. The first is that there is, as yet, no safe means of disposing of the wastes it produces. The second is that even if one were found, the monitoring and safe management of these wastes requires 250,000 years of political and economic stability. No government on earth can guarantee five." The route the return shipment will take if the legal challenge fails is still unknown, but whichever route it takes, a protest flotilla will be there to meet it. www.nuclearfreeflotilla.org

More info on nuclear transport see www.greenpeace.org

Brighton Briefs

Saturday 15th there's an Iraq sanction-busting action outside the Peace Centre, Gardner St. noon-4pm which will move down to the seafront from 4pm-6pm. People can come and get involved in wrapping and sending parcels to the Red Crescent in Iraq. Bring things to send to Iraq. Parcels will be sent from the Ship St Post Office on Friday 21st at 1pm, in defiance of the sanctions on Iraq. ** **Sunday 16th June Marxist Forum on Kashmir.** What is behind the Kashmir conflict? Starts 7pm at the Phoenix Brewery Community Centre, Phoenix Place, Brighton (on the small alley that runs down the left hand side of the Phoenix Gallery on Richmond Place). ** Tune in this weekend to **Radio 4A** on the new frequency of 107.8FM also online at www.piratetv.net ** Meeting to show opposition to Brighton's bid to be **European Capital of Culture**, next Wednesday (19) 7.30pm Brighthelm Community Centre, North Road. ** **Chalk Circle** squatted community centre in Hove opens its doors to all this Sunday from 2pm. There will be a raw food banquet and evening chill out from 4pm with assorted holistic fluff including massage, meditation and music and events running throughout the week. They are at Medina House on Hove seafront next to a café called Marrocco's.

GOLDEN SHOWER

While the TV news and the tabloids were stuffed with flag-waving God-bless-'er sentiment over the Golden Jubilee weekend, another story was unfolding behind the scenes. In London, police nicked around 40 people before an anti-monarchy protest, even pulling some out of pubs, apparently to 'prevent a breach of the peace'. A protester complained "The National Front are routinely allowed to march through sensitive areas - why not us? The cops tell us that we have to apply for permission to hold a protest - but what's the use when they'll never grant it in the first place?"

The police were understandably touchy though after an action by the London cell of the Biotic Baking Brigade. An operative calling herself Agent Royally Pissed Off launched a chocolate fudge cake at Prince Edward during a royal visit to Hackney. A press release was issued to press and public saying "We need resources not Royals". Meanwhile police pulled out all the stops to block an alternative Jubilee free festival. The festival was for a different royal anniversary, 10 years since Castlemorton, the King of Free Parties (see SchNEWS 354). Despite police bringing in roadblocks, dogs and helicopters, the Feeling of Life party went off anyway and ran for 4 days with thousands attending at Steart Beach on Somerset's sweeping Bridgewater Bay.

For info about this and other free parties/festivals that happened over the Jubilee weekend check out http://uk.indymedia.org

* The Queens Gallery in Buckingham Palace was renovated with rare rainforest woods despite Prince Philip being ex-president of the World Wildlife Fund and an outspoken opponent of unsustainable logging. More info from Greenpeace Forests campaigner Andy Tait 020 7865 8250.

UNITED COLORS OF BENETTON. WE OWN YOU. AND THEM.

www.nosweat.org.uk

Genetix Round Up

Instead of the backbreaking, muscle straining exercise of pulling up or snapping GM crops, a group calling itself the **Brassica Broadcasting Corporation** simply scattered conventional seeds on the ground over the top of a recently planted GM crop trial. The conventional and GM plants have since been growing up together, sabotaging the oilseed rape trial at Alderminster, Warwickshire. This new-style midnight operation went completely undetected at first and has changed the density of the control crop, added crop debris to the herbicide resistant crop, and rendered the results dubious, if not invalid. The group can be interviewed by email: brassicabroadcast@hotmail.com ** Last Saturday an estimated 250 people from across Scotland met at Wester Friarton Farm in Newport for a **"Tea in the Field"** protest. 70 anti-GM crop demonstrators trampled crops in the field. Four people were arrested during the trashing. ** **Victory for the Pink Castle!** The Pink Castle had been occupying a field in Dorset since April because the field was due to be planted with GM crops. But now the farmer's nephew says it is packing up because the Aventis trial has been written off and they now want to plant a non-GM commercial maize crop there. On June 15th-16th there'll be a 'tat down' weekend. They're going to need plenty of people power and vehicles – so please do go and help 'em out. There'll be a party on the Saturday evening. More info: 07773-640159 www.sayhi.to/thecastle

WEST PAPUA

The tribal people of West Papua have been fighting from independence from Indonesia since it 'absorbed' their country in 1969. Since then 300,000 West Papuans have been killed at the hands of the Indonesian army. Last year Dortheys Hiyo Eluay the Papuan political leader was kidnapped and murdered by Indonesian Special Forces. Benny Wenda, the Secretary General of Koteka Tribal Assembly, an important representative of the people of West Papua has now been arrested and could be the next person to die at their hands if action is not taken to obtain his release. There is a call for international support, see www.westpapua.net.

...and finally...

We always thought that Devon was practically another country, but a suggestion by the Mayor of a small town in Devon looks set to send the South West back into another century. Mayor Richard Brown, who isn't too impressed with the "vandalism, littering rowdyism, boy racing, and a nasty tendency to foul mouthed abuse" from the town's youth, has suggested the use of pillory (stocks) to deal with this "nasty sub-species of human" (i.e. any one that's younger than him). And it may appear that legally he'll be allowed to do it, as the use of stocks has never been formally abolished. SchNEWS ain't too sure if the kids of Devon really deserve this punishment, but we can think of quite a few politicians who could do with getting splattered with a mouldy tomato or two.

Disclaimer

SchNEWS warns all bug eyed snoops that we won't be spooked. Honest.

WAKE UP! IT'S YER SERIOUSLY PARCHED

www.schnews.org.uk

The Choice of a New Privatisation

Summer Solstice 2002   Free/Donation   Issue 360

CHOKER-COLA

As all SchNEWS readers will no doubt know the Coca-Cola Company "exists to benefit and refresh everyone it touches." Which will come as great news to the villagers in the Kerala State of India who, thanks to one of Coca-Cola's 'refreshing' factories, are suffering water contamination and shortages.

Coca Cola's bottling plant at Plachimada was set up three years ago in the middle of fertile agricultural land and has sucked the local aquifers dry. Worst hit are the indigenous and Dalit (oppressed castes) communities who live near the factory. They have seen their wells dry up while they wave goodbye to truck loads of soft drinks that are making their way from the factory to distant markets.

Barely six months after the factory set up, villagers and farmers living nearby began noticing changes in the quantity and quality of well water. Water from a well in Plachimada became unfit for drinking, cooking and bathing. Complaints and requests to the company and the Government repeatedly fell on deaf ears so on the 22nd April locals began an indefinite picket outside the factory gates demanding its closure. For 49 days the peaceful protests continued until police violently arrested 130 people including nine children and infants.

As Nityanand Jayaraman from CorpWatch India said "As the summer and the water crisis intensifies, the hardships of the local people have worsened. But Coca Cola has continued its production and groundwater extraction uninterrupted with police protection."

The water scarcity has now even hit Coke. Until recently, the company was drawing 1.5 million litres a day from the common groundwater resource – now it is only able to extract 800,000 litres. The remainder is brought in by truck from borewells in neighbouring villages. According to local estimates, Coke's water mining has now parched the lands of more than 2,000 people living within 1.2 miles of the factory.

Dr. S. Janakarajan, an economist working on groundwater issues said, "The trouble with Coke [in Plachimada] cannot be seen in isolation. In this case, a community may have lost its access to water for drinking or agricultural purposes for the sake of supplying Coca Cola. The same has happened in other places where industries have privatised common groundwater resources or polluted them… In this race, those who have the resources are the winners; the poor are the losers." Or as one famous French woman might once have said 'Let them drink Coke.'

For more on this story www.corpwatchindia.org/action/PAA.jsp?articleid=1703

THE REAL THING

The United Steelworkers of America have filed a law suit against Coca Cola accusing the company of failing to ensure that workers at the plants were protected against persecution of trade unionists. "This case involves the systematic intimidation, kidnapping, detention and murder of trade unionists in Colombia, South America, at the hands of paramilitaries working as agents of corporations doing business in that country," the lawsuit said.

"With respect to their business operations in Colombia, the Defendants hired, contracted with or otherwise directed paramilitary security forces that utilized extreme violence and murdered, tortured, unlawfully detained or otherwise silenced trade union leaders of the union representing workers at Defendants' facilities".

Colombia Solidarity Campaign 07950 923448 colombia_sc@hotmail.com

NO MAR DAMS

Four villagers from the Narmada Valley in India who had been fasting for 29 days in a suburb of Bhopal, ended their protest on Wednesday. All four, who have been directly affected by the huge Narmada Dam Project, began their fast to demand the fair resettlement of the 6,000 people who are going to be displaced when the Maan reservoir fills up during the monsoon season. All four were willing to die unless their demands were met.

The Maan dam is one of the dams in the Narmada Dam Project, a massive irrigation scheme that will according to the development crazy Indian government 'provide large amounts of water and electricity which are desperately required for the purposes of development'. In reality the project is sucking money from truly long term sustainable water solutions in this drought prone region, and will leave the majority of the people waterless, as big agricultural projects suck up the lion's share.

As the Maan reservoir fills up during the monsoon season 17 villages will be submerged, displacing 6,000 people. The villagers had been promised that they would be resettled land-for-land by December last year, but in reality as has happened with other villages in the Narmada valley, there is no resettlement package. Those affected by the Maan Dam have already

Villagers watch their homes go under water because of the Narmada Dam

20th Century Kashmir cont...

identified land that would be suitable for the resettlement of the villages. The local government though had refused to consider the option, which they thought would set a precedent.

Instead of being resettled, the villages were forcibly evicted in May when police and bulldozers moved in and sealed hand pumps, demolished school buildings and clear felled trees. The hunger strike began on the 21st May as part of a wider protest against these evictions. Finally on the 29th day the fast was called off after the Chairman of the Grievance Redressal Authority agreed to ensure that the rehabilitation of the Maan dam oustees would be completed no later than July 31st this year. Thousands of people face submergence over the coming monsoon, which will start next month and many have vowed to drown rather than leave their homes. Keep and eye out for solidarity actions happening around the globe. www.narmada.org

Arabunna people at Keepers Of Lake Eyre Camp

BLOOD FROM A STONE

"Since the mine started taking the water, the Mound Springs have gone right down and they don't function like they used to. Our traditional story is that if the water dries up, then so do the people." - *Kevin Buzzacott, of the Arabunna people.*

The Western Mining Corporation's Beverley Uranium mine in central Australia is sucking the life juice out of an area the size of Texas. Slurping a whopping 42 million litres of water a day from the Lake Eyre Basin, the mine affects hundreds of river systems, tributaries and creeks, and threatens the livelihoods of the aboriginal peoples in the vast desert area.

The uranium mine - the largest in the world - relies on underground water, using a process called 'in-situ leaching' where millions of litres of sulphuric acid is pumped into the groundwater to dissolve the uranium, which is then pumped out. This leads to the permanent radioactive contamination of the underground water system. To top it all, once they've used the water they put it back into the ground, radioactive as hell.

A protest camp of local traditional people, and others has been held since the mine started in 1999, though it has been trashed several times by the mining company security.

Earthdream are throwing a solstice party this weekend (20-21st) on mine land next to Lake Eyre, in support of local Arabunna people. For details contact: www.active.org.au/sydney

Inside SchNEWS

Great News! After 8 years of wrongful imprisonment anarchist prisoner, **Mark Barnsley** is due to be released next Monday (24). The Mark Barnsley campaign would like as many supporters as possible to be outside the prison to welcome Mark. Meet 9am, at HMP Whitemoor, Longhill Road, March Cambridgeshire. There is a slight chance he may be released earlier www.freemarkbarnsley.com for any updates. Transport is being organised from around the country, email: barnsleycampaign@hotmail.com for details.

On Tuesday **Satpal Ram** was freed after spending 15 years in jail. Satpal received a life sentence after he defended himself against a racist attack, his attacker later died. His release came after David Blunkett was forced by a European Court ruling to overturn a previous decision by former Home Secretary Jack Straw that kept Satpal in jail because of his refusal to admit his guilt. Satpal's release does not mean that his conviction has been quashed. There is still a massive legal battle to clear his name. www.appleonline.net/satpal/

* 1 year on from the EU summit in Gothenburg and 71 people have been prosecuted, mainly for rioting. The average length of the sentence has been 14 months. Many of the prisoners would appreciate letters, addresses are available from abc-stockholm@autonom.zzn.com. The Gothenberg Solidarity Group desperately need donations. All money will go directly to help the prisoners. Money payable to 'Nisse-Latts minnesfond' at Solidaritetsgruppen, c/o Syndikalistiskt Forum, Box 7267, 402 35 Göteborg , Sweden Tel +46(0)733-16 42 96

* The Infamous and outrageously moustached French farmer Jose Bove was ordered to turn up outside a French jail on Wednesday to serve his 3 month prison sentence for his part in the 1999 demolition of a McDonalds In true style he turned up on a tractor. His sentence has been postponed for two months as politicians feared his incarceration may effect the presidential elections. www.commondreams.org/headlines02/0617-07.htm

GRIZZLY GOINGS ON

The G8 summit, the annual meeting of the seven major industrialised nations plus Russia, is taking place next week in Kananaskis, Canada. As usual they will be plotting and scheming on how to take more from the world's poor by promoting slave labour and environmental destruction (AKA 'globalisation' and 'development') and claiming that they're good for us by branding them 'sustainable'. Devised by the big three, the WTO, IMF and World Bank, this year's lucky theme is Africa – lucky because the unholy trinity will focus all of their manipulative money making scams on it.

After last years massive protests in Genoa (see SchNEWS 314/5) it was decided to move to the remote-

J26 for the G8 - march on June 26th in Calgary followed by convoy to Kananaskis

ness of the Rockies for the summit and put up a security fence stretching 6 ½ kilometres. There will also be hundreds of police and soldiers, with a top-level military commander commenting, "we are very serious … we have lethal weapons and we will use force if we think there is a serious threat," warning that protesters and "limelight seekers" who intend to test summit security in Kananaskis will be risking their lives.

Potential terrorist threats – such as the native grizzly bears – are being used as an excuse to bring in these new hardcore security measures. Apparently the bears pose such a threat in the rockies that the cops will be kitted out in some very fetching outfits (check out www.onf.ca/grizzly/suit.html and drool). Activists are still urged to go to Kananaskis, to disrupt as much as possible using roadblocks and "Ewok" tactics such as tree climbing. Masses of demos will also be going on around the country and thousands of people will head to the capital.

Unfortunately Canadian cops are known to respond to anti-capitalist demos with the subtlety we'd expect, at the last one in Ottawa. protestors at the G20 summit, were zapped with stun guns, mauled by badly trained police dogs and threatened with rubber bullets as riot cops held loaded MP5 machine guns with their fingers on the triggers.

For more info on the various actions, different coloured blocs and tactics see www.takethecapital.net and http://g8.activist.ca/event/

It's a mad mad world: The G8 circus comes to Calgary

WOODSIDE

In 1997, 27 Gypsy families clubbed together to buy Woodside, a 17-acre touring caravan park with full planning permission. But when the Gypsies moved on to the park, Mid-Bedfordshire council claimed they did not have permission for permanent occupation and issued enforcement notices. In July last year the council set aside £230,000 to finance clearance of the community. On Monday (24), the council is going to the high court to be allowed to carry out its enforcement notices, forcing the community back on the road.

The Woodside caravan park is unlike any of the 325 council Gypsy sites in this country. It isn't surrounded by barbed wire fences designed to keep the inhabitants in. It hasn't even been built near a sewage works or any other industrial facility. It looks, in fact, more like a modern hamlet than a ghetto, except that the homes are on wheels rather than stone foundations.

At the centre of the community is a large green where children play in safety. Yet the council wants the site removed on the grounds that it is having an adverse impact on the environment. The Gypsies say the council is using an environmental smokescreen to hide their bigotry.

"They say we are out of character with the area, but how can we be when we've always been here?" says Woodside spokesman and National Traveller Action Group chairman Clifford Codona, who, like many Gypsies, once worked as a seasonal agricultural labourer. "They don't need us any more, so they want to expel us. They can't stand the fact that, for the first time ever, Gypsies have their own village green!"

Current government policy recommends that travellers should house themselves on their own land, yet Gypsy families who attempt to do so are often denied planning permission. While over 80% of planning applications from settled people are granted consent more than 90% of applications from Gypsies are refused.

If you believe it's time to stop shoving British Gypsies from pillar to post, they need your help to turn away the bailiffs. Come the night before the expected eviction attempt from Monday onwards. Enjoy a midsummer night of Gypsy singsong around the fires - and be ready to protest when the council and private contractors come. There's plenty of room for tents and caravans. Woodside is in the village of Hatch near Sandy, Bedfordshire just minutes off the A1. F or directions http://www.streetmap.co.uk/

If you can't get to the site send an email to andy.rayment@uk.uumail.com head of Mid Beds Council urging him to reconsider his intention to evict the community of Gypsies at Woodside Caravan Park, Sandy, Bedfordshire.

For more information on how British Gypsy sites policy has made many homeless, read "No Room to Move" www.guardian.co.uk/Archive/Article/0,4273,4427029,00.html

Campesinos in Tacna, Peru set up a road block on the main Panamericana highway

SWITCHEROO

It kicked off last week in Peru when the government decided to privatise two local power companies in the city of Arequipa – and the locals, looking at the privatisation disasters in neighbouring Bolivia and Argentina, weren't having it. What followed was a back-down from the sell-off - but only after five days of rioting which left two dead, hundreds injured and US$100 million of damage. The country's so-called shoeshine boy-turned-president, the "man of the poor," Alejandro Toledo was elected last year promising not to flog the power plants – but that's politicians for you. Egasa and Egesur, the two electrical companies, were to be "auctioned off" to the one bidder – Belgian firm Tractebel – for roughly half what they were worth.

Things started on June 11th when the central province of Pasco downed tools for a 48 hour general strike, followed by 24-hour general strikes in four other provinces including Arequipa, and a large demo in Lima.

Marches in Arequipa on the 13th and 14th started peaceful, but were then teargassed and attacked by police, by which stage the crowd of 20,000 - featuring workers, campesinos and students alike - kicked off and government buildings were smashed. General strikes and mass demonstrations took hold in the cities of Tacna, Juliaca and Puno, attacking and looting privatised businesses and banks; meanwhile large solidarity marches took place in Cusco, Iquitos and other cities.

On the last night, when the sale of the plants was suspended, 10,000 gathered in Arequipa's Plaza de Armas, and the pro-privatisation Interior Minister resigned.

Resistance is rock solid in Arequipa

SchNEWS in brief

Plans for **everyone and their dog** to spy on our every email/phonecall (see last years SchNEWS) have been shelved for the time being after massive protests. Still, as one our readers pointed out, we shouldn't forget about America's Echelon - the worlds greatest surveillance system, which captures and analyses virtually every phone call, fax, email and telex message sent anywhere in the world! http://fly.hiwaay.net/~pspoole/echelon.html ** On **Working Links?** Think it stinks? AWOL (Abolish Working Links) meeting for benefits claimants in Brighton and Hove this Thursday (27) at Queens Head Pub, Queens Road , Brighton 7.30pm. Info 540717 ** There's a meeting about the selling off of **Brighton's council housing**. It's at Leech Court, Albion Rd next Wednesday (26) 7pm 608704 for more details ** Go to www.huntingdonsucks.com/ecd/ and join in the online protest to shut down the website of **evil** vivisectors Huntingdon Life Sciences. ** Activists managed to halt work on a new **incinerator** in Basingstoke by suspending themselves in cargo nets for 3 days. The action was one of 50 held throughout the world on Global Anti-Incineration Day www.greenpeace.org.uk

POSITIVE SchNEWS

Three hundred people, ten marquees, three days, countless workshops, discussions, advice sessions and a chance to meet people from all over the UK who are changing their own and others' lives. No, its not a Christian summer camp it's… the Groundswell self-help forum! From 16-18 July, Groundswell will be hosting the fourth national self-help forum in Sheffield, featuring loads of practical workshops to learn new skills. Groundswell are a group that promotes and supports a self-help network with people who are homeless, landless, or living in poverty. Groundswell 020 7737 5500 www.groundswell.org.uk/

Disclaimer

SchNEWS warns all Stonedhengers looking for a golden age goal when it comes to a world cup full of coke y'knows the score. Honest, ref!

WAKE UP! IT'S YER GLASTONBURY MUD SLINGIN'...

weekly **SchNEWS**
www.schnews.org.uk

Friday 27th June 2002   Free/Donation   Issue 361/362

SUMMIT OUTTA NUFFIN

"It is dangerous to assume that the goals of the private sector are somehow synonymous with those of the United Nations, because most emphatically they are not. Business and industry are driven by the profit motive…The work of the United Nations, on the other hand, is driven by a set of ethical principles." - Carol Bellamy, Executive Director UNICEF.

Oil companies, chemical corporations and mining multinationals will be heading to Johannesburg, South Africa in the next few months – because they want to help save the planet with a new brand of greenwash.

The biggest United Nations Conference for a decade will take place from August 26th to September 4th when over 60,000 delegates are expected to attend the World Summit on Sustainable Development – or Rio + 10 because it is 10 years since the first UN Earth Summit in Rio, Brazil. Ten years on and the planet is in more of a mess than ever.

Issues on the agenda include poverty eradication, unsustainable patterns of consumption, sustainable management of resources and how to make globalisation work for everyone, but it's the profit-hungry corporations who are muscling-in to make sure that instead of agreeing real solutions it will be 'carry on profiteering' for big business.

Major lobby groups like the International Chamber of Commerce, the World Business Council for Sustainable Development and their latest offspring, Business Action for Sustainable Development (BASD) will be flying the corporate flag. BASD's main task is to make sure that business interests are secured at the summit, so they've been busy finding examples of good business practice to use as proof of good 'corporate citizenship'. Just because there are some examples of companies doing some good, for the sake of PR doesn't mean they promote these values all the time. Still, who cares about all that – these good examples are being aggressively marketed to show these companies as 'good guys' and used to demand that there is no need for any legally binding agreements at the summit, because the environment is safe in their hands. It's all about partnerships, but as Erik Wesselius from Corporate Europe Observatory comments "The most vocal supporters of the partnership approach are generally corporations from some of the most environmental and socially dodgy industries - namely oil, gas, chemicals and mining." For them the so-called partnership approach is an ideal marketing opportunity for what is known in the business as greenwashing.

Green-wash is the term used for corporations who spend millions on adverts telling the world how green they are, while behind the scenes they do everything they can to oppose or avoid any social or environmental law that might harm their profits.

Former Shell boss Sir Mark Moody Stuart is now head of BASD and knows a thing or two about greenwashing. After being taken to the cleaners over the proposal to dump the Brent Spar oil rig in the sea and its oil exploration of Ogoni land in Nigeria, Shell have been busy re-branding themselves as a responsible company. Their 'People,

Planet, and Profits' report has been heralded as 'ground-breaking', with this new type of 'environmental and social reporting' all part of the greenwash process. As one of the business lobby groups admits, the reports give "increased credibility" while not requiring companies to fundamentally change anything.

Green Wash and Go

So in the lead up to Johannesburg we get BASD pushing partnerships like the Energy and Biodiversity Initiative, the Global Mining Initiative, and the Responsible Care program. But as Corporate Europe Observatory point out "These projects are largely an attempt to improve the corporate members' tarnished images. They are also a reaction to pressure by campaign and community groups or as a move to pre-empt binding regulation." For example, the Responsible Care program, long criticised as greenwash by campaign groups and academics, was established by the chemical industry after the Bhopal disaster where a Union Carbide plant leaked poisonous gas killing 4,000 people instantly and injuring tens of thousands more (see SchNEWS 238). The move effectively killed off efforts to toughen regulations.

We get sustainable mining reports funded by er... mining companies, among them notorious

FESTIVAL GUIDE INSIDE

Green Wash and Go cont...

companies such as Rio Tinto and Freeport McMoran.

We get the European Union pushing the World Trade Organisation's so called 'Doha Development Agenda' (SchNEWS 332) agreed back in November last year, with claims that it will benefit the world's poorest countries and so contribute to 'sustainable development'. Forget the fact that corporate globalisation has increased poverty and environmental degradation around the world.

We get the UN, working with some of the world's most notorious human rights and environment abusers.

We get warnings from BASD that anyone who dares calls for tougher regulations on corporations must be part of the lunatic fringe.

And we get thousands of delegates being wined and dined and put up in posh Sheraton hotels, nextdoor to the black shanty towns of Alexandra and Soweto.

In fact we're sick of it. - As Corporate Europe Observatory tell us "The world's leaders need to start listening to the demands by civil society groups and ordinary people, that business can not be allowed to continue as usual. Unless a dramatic U-turn in policy and approach is made soon, Johannesburg risks becoming little more than a propaganda circus." Or as Jens from ASEED puts it "The World Summit promises to be a shambles but will no doubt be promoted as a success…the immense amount of money and time could have been spent on something a lot more useful."

*For more of the above see www.corporateeurope.org/observer11/rio

* Recommended reading: Codes in Context by Corner House 01258 473795 http://cornerhouse.icaap.org

* A SEED have called for a Global Day of Action on August 31st against big business muscling in on sustainable development. www.aseed.net. To find about more about their campaign against the privatisation of the UN email uncorp@aseed.antenna.nl

* The Greenwash Academy are looking for nominations. www.earthsummit.biz

* The South African government has warned groups not to protest and spoil the Earth Summit, but demonstrations will happen whether they like it or not. Keep an eye on http://southafrica.indymedia.org

* The recently published Global Environment Outlook predicts the destruction of 70% of the natural world, mass extinction of species and the collapse of human society in many countries in the next 30 years unless radical action is taken. Written by over a thousand scientists and compiled for the UN, partly as a wake up call to world leaders in the run up to the Johannesburg summit, the report also paints 'four environmental scenarios'. One includes the current pattern of free trade and short term profit at the expense of the environment, which they say will lead to disaster. www.un-ep.org. Copies available from Earthscan 0207 278 0433 www.earthscan.co.uk

SchNEWS in brief

Can't afford a ticket or unimpressed with **Glastonbury** going to the Mean Fiddler Dogs? Check out a multi-rig gathering for the right to party... Call 07092310245, 07813620336 or 07811906642 after 11pm on Saturday night Expected to be on a piece of land not far from the Pilton Farm site. And the Druids of Kaos present a Midsummer Nights Moot, phone 07870 489123 www.systemprojectmayhem.cjb.net. However, after the 10,000 strong free festival on Steart beach during Jubilee weekend the Chief Superintendent of Somerset got so much shit that he's apparently on a personal mission to nick rigs. www.network23.org. Has Glastonbury sold out? See www.corporatewatch.org/news/glastonbury.htm. Why the Mean Fiddler are such tossers www.urban75.com/Rave/raverant ** Don't know what to do after Solstice? Free party soundsystems are promising a huge party somewhere in the South West this weekend. Call 07980401646/07815627676/ 07816984913 from Friday morning or www.guilfin.net/ ** **The London Social Centres Network** have set up two new email lists. To subscribe to the discussion group send an email to londonscn-forum-subscribe@lists.riseup.net. For the events listings and newsletter group e-mail: londonscn-events-subscribe@lists.riseup.net ** To Coincide with the EU Summit in Sevilla over 1000 people Occupied a **Dutch Motorway** in Utrect for seven hours. The protest was in response to the Dutch governments plans to expand the motorway network www.groenfront.nl/english ** **Ned Ludd's News** the independent radical newsletter in Nottingham has been resurrected and is available from the Sumac Centre (245 Gladstone Street) info: nottingham_freedom@hotmail.com. ** **Globalisation and the Media** is a new video from undercurrents exploring the role of the media in the corporate led take over of the planets natural resources. It's £10 - details from www.cultureshop.org

BOOKED

Two independent bookshops, Housmans and Bookmarks, in London are currently in the middle of fighting a libel case, which if they lose will ruin 'em. The case is one of a number filed against them by someone criticised in a 1993 edition of the anti-facist magazine, Searchlight. At the time both bookshops stocked Searchlight and under a warped British law it is possible for the person who thinks they've been libelled to sue a shop, distributor or library handling the alleged libellous publication, as well as or instead of suing the author, editor and publisher. Both bookshops feel it is important for them to make a stand on behalf of other independent bookshops, which are few and far between these days. But this will mean massive legal bills. A legal fund has been set up and contributions are desperately needed. Send money to the "Bookshop Libel Fund" c/o Housmans Bookshop, 5 Caledonian Road, London N1 9DX. Phone 020-7278 4474 blf@housmans.idps.co.uk

Howzat For A Work Of Art

Forget the faddish fluff of the Turner Prize nominees - this was art event of the year. On the 3rd July Paul Kelleher took performance art in an exciting new direction when he knocked the head off a statue of Margaret Thatcher.

Five days after conducting a "reccy", Paul entered London's Guildhall where the statue was being displayed armed with a cricket bat. When that didn't work a metal bar across the nose did.

After performing the act - which will take its place in art history somewhere between Duchamp's urinal and Winston's mohawk - he chose not to make a run for it and waited quietly by the statue to be arrested. When police arrived, he told them, "I think it looks better like that."

Defending himself in court, Kelleher insisted he had a "lawful excuse" for his actions since he believed 'his young son was in "immediate need of protection" from "this stupid world" and the political system represented by Lady Thatcher.

Later, in February 2003 he was sentenced to three months imprisonment at Southwark Crown Court for decapitating the £150,000 statue (see also SchNEWS 394). The judge said, "I don't doubt the sincerity of your beliefs. Many people share them, particularly in relation to what is happening in Third World countries ... and I would be the last person to deny any person the right to freedom of speech and the right to protest against matters which support his beliefs." But he concluded... "The way you acted to knock the head off a valuable statue of a politician who left power over 10 years ago and whose party is no longer the party of government, was very much the wrong way." (That's right - Blair and Neo Labour are the current enemy.)

Kelleher reiterated to the judge, "I am becoming increasingly worried as to what sort of world I have brought my son into."

She was always off her head

The prosecution had described the attack as an "ill-conceived publicity stunt" carried out by a man who was "not an avid fan of the former prime minister".

The court heard that on the day of the attack Mr Kelleher arranged a babysitter for his son and purchased a Slazenger V600 cricket bat. Once in the gallery he waited for his "window of opportunity". When the cricket bat "pinged off" the statue, Kelleher picked up a metal crowd barrier and successfully beheaded the statue.

Note: We tried but failed to get a contact address for Paul while he was in prison - as we always post SchNEWS free to prisoners. If Paul could contact us we will gladly send him a copy of this book.

Daily Refugee

Another EU Summit - this time in the Spanish city of Seville. There were massive protests against a 'Europe of Capital', and a Spanish general strike against welfare cuts.

Tony Blair's plan to use "financial and economic clout" against countries that did not co-operate on migrants was rejected but plans for a Fortress Europe march ahead. Because it's OK for governments to go on about the free movement of goods – but not the free movement of people. OK to sell arms to countries, helping to fuel conflicts, displace people and create refugees, but not OK for those refugees to try and come over here. OK for industrialised nations to pump greenhouses gases into the atmosphere, but not OK for environmental refugees whose land has been devastated by climate change to try and find somewhere else to live.

Seven of the top ten countries of asylum seekers arriving in the European Union over the past decade have been from war-torn regions, according to the data from the office of the UN High Commissioner for Refugees. And in any case, if you look at the numbers of asylum seekers coming to Europe, you'll see that this is nothing if you compare them with developing countries that receive hundreds of thousands, or in the cases of Iran and Pakistan, millions of refugees. If people had a bright, rosy future in their homelands, would they need to seek asylum elsewhere?

* **A Palestinian held without charge for six months in Belmarsh high security prison** under all the UK's new Terrorism Act is too seriously mentally ill to remain there a judge has ruled. Mr Rideh came to Britain in 1995 as an asylum seeker and was being treated for severe post-traumatic stress disorder following torture at the hands of Israelis when he was a teenager living in Gaza. His detention in Belmarsh caused flashbacks: the rattling of keys and the sight of guard uniforms brought back memories of torture. His illness was not taken seriously by prison staff and he had been described as a "malingerer".

* **Who said this?** "'The way stateless Jews from Germany are pouring in from every port of this country is becoming an outrage.' In these words, Mr Herbert Metcalf, the Old Street magistrate, yesterday referred to the number of aliens entering the country through the 'back door' a problem to which the Daily Mail has repeatedly pointed." Why it was the Daily Mail in 1938. Now go and read the bile from them now about refugees and see how much has changed.

* There will be a No Borders action camp in Strasbourg 19-28 July www.noborder.org

51

IT'S YER SCHNEWS PARTY AND PROTEST GUIDE

The film NOT THIS TIME - THE STORY OF THE SIMON JONES MEMORIAL CAMPAIGN chronicles the death of Simon Jones on his first day as a casual worker - and the fightback, involving direct action against government agencies and departments, that forced a prosecution of those responsible for Simon's death.

The 20 date film tour has its first British date at the **Glastonbury Festival** Left field stage on Saturday night on the same bill as Billy Bragg and Mark Thomas. Dates in July: **London (3)** National Probation Service, 71-73 Great Peter Street (nearest tube St James Park) 1.30 pm **Banbury (3)** St John's Catholic Club, under St John's Church, South Bar 7.30pm, **Battersea (8)** Lara Community Centre, St Paul's Church, 92c St John's Hill (nearest rail Clapham Junction) 7.30pm, **East London (9)** London action resource centre, 62 Fieldgate Street (nearest tube Aldgate East) 8pm, **Bristol (10)** Easton Community Centre, Kuburn Street, Easton 7.30pm **London (16)** RMT Union, Somerstown Coffee House, 60 Chalton Street (nearest tube Mornington Crescent) 5pm. **Sheffield (17)** The Red Dear, Titt Street 7pm, **South London (18)** Union Tavern, Camberwell new Road (nearest tube Oval, nearest rail Vauxhall) 7pm, **Reading (19)** Global cafe-bar, RISC, London Street 7pm, **Brighton (21)** Sussex Arts Club, Ship Street 7.30pm, **Stokesly (22)** Stokesley Community Centre, Station Road 7pm, **Worthing (23)** Upstairs at The Downview (opposite West Worthing railway station) 7.45pm, **Leicester (23)** City Rooms, Hotel Street 6.30pm, **Manchester (24)** Hare & Hounds, Shude Hill 8.30pm, **Leeds (25)** Roger Stevens lecture theatre 15, Leeds University 7pm, **Hull (26)** Kingston Social Club, Beverley Road 7.30pm, **Leicester (11 Aug)** Phoenix Theatre, Upper Brown Street 5pm.

The 25 minutes film is available for five pounds including postage from the Simon Jomes Memorial Campaign, PO Box 2,600, Brighton BN2 0EF. More information: www.simonjones.org.uk 01273-685913.

JULY

Unitl 10 July Peace camp Cape Wrath, Durness, North West Scotland where warships from the US, UK, France, Sweden and Denmark will be taking part in live firing at the Cape Wrath ranges. The US Navy have been stopped from using the ranges in Puerto Rico after protests following the killing of several locals and the discovery that they were using depleted uranium "by accident". 0141-4231222 www.banthebomb.org **4 The annual 'Independence From America' demonstration,** Main Entrance of NSA Menwith Hill, near Harrogate, North Yorkshire 12-4pm. 01943-466405 www.caab.org.uk **5-7 Winchester Hat Fair** FREE " The Hat Fair is Britain's longest running festival of street theatre, with oddball characters, breathtaking performance, unbelievable stunts, specialist circus, crazy clowning and new world music." 01962-849841 www.hatfair.co.uk **5-7 Big Chill Enchanted Garden**, Larmer Tree Gardens, Wiltshire. Sold Out 020-7503-7504 www.bigchill.net **5-7 Bracknell Festival - Out There**, Southhill Park. Seems to have shaken off its folk festie with Lamb, David Byrne and Stereo MC's among the acts. 01344-484123: www.outtherefestival.co.uk **6 London Mardi Gras**, Hackney Marshes, London. £17. www.londonmardigras.com **6 Thurrock Mu-** sic Festival, Orsett Showground, nr Orsett, Essex. A back-to-roots event for unsigned bands and DJs. 40+ live bands, two dance stages. Tickets £5 in advance (more on door). www.tmfonline.co.uk **6-7 Diaspora free festival**, Regent's Park, London. noon-9pm 020-7456-0404 www.culturalcooperation.org **6-7 Ocean FM Balloon and Flower Festival**, Southampton Common. Free. www.southampton.gov.uk **7 Ambient Green Picnic**, Shalford Park, Guildford, Surrey. www.ambientpicnic.co.uk **7 Peace Messenger Fair**, Hove Lawns. 01273 671213 peacemessengeruk@yahoo.com **7 Carnival against GM crops** Assemble 12.30pm outside the Black Boy Pub, Weeley, Essex. March and parade past GM crop farm to village fete against GM crops with Kids bouncy castle, music, car boot sale, tea and cakes, open forum on GM, organic produce, morris dancing, beer and much much more! 07931-638938 www.nogm.cjb.net **7 Israel-Palestine day long event** bringing together individuals from the region and from diaspora community (include music and poetry) Institute of Contemporary Arts The Mall, London 10am-7pm **7-8 Protest at the Manchester Military Tattoo at the M.E.N. Arena**. The event glorifies war, and in its literature, shows glossy photos of our trooops in Afghanistan. Meet Friday 7th 6.30pm at the Post Office by Victoria Station. Contact 0161-273-8283 for details of possible pickets on the Saturday shows. **8-14 National Vegetarian Week** 0161-925-2000 www.vegsoc.org

10-14 Earth First! Summer Gathering, West Country. An opportunity for anyone interested in non-hierarchical environmental direct action to get together and spend Five days in the countryside learning new skills and discussing campaigns. With a range of practical workshops and theoretical discussions on everything from 'how to do an office occupation', facilitate meetings and run a newsletter to self defence, land collectives and community organising. Discussions on past, present and future UK campaigns, the implications of the global economy and building international resistance. www.eco-action.org/gathering

11 Nought for Conduct film night. Matewan - true story of a West Virginia mining town that formed an unlikely union between striking hillbilly miners and black and Italian scabs in the 1920s. 7.30pm, Marchmont St Community Centre, Marchmont St, London. £2/£1. 07946-214590 noughtforconduct@hotmail.com **12-14 Anarchist Youth Network first national conference/gathering**. Meet midday outside Holborn Tube Station. Free accommodation for those coming from outside of London. 07814-629780 www.anarchistyouth.net **12-14 Positive News Readers Weekend**, Herefordshire. 0845-458 4758 **12-14 Willow Fesitval** FREE The "region's largest rock and pop extravaganza set within the beautiful surroundings of the Embankment of the River Nene in Peterborough and is the culmination of the Peterborough Festival." 120 bands on six stages over three days - just avoid the Queens Jubilee bullshit. Volunteers needed. Limited camping 01733-346529 www.willowfestival.co.uk **12-19 5th No one is Illegal-Camp** in Jena/Thuringia/Germany, on the 19th July a convoy will start from Jena to Strasbourg. www.nadir.org/nadir/kampagnen/camp02/aufrufle.htm **13 Food for Life Festival**, Camden Centre, Judd St., London. 11am-7pm. 01273-777688 www.factoryfarming.org.uk **13 Hornsey**

www.schnews.org.uk

Visit our website for a comprehensive and regularly updated party and protest guide throughout the year. Plus Critical Mass bike rides, protest camps, free party hotlines, DIY Guides, what's happening in your area, prisoner support...

History Bike Ride 2pm Great Northern Railway Tavern, Hornsey High St, London **13- 14 Compost Toilet Design & Building Workshop**, Dial House North Essex (home of CRASS). grahamburnett@blueyonder.co.uk 01702-303259 **13-14 Diaspora free festival**, Greenwich Park, London. noon-9pm. 020-7456-0404 www.culturalco-operation.org **13-14 T in the Park**, Balado, by Kinross. £37.50 per day, or £74 for the weekend with camping. www.tinthepark.com **13-14 Leicester Belgrave Mela**, Abbey Park. Asian arts and culture. Free www.leicester-mela.co.uk **14 Finfest 2002**, Finsbury Park Community Festival 1-7 pm. World stage, youth entertainment; a photography contest; sports contest; a space for acoustic music and poetry; a children's village; market stalls; and a grand finale of a carnival procession. **16 INJUSTICE** - feature length documentary about struggles for justice by the families of people who have died in police custody in the UK - will have a special public screening at which the Attorney General, Lord Goldsmith QC, will be present to take part in a Q&A session after the film. 6.30pm at Prince Charles Cinema, 7 Leicester Place, London. 020-7494-3654 www.injusticefilm.co.uk **16-4 August Crisis -** an exhibition offering critical perspectives on the political upheavals of globalisation and the struggle against war, violence and injustice. Vaults at The Foundry 84-86 Great Eastern Street, Shoreditch, London. 020-7515-6291 **16-18 Tools for Change**. The 4th Groundswell self help forum. Bringing together homeless people, activists and housing professionals. At the Poderosa, Sheffield. 020-7737-5500 www.groundswell.org.uk **17-21 Buddhafield Gathering**, Devon. Advance booking only 020-8671-7144 www.buddhafield.com **18-21 Larmer Tree Festival**, Larmer Tree Gardens, Wiltshire. Family folk festival in 11 acres of garden, surrounded by eastern temples, peacocks and Nepalese pagodas. Weekend adult tickets with camping £68. www.larmertree.demon.co.uk **19-20 Wickerman Festival**. Main stage, campsite, dance and cult music tents, children's area, trade stalls, alternative area, bars, a talent stage and food stalls. And Yes, they will burn a wickerman on both Friday and Saturday night. www.thewickermanfestival.co.uk **19-21 Guildford Festival**, Stoke Park, Guildford. A main stage, comedy and dance tents, Aladdin's Cave - full of classic musical gems, comprehensive children's area and over 100 craft stalls. The Guilfin Ambient Lounge offers a 24-hour mellow performance zone, a daily open stage slot encourages participation from budding young and unknown musicians. £30 per day or £90 for the weekend, including camping. 01483 536270 www.guildford-live.co.uk **19-21 Video Activist Training Weekend**, Oxford. A few places left for a video activism residential course in Oxford - and its free. 01865-203661 hamish_campbell@hotmail.com **19-21 Festival at the Edge**, Stoke Barns, Much Wenlock, Shropshire. Storytelling festival. Weekend ticket including camping £35. www.festivalattheedge.org **20 Respect Festival**, Victoria Park, Tower Hamlets, London. Free anti-racist festie. 020-7983-4000 www.london.gov.uk/respect **20 Rally against GM crops in Cheshire**. 0161

232 0860 **20-27 Blitz Festival** "A radical political arts festival will be held in Manchester UK, timed to coincide with the opening celebrations of the Commonwealth Games. The 20th will be a big opening party with Undercurrents, BeyondTV and others showing films and bands playing right through the day. The end celebrations on the 27th will be more spontaneous and bizarre. www.nato.uk.net No Sweat - the anti sweatshop campaign - will also be doing actions before, during and after the games. 0161-861-7160 manchester@nosweat.org **20-21 Truck Festival**, Hill Farm, Near Abingdon, Steventon, Oxfordshire. 07979 646 815 "There is no cut throat capitalism here, no huge entry fees, and huge advertising boards. It's a nice day out in the country side with a few bevies and a plethora of bands." www.truckrecords.com **20-21 Ashton Court Festival**, Bristol - finest free event in the West Country www.ashtoncourtfestival.com **20-21 Organic & Real Food Festival**, Powderham Castle, Kenton, nr. Exeter. 01934-813407 www.naturalhealthshows.co.uk **20-21 Home Herbal Training**. Skills and Inspirations for a greener future. 01503 250135 ediblewolfpeaches@btinternet.com **21 A year to the day that protester Carlo Guiliani was shot dead by Italian riot police**, Jonathan Neale will talk about his new book describing the dramatic events at the Genoa G8 summit. The Foundry 84-86 Great Eastern Street, Shoreditch, London, 7pm 020 7515 6291 **24 No to GM Crop commercialisation**. 12 noon Victoria Tower Gardens, next to Houses of Parliament Bring your own picnic 2pm DEFRA, Smiths Square, Westminster. 01273-628441 or 020-7272-1586. **24-28 The Big Green Gathering** 01932 229911 www.big-green-gathering.com **25 5-a-Side No Sweat Challenge Fundraiser** at Fulham's Craven Cottage Minimum £50 to enter, 32 teams and you will each play at least 3 games, more if yer any good. 07904-431959 for an application pack www.nosweat.org.uk **26- 28 WOMAD Rivermead**, Reading. Ticket bookings 0118-939-0930 www.womad.org **26- 28 VooV-Experience**, northern Germany. Open Air Trance Festival. 35 Euro's www.voov-experience.de **27 Godskitchen**, Long Marston Airfield, nr Stoke-Upon-Trent, Dance Festival 4pm-7am £45 www.godskitchen.com **27 Skate Attack and Critical Mass!** "Skateboarding in Manchester city centre is banned, cycling in Manchester is dangerous and not particularly pleasant! On Saturday the skaters and cyclists are invited to take part in simultaneous reclaiming of space and celebration of cycling and skating." Meet 1pm in St Peters Square by the Central Library, anyone with wheels, without an engine is welcome to join in. 07763740453 **27 War Tax Resistance** public conference. Friends Meeting House, 120 Heath St, Hampstead, London 10.30 am-3.30pm 0870-7773223 lobby@conscienceonline.org.uk **27-4 Aug Woodcraft Folk camp**, Lurgashall in Sussex. "We're an educational movement for children and young people, designed to develop self-confidence and activity in society, with the aim of building a world based on equality, peace, social justice and co-operation." 020-8672-6031 www.woodcraft.org.uk/venturercamp **31- 4 August** Goddess Conference, Glastonbury (where else) Celebrating "with ceremonies, adorations and praise songs, talks, workshops, beautiful womanspirit exhibitions, music, stalls, fun and dance." 01458-833933 goddessconference @ukonline.co.uk **31- 8 Aug** Szeiget 2002, Hungary £7 per day Bands inc: Pulp, Muse, The Cure, Mambo Kurt, Transglobal Underground, Stereo MC's, Herbalizer "Wipes the floor with a lot of the moneymaking mainstream festies in the UK." www.diaksziget.com

YEW FOOLS

Campaigners against the Stourbridge, Wolverhampton and Southern Dudley Bypasses are mourning the death of a 2,000+ year old yew tree which was on the proposed route. The tree was on top of Wychbury Hill, site of an Iron-Age Hill Fort, on the site are another 28 yew trees up to 2,000 years old. The bypasses run virtually exclusively through the region's green belt and link with the Birmingham Northern Relief Road and the M5/M42 to form a massive Super-Highway around Black Country and Birmingham. Once again the authorities are building a road that is environmentally damaging and won't solve traffic problems. The Anti-Bypass Campaign meet every Thursday at 8pm in The Crispin, Church Street, Stourbridge. Or Phone 0789 0973458. www.tararabeat.worldonline.co.uk www.antibypasscampaign.pwp.blueyonder.co.uk

* Get a copy of all the lovely new proposed road schemes by emailing andreww@transport2000.org.uk

ANIMAL FACTORY

After a year of undercover filming across the country, a coalition of animal rights groups are marching to demand an end to factory farms. The march coincides with the release of the shocking film which shows the horrific conditions endured by billions of animals all over the world. As well as the usual offenders the film rips the lid off the RSPCA's "Freedom Farms" and the bogus quality assurance stamps that supermarket suppliers slap onto every corpse that comes their way.

Viva!'s national march and rally against factory farming will be held on Saturday July 13th, noon at Kennington Park, London WC1. Info: 01273 777688 www.viva.org.uk

* Badger killing is expected to start soon on Exmoor National Park and North Wiltshire. Find out how you can help stop it: 07779 442395 www.badger-killers.co.uk

E$$OLES

Oil giant Esso, the world's richest corporation and premier league polluters, are suing Greenpeace about the French StopE$$o campaigners using their logo. The StopE$$o campaign is a world-wide alliance united against Esso's dirty fuels, tricks, money and lies. Esso has a history of throwing money around to buy researchers to deny the existence of global warming. They also bought themselves a president by donating more cash to the Republicans than anyone else.

The company says the replacement of the middle two letters of Esso with dollar signs makes it resemble the Gothic-scripted symbol of the SS and this is confusing to the public.

Stephen Tindale, Greenpeace UK director, explains: 'We simply replaced two letters in Esso's logo with the internationally recognised symbol for the US dollar. We find it ironic that the richest corporation in the world can't recognise the dollar sign and confuses it with a Nazi symbol.'"

Esso (or ExxonMobil in America) pressured Bush into backing out of the Kyoto agreement on global warming and were caught out this April when secret memos to the White House were leaked. One asked Bush Jr to get rid of top UN climate scientist Dr Watson and replace him with someone "less biased". Under Watson the Intergovernmental Panel on Climate Change had concluded that "most of the warming observed over the last 50 years is attributable to human activities" and predicted that average global temperatures will rise between 3°C and 10°C by the end of the century.

Bush did just as his oily friends told him and led the charge to get Watson out. He has now been thrown out of his job and is not even allowed a position on the panel. Bush's top climate negotiator now refuses to take stock of climate change until 2012.

Inside SchNEWS

Malachie Nichols has been sentenced to nine months imprisonment for trying to stop a fascist paper sale in Leeds. Please send letters of support to: Malachie Nichols, JN4126, HMP Wealstun, Weatherby, W Yorkshire, LS23 7AJ.

...and finally...

SchNEWS has found a web site concerning genetically modified (GM) crops but this one won't tell you where the frankenstein 'food' is being grown - quite the opposite. This site was set up by a PR company who go by the name of the Centre for Food and Agricultural Research (CFFAR), a shadowy organisation who are funded by, amongst others, our old muckers Monsanto, the bio tech multinational. With their liberal usage of terms like "terrorism" "violence" and "acts of terror" the real purpose of this site is to associate anti-GM activists with something like Al-Qaida.

In one ridiculous statement CFFAR likens people who pull up dodgy crops to rapists. While talking about newsletters like Genetix Update and how they write about actions on GM food, CFFAR says it's like them saying "I do not approve of rape but I'm going to give you some tips on how to find your victim and pin her to the ground. Then you can tell me about it and I'll tell the world". How sick is that? Surely pulling up GM crops is better than being on the pull. Anyway SchNEWS always thought that multinational corporations like Monsanto were the real earth rapists and just what are they pulling? The tossers. Check it out. www.cffar.org/vandalwatch

Psychodelic Disclaimer

SchNEWS warns all greenies not to get browned off and feel blue when the future looks black and nothing's going white. If you're seeing red about the grey monotone around you, don't be yellow – be purple with rage. It's crystal-clear. Honest.

Subscribe! _____

Keep SchNEWS FREE! Send 1st Class stamps (e.g. 10 for next 9 issues) or donations (payable to Justice?) Ask for "Originals" if you can make copies. Post *free* to all prisoners. SchNEWS, c/o on-the-fiddle, P.O. Box 2600, Brighton, East Sussex, BN2 0EF.
Tel/Autofax +44 (0)1273 685913 *Email* **schnews@brighton.co.uk** *Download a* **PDF** *of this issue or subscribe at* **www.schnews.org.uk**

Regardless of what the United Nations did, a deranged meglomaniac (more about him later) and his rascally associates in their underground lair had already decided to invade Iraq to gain control of its oil. Now nothing could prevent the unswerving march towards war - neither the distinct lack of evidence of Iraqi weapons nor the moral fibre of the chief weapons inspector...

ARE YOU GOING TO DO A FULL INSPECTION MR BLIX?

WELL THEY DON'T CALL ME HANS FOR NOTHING YOU KNOW

TONY - WE NEED YOU TO PUBLISH A DOSSIER SHOWING THAT SADDAM'S GOT THE WEAPONS. BUT THE CATCH IS YOU'LL HAVE TO MAKE ALL OF IT UP... AND... 'SEX IT UP' A LITTLE WILL YOU

To write the dossier Downing Street brought in the expert research of 16 year old Tammy from Croydon and borrowed heavily from the contents of one of her human biology projects...

Blair's Dossier

Weapons of Mass Destruction In Iraq

...and ended up with something which was suitably sexed up - but didn't contain anything in particular about Iraq's weapons of mass destruction

Meanwhile Tony paced about his office, taking calls from Dubya and his mysterious henchman, bossing his minions around, organising press releases with his spin doctors and rubber stamping extra funding for the department of defence.
Occasionally he would look outside his window to see how many hundred thousand were protesting against his policies.

I NEED ANOTHER STIFF ONE

TORQUAY SUMMIT

On the brink of war, the leaders of the two countries leading the euphemistically titled 'coalition' met at Torquay for a war summit, hosted by Manuel Aznar, the leader of Torquay. The main thing the three leaders had in common was that the populations in their countries had turned out in record numbers to oppose their war.

I'LL BE LUCKY TO COME OUT OF THIS WITH MY JOB. PUBLIC SUPPORT FOR ME IS AT 41%

YOU'RE LUCKY - WE'RE DOWN TO 35%

HIN HMY HCOUNTRY HWE HAVE THE HBIGGEST PROTESTS HIN THE HWORLD HHI HAM HVERY PROUD

DON'T YOU THINK THIS WAR ON TERRORISM HAS SENT US ALL BACK 40 YEARS?

Every opportunity for a contrived display of public unity was seize upon...

TONY - THE SPECIAL RELATIONSHIP DOESN'T GO AS FAR AS HOLDING HANDS

While the mysterious phone calls continued...

DON'T GO SOFT ON US NOW, TONY. FORGET THE FRENCH - THEY'RE JUST SORE LOSERS. TELL JACK HE'S DOING FINE - THE LISP MAKES HIM SOUND SINCERE AND GENUINE.

Tony Blair and Jack Straw put the full neo - labour spin machine behind the war

YOU LYING SLIMEBALL TONY - HOW ARE YOU GOING TO KEEP THIS UP?

SCOUT'S HONOUR THAT SADDAM HAS THE WEAPONS AND WE ARE RIGHT TO SUPPORT A GENOCIDAL ATTACK

YOU KNOW HOW LARGE MY MAJORITY IS DON'T YOU...

57

I LONG FOR THE GOOD OLD DAYS... OF THE COLD WAR WHEN YOU KNEW WHO THE ENEMY WERE, WHEN OIL SUPPLIES WERE MORE CERTAIN, AND IT WAS POSSIBLE TO BE A SEXIST CREEP AND GET AWAY WITH IT

GO AND BE USEFUL AZNAR AND MAKE ME A CUP OF TEA

HANYTHING TO HELP THE HWAR START HMISTER BLAIR. I HLEARN HABOUT HIRAQ. I HREAD HIT HIN HA BOOK.

YOU LOOK SMASHING IN A UNIFORM GEORGE - SHAME YOU NEVER SHOWED UP FOR DUTY WHEN YOU WERE IN THE NATIONAL GUARD

YOU'RE JUST JEALOUS YOU WEREN'T BORN AN OVERPRIVILEGED BRAT LIKE ME COLIN. AND ANYWAY - I ALWAYS END UP GETTING MY HANDS DIRTY WHEN I DRESS UP LIKE THIS IN FRONT OF THE TROOPS.

As the American war machine built up on the perimeters of the Middle East, the British committed as many troops as it could to the invasion - but kept a few back to cover for the firefighters who were on strike.

NOW GENTLEMEN - WE ARE STANDING IN FOR STRIKING FIREMEN SO WE WILL BE MANNING THE GREEN GODDESSES. THE CATCH IS THAT THEY'RE OLDER THAN MOST OF YOU ARE.

The mysterious man known only as Dr Evil continued calling, but the deals Blair was making with him were really beginning to stretch Tony's thin morals to the limit...

DON'T WORRY ABOUT PUBLIC OPINION TONY - I'LL HAVE A WORD WITH RUPERT FOR YOU

TELEPHONE

Then one day he got fed up with the pressure coming from both sides and rang up Dubya wanting answers...

LOOK DUBYA YOU PROMISED I'D COME OUT LOOKING LIKE A CHURCHILL OR A THATCHER IF I DID YOUR BIDDING IN THE U.N. AND GOT COUNTRIES TO AGREE TO WAR. NOW YOU'RE SAYING THAT AFTER THE INVASION ALL THE CONTRACTS TO REBUILD IRAQ WILL GO TO AMERICANS.

YEP THAT'S RIGHT - DIDN'T I MENTION THAT? BUT THANKS VERY MUCH FOR ALL YOU'VE DONE - COULDN'T HAVE DONE IT WITHOUT YOU

EVERY DAY I GET TOLD WHAT TO DO OVER THE PHONE BY A MYSTERIOUS MAN WITH A HUSKY VOICE. AND THAT'S JUST MY SHRINK... BY THE WAY WHO IS DR EVIL?

I THINK IT'S ABOUT TIME YOU MET THIS DR EVIL. I'LL ARRANGE A MEETING ON THE FRONT LAWN OF THE WHITE HOUSE FOR YOU...

So Tony and Jack flew over to Washington to pay a visit to the White House. At the designated time they crept around the lawns looking for signs of Dr Evil...

TONY, TONY, DO YOU SEE WHAT I SEE?

YERRS. IT LOOKS SOME SORT OF ORIFICE. I WONDER IF WE CAN GO DOWN INTO IT...

LOOK THERE'S A MAN COMING OUT POINTING HIS GUN. PERHAPS HE IS ONE OF DR EVIL'S HENCHMEN AND THE HOLE LEADS TO A SECRET UNDERGROUND LAIR. HOW EXCITING!

OOH HEAVEN FORBID WE'RE NOT HERE TO MIX BUSINESS WITH PLEASURE

MR BLAIR I SWEAR I CAN HEAR COUNTRY AND WESTERN MUSIC THROUGH THIS WALL

"STAND BY YOUR MAN" - ONE OF MY FAVOURITES. THEY MUST KNOW I'M COMING

NOW LET'S SEE - THAT LAST TRAIN WAS THE NINE O'CLOCK FROM...

The intrepid Carry On Bombing team descend into the manhole and - predictably - are immediately in the corridors of an underground complex....

OOH I WONDER WHERE THIS TUNNEL LEADS TO... MAYBE WE'LL FIND SOME WEAPONS OF MASS DESTRUCTION

JACK - WE AREN'T IN SADDAM'S PALACES YET - THIS IS THE HIDE-OUT OF THE AMERICANS. IN FACT IF YOU SEE ANY WEAPONS OF MASS DESTRUCTION - WHICH YOU MAY WELL DO - LOOK THE OTHER WAY!

Eventually they are greeted by one of Dr Evil's assistants...

WELCOME MR BLAIR - DR EVIL HAS BEEN EXPECTING YOU - NOW GO DOWN THE CORRIDOR AND IT'S FIRST DOOR ON THE LEFT AFTER THE COLLECTION OF BODIES RECOVERED FROM ALIEN SPACECRAFT...

OOOH IS THAT YOU MONICA? - YOU'VE GROWN INTO SUCH A BIG GIRL. WHAT REALLY HAPPENED BETWEEN YOU AND BILL?

THE ORGANISATION NEEDED A SMOKE-SCREEN WHEN WE PLANNED THE BOMBING OF IRAQ IN 1998. AND THAT INVOLVED ME GOING DOWN ON THE PRESIDENT. BILL WAS A MAN WITH HIS WEAKNESSES.

OH MY WORD - THIS IS A PROPER UNDERGROUND COMPLEX. IT'S A BIT LIKE DOWNSTAIRS AT RAF NORTHWOOD ONLY MUCH BIGGER

THESE MUST BE THE VERY ROOMS WHERE THEY PLANNED THE FAKING OF THE MOON LANDING, THE SHOOTING OF THE KENNEDYS AND...

...AND THE SHOOTING OF MARTIN LUTHER KING! YUP. THE PLANE CRASHES ON SEPTEMBER 11 - PLUS ALL THE COUPS AND REGIME INSTALLATIONS, PROXY WARS AND COUNTLESS ASSASSINATIONS - ALL PLANNED RIGHT HERE IN THIS ROOM, BY MYSELF OR MY ESTEEMED PREDECESSORS. WELCOME BOYS - I AM THE CURRENT... DR EVIL

DR EVIL... IT'S REALLY YOU.

I PREFER TO BE CALLED DR EVILSFELD - AND THIS HERE IS MY LITTLE CLONE, DONALD W. WELCOME TO MY LAIR. YOU KNOW YOU GUYS HAVE DONE BRILLIANTLY. I COULDN'T HAVE COMPLETED MY WARPED PLANS FOR WORLD DOMINATION WITHOUT YOU. BUT FIRST - COME AND MEET THE CHILDREN...

WE ARE CLONING OUR NEXT ADMINISTRATION. ONE DAY THESE KIDS WILL RULE THE PLANET... GEORGIE, DICKY, PERLY, WOLFY AND CONDY

Usually when the meglomaniac reveals his mad plan, the hero does something about it. Not this time...

HELLO - AND WHAT DO YOU WANT TO BE WHEN YOU GROW UP THEN?

SIR I WANT TO BE A GENOCIDAL MEGLOMANIAC SIR

PERFECTLY CHARMING BOY

THEY'RE ALL VERY EXCITED ABOUT THE UP-COMING INVASION OF IRAQ YOU KNOW

TWO MONTHS LATER , after the invasion of Iraq, the two leaders met to discuss the next stage of the war...

LOOK TONY - THANKS A LOT. TO SHOW OUR GRATITUDE HERE ARE SOME TREASURES FROM THE IRAQI NATIONAL MUSEUM FOR YOUR MANTLEPIECE. AND WE CAN'T OFFER YOUR COUNTRY ANY OF THE CONTRACTS FOR THE REBUILDING OF IRAQ BUT WHAT WE CAN OFFER - AS A PERSONAL REWARD FOR YOU - IS A PROMISE THAT YOUR PLACE IN HISTORY WILL BE ASSURED - FOREVER.

OOOH GEORGE - I DON'T ACTUALLY CARE WHAT HAPPENS TO IRAQ NOW, I JUST WANT TO GO DOWN IN HISTORY AS A GREAT PRIME MINISTER WHO LED BRITAIN TO VICTORY AGAINST A COUNTRY WHICH HAD WEAPONS OF MASS DESTRUCTION. AND I WANT THIS STORY TO BE REPEATED ON TELEVISION EVERY BOXING DAY FROM NOW UNTIL ETERNITY.

THERE'S ALWAYS A GAP AT 3AM BETWEEN 'DR NO' AND 'ON THE BUSES'

weekly SchNEWS

www.schnews.org.uk

Friday 5th July 2002   Free/Donation   Issue 363

IF YOU'VE DONE NOTHING WRONG, YOU'VE GOT NOTHING TO HIDE

ENTITLEMENT CARD

BLAIR, TONY
DOB: 6 May/Mai 1954
Nationality: GLOBAL CITIZEN
CRIMINAL RECORD:
* War Crimes in Kosova 1999
* War Crimes in Afghanistan 2001
* Fucked up transport, education, housing & health in UK 1997-
* Knowingly sold arms to terrorists 1997-
* and the rest...

IDENTITY CRISIS

"Since Labour came to power they have introduced draconian surveillance laws on email, the recent anti-terrorism legislation, new proposals to extend data-sharing between government departments and the "Snooper's Charter", abandoned two weeks ago. A worrying trend is emerging" - **Karen Bartlett, Charter 88.**

ID cards are back on the agenda – or as the government would like us to call them 'Entitlement Cards', which must mean the government and police are entitled to find out everything about you whenever they like.

On your funky new card will be your fingerprints, digital photo, name, address and an ID number. To make sure people are who they claim to be, the cards will probably incorporate a chip containing the "biometric" - a fingerprint, retina or hand scan of the holder. The card and the finger are placed into a reader, and the person is "validated".

The government argue that it won't be compulsory to carry a card but as it would be required for just about everything then not carrying it will be a major hassle.

Neo-Labour says the cards are needed in the fight against crime, terrorism, illegal immigration and dog fouling. Privacy International on the other hand reckon they will actually make some of these things worse. For the past 12 years the Big Brother busting watchdog has studied the world-wide implications of ID cards and concluded that they have no effect on the reduction of crime or fraud, and instead introduce additional problems of discrimination, criminal false identity and administrative chaos!

Their survey also found claims of abuse in virtually every country with the question of who is targeted for ID checks left largely to the discretion of the police. And what happens if your card is lost or stolen? In nearly all countries with ID cards this causes immense problems with services and benefits being denied. So with all these problems and costs estimated to be up to £3 billion why the hell does the government want to carry on with this IDiocy?

Well Privacy International believes that the proposal has little to do with the government's stated objectives of reducing crime but part of a broader objective outlined in the Cabinet Office report "Privacy & Data Sharing". As Mark Littlewood from Liberty points out "Any form of ID card scheme would require a national database storing vast amounts of sensitive information on every one of us. You would have to be supremely uncynical or incredibly naïve to believe that the database will only be deployed in catching the guilty."

* For more on why ID cards are such a great idea see www.privacyinternational.org

* A report by the NACRO has found that CCTV only has a limited effect in cutting crime, and that other measures such as better street lighting, could be up to four times more effective. A Home Office evaluation of 24 CCTV schemes across the country showed that in four cases crime rates had risen significantly and in seven there was no effect at all. Yet this didn't stop Lord Falconer, the Home Office minister contradicting his own department's evidence and say "What the research indicates is that in every area there is a statistical reduction in crime." Now SchNEWS isn't surprised to hear politicians spin out lies, but we think that saying a success rate of marginally more than 50% is a total success really takes the piss.

* 11th September is International Day Against Video Surveillance. www.notbored.org

CRAP ARRESTS OF THE WEEK

For returning a library book late. 12-year-old Marisa Gohr must appear in an American court next Tuesday after failing to return one of the books she borrowed for a research project on dolphins. Her mum went to the original trial and told the court the book had now been taken back and a $9 fine paid. But that wasn't good enough for the Judge who wants to see Marisa because its her who's named on the court summons.

INTERNAL STRUGGLE

"Internment is clearly intended to deter political activity and dissent by foreigners in the UK. It intimidates the prisoners, their families, associates and indeed, entire communities - who are left wondering who will be next." - **Campaign Against Criminalising Communities.**

Seven people have been interned (that's a sanitised way of saying banged up in prison without charge, something that isn't supposed to happen in democracies) in the UK thanks to the Anti-Terrorism Crime & Security Act 2001. We are not allowed to know who they are, they are not allowed to know what they are accused of - and have not been charged with any crime. The government does not have to offer any reasons to the prisoners or the public.

All of the prisoners are being held in maximum-security prisons with severe restrictions on space, sunlight, and visitors, described by lawyer Gareth Peirce as "concrete coffins". For those who have already been subjected to torture and imprisonment in their own countries, it will feel like a home from home.

Identity Crisis cont...

From the 17th to the 20th of July the Home Office will present secret evidence to keep the unnamed seven locked up without charge and still without giving them a chance to defend themselves in court. Anonymous, voiceless and unaware of what crime they are supposed to have committed, they could be sentenced in their absence to years in prison.

This treatment can be inflicted only on foreign nationals who are in danger in their own countries and so cannot be deported. It ignores not only the centuries old right to Habeas Corpus*, but also the Human Rights Act 2000 and international law like the European Convention on Human Rights. The government justifies this racist and illegal behaviour by claiming the UK is currently under a state of emergency, about to be blown up any second by terrorists.

Similar abuses were perpetrated in the past against black and Irish people in Britain, with similar justifications, and we have since learned that surprise, surprise many of those interned were innocent. In Northern Ireland in August 1971, in an attempt to crush the IRA, the Army raided homes and abducted hundreds of Catholics, who were interned without trial. All were subjected to brutal treatment and 'ringleaders' were singled out, isolated and systematically tortured. In all 924 people were interned and the vast majority released without charge (see SchNEWS 331).

The same treatment is being directed at Muslims in Britain and the USA today. In America 325 Muslims have been interned since Sept 11th and only one has been charged with terrorism.

The Campaign Against Criminalising Communities have called for a protest on Wednesday, 17th at 9am at the Special Immigration Appeals Commission, 15-25 Field House, Breams Building, off Chancery Lane (nearest tube: Chancery Lane) 020-7586-5892 www.cacc.org.uk

* SchNEWS Vocab Watch: Habeas Corpus – the right to Habeas Corpus is the right not be imprisoned without appearing before a court.

PIQUETEROS PICKED OFF

Last Thursday Dario Santillan and Maximiliano Costeki from the piqueteros (unemployed workers' movements) of Argentina became the latest casualties in the country's economic meltdown (SchNEWS 350) after taking part in a roadblock to demand food and jobs.

Two cops have been arrested and 100 more suspended, but while the government have blamed the police, it is the government who have been busy telling the piqueteros that their road blocking tactics will no longer be tolerated. This resulted in two people dead, 60 injured, four of them severely, and more than 150 arrested.

Dario was a 21 year old, who worked every day in a factory making bricks for a new community hall. He lived on land taken a few months ago, on a vacant farm.

On Wednesday 50,000 people gathered at the Plaza de Mayo in heavy rain to denounce the murders and state repression with banners such as 'Maxi, Dario, always present, your comrades won't forget you'. http://argentina.indymedia.org/features/english/

SchNEWS in brief

Help! SchNEWS is always on the hunt for some people to help with the mail out on a Friday, but we're desperate for some volunteers over the next couple of weeks. Wanna DTP a copy? Give us a call for details ** **La Vielle Vallette** a French squatted eco-village is facing eviction at the end of month, and they desperately need help. There's plenty of space and even empty houses. The village is in the South of France near Nimes-Ales. Tel: 00 334 66 25 32 62 http://collectif.valette.free.fr ** **The Future of Freedom** – have your say about the anarchist mag Saturday 6th 3pm at Freedom Press, 84b Whitechapel High St, London. 020-7247-9249 ** **The Bristolian**, Bristol's excellent weekly free paper is celebrating it's 50th issue. They're now trying to increase their circulation to an amazing 20,000. Check 'em out, send an SAE to Box 3, Green Leaf bookshop, 82 Colston Street, Bristol, BS1 5BB. www.bristolian.org.uk ** A Dutch Judge has ordered **Netherlands Indymedia** to remove links on their site to German magazine 'Radikal' which contains articles suggesting ways protesters might stop the transport of nuclear waste in Germany. They face a fine if they do not comply www.statewatch.org/news/2002/may/03dutch.htm ** **Cultureshop** the online independent video store are looking for new political, social, independent videos to distribute on their site. If you have any contact them: ben@videonetwork.org ** Demonstration this Sat (6th) 1:30pm outside **Lewes Prison** in protest at restrictions on visiting times. Transport from St Peter's Church in Brighton at 12:30pm. ** A **new 4-lane bypass** is being built between Bilston and Penicuik, in Scotland, 8 miles south of Edinburgh This will involve the destruction of woods in Bilston and will also destroy sites of local historical interest. Construction has already begun, but it's not too late to show opposition: 07753 808709 spikesay swoof@ihateclowns.com ** Gaelic language campaigners have been painting road signs in the Highlands with snappy slogans such as **'Ceartas dhan Ghàidhlig'** (Justice for Gaelic) to protest at the authorities refusal to recognise the language. According to the powers that be Gaelic language signs are 'dangerous' to road-safety! http://groups.yahoo.com/group/Iomairtean_Gaidhlig/ ** Just 2 hours before a High Court Judge in London was due to decide whether to allow a dangerous **cargo of nuclear waste** to be shipped back to the UK from Japan, the ships in defiance set sail anyway. The two ships are now travelling half the way around the world with enough plutonium to make 50 nuclear bombs. www.greenpeace.org.uk ** **Survivors of the Bhopal disaster** in India, where poisonous gas from Union Carbide's pesticide factory has so far killed more than 20,000, and at least 150,000 continue to suffer serious health effects, (See SchNEWS 238), last week set up a permanent picket in New Delhi calling for the fair distribution of the compensation funds that Union Carbide have been ordered to pay. Find out more at Bhopal Express a film exploring the story of the disaster is showing 14th July, Duke of York's cinema, Preston Circus, Brighton, 2pm. ** Last week activists helped free 34 asylum seekers from the infamous Australian Concentration Camp, the **Woomera** detention centre, using a car to drag down fences. Next Wednesday (10th) there's a solidarity picket/fast outside Australia House in London. 5-9pm no food or drink apart from water. info@chilout.org.uk ** **God Save the Guillotine** 7 incher out now by LSDS on Scrap Records www.dirtysquatters.com

PARTY ANIMALS?

Smeatharpe

Despite the best efforts of the cops backed up with roadblocks and the trusty old Criminal Justice and Public Order Act (1994), free parties just won't go away. Usually low key attracting a few hundred with no one taking much notice, over the past few months some have become festival size. The problem of trying to put on anything (ask the Welsh Green Gathering lot, SchNEWS 354) you've got to jump through a million licensing hoops, or like Glastonbury forced to work with corporate cock suckers like Mean Fiddler.

Take Stonehenge where for the past few summers people have tried to sort out a festival afterwards – last year the MOD pulled out at the last minute, this year there were rumours that farmers who were up for renting their land were warned off by the cops. So instead of free festivals being at least a bit planned, and stuff like provision of toilets and wood for fires, it becomes a game of cat and mouse with the cops, with the result that parties end up on sites that aren't always suited.

One local complained to SchNEWS about the festival in Steart over the Jubilee weekend "Over ten thousand of you arrived at a nature reserve and birdlife sanctuary - at the height of the wading birds nesting season. For three days, you terrorised the local inhabitants, and destroyed the nests and the fledglings." Guilfin responded "The site wasn't the one chosen, confusion, abounded, a few rigs took the previously used beach, then everybody else followed. It's not on to use somewhere like that, but if you're not aware of it's sensitivity, and the police are chasing down convoys, then it's not surprising someone made a snap decision to take the site. What we need is places to party safely and responsibly. Dancing shouldn't be an outlaw activity."

So beyond the roadblocks the parties continue. Here's one report from someone outside The Great Wall of Glasto plc: "Several thousand people in a field, dancing to underground music from sound systems to live bands, taking whatever drugs they want as the party continues 24 hours a day, and making new connections outside capitalism's reign of terror. Sound idyllic? This was the scene at Smeatharpe, a former airbase some twenty miles from Glastonbury last weekend. Worlds apart? Well actually maybe not.

Smeatharpe should be the ideal spot for a free party. It's in the middle of nowhere. The neighbouring farmer had no problem with the party as long as people showed him the basic respect of not using the fences for firewood (it's lambing season at the moment) or trashing his crops. Not so tricky really, but that, unfortunately, is what happened, as well as kids burning a car left behind 10 years ago and sending a smoke signal of filth over the surrounding countryside.

Free parties and festivals are great cos they rely on the people there to sort out everything themselves – there's no gap between organisers who sort out infrastructure and the punters. Everyone's on the same vibe - in theory. No one will look after your land for you, toilets and bins won't be provided. So it's best to take a shovel (or even a trowel if you're hitching), clear your rubbish and take it with you, and if there are people who don't know the score, let them benefit from your experience. Free events are a great opportunity for our culture to make the connections between free space and the environment we live in. Let's create the world we want to live in – all of us, together."

* Saturday 13th July Truth and Reconciliation Commission for Stonehenge, George Hotel, Amesbury 10am. 0117 9542273 www.greenleaf.demon.co.uk
* For more information about the Steart festival see www.squall.co.uk/squall.cfm?sq=2002061403&ct=9
* For free party hotlines, reports and pictures www.guilfin.net

Inside SchNEWS

5 anti-fascist activists have all been sentenced to 9 months in prison for affray. They were arrested when they tried to stop fascists from selling papers in Bristol. Letters of support appreciated to Michael Davison JN4124, Callum Currie JN4121, John Whinfrau JN4123, Malachi Nicholls JN4126 via the Prisoner Support Group, Bradford Art and Resource Centre, 17-21 Chapel St, Bradford, BD1 5DT. Please write your name and address on the envelope otherwise they won't be accepted at the prisons.

Positive SchNEWS

The newly elected President of Costa Rica, Dr. Abel Pacheco de la Espriella, has decided that he likes his country the way it is- with pristine coastlines, fragile coral reef systems and lush rainforests. He's banned all offshore oil explorations and large scale mining and vowed to ensure its "absolute protection" from the greedy claws of the oil and mining companies who are clambering to destroy it. Pachecho is continuing a Costa Rican tradition of making unconventional decisions as Costa Ricans take pride in being the only Central American nation without an army, and one of the most peaceful countries in the region. You can bet he will have to fight every inch as pressure is already mounting on him from the oil guzzling US. You can write and urge him to hold firm at presidente@casapres.go.cr or visit www.elaw.org/campaigns/info.asp?id=495

...and finally...

Anarchist librarians in America are fighting to ensure that the US doesn't become a nation of illiterates. Under the new USA Patriot Act, the FBI has been given rights to snoop on people's reading habits, under the pretence of fighting terrorism. SchNEWS can't help but wonder though whether the Act is just a ploy to bring everyone down to the same level of ignorance as George W.

Librarians around the USA are vowing to do all they can to make sure that people's reading habitats are kept secret. In the meantime they'd advise everybody to return that flying for beginners book as soon as possible. www.infoshop.org/library2/stories.php?topic=2

Disclaimer

SchNEWS warns all readers beware of unidentified flying entitlements.

QUICK - CHANGE CHANNELS - THE FOOTY'S STARTED

...ARE CALLING THIS FAMINE A HUMANITARIAN DISASTER

weekly SchNEWS

www.schnews.org.uk

Friday 12th July 2002   Free/Donation   Issue 364

LAST SUPPER

"That there are, today, still 815 million hungry people in the world is truly a crime. That the proposals we made nearly six years ago are now even further from being achieved is [even more] shameful." - Sr. D. Felipe Pérez Roque, Cuban Foreign Minister.

In 1996 world leaders met at the World Food Summit to talk about how they might be able to reduce world hunger, a time when there were 800 million starving people. They made commitments to halve world hunger by 2015. Last month, nearly 6 years later, the follow on summit took place in Rome.

This year's summit was never going to get off to a good start, with the number of starving people in the world pretty much the same as at the time of the last Summit, and a massive famine looming in southern Africa. But rather than take the bull by the horns and do something for the poor, the leaders of the world's richest countries decided to stay at home and count their weapons. Only two managed to attend, and one of them Silvio Berlusconi – the Summit's host, even managed to wrap it up early so he could watch the footie.

This is in sharp contrast to the NATO- Russia Summit, also in Rome, five and a half weeks earlier, where 20 world leaders met and agreed effectively to sustain the $800 billion a year global arms industry without a mention of the needs of the poor. In fact as Patrick Mulvany from Intermediate Technology Development Group (ITDG) points out "Apart from Berlusconi and José Maria Aznar, the Spanish Premier,

the only common link between the two Summits was the military operation of 16,000 police, carabinieri and soldiers put in place to contain the politicians and exclude the people. Many people from Civil Society were unable to enter the exclusion zone of half a kilometre around the building, which kept away the 30,000 person 'March for Food Sovereignty: land and dignity'. [The Food Summit] became a military zone. And this emphasised the sense of oppression in the summit."

In the absence of world leaders the summit was gobbled up by corporations, who made sure they didn't leave it empty handed. The final declaration was extremely bad news for the poor with a US imposed acceptance of genetically modified (GM) crops as a solution to world hunger, and an abandonment of any reference to the precautionary principle when it comes to GM food. The declaration also deleted any reference to a legally binding code of conduct on the right to food (the right to produce and consume food), and watered down the call to ratify the International Seed Treaty (ITPGFRA- see SchNEWS 329), which should stop the patenting of crops, to something that countries "should consider".

So if you're starving from now on it seems that it's going to be the same but worse, with little hope for anything but GM food landing on your plate in the future. Food aid spiked with GM maize will now be dumped on the ravaged countries of southern Africa by Uncle Sam. This cleverly pollute all the crops in the region, making any sustainable GM-free op-

tion a dead duck - so much for the World Summit on Sustainable Development being held in Johannesburg in August/September.

Meal Ticket

Six Hundred people took part in the Civil Society Forum for Food Sovereignty, also in Rome, at the same time as the official Food Summit. This Forum was attended by many that were excluded from the main Summit: farmers, fisherfolk, pastoralists, indigenous peoples, environmentalists, women's organizations, trade unions, and NGOs. They came up with their own 'Action Agenda' that totally rejected the declaration made at the formal summit. Instead they called for a radical change in ap-

Last Supper cont...

proach to address the real cause of hunger – international trade rules. Their agenda calls for the removal of food and agriculture from the control of the World Trade Organisation, an end to dumping of cheap food in poor countries, the total rejection of GMOs and patents on life, and investment in more sustainable locally controlled small-scale agriecology (sustainable agriculture).

Part of their press release read: "The 1996 Plan of Action has not failed because of a lack of political will and resources, but rather it has failed because it supports policies that lead to hunger, policies that support economic liberalisation for the South and cultural homogeneity, which are backed by military force if the first wave of prescriptive actions fail. Only fundamentally different policies, which are based on the dignity and livelihoods of communities can end hunger. We affirm our belief that this is possible and urgently needed."

The fact that anybody is hungry in the world today is a scandal: there is no scarcity of food overall. In fact we've never grown so much food; and food has rarely been so cheap. But as trade liberalisation has increased there's been increasing levels of hunger amongst growing mounds of plenty, now spiked with GMOs. The bottom line has become that if you want to eat then you've got to pay, and that goes just as much for those in Europe and the USA as in poorer countries. Unless the situation changes by 2015 it's predicted 122 million people will have died needlessly of hunger.

As Patrick Mulvany, from ITDG says "It is our Global Shame that nearly a quarter of the population goes to bed hungry in a world that has never before produced so much food. The sad reflection on the formal summit is that governments will do little to eradicate hunger and corporations will continue to be allowed to extend their control over who gets to eat. And there is little profit in providing for the poor."

* Check out the Forum for Food Sovereignty Action Agenda: www.forumfoodsovereignty.org
* For analysis of the summit and information on sustainable agriculture check out www.ukabc.org/wfs5+.htm or www.itdg.org
* For the low down on aid and food dumping check out www.globalissues.org/TradeRelated/Poverty/FoodDumping.asp
*An Andean root crop has become the latest victim of biopiracy by a US corporation. Extracts of the Maca, a crop that has been grown

IRAQI SUV JUICE! NOW ON SALE CHEAP!

President Bush & Vice President Cheney are proud to offer land yacht-driving Americans a wonderful new brand of discount petroleum, freshly pumped from beneath the ashes of that bombed-out, Godless, formerly sovereign armpit called Iraq.

for centuries by indigenous people in the Puna highlands in Peru, have been patented for their viagra like (sexual potency) and natural fertility properties. Indigenous people's and farmers organisations are vowing to ignore the patent, and last month held a protest outside the offices of the Ecological Forum in Lima denouncing the biopiracy. Full story at www.etcgroup.org
* The 18 sites that will be used for the last 3 years of farm scale GM trials have just been announced. Check them out at www.geneticsaction.org.uk/testsites.

Polyp

BLITZED

Blitz promises to be "a kick-ass anti-corporate extravaganza" to coincide with the Commonwealth Games being held in Manchester later this month.

Organised by NATO – that's Northern Arts Tactical Offensive, the festival covers a week of shows, actions and events kicking off on Sat 20th July with an open air music event, and the opening of two exhibitions. One is AgiTATE being held in a spanking new shopping mall who failed in their bid to ban it once they realised what was happening! Throughout the week there will be film and multimedia events organised by Beyond TV. The week will end with a skate attack and critical mass plus political street theatre on Saturday 27th. NATO has also produced a spoof guide to the city to guide tourists to their events.

During that week there will also be a GM trashing nearby, Manchester People's open seminar for the Anti Commonwealth Games Coalition and lots of anti sweatshop actions. For a full programme see www.nato.uk.net

Direct action magazine Loombreaker reports "the Commonwealth Games are being used to launch a new Corporate Manchester - a posh apartment playground for coke-sniffing yuppies, ... The cost of the games are astronomical - the stadium alone accounts for a cool £120 million - but you won't hear too much about £80m of public money the council has committed to paying... So if you're wondering why there are cutbacks in schools and housing, or where your local swimming pools and other public amenities have all gone when your council rents and tax are rising, there's not much need to look any further really."

Inside SchNEWS

The 3p three (See Crap Arrest)

Sarah Gisborne HR4337 & Kate Simpson GN8957, HMP High Point, Stradishall, Newmarket, Suffolk, CB8 9YG

Madeline Buckler HR4338, YO Bullwood Hall, High Road, Hockley, Essex, SS5 4TE

GHOSTBUSTERS

Gabriel Nkwelle, a human rights activist and asylum seeker will be starting his appeal against his deportation on Monday 29th July at Bromley Magistrates Court. He is urging people to turn up and show some support. Gabriel arrived in Britain in May 2000 to claim asylum after exposing massive electoral fraud in his native Cameroon, but was promptly thrown in jail . Since then he has been 'ghosted' (moved) from prison to prison and detention centre to detention centre a total of ten times. While inside he was a tireless campaigner for other asylum seekers, a lot of whom couldn't speak very good English, and was a thorn in the side of the establishment, before being released late last year. So get down to Bromley at 10am on 29th July in the Immigration Appellate Authority Section, First Floor, 1 London Road, Bromley, Kent and make some noise.

*For the past 16 days the inmates at Woomera detention/concentration camp in the outback of Australia have been on hunger strike in protest at the appalling conditions they have to endure. In solidarity people have been fasting all over the world – Mexico, India, the U.S. and Israel outside their Australian embassies. On Wednesday in London around 100 people turned up for a rally in support of the detainees.

STOP PRESS –The hunger strike has now been called off because the authorities at Woomera stopped all medical treatment for the inmates and because of this all the solidarity fasts have now finished. For more info check out http://autonomous.org/refugee/ or www.rran.dhs.org

BARON BOOKBURNER

A man who targeted a radical bookshop because it didn't like the material they stocked walked away from the High Court last week with just £14 in damages – but the case leaves two of London's last remaining radical bookshops facing potentially crippling legal bills.

The case was brought nearly 2 years ago against Housmans Bookshop by Alexander Baron, a right-wing anti-gay litigant who had been referred to as a plagiarist in one sentence in a 136-page pamphlet stocked in the shop. Baron decided not to sue the author or publisher, but the shop, at one point asking them to pay him £50,000 to drop the case.

This case is the first time the defence of "innocent dissemination" has been used, where it was argued that it is impossible for bookshops, particularly small independents, to check - and take responsibility - for the content of the thousands of publications in stock at any one time. As Albert Beale from Housmans said "We feel it is important to try to take a stand, otherwise there might be no end to this sort of legal intimidation."

This action against Housmans was one of a series, dating back to 1996, brought against them, Bookmarks (also in London) and others, by people criticised in Searchlight magazine. The next case is due in court this autumn and the bookshops need donations for legal costs. Send cheques (payable to the "Bookshop Libel Fund"), 5 Caledonian Road, London, N1 9DX, 020 7278 4474 On-line donations at www.apoogee.com/Housmans

SchNEWS in brief

Albion Community Arts Trust have a two day festival fundraiser for a Norwich Free festival. Norwich Playhouse 19-20th July. 01603-717074 www.albionarts.org ** Benefit for **Walthamstow Anarchist Group** featuring Thatcher's Children plus others. 19th upstairs, Chestnut Tree, 757 Lea Bridge Rd, London E17. £3 info@walthamstowanarchy.org.uk ** If you've ever worked with **Veggies** catering campaign (even if it was just once) they want to speak to you for a book. Write to PO Box 2284, London,W1 5HU Or ronny.garlic@blueyonder.co.uk ** **Want some SchNEWS stickers?** Send the office an SAE to help spread the word. ** **Reclaim the Beach 9** - more urban free-party-in-posh-looking-venue-nonsense, Saturday 13th 8pm, Royal Festival Hall Beach south bank www.swarming.org.uk ** **No War But Class War** political discussion Saturday 13th 2-5pm Rutland Arms, Brown St, Sheffield (nr.Sheffield Railway Station) SheffieldNWBCW@aol.com ** **Interested in development of alternative education?** Meeting at the Brighthelm Centre, North Rd.,

Brighton 23rd July 7pm ** Campaign Against Arms Trade protest against **Farnborough Air Show**, 22nd-28th July. "Whilst the public days are championed as fun days out for all the family, the reality is very different. Farnborough is an arms fair and a very important date in the defence industry calendar." 020 7281 0297 www.caat.org.uk ** Brighton's **Radio4A** is back on the airwaves this weekend on 107.8 FM and www.piratetv.net ** A **protest camp has been set up near Edinburgh** to stop a bypass destroying an SSSI. Help urgently needed. 07753808709 ** **Woodside Traveller Site latest**: The Romany travellers at Woodside caravan park in Bedfordshire (see SchNEWS 360) have be been given their eviction date, its 1st November, they want people to come down to resist. Tents, campfires, cups of tea and music will be provided. More info: Clifford Codona 01206 523528 (mornings only) ** **Protest against Working Links** exploitation of uemployed people. Meet 10am Wednesday 17th Pavillion Gardens Cafe, New Road, Brighton.

PIPING HOT NEWS

A consortium of oil companies led by BP has big plans to build a 1,777km long oil pipeline from Baku in Azerbaijan, to Ceyhan, Turkey via Georgia, so that Caspian Sea oil can be exported to the US. BP, the world's third largest oil company, are begging the World Bank and other national export credit departments to provide them with credit for this environmentally disastrous scheme.

Campaigners against the pipeline are pressing these institutions to refuse credit, cos' apart from the obvious pollution the oil will cause when burned, they believe the pipeline may well exacerbate tension in a region recovering from conflict, and will provide no benefit to local people. The pipeline passes through several Kurdish regions in Turkey, according to Kerim Yildiz of the Kurdish Human Rights Project

"This pipeline would militarise a corridor running from the Caspian to the Mediterranean. This could threaten the fragile cease fire in the Kurdish region through which the pipeline will pass." For more information see www.bankwatch.org

* **Rising Tide weekend summer school on climate change** 26-28th July. Booking a space essential: 01865 554331 george@risingtide.org.uk

* **Climate Criminals Critical Mass** will pay a visit to the perpetrators of the pipeline on 15th July. Meet 2pm outside the National Film Theatre, South Bank, London.

* **The Ecotopia Biketour** is coming to the UK this summer along their route they will be doing actions and giving workshops. www.thebiketour.net
SEE ARTICLE IN THIS BOOK

Positive SchNEWS

Vegan-organic gardening is organic gardening, which avoids the use of any animal products, such as manure and animal remains, which many people use to fertilise the soil. The advantage of this type of gardening is that there's no animal exploitation at all, instead you can enjoy piling your vegetable beds high with home made vegetable compost.

If you're interested in learning vegan-organic skills the Vegan Organic Network have a training weekend, 20-21st July in Bolton. Only £15 for a day, £25 for the whole weekend. Contact Jenny Hall, 20 Hawthorn Ave, Orrell, Wigan, WN5 8NQ. Phone 07855 392037 email jennymosscentre@hotmail.com www.veganorganic.net

...and finally...

"This is the first-ever in-depth research into the health risks of anorak wearing," Professor Philip Murray announced at a press conference at Birmingham City Hospital, "and the results are remarkable. Campaigns to reduce road traffic accidents have hitherto paid little attention to the subject, but our findings prove what many people have long suspected. Put simply, the wearing of anoraks can be dangerous, and injurious to health.

"Our researchers measured the binocular visual field of healthy volunteers while they were wearing four different styles of anorak. Most wearers habitually pull the hood over their head, and our ophthalmologists discovered that, with the hood up, the field of vision is more than halved. The biggest danger comes when an anorak wearer tries to cross the road, because their vision is severely impaired, and they simply cannot see as well as other people. Our results prove beyond doubt that people need to be far more careful in their choice of headgear. And quite apart from that, they look ridiculous." *(Journal of the Royal Society of Medicine, 2002.)*
Shamelessly stolen from Private Eye.

Disclaimer
SchNEWS warns all greedy pigs we'll huff and puff on puff till yer Tower of Babylon falls down. Honest.

The Anus

If it's happening... it's up The Anus!

Free   Friday, July 19, 2002   www.brightonsucks.com

Beach Bummers Boozy Bottleneck

REVELLERS partied the night away on Brighton seafront last Saturday to the sound of overhead police helicopter display teams, traffic chaos, stranded emergency vehicles and the ecstatic screams of a quarter of a million happily crushed ravers.

The event, hosted by the Big Beached Buttock, featured the huge talent of disk jockey Fate By Slime who played some records to approximately 3000 people in front of Brighton West Pier. Meanwhile the remaining 247,000 party-goers looked on in awe and jubilation, but couldn't hear a bloody thing.

Party animals had been bussed in from as far afield as the Highlands of Scotland where whole hillsides had been cleared of trees and vegetation to make way for huge billboard posters for the event of the century. Welsh revellers talked of sheep that had been used as walking adverts for the gig with directions written in Welsh and English branded onto their once snow white bodies. Council 'helper' Simone Franchise stated that the massive advertising campaign had been essential in order to make the Flat Boy Scam gig the huge success that it was: "Everyone knows that an event of this magnitude has to be hugely over-attended. Some people have moaned about litter and broken glass on the beach but let's face it, where do you think all that rubbish came from? Mostly from our shops and therefore using our beach as a landfill site is good for business and good for everyone in Brighton."

Life's a Beach

Despite a handful of tragedies relating to the event, the police immediately ruled out any talk of an enquiry into the fantastically financially successful maritime pop show. Police spokesman Superindented Death Ray stated that the problems relating to the salty extravaganza were 'fairly obvious' and an inquiry would tell organisers nothing they did not already know about the event. Luckily there had been only one death relating directly to the event

and a mere 160 injuries during the night and as such the event had been 'as safe as houses.' Death added that having 250,000 drunk people and children trapped on a darkened Brighton beach in dangerously overcrowded conditions surrounded by broken glass and urine and unattended by emergency services was 'character building', creating a sense of community and togetherness reminiscent of the Blitz. Eyewitness reports that anarchy broke out as revellers threw bottles into the crowd and at emergency personnel have been dismissed as 'unproductive' criticism. As a result of the spectacular safety record and outstanding organisational skills displayed throughout Saturday evening by the police, officials felt questions raised by a handful of moaning locals were largely irrelevant. Brighton and Hove Council agreed whole-heartedly as did event organisers Big Beached Blunder.

Free for all party

Event Organisers The Big Blunder joined forces with the council and police to stress that in no way should the Filled By Slime gig be confused with the illegal free parties that have historically occurred on Brighton and Shoreham beaches. "We have gone to great lengths to stamp out the scourge that is the local free party scene; that cancerous rash that blights our cultural landscape should in no way be confused with legitimate council-backed beach-trashing events, all of which are wonderful and never go wrong". Council spokesthing Simian Fanfare added that "The council only supports events that are much, much larger and more corporate than free parties and therefore better. More mindless consumers visiting Brighton means more beer and chips being sold everywhere, as well as silly hats, sales of which have gone through the roof, and that's very important for our City of Culture Bid." Mr Fiasco also pointed out that the costs of policing this particular event as well as the impact of a quarter of a million guests descending on the city meant the event was far from free to local residents - unlike the vast ma-

jority of free parties which have done nothing to improve the corporate worth of Brand Brighton.

Meanwhile free party organisers are said to be fleeing the country in fear of their lives as Brighton Council death squads are being mobilised to further enforce their 'say no to unlicensed fun' campaign. One free party organiser who prefers to remain nameless stated that: "We're being persecuted because we keep throwing underground free parties for a few hundred locals without adequate advertising. Several of our crew were arrested last weekend for picking up litter and giving away free water to party-goers at an unlicensed free party. When they were eventually released, all they could do was dribble while reciting the Brighton and Hove mission statement over and over again." The drugged up squat rave organiser later added that "Finding sites with adequate parking well away from the public scrutiny has just got us in the worst kind of trouble – maybe in future we should just organise Dresden style leaflet drops and invite everyone to come and piss on our beach; it seems to work OK for the council."

After the unmitigated success of the gig on the beach, DJ Fete Boy (real name Naomi Coke) spent the remainder of the night guzzling Champagne and playing even more records for all of his celebrity friends in an exclusive Brighton nightspot. In the small hours, the exhausted DJ and his beautiful wife were whisked away in a limousine to their sparkling luxury condominium love pad with its private beach, which remains, as ever, beautifully clean.

Meanwhile, some people in our lovely new broken-glass-sparkly City, the ones who actually do useful jobs like clean the litter and look after sick people, have complained that they can't actually afford to live here anymore. Some even joined the nationwide strike on Wednesday, complaining, "It's time they (the Council) decided whether this is a playground for Londoners or a city for its own people." Council spokesperson Simpering Fanatic told the Anus "Why don't the poor people all just fuck off to Hastings?"

WAKE UP! WAKE UP! IT'S YER ON THE DECKS

weekly SchNEWS

www.schnews.org.uk

Friday 19th July 2002   Free/Donation   Issue 365

Not This Time – the Story of the Simon Jones Memorial Campaign, film showing in Brighton this Sunday as part of a nationwide tour. The film will be followed by a discussion with members of the Memorial Campaign and the film 'Globalisation and The Media' by Undercurrents. 7.30pm, Sussex Arts Club, Ship Street. Entrance is free.

UNCORPORATION

Hundreds of angry Nigerian women have pulled off something we here in the West can only dream of - they've managed to shut down a huge multinational oil company's operations for nearly two weeks, armed with nothing but their bare hands. On Monday, July 8th, a band of women from the Ugborodo and Arutan tribes in southern Nigeria pirated a ChevronTexaco staff ferry to sneak into the company's Escravos pipeline terminal. The unarmed women have occupied the terminal ever since, stopping exports and trapping about 700 workers, including Americans, Britons, Canadians and Nigerians, inside.

The women are demanding that ChevronTexaco hire more local workers, and provide water, electricity, schools and clinics for their villages, some of which are less than 100 yards from the terminal. They are angered that previous company promises to transform the villages surrounding the facility into modern towns have not been realized.

On Wednesday (10th), about 100 police and soldiers armed with assault rifles were sent to the terminal to protect the facility, but Anunu Uwawah, one of the women occupying the building, said the women weren't intimidated by security forces. "If we die, Chevron will die with us," she said. The women began talks with senior ChevronTexaco management in Nigeria on Friday (12th) after days of false starts, but Uwawah and other leaders in the group say they wouldn't leave the terminal until the company commits to hiring people from the neighbouring villages and helps them build better infrastructure.

* As of Wednesday, July 17th, various newsgroups are reporting that women from the Ijaw tribe have now occupied four ChevronTexaco oil facilities in the same area as the Escravos oil terminal, which is still occupied by the same kick-ass group of Ugborodo and Arutan women.

* In Mexico, hundreds of irate farmers armed with machetes and petrol bombs and holding 10 hostages are protesting against plans to build a new international airport outside of Mexico City. Why do the farmers feel so strongly about the new airport? Because it just so happens that its scheduled location is smack in the middle of their land. In return for the hostages, protestors are demanding that they be allowed to keep their land. Sounds reasonable enough to us, but the pro-business government of Mexican President Vicente Fox has ruled out any changes to its plans to build the £1.3 billion airport.

Positive SchNEWS

At the end of May, a Football Association Commission granted the owners of Wimbledon FC permission to relocate to Milton Keynes. Wimbledon, the fairy tale football club that had gone from non-league to FA Cup winners, had been without a home for years and was now being moved lock stock and barrel to a site 70 miles away. Six weeks later, disgruntled fans set up a new club called AFC Wimbledon, found a new place to ground share and a new league to play in, had 230 hopefuls turning up for trials on Wimbledon Common, sold 600 season tickets and had nearly 5,000 fans cheering them on at their first match, a friendly against Sutton. One fan commented "This is something very special here; A cottage industry in the middle of a globalised trading estate. A corner shop perched between hypermarkets. A community football club in the midst of greed and desperation." The new AFC Wimbledon will be kicking off a season-long boycott of their old club with a human chain round Selhurst Park on the first game against Gillingham. www.afcwimbledon.co.uk

CRAP ARRESTS OF THE WEEK
For having the wrong views

Late last year, American high school student Katie Sierra was suspended for 3 days after she tried to start an anarchy club. Now a jury has decided that the school was wrong to ban an anarchy club, but right to suspend her for proposing it in the wake of the September 11th attacks! The jury also sided with the school's ban on some of Katie's homemade T-shirts, one of which read, "When I saw the dead and dying Afghani children on TV, I felt a newly recovered sense of national security. God Bless America." The jury apparently felt that such messages "disrupted" other students' patriotic brainwashing, er, education - although students are routinely allowed to wear shirts that blatantly display corporate logos, slogans, and messages.

SICK AS A PARAGUAY

The people of Paraguay, pissed off with their corrupt government and their collapsing economy, took to the streets last week calling for the President to resign. (see pic right) Protected by the army and police officers with water cannons, the president responded on Monday by declaring a 5-day state of emergency which allowed the government to ban demonstrations, search homes and arrest hundreds of individuals. At least 2 people have been killed.

Paraguay is the latest of the South American countries to be crumbling under pressure from the International Monetary Fund, who've been telling them to privatise their public services in order to make their loan repayments. Massive opposition to such tactics has meant that privatisation plans have been put on the back burner. Instead the government are now turning to the World Bank for a loan which will plunge them even further into debt. Check out the latest at http://argentina.indymedia.org/

SchNEWS in brief

The **Community Activism Workshop** takes place Saturday 27th with a wide range of speakers from NoBorders to the Social Centres Network. The day is "an opportunity to share practical skills gained through community struggles - to learn from the experiences of others in organising grassroots campaigns and developing effective community activity." At the Radical Dairy, 47 Kynaston Road, London N16. from 2pm. 07944 586416 www.temporary.org.uk ** **Plans for a second nuclear reactor at Hinkley Point** (site of the Jubilee free festival on Steart Beach-see SchNews 359) rumble on despite a recent survey conducted by concerned parents which found rates of cancer in the area were four times the national average. There's a public meeting 'Stopping the drive for New Nuclear Power Stations', 7.30pm 25th July, Temple of Peace, Cathays Park, Cardiff 01984 632109 stophinkley@aol.com ** **No to GM Crop Commercialisation**, **protest outside DEFRA**. Wednesday 24th 12 noon for a Picnic at Victoria Tower gardens then 2pm demo on the steps of DEFRA, Smiths Sq, Westminster. 020 7272 1586 www.geneticsaction.org.uk ** **Genoa - Red Zone anniversary film screenings** happening in London (24th July, Ritzy Cinema, Brixton £5), and Glasgow (28th July - Glasgow Film Theatre). Copies will soon be available through www.cultureshop.org ** Local campaigners desperately need help to take **direct action to stop a mobile phone mast and access** road being erected in Maple, Cheshire. Info 0161 427 7789 ** **Ecotopia 2002** the annual European environmental festival takes place this year in County Clare, Ireland 10th-24th August. Info 00 353 86 3097622 www.ecotopia2002.org ** For the first time since the Foot and Mouth crisis last year, **live animal exports have resumed from UK ports**. Protests are being organised. 24 hour hotline live export hotline 01730 237379 www.ciwf.org.uk ** Want to check out what happens at **Fylingdales** – which could soon be home to Star Wars II? Check out www.fylingdales.ukf.net ** **Ladyfest London** (August 1st-4th) is a celebration of the achievements of women, primarily in music and the arts. With the exception of some workshops, the festival is open to women and men alike, with highlights including performances by The Gossip, The Haggard, Gertrude, and Sara Dougher. www.ladyfestlondon.org ** **The trial of campaigners arrested at Simon Jones Memorial Campaign** occupation of Euromin Docks in December last year takes place 29th-31st July in Worthing. The protesters who are accused of "besetting" would like support and are asking campaigners to meet at 8am at Brighton Station at the start of each day to travel together to Worthing Court. www.simonjones.org.uk ** **The Americans are coming!!** Okay, just one. A surprisingly anti-American one. On July 30th, political artist Seth Tobocman will visit Brighton to do a slide show of his work and talk about his life and times as a New York squatter. His kick-ass books include "War in the Neighbourhood" and "You Don't Have to Fuck People Over to Survive." For venue info (still being sorted out), contact sethtobocmaninbrighton@hotmail.com

BLANC CHEQUE

After a three year ban, lorries are once again being allowed to wreak their noxious fumes in the Mont Blanc tunnel. Many lorries ignore posted speed limits, but local police argue they don't have enough personnel to police speeding vehicles, although they were mysteriously able to rally more than a hundred riot cops to harass a peaceful anti-lorry protest held near the tunnel on June 25th. If you're interested in getting involved with the anti-truckers, contact noragallieni@mac.com, or info@arsmb.com

...and finally...

Corrupt, lying, dodgy Freemasons deserve human rights too! That's the claim made by the United Grand Lodge, the London headquarters of the secret brotherhood. With no apparent sense of irony the funny hand shake brigade is planning on using the Human Rights Act to stop the government making freemasons in public office declare that they are on the 'square' – or is that the make. Here at SchNEWS we had this strange idea that the Human Rights Act might give people a bit of leverage against the powers that run our lives and NOT be used by pro-establishment secret societies to cover up their shady deals- especially ones with initiation rituals pretty similar to the Cosa Nostra. So don't go kissing any freemasons as ya don't know what their hands have been shaking.

Disclaimer
SchNEWS warns all readers listening to repetitive bleats that they can make you sheepish. Honest. There's not going to be SchNEWS next week 'cos we'll all be at the Big Green Gathering.

Paraguay, July 15th: Boot boys attack people who have blocked major roads around the country calling for the president to resign.

IT'S YER SCHNEWS PARTY AND PROTEST GUIDE
AUGUST

1-4 Cambridge Folk Festival. Weekend tickets £62, plus camping at £27 or £18. www.cam-folkfest.co.uk **2 No Sweat benefit** to raise funds for Dita Sari and the Indonesian union federation that organises clothing workers Manchester Met Students Union. 0161-861-7160 manchester@nosweat.**org 2- 4 Essential Music Festival**, Hackney Marshes, London www.essentialfestival.com **2-4 The Big Weekend**, Cardiff. FREE www.cardiff.gov.uk **2-5 Healingfield Gathering** "our vision now is to bring the Healing Field to a beautiful secluded Somerset location" www.healingfield.btinternet.co.uk **2-9 Devon Sidmouth Festival** www.sidmouthfestival.com **3 March and rally in support of sweatshop workers around the world**, demanding the Commonweath Games organisers in Manchester make a stand against exploitation. 11.30am All Saints' Park, Oxford Road. 0161-861-7160 manchester@nosweat.org **3 Stanmer Organics Open Day**, Stanmer Park, Brighton 11am-4.00pm 01273-620486 info@stanmerorganics.org.uk **3-4 Nottingham Riverside Festival** www.nottinghamevents.org **3-17 Vegan Camp**, Park Foot caravan and camping park, Howtown Rd., Pooley Bridge, Penrith, Cumbria. www.vegancamp.org **3-11 Crossover Summer Camp**. Camp to bring people together from a variety of backgrounds to find intersections and make new alliances. Event will take place near Cottbus, Germany. www.summercamp.squat.net **4-11 Ealing Jazz Festival**, Walpole Park, Ealing. www.ealing.gov.uk **4-19 Trident Ploughshares Disarmament camp** at Peaton Glen Wood, near Coulport, Scotland. Fifteen days of direct disarmament action and campaign workshops at the Faslane and Coulport nuclear weapon bases. 0845-4588366 www.tridentploughshares.org **8-11 Welsh Green Gathering**, Margham Country Park, near Port Talbot. www.big-green-gathering.com/wgg CANCELLED cos the Welsh Police don't like wind turbines and recycling, see SchNEWS 354. **8-11 Cropredy Festival** nr Banbury, Oxfordshire. Fun with Fairport Convention. £55 for the weekend but bikers and backpackers go free. www.fairportconvention.co.**uk 9 International Day of Indigenous People** www.ifad.org/media/events/indigenous **9-12 Shambala Festival**, mystery countryside location, revealed with ticket purchase £30 www.shambalafestival.org **9-16 Broadstairs Folk Week**, Kent www.broadstairsfolkweek.com **10 Gay Pride festival**, Preston Park, Brighton. Parade begins at 11am. www.prideinbrightonandhove.com **10-11 Eden Festival**, Arrowe Park, Wirral FREE "Indie / Rock festival with an environmental theme, a northern Glastonbury, held on behalf of Wirral Green Alliance and Friends of the Earth. An estimated 60,000 plus crowd is expected." www.wga.merseyside.org **10-24 Ecotopia 2002** two-week environmental festival, Glentenassig, Co. Kerry, Ireland. 00 353 86 3097622 www.ecotopia2002.org Also an "Eco-topia" biketour, crossing England and Wales. 07870-467231 www.thebiketour.net **15-30 Earth Activ-**

ist Training Ragmans Lane Farm, Gloucestershire, with Starhawk & Penny Livingston-Stark. A permaculture design course for visionary activists. £400 waged £200 low income £100 unwaged c/o 3 Yew Tree Cottages Pitt Court North Nibley Glos Gl11 6EB earthactuk@yahoo.com **16-18 Big Chill festival**, Eastnor Castle, Herefordshire "Cinema, cafe culture, poetry recitals and performance art blend with the cool vibe music." www.bigchill.net **17- 18 Swaines Green Festival**. A green event powered by solar energy, with music, sundials, workshops and poetry. The aim of the festival is to help save the meadows and woodland which lies adjacent to the festival fields. The festival will take place in Epping. Further details from Paul Flack, 56 St Johns Rd, Epping Essex CM16 5DP **20-26 Tribe of Doris**, Blackdown Hill, Somerset. "We use the arts of music, dance, song and ceremony to bring people together, to raise awareness and to encourage respect and understanding of different cultures and musical origins." Everything from Animal Spirit Dance to Ghanaian Zylophone, Brazilian Samba, tablas and Innutitut Throat Singing! 0845-4580190 www.tribeofdoris.co.uk **21-24 Boom Festival**, Portugal. If you like psychedilic trance... www.boomfestival2000.com **22 - 26 Sustain Up North! - Northern Green Gathering**. West Yorkshire. www.ngg.org.uk **22-26 Samothraki Dance Festival**, Greece. Featuring 35 Live Acts and 60 Djs on 3 Stages. www.samothrakidancefestival.com **23 Canterbury Festival**, Mount Ephraim Gardens, Hernhill, Kent The Stranglers, The Damned, Rick Wakeman, Pretty Things, 21st Century Schizoid Band £80 (children under 14 free), including camping, no day tickets available www.canterburyfestival.com **24 Creamfields**, Old Liverpool Airfield 2pm-6am £46 plus booking fee. www.cream.co.uk **24-25 Deepdale Jazz Festival** 01485-210404 www.deepdalejazzfestival.co.uk **24-26 Notting Hill Carnival**. Second largest carnival in the world after Rio - and it's all FREE. www.rbkc.gov.uk/NottingHill **25-26 The Big Green Road Show**. Displays of sustainable woodland craft, renewable energy sources and elements of sustainable living. South of England Rare Breeds Centre, Ashford, Kent. 01233 861493, ext.224. visit@rarebreeds.org.uk **26 Colchester Free Festival**, massive free community arts festival held in Castle Park, Colchester 10.30am-7pm 01206 531185 www.colchesterfreefestival.co.uk **29-31 Eastern Green Gathering** near Bury St Edmunds, Suffolk 01284 728253 www.easterngreengathering.com **30-1 Sept Off The Tracks Festival**, Donnington Park. Folk, roots, dance and fusion 01332-384518 www.offthetracks.co.uk **31 Global Day of Action against a corporate influence on our lives** www.aseed.net/un-corporated **31 Edinburgh Mela**, Pilrig Park, Edinburgh. Free. www.edinburgh-mela.co.uk **31-4 Sept 2nd European Conference of the Peoples' Global Action** network in Leiden, the Netherlands. www.pgaconference.org

RIO +10 SUNBLOCK PROTECTION FROM CLIMATE CHANGE

SEPTEMBER

2 Countryside Alliance will be marching in London - counter demonstrations planned **6-9 Centre for Alernative Technology Conference**. "A climate for change: effective strategies for building a more sustainable and secure world - and one that is based on principles of universal human values and mutual support - could not be more urgent." 01654 705950 www.cat.org.uk **11 Second International Day Against Video Surveillance**. More details at www.notbored.org **20 Car Free Day** www.carbusters.ecn.cz **20 -21 Diaries of Despair protests** mark the second anniversary of the still-injuncted Diaries of Despair report into Imutran's pig-to-primate organ transplant experiments at Huntingdon Life Sciences. www.xenodiaries.org 0114 2722220 **21 Peace One Day**. Idea for one-day truce in all armed conflicts on UN's International Day of Peace, plus celebratory events. 020-7456-9181 info@peaceoneday.org **21 London Peace Trail**. Includes Mystery Walk for children - get your peace passport stamped at eight sites, learning about our peace heritage. 020-7609-2777 twallis@mail.com **23 Autumn Equinox -** for the next six months days will be shorter than nights, don't get too depressed. **28 International Rabbit Day** 020-8888-0001 info@bunny.org.uk **28 Demo against Bush and Blair's proposed war against Iraq**, ending in Trafalgar Square (for a change) Organised by Stop the War Coalition. **29 National Vegan Festival**, Conway Hall, Red Lion Square, London 020-8670-9585

FREE PARTY QUICKIE GUIDE

Despite the best attempts of the authorities free parties still happen up and down the country every week. Here's a few quick dos and don'ts:
- Be prepared to be self sufficient, facilities could be minimal
- Park sensibly, keep site roads clear
- Don't be a dirty scumbag - bury your shit and don't drop litter
- Fires - use dead wood, not green (which won't burn anyway)
- Make a donation - if someone passes round a bucket don't be sick in it, but hand over some cash. It costs money to put on free parties.

More helpful tips www.schnews.org.uk/diyguide/howtohaveafreeparty.htm

To get in touch with free party systems around the country see www.guilfin.net/extra/freeparties.php3

REPETITIVE BEATS

From Bristle www.bristle.org.uk

Who says that police are petty minded and violent? Last year the free party massive had one over on Avon and Somerset constabulary when they were forced to let a massive 5-day teknival go ahead on their doorstep (See Common Ground). Pissed off at being made to look stupid by a bunch of cheesy quavers the boys in blue decided to crack down heavily on the 'people having fun' menace when Mutant Dance put on a party in Cumberland Basin, Bristol, in July. This report comes from Bristle magazine.

The party began just after midnight. As people arrived there was no sign of trouble. The site has been used for years without any problems. Half a dozen cops stood by, watching the partygoers arrive. The crowd quickly grew and the atmosphere was friendly.

At around 1am at least 10 riot vans appeared and hordes of cops began putting on riot gear as a police helicopter circled overhead. Attempts were made by several partygoers to communicate with the police and to prevent any agro. One organiser offered to move the party elsewhere if there was a problem with the site. He was subsequently arrested for `conspiracy to cause a public nuisance' (charges later dropped). There was no attempt by officers to address the crowd and at no point did they make it clear that the party was illegal. Instead, at 2am, around 30 officers came to attack the party.

By this time word had gone around and many people formed a human chain around the DJs and sound systems to protect them. Many officers wore masks and no ID numbers. They drew batons and assaulted a few people but didn't break the lines of people standing their ground. The strength and unity of the crowd was impressive, but one person was dragged away under a rain of baton blows. After a stand-off the order was given to withdraw. People were shaken but the party continued until sunrise.

And then the police came back, en masse and with dogs. This is when the worst attack began. Cops came from both sides of the party and began trashing the sound system and indiscriminately beating people. One eyewitness recounts, "The police charged at everyone, hitting them with truncheons and trampling anyone in their way. I saw at least 15 people being hit, some were young women doing absolutely nothing. I saw one woman around 18 years old being hit while on the floor by at least five police officers." Injuries ranged from bruises and bleeding noses to neck injuries, fractured wrists and broken arms.

Most of those on the receiving end were young women.

A benefit night in October raised enough money to replace the damaged sound kit. Clearly, people refuse to be intimidated and will carry on partying. The party crews will continue to regularly organise unlicensed, free gatherings. Bristol has a strong network of sound systems up for organising entertainment on our own terms, without profit and controls

WORST BRITONS

Irritated to the point of violence by the BBC's Great Britons wankathon, SchNews decided to let our readers compile their own 'Worst Britons' list. Then, just after we'd put our poll on-line we found that Channel 4 were doing the same thing - and even using the same name (the only difference was that their Britons had to still be alive). We thought that had blown our idea, and let it slide. It was when Channel 4 broadcast their list - which was a totally piss-weak load of spurious TV distractions (Jordan at no. 2? Never heard of her) - that we dusted off our results to find our readers had been busy giving it their sarcastic best about the Brits they loved to hate - and it packed a punch! Basically Blair and Thatch predictably stole the best of it, with Churchill getting a good few kneejerks to the groin too. But there were some surprise choices. Here's the top twenty...

20. Lord Elgin (1766-1841)

"Partly responsible for the Opium Wars in China. The Chinese didn't want opium grown in their country but the Brits wanted it for trading (surprise, surprise) so on a diplomatic visit to the Chinese palace, he started a fire, which burnt it down and sent out the poppy planters anyway. What a selfish cunt, statesmen never change, do they?"

He's also the bloke responsible for 'finding' the famous 'Elgin' marbles in Greece, which he promptly stole. Those once beautifully carved stones were rediscovered by the Greeks a couple of years ago, rotting in a cellar of the 'British' museum. This clearly came as a huge embarrassment to the BM who usually argue that they can't return treasures stolen during the British colonial rampage 'cos foreigners don't have the proper facilities to look after them. They still have the cheek to call it the 'British' museum.

19. 'Hanging' Judge Jeffreys (1648-1689)

Made a name for himself by hanging most of the rebels who'd fought against the reign of James II in the 17th century.

18. Captain Cook (1728-1779)

More than just hoisting the jolly roger for British imperialism, he was also possibly the first person to use biological weapons for genocidal purposes: He gave clothes to Australian Aboriginals deliberately contaminated with smallpox, with catastrophic consequences.

17. Matthew Hopkins (1620's-1647)

Perhaps the most famous witch hunter of 17th century Britain. During his short career he had between 200 and 400 people executed for witchcraft.

"Roamed southern England fingering hundreds of people as witches, tortured the hell (sic) out of them, hanged the lucky ones".

16. Oswald Mosely (1896-1980)

Upper class playboy and leader of the failed British Union of Fascists party. Youngest MP in his day, and you thought Blair was as right wing as the Labour party had ever got...okay maybe he is. But, Mosely's anti-semitic, anti commonwealth-immigration rants and private army of bonehead thugs came close. We can thank him for instigating 1936 public order act and the 'battle of Cable Street'.

"Oswald Mosely. Maybe more representative of British thinking of the day than many would admit to once the tanks started rolling over Poland. An ugly national characteristic - good to see them getting the shit kicked out of them by the East London working class of the day."

15. George Granville Leveson-Gower 1st Duke of Sutherland (1758-1833)

A dead cert winner as worst Scot, he symbolises the highland clearances, perhaps the most devastating case of ethnic cleansing Britain has seen. Tens of thousands of Scots were driven from their homes by agents of the Duke of Sutherland in the early years of the 19th century, often by the burning down of their houses, to make way for sheep - an ecological and social disaster whose impact is still being felt.

14. Julie Burchill (1959-   )

"For being a stupid, shallow, self-ag-grandising, opinionated no-body. It's time the Guardian stopped giving her the Alf Garnet ironic humour platform because unlike him she appears not to be acting".

13. Cecil Rhodes (1853-1902)

Tricked and connived his way into power in Southern Africa in the late 19th Century - and set about stealing the continents natural resources "for his health"... no shit. Surrounded himself with strapping bodyguards in order to while away the hot afternoons and keep the natives at bay. Sparked a chain of events of theft and bloodshed that can be traced to the bloody mess that is present day Zimbabwe.

"For his involvement in colonial expansionist terror and the unbelievable arrogance to name an entire African country after himself."

12. William the Conquerer (1027-1087)

[er, French ain't he?] *"He and his descendents stole the 'common land' from the people of England. The ruling classes are still Normans with names such as Bowes-Lyons."*

11. Peter Stringfellow (1940 -   )

"For giving wankers a bad name."

10. General Dyer (1864-1927)

"Monster of the British Raj who, on April 13th, 1919, ordered his troops to open fire on thousands of unarmed, peaceful Indians in Amritsar. For 10 to 15 minutes 1,650 rounds of ammunition were unloaded into the screaming, terrified crowd, who were desperately trying to escape (Dyer had blocked the only exit). Dyer admitted that the firing would have continued had more ammunition been available, and said he would have used his machine guns if he could have got them into the enclosure, but these were mounted on armoured cars. He returned a hero to many in Britain, especially conservatives, who presented him with a jewelled sword inscribed 'Saviour of the Punjab.' Though his actions have obviously been imitated plenty of times since by British army personnel, from Ulster, to Iraq, Dyer set a precedent for the rest to follow."

9. Richard Littlejohn (1954-   )

Captain reactionary. Tenth rate Sun columnist. Dislikes: foreigners, lefties, tree-huggers, asylum seekers, poor people, the unemployed, blacks, Asians, northerners, Scottish people... Likes: big tits and football.

"Littlejohn constantly emits huge waves of conformist bile towards anyone who doesn't proscribe to the Sun's blend of cutting-edge, unbiased reportage."

"Why does Five Live insist on having these wankers introduce 6.06. Bring back Danny Baker...shit, did I really say that?"

8. Oliver Cromwell (1649-1658)

"Puritan, tyrant and killer of people. Possibly indirectly responsible for the emergence of capitalism (the protestant ethic or something). Invaded Ireland and responsible for much of the conflict today. Banned Christmas!!! Redeeming feature: killed monarch."

"I know it's pointless voting for him but well, I'd at least like the chance for a no holds barred match with him as long as I could wear my steel toes - because, well, I'm from Connaught - nuff said!"

7. Paul Dacre (1949-   )

"I'd have to say Paul Dacre is the worst Briton, cos he's partly responsible for the increasing level of racial tension in this country and making the right-wing petty bourgeoisie think that they actually have an intelligent viewpoint, which they obviously don't. Oh yeah, and my mum reads the fucking mail and I have to listen to the shit she reads in that rag, so hang the bastard! And get Titchmarsh to dig his grave and throw him in after... Sorry, I've had a boring day!!"

"He wins because, unlike the other two, he's still alive - for the time being…"

6. Robert Peel (1788-1850)

"For creating The Old Bill, and for causing the deaths of millions of Irish during the potato famine by refusing to repeal the Corn Laws, and insisting any aid offered to the starving had to be earned by hard physical work because the Irish were well known for being lazy scroungers (first 'workfare'?) Didn't work and thousands starved."

TURN OVER FOR YER TOP 5!

5. Ian Paisley (1926-   )

"Has encouraged sectarian gangs to torture and murder, earned a fortune for his misdeeds and has been protected in his crimes by the British state. If he were a Muslim the British Propaganda machine would have torn his character apart before imprisoning him and he would've been tortured in Cuba by now."

4. The Queen (1926-   )

Okay we're just using her as a figurehead here for all royalty before and since. While the pack of French, Danish, Russian and German parasites that have installed themselves on Britain/England/Scotland's thrones over the years don't really fit the worst 'Briton' criteria - they could all do with a slating; Henry VIII, Charles I, 'Bloody' Mary and Victoria, to name but a few.

"The queen for being an outstanding reminder that class is still a very important issue, bitch."

"The Queen, Charles, Camilla and the rest of the family. Bring back the fucking guillotine!"

3. Winston Churchill (1874-1965)

Big Fat Havana chuffing Tory Freemason credited with winning World War II everywhere outside of Russia. Expanded British Empire throughout Middle East and beyond. The first to gas the Kurds and the last to get a drink in. Sometimes seen sporting a grass Mohawk.

"He was a member of the eugenics society, and probably aware that he agreed with Hitler on that score, was friends with the international bankers that funded both sides of WWII"

"Because he was voted 'Greatest Briton' by a BBC TV audience I would like to nominate the British TV viewer for ignorance and bigotry beyond the call of duty. Churchill also fought in the Boer War 1899-1902 where he helped round up the Boer population and put 'em in concentration camps. Britain's final solution to its own Vietnam."

2. Margaret Thatcher (1925-   )

What can you say? No society, no jobs, no future, no fun. Gave us: the poll tax, yuppies, the 'it's okay to shit on anyone in order to get rich mentality', sink estates and punk rock. Credited with politicising more young people than Crass, Class War or the entire Chomsky back catalogue put together.

"The worst Prime Minister we've ever had she was responsible for the unnecessary Falklands War and saw working class people as scum."

"School milk, YOP, YTS, anti union laws, Poll tax, council tax, Pinochet, Falklands, Northern Ireland. Classic sociopath."

"Don't you remember the day she left office - it was a great day - after 12 years of job loses, miners strikes, destruction of the UK industry and giving away national assets to the Tory's friends." [er... bit like the next 12 then...]

"Thatcher's the worst - for destroying the idea of communities and throwing away coal and squandering money from North Sea oil - on tax cuts for the rich."

SchNEWS WORST BRITON NUMBER 1

Tony Blair (1953-   )

Planted in the Labour party by the CIA while still at university, given long hair and dubious rock guitar tuition at School of the Americas. Kept lowish profile until Tories displayed imminent-implosion status. Old skool Labour predecessor John Smith is offed by the Pentagon in pseudo heart-attack scenario - Blair slides into the limelight. Despite obvious corporate/right wing fundamentalism of "New" Labour, old left sheepishly elect said tosspot, not once but twice. Last vestige of hope for a working class/labour electoral alternative to hit-and-run capitalism is extinguished. As true blue blend of his blood is exposed, Blair does no-return sale of UK and all who sail in her to Washington. History may judge him, but then again, his mates are writing the history books...

"Blair's the worst...what a cunt!"

"A lickspittle and congenital liar. A phoney Christian who purports to pray to the Prince of Peace whilst showering innocent civilians with cluster bombs."

"Oooh. It's almost impossible to choose but given the present climate and that he is unfortunately still breathing our valuable Oxygen. I would have to vote for the Right Arseonrable Satan Blair."

"Not in my name, you fascist, capitalist, war-mongering git!"

"Tony Blair for being a cunt and licking any arse he can reach plus following on from Thatcher."

"Iraq War, Afgan War, PFI, Foundation Hospitals, Tuition Fees, US Poodle, Sainsbury, Straw, Blunkett, BAE, Fox Hunting goes on, Right to roam forgotten, Fear Mongerer, Single Mother Benefit Cuts, Welfare to Work, God Fearing Facist!"

Disclaimer
The comments here come from SchNEWS readers, and all this libellous slander is nothing to do with us. Honest.

Official: Britain's biggest tosser

WELCOME TO FORTRESS EUROPE

X-RAY   IRIS   FINGERPRINT   SIS

Just a few quick questions

weekly SchNEWS
www.schnews.org.uk

Friday 2nd August 2002   Free/Donation   Issue 366

BORDERLINE CASE

"War, environmental exploitation, poverty, economic conditions, dictatorships, all of these situations create refugees. The cause of refugees, whether it is economic reasons or war, is capitalism."
– Osaren, The Voice Refugee Forum, Germany.

In a group of actions spanning ten days (19-28 July), people from all over Europe hooked up with migrants without papers to reclaim the city of Strasbourg, on the French/German border for a No Border action camp. The focus was a resistance to Europe's draconian policy of treating refugees as criminals. Home to the European Parliament and the European Court of Human Rights as well as the Shengen Information System, or SIS, (SchNEWS 312) as well as its very own detention centre, Strasbourg truly represents failed democracy. People were spoilt for choice. Amongst chosen targets was the Accor hotel group who own detention centres in France and supermarkets in migrant 'zones' in Germany. They up the prices in their supermarkets so that migrants, who have to shop there, get even less for their 40 Euros a month (£27). A large part of their workforce is made up of undocumented migrants, on strike since March about low pay and bad conditions. Other actions included the usual trashings of institutions and corporations as well as cyberactivism, where hackers broke into the SIS.

The camp was based on self-organisation. People sorted out kitchens, showers and toilets as well as going on daily skipping runs to feed the camp. "I like it that people are so open here and that it's well organised. It's decentralised and provides a platform for resistance and engagement in Europe" Gaston, an asylum seeker, told SchNEWS. Everyone got together in their immediate areas to form barrios, which centred around a kitchen/meeting area. Someone from each barrio could then go to an inter-barrio meeting to make more general decisions about the camp, actions and broader political aims.

ALIENATED

One of the biggest, fattest, most vicious lies we've been told is that asylum seekers are stealing our jobs and invading our lives out of choice. The opposite is true: they don't want to die, it's as simple as that. There are an estimated 22 million refugees worldwide, according to the UN High Commissioner for Refugees (UNHCR) in May 2002 and the situation most refugees find themselves in is desperate. As Osaren told SchNEWS, "They borrow money, sell things, cars, homes if they have them before they leave to seek asylum in another country. If they are lucky they get a bad job and can start to pay back the money they have borrowed."

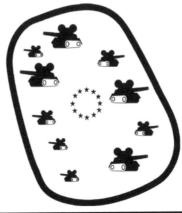

In Germany, people who've been granted asylum are restricted to a specific area or part of town. In some cases they're tagged but usually they're just monitored to make sure they don't nip across a boundary to make a phone call or go to the supermarket or something. So far this system of separation where refugees are kept in isolation and require special permission to leave their 'area' is unique to Germany. Children have no right to education and there's no right to healthcare or work. "All we can do is sit, maybe eat something, and think. Those of us who can go home will probably have to in a year or two if we don't get any chances to live here. Those who cannot return will just self-destruct. Their strategy is to separate and persecute us." - Abdul, asylum seeker in Germany.

As the WTO (World Trade Organisation) threatens to have a scrap with anyone blocking free trade and the 'free movement' of money, people find themselves confined to ever smaller areas, watched for their every move. For these reasons the No Bor-

Alienated cont...

ders network are demanding the right to freedom of movement without any limitations for all the people of the world. At the heart of the problem is SIS - a centralised database used to collate info on Europe's unwanted. At the same time as the action camp in Strasbourg an Afgani family in the UK who had been sheltering in a Mosque were violently removed by riot cops and banged up in a detention centre. This was because their asylum application in Germany had been turned down – information that the UK got from their finger prints.

Germany is the model for Fortress Europe and Britain is trying to push through tougher laws this autumn to keep up with their fascist policy. The government's latest white paper 'Secure Borders, Safe Haven' states that the already racist border controls are to be tightened using the SIS database, iris recognition, ID checks and increased powers to screen passengers. It doesn't take a genius to guess the colour of the skin of people most likely to be harassed by immigration cops. The Secure Borders white paper states that the govt target is to deport 30,000 refugees by spring 2003 – that's 2,500 a month. All new asylum seekers are to be housed in four planned accommodation centres to further segregate them from our society.

Talking about his experience of the camp, Osaren from the self-organised migrants Voice Refugee Forum told us, "The distance between the activists and refugees is very wide. Very few activists engage with refugees on a daily

Strasbourg Noborders July 2003

basis. My advice would be for activists to get closer to the most repressed people in society, find out where they are and support them from below. The struggle can't have a base unless this has happened. We need to re-evaluate support and resistance from the base."

NON au SIS

« SYSTEME D'INFORMATION SCHENGEN INSTRUMENT DE CONTRÔLE ET DE REPRESSION

NI FRONTIERES NI NATIONS NI CONTRÔLE SOCIAL . ACTION . INFORMATION . DEBATS

CAMPEMENT CONTRE LE SIS A STRASBOURG DU 19 au 28 JUILLET 2002
WWW.NOBORDER.ORG

Here's some of that resistance ...

* **Italy**: "We have occupied houses with Italian activists and migrants working together, we are now 500 people strong and have 10 houses with 100 migrants and people without papers. Last Tuesday the Italian military sank a ship carrying 60 Albanian migrants. There will be no investigation.

* **Lyons, France** "Despite police repression we have been fighting for a year, occupying buildings and orgaanising demonstrations."

* **Seville, Spain**: "We come from a place where 7,000 migrants live and work with no water, no food, no medicine - we are living in plastic shelters. Because of these conditions we decided to organise ourselves. We have occupied the Seville University for the last 2 months. Info: solidarity@hotmail.com

* **Belgium**: "Over 25 people are occupying the ex-Somalian embassy in the capital Bruges.

*__Germany__: From 17 Aug – 21 Sept there will be a caravan tour of Germany campaigning for the rights of refugees and immigrants. To find out dates and places check www.humanrights. de.caravan/index_de.html.

*__Britain:__ Shut the Dover removals centre picket on Sat Oct 19th. Meet 10am Western Heights, Dover and move on to Sangatte Red Cross Centre. – contact Kent Committee to defend asylum seekers.

For more about actions and camps around the world www.noborder.org or info on prison building contact: CAGE 07931 401962

GENOA G8: One Year On...

It's a year since the G8 summit in Genoa (See SchNEWS 314/5), when the Italian city became a militarised zone, with police cruising round in armoured cars and the city centre ringed with a 15ft steel fence. The 250,000 people who marched through the streets opposing the eight most powerful leaders in the world faced massive police repression, with over 6,000 tear gas canisters fired by cops who also used live ammunition with which they killed Carlo Giuliani.

One year on, up to 100,000 took the streets of Genoa on Saturday 20th to remember Carlo Giuliani - much more than the 30-40,000 expected, which shows the anti-capitalist movement is still alive and well after September 11th. At 5:27 p.m., the time that Giuliani was shot by a young police trainee (Officer Plannica) trapped in a paramilitary police jeep, the crowds broke into a prolonged cheer and released hundreds of coloured balloons into the sky. "This is not a funeral. We wanted to have a celebration of life, of the right to live and of so many rights that are denied in the world and in Italy," said Giuliani's father in the piazza where his son was shot.

But as a final sickening note to Carlo's murder, Officer Plannica sold his story for 30,000 euros (£20,000) to one of Italian Prime Minister Berlusconi's TV channels, claiming he was not guilty of murder or manslaughter.

The worst aspect of pre-meditated police violence a year ago was a raid on the Indymedia Centre and Diaz School where some protestors were staying. During the raid 93 people were arrested with 63 put in hospital, but none of those arrested have been charged with any offence. This year a press conference by many people beaten and arrested at the Diaz School called for deputy prime minister Gianfranco Fini, leader of the fascist National Alliance party, to be held accountable for the brutal raid. During the raid police produced two molotov cocktails as evidence that the School was a base for violent protesters. Since then it has emerged that these molotovs were in fact recovered seven hours earlier hidden in Genoa city centre, with a policeman confessing that he planted the explosives: "I brought the molotov cocktail to the Diaz school. I obeyed the order of one of my superiors." His superior, Pietro Troiani, from a mobile police unit in Rome, is already being investigated after another colleague accused him of providing false information to justify the raids.

The Italian Government has come under fire for failing to prosecute those responsible for police brutality against demonstrators and Amnesty International has criticised the police. MPs in Rome are calling for another enquiry. 77 police officers are under investigation, including the one who shot Carlo Giuliani. Genoa police chief Gianni De Gennaro was demoted after admitting some of his men might have used ''excessive force.''

In Italy the cops may be blatantly fascist, but in Britain the situation isn't much different. Two people arrested at a demo outside the London Italian Embassy last February recently had their charges dropped. Police at the demo had punched and kicked protestors and one cop (PC D343) was heard to say "I don't give a fuck about the law". That's because, like in Italy, the police can get away with being violent towards protestors and never get punished.

* Indymedia have produced a video, Genoa Red Zone. Copies from www.cultureshop.org
* Read "On Fire: Genoa and the Anti-Capitalist Movement" published by AK Press for £3 a go. www.akuk.com.

SchNEWS in brief

This Saturday sees the beginning of the **National Week of Action Against War and Sanctions on Iraq.** Info 0845 458 2564 www.viwuk.freeserve.co.uk ** Last Saturday over 150 people demonstrated outside the Department for Environment, Food and Rural Affairs in London calling for the government to abandon the testing and possible future commercialisation of **GM crops**. 17 bags of crops from GM test sites that have been destroyed this year were dumped on the steps of the building. www.geneticsaction.org.uk ** **Direct Action Against War Now** are organising a demo and occupation of Oxford Street Selfridges who sell products produced in illegal Israeli settlements. Sat 3rd, 1pm at the entrance – or dress as shoppers and do what you have to do once you're inside. 07817 061 183 stopselfridges@soon.com** There's a Justice for Mark Barnsley national meeting and social this Saturday (3rd) to discuss the future of the campaign. 1.30pm, at The 1in12 Club, 21-23 Albion Street, Bradford. www.freemarkbarnsley.com ** A **new protest camp** set up to protect Bilston Woods, Penicuik, near Edinburgh from being destroyed to make way for a bypass is now up and running and urgently needs people and tat. 07753 808709 ** **Trident Ploughshares** have a two week (4th-19th August) disarmament camp at Coulport, near to the Trident nuclear warhead depot on Loch Long. Info: 0870 4583117 www.tridentploughshares.org ** Demonstration against the **Draft Mental Health Bill**, noon 12th August at the Department of Health, Richmond House, Whitehall. ** The Nigerian Women occupying a **Chevron oil pipeline terminal** (see last week's SchNEWS) have ended their occupation after reaching an agreement with the company http://nigeria.indymedia.org

APPEALING

Nine unnamed prisoners who have been locked up in the high security Belmarsh Prison, without trial since September 2001 have won an appeal against their imprisonment. They were interned under the knee-jerk Anti-Terrorism, Crime and Security Act (see Schnews 363). The Act makes it legal for the government to imprison non-UK nationals who they believe to be involved in 'terrorist activities' and whom they are unable to deport – because for example, they could face degrading treatment or death. Those detained are not given a reason for their internment, and they can't defend themselves in court. The appeal was upheld because the Act breaches the European Convention on Human Rights. Unfortunately the ruling does not make the detention unlawful, and the nine individuals are still behind bars. The Foreign Office will appeal against the verdict on Oct 7th. www.blagged.freeserve.co.uk/ta2000/index.htm

Positive SchNEWS

England's first ever earthship is to be built in Brighton. An earthship is a building made of rammed earth and used car tyres and solar energy and rain provide heat, power and water. They also have their own sewage systems. Not only do they help solve the problem of a growing tyre mountain, but provide low cost homes as they are cheaper to build than conventional houses. The earthship will be built in Stanmer Park as part of the Stanmer Organics project and it will be a meeting place for groups and a model for future houses. There's an open day at Stanmer Organics this Saturday (3) where you can see the earthship site, learn about permaculture techniques, organic food and green-recycling as well as crafts and music. 11 – 4pm 01273 620486. E-mail: info@stanmerorganic.org.uk For more about earthships: www.lowcarbon.co.uk

Subscribe!

BRISTOL FASHION

People are considering legal action against Avon and Somerset Constabulary after 50 officers in full riot gear broke up a free dance party at Cumberland Basin, near Bristol a couple of weekends back, seriously injuring at least nine people. Cops made no attempt to negotiate with party-goers, telling them "If you're down there, you're going to get hurt." The police had even thoughtfully brought an ambulance with them just in case they kicked anyone's head in - which they did. Police blamed party-goers for the injuries commenting "It was clear a rave at this location would put a risk of harm to those attending." The 'location' was under a motorway flyover, far away from residential housing, which had been used as a party site on numerous occasions before. Avon and Somerset Police seriously got their fingers burnt over the massive Steart beach party over the Jubilee weekend (SchNEWS 363) and local media have been busy whipping up a frenzy as "hooligan ravers" descend on the countryside to have fun. One party organiser told SchNEWS "We reckon the cops decided it was pay-back time."

The Free Party Defence Collective is now appealing for witnesses to mount legal action 07810 601703 www.guilfin.net

* Four Brighton based sound systems have finally been charged after having rigs seized from a Shoreham warehouse during Easter bank holiday. Despite never getting to turn on sound systems, attract a crowd or actually disturb anyone other than local plod, party organisers have been charged with 'Conspiracy to cause public nuisance' - and all for not quite getting to throw a free party.

* Thanks to the cops and the local council this year's Welsh Green Gathering was cancelled, and so a Greenwar Gathering is being organised. It's on an urban common in Glamorgan starting 8th August. For details of how to find it see the environment pages on www.protest.net or email: Plebs.Col@ntlworld.com

Inside SchNEWS

A 22 year old man from Stockholm has received 5 years prison for actions at the EU Summit in Gothenburg last year. Five others are still in prison. Send letters of support and money to: Solidarity Group GBG, c/o Syndikalistiskt forum, Box 7267, SE-402 35 Gothenburg, Sweden. e-mail: solidaritetsgruppen@hotmail.com

...and finally...

So what is it with asylum seekers that make them want to come to our shores? The hospitality and all year sunshine? Our generous benefits system and friendly immigration officials?

Er, no. According to research after interviewing 65 asylum seekers, the main reasons people come here include: Margaret Thatcher, because the old bag gave the impression of the UK being a powerful country; Manchester United football club as evidence that Britain is loaded: and the Beatles and the Spice Girls contributing to the idea that this is a progressive and tolerant place.

The authors also mentioned that many of the asylum seekers they interviewed were fleeing persecution and were more concerned about escaping their own country than about where they would end up, and get this, few knew much about British asylum policy or had any detailed knowledge of benefit levels they might receive, let alone how they compared with other European countries. Funny that, SchNEWS always had the impression that before coming here refugees would be surfing the Net trying to find out the best location to come and sponge off taxpayers, before legging it out the backdoor just in time to escape torture and death.

Disclaimer

SchNEWS warns all asylum seekers you would be bordering on the insane to think there is any refuge in this country. Honest.

Iraq Sanctions: Suspected Dual Use

"Sanctions target the weakest and most vulnerable members of the Iraqi society – the poor, elderly, newborn, sick and young." – **Voices in the Wilderness**

"The sanctions have decimated the Iraqi people, driven most Iraqis into a dependent relationship to the government, shattered institutions that could sustain opposition and increased nationalism." **Anthony Arnove, Iraq Speakers Bureau**

In the buildup to war, liberal anti-war groups got far too worked-up about the UN confrontation with the US/UK coalition over their plan to attack Iraq. It was as if America was the Source Of All Evil and the UN Security Council was heroically standing up for innocent Iraqis. But it's unlikely that the Security Council was any more concerned about Iraqi lives than George Dubya – they just didn't want to hand over all control of the region to the US. If there's any doubt about this, we only need to recall the UN's preferred method for keeping Iraq under thumb: the sanctions regime that has been imposed on the country for over 12 years.

It's hard to imagine the shit that ordinary Iraqis have had to put up with since the imposition of sanctions. In 1991 Iraq was recovering from an 8-year war with Iran that had left over 500,000 dead, the first Gulf War in which perhaps another 250,000 were killed, and a brutal counter-insurgency by the Baathist regime, after the US pulled its troops out to allow them to put down the uprisings that began early that year (see *Milan Rai article*). The Gulf War had destroyed the country's infrastructure. At this time, the UN decided to continue with a program of economic sanctions so extreme that health, energy, education and sanitation services virtually fell apart, unemployment rose to critical levels, and rationing had to be introduced. Before the Gulf war Iraq had the best public health system in the region. In 1996, Kathy Kelly from US direct action group Raising Voices visited Dr Tarik Hasim Habeh at the Basra pediatrics and gynecology hospital. He told her that doctors couldn't earn enough to feed their families, sometimes making no more than $3 a month, so some had had to find work as taxi drivers, street vendors or waiters. He took her through several wards where infant after infant lay wasting in squalid conditions. They were suffering severe malnutrition, respiratory diseases, leukemia and kidney disease. In one room 14 incubators were stacked against a wall, useless because of the lack of repair parts available under sanctions.

The UN Security Council first imposed economic sanctions on Iraq in August 1990, following the country's invasion of Kuwait. They were originally intended to force Iraq to end the occupation. After the Gulf War forced Iraq out of Kuwait the decision was made to re-impose the sanctions. The official reason given for this was to force Iraq to give up its Weapons of Mass Destruction programs, but there was also clearly an intention to punish the Iraqi government for its disobedience. The wording of the new resolution, "one of the longest and most complex…ever passed" was so vague that it allowed Security Council members – particularly the US and the UK – to constantly shift the goalposts over what counted as co-operation with UN demands.

Sanctions are basically barriers to trade, where no goods are allowed in or out of the country without the permission of the UN. The scope of the sanctions program was so broad that it almost completely shut down the country's economy. Many items were banned from import because of their "Suspected Dual Use" – the threat that they could have military as well as civilian uses. The list of these supposedly deadly items was long and ridiculous. It included wheelbarrows, aspirin, chlorine for purifying water, brake pads for various makes of car, cuddly toys, pencils and detergent. The banning or stalling of most necessary items meant that cars lay abandoned on roadsides, hospital staff had nothing to clean the floors with but petrol, children had nothing to write with, and most drinking water became contaminated. Where needed items were not banned, the restrictions placed on exports meant that the country simply didn't have the cash to buy adequate supplies.

The sanctions prevented the reconstruction of essential infrastructure such as water works, sanitation plants, schools, hospitals, roads and electricity generating plants that were bombed during the first Gulf War. In stark contrast to the fairly swift reconstruction following the Iran/Iraq war in 1989, reconstruction after the 1991 war was more or less non-existent. Not only did sanctions prevent effective reconstruction, they prevented the day-to-day maintenance of those facilities that hadn't been destroyed by bombs.

Holding back the supplies needed to repair water and sewage works amounted to germ warfare. By 1999 the UN's own staff estimated that "access to potable water [in Iraq] is currently 50% of the 1990 level in urban areas and only 33% in rural areas." Public health deteriorated massively, in large part because of lack of access to clean water. The Humanitarian Panel of UNICEF reported in their 1999 study, "Communicable diseases, such as water borne diseases and

Second hand book market in Baghdad - under sanctions people were forced to sell what possesions they could to survive.

Malaria, which had been under control, came back as an epidemic in 1993 and have now become part of the endemic pattern of the precarious health situation."

By 1997 it was estimated that over half a million people had died because of the sanctions, more than were killed in the Iran/Iraq war. According to Amatzia Baram, Director of the Jewish-Arab Centre at the University of Haifa, it's been civilians and "mainly young children and the elderly [who've] paid the price." In southern and central Iraq - home to most of the country's population - under-5 mortality more than doubled, from 56 deaths per 1000 live births during 1984-9, to 131 between 1994-9. Likewise infant mortality - the death of children in their first year - increased from 47 per 1000 live births to 108 within the same time frame. Maternal death during childbirth also increased.

Unemployment became unimaginably high. For example, by 1996 only six people in every hundred were working in the area around Basra. School enrolment halved since 1990 and the schools that were able to operate became massively overfilled. UNICEFs Humanitarian Panel wrote at the time, "The rising number of street children and children who work can be explained in part as a result of increasing rates of school drop-outs and repitition, as more families are forced to rely on children to secure household incomes."

Once the cultural hub of the Middle East, Iraqi culture was stifled. Nasra Al-Sa'adoon, an Iraqi writer explains, "...most painters, archaeologists, musicians and professors either died or moved away, or became too depressed or impoverished to continue."

The only section of Iraqi society that didn't suffer was the Baath Party. Weakened by poverty and made dependent on the regime for food rations, Iraqis had little hope of repeating the uprisings that nearly brought down Saddam Hussein in 1991. A clique of doting dependents formed around Hussein, who played on the nationalism that increased with people's resentment of the sanctions.

For ordinary Iraqis, the sanctions meant daily reminders that they were living under siege. Even trying to walk down the street became a major health hazard. In Basra, Iraq's second largest city Kathy Kelly describes a scene, "Basrans trudge through streets fouled with piles of human waste. The piles, five to six feet tall, spaced every thirty feet, are left to dry. Adults negotiate residential sidewalks with care, stepping over human feces, and wastewater spills from the streets into nearby homes."

In 1996, Madeleine Albright, the then US secretary of state, was asked what she felt about the fact that 500,000 Iraqi children had died as a result of US-backed economic sanctions. She replied that it was 'a very hard choice,' but that, all things considered, 'the price is worth it.' This judgment came at a time when many UN members favoured easing the sanctions. The US position is thought to have swayed many UN officials and kept them quiet about the deadly effects of the sanctions. It was two more years before Denis Haliday resigned his post as UN coordinator for humanitarian aid to Iraq, for example. When he did resign, he said the sanctions were "... ignoring the human rights of ordinary Iraqis

and turning a whole generation against the west." On a later occasion he said, "The member states know full well what they're doing and what the impact is."

In October 1999, in a letter to the president of the UN Security Council, even Kofi Annan, the UN Secretary General complained about unnecessary 'holds' on food and equipment that had been preventing the reconstruction of water, sanitation and electricity plants as well as the communications infrastructure in Iraq. Meanwhile an American official boasted to the Washington Post, "The longer we can fool around in the [UN Security] Council and keep things static, the better." An example of this lethal 'fooling around' was given by Anthony Arnove, US writer and activist, "When the Iraqis asked for 500 ambulances, these were initially blocked in their entirety and then slowly, over a period of months were released – 100, 200 ambulances."

A major problem with the UN seems to have been their complete inability to consider the Iraqi people living under sanctions as human at all. As John Pilger put it, "Peter Van Walsum, Netherlands Ambassador to the UN and chair of the sanctions committee ... seemed to associate Iraq, the civilized society, with Saddam Hussein, the murderer as if they were one and the same. He also seemed to believe in holding innocent people hostage to the compliance of a dictator over whom they [had] no control."

At the time of writing, the US and the UK, having been the main obstacle to lifting the sanctions for years, have presented a new resolution to the UN calling for them to be lifted. White House spokesman, Ari Fleicher, announced, "There is no reason for the people of Iraq to suffer sanctions any longer" – although the US consistently denied that the sanctions were causing suffering throughout the 90s. Of course the White House couldn't give a toss whether Iraqis are suffering or not, but they know that unless oil revenues are released there won't be any money for the lucrative post-war reconstruction contracts that are already being farmed-out to US companies. The last word on the new resolution goes to Voices in the Wilderness, the direct action group who organised illegal deliveries of medical supplies to Iraq throughout the sanctions regime. On the day the resolution was presented, they said, "We support their removal...and the recognition of economic sanctions as both a failed and genocidal policy. We continue to oppose the umbrella of military violence, occupation, corporate control, and foreign developed leadership that Iraqis have been told is their 'liberation.'"

Useful sources
Voices In The Wilderness:
www.viwuk.freeserve.co.uk
Middle East Institute: www.mideasti.org
Campaign against sanctions on Iraq: www.casi.org.uk
Human rights watch:
www.hrw.org/reports/1991/iraq
UN Food & Agriculture Organisation:
www.fao.org/giews
Electronic Iraq: http://electroniciraq.net
Arnove, A (Ed) 2003 <u>Iraq Under Siege</u>,
Pluto Press, London

WAKE UP! IT'S YER WEAPON OF MASS DISTRACTION

Mr President, this is a nuclear reactor and four missile launchers and they're all over Iraq Sir.

weekly SchNEWS

www.schnews.org.uk

Friday 9th August 2002   Free/Donation   Issue 367

IT'S A NUKE OUT

Tuesday was the anniversary of the bombing of Hiroshima. Fifty-seven years since the USA dropped a nuclear bomb on the Japanese city which eventually killed an estimated 200,000 people.

Tuesday was also the 12th anniversary of the imposition of sanctions on Iraq - where another Hiroshima is taking place. In a report published three years ago, the United Nations Children's Fund said that between 1991 and 1998 economic sanctions contributed to the deaths of half a million Iraqi children under the age of five.

These deaths weren't caused by sanctions alone, however. Other factors have also contributed to the high child mortality rate, including the after-effects of the Gulf War, where the country's infrastructure, namely water and sewage treatment facilities, was deliberately destroyed. In addition, depleted uranium from tank shells and bombs used in the Gulf War has caused cancer in many children. This situation was worsened by the Iraqi government not taking all available measures to prevent the massive increase in child mortality. Dr. Ginan Ghalib Hassen, an Iraq paediatrician said, "I have studied what happened in Hiroshima. It is almost exactly the same here; we have an increased percentage of congenital malformation, an increase of malignancy, leukaemia, and brain tumours."

During the Gulf War, more than 300 tons of depleted uranium was used in weapons against the country. On impact, they left a residue of radioactive dust. This dust, travelling where the wind blows, remains radioactive for 4,500 million years and as a result, there is now an epidemic of cancer throughout Iraq causing babies to be born without eyes, limbs, genitalia, and sometimes with their organs on the outside of their bodies.

Professor Doug Rokke was the army physicist responsible for cleaning up Kuwait. He now has 5,000 times the recommended level of radiation in his body. He wonders why the United States and Britain decided to use a 'weapon of mass destruction', "What happened in the Gulf was a form of nuclear warfare," he maintains.

As if the death of innocent civilians from cancer wasn't enough, Britain and the US have also been bombing the country on and off since 1991 to protect the so called 'no fly zones'. During 1999 alone the two countries dropped more than 1,800 bombs and hit 450 targets. Bombing happens almost every day, yet to read the mainstream media you wouldn't know it was happening.

OIL SLIP

For 50-odd years, Iraq relied on its oil exports for national earnings. In 1990, its ability to export was cut off overnight and its oil facilities decimated by bombing. Although the country can now export oil, it can only spend the bulk of the revenues on humanitarian imports. "What this means" Dr Glen Rangwala from the Campaign Against Sanctions on Iraq told SchNEWS "is three things: Iraq can't rebuild its country's public services; it can't rebuild its oil sector, so it earns less than a fifth of what it was earning in 1980 with double the population

to provide for. The Iraqi people don't have jobs that pay anything like adequate salaries, because the Government can't use its oil revenues to pay its people - which means that people aren't able to afford any of the necessities of life. They receive the bulk of their food in a government ration - the whole country has been run like a refugee camp for the past 12 years. Lastly, it also means that if we invade, the ration distribution system will probably collapse and we'll see mass starvation."

Bush and Blair say Saddam Hussein is still a threat to the world but Scott Ritter, for five years a senior weapons inspector in Iraq who meticulously checked out the country's chemical, biological and weapons infrastructure, said "If I had to quantify Iraq's threat, I would say (it is) zero."

It was the CIA who helped put Saddam in power and it was the West who helped keep him there.

Oil Slip cont...

It was the US who sold materials that it knew could easily be used to make nuclear, biological and chemical weapons, even after the Iraqi government had slaughtered 6,000 Kurds in its chemical bombardment of Halabja in 1988. A year later John Kelly, US Assistant Secretary of State, visited Baghdad and told Hussein "You are a force for moderation in the region, and the United States wants to broaden her relationship with Iraq."

Saddam's problem was not that he tortured and murdered thousands of his people, gassed and bombed the Kurds and made war with Iran, but that he invaded Kuwait and now refuses to toe the American line. As Rahul Mahajan, author and Green Party candidate for Governor of Texas points out, "The Bush administration wants a war…replacing Saddam with a U.S.-friendly dictator who will make deals with American companies and follow American dictates."

On any given day, U.S. troops are in 140 countries around the world with permanent bases in more than half of those. This is the reality of the so called war on terror, a war that will never end, until every country bows to the might of the United States.

* A lot of this material was lifted shamelessly from John Pilger's excellent new book 'The New Rulers of the World' published by Verso. Essential reading.

* **Campaign Against Sanctions on Iraq** have produced a booklet giving twelve suggested actions for twelve years of sanctions 0845 330 4520 www.casi.org.uk

* **A doctor from Oxford** has begun withholding 7% of her tax bill in protest against sanctions on Iraq and instead donating the amount which would usually go to the military to the UK charity Medical Aid for Iraqi Children.

* **24 August: Citizen's Inspection** at Welford US munitions store to highlight the hypocrisy of US demands for arms inspections. Meet 10 am Reading station. 0118 966 8328 readingpeacegroup@hotmail.com

* **Sellafield Peace Camp** 29-31 August The Sellafield site is implicitly involved in the nuclear weapons industry. 0773 2928780

* **Don't Attack Iraq** demonstration Saturday 28 September. 12noon Speaker's Corner, Hyde Park, Central London CND 020 7700 2393 www.cnd.org.uk

* **Two ships carrying rejected MOX fuel** from Japan are due to arrive in the UK at the end of the month. A nuclear-free flotilla is going to sail out to greet it, and a protest is being organised in Barrow-on-Furness. Info: fgod@hotpop.com www.nuclearfreeflotilla.org

SchNEWS in brief

Brighton's **Radio 4A** is back on the airwaves this weekend, followed by a Reclaim the Beach party on Saturday night. 'Bring your ghetto blaster - you are the sound system.' 107.8 FM www.piratetv.net ** **Random Artists** have opened a building as a café, gallery space and record shop at 282 Richmond Rd. London E8. Open Thurs-Sat midday-late. 07092 012299 ** Sunday 11th is the 9th **Portsmouth Smokey Bears Picnic** for those who like a joint or twenty. 2pm on Southsea Common. 07753 219135 ** 87 activists who were arrested during a march to the Mayor of Johannesburg's house in protest against water privatisation, are being taken to court on 15th August. An international day of action is being called. **Picket of South Africa House**, Trafalgar Square, London, 4.30pm onwards.www.resist.org.uk ** Glasgow once again has it's own new radical bookshop and meeting space. **The John MacLean Centre** is a workers co-op run by volunteers, 34 Clarendon Place. 0141 332 6849. www.johnmacleancentre.org ** **A compilation video of various GM actions** from Stop the Crop in 1998 to last months DEFRA action is now available for £5 from ToGG 01803 840098. ** At **Hayle Beach in Cornwall** there is a series of protests against the destruction of the beach by the harbour company that manages the area. www.SOSHayle.fsnet.co.uk ** **Road Alert!** have a new website www.roadalert.org.uk created to provide a forum for those interested in a direct action response to the resurrection of the Government's road building program ** Demonstration against the resumption of **live exports** from Dover next Saturday (17th) midday, Pencester Gardens, Dover. Coaches from London and the Midlands 01730 264208 ** Last Saturday shoppers at **Selfridges** in Oxford Street faced a couple of hundred demonstrators protesting about the store continuing to stock goods made in illegal Israeli settlements in the West Bank and Gaza. The protest was organised by Direct Action Against War Now! www.daawn.cjb.net

SODS

Last week, 300 hospital workers at Glasgow's Royal Infirmary went on strike to demand a minimum of five pounds an hour and a return to NHS conditions of employment with holidays and sick pay. Ever since the French multinational Sodexho has officially employed the workers (when they won the contract from the NHS) the workers have been in a much weaker position to make any demands. Not content with treating workers like second class citizens, Sodexho has really taken the piss recently by offering to restore workers rights by 2005! No rush hey. This crap offer was unanimously voted out and there has been a three day strike this week and one planned for next week. The fact that public services are now run by profit is due to the Private Finance Initiative (PFI), which is basically privatisation by the back door, allowing corporations like Sodexho to get their hands on public services (see Schnews 240). Sodexho has its fingers in many pies--it has contracts with 120 public sector institutions, at least 4 of which are PFI profit-run NHS hospitals; it's subsidiary, UK Detention Centres Ltd., is a leader of the privatised prison service. This lovely company was also planning to pay asylum-seekers 34p an hour for cooking, cleaning and doing odd jobs at a detention centre near Heathrow, an offer which they eventually dropped under pressure from various groups.

More info: Sod Action, Box 95, 82 Colston Street, Bristol, BS1 5BB. sod-action@fsmail.net

AIRBORTED

In an astonishing victory for the residents of San Salvador Atenco, the Mexican government last week confirmed that they were abandoning plans to build a new international airport smack on top of the small farming community just outside of Mexico City.

The whole saga began last autumn when Mexican President Vicente Fox's government approved plans to build a six-runway, $2.3 billion airport that would gobble up much of San Salvador Atenco's farming land.

In October, a federal ruling offered villagers a mere 40 pence a square yard for the land - the land that served as the farmers' main source of food, income, and security. The residents of Atenco and the surrounding villages quickly dismissed this slap-in-the-face offer, and immediate protests and marches were organised.

Over the next 9 months, farmers mobilised themselves with few results - but things began to change on Thursday, July 11th, when a demo was organised to protest an official government announcement affirming the airport plans. Farmers travelling in a peaceful caravan to the demo were

Enjoy Autonomy - it's the real thing

attacked by police with clubs, tear gas, and live ammunition. Thirty protesters were injured, fifteen arrested, and five hospitalised—one of whom, Jose Enrique Espinoza Juarez, died in hospital two weeks later.

This brutal show of force inspired supporters in nearby Atenco to take immediate and radical direct action. Over the next few days, five police squad cars were burnt and used along with other seized vehicles (including some Coca-Cola trucks!) to block the nearby national highway. Thirteen government and police officials were taken hostage, and the Atenco farmers used these hostages as bargaining tools in their struggle with the authorities. On July 14, the last hostages were released in return for the release of all arrested farm workers. It has taken the government another three weeks to cancel plans for the airport altogether, but with last week's announcement; the Atenco workers' victory became certain.

Many people feel that the Atenco struggle has been a vital test of the ability of a community-based movement to stop projects that only serve the interests of a few, powerful and wealthy businesses. The administration of President Fox has a plethora of such projects, including the lofty Plan Puebla Panama (PPP), a plan to privatise the energy industry and support the Free Trade Area of the Americas.

The PPP is President Fox's crown jewel economic project, which seeks to transform south eastern Mexico into an industrialised factory centre where maquiladoras (sweatshops) can thrive, producing yet more raw materials for the developed countries in the Northern Hemisphere. The plan involves massive construction projects and generous factory building incentives in an attempt to attract more foreign investment from multinational corporations. But the PPP cuts right through the heart of a lot of indigenous land and territory in the poverty stricken southern Mexico State of Chiapas and beyond. Roberto Rivera, a student involved in a recent Atenco solidarity march, sees the protests in Atenco as "an important turning point, because the proposed airport is the first integral step in the process of implementing the Plan Puebla Panama . . . if the plans to build this new airport in Atenco are stopped, it will be a major blow to the PPP."

The events of Atenco have indeed sent a clear message to multi-national companies and the governments that seek only to protect their interests. "Even if they gave us all the gold in the world," said one Atenco woman, "We wouldn't leave our land because that is all we have." http://mexico.indy media.org/

Corporatewealth Games

"While big business is profiteering, local resources are cut. While poor areas of the city are given a paint job and abandoned shops covered over with corporate adverts, the real problems go unsolved and the real needs of the communities in these areas are ignored." - Manchester Biotic Baking Brigade.

The Blitz festival blew up in the streets of Manchester with a mind-expanding explosion of art and direct action. Running parallel to the Commonwealth Games, this well-organised, independent festival showed how cunningly the people of Manchester could attack the corporate games spectacle.

The simply splendid march FOR capitalism kicked off with cucumber sandwiches and G & T's in a park, where an impeccably dressed rabble held banners such as "Bomb Other Countries" and "the environment can kiss my ass." AgiTATE put on an art exhibition in a shopping mall, and cyclists and skaters teamed up for a skate-athon around Manchester City centre. Councillors were none too pleased with all this unpredictable activity, particularly when they eventually realised that tourists were wandering around with spoof alternative guides to the city.

The Commonwealth Games, like all major sporting events, was used to boost sales of advertising and sponsorship. Reebok sponsored UK Athletes. Chinese Labour Watch say the company encourages "illegal long hours, failure to pay the minimum wage, lack of social benefits, crowded living, short term contracts, and constant violation of both Chinese law and Reebok's own cosmetic Human Rights standards." Asda Walmart and Manchester Airport were two other sponsors who both have lousy labour rights records. In 2000, Walmart in the US was forced to pay $50 million to settle claims after 69,000 workers were forced to work unpaid overtime.

No Sweat organiser Mick Duncan said "Our campaign isn't about attacking the Games, or sport - it's about exposing the practices of firms who use sport and sporting events to make millions while paying next to nothing to the workers who make the products." www.nosweat.org.uk

For a copy of the splendid spoof booklet send 2 first class stamps on an SAE to NATO, c/o EF! Box 29, MERCi, Bridge 5 Mill, 22a Beswick Street, Manchester, M4 7HR

To keep the tourists informed an alternative guide to the city appeared for the Games, an exact replica of the offical guide. It gave the other side of the story - about how funds were diverted from local communities to pay for the Games, and on the positive side, pointing people to events in the Blitz festival.

Positive SchNEWS

'Land and Future' is the world's first guide for tribal people, with information on how tribes around the world can secure their lands and way of life. It advises tribes on how to conduct a campaign when faced with the invasion of their lands by nasty oil companies, loggers and colonists, and offers tips on their rights under international law, and how to secure them. The book is going to be printed in many languages and there are plans for it be sent out to the remotest parts of the world. www.survival-international.org

...and finally...

Cardiff Bay, once an expanse of tidal mud flats, was recently re-developed at a cost of billions cos' nature wasn't considered good for business. Instead of being home to wading birds, the Bay's new residents are thousands of rich people who flocked to the area hoping to spend their time sipping cocktails on their balconies whilst the sun set over the tidal barrage. It now seems however that nature is getting its revenge in the form of thousands of midges that are plaguing the area. Residents, who now have to lock themselves in their luxurious flats at dusk to avoid the swarms of midges, are now threatening to take legal action against the harbour authorities for their failure to understand mother nature. Gnats that then.

Disclaimer
SchNEWS warns all readers living in the atomonous zone - don't fall-out over the mushrooms. Honest.

States of Unrest III

The A-Z of global resistance to the IMF and the World Bank

"The rising tide of the global economy will create many economic winners, but it will not lift all boats. ... [It will] spawn conflicts at home and abroad, ensuring an ever wider gap between regional winners and losers than exists today.... [Globalisation's] evolution will be rocky, marked by chronic financial volatility and a widening economic divide. Regions, countries, and groups feeling left behind will face deepening economic stagnation, political instability, and cultural alienation." Central Intelligence Agency, 2000

Mobilisations in Europe and North America against the International Monetary Fund (IMF) and World Bank are only branches of a much larger movement – the fiercest opponents of IMF and World Bank policies have always been people in the poorest countries, i.e. those who are most affected by them. Despite massive popular protest over the past few years the IMF and World Bank continue to force privatisation and 'austerity' on indebted countries.

Most of the money owed by indebted countries is owed to private banks. Often these countries need to seek new loans just to keep up with the interest payments on old debt. The IMF acts as 'gatekeeper', deciding whether to open or shut the 'gate' between a borrowing government and all other lines of international credit. That means that before anyone will lend an indebted country money the IMF is sent in to get the government to push through 'reforms' that ensure a climate that's 'good for business'.

Needless to say, what's 'good for business' – hacking back social spending and privatising everything to provide global capital with a constant supply of new markets; cheap & impoverished labour, and bargain-basement raw materials – is bad news for almost everyone else.

IMF reform packages used to be called Structural Adjustment Programmes (SAPs). In 1999, just for a laugh, they were re-named Poverty Reduction Strategy Papers (PRSPs), as though that would stop anyone noticing that they were made up of the same poverty-increasing schemes as always. These include:
• *Reduced government spending, leading to public-sector lay-offs, freezing of salaries, and cutbacks in health, education and social welfare services;*
• *Privatisation of state-run industries, often leading to massive lay-offs with no social security provision and the loss of services to remote or poor areas;*
• *Currency devaluation and export promotion, leading to the soaring cost of imports, land use changed for cash crops, and reliance on international commodity markets;*
• *Raising interest rates to tackle inflation, putting small companies out of business;*
• *Removal of price controls, leading to rapid price rises for basic goods and services.*

This report is the third annual global round-up of its kind from the World Development Movement. For the unedited version see the website: www.wdm.org.uk

ARGENTINA

At the end of December 2001, Argentina defaulted on its public and private foreign debts, totalling some US$132 billion – the largest default in history – plunging the country into economic and social crisis. In early December, the IMF refused a request by Argentina for an emergency loan agreement to cover the country's increasing debt and so the country defaulted. Throughout December and into January 2002, Argentina imposed emergency, short-term polices to deal with the economic fall-out from the debt default crisis, including changing the exchange rate regime and freezing banking accounts. The IMF set a number of strict conditions including the cancelling of an anti-corruption law and commitments to reduce public spending by 60 per cent. By the end of 2002 the IMF had still not resumed lending to Argentina. A new programme was eventually signed in January 2003.

After massive riots and the subsequent collapse of President Fernando de la Rue's Government in December 2001 (States of Unrest II), Eduardo Duhalde assumed Argentina's Presidency on 1 January 2002. Duhalde was put in place by the Argentinean Congress to remain President until December 2003. As his first act as the new President, Duhalde announced a currency devaluation plan and the dismantling of the 'convertibility' regime that for 11 years had pegged the peso on par to the dollar. Hours after the announcement, more than 4,000 Argentineans, fed up with Argentina's politicians and the economic crisis, streamed onto the streets of Buenos Aires in a raucous protest that continued throughout the night.

10 January: Thousands of protesters, in at least 60 Buenos Aires neighbourhoods, took to the streets in reaction to new restrictions (known as the 'corralito') imposed on bank account transactions and withdrawals. The restrictions were first introduced on 3 December 2001 to maintain the integrity of the banking system, which faced a massive run on cash withdrawals as the public and foreign investors lost faith in the banking system (States of Unrest II). The demonstration ended with riot police firing rubber bullets at the crowd, and several properties being trashed or burned including shops, supermarkets, McDonald's and the pay phone booths of Spanish company Telefonica de Argentina.

15 January: In the Santa Fe town of Casilda, 7,000 people mobilised, throwing eggs at the local offices of the Credico-Op and Galicia banks, while others threw rocks at the Bisel Bank and nearby shops. Riot police used tear gas and rubber bullets on the protesters. In Jujuy province government employees who hadn't been paid their December wages held a demo during which at least five banks and a company that provides public services were attacked. The facade of the provincial energy company, which had repeatedly raised its rates despite complaints from local residents, was also destroyed.

22 January: Workers from 76 public hospitals in the central province of Buenos Aires held a strike in defence of the public health system, demanding the materials and drugs needed to treat patients, and calling for payment of back-wages.

30 January: Over 7,000 middle-class mortgage-holders staged an 'el llaverazo', or 'key-banging' protest in Buenos

Aires. This was a variation on the frequent "cacerolazos" or 'pot-and-pan-banging' protests of the poor. Many people's mortgages had remained in US dollars while their savings had turned into pesos. The Head of Argentina's Association for the Defence of Consumers and Users, Sandra Gonzalez, said "More than three million people have debts in dollars to construction firms and private finance companies and run the risk of losing their homes if the government does not take a hand in the matter."

20 February: Public employees, the unemployed, teachers, doctors, pensioners, account-holders and students held massive street protests in Buenos Aires and in at least 10 provinces, while the Government tried to minimise the impact of the falling peso and rising fuel prices. Workers from the 'Congreso de Trabajadores Argentinos', the central trade union, wrapped Congress in a 400-metre-long Argentine flag, while retired and jobless protesters gathered outside the central offices of Repsol-YPF (a multinational oil company), demanding "50,000 real jobs," and "urgent food aid". The Secretary-General of the teachers' union, Marta Maffei, commented, "Every day, another 1,700 workers are left without a job, and enter the circuit of poverty. And those of us who do not lose our jobs have to put up with salary cuts, unpaid wages, and restructuring."

Argentina's Economy Minister, Jorge Remes Lenicov, told reporters that without foreign financial support not only would the economic programme collapse, but so could the Government itself, and urged that aid must not be delayed too long. Observers attributed the IMF's reticence to the stance of the US Government, which, upon realising that the Argentine crisis was not having a "domino effect" in the region, withdrew support for a bailout.

23 April: Lenicov resigned because Congress refused to back a bill that would meet some of the IMF's demands. Congress failed to agree the bill because protestors had surrounded the Parliament building.

27 May: Argentina's savers demonstrated again outside the main offices of several banks. Clashes with the police resulted in the arrest of four women.

26 June: Over 50 people were arrested, 15 injured and two people shot dead in violent protests against the Government and IMF. Riot police used tear gas, rubber bullets and batons to disperse protesters, who took to the streets just before new Economy Minister, Roberto Lavagna, was due to travel to Washington to meet IMF officials.

9 July: Independence Day. Over 15,000 people demonstrated peacefully in Buenos Aires against the Government and IMF.

9 December: The Government lifted the 'corralito', or banking restrictions that limited cash withdrawals.

20 December: Thousands of protesters marched through Buenos Aires, to mark the first anniversary of the 2001 riots which had led to the downfall of elected President Fernando de la Rua. Demonstrators burnt effigies of politicians and hurled paint bombs at the stock exchange.

BANGLADESH

In May 2002, the IMF cautioned that, "the financial burden posed by state-owned enterprises" needed to be addressed and "urged the authorities to move ahead forcefully to strengthen and implement their plans for privatisation and closure or restructuring of non-viable enterprises."

9 January: The Awami League held a nationwide half-day general strike to protest against fuel and other utilities' price

hikes. The Awami League leaders said that the Government had increased the price of fuel, gas, electricity and water to maximum levels while the prices of these commodities on the international market remained at minimum levels.

BENIN

In August 2002, the IMF "stressed the need to…control spending in non-priority areas…In particular, Directors urged restraint in wage settlements…Further action is also needed to complete a thorough review of the civil service pension fund, aimed at ensuring its viability, and implement the long-delayed reform of the civil service compensation system."

29 January: Public sector workers in Benin started a series of rolling 72-hour strikes in response to the lack of progress made by the Government in response to their wage claims. Despite promises made before the last presidential elections in March 2001, salaries have remained blocked since 1996.

COLOMBIA

In January 2003, the IMF Directors "were encouraged by the authorities' commitment to wide-ranging structural reforms [and] supported the high priority assigned by the new administration to modernising and streamlining and introducing greater flexibility in public spending." In December 2002, the Colombian Government explained how it had "proposed to freeze a large part of the public sector's… primary spending for the next two years at the 2002 level... The proposal that the government submitted to congress should reduce labour costs by extending daytime working hours and reducing overtime charges and severance payments."

January 2002: The Colombian Government, the Mayor of Cali and trade union SINTRAEMCALI signed an agreement ending a 35-day office occupation by workers of EMCALI, the state water, telecoms and electricity company (States of Unrest II and SchNEWS 339, 354). The union occupied the offices after the government announced plans to sell the enterprise in December 2001, amidst allegations by the union of mismanagement and corruption. The agreement ensured that the enterprise would not be privatised, that rates would not be increased in 2002, and that an investigation would be started into those officials who had defrauded the enterprise in recent years.

6 September: The first of two national strikes attracted thousands of workers to protest against the new President's economic policies and the treatment of trade unions, particularly SINTRAEMCALI, which had been subjected to a campaign of violent intimidation since January. The President had announced that he was going to freeze salaries, abolish the offices of municipal inspectors general, cut more than 10,000 public sector jobs, and present to the Congress labour and pension reforms as a way of following more IMF policies. The strike disrupted air traffic, hospitals and the state oil company.

30 October: Public sector and other workers took to the streets in the second national protest against IMF prescribed policies.

ECUADOR

In May 2001, the Government stressed that, "Agreement has been reached with a consortium of private oil companies to construct a second oil pipeline from the Amazon to the coast" and highlighted plans to submit to "congress legislation that includes agreed reforms of the oil stabilisation fund, and elimination of all tax revenue earmarking not mandated by the constitution." In January 2003 an IMF Mission concluded,

"The new Ecuadorian government has been very courageous in its first few days… and has developed a comprehensive program of far-reaching structural reforms."

21 January: The United Workers' Front (FUT) organised demonstrations throughout the country to protest against the fuel price increase and repression against students. The protests coincided with the second anniversary of the overthrow of former President Jamil Mahuad in Jan 2000 (States of Unrest I).

20-25 February: In the north eastern provinces of Sucumbios and Orellana, indigenous people, peasant farmers and municipal authorities workers staged protests and occupied oil industry infrastructure to demand compensation for the environmental damage that would be caused by the Heavy Crude Pipeline (OCP) project (SchNEWS 346).

22 May: Congress amended and passed a law stating that 10% of revenues generated from the OCP pipeline must put towards health and education.

29 May: IMF withheld US$240 million because it opposed the 10% amendment. The IMF demanded that the revenues attained from the OCP pipeline should go exclusively towards servicing debt. Economic analyst, Wilma Salgado, said the Ecuadorian population would not benefit in the least from the rise in oil revenues if the government did what the IMF wanted them to, pointing out that "Under the new law, the creditors who hold Ecuador's public debt, most of which is external, will be the beneficiaries of 90% of the revenues from exports of oil transported by the OCP pipeline."

HONDURAS

In September 2001, the Honduran Government reported that "In April 2001, decrees were issued that established a…limit for the wage bill in 2001 and 2002." They said, "Further progress with privatisation is essential to promote faster poverty-reducing growth." The conditions attached to Honduras receiving debt relief under the Highly Indebted Poor Countries Initiative have included privatisation of water and sewage management and electricity distribution.

15 March: Around 2,000 members of 30 popular organisations protested against the IMF, urging the Honduran Government to learn its lesson from Argentina's mistakes. SITRASANAAYS, the National Water and Sewage Workers Union, together with other social organisations formed a grassroots network against privatisation. The network held a series of popular mobilisations to resist the privatisation of water services and to protest free trade negotiations. In late 2002 it was reported that Honduras was stalled in its debt relief programme for not adequately complying with IMF conditions.

INDIA

In August 2002, the IMF advised that " priority should be given to reducing subsidies and the wage bill, for which further progress on downsizing the civil service will be necessary, together with bringing remaining subsidies [on fuel] on budget and announcing a timetable for the elimination of these subsidies." They also noted "reform of labour laws would facilitate greater labour mobility."

February: Keralan government employees and teachers went on a 20-day strike protesting curbed benefits. Workers picketed government offices in the state capital and district headquarters - about 30 people were arrested. Rallies in support of the strike were also organised. Hundreds of activists marched on the residence of the chief minister.

26 February: In the Kolar district, a dawn-to-dusk strike was organised to protest the failure of the state government to supply adequate electricity to rural areas and also against the proposed hike in power tariffs.

16 April: A major nationwide strike over labour reforms and the Government's privatisation plans involved over 10 million workers from state-run firms, banks, as well as the insurance and financial sectors. The day of protest followed Indian Cabinet approval, in February 2002, of reforms to a 55-year-old labour law reducing the rights of workers. Unions also protested the Government's plan to push ahead with a programme to privatise state-run firms including banking, automobile, telecoms, petroleum, port and metal companies.

INDONESIA

In December 2001, the Government explained how key features in the 2002 budget included, "continued wage restraint in the public sector…lowering untargeted subsidies through planned increases in fuel and electricity prices; and capping the share of general allocation funds to the regions at 25% of domestic revenue. It stated that it "is also committed to maintaining a liberal trade regime. Privatisation of state-owned enterprises is a key part of the… reform effort aimed at improving economic performance and strengthening the public finances."

14 January: More than 1,000 protesters flocked into central Jakarta to protest Government plans to raise fuel prices, along with telephone and electricity fees. Some demonstrators also demanded a raise in the minimum wage and a reduction in prices of basic staples. It was reported that the Government planned to increase basic fees for electricity by up to 15%; fuel by 20-25%; and telephone fees by 15%.

16 January: Hundreds of students took to the streets in several cities, in protest at the planned increases in fuel, electricity and telephone costs.

18 January: Protests continued with two separate marches converging on the House of Representatives in central Jakarta and bringing traffic to a halt.

8 March: Around 500 protesters from three different organisations staged a simultaneous rally to commemorate International Women's Day. The protesters marched from the Hotel Indonesia to the State Palace in central Jakarta. A spokesperson said her group demanded an increase in the regional minimum wage, reinstatement of public health subsidies and greater employment opportunities for women.

13 March: The Government sold its 51% stake in Bank Central Asia to a consortium led by US investment firm Farillon Capital. The sale nearly collapsed when thousands of the bank's employees held a strike in protest. The sale was reported by the BBC as "the country's most significant privatisation since the Asian financial crisis in the late 1990s and a key requirement for International Monetary Fund (IMF) assistance."

April: More than 400 employees from state-owned water company, Banding City (West Java) went on strike rejecting the privatisation of the company to South Australian Water.

21 May: Several hundred students and activists clashed with police. The protest marked the fourth anniversary of Suharto's resignation, which heralded the start of Indonesia's transition to democracy. But the protesters claimed that reforms had gone astray. The groups argued that politicians had sunk into inter-party bickering and blindly followed IMF-led economic reforms that ignore the poor.

KENYA

In April 2002, the IMF advised that "to maintain the credibility of the PRSP process and reduce poverty in Kenya, budget execution should reflect the priorities identified in the PRSP, including the need to reduce the government wage bill." In July the Government said, "reforming the public service lies at the heart of tackling poverty ... The operational structure of the entire public sector will be rationalised and reduced."

10 April: Police fired teargas into a demonstration of farmers protesting the decision by Kenya's National Cereals and Produce Board (NCPB) to pay maize farmers with seed, fertilizer and fuel instead of cash. The NCPB initiated the 'in kind' payment system for small-scale maize farmers after it ran out of money. In the past, the NCPB played an important role in the Kenyan farming community by buying the crops of small farmers at a guaranteed minimum amount. Since the liberalisation of the cereals market and the commercialisation of the NCPB, the system had collapsed.

October: Over 240,000 teachers from the Kenya National Union of Teachers (KNUT) went on a four-week strike because the Government refused to pay them wage increases agreed in 1997.

LEBANON

In October 2001, the IMF advised that Lebanon should "restore competitiveness and spur economic growth" through "structural reforms", particularly "privatisation, tariff reductions, and improvements in the business environment more generally...[the IMF] stressed the key role that privatisation may play in this regard."

January: Workers began a strike to protest against the planned privatisation of public services and to remind the government of union demands, including re-organisation of some sectors, payment of transport bonuses, and the implementation of agreements that had already been made.

MOROCCO

In 2001, the IMF warned that, "Morocco faces important remaining challenges in raising growth sufficiently to reduce unemployment and poverty on a sustained basis, that would require further trade liberalisation and structural reforms." They emphasised that, "the highest priority" must be given to "fiscal consolidation... aimed at curbing the growth of the wage bill."

1 February: The National Federation of Employees and Civil Servants from Collective Localities, which is affiliated to the Moroccan Workers Union, went on strike. The strike followed two general strikes in December 2001 (see States of Unrest II). The unions were calling for a rise in wages, which had been the same since 1997 despite an increasing cost of living.

NIGER

In March 2002, the IMF "urged the [Niger] authorities to maintain their structural reform agenda, particularly the privatisation program, [and] encouraged the authorities to focus on improving the business environment and private sector development".

22-23 July: The health workers union, Syndicat unique de la santé et de l'action sociale (SUSAS), went on a 48-hour nationwide strike. Throughout the strike only minimal health services were provided. The union was calling for the granting of a housing allowance for health workers; the unfreezing of length of service allowance for auxiliary staff; and increased training.

NIGERIA

In January 2003, the IMF stated that, "Progress on structural reforms...has been mixed. On the positive side, the authorities on January 1, 2002, adjusted the maximum retail price of gasoline... and began charging the Nigeria National Petroleum Corporation US$18 per barrel for crude oil used for domestic consumption compared with the US$9.5 charged in 2001. The hike in the retail price of petroleum is a step forward in the deregulation of the downstream petroleum sector." They also "urged the authorities to renew their commitment to trade liberalisation [and] to strengthen expenditure control, especially with regard to the wage bill."

16 January: The Nigerian Labour Congress (NLC) organised a nation-wide strike against the increases in the cost of petroleum products. Fuel deregulation and the ending of subsidies had proved a rallying point for the NLC, which successfully forced President Obasanjo to climb down from a 50% price rise in 2000 when protests turned to riots that paralysed the economy for several days (see States of Unrest I). Earlier threats by the Government to use the security forces to prevent the strike went unheeded as protesters blockaded streets in Lagos, and forced the closure of banks, schools and street markets. Work in other cities also halted. More than 50 union leaders were arrested as a result of the strike, including the leader of the NLC.

February: The police went on strike because of non-payment of wages and allowances. A total of 185 junior officers were arrested because of the strike.

12 October: Workers from the local government employees' union, NULGE, took industrial action in order to secure back pay owed to local government workers in Adamawe State. The government finally agreed, but in Gombe State workers continued the strike over salary arrears at the same time after councils failed to respond to the unions.

PARAGUAY

In June 2001, the IMF "welcomed the progress made in the privatisation of the telecommunications and water and sewage companies [but] encouraged the authorities to complete these operations this year [2001/02], to privatise additional enterprises, and to improve the efficiency of the remaining state enterprises." The Government said "Fuel prices were recently increased to reflect increases in oil prices (Paraguay imports 100 per cent of its oil needs)...[and] The government has pressed ahead with the privatisation of the telecommunications and water and sanitation companies." In August 2002, the IMF announced it would provide Paraguay with a US$200 million loan.

4 June: In Coronel Oviedo City, police harshly cracked down on around 5,000 peasants marching on the Paraguayan capital to demand that a law on privatisation be overturned. Calixto Cabral, a 34-year-old farmer, was killed by a bullet to the head and another farmer, Teresio Velazquez, was critically wounded when he was shot in the stomach. At least five others were injured.

6 June: The Central Nacional de Trabajadores (CNT), the country's main trade union, announced a strike to demand changes in economic policy and the revocation of the law on privatisation, including the sale of the public telephone company, the Compania Paraguaya de Comunicaciones (Copaco). The President of Paraguay's Central Bank,

Raul Vera Bogado, stressed that the sale of Copaco was indispensable for reaching a US$60 million agreement with the IMF. However, in reaction to the strike's intensity, the President called an emergency cabinet meeting and a few hours later announced on television that he had decided to indefinitely postpone the sale of Copaco, scheduled for 14 June, in order to "calm things down."

18 June: Eight people were injured and six were detained on the first day of a strike by the Union of Municipal Workers, SITRAMA. The Union called the strike in reaction to the authorities' lack of compliance with their contract, and in protest against dismissals, unjustified transfers, and unpaid benefits. The Mayor sought to have the strike declared illegal and threatened to fire all strikers, offering overtime rates to anyone who wanted to work in their place.

15 July: Paraguay's President decreed a state of emergency, suspending civil rights, after escalating nationwide protests against his Government's economic policies. In the capital, baton-wielding police battled with 600 protesters who had blockaded roads and taken to the streets. Police officers used rubber bullets and water cannons while the army took up positions outside Congress. At least four people were shot, two people died and several were seriously injured and over 33 demonstrators were arrested. The protests also spread to Ciudad del Este, some 200 miles east of Asuncion. Four people, including an 11-year-old, were treated for bullet wounds after 800 protesters clashed with police, who used tear gas and water cannons to disperse them. The protest had blocked the Puente de la Amistad bridge, which links Paraguay to Brazil.

PERU

In January 2002, the Government outlined plans "to generate investor confidence [by implementing a] sizeable program of privatisation and granting of operating concessions to the private sector. Privatisations will focus in the energy sector, particularly in the generation, transmission and distribution of electricity. In infrastructure, the government will accelerate the transfer to the private sector of the operation of several state-owned assets, including regional seaports and airports and highway projects."

15-17 June: Thousands of protesters took to the streets to oppose the sale of Egasa and Egesur, two state-owned electricity companies. Protesters put up roadblocks and smashed up the airport as well as phone boxes and shop fronts. At least one man died in the protests and the police made over 30 arrests, with at least two officers injured.

17 June: After three days of rioting in Arequipa, the Government declared a state of emergency. President Alejandro Toledo ordered 1,700 heavily armed police and soldiers into Arequipa to repress the demonstrations. Rioting also spread to other provinces. In Cuzco, over 3,000 students marched in solidarity with the protesters in Arequipa. In Tacna, over 2,000 people took to the streets, closing the Pan-American Highway with blockades of burning tyres.

19 June: An official government mission sent to Arequipa under armed guard announced a temporary suspension of the privatisations.

December: The privatisation of state enterprises was re-started.

PHILIPPINES

In November 2002, the IMF noted, "During its first year, the new administration made significant progress... especially reviving the energy sector deregulation bill... Direc-

tors agreed that further structural reforms are needed to bolster growth. In this respect, they welcomed plans to privatise and deregulate the power sector, which hold out the promise of solving long-standing problems, while spurring large amounts of foreign direct investment".

15 May 2002: Nationwide protests were launched for the abolition of the Power Purchased Adjustment (PPA) charge. Hundreds of families living in Caloocan City participated in a 'noise barrage' and 'power off' protest. One spokesperson from poor residents said residents of depressed areas were mobilising against PPA. He cited the power-off protest of 2,000 residents of Sawata against the controversial billing of Manila Electric Co. (Meralco). Residents began to mark billing statements with "Under Protest."

June: Thousands in Metro Manila and surrounding provinces took part in a planned 'noise protest' against power rates and the PPA charge. Riot police were ordered to set up barricades as demonstrators marched on the presidential palace in the capital.

SOUTH AFRICA

In July 2002, the IMF highlighted that "reforms aimed at promoting private sector activity and attracting foreign investment will remain critical, and should focus on further progress with privatisation and trade liberalisation... Directors encouraged the authorities to persevere with structural reform [and] welcomed efforts to pick up the pace of privatisation... Directors also welcomed the steps taken to communicate the privatisation strategy more clearly to the public." They urged "the authorities to continue reviewing labour laws at frequent intervals."

March: The Soweto Electricity Crisis Committee and the Anti-Privatisation Forum, organised a protest march to demand the electricity company stop cutting off electricity to those who are too poor to pay and who have illegal power connections. The state power company, Eskom, was clamping down on the illegal connections practice because they claimed it to be dangerous and costing too much money. But the protesters claimed that the poor deserve free electricity and that the government was preparing Eskom for privatisation (SchNEWS 391).

July: For three weeks municipal workers from the South African Municipal Workers Union (SAMWU), were on national strike against rising inflation and low wages. Workers occupied Mayors' offices in several centres, including the economic heartland of Johannesburg. A worker was shot and killed in the town of Louis Trichaardt, the first casualty of a strike that saw other workers injured in clashes with security guards and police officers.

SOUTH KOREA

In February 2002, the IMF "noted that, despite progress, the corporate sector remains beleaguered by the continued operation of loss-making [state] companies. They stressed that the orderly exit of non-viable companies should be accelerated... Furthermore, many companies need to undertake deeper restructuring, close loss-making operations, and sell non-core assets to improve profitability and resolve debt levels."

26th February: Workers in state railway, power and gas sectors held massive nationwide strikes in protest against moves toward privatisation. The strike caused widespread disruption, especially to transport infrastructure. The President of the FKTU railway union was arrested and arrest warrants issued on 12 others. The strikes involved more than 50,000 workers in 94 workplaces. The Government planned to hand over the railway to a private company and sell most of its power generation operation.

March: The Electric Power Industry Union (EPIU) began a five-week stoppage to protest Government privatisation plans.

20 March: Leaders of the EPIU began a hunger strike at Myeong Dong Cathedral demanding the Government scrap plans to privatise power plants.

2 April: Tens of thousands of union members went on strike in support of the EPIU. Both public and private sectors were affected by the nationwide walkout, intensifying pressure on the Government to reconsider the planned privatisations.

17 April: Members of the Korean Confederation of Trade Unions (KCTU) clashed with police as they tried to storm a conference room to protest against the proposed conditions being attached to a five-day working week agreement. Demanding the unconditional adoption of the shorter working week for small businesses and part-time workers, KCTU members tried to force their way into the room where the labour commission was meeting.

23 May: The Korean Health and Medical Workers' Union (KHMWU) launched strikes in 16 hospitals. Two hospitals staged full-scale walkouts, while workers at 13 hospitals took part in partial strikes. Strikers called for more staff, demanding that the distinction between full-time and part-time workers be abolished. KCTU conducted a sit-in at Jongmyo Park in Seoul calling for the withdrawal of privatisation plans and the introduction of a five-day working week.

4-5 November: The Korean Government Employees Union (KGEU) held a public rally, with around 30,000 members taking to the streets. As soon as the rally started riot police broke it up violently, leaving many unionists injured. Thousands of KGEU members were arrested. The KGEU was against a draft government bill on labour rights aimed at denying civil service workers the right to organise. The protest came after 27 members of the KGEU were arrested on 1 and 2 November. Arrest warrants were issued against eight other leaders and riot police surrounded the KGEU offices, blocked the entrance and confiscated documents.

URUGUAY

In August 2002, the IMF agreed to bail out Uruguay's escalating financial and banking crisis. In doing so they "welcomed the Uruguayan authorities' decisive response to the continued deposit outflows [but noted that] significant challenges continue to lie ahead for the authorities, to restore financial stability, regain access to markets, and to return to economic growth. This [loan] programme provides the authorities with the opportunity to achieve these objectives, but sustained structural reform to reinvigorate the economy through privatisation and deregulation will be key in the months ahead."

16 April: Thousands of farmers held protests in the capital, Montevideo, and other cities, against the Government's economic policies.

May: Workers held a general strike protesting against the Government's economic polices and a bill which aimed to raise taxes on salaries and pensions.

29 May: Congress passed the bill that would raise taxes and which the IMF demanded as a condition of fresh loans. Congressional approval for the bill came a day after the IMF said it would be willing to loan Uruguay an extra US$1.5 billion.

20 June: Uruguay got rid of its currency-trading band, and announced the free flotation of the Uruguayan peso against the dollar. Immediately the peso plunged in value. IMF Deputy Managing Director, Eduardo Aninat, praised Uruguay's decision.

30 July: The Government ordered a halt to all financial activity for one day by creating a 'bank holiday'. The freeze aimed at stopping the free fall of the Central Bank's reserves, which plummeted from US$3.1 billion at the end of 2001 to US$725 million by July 2002. In the month of July capital flight totalled US$746 million, with at least $50 million withdrawn on 29 July alone. The President, Jorge Batlle, gave his word that the bank holiday would last only 24 hours. It was reported that government delegates were in Washington asking the IMF for an early disbursement of a loan approved at the end of May.

4 August: After four days of bank closures, public frustration and panic erupted into rioting on the streets of the capital, Montevideo. The protests were the largest the country had seen in a decade, as thousands joined a general strike called by 42 unions to protest at the closed banks and the country's three years of recession. Shops were looted and 20 people arrested.

6 August: US Treasury Secretary, Paul O'Neill, visited Uruguay as part of a four-day regional tour. When asked why Uruguay received a loan and not Argentina, Mr O'Neill said: "Why Uruguay? Because Uruguay is a country that has followed sound economic policies."

ZAMBIA

In May 2002 the IMF approved new loans to Zambia, praising " the recent re-advertisement inviting bids for an increase in the sale of the Zambia National Commercial Bank shares to 51%, which is indicative of the commitment to move forward with major structural reform policies." In 2000, the receipt of debt relief by Zambia under the HIPC initiative was made conditional on the privatisation of the state run telephone, electricity, bank and oil companies.

23 May: The Government announced that it was privatising 51% of the Zambia National Commercial Bank (ZNCB), after an offer for 35% attracted little interest from foreign investors. ZNCB has 43 branches and 1,440 employees, making it Zambia's biggest retail bank.

May 2002: Zambian President, Levy Mwanawasa, declared the country's food shortage a national disaster, saying four million people faced starvation. The food shortage was part of a wider pattern facing many other countries in the Southern Cone of Africa, including Malawi, Botswana and Namibia.

29 August: Unions reacted angrily to the Government's decision to suspend expense payments, including food and travel, to civil servants and public sector workers. The Primary School Teachers Association of Zambia and the Civil Servants Union of Zambia suggested cuts should be made to benefits paid to senior civil servants and politicians instead of the lowest paid workers and threatened strike action.

9 December: After strong opposition by unions, the President announced that the privatisation of ZNCB would be halted. In immediate retaliation, the IMF told the Zambian Government it would not receive debt relief worth US$1 billion (£633million) unless it went ahead with the privatisation. "If they don't sell, they will not get the money," said Mark Ellyne, the IMF resident representative to Zambia.

14 December: Thousands joined in a demo in the capital, Lusaka, to oppose the IMF and to call a halt to other privatisations, including telecom operator Zamtel and electricity operator Zesco Limited. The President of Zambia's Federation of Free Trade Unions (FFTUZ), Joyce Nonde, told the rally that the economic mistakes of the past 10 years had left people in abject poverty and deprivation. "Now let somebody out there tell us," she said, "having privatised 80% of our economy, why is it that we have become one of the poorest countries in Africa and the whole world?"

"We've finally reached the summit"

SchNEWS

weekly

www.schnews.org.uk

Friday 16th August 2002   **Free/Donation**   **Issue 368**

GRAVY PLANE

"South Africa is in the hands of global capital. That's why it can't meet the legitimate demands of its people." - *George Soros, money launderer*

It's all hitting the fan in South Africa and that's before 60,000 delegates fly in for the huge talking shop that will be the World Summit on Sustainable Development coming up at the end of this month.

It all started when the ANC government (yes the same people that fought against Apartheid) began implementing a World Bank-influenced development model for Johannesburg which included privatization of public services. When the ANC first came to power in 1994, its Freedom Charter promised one million houses, universal and affordable electricity, a national health scheme and social security. But in 1996, the ANC was forced by powerful investors and the International Monetary Fund to adapt itself to the 'realities' of the global economy. Since then, health, welfare, education, electricity and housing budgets have been slashed. The gap between rich and poor has increased since the end of apartheid, with around 1 in 4 South Africans unemployed.

Now the social force that helped bring down apartheid is once again active in townships across the country – and this time the ANC isn't taking too kindly to it.

Yesterday the trial began of 87 people arrested in April as part of an action organised by the Soweto Electricity Crisis Committee (SECC). The group had gathered in front of the mayor's house to protest about people's services being cut off. Some thought it would be good to give him a taste

of what they have to put up with and tried to cut off his water and electricity when one of his bodyguards fired eight shots into the crowd, wounding two people. The protestors were then all nicked for public violence and damage to property. Most of the damage was done to the Mayor's swimming pool, ironic since most of the people in Soweto can't even afford to pay for drinking water.

On the official summit website they talk of "hundreds of millions of people living under conditions of abject poverty or experiencing highly unequal access to resources, living in inadequate human settlements — characterised by over-crowding, lack of access to basic infrastructure, services and economic opportunities, inadequate resources, environmental degradation, homelessness and social exclusion."

And what would you do if some of these same people lived in your country, in townships just a few miles away from the conference centre? Well you would host a summit that costs £34 million pounds to talk about it of course! And who would you get this money from? From Eskom, the electricty company who've been busy helping people stay in abject poverty by pushing up bills past the point where people can afford to pay for them and then cutting their electricity supply off.

Sowoto?

Last September, 1800 houses in Tafelsig, a township near Cape Town, had their water cut off because they couldn't afford to pay the bills the recently privatised company was demanding, some of which had increased about 400%. People who resisted were shot with live ammunition while riot cops protected the people who were busy disconnecting. Within weeks, a major cholera epidemic broke out because people were forced to use rivers and stagnant ponds for water. To date there have been more than 100,000 cases of cholera and 250 deaths.

Meanwhile, the recently privatised electricity company, Eskom, started cutting off the electricity of people who couldn't pay their massively increased bills. Poor communities in Sowetan South Africa organised a boycott of their Eskom payments and the Soweto

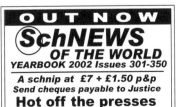

Sowoto? cont...

Electricity Crisis Committee began illegally reconnecting the power of families left in the dark. For their troubles one ANC minister called them a "criminal gang." For nine months it co-ordinated this campaign, until last October, when Eskom announced it would no longer disconnect those who couldn't pay:

The success of the campaign inspired a similar boycott of water payments, and thousands of Sowetans took to the streets.

With the telephone system also recently privatised, 40 per cent of the new phone lines that the company Telkom has delivered have been disconnected because the people can't afford the new rates that have gone up by 35%. In contrast, the price of domestic long- distance and international calls, used mainly by wealthy South Africans, has become 40% cheaper!

Earlier this month, hundreds of residents of Mandela Park in Cape Town occupied a house before a pensioner was 'rightsized' by the Servcon Housing Company. 'Rightsizing' is a legal process whereby vulnerable people such as pensioners, the disabled, and the unemployed who cannot afford to meet repayments on houses (some of which aren't even properly built) are forced to move to tiny houses. These tiny houses are described as 'dog kennels' and are often far from their community. One pensioner recently died after being forcibly evicted.

The township of Soweto will always be known for its own 'Spirit of '76' when a thousand students were killed in an uprising, an event which radicalized a generation of anti-apartheid activists. Resistance to privatisation has once again radicalized this and other communities across the country. As one campaigning group put it, "The Summit will offer the opportunity for the social movements to demonstrate with the whole world watching. This will be the time to show that the neo-liberal model aided by the international financial institutions and profit hungry corporations do not deliver social or ecological justice to those who need it most."

* Aug. 31 will be a global day of action against big business muscling in on sustainable development. www.aseed.net

* Also on Aug. 31, many of the social movements in South Africa have agreed on a common platform to organise what they hope will be the biggest independent political gathering since apartheid ended in 1994. To keep updated with the protests visit http://southafrica.indymedia.org

* For more:www.earthsummit.biz/

Batle Battered In Uruguay

And now boys and girls, it's time for another South American economic crisis brought to you by our old friends at the IMF and World Bank. By now it's a familiar story—the IMF lends money to an impoverished country, on condition that said impoverished country will agree to IMF demands for "structural readjustment," i.e. privitisation of public services, unlimited foreign investment (read: allowing Nike to build as many sweatshops as they like) and free trade agreements which allow local industries to be outdone and then overtaken by foreign multinationals. Once "structural adjustment" is up and running, large amounts of cash flow OUT of the country (into the bank accounts of aforementioned multinationals or corrupt local governments), causing the local currency to plummet and the price of goods and services to skyrocket.

At the beginning of August, Uruguay began to show signs of just such a disaster. President Batle closed banks and froze savings deposits in fear of bank runs amid a freefall in the value of the Uruguayan peso. Pressed to breaking point, the poor and starving population of Uruguay decided they'd had enough. In a recent statement, the Federación Anarquista Uruguaya (FAU) describes the situation, "The tariffs on essential services [water, electricity, etc.] had been raised, supermarkets increased prices scandalously... Basic items doubled their price in little time. Salaries stayed the same, however, and there were hardly any more "odd jobs" available. Quite simply, hunger had taken over the world of the poor." On August 2nd, the Uruguayan people took action— more than 13 supermarkets were looted in the poor neighborhoods of Montevideo to the shouts of "We are hungry!" The FAU letter explains, "Hundreds of people "looted" supermarkets in different areas. Children, women, the elderly, entire families entered and took what they could: sugar, rice, noodles, flour, oil, etc."

As a result of these "food liberations," the government and corporate media in Uruguay have started a campaign against alternative media sources, desperate to blame the situation on anyone but the truly responsible parties. On August 3, police raided and shut down the community radio station "El Quijote", also located in the neighborhood of Montevideo, blaming them for inciting the lootings. Mainstream newspapers have published articles accusing radio stations and even Uruguay Indymedia of inciting looting at supermarkets. In articles reminiscent of The Sun or The Daily Telegraph, one paper assured its readers that "The Minister of the Interior [blames] 'Anarchists' for the looting... These are people who want to destroy our style of life." ("Our style of life" which includes starvation, poverty, and suffering for the poor, of course). Meanwhile, President Batle has managed to re-open all banks. And just how did he manage this fantastic achievement?? Why, by securing a new £1 billion loan from the IMF, of course. For breaking news, visit:

http://www.indymedia.org/
(or if you can read Spanish):
http://uruguay.indymedia.org/

SchNEWS in brief

Check out the **new Lancaster Re-Source centre**, a fair trade café and local campaigns base, open every Wednesday 12-7pm. 78a Penny St., Lancaster Tel- 01524-383012 ****Another World is Possible** free festival is happening on 31st August from 1-9pm, Tankerton Slopes, Whitstable. 07753 822424 ** One of the last independent political bookshops in the country, **Little Thorn Books in Leicester** desperately needs money (or better still, people to go in and buy books) or they'll have to close. And of course you can always go and get the new SchNEWS book there that's out today so hurry! 73 Humberstone Gate, Leicester. Open 10-5.30 Tues-Sat 0116 251 2002 ** **The Green Blayde Fayre** which the Levellers were organising has been cancelled cos the nice people of Sidmouth in Devon didn't want a lot of "New age traveller" types staying there for weeks disrupting the local community ** **The Ministry of Defence** care so much about life that they're putting up birdboxes for ospreys at their Trident nuclear submarine base. On Wednesday activists from the nearby peace camp dressed up as birds, a cockroach and a dog commenting, "Nuclear weapons could make all life on the planet (with the possible exception of cockroaches) in danger of extinction. The ospreys have so far declined to take up residence, obviously they are aware of the dangers within the base." So far 53 have been nicked during the summer **Trident Ploughshare camp** including two who swam out to HMS Vigilant and spray-painted 'Vile' on both sides of the submarine! 0845 4588366 www.tridentploughshares.org ** **Several thousand Polish shipyard workers** last week broke into the Odra clothes factory in Szczecin where women workers have not received pay for several months and are on partial strike. The shipyard workers pelted the boss with eggs and then stuck him in a wheelbarrow – apparently an age old custom in Poland when firing your boss!** The world car-free days billed as **"Fifteen Days to End the Auto Age"** are coming up on September 13-27 for more info www.carbusters.org/carfreeday ** The International Longshore and Warehouse Union in San Francisco is under threat from the Bush administration who are threatening to bring in the National Guard (a division of the army) to break a threatened strike. Working for months under an expired contract, **10,000 dock workers face a threatened lockout** by their bosses who want to sack staff, cut healthcare, and attack workers' rights. http://sf.indymedia.org/

Reedy Business

On Tuesday a group of people occupied Reed Recruitment Agency to protest against the company's involvement in the privatisation of education, in particular the creation of a privatised 'City Academy' in Leicester. 16 people gathered outside Reed Recruitment Agency in Leicester's market square carrying banners with slogans such as, 'Keep Fat Cats Out of Education.' Several people entered the agency and refused to leave while Reed's window was decorated with banners and 'spoof' job vacancies– 'School Governor wanted: no previous experience necessary, must have lots of wonga, call inside and ask for Tony'. Staff kept asking people to leave but as one protestor said, "Alec Reed decided to interfere with education so we'll interfere with his business."

Alec Reed, owner of Reed Executive, already owns one school in London and has a fortune in the region of £50 million. He has argued that the present school curriculum should be 'torn up and thrown away' and that his investment 'buys him permission to interfere.' Alec Reed wants free enterprise to be taught in schools to children of all ages so that they can all grow up to be wankers like him. As part of the Labour Government's new privatisation policy, 10% of funding required to establish a new school comes from the private sector. Even though the remaining 90%, along with the running costs, is fronted by the taxpayer, the private backer is considered the owner and is handed control of the whole school. With "City Academies" being exempt from the national curriculum, this gives the owner free reign over what children can be taught. leicesterisr@yahoo.co.uk

HOLY AXIS OF EVIL, BATMAN!

Positive SchNEWS

A new squatted community art space will be opening at **282 Richmond Road in Hackney, London on the 24th August**, running for a week with workshops on sculpture/metalwork, woodwork/speaker cabinet building, web design, and desk top publishing, plus an array of the finest underground art in the capital. Running along side this event will be Riot Squad Records, a squatted record shop devoted to underground dance music and hoping to be a vital link between musicians, artists, producers and performers. "Finally there will be a friendly place to listen to tunes, with good prices and the opportunity to get some second hand classics," say the organisers. More info on 07092 012299 www.randomartists.org

* **The Edith Cavell building**, a huge modern office building in Hackney (between Enfield Road and Hertford Road, just off Kingsland Road) has just been squatted as a community centre.

* Parents at **St Johns nursery, Hackney** have organised a festival of resistance on Saturday 31 August as part of a campaign to fight its closure by the bankrupt council. The nursery is at 22 Milborne St Tel 07905 460472 or contact joeeamon@aol.com

On Tuesday a group of people occupied **Reed Recruitment Agency** to protest against the company's involvement in the privatisation of education, in particular the creation of a privatised 'City Academy' in Leicester. 16 people gathered outside Reed Recruitment Agency in Leicester's market square carrying banners with slogans such as, 'Keep Fat Cats Out of Education.' Several people entered the agency and refused to leave while Reed's window was decorated with banners and 'spoof' job vacancies– 'School Governor wanted: no previous experience necessary, must have lots of wonga, call inside and ask for Tony'. Staff kept asking people to leave but as one protestor said, "Alec Reed decided to interfere with education so we'll interfere with his business."

Alec Reed, owner of Reed Executive, already owns one school in London and has a fortune in the region of £50 million. He has argued that the present school curriculum should be 'torn up and thrown away' and that his investment 'buys him permission to interfere.' Alec Reed wants free enterprise to be taught in schools to children of all ages so that they can all grow up to be wankers like him. As part of the Labour Government's new privatisation policy, 10% of funding required to establish a new school comes from the private sector. Even though the remaining 90%, along with the running costs, is fronted by the taxpayer, the private backer is considered the owner and is handed control of the whole school. With "City Academies" being exempt from the national curriculum, this gives the owner free reign over what children can be taught. leicesterisr@yahoo.co.uk

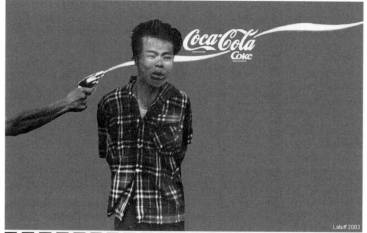
Latuff 2003

...and finally...

Still think the UN has people's best interest in mind? That the UN Children's Fund (UNICEF) really cares about the health of the world's children? SchNEWS (in co-operation with our corporate sponsors McDonald's) begs you to reconsider. Last month UNICEF and McDonald's announced plans "to team up to raise money on behalf of the world's children as part of a new McDonald's fundraising initiative called 'World Children's Day'" to be held on November 20th.

How sweet…Too bad McDonald's is a global leader in the marketing of junk food that creates soaring rates of childhood obesity and diabetes. Too bad that its type of nutritionless convenience crap is disrupting traditional ways of food preparation in families and cultures, and its Golden Arches are branded on urban and rural landscapes from Bangkok to Mexico City, bright shiny symbols of a country whose children throw away more food in a year than the children of some other nations eat. The initiative, which aims to raise money for McDonald's charitable arm and a dozen UNICEF programmes, includes a pop concert in China which will be broadcast over the internet—access to which can only be obtained by buying a Big Mac burger! Conveniently, UNICEF will receive a cut of the profits from each Big Mac sold.

Sensing a slight inconsistency in the alliance, an international coalition of public-health professionals and activists has asked UNICEF to withdraw from the partnership. The charity, which stands to make millions of pounds by lending both its name and resources to the event, responded to the coalition by saying that, "The partnership does not mean that UNICEF endorses McDonald's or its products." But if this "Buy a Big Mac and Help UNICEF" arrangement isn't an endorsement, we at Schnews wonder what is? Perhaps "Buy a Happy Meal and Support Global Destruction" would have been a bit more appropriate.

Disclaimer

Schnews warns all conference goers to stay at home and watch TV and not to go to any legal gathering, honest.

weekly SchNEWS

www.schnews.org.uk

Friday 23rd August 2002   Free/Donation Issue 369

RETURN TO SENDER

"The least important global environmental issue is potential global warming, and we hope that your negotiators at Johannesburg can keep it off the table and out of the spotlight."

- Excerpt from a letter sent to George W. Bush by a group of Exxon Mobil funded lobbyists.

As if dodging out of the Kyoto treaty, supporting rabid fossil fuel consumption, and making money at the expense of all forms of life on earth weren't enough to keep them busy, it now seems that some of the big business lapdogs in Washington have taken it upon themselves to sabotage the upcoming Earth Summit in Johannesburg.

In a letter to George W. recently leaked to the media by Friends of the Earth, thirty-one lobbyists – many funded by Exxon Mobil – told Bush that "we applaud your decision not to attend the Summit in person … the Johannesburg Summit will provide a global media stage for many of the most irresponsible and destructive elements involved in environmental issues. Your presence would only help to publicise and make more credible various anti-freedom, anti-people, anti-globalisation, and anti-Western agendas."

So let's get this straight—this lot doesn't want Bush to attend the conference because they think it's been taken over by irresponsible and destructive tree-huggers who, unlike them, wouldn't sell their own grandmothers to make a buck. They're upset because they think the Earth Summit is actually going to be a meeting of concerned environmentalists, gathering to discuss what can be done about the impending ecological disaster brought on by capitalism and free trade. They think the Summit is a threat to all the things they hold

dear—greed, gain, and globalisation. But for once, dear readers, the joke's on the corporate whores. They needn't bother sabotaging the conference because it's already been sabotaged by their favourite things—multinational greed, corporate gain, and the push for globalisation at any cost.

If the American big business butt kissers would simply pause a moment to review some of the people who are planning to attend the Summit, they'd quickly realise they have nothing to fear. Just for kicks, let's look at some of Blair's hand-picked delegates. Blair's posse contains a number of his Big Business cronies including Bill Alexander, chief executive of Thames Water. The largest water company in the UK, Thames Water has been prosecuted for pollution over 20 times since 1996. Just two days after it was announced that Thames Water would become an official defender of the global environment in Johannesburg, its parent company, RWE, threatened to cancel the creation of 4,000 new jobs unless the European commission dropped its plans to impose stricter controls on carbon dioxide emissions. During the Summit, Bill Alexander will be making a speech outlining how private water companies can make immense contributions to environmental and humanitarian interests. Try telling that to the hundreds of South Africans who contracted cholera from drinking polluted river water after their unaffordable privatised water was cut off (See Schnews 368).

Chris Fay, another of Blair's prime choices, is not only a non-executive director of Anglo America, another of the world's mining giants, but he's also a director of British Airways and was formerly the chairman of Shell—mining, aviation, and oil being three of the most sustainable

industries, of course. This is a particularly sensitive choice on Blair's part, as many South African communities are currently involved in seeking compensation from Shell and BP following leaks from an oil refinery. Fay is also a director of Weir Group Plc., whose subsidiary, Weir Pumps, has been implicated in human rights abuses and genocide in Sudan.

And last, but certainly not least on Blair's stunning list of eco-warriors, is Sir Robert Wilson, executive chairman of mining company Rio Tinto. As the world's largest mining conglomerate, Rio Tinto has destroyed ecosystems the world over and is currently the focus of one of Australia's highest profile environmental rows ever. The company's plans to mine uranium in one of the planet's most valuable wildlife sites – Kakadu National Park, a World Heritage Site – has sparked protests that have led

EARTH SUMMIT ACTIONS:
Global Day of Action has been called by ASEED 31st August. www.aseed.net
Brighton "Sunny Day" Sept 1st at the Ellipse on Brighton seafront (11-4pm). Energy efficiency, climate change, electric bicycles, biodiesel, Brighton's earthship, Rising Tide, bands and music. 01273 725077 RTtrad@aol.com
For more Earth Summit stuff visit:
* http://climate.indymedia.org/
* http://southafrica.indymedia.org/
* www.corporatewatch.org.uk/news/blair_and_earth_summit.htm
* www.corporateeurope.org/observer12/wssdlobby.html
* www.monbiot.com

to more than 500 arrests.

Speaking sensitively about environmental issues in underdeveloped countries, Hugh Leggat, a Rio Tinto spokeman, has remarked:

"When you get there, you can find the locals have chopped all the trees down. So perhaps it would be advantageous to allow in a mining firm which could then in return promise to do regeneration work." Cross your heart and hope to die, Mr. Leggat? But, as Leggatt has pointed out, "We are already just about the most regulated industry in the world." Apparently he doesn't remember his company's brilliant track record in Bougainville.

Deadbeat Delegates

With a group of delegates like this, one might wonder just what kind of an environmental conference Blair's going to? But at the heart of Blair's seemingly contradictory delegate choices lurks his pet project - public-private partnerships. He, along with many other Western governments, seems to think that by inviting reckless corporations to the party and allowing them to control things like water, energy, and forests, they will then start to behave sensibly, protect these crucial resources, and sustainable development will naturally follow.

But the craziest part is this - even if corporations weren't in the thick of the decision-making process, it would still be a bogus summit. Why? Because none of the agreements that the involved parties sign will be legally binding. Legal regulations (covering such issues as human rights and the environment) have been dropped in favour of voluntary codes. The draft plan now calls only for the "promotion of corporate accountability and responsibility and the exchange of best practices." Believing in the actual existence of "corporate accountability and responsibility," the powers that be have decided that voluntary self-regulation is all that's needed to fix the environmental problems caused by free trade. As George Monbiot says, "To defend the world from the destruction brokered by multinational capital, governments will tie a ribbon round it and hand it to multinational capital."

SchNEWS in brief

Catch up with everyone's direct action summer adventures at the next **Rebel Alliance**, 4th September 7.30pm upstairs at the Albert Pub, Trafalger St. Brighton. ** On the same night, SchNEWS will be hosting our annual **Book Launch Party** at the Volks, Madeira Drive, Brighton 9pm. Please arrive early! ** Great news - **Steward Community Woodland** in Devon has been given a 5 year temporary planning permission to continue their sustainable woodland low-impact living project www.stewardwood.org ** Film premiere of **'Drowned Out'** about the **Narmada Dam** protests in India. It's on at Curzon Soho Cinema, Shaftesbury Ave, London W1 £7/5,Wed 28th, 7pm, the screening will be followed by a Q&A session. www.spannerfilms.net ** **The Colchester Radical Collective** have opened a social centre in a Grade 2 listed building. The building had been left empty by Capita (big friends of New Labour's Private Finance Initiative) who have been trying to turn it into posh flats. Capita is taking the squatters to court today (23rd). If you're going to the **Colchester Free Festival** (www.colchesterfreefestival.co.uk) this bank holiday Monday, why not pay the centre a visit? 87 East Hill, 0798 6654583 squat@nogm.cjb.net ** Meanwhile in nearby **Southend,** two people let everyone know about a road widening scheme that could destroy 100 trees by spending eight hours in the threatened trees' branches www.ppps.org.uk ** Worthing cops are continuing to hassle people they suspect might be 'ringleaders' of the campaign to stop the destruction of ancient **Titnore Woods** by property developers. The next action planned on September 1st is delivery of a letter to the landowner urging him to consider preserving the area as a nature reserve. Fancy dress if you can. Meet 1pm Coach and Horses on the A27 Arundel Road www.worthinga27.freeserve.co.uk ** Copies of our new **SchNEWS OF THE WORLD** book will be on sale at a S.C.R.A.P. Records music alldayer next Saturday (31st) at Windmill Pub, 22 Blenhelm Gardens, Brixton, London. 3pm onwards www.dirtysquatters.com ** **The Fylingdales Star Peace Camp** in the North Yorkshire Moors is desperate for more people to come and stay – otherwise they might have to shut up shop. 01274 730795 cndyorks@gn.apc.org

Positive SchNEWS

In a time when everywhere is being McStandardised, Common Ground is working on a big encyclopaedia all about 'Local Distinctiveness,' championing the regional differences still to be found across England. They tell all Schnews readers,"You know much more than we do, and with your knowledge and help, we can bring the book and the web-site alive. We would like to hear your local stories, details, examples, and observations about the particularity of everyday places: from houses and woods to food and legends, from dialect words and endemic wild life to vernacular greetings and breeds of sheep." If you've got something to contribute visit http://www.england-in-particular.info/

Justice?

* **The 'Fair Justice For All campaign' which represents the families of people imprisoned after the Bradford riots last year** (SchNEWS 313) are holding a rally on bank holiday Monday outside the city court house. They are protesting against harsh sentences given to 94 people convicted of riot, people such as Istifar Iqbal, who received 11 months for picking up, but not throwing, two stones and Ashraf Hussain, who got four years for throwing three stones.

Campaigners contrasted the length of the sentences with maximum terms of 18 months given to white youths who rioted on the Ravenscliffe estate the day after the disturbances in Bradford.

This 'special treatment' is also reflected in the team that was appointed to look into the causes of last years riots. Muslims on the community cohesion review team told one member of the review team "At the first team meeting we were informed our purpose was not to focus on any one community, but to look for solutions to bring communities together. This was disappointing, as I felt that the specific issues of the Muslim community needed to be investigated and dealt with. Often Muslim participants would tell me in private of their frustration with this review. When I asked why they didn't speak up at the meetings they answered: "What's the point? They're not going to listen."

Mobil Phoney

Eleven Indonesian villagers, backed by the International Labor Rights Fund, are trying to sue oil giants Exxon Mobil in an American court claiming that the company knew of the murder, torture and rape of residents near its natural gas plant in the northern province of Aceh.

Since 1990, there has been a bitter war of independence being fought in Indonesia. Human Rights Watch reports that in the last decade, "Over 1000 people were killed, tortured or have 'disappeared' ... Thousands of Acehnese were detained without charge, often for years at a time, in military camps; Many never returned." The current law suit says that under an agreement with General Suharto, the former military dictator of Indonesia, Mobil paid the Indonesian military for protecting its facilities. One of the plaintiffs described how troops held him in a building at a Mobil plant and tortured him for three months. Before they released him, the soldiers showed him a large pile of human heads. Another plaintiff claims he was tortured by soldiers at a building inside the company's compound. Others have reported similar accounts of abuse.

BIG BAD WORLD

'Cartoon Molotovs In The Face Of Corporate Rule' a cartoon book by Polyp
"Anti-American, unbalanced and unreasonable"
- Coca Cola Company.
Get yours for £6 from NI Publications,
01858 438896 ISBN 09540499-3-4

This legal wrangle all started in 1998 when several Indonesian human rights groups accused the company of sponsoring the violence because it had provided the army with earth-moving equipment used to dig mass graves.

In April, addressing a US federal district judge, an Exxon Mobil lawyer said "This is a very difficult time in Indonesian-American relations because al Qaeda fighters are residing in that large Muslim nation." He continued that it would be bad for trade relations and bad for the so-called war on terror if a US court accused Exxon Mobil and the Indonesian government of murder. The judge's decision on whether to proceed with the trial is still pending.

After the bankrupt Enron corporation, Exxon Mobil were the second largest campaign contributor to the Bush administration. In 2000, Exxon Mobil refused to sign a code of conduct for businesses working in developing nations where governments might commit human rights abuses. They have constantly denied that global warming is happening and even claim that covering ourselves in crude oil is actually good for us.

The lawsuit against Exxon Mobil is one of a series of suits brought to U.S. courts by human rights groups against multinational companies under the Alien Tort law, which allows victims to sue in US Courts for alleged human rights violations perpetrated in other countries.

Corporations like NatWest, Barclays Bank, ICL and Vickers are currently facing a multibillion pound lawsuit claiming they profited from collaborating with apartheid in South Africa. One of the lead plaintiffs in the campaign for compensation said, "We want reparations from those international companies and banks that profited from the blood and misery of our fathers and mothers, our brothers and sisters."

Inside SchNEWS

At a demo during the recent No Borders protest camp in Strasbourg (SchNEWS 366) Ahmed Meguini, co-founder of the French anti-racist group Mouvement Spontane (Spontaneous Movement), was violently arrested, receiving a broken wrist from the French riot squad. From his arrest on 24th July to his trial date on 21st August, Ahmed was held in solitary confinement, which meant, amongst other things, he was not allowed to receive visitors. At his trial, Ahmed was sentenced to 8 months but luckily 5 of these will be probation which means he will be out in 3months. He also received a fine of 700 Euros (£500). Incidentally Ahmed was the only person from the No Borders camp who was locked up the entire time before his trial and the charges against him were the heaviest. This Saturday (24th Aug) there will be a benefit to help pay his fines at the Radical Dairy, 47 Kynaston Rd, Stoke Newington, London, with food and DJs. www.noborder.org

...and finally...

After banging on and on about the leaked letter to Bush on the front page, we thought you might be interested in who it was exactly that sent the letter. Many of these organisations have been involved in anti-environmental activities before. More to the point seven of them are known to be funded by Exxon Mobil. Signatories include:
* Fred L Smith and Myron Ebell of the Competitive Enterprise Institute - *funding from Exxon $280,000 in 2001* ** Craig Rucker from the Committee for a Constructive Tomorrow (CFACT) - *funding from*

OUT NOW
SchNEWS
OF THE WORLD

What a year it was... Genoa, September 11, Argentina, Palestine, Gothenburg and the rest. Phew. All in one book. Issues 301-350 of SchNEWS plus 200 pages of articles, satire, cartoons, photos, subverts, the direct action yellow pages and loadsmore. Order yours from us now - £8.50 including p&p (cheques to Justice). ISBN 09529748-6-X

Exxon $35,000 in 2001 ** Steven Hayward from the American Enterprise Institute - *funding from Exxon $230,000 in 2001* ** Terrence Scanlon from the Capital Research Center - *funding from Exxon $25,000 in 2001* ** Joseph L Bast of the Heartland Institute - *funding from Exxon $90,000 in 2001* ** Deroy Murdock of the Atlas Economic Research Foundation (AERF) - *funding from Exxon $150,000 in 2001* ** H Stirling Burnett of the National Center for Policy Analysis - *funding from Exxon $20,000 in 2001*

This is, of course, absolutely typical of the way Exxon works....... They pay other people to do their dirty work and then—with breathtaking hypocrisy—deny that they are trying to influence anybody or are the tiniest bit anti-environmental!!

Disclaimer

SchNEWS warns all readers to not take everything we say letterally. Honest.

Subscribe!
Keep SchNEWS FREE! Send 1st Class stamps (e.g. 10 for next 9 issues) or donations (payable to Justice?) Ask for "Originals" if you can make copies. Post *free* to all prisoners. SchNEWS, c/o on-the-fiddle, P.O. Box 2600, Brighton, East Sussex, BN2 0EF.
Tel/Autofax +44 (0)1273 685913 *Email* schnews@brighton.co.uk *Download a* **PDF** *of this issue or subscribe at* www.schnews.org.uk

Scotch Wrath

This is a round-up of direct action and stuff that's been going on in Scotland in the build up to the war on Iraq...

On June 10 2002, as part of Faslane Peace Camp's 20th birthday celebrations, a group of Faslane peace campers and associates successfully blockaded BAe Systems's headquarters in Edinburgh using lock-on

Anti-war demonstration in Glasgow

tubes and a D-lock. Flyers were given out to passers by which gave an extensive list of BAe's dodgy deals, highlighting how the site has been involved in refurbishing the laser sighting for guns that shoot depleted uranium shells. No arrests were made, perhaps because BAe didn't want the bad publicity. All the better for us - we went and did it again the following January, shutting the place down for five or six hours.

August 2002 saw another Trident Ploughshares disarmament camp at Coulport, in which diverse groups of people took part in actions including blockades, fence cutting, spray painting, and swimming and canoeing out to visit nuclear submarines.

In January 2003 a series of actions took place against the Ark Royal aircraft carrier, at Glen Mallon near Faslane being loaded with troops and equipment to go to the Gulf. On 15th January the only gate to the jetty was blockaded by three activists who locked on to each other and locked themselves inside a car, which they parked across the gate for over three hours. The MOD eventually got the activists out by taking off the back window, and the car was impounded.

There was less than an hour's gap between their removal and another group of protestors going to Ark Royal. A Peace Camp resident managed to climb the fence, then walk along it to the gate, where he D-locked the gate shut and locked himself to the top, keeping it shut for another 4 hours.

The following morning, half an hour before the Ark Royal was set to leave, two other peace camp residents got into the water and D-locked their necks to the mooring ropes of the ship under the jetty. The MOD went into the water after them and managed to cut the ropes, which must have cost them a few bob. One of the activists was arrested but the other managed to swim away, having sucessfully delayed the ship's leaving.

The war against Iraq involved the Tornado war planes at Leuchars in Fife, near Edinburgh. The Leuchars RAF base, whose motto is "Attack and Protect", is believed to have been involved in the bombing of Iraq since 1991.

Early on the morning of Monday 10th March two anti-war activists were arrested at the base, which they were inspecting ahead of its illegal use in war on Iraq. The two were able to get in and 'inspect' the base for over two hours before being discovered, even though one was in a wheelchair. Both are charged with two sets of Malicious Mischief for alleged fence-cutting, and for spray painting anti-war messages on three army trucks and an empty

aircraft hanger. They were both let out on bail, but on the condition that one of them, who is from Sweden, handed in his passport. Both are under "Petition" which means they have closed hearings in court and the police have more rights over searching them. (Airbases were discovered to be very wheelchair friendly once you get inside!)

The following day Trident Ploughshares activist Ulla Roder entered RAF Leuchars to disarm a Tornado. She was arrested having successfully carried out her action and is now on remand awaiting trial. It's possible that she will be in jail for some time so letters of support would be good. Her address is: Ulla Roder, HMP Cornton Vale, Cornton Road, Stirling FK9 5NY.

The day war was declared the army recruitment office in Glasgow was decorated with fake blood. Unfortunately the decorators were not able to make a swift getaway and one received a few punches and kicks from the local constabulary; rather ridiculously he was done with 7 charges of police assault for getting fake blood on their nice clean uniforms.

Since the start of the war there have been regular demonstrations in Glasgow and Edinburgh, some invlving civil disobedience in the form of blocking roads and junctions. On some occasions roads were sucessfully shut down in spite of attempts by demonstration 'organisers' to maintain obedience.

On Tuesday 22nd April some 500 people from all over Europe went to a blockade of Faslane naval base. The turnout was lower than hoped, maybe due to the media's repetition that the war was 'over'. However 160 arrests were made, the majority for blockading the base but some for cutting the fence in an attempt to 'inspect' the UK's weapons of mass destruction.

Protestor locked to the gates at Glen Mallon

McAfrica

weekly SchNEWS

www.schnews.org.uk

Friday 30th August 2002   Free/Donation   **Issue 370**   Because we wouldn't want you to starve

APOCALYPSE SOON?

"It should now be crystal clear that the South African government is hell-bent on smashing legitimate dissent by whatever means they deem appropriate, including attacking peaceful marchers and terrorising children. The ghosts of the South African past are returning with a vengeance." *Johannesburg demonstrator, outside the Earth Summit, this week.*

Tanks in townships, tooled up riot cops firing teargas and stun grenades into crowds of people, mass arrests, threats of deportation, laws against group assembly, the secret police spying on people … South Africa ten years ago?? Try South Africa this week — just a small dose of what's in store for anyone who has the cheek to criticise the hijacking of the Earth Summit by Big Business.

And while the fat cat delegates hob nob in air-conditioned grandeur inside the summit, ignoring any and all voices of dissent outside, the world continues to melt away. Since the Earth Summit ten years ago in Rio, 10% of the earth's remaining forests have been destroyed. Over the next 18 years, carbon dioxide emissions leading to global warming are expected to rise by a third in rich countries and to double in the rest of the world. These are not facts from some loony lefty environmental organisation, but reports written by the fat cats themselves.

This week, a report from last month's Organisation for Economic Co-operation and Development (OECD) meeting was leaked to the press. The report had been written in preparation for the Earth Summit, to inform people going to the OECD meeting about the state of the world before going to Jo'burg to do nothing about it. A flock of suits who push for salvation through privatisation, the OECD is a group that works along the same lines as the G8 or WTO—a think-tank (wank tank) made up of 22 of the world's richest countries who like to influence world-wide economic policy. Most of the OECD's members are in the rich North, but some lucky industrialised outsiders such as Mexico and South Korea have been invited to send reps too. Their report just goes to show something we've suspected all along — heads of state and powerful corporate CEOs know how fucked the world is, their own research supports it, and yet they refuse to do anything except push more of the same thing that got us in this whole mess to begin with.

"Through the provision of subsidies on fossil fuels, governments are effectively subsidising pollution and global warming as more than 60% of all subsidies flow to oil, coal and gas."
- Leaked OECD report.

For all the conventions, treaties and intergovernmental agreements of the last 30 years, little has actually changed. Warnings that air pollution has already reached crisis point in many cities, and that there is not really anything anyone can do anymore to reverse climate change are being ignored, even when these subjects are contained in corporate reports like the one written by the OECD.

Other info from the report: The current demand for fresh water will continue to increase and already 40% of the world's population is short of fresh water. Tying into global warming, the report also says that the number of people affected by weather related disasters has risen by half in the last decade.

But while the OECD report highlights these facts, it tends to hush up how these disasters have come about. Take Coca Cola, for instance, who are still forging into Kerala, South India sucking up all their ground water or Shell, who is still in Nigeria polluting all water supplies with their regular oil leaks. And in Brazil, the government is pushing ahead with Advance Brazil, a rainforest development project set to destroy 42% of the forest by 2020. All the while, the OECD report tells us, more and more land, unprotected from the sun and the rain and destroyed by intensive agriculture is turning to desert or rendered unusable. Plant, insect and animal species are being made extinct at a rate never seen before as habitats are destroyed or polluted, or cooked to death by climate change.

Apocolypse Soon? cont...
UN Sustainable

Not only have governments and businesses seen the OECD report, they've also been given a huge UN report, the Global Environment Outlook, each presented in a fruitless attempt to make them actually do something.

This UN report looks back over the last thirty years of Earth Summits and makes some predictions for the future. Unsurprisingly, the conclusion the report reaches is that more "sustainable development," is needed. All of this while admitting that full scale emergencies already exist: water shortages hampering developing countries, land degradation reducing fertility and agricultural potential, and destruction of the tropical rainforest that, according to the report, has gone too far to be reversed.

Okay, so let's recap: The big business friendly OECD and the West obsessed UN are saying that enough is enough. And what will they do with these conclusions? Probably just make up another set of hollow pledges to "defend" the environment against themselves – missing the point that you would actually have to dismantle capitalism to do this. The fact is there are things that can be done.

Trying to link global problems with local ones is vital when governments and big businesses only care about lining their pockets. Through direct action and community-based resistance, there ARE ways that we can battle against the destruction of our environment. We can support resistance in other countries in many ways. In West Papua, local groups such as the OPM are fighting against oppressive mining companies like Rio Tinto and BP. Activists in the UK have been targeting offices owned by these companies for protests and actions; they have also made concrete links with communities in West Papua by going there and also by raising money to give directly to the OPM.

As well as supporting struggle in other countries, looking in our own backyards is still important. In the UK, people have been targeting the destructive extraction of peat from three moors, Hatfield, Thorne and Wedholme Flow. This successful direct action campaign has fought the mining of peat by the US multinational Scotts and has been instrumental in the recent agreement between Scotts and the UK Government to halt mining in Thorne and Wedholme Flow immediately. There are many more projects like these that need people's help. As one ecological activist told Schnews, "I am not going into detail about what tactics are needed in local battles. After 10 years it's pretty obvious. Community mobilising, occupations, blockades, bulldozer pledges, sabotage. Threatening destroyers with costly chaos and giving it to them if they try it on."

To find out more about direct action in your area check out the Party and Protest guide on the SchNEWS website.

Summit info: http://southafrica.indymedia.org

West Papua info www.eco-action.org/sst

UK Biodiversity Website: www.ukbap.org.uk

For many people it is the

Freedom of

Cheap Flights

which makes them so

Appealing

But they're only cheap if you ignore the hidden costs... Airlines don't pay any tax on the fuel they use, the tickets they sell or the new planes they build. They also receive large money handouts from governments. This keeps prices low, which means more flights and more pollution.

CO_2

Airplanes produce large amounts of carbon dioxide, the gas most closely linked to global warming. In one year more carbon dioxide is produced by all the planes in the world than the total output of Africa and South America combined.

HC NO_x

Spilling fuel releases Hydrocarbons.

Nitrogen oxides are emitted while planes are on the runway or taking-off. Engine efficiency has been improved in recent years, but already any reduction in NOx has been eclipsed by the increase in flight numbers.

ozone

New supersonic planes fly high in the atmosphere, and their emissions destroy the ozone layer.

Chemistry Set-up

A court in the city of Bhopal, India has rejected an appeal made by the Indian government to reduce charges against the former CEO of Union Carbide. Warren Anderson if convicted faces 20 years in prison – that's if they can find him. Nearly 18 years after the fact, the disaster at the Union Carbide pesticide factory is still a nightmare for the people of Bhopal. More than 3,000 people died on the day of the actual disaster, when a storage tank in the factory burst, sending tonnes of poison gas over the city. Now more than 100,000 people continue to get ill as a result, including babies born to survivors.

Meanwhile, CEO Anderson hasn't been turning up to court for some reason and is classified as an 'absconder' under Indian Law. Apparently he's been photographed in the US, although Law enforcement agencies there say they have not been able to locate him. SchNEWS wonders if that would be the case if thousands of Americans had died? www.bhopal.net

**Yesterday Greenpeace put the spotlight on Dow Chemicals, who bought Union Carbide, by fencing off an open discharge pipe for toxic waste at the company's manufacturing facility in South Africa. www.greenpeace.org

Hit On Hinton

14 people were nicked last weekend after a GM rape seed oil crop site was trashed at Hinton, in Dorset. For 4 years the biotech company Aventis Cropsciences (now owned by the German Chemicals giant Bayer) has been using rape seed illegally contaminated with antibiotic 'marker' genes. The use of antibiotic markers in crops was banned because the British Medical Association feared that the genes could possibly cross to bacteria in human or animal guts, making common diseases and infections as well as already life-threatening illnesses immune to antibiotics. Planted at twelve sites around the country, these crops are set to be harvested in September, which means now is the time they are most able to cross contaminate the soil, other plants, and animals. The government says it is 'very annoyed' with this activity, but plans to let Aventis leave the crops in the ground anyway!

With only paper inspections, it's hardly surprising no one spotted the contamination earlier. As Friends of the Earth's Adrian Bebb said: "This is yet another biotech blunder from the GM industry. How can we trust them to produce our food if they cannot even run a GM test site?" Totnes Genetics Group: 01803 868523 www.genewatch.org/Publications/Briefs/Brief3.htm

Positive SchNEWS

While SchNEWS doesn't hold out much hope of the Earth Summit coming up with the goods, it does seem to be inspiring some people to think about the state of the planet. RioKids is one such group. Children from four primary schools in Bristol who were born in 1992, the year of the first Earth Summit, spent time recently researching some of the issues raised by the Summit, issues such as recycling, protecting coastal environments, and caring for natural habitats. They then went on to make pictures, writing and photography expressing how they felt about the issues and how they thought the issues to affected them personally and in their own locality. Check it out at www.riokids.net

AMAIZED?

"Africa is treated as the dustbin of the world. To donate untested food and seed to Africa is not an act of kindness but an attempt to lure Africa into further dependence on foreign aid." – *Africa's Biowatch.*

The US has come up with a grand scheme to get rid of its excess GM crops–dumping them in Africa, while claiming to 'save' the starving. Last week the US told Zambia that it would have to borrow money in order to buy $50 million worth of GM maize from the World Food Programme - or face starvation. While India has vast stocks of rice - 65 times as much as Africa needs - available at half the cost of the US maize, Zambia has been "strongly advised" by US interests not to buy it. Zimbabwe, Lesotho, Mozambique and Malawi have all been offered similar threats, er, deals. Many countries have outright refused to buy the GM maize.

But with the EU standing firm on the strict labelling of GM food in supermarkets, the US is getting desperate to unload its GM food somewhere a bit more label-free. The US along wiht the biotech firm Monsanto, claim that environmentalists and scientists opposed to giving GM food the green light stand in the way of feeding the poor. The truth is, none of the countries suffering from famine want to import subsidised GM crops or to accept GM food 'aid'.

Four years ago every African nation – apart from South Africa - signed a statement saying "[We] strongly object that the image of the poor and hungry from our countries is being used by giant multinational corporations to push a technology that is neither safe, environmentally friendly, nor economically beneficial to us."

Meanwhile, the millions of tons of surplus Indian rice that the Zambians are not supposed to buy is rotting in warehouses because the poor of India can't afford to buy it either. Malawi also had non-GM surpluses until a few months ago, but was required by the International Monetary Fund to sell them to pay off its debt. As Ethiopia's Food and Agriculture spokesman, Dr Tewolde Egziabher, put it, "this notion that genetically engineered crops will save developing countries misses the real point. The world has never grown as much food per capita as it is doing now, yet the world has also never had as many hungry. The problem is not the amount of food produced, but how it is both produced and distributed."

IF ORDINARY PEOPLE BEHAVED LIKE- MONSANTO

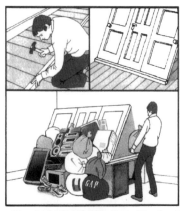

SchNEWS in Brief

'Argentina & Venezuela: Organizing for survival and revolution - The truth behind the headlines' Public meeting next Thursday (5) at Conway Hall, 25 Red Lion Square, London WC1 (Holborn tube) 7pm. Two women from Argentina's grassroots women's assemblies and the highly respected housewives union will be speaking – as well as the video premiere of **'The Global Women's Strike & the Venezuelan Revolution.'** 020 7482 2496 http://womenstrike8m.server101.com/ ** Speakers from the Sante Fe Neighbourhood Network in **Argentina** will be at the Easton Community Centre in Bristol next Wednesday (4) 7pm 0117 9399469 www.marsbard.com/kebele ** **American Indian** activist Rod Coronado will be kicking off a speaking tour of the UK in Brighton on Monday 9th September 7.30pm in the Hanover Room, Brighthelm Centre, North Road. From sinking Icelandic whaling ships to defending old growth forests, Rod has engaged in militant and uncompromising direct action and in 1995 was jailed for some of his actions. Recently released, he lives on the Pascua Yaqui reservation in Arizona, USA. Other confirmed dates on his speaking tour are London (11), Nottingham (12) Sheffield (16) Manchester (17) and Leeds (19). For more info 07763 552 627 ** **Compassion in World Farming** have released a major report proving that the introduction of industrial animal farming into developing countries will be a disaster. Crowding thousands of animals together in disease-prone sheds uses very little local labour, uses scarce water and electricity, creates reliance on imports for cereals and farming equipment, causes pollution and after all that ends with a product which the poor cannot afford! For copies 01730 233 904 www.ciwf.co.uk ** There's a **free festival** this Saturday (31) in Tankerton Whitstable, Kent from 1-10pm. "One of music & resistance organised by the European Social Forum Mobilise Kent." 07950 610257 ** Since October 2000, hundreds of thousands of Palestinian trees have been bulldozed, uprooted or set ablaze by Israeli soldiers and settlers. Many of these were olive trees. **Olive trees** are an important symbol to Palestinians as well as massively important economically. So this year the International Solidarity Movement are calling on people to join them for the olive harvest from October 15 – November 15. More info www.palsolidarity.org ** Anti-fascists last week attacked a shop in **Burnley** owned by Steve Smith, the **BNP** organiser for Burnley. The shop actually sells very little and is mainly used as a base for BNP organising

...and finally...

While 12 million people starve to death in Africa, McDonald's has just dreamed up a stunningly sensitive new product--the McAfrica burger. With no apparent sense of irony, these burgers are currenly on sale at McShit branches in one of the most expensive and comfortable countries in the West, Norway. Aid agencies are understandably a bit wound up with this bit of McMarketing. As Linn Aas-Hansen of Norwegian Church Aid says "It's inappropriate and distasteful to launch a hamburger called McAfrica when large portions of Southern Africa are on the verge of starvation." Initially, McTosser's spokeswoman Margaret Brusletto said the company would consider sharing the proceeds of its sale with aid agencies(!) but a meeting with Norwegian Red Cross came to no agreement. Instead, after getting loads of protests about this McScam, McDonald's have agreed to place collection boxes for Africa in the participating stores while the promotion lasts--but no longer. We wonder if stuffing the boxes with McAfrica burgers would help to fill the stomachs of Africa's starving.

Disclaimer

Inside SchNEWS

17 supporters of Ahmed Meguini, who was jailed for eight months last week after taking part in the No Borders protest in Strasbourg (SchNEWS 366), were nicked last Friday during an occupation of the local Ministry of Justice the day after his trial. They were demanding Ahmed be taken out of solitary confinement and allowed visitors. They have all been charged with 'kidnapping' after three members of the Ministry of Justice staff refused to leave the building. Now Meguini's supporters could be facing prison sentences of up to five years themselves. Find out how to support them at www.noborder.org

Landside Victory

With the **Countryside Alliance** promising the biggest demonstration London has seen since the Poll Tax Riots of 1381, a group of people have decided while the aristocracy are in the Capital on September 22nd they'll target one of the Alliance's prime movers. In their own words, they plan to "Move onto his estate... (and) establish an autonomous community in the spirit of Winstanley and the Diggers."

They are calling on other groups to organise as well, with the aim of reoccupying stolen common heritage."If you really want to stop the Alliance," the squatters say, "Don't go to London to yah-boo them, get out into the countryside and hit them where it really hurts - in their own back yard!"

Catch up with everyone's direct action summer adventures at the **REBEL ALLIANCE** next Wednesday (4th) 7.30pm upstairs at the Albert Pub, Trafalger St. Brighton. Followed by SchNEWS of the World Book Launch at the Volks, Madeira Drive, Brighton. Donations on the door

Subscribe!

Keep SchNEWS FREE! Send 1st Class stamps (e.g. 10 for next 9 issues) or donations (payable to Justice?) Ask for "Originals" if you can make copies. Post *free* to all prisoners. SchNEWS, c/o on-the-fiddle, P.O. Box 2600, Brighton, East Sussex, BN2 0EF.
Tel/Autofax +44 (0)1273 685913 *Email* **schnews@brighton.co.uk** *Download a* **PDF** *of this issue or subscribe at* **www.schnews.org.uk**

WAKE UP! IT'S YER MAD, BAD AND SAD....

weekly SchNEWS

www.schnews.org.uk

Friday 6th September 2002   **Free/Donation**   **Issue 371**   **DISASTER RELIEF**

THANK GOD - IT'S A PANEL OF EXPERTS.

SUMMIT ROTTEN

"...These people at the summit are not kind. We earn peanuts and they don't even tip us. They think they are so important, they fly around the world having meetings and getting waited on, but they know nothing of how we live. I came here from Zimbabwe because my people are very desperate there. I live in a shack in Soweto now, one room with two children, no privacy, trying to earn money to send home. For months the government has talked about cleaning up the city for the summit, but when these people go home, everything will be back like it always was. They will still be rich, we will still be poor. It's not right that they say they meet for our sake. It's all for their benefit, not ours."

- Rosemary, a Zimbabwean refugee waiting tables under the shining towers of Sandton, South Africa, where the conference was held.

SchNEWS would never snipe at the sidelines telling anyone who'd listen 'we told you so' but as the Johannesburg Earth Summit finishes, the new blueprint to save the planet is about as useful as waterproof bogroll.

Corporations hailed it a success (horray – no strings, we can carry on polluting), there was fine words from politicians (like Vice-President Blair banging on about climate change then promising to improve the people of Iraq's climate by bombing them), plenty of NGO hand wringing and muttering in Victor Meldrew 'I don't believe it' style disbelief and demonstrators being given a good kick in the privates so they don't feel left out in the new era of global partnerships. SchNEWS has sifted through the final 65 page document with its eight key commitments and come up with summit of the highlights.

* Dropping all renewable energy targets, because oil rich nations argued that until

they figure a way of charging us for the sun and wind they aren't interested in bloody solar panels and windmills.

* Promising to increase the number of people cut off from essential services like water and electricity by privatising services immediately.

* Getting rid of poor people, or at least making them disappear out of view, with the use of very big fences surrounded by razor wire and men with machine guns (hey, just like the Earth Summit).

* Making people re-use envelopes and dig ponds in their back gardens to preserve fish stocks.

* Handing out free umbrellas and suntan lotion to help lessen the effects of climate change.

*A pledge to stop species extinction through gene transfer and cloning of profitable animal and plant crops.

* A free market monopoly in exchange for eternal debt and gratitude plus spontaneous culling of various groups as and when necessary all done in the best possible taste.

Er, that's it.

But perhaps the 'major triumph' of the Summit was the creation of "partnership agreements." Corporations promise to respect the environment and peoples' human rights, as long as they can do it voluntarily and with none of that silly red tape that spoils it for everyone. As an ecstatic spokesman for Business Action for Sustainable Development (BASD - see SchNEWS 361/2), a powerful new lobby group stuffed full of fat cats, told SchNEWS "We can't believe those suckers expect us, the very people who are destroying

---

CRAP ARRESTS OF THE WEEK
For asking a question...
Indymedia reporter and former political prisoner Chris Plummer was arrested last month at a Conference organised by the Texas Dept. of Criminal Justices. Billed as a forum for the exchange of information between families and prison officials, he was arrested after asking the riot-inducing question, "What percent of grievances get a not guilty verdict?" Chris is still on parole for his antifascist actions in the 90's, and this arrest could be used as an excuse to revoke his parole and send him back to prison.

---

the planet to come up with a grand plan of how to save it!"

BASDtardly Deeds

During one of the BASDtards Summit knees-up Shell Chairman Philip Watts reluctantly accepted a Greenwash Lifetime Achievement Award, muttering something about the good work his company has done in Nigeria and the report his company had produced which said how responsible they now were. Isaac Osuoka of Environmental Rights Action, a Nigerian group that has documented Shell's pioneering human rights and environmental work in the Niger Delta pointed out "How can we talk of partnership and trust with business leaders who do not recognise the most blatant corporate crimes?"

Other Greenwash Award winners include BP, who spent £20 million on their new sunflower logo to show the world how much they like flowers, Nestle who continue to defend the rights of mothers in the developing world to use powered milk, Enron for Best Makeup, and accountants (and we use the term in the loosest possible manner) Arthur Andersen for Best

Summit Rotten cont...

Documentary Destruction. As author Naomi Klein puts it "Post Enron it's hard to believe that companies can be trusted to keep their own books, let along save the world." Or as Kenny Bruno co-author of Earthsummit.biz says, "Most corporations, when left to their own devices, are attracted to irresponsible behaviour like moths to a flame."

So, without wanting to become the pub bore going on and on about what's to be done, we at SchNEWS Towers repeat it's only when people get together to solve problems, offer solutions and take direct action against those who are destroying the planet, that life will ever change.

Capita Punishment

The school year has begun with a right neo-labour cock-up. Thousands of lucky kids have been turned away from school because not all staff have been cleared by the new Criminal Records Bureau (CRB). And just who's behind this mess? Why our old friends Capita (see Schnews 335) who got control of the bureau thanks to the PFI (Private Finance Initative).

Launched in April, the CRB is a system for checking the background of all people who work with children or vulnerable adults in schools, voluntary organisations or professional bodies. Collating information from the police and government agencies, the CRB is run by Capita, which charges £12 for each check. Initially, Capita promised to respond to 90% of high-level enquiries - those required for the teaching profession - but within three weeks this promise had slipped back to the end of the year "if yer lucky".

The problem was that poor Capita were expecting 75% of the applications to come by phone and were surprised that so many came in hand-written through the post - actually not all that surprising since applications from local authorities need to be signed by a designated officer and so can't really be phoned in. The real reason for the mess up is that Capita set up a system to scan the applications using optical character recognition which can't read handwriting so all the data had to be input manually (I don't believe it!) and they just didn't have the staff to handle such a tall order. Capita have since shipped off all the applications to India! So the education Secretary Estelle Morris was left a 'very dissatisfied customer'.

But of course unlike failing schools, Capita is under no threat of the government taking them over or even giving them a slap on the wrist. Instead, Capita, who cocked up the Individual Learning Accounts Scheme earlier this year and left £260 million of tax payers money open to fraud, have continually been fed more and more contracts – over £1 billion worth in the first half of the year alone including a 10-year contract to collect TV licence fees (which should make SchNEWS readers without licenses breath a sigh of relief) and a five-year contract to run the congestion-charging scheme in London. Maybe that's why they've had a 38% rise in profits for the first half of the year, with three of their top exec's sharing a £7.5million payoff.

Meanwhile, hospitals, care homes and social services dept's trying to recruit struggled with delays that have built up in vetting potential staff. The whole social services system had "slowed down dramatically", said one director of social services. A care worker told Schnews she'd spent 18 weeks waiting to be cleared and unable to work.

SchNEWS in brief

This weekend (6-8) is **Big Blether 3**. "A weekend for those interested in direct action, environmental issues and campaigning in Scotland" at the Talamh Life Centre, Lanarkshire, Scotland. Workshops on greenwashing vs. corporate responsibility, herbal medicine, alternative technology etc. Cheap vegan food avaliable but come as self sufficient as possible. Donations of £5-20 depending on income. 0131 557 6242, www.j12.org/bigblether/ ** Next Wednesday (11) there's a **Peace Walk**. Meet at the Peace statue in **Hove**, 12 noon. Walk silently through Brighton, no banners or placards please ** Film, talk and discussion with **North American Indian activist Rod Coronado** this Monday (9th) in Brighton, 7PM, Brighthelm Centre, North Road , also London Wednesday (11th) at LARC 62 Fieldgate Street. Aldgate East tube, Whitechapel. 7.30pm 020 7377 9088 www.londonarc.org ** All charges against the five protesters who occupied the Shoreham docks of Euromin, the company responsible for killing **Simon Jones**, have been dropped. www.simonjones.org.uk ** **Reclaim the Future** 20-22 September, includes all day event on the Saturday with workshops, kids area, inspiring films, spoken word and cabaret followed by party. 07931 560 569 rtsparty2002@yahoo.co.uk ** **INJUSTICE**, the documentary about struggles for justice by the families of people who have died in police custody, has won Best Documentary at the BFM Film and Television Awards, which will take place in London next Monday. The awards are an annual celebration of achievement in black cinema and television. Between 1969 and 1999 over one thousand people died in police custody in England, with not one officer ever being convicted. www.injusticefilm.co.uk ** In protest against the Nike "Run London" event in Richmond Park on Sept 22nd, **No Sweat**, the UK campaign against sweatshops, will be holding its own events to expose the poor working conditions in the Niketown shops, and on factory floors. Get "No to Nike Naked Greed" posters to post over Nike's ads on your local high street. 07904 431 959 www.nosweat.org.uk ** The radical video collective cultureshop.org are now selling **Drowned Out - The Narmada Dam Story**. The film will be showing at the Cube, Bristol next Tuesday (10) 7 pm £2 door tax ** Lancaster City Council have just voted against the Lancaster University / Jarvis Greenfields Expansion Plan and A6 link road. Interested in setting up a protest camp? grandlaf@lineone.net ** **Critical Mass North London Ride**, 14 September. Critical Mass is a rolling party encouraging a better deal for London's cyclists, pedestrians and public transport users. Bring a bike, roller blades, skateboard, pogo stick or any non-motorised transport. Starts 2pm Finsbury Park main gate (Seven Sisters Road).

Suit Up!

In America, the land where obese people recently sued the inventors of burgers and fries, now it's the environmentally disadvantaged suing the inventors of global warming....

Friends of the Earth, Greenpeace and the City of Boulder, Colorado are filing a lawsuit on behalf of their members who are victims of global warming. The suit has been filed against two US government agencies - the Export Import Bank (ExIm) and the Overseas Private Investment Corporation (OPIC) - who use taxpayers' money to fund loans to US corporations for overseas projects that other banks have deemed too dodgy. In partnership with the Bush Administration, virtually every major energy, oil and gas company has received subsidisation by these two in the last ten years. Edison, Citicorp, ExxonMobil, Enron, Westinghouse, GE, Chase Manhattan, Bank of America and many others receive billions in taxpayer support from them.

The lawsuit claims that through this subsidisation, OPIC and Ex-Im have illegally provided over $32 billion in financing and insurance for oil fields, pipelines and coal-fired power plants over the past ten years "without assessing their contribution to global warming and their impact on the U.S. environment." Or, more to the point, without giving a toss.

The lawsuit website goes on to say that, "OPIC and Ex-Im are using taxpayer dollars to support fossil fuel extraction projects around the world, primarily to take oil from developing countries and bring it back to the United States. 56% of U.S. oil consumed comes from other countries like Nigeria, Venezuela, the Middle East and Mexico. Chapter 8 of the Bush/Cheney Energy Plan seeks to expand that even further. OPIC and Ex-Im are involved in virtually every major fossil fuel extraction project in the world. Despite requirements under the National Environmental Policy Act to assess the climate change impacts of these projects, the Bush Administration is not in compliance and U.S.-caused greenhouse gas emissions continue to rise. Private citizens, environmental organizations, states and cities in the U.S. are being harmed by climate change and therefore

are bringing this legal action."

Which all sounds well and good, but becomes a bit disappointing when you learn what the plaintiffs hope to accomplish through their lawsuit — they want OPIC and Ex-Im to simply fill out more paperwork, believing this will make them into better environmental stewards. The lawsuit pushes for, "Environmental Assessments to see if an action will significantly affect the environment and if the answer is affirmative to prepare an Environmental Impact Statement (EIS) detailing the effects and options for alternative actions." More red-tape and bureaucratic greenwash anyone?

And while attacks on meanies like OPIC and Ex-Im are never a completely bad thing, one has to wonder when the rest of world's population (i.e. those of us who can't afford costly lawyers but are still affected by climate change) will get our day in court. Maybe OPIC will lend us some money for a lawsuit.....
www.climatelawsuit.org

Positive SchNEWS

Meanwhile Gardens in West London is a project aimed at helping people who have severe or enduring mental health problems learn about gardening and allotments. Originally set up in the early 1970s when a group of local residents managed to save it from developers, Meanwhile Gardens is a half acre site on a small strip of land between the canal and the A40 Westway and tower-blocks. Its achievements include ponds, a bog garden, a meadow area, herb garden and the promotion of a variety of species such as alder, hazel, birch, oak and beech. The success of the project has enabled it to thrive and currently to challenge yet more encroachment on the land by potential developers. "Experience gained at the Gardens can boost the confidence of trainees who may have been out of work for a long time, and show both them and potential employers that they can commit to a project, interact with a group of people and gain nationally recognised qualifications in the process." Contact: Kensington and Chelsea Mind, 020 8960 6336

The Chiapas Are Down

Things have been hotting up in Chiapas, Mexico over the last few weeks, with at least 5 Zapatistas murdered by paramilitary groups and many civillians from the autonomous zones seriously injured. The first co-ordinated assault on the communities since the brutal massacre at Acteal in 1997, Zapatistas and aid agencies are eager to find out what has sparked these recent killings. New and existing paramilitary groups, along with police have stepped up the violence. Hundreds of additional Mexican soldiers have also been deployed in the conflict zone around Monte Azules and the Lacondon jungle. Several Zapatista communities have had to flee from paramilitary violence, and human rights observers are accompanying threatened communities. Zapatistas and human rights groups are calling for action and support. www.chiapas link.ukgateway.net
* 'Fiesta Zapatista' benefit night next Monday (9) upstairs at the Albert pub, Brighton. Includes the film 'Storm From the Mountain' at 7pm. Money raised will go towards re-painting a mural in a Zapatista autonomous co-op.

...and finally...

Most wanted fugitive found in New York. No its not that bin liner bloke, but international fugitive Warren Anderson, the former Chief Executive of Union Carbide responsible for the deaths of thousands of people after the Bhopal poison gas disaster (see Schnews 371). Apparently the US law enforcement agencies couldn't track him down so instead it was left to a team of crack commandos from Greenpeace to go to his house. Anderson is now facing extradition to India to face charges of culpable homicide. Not having a good time of it really are they?

Disclaimer

A Really Brief History of Iraq

There's nothing new about the US and Britain's use of military force to secure 'regime change' and control of oil reserves in Iraq. Since before Iraq existed the history of the region has been dominated by Western imperialists and local gangsters fighting for control of its people and resources. But Iraq also has a history of popular rebellion against all forms of exploitation, homegrown or imported; and people's uprisings have brought down governments, thrown repressive regimes into chaos, and forced out a British occupation. This timeline was nicked from Practical History, and heavily cut down. To read the complete version, Iraq: a history of war and rebellion, see their website: http://www.geocities.com/CapitolHill/Senate/7672/

1900: Iraq doesn't exist. Since the 16th century the area that will become Iraq has formed part of the Turkish-based Ottoman Empire. The Empire's rule is based in the cities; the countryside remains dominated by rural tribal groups, some of them nomadic.

1912: The Turkish Petroleum Company, formed by British, Dutch and German interests, acquires concessions to prospect for oil in the Ottoman provinces of Baghdad and Mosul.

1914-18: Turkey sides with Germany in WWI. To protect strategic interests and potential oil fields, Britain occupies Basra in November 1914, eventually capturing Baghdad in 1917. By the end of the war, most of the provinces of Iraq are occupied by British forces although some areas remain "unpacified". Colonial rule is established, with top levels of the administration in British hands.

1919: Throughout 1919 and 1920 there are constant uprisings in northern Iraq, with British officers and officials being killed. The tribes in this area share a common Kurdish language and culture, but at this stage there is little demand for a separate Kurdish state. The main issue is resistance to external state authority.

The RAF bomb Kurdish areas. Wing-Commander Arthur Harris (later known as "Bomber Harris" for his role in the destruction of Dresden in WW2) boasts: "The Arab and the Kurd now know what real bombing means. Within 45 minutes a full-size village can be practically wiped out and a third of its inhabitants killed or injured".

A leading British officer declares that the only way to deal with the tribes is "wholesale slaughter". RAF Middle Eastern Command requests chemical weapons to use "against recalcitrant Arabs as (an) experiment". Winston Churchill, Secretary of State for War says, "I am strongly in favour of using poisonous gas against uncivilised tribes... It is not necessary only to use the most deadly gases: gases can be used which cause great inconvenience and would spread a lively terror and yet would leave no serious permanent effects on most of those affected".

1920: In the post-war carve up between the victorious imperialist powers, Britain gets Iraq (as well as Palestine), France gets Syria and Lebanon. The borders of the new state of Iraq are set by the great powers, setting the scene for a century of border conflicts.

The British authorities impose tight controls, collecting taxes more rigorously than their predecessors and operating forced labour schemes. In June an armed revolt against British rule ("the Revolution of 1920") spreads across southern and central Iraq. For three months Britain loses control of large areas of the countryside.

1921: By February the rebellion has been crushed, with 9,000 rebels killed or wounded. Whole villages are destroyed and suspected rebels shot without trial.

Britain decides to replace direct colonial rule with an Arab administration which it hopes will serve British interests. Britain creates a monarchy with Faysal as Iraq's first King. Iraqis now fill senior positions, but ultimate control lies with their British advisers.

1924: Britain's Labour Government sanctions the use of the RAF against the Kurds, dropping bombs and gas. The effects are described as "appalling" with panic-stricken tribespeople fleeing "into the desert where hundreds more must have perished of thirst".

1927: The British-controlled Iraq Petroleum Company (IPC, successor to the TPC) opens its first substantial oil well near Kirkuk. Tons of oil decimate local countryside before the well is capped.

1930: The Anglo-Iraq Treaty paves the way for independence. The Treaty provides for Britain to maintain 2 air bases, and an influence on Iraq's foreign policy until 1957.

Kurdish uprisings, prompted by fears of their place in the new state, are put down with the help of the RAF.

1931: General strike against the Municipal Fees Law, which imposes new taxes three times heavier than before, and for unemployment compensation. Thousands, including 3,000 petroleum workers, take part and there are clashes with the police. The RAF flies over urban centres to intimidate strikers.

> **"I am strongly in favour of using poisonous gas against uncivilised tribes"**
> Winston Churchill

1933: The Artisans Association (a union) organise a month-long boycott of the British-owned Baghdad Electric Light and Power Company. After this, unions and workers' organisations are banned and forced underground for the next ten years.

King Faysal dies and is succeeded by his son Ghazi.

1935-36: Sporadic tribal rebellions, mainly in the south. Causes include an attempt to introduce conscription and the dispossession of peasants, as tribal lands are placed in private hands. The revolts are crushed with bombing and summary executions.

1936-37: General Bakr Sidqi, an admirer of Mussolini, installs a military government and launches a repression of the left. There are protest strikes throughout the country including at the IPC in Kirkuk and the National Cigarette Factory in Baghdad.

1940: Rashid Ali becomes Prime Minister after a coup, at the expense of pro-Brit politicians. The new government takes a position of neutrality in WW2, refusing to support Britain unless it grants independence to Syria and Palestine. Links are made with Germany.

1941: Britain re-invades Iraq and restores its supporters to power in the '30 days war'. During the occupation, martial law is declared. Arab nationalists are hanged or imprisoned. Despite this, British forces don't stop Rashid supporters from staging a pogrom in the Jewish area of Baghdad, killing 150.

1946: Strike by oil workers at the British-controlled IPC in Kirkuk. Workers clash with police, and 10 are killed when police open fire on a mass meeting. The following month there is a strike by oil workers in the Iranian port of Abadan and Britain moves troops near to the Iranian border. The Iraqi government suppresses papers criticising this move, prompting strikes by printers and railway workers. The cabinet is forced to resign.

1948: The Iraqi government negotiates a new treaty with Britain which would have extended Britain's say in military policy until 1973. British troops would be withdrawn, but would have the right to return. The day after this is agreed police shoot dead four students demonstrating against the Treaty. This prompts an uprising that becomes known as al-Wathba (the leap). Riots spread across the country, directed not just against the Treaty but also bread shortages and rising prices. More are killed a few days later when police open fire on a mass march of railway workers and slum dwellers. On 27 January 3-400 people are killed by the police and military as demonstrators erect barricades of burning cars. The cabinet resigns and the Treaty is torn up.

In May, 3,000 workers at IPC's K3 pumping station go on strike, bringing the station to a halt. The government and IPC cut off supplies of food and water to the strikers, who then decide to march on Baghdad, 250km away. On what becomes known as 'the great march' strikers are fed and sheltered by people in the towns and villages en route before being arrested 70km from Baghdad.

The British military is withdrawn from Iraq. Martial law is declared and demonstrations are banned.

1949: Communist Party leaders are publicly hanged in Baghdad, their bodies left hanging for hours as a warning to opponents of the regime.

1952: Students strike over changes in exam rules. The movement spreads to mass riots in most urban centres, known as al-Intifada (the tremor). In Baghdad a police station and the American Information Office are burned down. A military government takes over, declaring martial law. 18 demonstrators are killed in military action.

1954: Government decrees permit to deport persons convicted of communism, anarchism or working for a foreign government.

1958: Popular unrest throughout the country, including in Diwaniyah, where in June 43 police and an unknown number of demonstrators are killed in a three-hour battle.

A month later the "14 July Revolution" brings to an end the old regime. A coup led by members of the Free Officers seizes power, denounces imperialism and proclaims a republic. The royal family are shot. Crowds take to the streets and a number of US businessmen and Jordanian ministers are killed. People take food from the shops without paying, thinking that money is now obsolete. To prevent the revolution spreading out of control, the new government imposes a curfew. After a brief power struggle, Abd al-Karim Quasim becomes prime minister and continues to rule with the support of the Iraqi Communist Party (ICP) and other leftists.

Although Islamic influence remains strong, there are public expressions of anti-clericalism including public burning of the Koran.

Without waiting for Quasim to deliver on land reform promises, peasants take matters into their own hands. In al-Kut and al-'Amarah they loot landlords' property, burn down their houses, and destroy accounts and land registers. Fearing the spread of rebellion throughout the region, the US sends 14,000 marines to Lebanon. Plans for a joint US/British invasion fall flat because "nobody could be found in Iraq to collaborate with".

1959: Baathists and nationalists form underground anti-communist hit squads, assassinating ICP members and other radical workers. By 1961 up to 300 people have been murdered in this way in Baghdad and around 400 in Mosul.

In Mosul, Arab nationalist officers stage an unsuccessful coup, prompted largely by anti-communism. Popular resistance goes beyond suppressing the coup: the rich are attacked and their houses looted. There are similar scenes in Kirkuk where 90 generals, capitalists and landlords are killed in violent clashes.

1960: Quasim cracks down on radical opposition. 6000 militant workers are sacked. Several communists are sentenced to death for their role in the Kirkuk clashes. Despite this the ICP leadership continues to support the government.

1961: War breaks out between the government and Kurds, lasting on and off until 1975.

1963: The Baathists seize power in a January coup. They strengthen links with the US, suspected by many of encouraging the coup. During the coup, demonstrators are mown down by tanks, initiating a period of ruthless persecution during which up to 10,000 are imprisoned, many of them tortured. The CIA supply intelligence on communists and radicals to be rounded up. Up to 5,000 are killed in the terror, many buried alive in mass graves. The new government continues war on the Kurds.

In November the Baath are removed from power in a coup by supporters of the Egyptian Arab nationalist, Nasser.

1968: The Baath Party returns to power after a July coup. It creates a state apparatus systematically dominated by the Baath party that enables it to remain in power for at least the next 33 years.

1969: The regime begins rounding up suspected communists.

The air force bombs Kurdish areas, but military stalemate remains until the following year when Saddam Hussein negotiates an agreement with the Kurdish Democratic Party. In exchange for limited autonomy, the KDP leadership agrees to integrate its peshmerga fighters into the Iraqi army.

1973: The Iraqi oil industry is nationalized.

1974: The ICP joins the pro-government National Progressive Front along with the Baath, but the Baath remain in sole control of the state.

War breaks out again in Kurdistan as the agreement with the KDP breaks down. The KDP is deprived of its traditional allies in the CP and the Soviet Union, now supporting the Baath. Instead it seeks and receives aid from the USA and the Shah of Iran. The Baathists launch napalm attacks on Halabja and Kalalze.

1975: The Iraqi military continues bombing civilian areas in Kurdistan.

Iraq negotiates an agreement with Iran, withdrawing help from Iranian Kurds and other anti-Shah forces in return for Iran stopping support to the Iraqi KDP. Iran takes back the military equipment it had given to the KDP, leaving the field open for the Iraqi army to conquer Kurdistan.

1978: All non-Baathist political activity in the army (such as reading a political newspaper), or by former members of the armed forces is banned under sentence of death. With universal conscription, this means that all adult males are threatened with death for political activity.

1979: Saddam Hussein becomes president of the republic.

1980: War breaks out between Iraq and the new Iranian regime lead by Ayatollah Khomeni. The conflict centres on border disputes and the prospect of the Islamic revolution spreading to Iraq.

1982: Popular anti-government uprising in Kurdish areas. The government decrees that deserters from the army (anyone who has gone AWOL for more than 5 days) will be executed.

In the southern marsh regions, the Iraqi army launches a massive military operation to flush out the thousands of deserters and their supporters in the area. Rebels not only run away from the war, but also organise sabotage actions such as blowing up an arsenal near the town of Amara. In the village of Douru armed inhabitants resist the police to prevent house-to-house searches for deserters. Villages supporting the rebels are destroyed and their inhabitants massacred.

1984: US support for Iraq in the war is reflected in the restoration of diplomatic relations between the two countries. Iraq has received military planes from France, and missiles from the Soviet Union. Saudi Arabia and Kuwait fund the Iraqi war effort. West and East are united in a wish to see Iraq push back the influence of Iran and Islamic fundamentalism.

The Patriotic Union of Kurdistan calls a truce, with its troops fighting alongside the Baath.

1987: In May there is an uprising in the Kurdish town of Halabja led by the many army deserters living there. One eye-witness reports: "governmental forces were toppled. The people had taken over and the police and army had to go into hiding, only being able to move around in tanks and armoured divisions". Hundreds are killed when the rebellion is crushed.

1988: Armed deserters take over the town of Sirwan (near Halabja). The Iraqi air force destroys the town. On 13 March the Iraqi government attacks Halabja with chemical weapons killing at least 5,000 civilians. Poor people attempting to flee the town for Iran before the massacre are stopped from doing so by Kurdish nationalist peshmerga. Throughout this period of insurgency there is widespread suspicion of the Kurdish nationalist parties because of their history of collaboration with the state.

The US sends a naval force to the Gulf after attacks on oil tankers. It effectively takes the Iraqi side, shooting down an Iranian passenger jet, killing nearly 300, and attacking Iranian oil platforms, killing another 200. In August Iran and Iraq agree a ceasefire.

1990: Iraq invades Kuwait.

1991: In January the US military, with support from Britain and the other 'Coalition Forces' launches Operation Desert Storm, a massive attack on Iraq and its forces in Kuwait. The conflict is less of a war than what John Pilger calls "a one-sided bloodfest". Allied forces suffer only 131 deaths (many by 'friendly fire'), compared with up to 250,000 Iraqi dead.

Despite public statements by the US army that the allies will not attack Iraqis in retreat, Iraqi conscripts are slaughtered even after the unconditional withdrawal from Kuwait has begun. The day before 'war' comes to an end troops retreating from Kuwait City on the Basra highway are mas-

sacred, in what US pilots call a 'duck shoot'. For miles the road is filled with charred bodies and tangled wreckage. An eye witness writes that "In many instances the human form has been reduced to nothing more than a shapeless black lump, the colour of coal, the texture of ash".

Many civilians are also killed, most famously at the Amiriya bunker in Baghdad where hundreds sheltering from allied bombs are killed when it receives a direct hit from 2 missiles.

In February and March, popular uprisings against the Iraqi government spread across the country. It starts at Basra, sparked by rebels using a tank to fire at huge pictures of Hussein. Inspired by southern rebellion, people in Kurdish areas join in. Police stations, army bases and other government buildings are wrecked. Shops are looted. Food warehouses are occupied and the food distributed. In Sulliemania, rebels smash up the prison, set the prisoners free and then storm the secret police HQ. Baathist officials and secret police are shot. In some areas, self-organised workers' councils (shoras) are set up to run things. They set up their own radio stations, medical posts, and militia to resist government forces.

After a brutal repression of the rebellion in the South (made easier by the Allied massacre of mutinous conscripts on the Basra highway), Government forces focus on Kurdistan. They reoccupy Sulliemania in April, but the city is deserted with almost all inhabitants having fled to the mountains.

The Western media present the uprisings as the work of Kurdish nationalists in the north and Shiite Muslims in the south, but they are in fact mass revolts of the poor. The main Kurdish nationalist parties (the KDP and the PUK) oppose radical aspects of the uprisings and try to destroy the shora movement. True to form they announce a new negotiated agreement with Hussein soon after the uprisings are crushed.

> During the 1991 uprisings, rebels in Sulliemania smashed up the prison and set the prisoners free, then stormed the secret police HQ.

1991- 2003: Desert Storm comes to an end but the war on Iraqi people is continued by other means - sanctions. The destruction of water pumping stations and sewage filtration plants by allied bombing is compounded by sanctions, which prevent reconstruction. This amounts to germ warfare, as the inevitable consequences are epidemics of dysentery, typhoid and cholera. In 1997, the UN estimates that 1.2 million people, including 750,000 children below the age of five, have died because of food and medicine shortages.

1996: The US launches 27 cruise missiles against Iraq.

1998: In February there is a massive military build up of US and British forces in the Gulf, threatening a new war on Iraq. Conflict is avoided after a last minute deal on UN Weapons Inspectors.

In December, after weapons inspectors are forced to leave, being told that bombing is imminent, the US launches Operation Desert Fox. Over a 4-day period, 400 cruise missiles are launched, along with 600 air attack sorties. British aircraft also take part. Thousands are killed or wounded.

1999: Western military attacks continue. On April 11, two people are killed when Western warplanes bomb targets in Quadissiya. On 27 April, four are killed by US planes in the northern no-fly zone. On May 9, four are killed in Basra province, including three in a farmer's house in Qurna. On May 12, 12 people are killed in the northern city of Mosul.

2003: ...see rest of book.

WAKE UP! WAKE UP! IT'S YER BOMBED OUT

weekly SchNEWS

www.schnews.org.uk

Friday 13th September 2002   Free/Donation   Issue 372

Number of people killed in NY on 9-11

Number of Afghani civilians killed by US led bombing (approximately another 20,000 have been killed indirectly, and over 500,000 have been made refugees)

8000
7000
6000
5000
4000
3000
2000
1000

SILENT BUT DEADLY

"As a Native American, every time I see the American flag I feel the same way I imagine Jewish people must feel when looking at the Nazi flag. The American flag is a flag of oppression and genocide. Because that's what America is built on — from the very beginning when the first European settlers landed in North America, it has been a country built on blood." *Rod Coronado, Native American activist, speaking in Brighton last week.*

"It's really not a number I'm terribly interested in." *General Colin Powell, when asked about the number of Iraqi people who were killed by Americans in the 1991 Desert Storm campaign (200,000 people, incidentally)*

September 11th is an anniversary. And if you've watched too much telly or read too many newspapers this week, you may have been fooled into believing that September 11th is only the anniversary of one tragedy, in one nation. But it's not. On the same day in 1973, Salvador Allende, the socialist President of Chile, was killed in a violent, American-sponsored coup, led by General Augusto Pinochet. Pinochet's rise to power,

dreamt-up and orchestrated by a Red-paranoid CIA and Mr. Henry Kissinger, began nearly twenty years of military dictatorship that led to thousands of deaths and countless incidences of oppression and torture. 30,000 people were massacred in the weeks following this other September 11th, as Pinochet tried to wipe out an entire layer of society who had identified with the left. Even in exile, many who had associated with the Allende government (or were vaguely perceived as some sort of communist threat) were assassinated by Pinochet's secret service. And all of this sponsored in the name of Freedom and Democracy.

So when we're having a minute of silence for the people who died in the Twin Towers, why not a minute of silence for those who died at the hands of Pinochet's CIA-sponsored death squads? Or while we're at it, we could have a minute of silence for the people of the Congo, also subjected to a military dictatorship thanks to the CIA assassination of evil lefty Patrice Lumumba. Or how about Cambodia, which deserves at least two minutes of silence when one considers that America (and Britain) backed Khmer Rouge

leader Pol Pot to the tune of $85 million in his genocidal rampage which killed nearly 2 million Cambodians. Or what about a few minutes of silence for Nicaragua, where in 1936, the American National Guard helped Anastasio Somoza to establish and maintain a family dynasty which would rule over Nicaragua for the next 43 years. While the National Guardsmen, consistently maintained by the US, passed their time with rape, torture, murder of the opposition, and massacres of peasants, as well as less violent pursuits such as robbery, extortion, contraband, running brothels and other government functions, the Somoza clan laid claim to the lion's share of Nicaragua's land and businesses. Love that Freedom & Democracy, don't ya?

The problem with this list is that it could go on and on — Brazil, Guatemala, El Salvador, Ecuador, Uruguay, the Dominican Republic, Cuba, Haiti, Iraq, Iran, Laos, East

"What might be the effect upon the American psyche if the true-believers were compelled to witness the consequences of the past half-century of US foreign policy close up? What if all the nice, clean-cut, wholesome American boys who dropped an infinite tonnage of bombs, on a dozen different countries, on people they knew nothing about - characters in a video game - had to come down to earth and look upon and smell the burning flesh?"

From the book *"Killing Hope: U.S. Military and CIA Interventions Since World War II"* by William Blum... For more info on Blum's books: www.thirdworldtraveler.com/Blum/KillingHope_page.html or http://members.aol.com/bblum6/American_holocaust.htm

111

Silent but Deadly cont...

Timor, Grenada, Greece... All of these and more are countries who have suffered from oppression, torture, starvation, and death at the hands of American "intervention," whether it takes the form of bombs, sanctions, or our personal favourite, CIA sponsored military regimes.

As ex-State Department employee and author William Blum writes, "An American holocaust has taken place... So great and deep is the denial of the American holocaust that the deniers are not even aware that the claimers or their claims exist. Yet, a few million people have died in the American holocaust and many more millions have been condemned to lives of misery and torture as a result of US interventions extending from China and Greece in the 1940s to Afghanistan and Iraq in the 1990s."

"I will never apologise for the United States of America - I don't care what the facts are," said President George Bush Sr. in 1988, when the U.S. Navy warship Vincennes shot down an Iranian commercial airliner. The plane was on a routine flight in a commercial corridor in Iranian airspace. All 290 civilians on board the aircraft were killed.

So while George Bush Jr. demands that the world observe a minute of silence for the dead and injured civilians of September 11th, the 290 dead Iranian civilians of 1988 didn't even get an apology. Neither did the nearly 8,000 Afghani civilians who have died in the last year as a result of U.S. led air strikes in Afghanistan, a campaign appropriately titled "Enduring Freedom."

To the best of our knowledge, none of the victims of bombings in these countries have ever received any apologies, memorial funds, or commemorative minutes of silence. Yes, it is a tragedy when 3,000 people lose their lives on a single day as the result of madmen. But it is also a tragedy that takes place in many countries around the world on a daily basis, often times as a result of the madmen in Washington. And when this fact is not acknowledged, anniversary observances of September 11th sound hollow at best, and grossly hypocritical and offensive at worst. As one American activist told Schnews, "If we had to observe a moment of silence for all of the victims of American foreign policy, we'd be silent for the rest of our lives." www.geocities.com/ americanterrorism/ www.users.bigpond. com/ nlevine/thearchive.html

> *While we're on the subject of bombs, let's remember that since the Second World War, the US government has bombed 21 countries: China in 1945-46 and again in 1950-53, Korea in 1950-53, Guatemala in 1954, 1960, and 1967-69, Indonesia in 1958, Vietnam in 1961-73, Congo in 1964, Laos in 1964-73, Peru in 1965, Cambodia in 1969-70, El Salvador throughout the 1980s, Nicaragua throughout the 1980s, Lebanon in 1983-84, Grenada in 1983, Bosnia in 1985, Libya in 1986, Panama in 1989, Iraq in 1991-20??, Sudan in 1998, Former Yugoslavia in 1999, and Afghanistan in 1998 and 2002.*

Atenco Update

Having successfully fought off government plans to build an airport on their land, farmers in the Mexican town of **San Salvador Atenco** have now declared the town the first 'autonomous municipality' outside of Chiapas, electing a people's council and seizing all government vehicles trying to enter the area. This is the latest episode in an uprising that began on July 11, when the government tried to violently suppress a protest organised by farmers against the airport proposals. The residents of Atenco responded to police clubs, tear gas, and bullets by burning police vehicles, barricading the national highway, and taking 13 government and police officials hostage. The result was a five-day stand off between residents and the authorities, which ended in the government releasing all prisoners they had taken during the protests and abandoning their plans for the new airport (see Schnews 367).

Since their victory, residents have made the town a no-go area for police and federal authorities. Their declaration of autonomy is the most recent expression of a new unwillingness on their part to allow the Mexican government to dictate the organisation of their community. The 'people's council', described by the town's former mayor as 'frankly illegal', is seen by residents not as an attempt to withdraw from Mexico, but as an effort to decide for themselves how to meet their communities needs. "They try to scare people off with the word 'autonomous' ", said one resident, "but what it means is that the people's will is respected. It doesn't mean we want to close ourselves off. The people are just going to decide how to police the town".

We Won't Bet The Farm: Atenco

On September 11th 2002 a peoples council voted on making the town of Atenco an autonomous municipality. Neighbourhood assemblies were set up and a 14 member Peoples Council said in a statement read at their swearing-in ceremony, "We are aware that that the government will not recognize this action by the people, but they have no choice but to respect our decision". A declaration stated that police and government officials would no longer be allowed to enter the town and Atenco will continue to be self-policing.

The people managed to keep all police and other government authorities out of the town, but March 9th 2003 was local election day in and around Mexico City. The elections went without a hitch for the large part elsewhere in Mexico's largest state but for Atenco it was an affront to their declared independence. The authorities could only look on helplessly from police helicopters as protesters burnt ballots and demolished the polling booths. This time there were no serious injuries and the people celebrated the destruction of all the voting booths by firing off a cannon. Some of the townspeople went to outlying areas to vote but farming leader Ignacio Del Valle insisted, "We are right and we have the force of the people behind us".

The struggle in Atenco has continued to inspire imperilled or dispossessed Latin Americans even more than the Zapatistas, as it has proved how unified community action can overcome even the most fierce and well-funded adversity.

Organ Play

Next Saturday (21st) people will be marching to the Home Office to protest against **xenotransplantation** - the transplanting of animal organs into humans. Two years ago the High Court, following legal action by research company Imutran, put a stop to a report written by Uncaged entitled 'Diaries of Despair'. The report exposed the negligent and cruel research methods used by Imutran, a subsidiary of the biotechnology giant Novartis.

Research mostly involved the transplantation of hearts and kidneys from genetically-engineered pigs into macaque monkeys and baboons caught in the wild. In some of the most horrific experiments, Imutran researchers implanted hearts from transgenic piglets into the necks of baboons. One of these primates was observed holding the transplant, which was 'swollen red' and 'seeping yellow fluid', for most of the last days of its life. Animals are often 'sacrificed'- jargon for being killed - both as a direct result of the experiments and due to sloppy lab practice. A baboon quickly got the chop when scientists discovered, mid operation, that the pig's heart it was supposed to receive was still in the freezer.

Imutran, who have used thousands of pigs, monkeys and baboons in their five years of research, claim to be on the verge of conquering the problem of 'organ rejection'- where the immune system sees the 'new' heart or liver as a foreign object, and attacks it. But the documents tell a different story. In one experiment, two baboons, who suffered 'hyperacute' organ rejection and quickly died, were left out of the published results which had claimed success. In another, the animals were pumped full of immuno-suppressant drugs to make sure their bodies didn't reject the 'new' parts.

Many scientists are worried about the safety of xenotransplantation itself. They believe there is a danger that putting bits from one species into another could easily trigger new and unheard of diseases. While scientists routinely screen transplant organs for viruses, they can only screen for those they know the existence of. And there may be many viruses which lie harmless and undetected in pigs but which could kill humans. Pigs are known to contain

600 go ape-shit around central London on September 21st, visiting the Home Office for a die-in to bring attention to the primates held by the bio-tech company Imutran. Pic: Corin Jeavons

certain viruses closely related to human ones that cause blood leukemia.

An obvious alternative to cross-species transplants would be a decent diet and improved living standards for everyone. It would also make more sense if everyone just used 'Opt Out' donor cards instead of what we have at the moment. People would have to carry an 'opt out' card to show that in the event of their death they didn't want certain or all of their organs to be used, as is the case in some other European countries.

The march next Saturday starts 12 noon in Temple Place, Central London. 0114 272 2220 www.xenodiaries.org

Taking the peace

The Brighton Peace and Environment Centre, North Laines' own radical book and re-usable nappy shop, is closing this weekend due to rising rents. BPEC will be moving to temporary office space, from which it hopes to attract new volunteers and funding by dropping the bit about peace cos it just doesn't sell. If you can help in the search for new premises, or want a say in BPEC's future, e-mail them at info@bpec.org With the Peace and Environment Centre closing, pick up your copies of SchNEWS from Infinity Foods in North St.

Why the dinosaurs died out.

"Don't worry about the coming Ice Age. The important thing is to deal with the terroradactylist threat!"

SchNEWS in brief

Radio 4A, Brighton's Premier pirate station is back on the airwaves this weekend 107.8 FM across Brighton and worldwide on www.piratetv.net ** There's a noise demo outside HMP Frankland, Brasside, Durham this Saturday (14) 2-4pm in support of four prisoners who are on a 'dirty protest', and are 'down the block' (in segregation/solitary confinement)at Frankland.07944522001 nicki.rensten@prisonersadvice.demon.co.uk ** John Pilger's new documentary, 'Palestine is still the Issue', is on ITV next Monday (16) 11pm ** From sinking Icelandic whaling ships to burning down fur industry buildings, Native American Rod Coronado has engaged in militant and uncompromising direct action which eventually led to prison. Listen to his engaging stories in Sheffield next Monday (16) at the Showroom Cinema, Pater Noster Road; Manchester (17) at Briton's Protection Pub, Great Bridgewater Street, 8pm; Leeds (19) Woodhouse Community Centre, Woodhouse Street 7pm ** People are urgently needed at the Lappersfort protest camp in Brugge, Belgium which has just been given its eviction notice. Protestors are trying to prevent the destruction of a green oasis in the city by a new motorway bypass and industrial zone. For directions call 0032 494 59 14 67 lappersfort@ziplip.com ** Volunteers are needed to help with the Reclaim The Future event happening the weekend 20-22 September, everything from cooking to building work to help on the Saturday. Call 07931 560 569 rtsparty2002@yahoo.co.uk. They are also looking for old Reclaim The Streets/direct action exhibition materials e-mail maxsvoboda@hotmail.com if you've got any stashed under your bed ** No Sweat, the anti sweatshop group, are asking people to get their kit off during the Nike Fun Run in Richmond Park on Sunday 22 September. Meet at Barnes train station 9am. 07979 046 219 Email yesgaryjarvis@hotmail.com www.nosweat.org.uk ** A massive campaign has been launched to stop Redditch Borough Council giving the go ahead to an animal carcass incinerator in the village of Astwood Bank. The incinerator would be next to the village school, with the chimney 100 yards from the kids' playing field! The incinerator would burn up to 1 tonne of animal carcasses per hour, 24 hours a day. www.abai.org.uk ** Villagers in Kingskerswell, Devon are fighting a dual carriageway proposal and 600 new homes www.kingskerswellalliance.org.uk ** A McDonalds in Linkoping, Sweden was recently completely burnt down by animal rights activists ** An anti-fascist phone tree is being set up in Brighton in response to the lack of opposition to anti-Islamic fascist demonstrations which took place in London on Wednesday the 11th. Call 01273 540717 ** Battersea and Wandsworth TUC are holding a demo outside Balfour Beatty Offices at 130 Wilton Road, Victoria next Monday (16) 9am to coincide with the launch of their report 'Corporate Killers in Wandsworth'. The report, which focuses on the deaths caused by casualisation, is being launched at the Bread and Roses in Clapham at 7pm the same evening. Speakers include Bob Crow and Mark Thomas 020 8682 4224 ** After development plans were stopped by local protests 4 years ago (SchNEWS 203), Bromley Council has again fenced off part of Crystal Palace Park with unsightly 2.4m high wooden hoardings and are preparing to sell it off. Local opposition is organising and a candle-lit vigil is being held on the 21st Sept from 7.30 - 8.30pm near Crystal Palace Parade beside the fence (you can't miss it!). save crystalpalacepark@yahoo.co.uk ** "Battle For Chile" video showing, Sept 15, Conway Hall, Red Lion Square, London, 2pm, £5

Lode of crap

Rio Tinto, one of the world's biggest mining corporations, has pulled out of plans for the Jabiluka uranium mine in the Northern Territory, Australia. The mine is in the ancestral homeland of the Aboriginal Mirrar people and would have contaminated huge parts of their land which is also part of Kakadu National Park, a listed World Heritage Site.

Since uranium was first found there in the early seventies, the Mirrar have been fighting to stop mining on their land. The struggle escalated in 1998 after the government reversed long-standing environmental policies permitting new uranium mines to be built. A protest camp then sprang up, blockading the site for several months and resulting in hundreds of arrests. This, along with constant acts of sabotage on site and pressure on the government from UNESCO (UN environment quango) and the World Heritage Organisation, forced Rio Tinto to pull out of Jabiluka. www.jag.org.au/_

...and finally...

We at SchNEWS Towers are facing meltdown! We're staring at ground zero as all our support staff leave us for better jobs in the City, sun themselves in tropical climates, or leg it from the bailiffs, leaving the remainder of us drowning in deadlines, emails and uneaten biscuits.

So we are looking for new volunteers to pen some articles, help with our mail-out and do a bit of desk top publishing. Rates of pay are crap but the fringe benefits make up for it (honest). To make sure you don't miss this opportunity of a lifetime call our hotline now -- 01273 685913.

Disclaimer

Subscribe!
Keep SchNEWS FREE! Send 1st Class stamps (e.g. 10 for next 9 issues) or donations (payable to Justice?) Ask for "Originals" if you can make copies. Post *free* to all prisoners. SchNEWS, c/o on-the-fiddle, P.O. Box 2600, Brighton, East Sussex, BN2 0EF. *Tel/Autofax* +44 (0)1273 685913 *Email* **schnews@brighton.co.uk** *Download a PDF* of this issue or subscribe at **www.schnews.org.uk**

I GAVE AWAY ALL I HAD...

weekly SchNEWS

www.schnews.org.uk

Friday 27th September 2002   Free/Donation   Issue 373/374

WEAPON OF MASS DECEPTION

"They know we own their country. We own their airspace... We dictate the way they live and talk. And that's what's great about America right now. It's a good thing, especially when there's a lot of oil out there we need." - *U.S. Brig. General William Looney (Interview Washington Post 1999)*

"While the unresolved conflict with Iraq provides the immediate justification, the need for a substantial American force presence in the Gulf transcends the issue of the regime of Saddam Hussein." - *Washington think-tank report, September 2000*

The first world war of the 21st century is already underway. Bush and the oilmen who run his government have given orders to make the oilfields of the Middle East safe for America. The US military are deploying their unimaginably powerful flotilla of death against Iraq, a country they have been bombing and denying medicine to for over 10 years. The corporate media are spinning their lies and whipping up war fever in exactly the way they always do. With its overwhelming military superiority, and without the Soviet Union or any other competing superpower to restrain its ambitions of world domination, the United States is not even pretending to conform to international law. It is left to Blair, like a gangster's shiny-suited lawyer, to come up with pseudo-legal justifications for the violence that's already been agreed on. Capitalism doesn't get much more naked than this.

For the vast majority of humanity it's perfectly clear what the United States is doing. The most powerful nation on earth, and capitalism in general, is totally dependent on oil to keep it running - and most of that oil is in the Middle East. Since 1945, the US has armed and relied on puppet Arab regimes like Saudi Arabia to ensure the cheap oil has kept flowing for the West's ecologically suicidal way of life. It has armed the Israeli State to terrorise its Arab neighbours and ensure that the people of the potentially richest region in the world (the Middle East) are kept in poverty.

Iraq has the second largest oil reserves after Saudi Arabia, and for years Saddam Hussein was given western support to keep it flowing. For years, Bush Senior gave Saddam loans and sold him advanced technology with clear applications for weapons of mass destruction (WMD). Britain was still authorising export of military equipment and radioactive materials to Iraq even after Iraq invaded Kuwait. Iraq has been so important to the US that Saddam was able to get away with attacking a US naval vessel, the USS Stark, at the cost of dozens of American lives without any comeback.

ISRAEL POLITIK

But things are changing. The level of oppression in the Arab world is so great that capitalism fears popular uprisings in the region will overthrow its puppet regimes and threaten its oil supplies. Israel has been armed to the teeth but has been unable to defeat the risen Palestinian people. The Saudi Royal family have been bankrolled to maintain their brutal regime but popular opposition to their rule is growing. The oilmen in the White House live in fear of being unable to control a region they have become so dependent on. Direct military intervention, shrouded by a thick layer of propaganda for the public, has become the preferred tactic for the new century.

Saddam is, of course, a brutal dictator - like Suharto, Pinochet, and all the others the US has payrolled. But the excuse for invasion, that he may have weapons of mass destruction and

---

Over a thousand people have signed a **Pledge of Resistance**, committing themselves to taking part in acts of nonviolent civil disobedience should Iraq - or any other country - be attacked in the course of the 'War on Terrorism.' Hundreds more have pledged to support them.

Sign the Pledge on-line at www.justicenotvengeance.org or call 0845 4582564. Also check their website out for a list of regular anti-war protests across the country.

Stop the War, Stop the City: direct action against the war in Brighton. Meet the day after ground troops enter Iraq. Churchill Square, 5.30pm bring pots and pans to bang for "rough music." Make your voice heard. brightonagainstwar@hotmail.com

---

Weapons of Mass Deception cont...

be a danger to his neighbours and others, is clearly just that - an excuse. The terrorist state of Israel has 200 nuclear weapons targetted at Arab capitals. It has illegally occupied Palestine for 35 years and breached dozens of United Nations resolutions – yet it wouldn't exist without US support. When Saddam invaded Iran and gassed Kurds, the West just made money out of it, because its strategic interests were not threatened. The terrorist attacks of September 11th were carried out by an organisation payrolled not by Saddam Hussein but by the United States itself to fight its war against the Soviet Union in the 1980s. Anyone who thinks this new war will be a war to make the world a safer place just hasn't been paying much attention.

BLAIRY-EYED

The vast majority of humanity is against this war. If the United Nations votes to support it, it will only be because Washington has bullied, bribed or terrorised poorer countries into supporting its plans. In the US, millions oppose Bush's imperialism. In Britain, despite Labour and Tory support for Bush and the usual media bullshit, half the population is against the war. If we wanna put a spoke in the wheel of capitalism's war machine, we've got a lot of friends.

But we won't achieve anything unless we really make a noise. When Blair gave a warmongering speech to the Trade Union Congress last month, he wasn't even heckled – this pathetic response allowed Blair to appear statesmanlike and led directly to increased public support for the war in the following week. If even one person had stood up and refused to shut up it would have resonated around the world – but no one did. We won't oppose this war effectively with that sort of cowardice.

It won't be union leaders or paper sellers or 'organisers' that will stop this war. It will be ordinary, angry, active people – us, you, your neighbours, your mates – taking direct action. Stopping high streets at rush hour. Shutting down government and military buildings. Having sit down protests on marches instead of moving on whenever the police tell us to. As Mukhtar Dai of the Birmingham South Asian Alliance said recently, "If it means disruption by our people who work in various service industries that will happen. People working in taxis and buses will stop work and there should also be strikes in factories." As even one ex-Labour MP said "The moment the bombing of Iraq begins we should stop for one hour. We should remember the women of Baghdad who will be widows, the children who will become orphans. I've never said this before. Non-violent resistance to the government will show they cannot claim to do this in our name. We should stop the buses, the trains, the schools. Everyone here should raise the threat of war in their schools, places of worship, where they work & live. We could be facing a Third World war triggered by stupid men."

Anti-War Actions

Saturday 28th **Stop the War, Don't Attack Iraq Demo**. Huge anti-war demonstration meeting at the Embankment @ 1pm then going to Hyde Park. www.stopwar.org.uk Buses from Brighton 01273 502241. Join the **Anti-capitalist Bloc**: Meet at Cleopatra's needle on the Embankment 1pm. anticapbloc@mail.com Or join the **SchNEWS Bloc** Meet 11am Brighton Station – and help us hand out these bloody newsletters. ** A **Peace Camp** has been set up outside the Imperial museum in London. 07986 465552. ** Sunday 6 Oct, **No Nukes, No War action** at USAF Lakenheath 11am - 3pm, A1065, near Thetford. Lakenheath is the main American tactical airbase in Europe, armed with nuclear weapons and hosting the 48th Fighter Wing of the U.S.A.F. This wing has been heavily involved in attacks on Iraq in the past, including campaigns from 1991 to 1994 and 1999. There are around 30 tactical nuclear weapons deployed at Lakenheath, the last remaining American nuclear weapons in Britain. These bombs each have a maximum explosive yield of 80 kilotons. The Hiroshima bomb had a 13 kiloton yield. 01508-550446 www.lakenheathaction.org ** 6th October **Protest against war with Iraq**, Southsea Common, Portsmouth 3pm 023 9229 3673 ** **Scrap Trident Demo**, 12th October, 12 noon Plymouth Hoe www.cnduk.org ** For other anti war events check the **SchNEWS party and protest** bit on our website.

* **For those of you wanting to take direct action against the war**, here's a few resources we thought you might find useful: ** For the addresses of all 123 Army and Navy Recruitment Offices in the UK visit: www.army.mod.uk/careers/recruit_office/a_z_results.htm#a ** For addresses of the MoD Bases in the UK, listed by area: www.100megsfree4.com/farshores/ukufobas.htm ** Addresses and maps of US Military Bases world-wide: www.globemaster.de/regbases.html ** The Defence Procurement Agency proclaim, "Our mission: To Equip the Armed Forces". Their website lists their 'projects' to design and build equipment for the Army, Navy and Air Force. Follow the links to find out which company is building what: www.mod.uk/dpa/projects/index.htm

* **Stuff to get you going:** ** Get hold of the CD **'The Fire This Time'** "Deconstructing the Gulf War and revealing the devastating effect of sanctions on Iraq" www.firethistime.org ** **'Hidden Wars of Desert Storm'** Essential viewing for anyone wanting to understand issues such as Oil, weapons inspectors, depleted uranium, Gulf War Syndrome and why America is now including Iraq in its so called 'War on Terrorism.' www.Cultureshop.org ** A new tune **"The Evil Plans of George W Bush IIIrd"** has just been released under Copyleft license so people can copy it, give it out, play it out and remix it as long as they give credit. www.twisted.co.nz/djdb/viewdj.php?dj_id=18

SchNEWS in brief

Imagine an area bigger than Brighton and Hove closed to traffic; Brussels managed it last Sunday and shut 160 square kilometres to traffic during **International Car Free Day**. 1,400 cities around Europe also took part. www.carbusters.ecn.cz. ** Speaking of cars (and the climate change they cause), **Rising Tide** are holding a gathering in Manchester next weekend (4-6th Oct) looking at global warming, oil, pipelines, corruption, water privatisation and other dodgy practices. 01865-241097 www.risingtide.org. ** Last Saturday, angry residents tore down fences in **Crystal Palace park**. The barriers were erected by Bromley Council who want to sell off some of the historic parkland for re-development. savecrystalpalacepark@yahoo.co.uk ** Authorities estimate 20,000 people will welcome the ringleaders of globalisation, the International Monetary Fund and World Bank to Washington next week. www.infoshop.org have organised a spoof **"anarchist scavenger hunt"** to amuse protesters: 300 points for smashing the window of a McDonald's or 400 points for a pie in the face of a corporate executive or World Bank delegate! Follow the protests at www.dc.indymedia.org. ** **"About Anarchism"** by Nicholas Walter has just been reprinted and is well worth reading. Copies from Freedom Press for £3.50,

020-7247-9249 www.ecn.org/freedom ** As part of the regular **international day of action against McDonalds** on October 16th, McDonald's workers have organised the first ever international industrial day of action. Burger flippers the world over are being encouraged to check out the website - http://mwr.org.uk ** **Zut Alors!** Millions of French teenagers are in for a shock if they swear at their teachers. New legislation means pupils could face fines of up to 7,500 euros and even custodial sentences for such serious misdemeanours as unruly behaviour and that most heinous of crimes – swearing at rail guards. ** This Sunday there's an **Earth First Strategy and Action** Discussion Group meeting, near Norwich Which will discuss the direct action and anti-capitalist movement in present form and where it's going. For a copy of the agenda and to book, call 01986 781 789. ** A new road construction project that is being proposed near **Stonehenge** in Wiltshire could pose a real threat to the World Heritage site. At the moment they can't decide whether to go overland or underground, but either way, if the road-building goes ahead, the land surrounding the stone circle which also has World Heritage status and includes important archaeological remains will be destroyed to make room for a new four lane highway. www.savestonehenge.org.uk ** There's a **benefit gig** at the Concorde 2, Brighton, for the street kids of Cape Town, South Africa next Tuesday (1 October) 9pm Tickets £4 ** The following day (2) there's another **Fun raiser** at the Volks, Maderia Drive, Brighton supporting Zapatista communities in Mexico.

ARIEL

MASSIVE POWER OF CLEANSING...

THIS PERSON DESERVES $692 AN HOUR FOR THEIR WORK

THIS PERSON DESERVES 8¢ AN HOUR FOR THEIR WORK

AND ANYONE WHO SAYS OTHERWISE IS A DANGEROUS, NAÏVE, WOOLY MINDED, BLEEDING HEART TROUBLEMAKER

OCCUPATIONAL HAZARD

Reprinted here are a selection of excerpts from the diary of a British activist in Palestine, who has spent the past two months working with the International Solidarity Movement (ISM) and other groups, to monitor the conditions of life for Palestinians living under the occupation and to offer physical and moral support.

I've been in Askar refugee camp, Nablus for the past eleven days now. Four of us internationals (our numbers here are TINY now, we really need more people) travelled up here after completing our training as 'official' ISM volunteers. Official in that you have to sign a contract committing yourself to no drugs, alcohol, violence - that includes NO stone throwing at the soldiers Even if the kids are all bang on it and you're standing in – literally – piles of stones: hand-sized, hard, easily reached stones.

Our main co-ordinator for the training was a small, earnest Japanese woman named Maki. As we are going to be staying in the houses of local Palestinians - mainly the homes of the families of suicide bombers and martyrs which are under threat of revenge attacks - usually a total bulldozing, we were taken through the do's and don'ts of Palestinian culture: don't sit with your leg up at a right angle , crossed over your knee - showing the bottom of your foot is considered very disrespectful. If you bring a gift to the family - make sure it's never bread - they will think you think they haven't even got enough cash for bread and are destitute - better to make it chocolates and coffee and then give it very matter-of-fact, don't make a song and dance about it, otherwise you might embarass the family; give the gift to the father of the house; no low-cut tops, vests or shorts; and do not kiss or touch men in public.

We also get an introduction to the politics and roots of ISM. The first ever ISM action, December 2000 saw locals and internationals march up to an Israeli Military base, walk straight past the soldiers guarding it, march raucously through, banners and Palestinian flags aloft, and up to the top where they took down the Israeli flag and raised the Green, White, Black and Red. That's quite an achievement in an occupied police state. The Israeli media have tried to discredit the ISM by saying its full of anarchists and communists. Everyone from Anarchist Youth Network UK people, Wombles, huge Ya Basta! Italy contingents, comedian Jeremy Hardy, and McDonald's smashing, GM crop-torching farmer Jose Bove have come out on ISM missions. The most interesting part of the training is handling the various projectiles the Israeli Army is likely to shoot at us… After passing round some weighty sound bomb shells, tear gas canisters, rubber bullets (rubber-coated steel balls), sharp pointed M16 bullets, Uzi bullets, and tank shells, Maki adopts a very stern, serious voice. We pay attention. 'What you will see here is very, very depressing. Many people feel very upset by what they see. You may get beaten or shot. You may see your friends get shot and Palestinian people shot or beaten very, very badly. You may need counselling after this

[nods up and down]. Yes. And the counselling, it might work. [nod, nod] It might work'.

Since the curfew was imposed, Nablus residents (numbering around 150,000 - making it the largest city in the West Bank outside of Jerusalem) have been allowed to leave their homes for an average of four hours a week. The lifting of the curfew is erratic and unpredictable. It was lifted for the first day of school just last week (Aug 31) but then re-imposed again, and hasn't been lifted since. Children are unable to get to school. It's a problem for them and their parents. A similar tactic of intellectually impoverishing whole generations was adopted by the South African apartheid regime. Demonising those living under an internal colonialism as inherently backward, retarded, and unmanageable, the state attempts to make this image a reality through the routine prevention and denial of education.

The Israeli Defence Force(IDF) has also occupied the homes of those unlucky enough to live on the outskirts of camps, who are positioned at good vantage points for snipers and provide key locations for military operation launches. One such family is the Alar Samfeh family, living on the edge of Askar. The house was forcibly occupied by soldiers in June to be used as a make-shift base for terrestrial operations in the area. The 19 people living in the home were prevented from leaving and as a result lost their livelihoods - builders, land surveyors- for the past three months. During the occupation, if the father of the family wanted to move from one part of the house to another he was forcibly blindfolded. Soldiers destroyed chairs, tables and a music system, and towels and linen were regularly used to clean oily guns.

Tank Dust Lunch - September 2nd

The idea is to march from the Askar Mosque, out to the house (only a 20 minute walk) and have a picnic outside the house/military base, and try if possible to deliver food to the family. We bring 100 falafel, houmous and salad pittas for the kids. The women from the Askar community women's centre come too - they control the megaphone, and the kids who are yip yipping around, all excited and carrying the placards we made last night: 'Zolnierze WON, Dzieci do Szkoly' - Soldiers OUT, Children Back to School (Polish), Japanese peace symbols, the word peace in Arabic and many others. There are about 200 of us. We manage to get as far as the first intersection before the house when the sound of a tank begins to grind against our ears. All of us internationals (about 10) are at the front holding hands, to act as a barrier between the soldiers and the kids. We brace ourselves for the tank. It comes roaring up to us, stops, spins its barrel round and round and then points it squarely at us. It then begins to rotate its entire body in circles churning up dust and spewing out bilious clouds of carbon monoxide. It disappears in its own thick grey exhaust. People cover their mouths with their t-shirts, turn away, cover their eyes, cough and splutter, but all stand firm. It eventually stops, gradually reappearing as the noxious fumes clear. The military plod turn up in a jeep. Negotiators, an international and a Palestinian, step straight up. We can't go to the occupied house. We end up staying where we are and eating the falafel's while kids take turns on the megaphone - singing freedom songs, shouting out demands, slinging the odd stone. We chant along to. 'Mur-der-ers!' 'Mur-der-ers!' 'Let the child-ren go to sch-ool!'

We don't retreat, we just all take the decision that we'll go. Although we didn't make it to the house, the kids are jubilant We weren't even supposed to stay at the intersection, let alone sit down and have a picnic. Everybody agrees that the demo was a great success. People have barely left their houses for months, let alone taken back their streets collectively and had the chance to give the soldiers a piece of their minds.

Checkpoint Demonstration

A military checkpoint has been in operation opposite Mukhata – the Palestinian Authority prison in Nablus that was destroyed by the IDF - for nine days now. A tank and Armoured Personnel stand at the dust-bowl junction between Old Nablus and the Ballata refugee camp. Directly behind the checkpoint are three blocks of flats and a number of homes nestled into Askar Mountain. Checkpoints are crucial to IDF (Israeli Defence Force - Israeli Army) operations in the Palestinian territories. They are the lynchpins of the occupation.

Checkpoints curtail all movement. Daily tasks and activities are criminalised or made nearly impossible by endless checks and searches. According to the IDF, the searches are necessary to prevent terrorists moving weapons around. One suicide bomb-belt was found - in front of much media, this year. No other armaments have been reported since. Meanwhile, over 80 people have died since the second intifada began, after being held up at checkpoints and prevented from accessing essential medical attention: cancer the new term started: August 31. Normally, during the occupation, they have had nowhere to go, and no education, although work is being done to set up schooling spaces in the refugee camps. The economy in Nablus has ground to a halt. Once the industrial heartland of the Palestinian territories it is now a daily ghost-town. Many people cannot go to work, cannot earn money, cannot obtain medicine or groceries, and can barely feed their families. This applies more stringently to the people forced to actually live amongst Israeli soldiers who've set up camp, inside their homes, using them as look-out points, human shields and operations bases, plus the people who have the soldiers on their doorstep, such as those living above the checkpoint at Mukhata.

We'd been doing checkpoint-watch every day there for the past nine days, monitoring the soldier's activities. Children from the surrounding area regularly gather by the wrecked prison to throw rocks (Plenty of them around - the IDF regularly makes roadblocks using Caterpillar and local Palestinian bulldozers. Roads are simply cracked open, dug up, and rock and cement piled up into mini mountains.) It's a depressing ritual. The kids detest the occupation, they are oppressed daily by Israeli soldiers. The soldiers regularly shoot at children. I got a taste of this last week, whilst I was hanging out with the stone-throwing streetfighter

kids. An Israeli commander and his colleague were using the exhaust fumes of an advancing tank as cover to get closer to the kids, all young raggedy boys aged 10-17. As the tank pulled back up to its position in front of the flats, the kids pointed wildly to a white square building in between the Mukhata and the checkpoint. 'Soldiers, soldiers' they shouted, pointing at the white building. 'I know I know', I said, pointing up at the checkpoint. 'No No No!' (cue sound of machinegun fire and more manic pointing at the white building). It was only then that I realised what they were doing. They opened fire, and we ducked behind a trench of rubble. The kids ran to hide behind some broken rocks. I got up and ran over to them. They were taking aim. I direct my question at the commander - a young, good-looking Israeli. 'You're not really going to shoot those....' 'FUCK OFF'. It's a curt acid command. 'Oh right, so, tell me, how many kids have you killed in your service?' His response was a round of ear-searing rapid fire at the scattering kids. He put the gun down, keeping his gaze trained straight ahead, and said '27'.

A demonstration is organised by ISM volunteers and local block residents against the checkpoint. The idea is to reclaim the area in front of the flats and have children play games, draw posters and generally have a laugh as an act of resistance to the occupation. It's a way of showing kids that there are alternative forms of resistance to the usual stone-chucking ritual, and it's good to flummox the soldiers. The ones on shift today are the same lot which policed our last kids' demo to the occupied house. As kids tried to gather for the demo outside before we all came up they were shooting at them. Only yesterday they were firing intimidation shots at us. Before we even start the tank's barrel is trained squarely at us. Around 100 kids turn up, tentatively at first, holding the placards we drew together yesterday. They chant at the soldiers. They are all over the shop but they're enjoying their chance to vent their frustration, as are the adults present. Demonstrations here are pretty much non-existent - how do you collectively protest against a military curfew? The presence of internationals is one of the only ways collective acts of civil disobedience can take place. The soldiers have orders not to shoot us. Palestinian civilians, yes. Internationals, no. Bad PR.

Following a bout of shouting and general fist-shaking, we have a drawing and painting session and a plastic sack race. The kids hop, leap and wriggle in white plastic sacks, whipping up dust and getting breathless with exertion. We join in too. Everybody is clapping and laughing and the atmosphere is festive. Neighbours bring us out trays laden with tiny china cups of Arabic coffee and glasses of sweet tea - it's surreal, sipping tea at an impromptu kids' sports day amidst swirling clouds of grey dust, under the gun barrel gaze of a forbidding Israeli tank, and soldiers standing around armed to the hilt. But we're having a laugh…

119

www.mahjoob.com

Baha

"Baha is an energetic, vibrant local kid, 14 years-old, with twinkly green eyes, all 'mush mushkele - No Problems', and as capable as an adult, looking after international activists staying in the old city by doubling up as guide and mediator between hostile kids and us. He takes time out to explain who we are and why we're in their town when our governments are funding the occupation.

We go out on the tank-hunt. Baha in tow. It's the usual. The APC and tank out on curfew patrol. We stay back at a street corner on our way into the old city, a warren of sandy big-rocked houses, archways, and piles of rubble (bulldozed ex-homes, factories, workshops). The April attack saw 25,000 soldiers, approx. 400 tanks, and multiple apache rocket-fire hit the city and surrounding camps. The 4th strongest army on the planet doesn't fuck about when it goes in for the kill. 87 Nablus residents were slaughtered within 4 days. Over 200 people were used as human shields.

Back to the present...The APC soldier gets on his phone. Nablus was declared a closed military zone about an hour ago. We could be nicked and dumped in Tel Aviv or deported. Whatever. We stay put. Kids pelt the APC with stones, a couple, chucked over from behind the safety of a wall, clop the soldier on the top. He responds with a round of live ammo. A family wants to cross the road, right in front of the tank's line of fire. They're in a hurry and looking fraught, mother father, and four kids. Baha helps them across. We rush up to be in front of him and them at once. Baha's brave, just goes straight across, head-on, by their sides, defiant. Baha knows the city like the back of his hand. In the aftermath of the April incursion he was one of the most plucky volunteers, clearing rubble, helping the sick.

We make our way down the street to where we expect the APC and Tank to be but it seems like they've rumbled off. Just curfew enforcement we think. No big deal. Later we'll find out that it's illegal for the Israel Army to use anything stronger than teargas to enforce curfew. Definitely not live ammo. They do what they want anyway though. The entire occupation is illegal under the Oslo Accords, The Geneva Convention, multiple United Nations directives etc

We get a call... the tank and APC are outside. We decide to just check out what they're doing. As we make our way down the road we hear the sound of the two vehicles whurring towards us. It's blazing hot. The street is clear at this point. Nothing is being thrown. I see the soldier in the APC take aim. I think it's with his M16 but it could be the mounted gun. I'm not afraid. Guns are constantly being pointed at Palestinians in the territories - at their backs, in their faces, up at their windows, from the middle of the street, from the mountains. A shot rings out, whizzes straight past me. I feel the air rush and duck down instinctively. 'FUCK that was so close', I say, turning round. 'is...Oh my God.' Baha is lying on his back in the porchway of a closed shop. Blood is blooming from the right side of his chest. His eyes are bulged back in shock. A Palestinian man is instantly above him, pumping his chest with short sharp thrusts of his crossed hands. Blood is welling up in Baha's mouth, flowing freely, it streams fast from his nose, his ear. 'Turn his head, turn his head, he's going to choke' I yell. It's too late though. We all know...

The examining doctor at El Ethad Hospital said that the massive internal damage caused by the "dumdum" bullet was consistent with an intentional kill. Dumdum's explode and fragment on impact causing maximum multiple injuries.

The Israeli army initially stated that Baha was carrying a bomb at the time of his assassination. This is not true. The statement then changed to accuse Baha of carrying a molotov cocktail. This was supposed to have exploded in his hand. Setting him on fire and killing him. 'It was his fault'. This is what the IDF said about the 17 year old boy they shot in the head in Balata the night before. He died when the ambulance carrying him was refused entry through a checkpoint to the hospital. They said he killed himself, shot himself. This a common statement released after the Army murders people here. All armies and police do it. Blame and demonise the victim. Here, it's because 'they're terrorists'. 328 children have been murdered by the Israeli army or armed settlers since September 2000."

Since the beginning of the second Intifada, people having been going to Palestine under the banner of the International Solidarity Movement (ISM). The ISM provide human shields against Israeli military crimes, break curfews to provide food and medical supplies, protest against Israeli tank blockades, and dismantle checkpoints and roadblocks – and this October they are looking for people to help pick olives.

In the past two years hundreds of thousands of Palestinian trees have been bulldozed, uprooted or set ablaze by Israeli soldiers and settlers - 200,000 of these olive trees. As the ISM point out "Olive trees are a symbol of the life of the Palestinian, and their destruction by Israeli forces is an attempt to de-root the Palestinians from their land. The economic impact of Israeli policies on the olive sector has been massive - over 10 million dollars lost to damage in the past two years, and millions more due to Israel's barring farmers from their land. And these policies are designed to have impact not just now, but for years to come - olive trees produce for generations. This year we are calling on you to join us for the olive harvest in Palestine."

To get involved 07817 554 814
www.ism-london.org/

TRIP OUT!

There's a day of action against immigration detention and deportation and racist border controls at 10am, 19th October outside Dover Immigration detention centre, The Citadel,Western Heights, Dover. Following on from the demo some of the protesters are crossing over the channel to the Sangatte detention centre to show solidarity with refugees there. Bring yer passport if you want to go. "The closure of Sangatte and the widespread incarceration of innocent people, men,women and children in prisons are actions of politicians that do not have respect for human life. It is up to us to ensure that refugees are given a voice until they have a chance to recover enough to tell us their stories themselves and to attempt to ensure they are treated with as much respect or dignity as we would hope for." noborder.org 07789-961744

ON THE CASE

Oil giant Unocal could be sued for forced labour, rape, and murder committed by Burmese soldiers who guarded a Unocal gas pipeline project. Because according to a US federal appeals court. "Unocal knew the acts of violence would probably be committed, it became liable as an aider and abettor''. Cases are also pending against Royal Dutch Shell, Texaco and ExxonMobil for various abuses by security forces "defending" their installations. www.burmadaily.com

*Burma Campaign UK has forced Premier Oil UK out of Burma after producing evidence that investors in the company were breaking UK and US sanctions. For more info 020 7272 3559 www.burmacampaign.org.uk.

DROP OUTS

Seems like while Bush and his cronies are foaming at the mouth waiting to create new wars they were unwilling to go down that road and put their own precious lives at risk. An independent newspaper in the US has published a list of 'Chickenhawks', high ranking politicians and other public figures who trumpet on about war and 'fighting for freedom' but were unwilling to get their own hands dirty. Their excuses to avoid service range from bad knees, to skin problems and our personal favourite 'anal cysts'. Does that mean that when he's trying to give the world a whole new war 'Dubya' is just talking out of his arse? See the whole list at www.nhgazette.com/chickenhawks.html

SKIN-UP!

Patients at Salisbury hospital are being asked to do their bit for the war effort by consenting to donate their "surplus skin" after surgery, to the notorious Porton Down "defence" research establishment in Wiltshire. Early last year the hospital was forced to stop supplying skin to Porton Down after it was revealed that it was being sold without patients knowledge. The Defence Evaluation and Research Agency (DERA) has now requested that the supplies are reinstated for their essential research into "defences against chemical warfare agents", the patients consent though will now be required.

The highly secretive Porton Down establishment has carried out the world's longest-running programme of chemical and biological experiments on humans and animals. Officials have always claimed that the tests are for purely defensive purposes - cos we is the nice guys - honest!.

...and finally...

Having given up on the ability of fast food, Mickey Mouse, and countless CIA-sponsored dictatorships to win them global love, the US has now decided to try and win world popularity the good old-fashioned way—by launching a multi-million dollar public relations campaign. According to senior white-house officials, the propaganda, er, public relations effort will be supervised by the newly formed, "Office of Global Communications," yet another shadowy Washington organisation set to ram the stars and stripes down everyone's throat.

Among the many pet projects the Office of GC will oversee—various pro-American radio stations throughout the Arab world, as well as the "American Room" concept, "corners of Americana established in existing local libraries or other cultural sites worldwide." Yippee!! Just what the world needs, more American cultural imperialism!!

Inspired by the events of 9/11, the Office of GC will attempt to get to the bottom of the mystifying question posed by George Dub'ya after the attacks, "Why do they hate us?" Well gee George, let's think about it for half a second… Could waging maniacal world war on anyone who doesn't bow down to you have anything to do with it?? Or could it be the last 60 years of terrorism and atrocity known as American foreign policy*….hmmm…. In a quote too good for us to have made up, Charlotte Beers, the advertising agency executive Bush appointed last year to the State Department's top public diplomacy job, said that America needed to "influence the attitudes of foreign audiences toward our country." Beers has pledged that all U.S. diplomats will receive more extensive training in the American "message" of democracy, personal freedom and free markets and learn how to spread it through local societies. Guess those bombs just don't speak loudly enough...

* see the last issue of SchNEWS for a variety of examples

Disclaimer

SchNEWS warns all readers it's Us or U.S. Honest.

FAST RELIEF FROM AUTHORITY

ANARCHISM 2002

EFFECTIVE AGAINST ALL FORMS OF DOMINATION

21ST ANNUAL ANARCHIST BOOKFAIR

Saturday 19th October 10am - 7pm Camden Centre, Euston Rd, London WC1 Nearest tube Kings Cross www.anarchistbookfair.org

Subscribe!

Keep SchNEWS FREE! Send 1st Class stamps (e.g. 10 for next 9 issues) or donations (payable to Justice?) Ask for "Originals" if you can make copies. Post *free* to all prisoners. SchNEWS, c/o on-the-fiddle, P.O. Box 2600, Brighton, East Sussex, BN2 0EF.
Tel/Autofax +44 (0)1273 685913 *Email* schnews@brighton.co.uk *Download a* **PDF** *of this issue or subscribe at* **www.schnews.org.uk**

There aren't many people who have worked as hard as Milan Rai, author of *War Plan Iraq*, to dig us out of the bullshit we've been buried in about the 'war on terror'. Active in Voices in the Wilderness, Justice Not Vengeance, and ARROW (Active Resistance to the Roots of War) his research has systematically cut through the lies about weapons of mass destruction, regime change, and democracy sent down the pipeline to justify the latest war in Iraq. SchNEWS caught up with him in April - a few days after US troops entered Baghdad - to talk about oil, uprisings, US power in Iraq, 'Vietnam Syndrome', and the anti-war movement in the West.

Sch: *Do you think that this war is the beginning of something new in the way that the US plans to maintain its global dominance, in the way that it disciplines weaker countries?*

Rai: Typically – and I think rightly – people divide US foreign policy since the Second World War into two phases; and now we're in a third phase. There's the phase up until the early 1970s, where you have a fairly free use of military power. Then you have the post-Vietnam period, where you have what they called the Vietnam Syndrome [massive anti-war feeling amongst the US population, which for decades after the war made it nearly impossible for the government to send troops into battle]. This forced the US to move much more clearly towards a 'proxy' system of controlling the world, [where the US armed and trained obedient states and used them to provide a military threat to anyone who threatened US interests in the region]. In the Gulf [at the time] it was Israel and Iran, 'the two guardians of the gulf', or whatever.

Now, Bush is hoping we're in phase 3: the post-Vietnam Syndrome era. So what the Vietnam Syndrome is, or was, is a crucial issue. From the point of view of US elites, it's what one neo-conservative called 'a sickly inhibition against the use of force'. That's why you call it a syndrome, because it's a disease, it's a bad thing. From the point of view of most of the world, and probably most of the US people as well, it's - as Noam Chomsky said - 'basically an aversion to massacring and slaughtering other people'. Reagan thought that the Vietnam Syndrome was cured by the Soviet Union's invasion of Afghanistan [in 1979]. That's why he was happy to start making noises about military action in Central America, [but this led to] a huge mobilisation in the US, which turned into the Central America solidarity movement, so they couldn't have a direct military intervention there.

What President Bush and the US political elite are thinking now is that September 11th has definitely cured the patient, and now the US can do stuff that it would have liked to have done years ago, decades ago, but couldn't because of public opinion, and the level of mobilisation which it could expect from the US public. So that's why this stuff is happening now, because they think that a traumatised US public is willing to, if not actively support, at least accept all kinds of brutality in the name of anti-terrorism which they wouldn't have done before the Twin Towers went down.

Sch: *At the moment people are saying that the US may even be planning to run Iraq as an old-fashioned colony. Do you think this is a possibility?*

Rai: In December 1989 the US invaded Panama, set up a puppet regime, and left. It still had its big base there, but it didn't have an official in each ministry or whatever. I think that we're seeing the same pattern now, which is why in War Plan Iraq I suggested that what the US was intending for Iraq should be called 'regime stabilisation and leadership change', rather than 'regime change'. I think the same goal, of basically keeping the same political and military establishment but changing the inner circle at the top, was the goal in 1991 and it was the goal this year. In 1991 they managed to stabilise the regime, by helping to destroy the rebellions, by authorising the flight of helicopter gunships, by refusing to hand over weapons which they'd captured from the Iraqi military to the rebels, and so on. So they achieved regime stabilisation but they didn't achieve leadership change.

In 2003 they achieved leadership change, because that's pretty much happened, but they fell down heavily on regime stabilisation. They were desperately hoping that – [with] the military build-up, all the threats about 'shock and awe', and all the talk about 'exile options' for Hussein and his family – they would be able to create a coup without firing a shot. [The US announcing before the war] that Saddam Hussein and his senior leadership should go into exile made it very clear that the people who they objected to in the regime [were] a very small group, and that the rest of the regime was basically going to be given immunity. And I think that both the US and Britain were deeply disappointed that they had to go to war.

What's happened is, because there wasn't a coup, and because the Iraqi forces didn't surrender en masse as [the US and Britain] were desperately hoping they would, they had to destroy, or disperse, the military forces who they wanted to hand power to, like the Republican Guard. The Republican Guard has been the backbone of the regime, and they were really hoping that the Republican Guard would remain an organised military unit, who would surrender and who they would then hand power to. There'd be some kind of integration of civilian exiles, [military] exiles, and Generals who were in power, some kind of pick-and-mix thing. But because the Iraqis didn't go to the script, they had to kill a lot of the people who they were going to put in power.

Why did they invade with so few soldiers, when they knew that if they won they'd be in charge of a whole country? Iraqis watching all the looting that's happening now are saying that these guys are terrible planners. No, they're not terrible planners: the plan was 'we'll hand it over to the military, we'll hand it over to the police, we'll hand it over to our troops – the Baathist regime'. They invaded with a small force, but they were expecting that at the end of the war they would be in charge of an enormous military machine, because there would be a continuation of the regime.

So, what's going to happen now? My guess is that they'll put something together out of the remains of the regime, but they're not going to be able to get out as fast as they would have liked to. So they're saying they might be in there for a year. I think they're desperately hoping that won't be the case, I think they're hoping they can put something together out of the military, out of the police, and get out of there faster. I don't think they want to have US officials or US officers in all the ministries for a moment longer then they have to. [They're hoping] it'll be like Saudi Arabia. Saudi Arabia's a dictatorship, [it's] run by these guys who wear funny clothes and things on their heads, but they've been to Harvard, they know how to take orders, and they know how things are supposed to run. In Iraq, as soon as they can get the personnel together, they'll just hand it all over; that's the plan, if it can possibly be done. As with everything to do with this war, the schedule is out, but I think it's entirely realistic for them to expect to be out of Iraq within a year.

Sch: *So you think they will be able to put together some kind of military/political structure that will be capable of putting down looting and uprisings and maintaining control?*

Rai: I think they can put something together. But, because the military/political structure is so weakened [by the war], the big question is 'what happens if there is a real nationalist uprising?' What if large parts of the general population have real uprisings and they say 'Yes, we want liberation, US, US puppets and Baathist torturers, get the hell out of our country'? In 1991 what we saw [when popular uprisings began against Hussein's regime] was the US tacitly enabling the Baathist repressive system to put down the rebellions. If there are rebellions again (and, at this point, I'd say it's unlikely but it's possible) we might see the US not tacitly enabling, but actually directing, arming and empowering the remains of the Baathist repressive system in putting them down, and that'll be a very ugly sight. It'll be dressed up in all sorts of ways, like 'we're stopping Iranian revolutionaries...'

Sch: *Or 'terrorists'...*

Rai: ... 'terrorists', and stuff like that.

Given that, I would guess, the US would have to

'Airlifting in the new regime'

fight that with their hands tied behind their backs because of all the sensitivities around it. I think if it did happen sometime this year it's not at all clear that the remains of the Baathist system would survive that, because they've had a lot of damage done to them and they're in a pretty demoralised state. I think that's the big danger for the US. I think they can put something together, but if that rickety system is challenged, seriously, then they've got lots of problems.

What they've got to do is they've got to make sure they bring enough of the opposition inside, they co-opt enough of the opposition, so that there isn't a real, strong, unified challenge to their designs for Iraq. And I think they've got a good chance of doing that, especially with the lifting of economic sanctions. With the lifting of sanctions everyone's going to be saying 'how can I earn a living for my family?' that's going to be the number one priority for everybody in Iraq. I think that's going to be their main help in diffusing political challenges.

Sch: *There's been a lot of talk about the US's obvious need to have obedient leaders in the Middle East, but less about the 'problem' of disobedient populations. So could you go back and explain a bit more about the uprisings that happened in Iraq in 1991, during the first Gulf War: where did they come from and when did they happen?*

Rai: OK, in terms of the timing, the uprisings happened after Iraq had basically been driven out of Kuwait. A large part of [the people involved were] Iraqi conscripts, coming back into Iraq extremely fed up with the whole fiasco, because what was the point of all of their friends getting killed? There turned out to be no point at all, they didn't even really fight. That was one major spark for the whole thing in the south [where] there was something of a spontaneous uprising. A strong element of the Shia population became involved in that, because they're 60% of the population but they've been excluded from political and economic power since the beginning of the Iraqi state, so they have a lot of grievances. In the north, the Kurds had been organising for some kind of uprising, so once things started in the south they launched their own semi-organised thing but, again, events outran the 'organisers' there.

Fourteen of the eighteen governorates, or counties,

of Iraq fell to the rebels. It was just the heartland, Baghdad and Tikrit basically, that were still under government control. So the regime was hanging by a thread.

Sch: *And what was America's response?*

Rai: One of the things which triggered the uprisings was President Bush Senior saying that 'the Iraqi people and the Iraqi army should make their leader stand aside'. Now, according to one account Bush had just been going to say 'it's up to the Iraqi military to make their leader stand aside' but he chucked in the bit about 'the Iraqi people' as a populist touch. Whatever its origins, this was taken by a lot of the people of Iraq as a signal that if they rose up they would be backed to the hilt by the government who had just inflicted this humiliating defeat on Saddam Hussein. So they rose up, they took most of the country and, just before the uprisings really got going, the US civilian leadership took the decision to let the Republican Guard survive the war.

A large part of the Republican Guard had been boxed in by the US military and were about to be destroyed, and the war was called to an end hours before that final onslaught. They were released, they were allowed to slip away [and] help put down the uprisings. The US military allowed Iraq to fly helicopter gunships and watched as they cut down the rebels and columns of refugees. They refused to release weapons which were captured from the Iraqi military: you see, sometimes the rebels were the soldiers from the barracks, they were going back to their own barracks and saying can we have our weapons, we want to fight the regime. The US said no.

So the rebellion was crushed, brutally, and the US played a very important role in that. If they hadn't allowed the gunships to fly, if they'd withdrawn and let the rebels get their hands on weapons, then probably the regime would have gone down. But the US didn't want that to happen, the US wanted there to be a military coup and a continuation of the regime. The National Security Advisor at the time, Brent Scowcroft, said very candidly afterwards in a US TV interview that he regretted the fact that the uprisings took place because he'd looked forward to a military government. But because the uprisings took place the Iraqi military elite realised they had to hang together, because if they started turning on each other they'd all go down.

Sch: *Can you explain the difference between a war for access to oil and a war to control the flow of profits that come from oil?*

Rai: If the US just wanted to get as much Iraqi oil out of Iraq as possible, and on to the world market so that [the US] could buy it, the easiest way to do that would be to lift the economic sanctions, which I guess is going to happen pretty soon. But the US isn't dependent on Middle Eastern oil, it's mainly dependent on Venezuela and Latin America. It's not a question of the US needing a physical supply of oil so that millions of cars can continue to roam around on the freeways; and if that were the case, then with

serious energy-saving measures, investment in the energy industries, changes in public transportation, whatever, they could probably deal with a lot of those problems, they could probably [get rid of] the need for Middle Eastern oil altogether.

That's not the issue. The issue is, firstly, that US-based oil companies have to secure a 'proper' share of the profits flowing from oil, and, secondly, that the profits from oil that are garnered by Middle Eastern states have to be put in the right places.

The first count is pretty straightforward: I mean everyone's presuming that the oil resources of Iraq are going to be largely handed over to US and perhaps British-based oil companies, and they're going to have these incredibly favourable production-sharing agreements, in which the rest of the world is left behind, because of their kind of colonial relationship. They're probably going to have these incredibly favourable deals, there'll be huge profits from that. That's pretty straightforward.

The other thing you need to do is to make sure that whatever revenues the oil producing state gets [are] used in the 'correct' way, i.e. the problem with Iraq under the Baathist regime [was that], despite their appalling record on human rights and civil rights, the Baathists actually invested their oil wealth in the social fabric of the country. That's why they had one of the best health sectors in the Middle East, they had one of the best education systems in the world – they won literacy prizes, and so on. That's why child mortality declined in a straight line from 1960 to 1990. There was a real investment in the social fabric of Iraq and that's how they legitimised their rule. That kind of stuff is wrong, that's the wrong priorities. The right priorities [involve] that money [being turned] into profits for western companies, and… [being] used to prop up western financial markets. What they have to do is 'recycle' petrodollars or petrosterling [i.e. western currency that is paid to oil-producing states].

There are two basic routes for doing that. One is for [western countries to] sell stuff to oil producers. Preferably it's high technology, because there's lots of profit there, it's rapidly obsolescing so you have to keep selling more and more of it, and also economically it's wasteful, so they won't actually start producing any competitive goods for you. The ideal thing is weapons, which fit all those criteria. You want a country which will buy a whole lot of weapons, and keep buying them in a steady stream. The other thing that you want to do is… get them to invest their treasuries in western financial markets. We can see this discussed very candidly by Foreign Secretary Selwyn Lloyd in 1957 in Britain: he [said] that one of Britain's main interests in relation to Kuwait [was] to get them to invest their money in the British stock market, because Britain's economy [was failing and it needed that] kind of support. The US economy isn't doing great [at the moment]: it relies heavily on investments from the rest of the world in order to keep afloat. So you have to get these countries to do that as well.

So that's the distinction between the flow of oil – which is energy in liquid form – and the flow of profits – which is power. That [power] is derived from oil sales, but it's a very different stream and that's the crucial stream really. The oil itself, the price of oil, these are secondary matters.

Sch: *Finally I wanted to ask you about the anti-war movement in this country. We're now looking at a situation where the war is becoming an occupation, and it's possible that the US/Britain now have the political strength that they need to use this attack as a model for other countries, like Syria or Iran. In this situation, what do you hope will happen to the anti-war movement: where do you think all that energy and feeling should be channelled?*

Rai: Firstly, because I'm sure that most people in the anti-war movement are feeling extremely depressed and unhappy about the way things have gone, that's my guess, I think it's really important for us to realise how close we came to getting Britain out of this war. On the 12th of March, when Rumsfeld made his remark about 'we can go to war without Britain', he made [it] because at that moment, in the Ministry of Defence, they were drawing up contingency plans for pulling Britain out of the invasion force and relegating them to peacekeeping and stuff like that after the war. It's now said that when Tony Blair went to the House of Commons for the final vote he had those plans in his back pocket: [it all depended] on how the vote went that night.

I haven't heard of an anti-war movement in the western world doing that [before]: before a war is started, forcing the government which is about to launch the war to draw-up contingency plans and to seriously consider pulling out its major foreign policy commitment of the decade. That's how close we came. There were all sorts of forces that went into that: the fracturing of the establishment; the problems in terms of legality; the way that the rest of the world denied the US and Britain the second resolution which would have been some kind of fig leaf of legitimacy... all sorts of factors, but one of the big factors was the anti-war movement in this country combined with the anti-war movements around the world.

We came incredibly close to pulling Britain out of this, and really it came down to the fact that a whole load of Labour MPs preferred to sacrifice the people of Iraq rather than sacrifice Tony Blair. That's what it came down to in the end, but it needn't have been that way: in Turkey the Turkish parliamentarians were under such enormous pressure that they didn't give way in their major turning-point vote. If we'd put our [government] under a similar amount of pressure, things could have been different. I think that's a sad, but accurate judgement about it.

What happens now? Well, at the core of the movement is a fear about what kind of world it's going to be for us to live in if there's this unchecked, unilateral US vandalism and rampage. So there's a fear about the US as a rogue state and there's also compassion and concern for the people who could get trampled underneath in other countries. I think that if the anti-war movement is going to grow, they will continue to be at the heart of the… movement. So exposing the claims about liberation, exposing the claims about WMDs being the core issue, these will be very important things for the movement to continue doing. However, there will also be elements of the movement which are trying to deepen people's understanding of the deeper issues which have brought us into this and what this war is all about. And I think that's a really important part of it. Educating people about the roots of this kind of imperialism, about why the US and Britain have this pattern of assault on other countries. And of course that leads very quickly into questions about globalisation and about corporate rule and so on and I think that's all a very important part of the agenda for one element within the movement.

I think that movements to develop and build resistance and civil disobedience to future assaults are going to be really important. We should be aiming to revive the movement, to make the movement grow, and we should be making it so the natural destination for people, and I'm quoting something Michael Albert said in Znotes, is to grow in their understanding and their militancy and that they're heading towards supporting, being closely involved in, or taking part in non-violent civil disobedience against these kinds of assaults. I think that's a natural way for things to develop.

The ARROW anti-war briefings are available on the Justice Not Vengeance website, www.j-n-v.org

September 28th
"Biggest peace protest in a generation in London"
- UK Indymedia.

28th Sept: In a powerful turnout of the opposition to the proposals for war on Iraq, the anti-war demo organised by the Stop The War Coalition and the Muslim Association of Britain, and supported by CND attracted around 400,000 demonstrators. The numbers at least equalled the numbers on the right-wing Countryside Alliance march a week earlier, when (probably for the first time in history) police and organisers agreed on the same number of 'disaffected rural protesters' which included members of the Tory party, aristocracy and the BNP. That march was prepared for two years and cost 2 million pounds. Police had yesterday informed City of London Security that they were expecting 30-40,000 people on today's anti-war march, but by the afternoon had counted 'more than 150,000 people', adding there had been two arrests for minor public order offences.
- uk.indymedia.org

"Have you got the time officer?"

Pic Jeff Brewster www.graphicattack.org.uk

I DON'T MIND A BIT OF BLOOD SPORTS

SchNEWS

weekly

www.schnews.org.uk

Friday 4th October 2002   **Free/Donation**   **Issue 375**

ACRES AND PAIN

Two large marches in a week sounds like a good thing - politics out on the street where it belongs. But according to most of the media, making sure foxes die is more important than making sure innocent Iraqi civilians don't.

It was a tale of two very contrasting marches: The Countryside Alliance's 'Liberty and Livelihood' march attracted mass media hype for the three weeks leading up to it and plenty after it, while the Stop The War demo was draped with a raft of 'conservative' estimates of numbers in the papers – think of the police estimate and halve it. The Stop The War march brought together a 400,000 strong crowd - the most racially diverse group SchNEWS has ever seen on a demo - with the clear message that Iraq must not be bombed, and supporting the related issue of ending Israel's occupation of Palestine. The Countryside Alliance could hardly claim the same clarity of purpose. They were out on the streets for… er apart from being pro-fox hunting what the fox were they on about?

The supposed Liberty and Livelihood message was that the Countryside Alliance are the guardians of the misunderstood rural way of life championing 'country ways', one of which just so happens to be killing for fun… but hey, they've been doing it for ages so doesn't that make it a minority right? The Alliance claim to be finding time to fight just about every rural issue that springs to mind, whether it be broadband internet access for rural poor, questioning pricing practices of supermarkets or campaigning for the provision of public services throughout our green and pleasant land.

The truth is far more sinister. The Countryside Alliance does little more than pay lip-service to major countryside issues by creating a broad base of touchy-feely policies muddying rural issues with the political dead dog that is bloodsports.

Last year the Countryside Alliance spent three million pounds on their pro-bloodsports campaign, compared to £200,000 on all other campaigns. Yet the CA policy statement only mentions the hunting issue once – why? What do the CA have to hide, other than the fact that they know that the media war surrounding the hunting issue is all but lost, that the great British public will never come to accept the hunting of wild animals and that the only way to stop the ban is through the back door? Under such circumstances it should come as no surprise that the CA are keen to wrap themselves in just about any rural flag they can lay their hands on, whether it be protecting rural post offices or fighting modern threats to the tweed industry.

It's when the Countryside Alliance claim to represent *all* country folk - including the small farmers and rural labourers - that the smell of manure really wafts in. How can the CA justify putting so much into fighting to protect the bloodlust of an elite landed gentry with huge arable estates funded by massive subsidies? According to ActionAid's *Farmgate report: the developing impact of agricultural subsidies,*

80% of subsidies are swallowed up by 20% of the richest 'farmers'. Meanwhile the remaining majority are being driven against the wall as they try to cope with inadequate subsidies and farm gate prices lower than those of production.

RURAL WARRIOR

As Charles Secrett of Friends of the Earth, put it: "the Countryside Alliance spends way too much time worrying about hunting, and not nearly enough working on the major threats to rural life… Unless there is a new system of sustainable food production, the next Countryside March may find there are very few farmers left to mobilise."

Well what are the real issues facing country folk on a daily basis? The right to hunt foxes? Spokesman for the foxes, Basil Brush, said "Not in

Acres and Pain cont...

my back yard old boy! Boom boom." Brendan Boal recently spent nine days interviewing small farmers in Devon and Dorset, who voiced concerns over issues as diverse as low milk prices, abusive business practices of supermarkets and the impact of rich urban 'incomers' buying up their 'weekend country retreats' and destroying the social structure of rural communities. When asked about the significance of the Countryside Alliance, however, Brendan said that the overwhelming response was very much to the effect: "they're nothing to do with the likes of us, the whole thing is for... hunting people". While Brendon and his team travelled from farm to farm (sustainably by bicycle you'll be pleased to know) he observed that "what was noticeable on our travels was the preponderance of Alliance placards outside of expensive homes that were clearly no longer working farms. In short, the very incomers [that] farmers feel alienated from are the ones that are providing a large measure of support for the CA".

Last week some country folk from the Wye Valley told SchNEWS about the plight of rural and farm labourers – those who have worked on the land over generations but are not farm owners - who are in fact the majority of rural folk. "The large scale argo-businesses, and the massive supermarket food distribution stitch up crushs small farms who can't compete with the economies of scale, and the intense mechanisation takes away many rural jobs." "We know of rural workers who were threatened with the sack if they didn't come down for the march last week". A MORI poll at the march found that 73% of marchers thought that hunting should not be the key concern of the Countryside Alliance.

Next week half a million foxes are marching to Hyde Park to hear Basil Brush talk about the ban on chicken hunting, but apparently most foxes are more worried about the threat of hunting. Boom boom.

Recommended reading

'The rich at Play: Fox hunting, land ownership and the countryside alliance' by RPM 07967 886257 www.red-star-research.org.uk
'The World is Not For Sale: farmers against junk food' by Jose Bove and Francois Dufour. (Verso 2001)
'Farmgate: The developmental impact of agricultural subsidies' compiled by ActionAid. 0207 561 7614 www.actionaid.org

No Dutch Luck!

On Thursday (3rd Oct), Colin Davies, owner of The Dutch Experience Café in Stockport was sentenced to three years in prison at Manchester's Minshull Street Crown Court, after being found guilty on all eight of the charges he was facing. The heaviest sentences were for the November 20th offences because he'd carried on opening the café after the September busts. Colin Davies "persistently flouted the law" by being involved with cannabis even while he was on bail for other drug-related offences, even though he uses it a pain killer for back injuries he sustained in a work accident in 1995.

There may be an appeal, but in the meantime, when we know which prison Colin is going to end up in we will give details for letters of support. After already doing 9 months on remand, he will have another 9 to still do. Colin's dad was also in court to face charges of perjury.

Just to rub it in, that afternoon The Dutch Experience Café was raided by hoards of police, including the 'Special Colin Squad', who spent the afternoon preventing the café from re-opening. www.dutchexperience.org

---

Fight War, Not Wars

The Stop The War Coalition has called for a day of action on the 31st October to oppose the possibility of full-scale war on Iraq. They have suggested occupations, teach-ins and blockades as suitable actions for the day.

A London-based group of activists have called for help organising a series of proposed actions on the day including an anti-war themed Critical Mass, a tour of London's military offices, and a set of moving blockades. Until they get more help with organisation these suggestions will remain merely ideas, so if you've got any time or ideas to contribute get in touch. http://www.cm-london.cjb.net

* There's lots of other anti-war events planned for this month, including a 'stop 'star wars' and stop the bombing of Iraq' demonstration at US spy-base Menwith Hill, North Yorkshire, on 12th October 12noon-4pm, organised by the Campaign for the Accountability of American Bases 01943 466405 www.caab.org.uk. On the same day there's a Stop the War Teach-in at London's SOAS University: a day of lectures, discussion, debates and film covering all aspects of Bush and Blair's "War on Terror". In the Main Building from 11am-7pm www.soasstopwar.org/events.htm#disc

* For full listings of regular anti-war activities check out www.justicenotvengance.org

SchNEWS in brief

Last chance to hear Native American activist **Rod Coronado**'s perspective on ecological direct action next Thursday (10) at the Friends Meeting House, Hill St., (off Corporation St. in the city centre) Coventry. ** This Sunday (6) there's a Leeds **Underground Film Festival**- Another World is Possible running from 1-9 pm @ City Art Gallery, The Headrow, Leeds, LS1. Films include 'Argentina In Revolt,' 'Gaza Strip' and 'Another World Is Possible' made by 33 Italian Directors about G8 summit in Genoa. Admission free. www.leedsundergroundfilm.org.uk ** There's a national demo this Saturday (5) in support of the **Hackney Library strike** – meet 12 noon, Hackney Town Hall. The bankrupt Labour led council is currently recruiting scabs to break the 10-month-old strike. 0207 8356 8710 unilibs@yahoo.com ** An Orwellian political satire book **'Hard Choices'** by Brighton writer Carol Hayman is now on the web after being dropped by publishers Times-Warner because it was too close to the bone post 9-11. Read it at www.hardchoices.co.uk ** A new email list has been set up to discuss **Solstice celebrations** "that include the possibility of amplified music in the Wiltshire area and near Stonehenge if at all possible!" http://groups.yahoo.com/group/stonehengeentertaimentsdiscussion ** Party this weekend at **Squatgate Park**, 167 London Road, Brighton 12noon to 9pm – bring your own CD's and vinyl ** And don't forget pre **SchNEWS 8th birthday benefit night** upstairs at the Albert Pub, Trafalgar St on October 14th with L.S.D.S, Miss CMC & MAMA, Judge Trev, Jelly & more. ** **RIP Martin Callaghan**, much loved Liverpool activist - who once spent a year in a tree-house at the M65 Stanworth Valley road protest, and later worked on festivals, allotments and community direct action with Greenloops.

"OK I admit it! I am a member of the IMF!!!"

Polish Top TEN

Missed out on Newbury? Well get over to Poland where the country is having a huge road building programme inflicted upon it – and the environmental and social costs of being in 'Europe' mount up. The rail system which served the country for years is being starved of funds, and the tentacles of TEN are extending eastward. TEN – the Trans Europe Network – is the world's biggest transport project pushed by the transport and oil industry to help the movement of consumer goods across Europe, and is currently reaching the new frontiers of countries soon to join the EU like Poland. The Poles are bringing in new legislation which will enable roads to be built without environmental impact studies and force people in their paths to sell at a price offered to them. As service stations, concrete ramps and truck parks spew forth over Poland, the average Pole had better consider getting a car and ditching public transport if they want to be like us in the EU club. So - if you're up for a bit of digger diving... pbielski@ore.most.org.pl www.aseed.net

* Bialowieza Forest, Poland – Europe's last primeval forest of high bio-diverstiy including bison, wolf, lynx, and much more is under threat from logging. www.zb.eco.pl/gb/3/workshop.htm

Inside SchNEWS

On 4th September, anarchist George Karakasian was sentenced by a Cyprus court to 7 months in prison for 'assaulting a police officer' at a demo outside the Israeli ambassador's home. George also received a fine for 'possession of an explosive device': an old bullet found when his home was raided following the demo.

The charge of 'causing serious physical injury to a police officer' was incurred by no more than a grasp at the cop's hat; by contrast, George was then dragged inside the ambassador's home and beaten by five state riotcops, whilst they shouted 'fuck your anarchy' at him. After being hospitalised with his injuries, he discovered when he attempted to pick up his case notes that his medical records had mysteriously 'disappeared'. Send letters of support to George to Leukosia, Central Prison of Cyprus, Wing 2B 6523, Nicosia, Cyprus.

* Did anyone see Philip Paden, get arrested in Wardour Street at 8.50pm during this years Mayday demonstrations? He's charged with affray and accused of using a plastic dustbin lid to hit police officer's shields. Philip was wearing a white paper suit, white arm guard and holding a pink plastic dustbin lid. If you can help call his solicitor Andrew Katzen 0208 986 8336.

Lancaster Bombers

Last Friday more than a hundred protesters on skateboards, bikes and feet reclaimed the streets in protest against plans that will destroy parts of Lancaster (pic above). Chelverton, a mega construction company backed by Carillion (formerly known as Tarmac), and Richardson Developments are planning to rip the soul out of Lancaster by building a 63,000 square feet super-store, dozens of "large-scale" retail units and a major new road on land between the tranquil Lancaster canal and the city centre. According to the council's own studies this would close down local traders in the city centre as well as in neighbouring Morecambe, never mind more traffic, noise and pollution. The plans also threaten the Homeless Action Centre, the Polish Centre and the Musician's Co-op (well-used rehearsal rooms and recording studio). Stop Chelverton! really need to hear from anyone who is fighting the company elsewhere or knows anything about them. 01524 383 012. stopchelverton@gmx.net www.nephridium.org/lancaster

UPDATE FROM CAMPAIGN: Chelverton went bankrupt and the project has been taken over by our old friends Carillion (aka Tarmac - those road building tree haters who we met on the M65, Newbury and now the Birmingham North Relief Rd). It is believed that they're using

this to test the strength of local opposition before they start their real project - a toll road bypass through SSSI, international bird reserves and the beautiful Lune estuary (secret negotiations have already started with one of the local MPs)...

The council have passed a resolution to prevent council land being sold off for warehouse retailing outlets or a road along the canal, but local people are worried that when Carillion pile on the pressure they may cave in.

A group called Real Planning for Lancaster has been set up by locals to work on a plan for the threatened area with the community, and planning officials at the council love it - they can use it to fend off Carillion's destructive plans.

Carillion are lying low, preparing their plans, and will probably ask for planning permission in spring or summer this year. In the meantime locals are preparing to occupy the threatened area. www.eco-action.org/lancaster www.realplanningforlancaster.org.uk

*A group has been set up to campaign against a planned Safeway's expansion in **Bridport**, because they know that the store would add to problems of rural exclusion, reducing access for those who use public transport and leading to the closure of local shops. The campaign group has organised a benefit gig with Billy Bragg and local performers for 12th October @ Bridport Arts Centre, 7.30pm.

* The revised plans for redevelopment of land at **Brighton Station** including a giant Sainsbury's can be seen at the council offices in Bartholomew Square from next Wednesday. BUDD (Brighton Urban Design & Development) have organised a public meeting on October 24th at the Brighthelm Centre, North Rd, Brighton 7.30pm to discuss the revised application. 07966 528944 www.buddbrighton.org

Positive SchNEWS

Congratulations to Greenleaf Bookshop of Bristol, who celebrated their 20th anniversary last month. Give them, and other independent bookstores, your support. Greenleaf, 82 Colston St, Bristol, BS1 5BB 0117 921 1369

* SchNEWS now has a list of radical bookshops and distributers on our website – let us know if we've missed any.

...and finally...

It would be funny -if it wasn't so tragic- the way British justice works. Martin Maynard, the man who nearly killed the hunt sab Steve Christmas (see SchNEWS 274) by deliberately running him over in his Land Rover had his court case last week.

Steve, who was very lucky not to die, suffered a crushed pelvis, four broken ribs, a damaged lung and severe internal bleeding. He also had a metre of intestine removed and metal plate fitted in two different operations in hospital where he was on the critical list for months. So after Maynard was arrested you would have bet your last quid on him going down for a long time. But no. After not turning up for court a total of four times, and the police not bothering with an arrest warrant, last week he finally made it into the dock. He must have been the judges best mate because the charges of GBH with intent were dropped to driving without insurance or license and he was fined the sum total of £75 plus costs. Meanwhile four women could be going to jail when their court case begins next week.

After Maynard tried to kill Steve, other hunt sabs were quite understandably angry and held a demo outside the hunt's kennel. A few windows were broken by people unknown but the women have been caught by the catch all conspiracy laws. www.sahc.org.uk

Disclaimer

Subscribe! _ _ _ _ _ _ _ _ _ _ _

MAD MAX MINDS THE GAP

In October over 500 people travelled thousands of kilometres to converge on Pine Gap - the top secret military intelligence base at its remote desert location somewhere near Alice Springs in central Australia. It is a key part of the US communications satellite network - playing a role in all US military campaigns including the first Gulf War and would be used extensively in a second invasion.

After sunset on Sunday 6th October a mysterious UFO containing an Intergalactic Cosmic Powered Sound System (called the Unified Gallactic Body Of Ontological Terrorists or UGBOOT for short) landed on the road in front of the infamous spying facility. On board were strange alien life forms playing crazy alien beats for a group of even stranger humans. They pumped out tunes from outer space places until 8am the next morning.

At that time another mob of strange red and blue lights appeared on the horizon. Unfortunately, at a closer look it turned out to be the Northern Territory Police, carrying a range of not-so intergalactic riot shields and batons. The police charged onto the road from all directions pounding, tackling and maiming people at random.

The aliens in the space craft kept playing music until the police smashed their intergalactic power source. The cops then smashed a space ship window and snapped off the steering wheel, successfully ruining all the fun as usual. Eight people were arrested for having fun and once again the police looked like stupid party poopers. Still, the party protest had strategically blocked the facility for fifteen hours.

Earlier that day five protesters got inside Pine Gap and took video footage of the facility. Unfortunately they where arrested about 10km into the compound and their footage was confiscated. The only comment by police when asked about the video and the camera was "What camera?"

Later the Alien Space Craft visited the Alice Springs car wreckers where it found a new steering wheel and is now taking observational photos over Pine Gap for either another crazy inter-gallactic party on top of one of the facility's golf ball domes, or a roller disco in the main satellite dish." - *Sydney.Indymedia.org*

Bomspotting

Over 500 bomspotters broke into the Kleine Brogel military base in Belgium - where illegal nuclear weapons are based - for a picnic on 5th October. This was a good effort seeing as the Belgian government had put on 2,000 soldiers and 400 police with helicopters, dogs and the works to stop them. They got past the hoards of uniforms by going around the perimeter fence in groups of four, spreading themselves around, and helping each other over. Out of the 2,000 protesters who descended on the base that day, 1,117 were eventually arrested - all later released without charge.

Intergalactic Sound System lands at Pine Gap

NUNSENSE

On 6th October, three American nuns disabled a U.S. nuclear missile silo in northern Colorado. Dressed in white boiler suits with 'Disarmament Specialists' written on the front and 'CWIT' (Citizen Weapons Inspection Team) in big letters across the back, the Dominican sisters bashed up the silo lid and the tracks that carry the lid to its firing position, cut cables, and cut through the surrounding fence.

The action, which took place on the first anniversary of the U.S. bombing of Afghanistan, is the 79th ploughshares or related disarmament action since 1980 in the United States, Europe, and Australia.

In a statement carried with them onto the site, Carol Gilbert, Jackie Hudson, and Ardeth Platte stated that they had "come to Colorado to unmask the false religion and worship of national security... We hope in the light of [God's] Word to name things what they are, to unmask the lies, abuses, and racism hidden in the rhetoric of patriotism, security and moral superiority."

All three have been charged with Sabotage and Malicious Destruction of Property of the United States and each faces up to 30 years in jail. Write to them at: Clear Creek County Jail, Box 518, Georgetown, CO 80444, USA. For more info email: disarmnow@erols.com or visit http://baltimore.indymedia.org/newswire/display_printable/2065/index.php

Emerson, Lake'n'Heath

RAF Lakenheath is the largest US Air Force-operated base in England, and the most important tactical nuclear bombing base in Europe, which makes it in urgent need of weapons inspections:

7th October saw the biggest direct action at Lakenheath in a decade. Around 200 people were at the main gate closing it for the day, while nine people entered the base by cutting or climbing the fence.

Once inside one of the climbers scaled a water tower and draped a banner from it which said 'LAW NOT NUKES' (don't laugh she was a law lecturer from Southampton), while two others entered the base within yards of the main munitions store to get a closer look. Three of the 'inspectors' were arrested, but not charged, including one man who'd been a magistrate for 10 years, and while it may have been his first bit of arrestable direct action, it certainly wasn't for the perennial Margaret Jones, who'd cut her way through the fence with bolt-cutters.

People on the action reckoned the police were keen to avoid a mass arrest situation so as to not draw attention to the fact that the weapons facility is illegal under international law.

The protesters discussed politics and philosophy in the bus on the way home.

OCTOBER 4-11, 2002

KEEP SPACE FOR PEACE

INTERNATIONAL DAYS OF PROTEST TO STOP THE MILITARIZATION OF SPACE

Help us build this vital global movement to stop the nuclearization and weaponization of space by organizing local events throughout the week. Working together we can create a new consciousness about protecting space from the bad seed of war!

1.5 Million March In Italy

5th October: More than 1.5 million Italians took to the streets of dozens of cities on Saturday afternoon and evening to protest against possible U.S. military action in Iraq. Earlier in the day 60-80,000 marched in Milan, along with large rallies in Bologna, Florence, Naples and Palermo. About 100 activists surrounded the British consulate in Venice. The day culminated with as many as 200,000 gathering in Rome.

3,000 also demonstrated in Cagliari on the Mediterranean island of Sardinia.

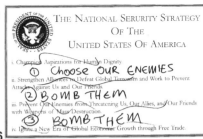

THE NATIONAL SERURITY STRATEGY
OF THE
UNITED STATES OF AMERICA

i. Champion Aspirations for Human Dignity.
① Choose OUR ENEMIES
ii. Strengthen Alliances to Defeat Global Terrorism and Work to Prevent Attacks Against Us and Our Friends.
② BOMB THEM
iii. Prevent Our Enemies from Threatening Us, Our Allies, and Our Friends with Weapons of Mass Destruction.
③ BOMB THEM
iv. Ignite a New Era of Global Economic Growth through Free Trade.

weekly SchNEWS

www.schnews.org.uk

Friday 11th October 2002   Free/Donation   Issue 376

DOCU-MENTAL!

"This is a time of opportunity for America. We will work to translate this moment of influence into decades of peace, prosperity, and liberty… We will actively work to bring the hope of democracy, development, free markets, and free trade to every corner of the world." From the recently published National Security Strategy of the USA.

We couldn't make it up if we tried, ladies and gentlemen. Last month, the Bush Administration released its new National Security Strategy of the United States of America. A document whose contents list included agenda items such as the obviously ironic, "Champion Aspirations for Human Dignity," the arrogant, "Ignite a New Era of Global Economic Growth through Free Markets and Free Trade," and the downright scary "Develop Agendas for Cooperative Action with the Other Main Centers of Global Power." The document also contained gems such as:

"Today, the United States enjoys a position of unparalleled military strength and great economic and political influence" (*and we will kill anyone and everyone who threatens this position*).

"We seek to create a balance of power that favours human freedom" (*and America*)

"We will defend the peace by fighting terrorists and tyrants" (*i.e. anyone who has the slightest criticism of America*).

"Free trade and free markets have proven their ability to lift whole societies out of poverty" (*and into our clutches*)

"The United States will work with individual nations, entire regions, and the entire global trading community to build a world that trades in freedom and therefore grows in prosperity" (too much bullshit to even parody).

"Freedom is…the birthright of every person—in every civilisation" (as long as we get to dictate 'freedom to do what?').

"Today, humanity holds in its hands the opportunity to further freedom's triumph over all its foes. The United States welcomes our responsibility to lead in this great mission" (and to cash in on all the profits that come with it).

The Bush Doctrine

This idiotic new document is already being hailed as the new Bush Doctrine. But the idiocy contains an evil little twist. Included in the paper is a section titled 'Prevent Our Enemies from Threatening Us, Our Allies, and Our Friends with Weapons of Mass Destruction'. The section basically says that the cold war strategies of 'containment' (preventing the spread of communism) and 'deterrence' (being so incredibly tough that no enemy could attack you without guaranteeing their own destruction) are no longer sufficient to guarantee US security. The US government now thinks it must reserve the right to use its overwhelming military might pre-emptively to attack and overthrow governments that it suspects of attempting to acquire WMDs, harbour terrorists, or contain any ill-will whatsoever towards the good ol' US of A. SchNEWS reckons

that pre-emptivity (read: kicking the shit out of everyone before they can make a peep) has always been America's policy (Vietnam anyone?). It's just that now, they've put it down in black and white.

And what's the justification for this newly publicised strategy? That the terrorists and rogue states that threaten America aren't motivated by a rational power-lust like the USSR was, oh no. Instead they are of course driven by an irrational hatred of justice, liberty, and freedom. According to the Bush Doctrine, because the new enemies of the US are not just evil, but also mental, it can't be assumed that they will act as 'responsibly' as previous forces of darkness have. And this, supposedly, is what justifies the Bush Doctrine of pre-emptive strikes—rogue states' sheer insanity.

On this basis, the Bush administration reckons that they can justify upsetting the UN by officially tearing up the rulebook on when it's acceptable to bomb the shit out of people in other countries. The problem is that no one, not the US's allies, 'citizens' or even their secret service is ready to buy the argument. According to the director of the CIA, George Tenet, there is no evidence that the rogue state currently in Bush's sights (Iraq) has any immediate desire to attack Western populations. He argues, however, that the kind of pre-emptive attack that Bush and his cronies are pushing for "could trigger the very things [Bush] has said he's trying to prevent—the use of chemical or biological weapons". The Bush government might think they're powerful enough to re-write the rules to justify their ambitions, but there's one rule that they would do well not to forget: playing with explosives makes you look hard, but if you don't know how they work, they just might blow up in your face. Tick, tick, tick…

For more ridiculous reading, see the full document at www.statewatch.org/news/2002/sep/nss.pdf

---

Positive SchNEWS

Radical Routes is a network of over 50 small co-operatives who work together to support collective ownership of houses and buildings for groups working for radical social change. It also aids small worker controlled businesses involved in socially useful work, supports and promotes de-schooling and home education, and helps facilitate the development of radical clubs and social centres. Radical Routes members meet four times a year. The next gathering is Manchester 26th-27th October. On the 26th there's an afternoon of discussions open to non-members who want to find out more about co-ops and the work of Radical Routes. Bridge 5 Mill, 22a Beswick St., Ancoats, Manchester www.radicalroutes.org.uk, info@radicalroutes.org.uk 0161 224 4846

LULA-LA LAND

Yer on-the-ball SchNEWS is in downtown Sao Paulo this week to give you the lowdown on the man they call Lula ("The Squid" in English, it's short for Luiz Inacio da Silva).

This week, Brazil's Workers Party (PT), led by Lula, won an unprecedented 4-2 victory against the US-backed government team in the first round of the Massively Important Presidential Championships of Latin America. The PT almost doubled their seats in the Senate, and at the final whistle, with 46.4 percent of the vote to his nearest rival Jose Serra's 23.2 percent, Lula was just short of outright victory. In the second and final leg, to be played on October 27th, the scores are back to 0-0 with everything to play for.

In Brazil, Lula is as recognisable a name as Pele or Ronaldo. He became famous as the leader of illegal metalworker strikes that helped bring an end to the military dictatorship in the mid-1970s. He has run for president and lost three times since becoming co-founder, in 1980, of the Workers Party.

GOOOOAAAAL!!! Lula opposes the Free Trade Area of the Americas, which he calls Bush's 'Annexation of Latin America.' He opposes Plan Columbia. He opposes sanctions on Cuba. He has the support of the landless movement in Brazil, Movimento Sem Terra He promises to end endemic corruption by getting people not aligned to politics or business in on the budget-making decisions.

There's talk of an axis between Lula, Castro and Hugo Chavez in Venezula, who foiled another attempted coup this week, timed to coincide with the Brazilian elections. With strong left gains in neighbouring Bolivia and Paraguay and elections in Argentina next March, Latin America's face could be unrecognisable from just 12 months ago, a complete rejection of the US-led free market reforms.

But however good all this may sound, Lula still may be foul. Because of his previous campaign defeats, Lula has changed much of his lefty tune this time around and many in the Workers Party

are angry but, for the moment, are keeping schtum.

DODGY KEEPER!!! Despite being locked-up and having his 1970s rallies buzzed by army choppers, Lula has made friends with the military, suggesting the signing of nuclear non-proliferation treaties was wrong. He is also supporting a move by Embraer, Brazil's massive aircraft maker, to develop a serious fighter jet and missile programme.

OVER THE BAR!! Despite previously fighting on a platform of defaulting on Brazil's crippling $260bn debt - more than half of what the country produces in a year - he now says they'll pay up. (But some people think he'll still default) Lula also says he'll work with the IMF and honour the new record-breaking $30bn loan. Lula has also attracted a few dodgy new geezers including his vice president and running mate, Jose Alencar, a textile baron worth $500M, from the centre-right Liberal Party. Seeing which way the wind is blowing, other business leaders have also backed Lula.

SchNEWS fought through the crowds last week at Lula's final emotional rally at the metalworkers union in the industrial suburbs of Sao Paulo, where he worked as a lathe operator and transformed the 100,000-strong union. "Everything that we have done until now hasn't been done to gain the Presidency, that is just a consequence," he told the crowds. "The most symbolic thing about me winning is that we will prove to anybody the truth of something that I said in 1979, which is that nobody will ever again be able to doubt the working classes." Does Lula deserve a Red Card? You make the call!

Inside SchNEWS

A new Zine is now avaliable to support Jeff 'Free' Luers, the US anarchist prisoner serving an amazing 22 years for burning a few cars. The zine called 'Let's Get Free'- includes writings for, by and about 'Free'. It's available for a donation of $5. Proceeds of the sale will (after paying copy costs) go to Jeff Luers directly. From NA-ELPSN, POB 50082, Eugene, OR 97405 USA. naelpsn@tao.ca. www.spiritoffreedom.org.uk/prisoners/fc/freezine.html

DAFT TAFT

We thought that full-scale global war and U.S.-instigated regime changes the world over would be enough to keep George Dub'ya busy, but no. Now Georgie has to take aim at unions as well. For the past two weeks, in 29 major docks up and down the American west coast, the International Longshore and Warehouse Union (ILWU) has been locked out by their bosses over contract disputes that have been raging since last June. The meanie bosses, the Pacific Maritime Association (PMA), want to sack a large number of dockers and attack workers' rights. Understandably, the ILWU have been threatening to strike and recently did a work 'slowdown', which lead to the lockout. Enter our old friend George. Deciding that the union shouldn't be allowed to use the lockout time to work out a better contract with PMA, as the whole dispute was costing the U.S. economy billions of dollars, Bush decided to call in the draconian Taft-Hartley Act.

The Daft Act was passed in 1947 as an anti-union law. It commands both the employers and the union to return back to work under the conditions of the old contract for 80 days. The act goes on to call for fines and prison sentences for those violating the terms of the contract (i.e. striking or engaging in slow-downs). This part of the bill is aimed at workers and effectively breaks the back of the union for the 80-day period, leaving them open to whatever the abusive bosses can come up with, with no real way to fight back. The 80 days of the Taft-Hartley injunction also gets PMA through the peak shipping season and to the slowest time of the year, thus relieving them of any urgency to bargain once the 80 days are over. PMA loved the government intervention, but labour unions were furious that the president had once again acted in the interests of big business. "PMA will start alleging supposed slowdowns straightaway. Taft-Hartley gives them 80 days of free shots at the union and we expect the employers will be dragging us to

"Unions? Fuck 'em!"
GET BACK TO WORK, YOU LAZY DEMOCRAT DOCK MONKEYS!
Corporations need their STUFF!

court daily, trying to bankrupt the union and throw our leaders in jail" said ILWU president James Spinosa. "No one should be surprised by the turn of these events," Spinosa said. "Bush has always actively sided with employers against workers. This collusion between the government and the employers was planned well in advance." www.labournet.net or http://sf.indymedia.org/

Lappersfort forest evicted

The Lappersfort Forest in Bruges, Belgium is a unique area. The 30 hectares of ground have lain undisturbed for such a long time that it had the chance to restore itself to its natural state, an example of what the whole of the northwest of Europe must have been like some 3000 years ago. It has become one of the last pieces of natural forest and marshland left in this part of the world. and unique in that it supports 7 different ecosystems.

One would expect a city that holds such richness within its limits to do its utmost to protect it. Not so Bruges. After a developer (the Fabricom group, part of the multinational company Tractebel) bought the land, it chose to let the terrain be developed for industrial purposes. The Mayor of the City, Patrick Moenaert, happens to be a member of the board of directors of Fluxys, another Tractebel company.

Since August 2001, activists have occupied this threatened forest. The goal of this permanent action camp was to save the forest from being chopped down for industry and a planned road and bus station. The occupation went on for more than a year, until NV Fabricom took the occupiers of the Lappersfort Forest to court to get them evicted. On 9th September 2002, the judge granted an eviction order, despite the fact that Fabricom bought the area 20 years ago and now wanted to sell it for a huge profit.

The eviction happened on Monday 14th October. Police stopped sympathisers and press from reaching the site as activists were violently removed from the

trees and tunnels, with the forest being heavily damaged in the process. Meanwhile, sympathisers who had travelled to Bruges to protest against the eviction were also arrested.

Since then, many people have demonstrated their support for the forest and have protested against the violent behaviour of the authorities. Actions have been held every evening against the eviction, and the police brutality. These solidarity actions achieved their climax in a big 'family' demonstration on 20th October when around 4000 people made it one of the biggest ever seen in Bruges.

Despite the eviction, the struggle for conservation of the Lappersfort Forest just goes on.

Indymedia West-Vlaanderen - www.lappersfront.tk

135

War BRIEFS

Last week 160 people shut down the gates of **US Air Base Lakenheath** in Suffolk where about 30 US nuclear war heads are kept. www.lakenheathaction.org ** **Some Americans don't agree with Bush!!** Last weekend 87,000 protestors took to the streets across America to protest against war on Iraq. www.indymedia.org ** An anti-war group has squatted the former **Brighton Peace Centre** in Gardner St. Open day Saturday 12th, check it out! ** Demo outside **Menwith Hill Spy Base.** Sat 12th, 12 - 4 pm, 01943 466405 www.caab.org.uk ** **Whose Terror?** Speakers from three countries facing "War on Terror" state terror--Palestine, Iraq, and Columbia. Sat 12th 2pm Friends Meeting House, Ship St, Brighton. ** **Films** against economic sanctions and war on Iraq. Sat 12th from 2.30pm, Rio Cinema, Kingsland High St., Dalston, London. £4/£2.50 0845 458 2564 voices@viwuk.freeserve.co.uk ** **Threat of War and Future of the Kurds** public meeting. Tue 15th 7pm, Committee Room 10, House of Commons, Westminster, SW1. 020 7435 4547 Liberation@btinternet.com ** **Why is the Anti-War movement ignoring Saddam's crimes?** With Peter Tatchell. Tue 15th 7:30pm, Upstairs Bar, Rugby Tavern, 19 Great James Street, London. www.newhumanist.org.uk * **Don't Attack Iraq** March & Rally, Sat 19th 11.30am George Square, Glasgow. 0141 423 1222 scnd@banthebomb.org ** **One SchNEWS reader** has been getting their anti-war message across by adorning bank notes with anti war messages - not a bad idea. ** **National day of action** against the war, 31st October, see www.stopwar.org.uk 020 7053 2155. In Brighton, a critical mass is planned, meet 3pm, University of Sussex. At 5:30pm there's an action planned, meet at the War Memorial, Old Steine. ** **Stop the War, Stop the City**. Meet on the day after war is announced against Iraq. 5:30pm in Churchill Square, Brighton. Bring pots and pans!!

SchNEWS in brief

SchNEWS nearly 8th Birthday Party, with LSDS, Miss C MC & Mama, Harry Diezel, Judge Trev and Jelly, 7-11pm, 14th, Albert Pub, Brighton. ** SchNEWS exculsive: we're the first to announce that **Noam Chomsky** speaks at St.Pauls Cathedral, 9th December as a benefit for the Kurdish Human Rights Project. Tickets £15/£8 will be snapped up quick, get yours from Hannah 020 7287 2772 ** **Gianfranco Fini**, the Italian Foreign Minister, well known fascist, and director of police operations at last years Genoa protests, is speaking in London on the 22nd. He'd love to see you!! Meet 8am onwards outside Claridge's Hotel, 53 Brook Street, London, W1 ** The offices of SHAC **(Stop Huntington Animal Cruelty)** were raided again by police last Friday. Five computers were confiscated and two people nicked. SHAC desperately need donations to replace the stolen property. Four other SHAC protestors, including a 70-year-old woman, have also been arrested in Kent and are on remand. SHAC, c/o Lynn Sawyer, 6 Boat Lane, Evesham, Worcestershire, WR11 4BP. 0845 458 0630 www.shac.net/resources.html ** Sat 12th is a silent demo in **Cambridge** against the University's proposed primate research lab. Noon, Guildhall, Market Square 01223 311828 info@x-cape.org.uk ** 1000 students are expected for next months **Shared Planet Conference**, speakers including Mark Thomas and George Monbiot are hoping to inspire students to start campaigning for a better world. 2-3 Nov. Warwick University Arts Centre. £16 (incl. accommodation) www.peopleandplanet.org/sharedplanet ** There's a **European Social Consulta** which aims to build activist networks across Europe in Barcelona, 19th-20th October. Info www.europeanconsulta.org encuentro@consultaeuropea.org ** 18th October is **Media Democracy Day**, a day dedicated to the promotion of independent media. Events in London see www.mediademocracyday.org.uk ** Special Screening of **McLibel** Two Worlds Collide film, 8pm 16th October, Cinematheque, Middle Street, Brighton.

...and finally...

What would you do if you'd got yourself a nice countryside pad with a sea view, but your neighbours, whose land your house is built on, keep making extensions that are reducing the price of your property? You could maybe move house, become more tolerant, or maybe even kill your neighbours!!

This last option may seem extreme, but for a family of badgers in Saltdean, East Sussex this is exactly what's going to happen. Residents in houses that were built on top of a badger sett have complained that the badgers subterranean extensions are undermining their foundations. And rather than look for alternative ways to cope with this problem, the Animal Welfare Minister, Elliot Morley, has granted a licence for the family of badgers to be killed under the 1992 Protection of Badger Act (Ummm). SchNEWS would like to suggest that a load of property developers out there be culled instead.

This Saturday there's a demonstration against the slaughter of the badgers at Saxon Close, Saltdean 10am- noon. www.geocities.com/wildlifeambulance/index.html

* The culling of badgers by the government in their long drawn out attempt to prove a link between badgers and the spread of TB in cattle is restarting in two areas of the UK. To get involved in stopping the culls contact 07773 572970 (Devon) or 07811 629846 (Derbyshire) www.badger-killers.co.uk

Disclaimer

Subscribe!

Keep SchNEWS FREE! Send 1st Class stamps (e.g. 10 for next 9 issues) or donations (payable to Justice?) Ask for "Originals" if you can make copies. Post *free* to all prisoners. SchNEWS, c/o on-the-fiddle, P.O. Box 2600, Brighton, East Sussex, BN2 0EF.
Tel/Autofax +44 (0)1273 685913 *Email* schnews@brighton.co.uk *Download a* **PDF** *of this issue or subscribe at* www.schnews.org.uk

Scenes Of Autonomous Resistance In Argentina

Faced with huge state debts, more than half the population living 'below the poverty line' and 30% unemployment, many people in Argentina rejected political solutions from both the left and the right and began taking steps to control their social, cultural and economic infrastructure.

The movement started in December 2001 as the country's social and political institutions collapsed under the weight of foreign debt (see SchNEWS 350 for coverage of the events of Dec 2001). Autonomous collectives sprung up across Argentina; neighbourhood groups were formed creating their own health clinics, education centres and other social services. Around 200 bankrupt and closed factories were re-opened under workers' control, supplying everything from food to farming equipment (see SchNEWS 383).

These ways of organising explicitly reject the hierarchies and centralisation of the political parties, as well as the 'shut up and join the party' left, who typically interpret demands for change as demands for a change of wording. What started as a survival tactic blossomed into self-empowerment based on solidarity, dignity and freedom of expression. When the police came to the occupied spaces demanding to speak to someone in charge, they were told, "We are all in charge".

El Padelai: Many examples of direct democracy came under threat in the build up to the elections in April 2003. On 25th February the repression began in Buenos Aires with the eviction of the squat El Padelai, a building occupied for the last 20 years, and home to around 500 people. Police fired rubber bullets and tear gas as the squatters tore down metal barriers and lobbed stones at a nearby police station. An elderly woman being evicted sobbed "I don't have thousands of pesos to buy a house."

Brukman Factory:
On 21st April 2003, six days before the presidential elections, police attacked the Bruckman factory in Buenos Aires, which was being run by 55 women textile workers who took over the bankrupt site two years ago. In solidarity, 7,000 of the town's population turned out to defend the factory. They were met with rubber bullets and live ammunition; some were chased into a children's hospital and tear gassed.

"Zanon belongs to the workers"

(above) 8th April 2003: Workers and supporters manage to fight off eviction by the police at Zanon Ceramics Factory.

The Zanon Ceramics Factory is a classic example of the 150 or so factories currently under worker control. The state, which had given massive subsidies to the factory when it was under the control of bosses, continually uses the police force to attack workers and try to throw them out. Even the official trade union sent scabs to break the occupation but the workers stood firm and proved they could run things without managers. An elected workers' committee now oversees the normal running of the factory and major decisions are made in an assembly of all the workers. Everyone has the right to speak and vote. The Zanon workers have strong links with the community, selling tiles at cost price so every house in Neuquen - many of which still had dirt floors - could have a tiled floor. The indigenous Mapuche people are letting the factory use their local clay having refused supplies to the previous owners, and now the factory has ditched the Italian styled tiles in favour of Mapuche designs.

(right) Protests in regional capital Neuquen on March 12th against imminent eviction of Zanon ceramics factory.
The lettering on the steps says: *"police prefecture – it's killing you, it's torturing you, it's repressing you, it's intimidating you , it's persecuting you , it's controlling you, it's watching you"*

4 ♣

GEORGE WALKER BUSH
Commander-in-Chief
President
Harken, Arbusto, Spectrum 7,
etc. ex-CEO

We all know that conspiracy theories don't explain why the world's fucked up. Capitalism isn't a conspiracy, and governments aren't really front organisations for the freemasons, aliens, or giant lizards. It would be nice if it turned out that war, exploitation, and environmental devastation were all just the work of a small, sinister group of complete bastards, but sadly life's more complicated than that. That said, it's hard to remember all this when you take a look at the current US president. From his rigged election to his CIA-poster-boy dad, from his oil-trading, arms-dealing cronies to his oil war and his plans for mini-nukes, it's clear that Dubya crosses the line from (normal) evil politician bastard to cartoonish, Dr Evil-style super-villain. So, for all you conspiracy theorists out there, here's a quick look at some of the big numbers in the SchNEWS deck of cards…

Keep it in the Family

Bush's granddad was a nazi.

In 1942 the US government seized a company called the Silesian American Corporation under the 1941 Trading with the Enemy Act. It was a steel and coal company, based in Poland, near Auschwitz, turning out artillery that would be turned on Allied soldiers, produced by a steady flow of slave labour in the form of healthy Jews, gypsies and trade union leaders. The company was owned by Union Banking Corporation, and Prescott Bush, the man responsible for the giving the world the two George's, was a director and share-holder. When the funds were finally free he passed them on to George Senior, who in turn passed them on to his son…

When it comes to business, no connection is too sordid if your name's Bush. It ain't what you know, it's who you know, which is exceptionally lucky if you've got the IQ of a twiglet, but have better connections in corporate America than Satan himself, eh Junior?

Before looking into the shark-infested waters of the Bush Administration, we'd better have a look at the man himself. Born (at the stroke of midnight?) in Connecticut, 1946, he went to Yale and then Harvard business school, with suspiciously average grades. Still

with a name like Bush, who needs to work for a living? After university he used his fathers contacts to launch a series of failed business ventures in the oil and mineral exploration game, starting with Arbusto Energy. He managed to get a reputation as "the only oil man in Texas who couldn't find oil". Arbusto was eventually bought up by Harken Oil, who kept Bush on as a director and gave him a tasty shares package.

During this time he made fantastic contacts in the oil scene, at home and abroad. One such contact, an investor at Harken, was Khaled Bin Mahfouz, who bought a 12% share in the business. Bin Mahfouz was known as the 'kings treasurer' to the house of Saud, with strong connections to Osama Bin Laden. He is currently under house arrest in Taef under the behest of American authorities.

Bush didn't actually make much money in oil. He got rich (basically) by buying a small part of a baseball stadium in Arlington, Texas, and getting the taxpayer to pay the rest. This made him popular with Texans (don't know why) and he was able to get himself appointed as Chief Executioner (erm… Governor) in 1994. And so began the career of another Great Man in American history. A few years and $190million in campaign contributions later, he became the most powerful vampire on the planet…

Look, we don't expect anyone to be surprised that politicians use their political connections for business advantage, and their business connections for political advantage. That's nothing new. But it's traditional for ruling class wankers to at least attempt to hide their dodgy connections. Usually they also like to make a pretence of trying to 'represent' those of us who don't have a couple hundred million stashed in a trust fund. On the other hand, the present US government actually seem to take pride in backscratching and backhanders – it's like they're trying to rub our faces in it. Do they think we're really stupid? Or have they just decided that they're now so powerful that they can afford to take the piss a bit? Either way, it's not funny. Let's take a look at some of the corporate interests currently ruling the planet.

Oil

When it comes to oil connections, you might as well start with the right-hand man, and bastard in chief. Dick Cheney has been darkening the corridors of the White House since Nixon, serving in almost all of the republican administrations up to the present. Cheney is the Father Christmas of American politics, having voted against the equal rights movement, the Head Start programme, a resolution calling for the release of Nelson Mandela, and federal funding for abortions, even in the case of rape.

When he wasn't voting against civil liberties or dropping bombs on the poor, Cheney enjoyed making a fortune as CEO of America's largest oil-services company, Halliburton. Like Bush, Cheney never lets politics get in the way of business. Under Cheney's leadership, Halliburton signed $30 million worth of contracts with Iraq through foreign subsidiaries. Cheney denied he knew about it. Likely. Halliburton is currently a leading bidder to 'restructure' Iraq's oil fields.

Listening to Cheney dribble on about liberating the 'people' of Iraq (that's people remember, not oil) it's funny to recall how, under him, Halliburton had few qualms about doing business in Burma. Or that in 1997, while Dick was still at the helm, the group Environmental Rights Action (ERA) alleged that Halliburton was behind an order for Nigeria's mobile police to shoot and kill activist Gidikumo Sule in Warri, where they were contracting for Chevron.

Reflecting on his transition from politics to business and back again in 1998 Cheney remarked, "in the oil and gas business, I deal with many of the same people." That's right… if you've got a moustache, a beard, and an oilfield and Dick's not selling you pipelines, the chances are he'll be bombing you. He is a vocal proponent of closer links between government and the energy business (if that's possible without penetrative sex), was a major player in quashing the Kyoto treaty, and is a big supporter of drilling in Alaskan nature reserves. He is also a member of far-right think tank Committee to Preserve American Security and Sovereignty (COMPASS), definitely one to watch if you're curious about the dark forces governing our world.

If you were in any doubt about the stranglehold that the energy business has on the current administration (which you're probably not, but if you were) then consider Miss Condaleeza Rice. As if having an oil tanker named after you weren't enough to give most right-thinking people the fear, Rice has achieved the kind of neo-conservative reputation that would make Enoch Powell look like some kind of Guardian-reading aromatherapist. As National Security Advisor her doctrine is to support only American interests, believing the 'international community' to be a myth. She has deep oil ties, serving a decade on the board of Chevron during their controversial penetrations into Nigeria, where there is an increasing US military presence. She has been known to describe environmental and human rights groups as "the enemy".

Cheney, Bush and Rice are by no means the only members of the administration to have oil ties, Rumsfeld and Wolfowitz both have ties to the black gold. Gale Norton, secretary to the interior started her career in the Mountain States Legal Foundation: sounds nice, but is in fact a conservative think-tank, funded by oil companies. She became notorious after entering her new government position by taking down the pictures of national parks and putting up photos of mining operations.

Not to mention Don Evans, Commerce Secretary, who was Bush's campaign manager (and secured the record-breaking funding), and who sat on the boards of Tom Brown Inc. and Sharp drilling. In his current post he is in charge of sustainable development and economic growth (!) and will be overseeing the National Oceans and Air Administration that protects coastlines. Nothing to worry about there then…

Cars

If you gotta sell oil, you gotta have something to burn it in. Cars. Lovely big ones. That's what Secretary of Energy Spencer Abraham deals in. Coming from Michigan, home of Detroit, it's little surprise that Daimler Chrysler, General Motors and Ford were major contributors to his campaign. He paid them back when he voted against legislation to improve fuel economy in SUV's, at a time when Daimler Chrysler brought out a model that does just 10 miles per gallon. He also voted against federal fuel tax and research into renewable energy.

White House Chief of Staff, Andrew Card Jnr is not only a good friend to the wheels industry, but one of the big hitters in the new administration. He worked as General Motors' chief lobbyist and as CEO of the former American Automobile Manufacturers Association, which lobbied against stricter fuel emissions and passenger safety, before landing his current job.

Enron

Talking of Energy, what happened to Enron? Well if the twin towers hadn't come down, you might have heard a lot more about Kenneth Lay, Director of Enron and shadow advisor to the president. Enron earned their White House privileges with massive electoral contributions, including the loan of their private jet. Consequently, when Cheney was formulating his National Energy Policy 'Kenny Boy' was lucky enough to be called in for a private consultation. When this came out before 9/11 the General Accounting Office was preparing to take it to court, then in all the excitement about the War on Terror the Enron scandal got kicked under the carpet. Sighs of relief all round about that, then..

The ties between Enron and the Bush administration are almost too numerous to go into. Altogether 32 administration officials held Enron stock, and many of the 'disgraced' executives were fast tracked straight into the administration. These included Enron Vice Chairman Thomas White, who made vast profits creating a false energy crisis in California, and even more when he sold his stock before the scandal broke. What do you do with a man like that? Offer him the post of Secretary of the Army.

Health, Fags and Pharmaceuticals

So the near future doesn't look too good if you in some way rely on clean air or unpolluted water. But if other members of the Bush administration have their way, you may not live that long anyway. Who better to head the department of Health and Human services in the US than Tommy Thomson, friend of fag-merchants. Thomson served on the Washington Legal Fund, an advisory board that campaigned on behalf of the tobacco giants, and went around the world promoting free trade sponsored by Phillip Morris.

RICHARD BRUCE "DICK" CHENEY
Vice-President
Halliburton ex-CEO

According to Corpwatch, he is not the only one to watch as far as smoking sponsorship goes in the White House. Karl Rove is one of the big guns along with the likes of Cheney – he fills the position of Senior Advisor to the president. He is a long-standing friend of George and helped secure his Texas victory. He worked as a consultant for Phillip Morris for 7 years in the nineties, and admitted that he steered Bush toward 'tort reform' in Texas, which made it harder for victims to sue the makers of harmful products. He has come under constant fire for abusing his position. Rove recently held a secret meeting with Intel executives about a prospective merger; two weeks later a merger was approved; two weeks after that Rove sold his inflated stock, valued at around $1.5million. Cha-ching!

The Director of the office of Management and Budget, Mitch Daniels Jnr sat on the board of Eli Lilly pharmaceuticals. Handily in his new position he will be overseeing any federal decisions concern- ing how much and what prescription drugs will come under the Medicare plan, the only free health-care in the US and something the big drug companies are fiercely opposed to.

Oh, and, let's not forget, the genetics and agribusiness giants have also got a foot in the door. Secretary of Agriculture Ann Veneman had a spell on the board of Calgene, one of the first companies to market genetically modified food, later bought out by Monsanto. Veneman has also served on the International Policy Council on Agriculture, an independent think tank, sponsored by Nestle.

Guns

OK so we're likely to see genetically modi-fied cigarettes, huge fucking cars and lots of drilling in the near future, but what about guns?

Yes, lots of guns too. Not only does the Attorney General find himself (against all odds) to the right of the National Rifle Association, but the administration has, unsurprisingly, formed a close, loving relationship with Lockheed Martin, the US's biggest arms manufacturer.

Probably most shocking though are the activities of the Carlyle Group, a multi-billion dollar private invest-ment firm that has fingers in just about every pie, but particularly communications and defence. Why? Because these are the most heavily government-regulated industries, and, well, looking at this company's payroll, they are the government.

Founded by ex-secretary of defence Frank Carlucci and ex-secretary of state James Baker, the firm uses its unbelievable contacts to secure unbelievable deals. Amongst those on their payroll are George Bush Senior, consultant to Asia, John Major, Ex-Thai and Philippine presidents and many, many more. The Group briefly courted scandal after 9/11 when it emerged that the Bin Laden family had major investments in the firm, ironically in the defence portfolio. The largest defence companies that are now under Carlyle's control are America's United Defence and Britain's own Qinetiq,

the research branch of the MoD, both doing rather well out of the war on terror.

Arch-bastards

No one's 'Big Book of Bastards' would be complete without a spot for Donald Rumsfeld, 'Defence' Secretary. 'Rummy', or 'Darth Vader' as he is commonly known, has been so fanatical in his incite-ment of international violence that even war criminal Henry Kissinger has described him as a 'despot'. Like every other fucker in the Bush administration he's loaded, to the tune of about $200 million, and shows the same respect for human life in business that he does international affairs. As head of one drug company he reputedly used his connections to get approval for a food supplement linked to brain cancer.

Rummy's initiation into American politics came as a Congressman in 1962, and he made staggering inroads by opposing food stamping, Medicare and a rise in the minimum wage. Making an impression with his obvious lack of a soul, he was snapped up by the Nixon administration, and later became a Defence advisor to Reagan. He is an avid supporter of son-of-star-wars and deploying nuclear capacity in space. He was influential in America refusing to sign a Chemical and Biological weapons treaty, and opposed a ban on testing of nuclear weapons, as that would make difficult the creation of the next generation of warheads. I know: the irony's a little too strong even to mention.

If you want to know what motivates Rumsfeld, then check out the plainly evil right wing think tanks he's linked to, like the Committee for the Present Danger, the International Rescue Com-mittee (Thunderbirds Are Go), the Centre for Security Policy, or the Committee for a Free World. Or look at the incubi who've got his ear on defence thinking, like Richard 'Prince of Darkness' Perle, who until the end of March this year was Chairman of the highly influential Defence Policy Board. Perle was forced to give up the post when it emerged that he was lobbying on behalf of Global Crossing, a bankrupt telecoms company who called on him to help 'overcome Defence Department resistance'.

This is not the first time Perle has been hit with the old conflict-of-interest fish. When he served as assist-ant secretary of defence in the Reagan presidency, he was caught urging the department to buy arms from a contractor who paid him a $50,000 'consulting' fee. He remains in contact with makers of big guns, as a non-executive director of Morgan Crucible (UK) and director of Memorex Corp. His role is questionable in the venture capital firm Trireme Partners, which invests in homeland security and defence projects.

Of course, none of this has anything to do with his advocacy of a defence policy that he touchingly de-scribes as "total war". He recently spoke at a confer-ence entitled "Implications of an Imminent War: Iraq Now, North Korea Next?", where his subject was the possible investment opportunities that might arise from future war. Well, if anybody, he should know...

DONALD HENRY RUMSFELD
Secretary of Defense
Gilead Sciences, GIC ex-Chairman

WAKE UP! IT'S YER BACKPACK OF LIES...

Weekly SchNEWS

www.schnews.org.uk

Friday 18th October 2002   Free/Donation   Issue 377

Mate - I reckon I'll be staying home for my holidays next year.

SARI SIGHT

The horrific bombing in Bali last weekend was not the first act of terror Indonesia has suffered. But somehow, other events that have claimed thousands of Indonesian lives have never managed to dominate the world's news pages. Australian tourists killed by terrorists must matter more than Indonesians killed by religious conflicts or an Australian and US-backed dictator.

In the wake of the bombing of the Sari night club, little has been said about the deaths of the Balianese men and women who make up 40% of the victims, or the injured locals who are left to suffer in third rate hospitals while westerners are flown out. It's the same with Iraqi civilians who are targeted by bombs, sanctions and depleted uranium and pronounced 'collatoral damage' because they have the wrong leader; or refugees fleeing in the hope of a better life jailed and sent back if they don't face *quite* enough hardship at home. It's September 11 all over again, kids - when Westerners die, people pay more attention. Here's one Australian's take on the unfolding events in Bali:

"There's a well known song in Australia titled 'I've been to Bali too'. 'Wired home for money, short of cash; A dose of Bali belly and a tropical rash; Daddy came through - American express; Bali t-shirts magic mushrooms Redgum bootlegs, I've been to Bali too,' go the lyrics.

"Bali has a special place in the hearts of many Australians. For most, two week holidays are cheaper there than to travel interstate – and the shopping!! Well, those locals really know how to please us Aussies. And then there's the cheap beer, cocktails, mushrooms and sexploitation. Bali really does epitomise the global consumerist tourist culture. A tiny island in the Indonesian archipelago, its entire social fabric has been irrevocably altered by Western tourism. The handicraft sector is now completely tourist-oriented, as well as about 80% of employment on the island. How do I know all this? Because I've been to Bali too – three times in fact – the first time as a very naive, very white, middle-class, Australian 14-year-old.

"Australia is now shocked by the events of the last 24 hours… Why us? The horror of it! We're being plied with images of 'our own' running down the streets (which many of us have been to), blood pouring down faces, skin peeling off bodies. And yes, it's horrid. But so was the drowning of 353 refugees off the coast of Australia only one year ago, while our government sat by and watched. Not only watched, but blamed those trying to save their children, for 'throwing them overboard'. Not only that, but our government has now been caught - and not fot the first time either - assisting in the sabotage of boats such as these...

INDOMNESIA

"This time around, however, the Government has jumped to the defence of innocents, with promises from the Prime Minister, John-munchkin-Howard, that 'all of the resources of the Air Force will be available for the task' of bringing the injured back to Australia for treatment. How blatant is our government's treating of some lives as more important than others? After being caught in the blast, Forbes Rugby Club President explained how important it was to get the injured Australians home, because 'he wouldn't admit his dog to the hospital he was treated in'.

"But the most worrying thing about these events is the ability of our government to use them to justify its slavish military support for the US-led, so-called 'War on Terror.' Already Howard is talking of a national review of security measures against terrorism. And of course we are now being bombarded with constant reminders that this, or something like it, could happen to any of us, anywhere, at any time. In practice this means the tightening of immigration border controls and even harsher treatment of refugees (who have become one of the Australian targets of the 'War on Terror'), a bolstering of the pro-

Sari Sight cont...

posed terror laws in Australia, and most importantly, a huge push for the war in the Gulf. But as demonstrated by the 40,000 people on the streets of Melbourne last Sunday, not all Australians back this war.

"Amid the current hysteria, one bright commentator is even claiming that 'This is the worst act of terror in Indonesia's history,' (Gen. Da'i Bachtiar, the national police chief). Please! We have such short memories!! It was only a few decades ago that the Indonesian Government, enthusiastically cheered on by Australia, the US and Western Europe, massacred millions of Communists, activists and anyone associated with them, as part of the coup that installed the hated Suharto regime in Indonesia. Sorry – not just cheered, but advised, encouraged, armed and even directed.

The Sari nightclub is not simply a random target. While the clientele may change throughout the year, the description is essentially the same – drunken, obnoxious, young(ish) Australians. It is a hated symbol of Western imperialism for many – no matter what the age of the 'revellers' inside. Every year thousands travel to the island, stay in their Western Hotels, visit their Western nightclubs, flaunt their money and feel like royalty for two weeks, then travel home to a country which supports the repressive regimes of the world. As the Sex Pistols put it, it's 'a cheap holiday in other people's misery'.

"That's not to say I support what happened last night. But let's be clear… as long as our governments continue to wage war on the world's poor and working class – whether through economic, diplomatic or military means – our government will develop enemies… enemies which unfortunately mistake us for our governments."

For the full article check out http://melbourne.indymedia.org/. The site also includes stories on the Indonesian military being linked to extreme Islamic groups including Jemaah Islamiyah, the group being blamed for the blast.

SchNEWS in brief

• **Sir Mark Moody-Stuart**, chairman of the ironically named Business Action for Sustainable Development (see SchNEWS 361/2) was **custard pied** in London last week before speaking at the Global Development Forum. The former Shell boss, now heading the corporate lobby group that likes to sound like Mother Teresa whilst making damn sure the Big Business profits keep rolling in at any cost, shrugged off the attack by protestors saying, "It was meant in good fun". Yeah right Mark, we love you really!

• **Lt General Shaul Mofaz, Israeli commander of the illegal occupation of Palestine** from May 98 to July this year, is coming for some dinners in the UK this month. He'll be in Glasgow (26), Liverpool (28) and Leeds (29). Contact Leeds Earth First! to make sure his tour goes off without a hitch. leedsef@ukf.net

• The second issue of **SchOUND OFF!**, Plymouth's direct action newsheet, is out now. To subscribe, email schound_off@hotmail.com

• This Sat (19) **London Animal Action** are celebrating **anti-McDonalds day** by having a demo at the Kings Cross branch of McD's, cnr Belgrove St and Euston Rd, WC1, from 4pm onwards – just up the road from the Anorak's Bookfair.

• The **Park Nook woodland protest site**, near Liverpool, has been squat-ted for the last five months and now has a 24-hour presence. An eviction is imminent and people are needed to defend the space! 0780 360 9721 http://rts.gn.apc.org/diary.htm

• Police tactics of mass arrests at **Faslane Blocades** have been undermined by the recent High Court ruling that Tommy Sheridan's breach of the peace charge doesn't stick, which will set a precedent for hundreds of others facing similar charges. www.tridentploughshares.org

• The folks at **Counter Information** news-sheet are holding meetings to discuss the future of the paper. If you're interested in going to a meeting or getting involved with the paper, contact them in Edinburgh on 0131 557 6242 (ask for CI) or email ci@counterinfo.org.uk

• There's still room on the Brighton mini-bus going to the **protest at the Dover Removal Centre** this Saturday (19). For a mere £3/£5, you get a seat on the bus, as well as a ferry ride across the Channel to attend a later protest at the Sangatte Red Cross Centre, soon to be shut down by the French government. The bus leaves early (7am!!) but plans to be back to Brighton on the same day. To book your spot, phone the Unemployment Centre on (01273) 540 717.

• **SchNEWS Of The World is now up on our website.** Or if paper's more your style grab a copy from us for £7 this weekend at the Anorak's Bookfair.

WAR BRIEFS

* **Read John Pilger's 'Lethal Hypocrisy'** about the Bali bombing http://pilger.carlton.com/

* **If you would like to financially help the Balinese victims** left in the chaotic and hopelessly overstretched hospitals with no medical insurance, no government support and few facilities email: idep@dps.centrin.net.id

* **The old Brighton Peace Centre** in Gardner St. is still being squatted by anti-war kidz. Visit them Friday (18) and Saturday (19) nights for radical films & good food. £1.50 7:30pm-10:30.

* **Last Saturday saw an anti-war demo at Shannon airport,** where US war planes land daily to refuel before heading to the Middle East. Around 10 people were arrested and then released without charge. http://struggle.ws/wsm/news/2002/shannonOCT.html

* **Anyone interested in anti-war propaganda** being put out in Manchester, take a look at: www.uhc-collective.org.uk/warpages/warpages.htm

* **An anonymous caller to a San Jose, California TV station** took credit for a pre-dawn fire at a military recruiting office on Monday. Three military cars were set on fire, and the words "pre-emptive strike" were painted across the front of the office in red lettering.

S-Pacific Target

The people of Bougainville are attempting to sue British mining giant Rio Tinto over the genocide and environmental devastation that were a regular part of Rio's 25 years of operations on the small South Pacific island. The lawsuit seeks compensation for every person who suffered during the nearly three decades of mining that went on at the giant, now-defunct Panguna copper mine located smack in the middle of Bougainville.

Bougainville is only a small island, but it's one that has been under siege since Papua New Guinea (PNG) took control of it from Australia in 1975. Even before this, CRA, an Australian subsidiary of Rio Tinto, had forced its way onto the island to build the Panguna mine. 220 hectares of rainforest were destroyed to build Panguna, and after 20 years, the mine had grown to a huge crater half a kilometre deep and nearly 7 km in circumference, creating over a billion tonnes of waste. This waste was dumped in the Jaba River Valley, creating a wall hundreds of metres high and turning one of the island's biggest river systems fluorescent blue.

By 1988, the islanders had started to fight back, successfully

closing the mine. The PNG government, which relied on the mining for 45% of its export earnings, responded swiftly and violently with Australia's help. But despite ten years of violent oppression, the Bougainville Revolutionary Army managed to keep the mine closed and eventually PNG got out. Bougainville is now in the midst of seeking its independence.

In solidarity with all indigenous peoples of the South Pacific, there was a week of actions from October 5-12 targeting companies and groups involved in ecological and cultural destruction in the region. Rio Tinto was the first to be targeted. Entrances to Anglesay Aluminium, a North Wales subsidiary of Rio Tinto, were blockaded for most of Thursday (10). A Toyota office in Redhill was paint-bombed, highlighting Toyota's involvement in logging in the South Pacific. On Wednesday, the Indonesian embassy in London was forcibly entered in protest over the country's continued occupation of West Papua and the murder of an estimated 100,000 indigenous people. And last but definitely not least, the New Tribes Mission offices were paid a visit at their UK headquarters in Grimsby. The missionary group has stated that it is their intent to reach and preach to every "dark corner" of the planet.

But the people of West Papua have declared missionaries to be one of the 4 biggest threats to free peoples-- one of the biggest reasons being that they build airstrips in remote jungles which are eventually used by businessmen, corporations and military personnel. First comes Christianity, then comes Coca Cola.

For more details on the week of actions, see www.eco-action.org/ssp For more Bougainville history, check out the excellent film "The Coconut War."

Inside SchNEWS

Please send letters of support to the 5 Stop Huntingdon Life Sciences protestors who are on remand and facing charges of "Conspiracy to Harass". This raucous, harassing mob include Gavin, who is partially sighted, and Rylma, a 70 year old pensioner...**Gavin Medd-Hall** [JK4564], **Kevin White** [JK4576] and **Paul Baker** [JK4584], HMP Canterbury, 46 Longport, Kent, CT1 1PJ, **Robert Lewis** [JK4563], HMP Elmley, Church Road, Eastchurch, Sheerness, Kent, ME12 4AY, and **Rylma White** [KV4069], HMP Holloway, Parkhurst Road, London, N7 0NU

The Jeff 'Free' Luers' zine we mentioned in last week's SchNEWS is available from Brighton ABC. Send 80p and a stamped self-addressed envelope to PO Box 74, Brighton, BN1 4ZQ, East Sussex.

One Sizewell Fits All

150 Greenpeace activists occupied the roof of Sizewell B nuclear power station this week. Greenpeace have produced a report showing that a quarter of the UK's energy demands can be supplied by offshore wind in East Anglia, but the nuclear industry insists that our ever increasing needs can only be met by them. www.greenpeace.org.uk

Sizewell B denies freak cloning accident of one of its workers at the nuclear plant.

Pain In The Ukraine

On September 30, anti-nuclear campaigner Ruslan Syninvsky was gunned down by an unidentified man in Kiev. One month earlier, Public Control, an organisation Syninvsky was deeply involved in, had filed a lawsuit against the Ukrainian government's plans to build two new nuclear reactors in a country still haunted by Chernobyl.

The police's official story is that Syninvsky was killed in a bungled robbery attempt, but the fact that the Ukrainian Secret Service has been harassing and threatening anyone who openly opposes the new reactors makes the official version kind of hard to swallow.

In the Ukraine, whose population suffered the world's worst nuclear disaster in 1986, the vast majority of people oppose nuclear energy. Knowing the opposition the project would face, Energoatom (the nuclear company contracted to build the new power stations) skirted the issue by neglecting to hold legally required public meetings on the topic, and didn't publish any information about the reactors in Ukrainian!

Funding for the proposed reactors would come from the European Bank for Reconstruction and Development (EBRD) and from one of the European Commission's 'EuroAtom' loans (set up to find new markets for Western Europe's stagnant nuclear industry). The whopping £400 million EuroAtom loan would be nearly impossible for the Ukrainian government to repay, not to mention that it comes with major strings attached—one of the loan conditions is that the Ukraine allow for privitisation of its energy industry as well as an immediate hike in energy rates. Bottom line—the average Ukrainian's energy bill would rise by 30% or more.

The EBRD's support for the project has been pure comedy. EBRD's president, Jean Lemierre, went on record as saying his bank would not support the reactors unless they were proven safe and economically feasible. To prove this point, EBRD hired their own team of experts to investigate. Unfortunately for Lemierre, the experts issued a report stating that the building of the two new reactors was neither safe nor affordable. Not being what the Bank wanted to hear, they then commissioned Stone and Webster, a US-based nuclear contracting company, to produce a second report. Surprise, surprise, the second report stated that the new reactors were a fantastic idea! www.aseed.net/publications/ebrdreader http://russia.indymedia.org/front.php3?article_id=3389&group=webcast

Doubled Dutch

When is a political refugee not a political refugee? When the Bush administration decides they're not. Prof Jose Maria Sison, founder of the Communist Party of the Philippines, has lived in the Netherlands since 1987, where he is seeking asylum as a political refugee. But now he's been labelled a terrorist by the American and Dutch governments, his 'funds' (a meagre joint bank account shared with his wife) have been frozen, and he is being threatened with extradition to the US. There is a meeting on Oct. 24, 4-9pm in support of Sison at the Tohum Cultural Center, 2A Belgrade Rd, London N16. There's also an action on Oct 21, 12-2pm, outside the Dutch Embassy, 38 Hyde Park Road, London. http://defendsison.be/

...and finally...

What goes around comes around... A local politician in a village near Lugansk, Ukraine, was out one night taking his dog for an evening pee when an over-zealous officer – albeit junior in rank to him – pointed out that his dog was in fact in breach of regulations by being off a lead, and unmuzzled. An argument broke out between the two men – culminating in the politician pulling a hand grenade from his pocket, pulling the pin, and throwing it at the young officer. What he didn't bargain for was his loyal pup running to chase the grenade... and faithfully bringing it back to his master. The macho man politician and his poor dog were both killed in the explosion.

Disclaimer

SchNEWS assures all readers - they'll never bomb Bognor Regis. Honest.

Subscribe!

Keep SchNEWS FREE! Send 1st Class stamps (e.g. 10 for next 9 issues) or donations (payable to Justice?) Ask for "Originals" if you can make copies. Post *free* to all prisoners. SchNEWS, c/o on-the-fiddle, P.O. Box 2600, Brighton, East Sussex, BN2 0EF.
Tel/Autofax +44 (0)1273 685913 *Email* **schnews@brighton.co.uk** *Download a PDF* of this issue or subscribe at **www.schnews.org.uk**

WAKE UP! WAKE UP! IT'S YER BIGGA + BETTA!

Welcome to the club - Transylvania

weekly SchNEWS

www.schnews.org.uk

Friday 25th October 2002   **Free/Donation**   **Issue 378**

TRICKY TREATY

"We are being asked to give more powers to the EU commission, an unelected, secretive body that is so corrupt it was forced to resign in its entirety in March 1999. We are being asked to give our support to the pro-business agenda of the EU, where the richer farmers receive enormous subsidies under the Common Agricultural Policy, where corporation taxes are slashed while public services are cut. Is this the Europe we want?" - Libertarians Against Nice.

Big business got its way when last Sunday Ireland finally voted "Yes" to the Nice Treaty. (Ireland had voted "No" a few months earlier, but as this was not the right answer, the powers that be gave it another go with even more "Yes" propaganda.) The yes vote now paves the way for ten more countries to join the European Union. While these countries are being ordered to privatise essential services if they want to climb aboard (see SchNEWS 287), the Nice treaty is an important step in the EU's privatisation agenda for those already part of the club.

Nice will, amongst other things, bring changes to Article 133 of the Treaty of Europe. Alarm bells should always start ringing when our old mates at the World Trade Organisation (WTO) give something the thumbs up. The WTO, who help eliminate 'barriers to trade' (silly things like workers rights and environmental laws), have admitted how important the changes to Article 133 are in their 'Trade Policy Review of the European Union,' a document which SchNEWS recommends any insomniac readers to rush out and buy. But this is how the bureaucrats work: boring us to death with gobbledegook so they can drive forward their business- friendly agenda while we yawn and check the footie scores.

Changing Article 133 means that, instead of national governments, the unelected EU Council bureaucrats and the unelected European Commission will be responsible for negotiating trade deals with organisations like the WTO, "fast-tracking" their deals behind everybody's backs. Fast-tracking is described by Pascal Lamy, the EU Trade Commissioner, as "modernising decision-making." That means swift, centralised decision-making that ensures that elected EU governments don't interfere with Big Business's deals as lobby groups push business demands through an already industry-friendly European bureaucracy.

GATS Piss

"The GATS is not just something that exists between governments. It is first and foremost an instrument for the benefit of business." - European Commission (1998)

For the past few years, the WTO have been trying to expand the General Agreement on Trades in Services (GATS – see SchNEWS 286), whose "privatise everything!" small print is a wet dream for corporations. Now with the Irish ratifying the Nice treaty, it's full steam ahead. Around 20 key basic services have been named by the WTO as ripe for privitisation. Postal, finance and banking, telecommunications, hospitals, transport – you name it, it's all gotta go private because, under WTO rules, government-run public services are a subsidy that 'discriminates' against foreign businesses and are an unfair 'barrier to trade.'

The problem for the WTO has been the mass protests whenever governments try to sell off essential services. But the Nice Treaty will take care of those pesky protestors! Article 133 lets the EU Council and Commission "act by a qualified majority." This means that, when they have made a

trade agreement, all member states have no choice but to go along with it. As one WTO official put it, GATS helps "overcome domestic resistance to change." Because even if a government wants to take back control of a failing private company, it won't be able to unless it is ready to face the trade sanction consequences. Take Britain's railways, for instance. Late trains, crap service, over the top prices – tough. A privatised rail network is here to stay, courtesy of agreements like GATS and Article 133.

Frights of the Round Table

It's estimated that Brussels – the home of the European Parliament – hosts some 500 industry lobby groups who employ some 10,000 professional lobbyists. Their job is to make the European Union more industry- friendly – and they do a good job. In 1999, for instance, there was a multi-million lobbying campaign by biotech companies that saw the introduction

Tricky Treaty cont...

of the industry-friendly 'Patents on Life' directive.

One of the most important lobbying groups is the European Round Table of Industrialists (ERT), made up of over 40 "European industrial leaders" from some of SchNEWS's favourite corporations. The ERT is fairly honest about the priviledge it enjoys, boasting on its web page that "The ERT has contacts with the European Commission, the Council of Ministers, and the European Parliament. ...Every six months the ERT meets with the government that holds the EU presidency to discuss priorities." And it usually gets what it wants. It was the ERT that wanted revisions to Article 133 for fast tracking – and hey presto!

As Andrew Flood of Ireland's Libertarians Against Nice says, "The message is clear. A substantial part of the Nice treaty, Article 133, has essentially been drafted by the European corporations to increase their profits at the expense of the people of Europe and those we trade with. The nature of these changes are things that huge numbers of Irish workers would oppose if they were presented in plain English in a referendum."

* Recommended reading: 'Diverse Voices of Struggle in Western Europe - Restructuring and Resistance' edited by Kolya Abramsky. AK Distribution 0131 555 5166 www.akuk.com
* For more on the Nice Irish Referendum, visit the Libertarians Against Nice website at: http://struggle.ws/anarchism/nice/index.html
* The World Development Movement is running a campaign against GATS 0800 328 2153 www.gatswatch.org
* Read all about the WTO's hidden agenda www.corpwatch.org/issues/PID.jsp?articleid=722
* With a few weeks to go till the WTO summit in Sydney (14/15 November), 3 anti-WTO websites face the prospect of being banned. Indymedia Melbourne is amongst the websites targeted by New South Wales Police Minister Michael Costa. Censoring the censorship lists? See www.melbourne.indymedia.org and www.nowto.cat.org.au

SchNEWS in brief

The Porkbolter, Worthing's 'radical local newspaper with a historically vindicated pig obsession' has a 5th birthday bash 7.45-midnight, Nov 1st at Vintners Parrot, Warwick St, Worthing, with live band Becomes The Water of Death, Attila the Stockbroker, and various DJs. Donations on door ** Planning meeting for protests against next years **DSEi arms fair**, 30th Oct, 7pm at St. Ann's Church Hall, Berwick Rd, Canning Town, London Info 0781 7652 029. Join the e-mail discussion at DSEi2003-subscribe@yahoogroups.com. www.dsei.org ** Where to next with the **Anarchist Bookfair**? Anyone with feedback/ideas for how it can be developed get y'self along to an open meeting, 17th Nov, Conway Hall, 25 Red Lion Square, London WC1R 4RL 6pm-9pm or e-mail comments to mail@anarchistbookfair.org ** **Protest against custody deaths** - Remembrance Procession organised by United Families and Friends Campaign. Sat 26th Oct, Trafalgar Sq 1pm. Please wear black. 07770 432 439 ** **Burger King** in Bristol found their locks glued and their windows repainted last week. The action was done as a protest against Burger King's continued profiteering from the stores they have opened in the Israeli occupied regions of Palestine ** Meeting about the **Baku-Ceyhan BP backed oil pipeline**. Thursday 31st with a speaker from Georgia, 7.30pm, Manchester University Student Union Main Hall, 1st Floor. ** The trial of **five antimilitarist activists** concludes in Watford today. The protestors are charged under the 1908 Public Meeting Act for "disrupting a public meeting", although the army presentation they disrupted was private invitation only. Two are also charged with criminal damage, although the Army has yet to say what was damaged. www.northwood.cjb.net/ ** Pickets are taking place outside supermarkets in Brighton, in support of the BIG (**Boycott Israeli Goods**) campaign. Saturday mornings 11 - 1 p.m. Currently at Sainsbury's, London Road ** **The Iraq Journal** website features reports of independent journalists Jeremy Scahill and Jacqueline Soohen, providing a forum for the distribution of independent information and views from Iraq. www.iraqjournal.org ** In New York this week 19 activists from the **No Blood for Oil Campaign** were arrested after occupying the UN General Assembly and demanding that the UN at no time give its support for the invasion of Iraq www.PeaceNoWar.net** **Work & Welfare, not Weapons Conference** organised by Greater Manchester and District Campaign for Nuclear Disarmament and Campaign Against Arms Trade @ Manchester Town Hall on 2nd November. Will look at diversification from military production and the creation of a non-military economy. 0161 273 8283 www.gmdcnd.org.uk/worknotweapons

STRIKE A LIGHT!

Remember how great firefighters were about a year ago? When it looked like the thought of merchant bankers leaping to their deaths on 9-11 might not be tragic enough to convince us of the importance of bombing the shit out of Afghanistan, we were treated to a stream of tear-jerking speeches and articles reminding us of all the firemen who lost their lives trying to rescue victims of the WTC attacks. Firefighters were heroes and the sacrifices they made were priceless.

Erm, well now it seems that all that was a bit of a misprint. It turns out that firefighters are actually lazy, greedy, and irresponsible and the sacrifices they make aren't worth very much at all. All this according to the same papers and politicians who were kissing their arses last year.

Why? Because the firefighters are now set to go on strike. And how dare they put other people's lives at risk to get the wages they deserve? The firefighter's union is calling for a 40% increase, the cheeky gits, which would take the wage for a qualified firefighter from £21,000 to £30,000. Don't they know that the country can't afford to actually pay a decent wage to workers who risk their lives every day?

For the Schnews reader's benefit, here's a short list of things the Labour government **can** afford:
* **A 40% pay increase for the Prime Minister**: 2 weeks after winning the last election, Blair congratulated himself with a £47, 000 pay increase, taking his salary to £173, 000.
* **A £20,000 pay increases for cabinet ministers**: Not wanting to be tight, Blair also handed out pay increases to Prescott and his mates, taking the cabinet minister's salary to £120,000. Cha-ching!
* **£3.4 billion** to underwrite arms exports in 2001 through the Export Credit Guarantee Scheme.
* **Approximately £1 billion** for 'low-intensity' bombing raids on Iraq since 1997.

...and remember, now we've really got to tighten those purse strings, cos we've got a **proper** war on the way.

WALK ON THE WOODSIDE

Tired of the powers-that-be yanking them about, a community of 200 Romany travellers and their supporters intend to resist eviction from Woodside caravan park in Bedfordshire on November 1st.

After years of being told to buy their own land and stop tresspassing on other people's land twenty-seven Gypsy families purchased Woodside, a 17-acre touring caravan park with full planning permission, for £300,000 in 1997. But when the families moved to the park, Mid-Bedfordshire council claimed they did not have permission for permanent occupation. The council have been trying to oust them from their land ever since, even allocating £230,000 of council money to finance clearance of the community!! After a long court battle, the council has been given the go ahead to evict the community.

Help and support is urgently needed!! There will be a protest outside the council offices (Dunstable St., Ampthill, Bedford) at 6:30 p.m. Thursday 31st during a meeting about the planned eviction. Demonstrators are then invited to camp at Woodside (at Hatch, near Sandy, off A1) and help defend the site on Friday 1st, when the council is scheduled to try to force the 52 families from their homes. The Gypsy Council is asking people to donate tents, bales of hay or straw, scrap wood and rope for the action. The travellers also are working on a last-minute legal appeal. More info: 01206 523528.

ANTI-WAR ACTIONS

There's a whole load of actions coming up on the 31st to oppose the possible war against Iraq. Here are just a couple:
London: Critical Mass Ride Against Death - meet 2pm by the peace camp at Imperial War Museum, Geraldine Mary Harmsworth Park, Lambeth Road, SE1. Move off 3pm. Dress scary - www.cm-london.cjb.net And Houses of Parliament, 6pm. Dress in white, disguised as ghosts, and converge on Parliament. 020 7377-9088 disobedience@riseup.net
Brighton: Critical Mass Ride starting from Sussex University at 3pm and 3.30pm from Moulescomb Wild Park. Stop the City Stop the War demonstration. Meet 5.30pm at the War Memorial, The Old Steine.**For your nearest action contact: Stop the War Coalition 020 7053 2155, www.stopwar.org.uk**

SQU'ART ATTACK!

On Saturday 12th October Russian police illegally evicted Moscow's only political squat giving one man a broken skull and hospitalising 3 others. The squat started out as a studio given to artist Evgeni Schetov two and a half years ago by the Moscow Union of Artists. Since then the space has become an important base for ecological activism. Not liking this turn of events, city officials and bureaucrats from the Union of Artists threatened to evict Schetov. In retaliation, Schetov stopped paying his rent - making the space the first political squat in Moscow since 1997. On the morning of Saturday the 12th, the police and members of the Union of Artists managed to smash the door down with axes and then violently attacked squatters inside. Everyone was arrested and all their property was thrown into the street. The squatters are launching a campaign against the eviction. Info: dikobrazi@lists.tao.ca

DIRTY MAC

October 16th was the annual worldwide anti-McDonalds day, where crappy fast food outlets the world over were picketed and free veggie burgers given away. But this year a load of workers got involved too: Workers at six McDonalds in France went on strike, there was a strike in Norfolk, attempts at strikes in three London stores and a walkout in Nottingham. McTrash was dumped back into stores in Australia, locks glued and stores painted in Austria, freezers and toasters sabotaged in Chicago, a mass resignation in Toronto... the list goes on: www.geocities.com/globaldayofaction

Unfortunately, there are serious repercussions for anti-Macs in Mexico: 94 protesters were arrested and detained following complaints from McDonalds. They were accused of damage to an umbrella and window and carrying explosives – i.e. fireworks. The state has set a bond of $14,000 for each protester, a fee which could buy untold numbers of replacement umbrellas. Financial help is now desperately needed. http://mexico.indymedia.org/front.php3?article_id=3486&group=webcast (In Spanish)

TUNNEL VISION

Europe's increasingly racist immigration policies have brought tighter border controls, higher surveillance, and more people being detained and deported.

Detention centres have been a focus of actions against these policies and last Saturday (19) people demonstrated outside the Dover removals centre. Later that day, they crossed the channel to join up with French activists at the Sangatte camp. Sangatte is a humanitarian Red Cross camp which is home to 1,500 people who are hoping to apply for asylum in Europe. Both the French and English governments have schemed together to close the camp by March 2003 because sheltering and feeding migrants was seen as far too liberal. The UN has very kindly offered to help sort the 'genuine' from the 'non-genuine' refugees and will be giving the 'non-genuine' the option of being sent back home with a bit of cash or living on the streets of Calais now that Sangatte will be shut down. On Saturday, many of the refugees came out of Sangatte to talk to the protesters. One protester told Schnews, "The hardest thing was meeting children who were telling us that England was their dream country when we really know the truth of what will happen to them when they come here."

For more information about the actions visit www.noborder.org, www.barbedwirebritain.org.uk and www.campsfield.org.uk
* Next demo at Sangatte is on Friday November 15th – the day that Sangatte closes its doors to newcomers. Info: goldfish1967@hotmail.com
* There will be a Brighton No Borders Meeting, 28th October, 7.30pm Tilbury Place. Unemployed Centre off Carlton Street.

...and finally...

Only weeks after announcing (then quickly retracting) that the solution to the annual 'fallen leaves' problem would be to fell all trees on the banks of their rail lines, it looks like Rail Track now have a new enemy. Taking the form of a giant inflatable hamburger, the new menace disrupted services from Newport to London on Tuesday. Rail Track have since announced a national cull of large inflatable hamburgers and of any giant inflatable clowns that might be making them. http://uk.indymedia.org/front.php3?article_id=44217&group=webcast

Disclaimer

SchNEWS warns all readers Bognor Regis is not Nice. Honest.

Subscribe!

DON'T BUY THE WAR TALK

Keep SchNEWS FREE! Send 1st Class stamps (e.g. 10 for next 9 issues) or donations (payable to Justice?) Ask for "Originals" if you can make copies. Post *free* to all prisoners. SchNEWS, c/o on-the-fiddle, P.O. Box 2600, Brighton, East Sussex, BN2 0EF.
Tel/Autofax +44 (0)1273 685913 *Email* **schnews@brighton.co.uk** *Download a PDF of this issue or subscribe at* **www.schnews.org.uk**

WAR IS BU$INE$$ A$ U$UAL

The strength of popular feeling against the UK's involvement in the war on Iraq led to actions and protests at military bases in this country on a scale that hadn't been seen since the Cold War. For many people these actions will have been the first time they visited a military base. But for others, direct action at the nerve centres of the military-industrial complex has been a familiar and regular part of life for years. As dodgy military establishments have been in place for so long, so have a lot of the networks that spread information and take direct action against military activity. However much the media persist in labelling anti-war protests 'echoes of the sixties', peace protest did not die at the end of the Vietnam War to be resuscitated after September 11; it never went away, and will not go away until it has achieved its aims.

See the map for military and anti-military stuff going on in your area.

1. Faslane Naval Base is where the Trident submarines, and some other British and American ships, are based. Britain has four Trident submarines, each of which can carry up to 48 nuclear warheads. For nearly 21 years, Faslane Peace Camp has been situated across the road from the base, as a permanent presence of opposition. The peace camp is both a focus for direct action and an attempt at a more positive way of life, using renewable energy and making decisions by consensus.

2. RNAD Coulport, five miles from Faslane, is an arms depot where Trident warheads are kept. For the last few years, Trident Ploughshares has held summer disarmament camps at Coulport.

3. Dundrennon is the only place in Britain where depleted uranium shells are tested. For more information contact the Campaign Against Depleted Uranium (CADU)

4. Cape Wrath is a NATO test bombing site. For more information contact Scottish CND or Faslane Peace Camp.

5. Sellafield is a nuclear reprocessing plant run by BNFL. There are women's peace camps on an irregular basis there, and occasional CND camps. Nuclear waste comes to Sellafield from all over Europe and beyond. Action has been taken at various places to try to stop the lorries and trains that carry it.

6. Menwith Hill is a US listening base. There was a women's peace camp there for many years. Contact the WoMenwith Hill Women's Peace Camp, Yorkshire CND or the Campaign for the Accountability of American Air Bases (CAAB).

7. RAF Fylingdales is another US base in North Yorkshire, soon to be upgraded for incorporation into America's National Missile Defence programme, AKA 'Son of Star Wars'. There have been regular protests at Fylingdales and since 2002 there has been a peace camp.

8. Rolls Royce, based in Derby, produces reactors and other equipment for nuclear submarines.

9 and 10. Lakenheath and Mildenhall are US military bases.

11. Situated next to a boring-looking town near Reading, **Atomic Weapons Establishment (AWE) Aldermaston** is a bomb factory which manufactures parts for Britain's nuclear arsenal. It was a focus for the early years of CND. Women continue to camp there one weekend every month, a campaign that has lasted since the Eighties. In recent years it has also been a focus for Trident Ploughshares disarmament camps, and Youth and Student CND camp there at least once a year to practice climbing fences.

12. AWE Burghfield works closely alongside Aldermaston, and is often another focus for the Aldermaston women's camp and Youth and Student CND camps.

13. Fairford is an air base that was used by the US in its recent attack on Iraq as a base for B52 bombers. *(see other articles in this book).*

14. Welford is a base that stores bombs to be taken to Fairford.

15. Devonport dockyard in Plymouth is where Trident submarines are refitted and refuelled with radioactive fuel. Trident Ploughshares held a disarma-

ment camp there in 2002 in which two people boarded a submarine. Seven people have been acquitted for blockading a gate to the dockyard.

16. Northwood is a British and NATO war command centre. (*See other articles in this book.*)

17. The MoD at Whitehall is where a lot of decisions are made ...

And the moving targets...

Nuclear convoys travel in groups of up to five carrying warheads for Britain's weapons of mass destruction. They drive on civilian roads, escorted by several support and police vehicles. They are not marked with radiation symbols, but they are still easy to identify. There have been a large number of mishaps involving these vehicles, and several near disasters.

Since the convoys began, people have been taking direct action against them. This is important – a major reason why American cruise missiles were removed from Britain in the 1980's was ordinary people persistently hindering their movements. In Scotland an attempt has been made to stop nearly every nuclear convoy that has passed through since 1982, sometimes with inspiring results. Nukewatch is a national network that keeps an eye on the movements of nuclear convoys.

It's fairly easy to stop a convoy by going out in front of it far enough in advance for it to stop. A place where the vehicles have to go slowly, such as a roundabout or junction, is good for this. Then people can attempt to climb on top of the vehicles, or lock on underneath or in front of them. In February 2003 a convoy was prevented from leaving Coulport for 2 – 3 hours when people locked on in front of the gates through which it was going to leave.

In 2002 a convoy was stopped in Balloch, a town in Western Scotland through which the convoy regularly travels. The town was leafleted that morning so local people knew what to expect. When the convoy arrived and was stopped, there was a large crowd of supportive onlookers - perhaps next time some of them will join in...

Convoy-stopping tactics have also been used recently to stop weapons convoys going from Welford and Fairford (see article in this book).

Convoy routes - which change regularly

Contacts: Scottish CND 0141 423 1222, www.banthebomb.org ** **Faslane Peace Camp** 01436 820901, www.faslanepeacecamp.org.uk ** **Nukewatch** www.gn.apc.org/ pmhp/convoys, 02380 554434 ** **Aldermaston Women's Peace Camp** 07904450307, www.aldermastonwpc.gn.apc.org ** **Trident Ploughshares** www.tridentploughshares. org, 0845 4588366 ** **Gloucester Weapons Inspectors** www.gwi.org.uk ** **Yorkshire CND** www.cndyorks.gn.apc.org ** **CAAB** www.caab.org.uk ** **WoMenwith Hill Women's Peace Camp** 01943 466825, www.cndyorks.gn.apc.org/mhs/wpc/wpcmhs.htm ** **Lakenheath Action Group** www.motherearth.org/lakenheathaction, 01508 550446 ** **Free Fylingdales Network** www.freefylingdalesnetwork.co.uk

We Can't Keep On Meeting Like This

They were called the "biggest anti-war demonstrations in the US since the Vietnam War". As part of an international day of action against the war, on October 26 more than 200,000 people formed a two mile long human mass through the streets of Washington, D.C. Meanwhile over 100,000 marched in San Francisco in addition to tens of thousands in other cities around the US.

San Francisco

(left) October 27: 3-4,000 visit the home of Donald Rumsfeld in Taos, New Mexico to give him some feedback about his push for war. Protesters said it was a bit difficult knowing which house to have a go at because he owns seven properties in the area.

(above) On October 25 at the US Embassy in Manilla, Philippines some argy-bargy broke out between protesters and police. A strong theme running through the protest was a demand that U.S. troops permanently go home. Washington has used the excuse of alleged terrorist organizations to reintroduce U.S. military forces into its former Pacific colony.

(above) In San Juan, Puerto Rico, hundreds gather in front of the Puerto Rican National Guard armoury to denounce a possible war and the continued U.S. Navy use of the Vieques bombing range.

In Germany US Airbases were targeted for direct action: at Spangdahlem, near Trier, several hundred converged on the airbase, while in Berlin 20,000 gathered in Alexanderplatz for a march which included large sections of the Muslim community. Despite rain and gale-force winds, thousands took to the streets in Frankfurt and Stuttgart, but a hurricane kept numbers down in Hamburg!

October 24th: Entrances to the US Spy Base at Menwith Hill are blocked for four and a half hours by a group braving the cold morning. D-locks and handcuffs in metal tubing were used to block the gate - with 1,000 employees at the base being turned away from work. Another gate was jammed using good-old superglue in the lock.

More Halloween Madness

The Spanish had it on the streets on October 26, with large crowds in Madrid, Barcelona, Bilbao, Oviedo, Valencia, Caceres and Sevilla as well as actions in many of the smaller towns and villages. The largest was in Barcelona with more than 30,000 (left).

Other events on October the 26th: In India the Kerala chapter of the All-India Anti-Imperialist Forum held a demonstration in front of the State Secretariat. ** In Holland, 10,000 came out in Amsterdam, and 1,200 in Rotterdam ** 3,000 gathered at the US Embassy in Copenhagen ** Another 1,500 hit the streets in Stockholm, Sweden and Oslo, Norway. ** In Italy 20,000 marched in Florence, 2,000 in Turin.

In Indonesia on October 24 demonstrators rallied at the U.S. Embassy in Jakarta. This Embassy was to become a very popular place in the coming months...

In Japan anti-war demos took place on October 20 in Hiroshima and Toyama, on the 21st in Tokyo, Osaka, Fukuoka, Hiroshima and Nagasaki, and then all over again in Tokyo on the 26th.

In Ankara, Turkey on October 21, students braved attacks by riot cops to protest a visit by U.S. Central Command Chief General Tommy Franks, who has been named as the regent of Iraq should the U.S. occupy the country.

Masking up for some direct action - Rotterdam, October 26th

WAKE UP! PUT THIS IS YER PIPELINE!

weekly SchNEWS
www.schnews.org.uk

Azerbaijan
Georgia
Turkey
Chechnya
SS War On Terror

Friday 1st November 2002   Free/Donation   Issue 379

PUTIN THE BOOT IN

"Is it a real victory - so many victims? The tragedy of the musical did not spring out of the blue. It is not the end, but the beginning. Now we shall live in fear, as we see our children and our elderly go out into the street. Perhaps this is how Chechen people live?" - Anna Politkovskaya, Russian journalist who went in to talk to the hostage takers.

Russia's very own war on terrorism came back to haunt it last weekend when Chechen rebels took hundreds of people hostage in a Moscow Theatre. Their demand was that Russia pull out of Chechnya which over the past few years has been bombed back to the iron age - retribution for a number of bomb attacks in Moscow that were blamed on the rebels. Russian troops captured the capital Grozny - already a pile of rubble after the last war with Russia five years earlier - and in the process killed up to 40,000 civilians. Although the 'conventional' war has largely ceased, human rights organisations have reported a rise in the disappearance, torture and summary executions, in what is called the 'Wild West' of Russia.

There is a catalogue of human rights abuses perpetrated by the Russian Army: In June, a ditch containing 50 mutilated bodies was discovered near the Russian army post in Chankala. The corpses were missing eyes, ears, limbs and genitals. In July in the village of Meskyer Yurt, 21 men, women and children were bound together and blown up, their remains were thrown into a ditch. The list goes on...

Some those who survive sometimes wish hadn't. In Zernovodsk this summer, townspeople say they were made to watch women being raped. When the men tried to defend them, 68 were handcuffed to an armoured truck and raped too. After this episode, 45 of them joined the guerrillas in the mountains. One older man, Nurdi Dayeyev, who was nearly blind, had nails driven through his hands and feet because it was suspected that he was in contact with the fighters. The Russians do not deny that these things happen, there's even an official order issued banning such abuses.

Theatre of War

Last weekend's tragedy has refocused attention on the conflict, which Russia has repeatedly claimed is winding down, even though its soldiers continue to die at a rate of two to three a day. Russia's President Putin has tried to sweep the embarrassing brutalities of the ongoing 'anti-terrorist' operations under the carpet, whilst the West has turned a blind eye so they could get Russian support for their own wars of terror in Afghanistan, Iraq and elsewhere.

The problem according to Krystyna Kurczab-Redlich, a Polish reporter is that "the brutality of the Russians has also resulted in a growing radicalisation of their opponents." Russia has tried to link the rebels to al-Qaeda, as some of the Chechen leaders no doubt see the conflict as a holy war. Now Chechen's everywhere face a further crackdown. Soldiers are surrounding refugee camps, while Chechen's in Russia are being rounded up and arrested. Russia has tried to stop the World Chechen Congress in Copenhagen, they persuaded Denmark to arrest Akhmed Zakayev, Chechnya's top European representative, who was to be the main speaker, who they accuse of playing a part in the theatre siege. As one Russian journalist commented "The search for participants in the terrorist act is turning into a cleansing operation to rid Moscow of all Chechens."

* For conspiracy theories that it was the Russian secret police who carried out the 1999 bombings of apartment blocks that sparked the latest war with Chechnya and swept Putin to power see http://uk.indymedia.org/front.php3?article_id=24275

* Amnesty International this week published a new report on the human rights situation in Russia and Chechnya. For copies 020 7814 6200 www.amnesty.org

More Shit in the Pipeline

Both Russia and the US are fighting the 'war on terror' to justify attacks on (largely) Islamic societies with racist rhetoric about the need to combat 'fundamentalism', but the real reason behind it is justification for anything the state does to protect

Putin the Boot In cont...

its interests. Nowhere is this more obvious than in the former Soviet republic of Georgia.

Back in July, this tiny country was granted $64 million of aid by the US government, making it the third largest recipient of US aid in the world. The reason? Both the US and Russia reckon that Georgia is in the frontline of the 'war on terror'. Russia argues that Georgia's mountainous Pankisi gorge, which sits along the border with Chechnya, is a hideout for Chechen rebels, who are able to move across the border to launch attacks on Russian troops. The US reckons that amongst these fighters there might be as many as a dozen Al-Qaeda members. The $64 million is for counter-insurgency training and equipment for the Georgian army, allegedly so that it can flush out these bad guys. Russia was furious about this move, which amounts to the US establishing a base for its Special Forces on the Russian border. Russia accused Georgia of 'complicity' with international terror and Putin wrote to the UN saying that Russia reserved the right to use 'pre-emptive strikes'

on Georgia to defend itself.

The US claim that it's pouring money on the Georgian military so that they can take out al-Qaeda just doesn't stand up. As one journalist wrote, 'why would the dozen or so suspected al-Qaeda terrorists hang around until a new force is trained?' But what other reason would there be for making sure the Georgian army is tooled-up like the Green Berets? Hmmm, maybe it's got something to do with the massive oil and gas pipelines that the US and Britain want to run through Georgia, to take oil from Baku, Azerbaijan, to Ceyhan in Turkey. For the last 10 years the US and Britain have been investing in central Asian oilfields, but have been struggling to find a way of getting the oil to the West without taking it through Iran or Russia. The proposed solution is the Baku-Ceyhan pipeline, which if built would transport 1 million barrels of oil a day along a route that runs across (amongst other things) 20 major rivers and 2 dense primary forests, and borders on several zones of conflict.

The consortium of companies backing the pipeline is only offering

to provide 30% of the £3 billion costs. BP, the company heading the consortium, has said that the project would not be possible without masses of 'free public money' (i.e. our money), including £65 million from the UK's own Export Credit Guarantee Scheme. It will also need military or paramilitary patrols all along the route to protect the pipe from sabotage and theft. Campaigners opposing the pipeline say that the proposed route 'as well as passing through war zones, cuts through villages and bisects peoples' lands. Many will be evicted, or forced to trespass on oil company property in order to lead their daily lives. Similar situations in other countries (such as BP's pipeline in Colombia) have led to major human rights atrocities.' Whilst Georgian peasants worry that Russia's 'new hard-line' approach to Chechnya will drag their villages back into conflict, Western greed for Central Asian oil is driving plans that, if carried out, will ensure that Georgia is threatened by war and environmental crisis for decades to come.

More info: www.bankwatch.org

Earth First! Baku-Ceyhan Action Briefing

If there was any doubt left in anyone's mind, the past year definitely made one thing clear: the oil industry's got it coming. At a time when some predict that oil reserves will run out within a couple of generations, when global warming is an imminent reality, the petrochemical giants are still one of the main forces standing in the way of developing sustainable energy, and are still scouring the globe for new sources of oil to burn. In the twisted logic of capitalism, the less oil there is left, the more profitable it will become for the energy barons to prevent investigation into alternatives. This isn't good for anyone, but it will be worst for people unlucky enough to live around areas where new wells and pipelines are being constructed. Extraction is a messy and expensive business: local environments are destroyed by leaks, and local people subjected to violence, as oil companies employ paramilitaries and support repressive governments to protect their massive investments. One oil company project threatening to make life nastier and shorter for a lot of people is the Baku-Ceyhan pipeline (see SchNEWS 379). In the following article activists working against the pipeline give an overview of the plan, and some of the stuff that's being done to stop it.

The Baku-Tblisi-Ceyhan (BTC) pipeline is BP's latest project. Running from the Caspian Sea through 8 conflict zones in Turkey, Georgia and Azerbaijan, this 1000-mile oil pipeline will bring 1 million barrels of oil a day to Europe and the US for the next 40 years, and will have a devastating impact on the climate, the environment and human rights.

The pipeline is the key to unlocking vast oil reserves, the burning of which directly contradicts Britain's Kyoto climate change commitments and will wreak havoc on the earth's climate. In terms of human rights, we only have to look at BP's track record (or that of any other oil company, such as Shell in Ogoniland) to know what this pipeline will mean for people on the ground. Pipelines invariably exacerbate conflict in the regions where they are built. BP funded paramilitaries in Colombia to protect its pipeline from local opposition and guerrilla activity, and to silence its own workers. Kurdish communities in Turkey have already been evicted from their land in preparation for the Baku pipeline. Militarisation is already happening along the length of the Baku pipeline (see SchNEWS 379): ABB recently won a security contract and use of US unmanned drones to patrol pipeline routes in Georgia.

Local communities will not see any benefit from

ence, their skills, and some will lose their lives. No one except BP and its project partners will benefit from this proposed pipelines system, yet BP is asking that 70% of the US$3.3 billion project be financed by public money. It is courting the UK government to influence banks such as the European Bank of Reconstruction and Development (EBRD) and the International Financial Corporation (IFC, an arm of the World Bank), which generate their funds from taxpayer's money. If these banks don't cough up the dough, the pipeline cannot go ahead.

Although these banks are 'minded' to give BP the money they need for the pipeline, and the construction company AMEC is in line for building it ($330 million contract so far), the project is not yet a dead cert. Which gives us an opportunity to stop it.

Earth First! and other concerned groups such as Rising Tide have been visiting many of the companies involved in the pipeline. In January, a group of people visited the offices of Environmental Resource Management (ERM) for a day. ERM are responsible for the Environmental and Social Impact Assessments that BP are required to do for greenwash purposes. These assessments are a joke. Independent researchers found that consultations had not been done in local languages, that many villages had been ignored and key locations excluded. The consultants from ERM claimed to have talked to 100% of villagers in Hacibayram in north-eastern Turkey - a village which was, at the time, completely abandoned following local conflict! The most recent Baku-Ceyhan Campaign fact-finding mission to northeast Turkey just returned having uncovered disturbing human rights abuses and it was itself detained by the Turkish gendarmerie.

In February, an Earth First! group occupied the offices of the European Bank of Reconstruction and Development (EBRD) in the city of London, interrupting an executive meeting about the pipeline. They refused to leave until they had spoken to those responsible for signing off the project and the very eager-to-appease directors attempted to 'dialogue' the group for four hours, confirming the group's understanding that the EBRD had already promised BP the money and were now just working out how to justify it! When asked to name one oil pipeline ever that had delivered the benefits promised to affected communities, they couldn't. An invitation to return as part of a focus group was declined.

a RSK in Cheshire, a greenwash company similar to ERM, with a client list that makes your blood run cold, but this time providing Cultural and Heritage Impact Assessments. Because not much was known about RSK - and because the group had no desire to listen to bullshit - the group decided on a silent occupation, refusing to engage with any of the staff and simply gathering whatever information they could from files and computers.

Also in March, the trading floor of the International Petroleum Exchange in the City of London was stormed and closed down for three hours in an action designed to crystallize the link between oil and the war in Iraq.

Action against the pipeline in the UK is also linking up with efforts to stop the pipeline in the countries which will be directly affected. As 16 Georgian, Azerbaijani and Russian NGOs presented their objections to the EBRD office in Tbilisi, Georgia, 120 people in the UK constructed their own pipeline starting at the EBRD in the Square Mile and passing the bank ABN Amro and ending up at BP headquarters in the City of London.

The Baku pipeline is a big deal, not only because it's a nasty project but because it is happening at a time when the first phase of the oil wars has begun. As for BP, it is already on shaky ground. Because of visits like those described above and due to pressure exerted by groups like Rising Tide and the broader Baku-Ceyhan Campaign, the Baku pipeline has already been put back by 6 months. At 1 million barrels of oil a day, every day's delay means the loss of millions of dollars. Furthermore, despite an aggressive greenwash strategy (including a BP-sponsored Ecology exhibition at the Natural History Museum!), concern about BP working practices in Alaska and in Colombia have already caused investors to question their involvement with BP. So get out there and shut BP down!

For information on the pipeline, contact Rising Tide (a UK grassroots network against climate change) at info@risingtide.org.uk or look at the following websites: Baku-Ceyan Campaign at www.bakuceyhan.org.uk and www.burningplanet.net Or get a group together and go and visit one of the following: ERM (London and Manchester), the EBRD (London), AMEC (London and Cheshire), RSK (Cheshire), Lazard Brothers (London) and any BP petrol station or office. Contact Manchester EF! for disk detailing companies involved or look on

Causing a climate of chaos at the Motor Show in Birmingham

STORMING

Last Tuesday (22nd October) workers on the Birmingham Northern Relief Road were able to enjoy an unscheduled break when a dozen people stormed the construction site of a bridge over a canal and disabled diggers and a crane. The protesters say it represents the start of a new phase of the campaign against car culture and climate change in the face of a renewed road building program under the Labour Government. The action happened one day before the start of the British International Motor Show and the UN climate conference in New Delhi, India (COP 8).

At the Motor Show in Birmingham, Europe's largest car show, actions continued highlighting how the car industry is part of the problem of climate change.

It's not just people in the west who have been protesting against climate change. Those communities most affected (mostly in southern countries) met at a Climate Justice Summit held at the same time as the UN climate conference to provide a platform for climate change impacted communities from around the world. "The negotiations to solve the climate change crisis have been hijacked by corporations and industrialised nations, especially the US. These meetings resemble a trade meeting to push globalisation over developing countries rather than a meeting to address the genuine needs of people," said Medha Patkar of the India Climate Justice Forum. The summit was followed by a 5, 000 strong rally in New Delhi.

And while the people directly affected by climate change met to discuss the issues affecting them the world's Governments met to carve-up another commodity - the earth's climate. The conference looks like being yet another failed opportunity, with the initial draft resolution in combating climate change being described as "unacceptable" and "worthless". Expect more storms and floods of hot air from the conference which finishes today. www.corpwatchindia Car show actions: www.anticarshow.net

* 600 protesters managed to shut down all 28 Esso petrol stations in Luxembourg last Saturday in a climate change protest by Greenpeace.

* **Protests at two Brighton Esso Stations** at Lewes Rd and Dyke Rd. Meet Sat 2nd 12pm.

* While our government's Environment Minister talks about cutting down greenhouse gases, there are plans for a massive extension of airports which will do nothing to curb air travel, the fastest growing source of greenhouse gases. A new Midlands airport would threaten the country's leading organic organisations gardens at Ryton (024-7630-3517 www.hdra.org.uk). And a new airport at Cliffe marshes in Kent would affect internationally important wetland sites that are home to 200,000 wading birds. The government has a consultation about air travel at www.aviation.dft.gov.uk or phone 0845 100 5554. You can email objections to the Department of Transport apd@dft.gsi.gov.uk for what its worth.

* **Runway No Way Demonstration** against Stanstead Airport, 2nd Nov Montessori School, Mole Hill Gn, nr Broxted. 07817 708113.

* Public meeting to discuss the current aviation consultation 14th November at Plants Brook School, Upper Holland Road, Sutton Coldfield, West Midlands 7.30pm.

* Remember the fuel blockades a couple of years ago by truckers and farmers? Welsh farmer Mr Brynle Williams one of its leaders claimed to have no political bias: "I'm not a politician, I'm just a simple farmer." Well guess who has been selected as Conservative candidate for Clwyd West? But then he did say "I don't want a career in politics at all" so maybe joining the dinosaur Conservative Party is the right thing to do.

LISTEN UP!

Last Thursday protestors used D-locks, Superglue and good ol' determination to blockade the US spy base in Menwith Hill, Yorkshire. The blockade started at 5am with protestors D-locking themselves to the main gates and then handcuffing themselves to each other. With alternative gates sealed off by Superglue and locks, all traffic was blocked and the 3 scheduled shift changes were disrupted. Most employees were prevented from entering the base to do their daily spying and so ended up heading back home. After 4 ½ hours the ever-friendly men in blue were threatening arrests and the protestors ended the blockade, happy with the results.

So what's this spy base about then? Well, it's an 'interception centre' that would be used to co-ordinate any bombing of Iraq. It's part of America's murky 'Echelon' programme set up during the Cold War – a network of 'listening posts' able to intercept millions of phone, fax and e-mail messages. Our upstanding government assures us that 'communication interception' is covered by strict legal guidelines - honest! But the EU parliamentary committee set up to investigate 'Echelon' reckons that Uncle Sam uses it for industrial espionage to benefit US companies. So the committee recommends that all EU capitalists encrypt everything…now!

* **Fylingdale Star Peace Camp**, outside the US airbase, which is now 5 months old, have received eviction papers and are appearing in court next week. Vigil outside the court 10.45am, 6th Nov, Whitby Law Court, Waterstead Lane, Whitby. The camp also urgently needs funds send money payable to 'WoMenwith Hill Women's Peace Camp', P.O. Box 105, Harrogate HG3 2FE. Tel 01947896481 www.FreeFylingdalesNetwork.co.uk.

SchNEWS in brief

Sick of prefab pop music? To help the sporadic network aimed at bringing down 'Pop Rivals' visit www.killpop.org ** The global arms trade has flourished since the end of the Cold War. Find out in the **'No-Nonsense Guide To The Arms Trade'** – available for £7 from CAAT, 11 Goodwin Street, London N4 3HQ www.caat.org.uk ** **Taking Aim** – a Revolutionary Conference for the liberatarian left, activists and other rebel-rousers, will be held in Bradford next year. To get involved email conference@riseup.net. ** **Sic** – Chumbawamba's very slick er 'zine' is out. All good stuff with Mark Thomas and others contributing, available now for a fiver www.chumba.com/_sic.htm ** To get a copy of **Que Se Vayan Todos**, the excellent newsprint publication about the events of the last 12 months in Argentina send SchNEWS a 41p SAE ** **Zapatista** - A benefit for Mayan autonmous communities, Tues 4th downstairs at the Sanctuary, Brunswick St, Hove. With food, info and world and rebel beats. Kicks off at 7pm with the film Zapatista ** **Remember Barry Horne**. Anniversary of the death of the animal rights prisoner who died on hunger strike against the government broken promises of animal welfare reform. Memorial demo Tues 5th 2pm followed by night vigil at HLS, Alconbury, Cambs.0845 458 0630 or 07899 775493 ** **Scottish Anarchist Day School** Sat 9th, Kinning Park Centre, Glasgow, Scotland. 10.30am-5pm. Workshops, discussions, and much more! £3/1. An-archo-scots@lists.mutualaid.org http://lists.mutualaid.org/mailman/listinfo/anarcho-scots

Inside SchNEWS

Pelle Strindlund from Bye Bye Meat Industry - a group that carries out "animal rights ploughshares type actions" - has been given 8 months for rescuing hens from a battery farm. He'd appreciate letters of support. Pelle Strindlund, Ostragård kriminalvardsanstalt, Box 215, SE462-23 Vanersborg, Sweden

Cassidy Wheeler an US anarcho-primitivist serving 8½ years for petty theft is looking for penpals to keep up with what's going on whilst he's inside. Cassidy Wheeler #1428456, SRCI, 777 Stanton Blvd., Ontario, Oregon 97914-8335, USA.

...and finally...

Boom, Boom... For those readers old enough to remember Basil Brush the country's favourite fox, you'll remember that he wasn't all sweetness and light. Well he's back on TV screens and he's still causing a bit of a stir, not only is he fatter and now allegedly a bit camp, but his fox's natural instinct to dislike farmers has resulted in an episode of his series being 'temporarily withdrawn' by the BBC. The episode, which featured Basil calling a bad-tempered farmer 'manure breath', and then ALF-style liberating the farmer's chickens from a chicken pie fate. The BBC insisted that the programme was not being screened because it was "not yet ready for transmission" and that it was nothing to do with complaints from Richard Haddock, a member of the National Farmers' Union council, who said: "I am absolutely disgusted. The BBC in London seems to be going down this anti-farm agenda." Which is obviously laughable considering the unquestionable support they gave to last month's Countryside Alliance March.

This story was stolen from October's brilliant Shoreham Protester-which includes loads of interesting info about the Countryside Alliance. 50p plus SAE from The Shoreham Protester, 7 Stoneham Road, Hove, BN3 5HJ. www.shoreham-protester.org.uk

Disclaimer

WOODSIDE LINED

The Woodside Caravan Park – a legitimate campsite in Bedfordshire bought in 1997 by 27 gypsy families – is under threat of eviction from this Friday (1). A protest camp has been set up to help the community resist eviction, and needs more people and tat. This comes a week after a gypsy from another camp, a 22 year old father of two, was subject to a murder attempt and dumped in a coma outside Woodside in a racially motivated act of intimidation. For Woodside residents this is even more reason to remain on the site as they feel safer together. Info. 01767 681 651 www.f-f-t.demon.co.uk/fft/WOODSIDE.HTM

BARRED FOR LIFE

The indefinite detention of 12 people without trial in the UK under last year's knee jerk Anti-Terrorism Crime and Security Act (see SchNEWS 363), has been deemed legal by the High Court. In July an appeal by those detained under the Act, led to an immigration appeals commission to rule that it contravened the European Convention on Human Rights. That decision has now been overturned by the High Court who believed the government that these 12 people are a threat to the nation's security in this 'time of emergency'. And what evidence did the government need to produce to show that we're in a state of emergency- well the evidence put forward by the government to back it's argument remained secret and was not considered by the court in it's decision. As according to the judges the government is in a better position than the courts to make such important decisions. Two of those detained have now left the country, the remainder now face indefinite imprisonment for the duration of the 'emergency'.

Subscribe!

WAKE UP! IT'S YER SERGEANT PEPPER'S SPICY

I'm sick of your middle-of-the-road politics!

NO WAR FOR OIL

weekly SchNEWS
www.schnews.org.uk

Friday 8th November 2002   **Free/Donation**   **Issue 380**

ASSAULT AND PEPPER

Police lose it on Brighton Seafront, Halloween

Thousands took part in last Thursday's nationwide day of action against the threat of war on Iraq. In Brighton, SchNEWS joined in with hundreds of others for the best bit of direct action on the city streets since the heady days of Reclaim The Streets parties way back in the mid 1990's.

The Brighton demo started at 3pm with a critical mass bike ride from Sussex University with the Peddlers for Peace blocking both lanes of traffic and, despite the best efforts of the cops, riding triumphantly all the way to the war memorial at the Old Steine. Over 500 people from a range of backgrounds - students, Christians, greens, socialists, anarchists and a peace choir were entertained with speeches, MCs and some crazy dancing people before they set off to block the main roundabout by Palace Pier.

Seeing as it was Halloween the cops, who had obviously done their PR training with the Seattle police department, were busy dishing out their own special trick or treats - a pre-emptive blast of pepper spray, boots and batons for all the poor protesters who were just too tired to carry on and ended up having

to sit down in the road. Still, what did the demonstrators expect? They were only trying to protest that thousands of innocent Iraqi civilians could be killed, while the police had the much more important task of keeping the traffic moving. And contrast this response to the City's small traders, who for the past few months have been disrupting traffic by driving through town at a snails pace in protest at increased parking fees, without a whiff of pepper spray or baton in sight.

One man was taken to casualty after being pepper sprayed twice. The weapon in his hand was a notebook in which he was recording police ID numbers, many of which weren't on display. He told SchNEWS "Ironically one of the justifications given for attacking oil-rich Iraq is Saddam's brutal treatment of dissenters in his country. He has been accused of using chemical

weapons such as mustard gas to suppress rebellion. How lucky we are to live in a civilised country where pepper spray is used instead."

According to their own rules cops can only spray when they are physically threatened – and apparently people sitting cross-legged in the road posed such a huge threat – but the heavy-handed tactics only succeeded in partly clearing the roundabout and nudging the crowd into going on a walkabout. The demo outmanoeuvred the cops for hours, heading towards key spots around the city, with riot wagons scurrying to get numbers to block-off roads.

Even the local rag, The Argus, said "The fact that so many people in Brighton alone were willing to take to the streets shows the strength of public opinion and that

HOT STUFF

Pepper Spray is not in fact made from pepper, but from a synthetic substance called PAVA which when sprayed causes burning to the skin, eyes, nose, mouth and breathing passages. The good news is that the effects are temporary. But for infants, the elderly, people who suffer from respiratory diseases, etc. the risks are possibly life-threatening.

If the police carry on behaving like

this on demos it would be a good idea to start carrying goggles. If you are sprayed the best treatment is to wash your eyes with a solution of half-liquid antacid (like Maalox) and half water, or failing that just use water. To treat skin wipe with a cloth saturated with vegetable oil, and immediately wipe off the oil with alcohol (But don't get alcohol in your eyes, it will hurt as much as the spray!) For more info on pepper spray and first aid see www.blackcrosscollective.org

Assault & Pepper cont...

cannot be ignored by politicians." The cops capped off a great day with the old chestnut that it was a small minority of troublemakers who had spoiled it for everybody. We agree and they are based at John Street Police Station.

* Next Wed (13) **Sussex Action for Peace Benefit Night** with various DJ's at Club New York, Dyke Road, Brighton £5/£3

* The next **Rebel Alliance**, Brightons get together of direct action groups, will also be about 'Peace and Pepper Spray' with a discussion and short film about the anti war demo. Monday 18th Nov Brighton Unemployed Centre, 6 Tilbury Place 7pm

* **March for Peace in Brighton** on 23rd November. Meet 12pm Preston Park. 07815 983022 sussexactionfor peace@hotmail.com

Were you baton charged or sprayed?

Under the Data Protection Act you have the right to see any CCTV footage of yourself. This would include both footage from static CCTV cameras (there are loads in Brighton, including one above the roundabout by the pier) and hand held cameras carried by police evidence gatherers. All you need to do is send a letter with your name and address, a description of yourself, where you were and at what time. You will also have to send £10 to cover costs. (cheques payable to S.P.A.) Send to Data Protection Officer, Sussex Police, Malling House, Church Lane, Lewes, East Sussex. Tel: 0845-6070999.

More info and a sample letter can be seen at www.mtcp.co.uk/campaigns/dataprotection.htm

This One's For Pa!

Our guess is that you've never heard of the investment firm the Carlyle Group. Well there's a reason for that—even Business Week describes it as, "One of the most powerful, well connected and secretive organisations in the world". Founded fifteen years ago by Ronald Reagan aide David Rubenstein, the company shot to the top when Frank Carlucci, former US Secretary of Defence, joined the team and started acquiring a list of staff that'll leave conspiracy theorists with unpleasant stains on their trousers.

Carlyle now boasts the likes of James Baker, former Secretary of State, Arthur Levitt, chairman of the Securities and Exchange Commission, and Karl Otto Pohl, former president of the Bundesbank. The list also includes former presidents of South Korea and the Philippines, and our own man of morality, John Major. But wait! There's more! CEO Carlucci is a 'close friend' of Donald Rumsfeld, current US Secretary of Defence, and also sits on a board of 'independent' defence analysts. Bush Senior also holds large interests in the company. Add to this the fact that Bush Jr himself was given a seat on the board of one of the Carlyle group's first companies in 1990, and you begin to wonder exactly how big this 'revolving door' between government and politics really is.

But this isn't just your average love affair between business and government. Carlucci and chums have used their extensive political connections to acquire control of heavily regulated industries at bargain prices, most notably *defence* companies. At present Carlyle owns United Defence, the fifth biggest arms contractor in America, Bofors, a Swiss munitions manufacturer, and since September the 3rd of this year, a substantial stake in Qineteq, the research branch of the MoD. What does this mean? Basically as the bombs fall and the sabers rattle, Bush's mates and his family are getting rich. Don't believe us? Ask them.

Carlyle sold United Defence stocks on the stock market only one day after Congress ratified Bush's new Defence Budget for the War Against Terrorism (a wee $11 billion more than the previous defence budget). Carlyle cleaned up $237 million in one day and spokesmen for the company admitted that the timing was fully intentional. Not to mention the renewed contracts that United Defence received to the tune of $2 billion.

So daddy Bush is doing very well out of the new crusade. Sickening, but not really unexpected, nor in this system of ours, illegal. What has got the watchdogs howling, however, is the fact that the Bin Laden family themselves were stakeholders in Carlyle until October of 2001, as part of a deal brokered by Bush Snr himself! Funny that when the administration was freezing the assets of any organization with links to terrorism this didn't include daddy's piggy bank! www.dyncorp-sucks.com/carlyle.html#Citigroup www.hereinreality.com/carlyle.html www.eco-action.org/porkbolter/carlyle.html

(right) Who you gonna call? Weaponsbusters! Gloucestershire Weapons Inspectors pay a visit to Fairford Airbase on October 31st - the base which the US Military have used in past conflicts to reload bombers, and which is about to feature strongly in an attack on Iraq. www.gwi.org.uk

SchNEWS in brief

SchNEWS is **really desperate** for people to help with the mailout for a couple of hours on Friday afternoons. Give the office a call if you can help ** On Wednesday, Clive Codona, Chair of the National Travellers Action Group, lost his appeal at the High Court and so the travellers who bought **Woodside** campsite in Bedfordshire are once again facing eviction. Bailiffs are expected 5pm today (8th) where Clive will ask them just where he and the other 27 families are supposed to go? Tel 01767 681 651 www.f-f-t.demon.co.uk/fft/WOODSIDE.HTM ** Brighton's premier pirate radio station **Radio 4A** is on the air this weekend (8th–10th). 107.8FM and www.piratetv.net, details at www.radio4a.org.uk ** **RIP. John Moore**, primitivist writer and poet, died suddenly on October 22. John was one of the UK's leading primitivists and frequently wrote articles for Green Anarchist and other publications. ** Around 200 people reclaimed the streets in **Copenhagen** last Friday, protesting against big business & private cars and demanding the right to party! ** Copenhagen is also the setting for mass protests against the **EU Summit** there from the 12-14 December. www.disobedience.dk ** **Greenpeace's Rainbow Warrior ship** is currently on a three month educational tour of UK ports including Trinity Quay Plymouth Wed 13th, Poole Quay 16th-17th, Liverpool, Greenock, Belfast, Dublin, Cardiff, Plymouth, Edinburgh, Newcastle, Ipswich and London. 020 7226 6059 www.greenpeace.org.uk/rainbowwarrior.htm ** The **Berkshire Citizens Inspection Agency (CIA)** will **be visiting 2 nuclear weapons establishments** this weekend, where they will demand to carry out inspections to ensure that the weapons establishments are complying with international law. The team will be visiting **Aldermaston** today and **RAF Welford** on Saturday. 0118 966 8328/07790 409339 **Support the **13 asylum seekers being fitted up for arson!!** Following the fire in **Yarl's Wood Detention Centre** last February, the Crown is bringing **charges of arson and violent disorder against 13 detainees** whom it is desparate to scapegoat for the blaze. On Sunday (10) there will be leafletting outside of Harrow Crown Court, Hailsham Drive, Harrow at 10am, followed by a planning meeting, then a drive over to Wormwood Scrubs to visit detainees. On **Friday the 15th there's a pre-trail hearing at Harrow Crown Court**. Meet at the court 9am for a demo & leafleting. Info: ginn_emma@hotmail.com / 07786 517379 ** Some people from Brighton will be taking a mini-bus up to Harrow on the 15th. If you're interested, come to the next **Brighton No Borders meeting**, Monday the 11th at 7:30pm, Unemployed Centre, Tilbury Pl.

COP8 & ROBBERS

The COP 8 UN Climate Change conference in New Delhi fizzled out last week – the latest in the series of meetings which benefit the five star hotel industry more than the environment. Each time the UN climate folks meet they tinker with their 'declaration' – and now it doesn't even mention the Kyoto protocol! Kyoto was supposed to be a pledge for the US, Europe, and Co. to reduce their greenhouse gas emissions by 5.2%. Sounds good, except when you consider that experts agree this figure should be 60-90%. In short, the New Delhi conference was a complete sham. But as a sidenote, the US—who cause 25% of worldwide emissions and aren't even signing up for Kyoto—were said to be happy with the 'progress'. 01865 241097 www.risingtide.org.uk

DARK AGES

Work has started on construction of a privately financed road at Bilston, 8 miles south of Edinburgh. The road will destroy a local woodland, part of which is an SSSI. The woods contain many mature trees and a medieval bridge and tower. A protest camp was set up in June this year—they desperately need more people and more tat! Directions by car - take the A701 towards Pennicuik until you get to Bilston. Search for a metal gate on your left (opposite VW garage), go through & follow the path. By bus - take the 37A from E'burgh towards Pennicuik, get off at the 1st bus stop in Bilston. Contact the site mobile 0798663249 or email: bilston.glen@dhmail.net

IF ORDINARY PEOPLE BEHAVED LIKE- **Microsoft**

THIS NEW WHEEL YOU SOLD ME- IT'S THE WRONG SIZE!

NO, NO, MADAM... IT'S THE RIGHT SIZE - IT'S JUST THAT IT'S GOT THE NEW 8.5 AXLE...

WELL THEN GIVE ME ONE WITH THE OLD AXLE!

I'M SORRY, MADAM- I'M AFRAID I CAN'T DO THAT... YOU'RE GOING TO NEED TO UPGRADE THE REST OF YOUR BIKE.

Projection on parliament Pic: Paola Desiderio

Nightmare At Palace Pier, Brighton

THE USUAL HAUNTS AT HALLOWEEN

Manchester

Bedford The Britons V Bush demonstration attracted 150 people – the largest protest in the towns recent history.

Cardiff On the 30th, protesters halted the Welsh Assembly and scattered Mass Destruction Flyers about. One of the protesters zip-tied himself to the speakers desk as security and police bundled the protesters out of the chamber.

Cambridge Women in Black supporters 'died' outside Great St Mary's, while 230 students occupied the Defence Evaluation and Research Agency building on New Museum's Site. Some lecturers cancelled their lessons in solidarity.

Essex University: Air raid sirens played over a sound system! Hundreds gathered to watch as the deafening crash of bombs rolled over the campus and 50 performed a die in.

Leeds Students disrupted lectures, occupied the Business School and local BBC studios, then joined the main Leeds protest outside Yorkshire TV.

Liverpool Students backed by the lecturers union walked out of lessons and some occupied Senate House, the main finance and administrative building of The University of Liverpool.

Manchester Despite heavy handed police and use of police horses Oxford Road (one of the main streets) was occupied for an hour by up to 1000 protestors, accompanied by a samba band.

Sheffield University occupied, Bikes not Bombs ride, large rally and a samba procession.

Walthamstow: A Territorial Army base graffitied with "Fight the rich not their wars".

More reports: http://uk.indymedia.org

* The Stop the War Coalition have called another mass London demo on February 15th 2003.

* Plans are still underway for widespread civil disobedience as soon as any military action against Iraq begins.

...Errr... I would just like to repeat what the previous ten speakers have already said...

NO BLOOD OiL!

FTAA Protests October 31, Quito, Ecuador

Quito Fooling

While thousands of UK residents took to the streets this Halloween to fight against the impending war, people in North and South America were making their voices heard against yet another Big Business trade agreement. In the Americas, October 31st was a Hemispheric day of action against the FTAA (Free Trade Area of the Americas), a pending trade agreement between every nation in North and South America barring Cuba. Based on the model of NAFTA and the WTO, the FTAA goes far beyond the trade liberalisation schemes brought about by those models, giving multinational corporations sweeping authority over virtually every aspect of life in the Americas.

By promoting IMF-style Structural Adjustment, the FTAA will bring about the privatisation and downsizing of public services such as health care and education and will also ensure that all public utilities - water, power, and telecommunications - come under the control of the private sector. Many in South America are certain that the FTAA will also wipe out small farmers and hand corporations a sweeping new set of tools to evade environmental and labour laws.

On October 31st, Quito, Ecuador was the unfortunate home of a FTAA Trade Ministers meeting. In response to this meeting, 15,000 people took to the streets. The crowd was nearly 90% campesinos (peasant farmers) and indigenous peoples, and chants of "No queremos, y no nos da la gana, ser una colonia, norteamericana," ("We don't want, and it doesn't do us any good, to be a North American colony") were heard everywhere. After being met by seas of teargas, the demonstrators marched to the Suissotel, where the trade ministers were meeting with assorted CEO's

and trade lobbyists. There the crowds stood outside the gates and demanded that some of their representatives be allowed to speak with the ministers.

Eventually, 40 representatives of social movements from across the hemisphere were allowed in. What followed were two amazing hours of the FTAA trade ministers being forced to stare real people in the face. The protestors who had been allowed in chanted and yelled at ministers, aiming much of their noise at Bob Zoellick, the US Trade Rep. One woman from Nicaragua seemed to sum it up when she addressed the trade ministers, "Don't think you can simply take your picture with us and push forward. We will stop the FTAA." www.indymedia.org www.stopftaa.org

* Solidarity demos against the FTAA Trade Ministers meeting in Quito took place in many cities across the Americas. On the 31st, 5,000 marched against the FTAA in Sao Paolo, Brazil. On the same day, 10,000 marched in Montreal, Canada. A few days earlier, on the 28th, 13 San Francisco activists occupied the entrance to the world headquarters of Bechtel Corporation. Bechtel, one of the world's largest engineering firms, was targeted by the San Francisco activists because of its strong support for the Free Trade Area of the Americas and its frontline position in the rush to commodify and privatise the world's dwindling supply of fresh water.

...and finally...

During last week's anti-war actions, protesters in Swansea chose Sainsbury's to make their protest taste better. They invaded the store and occupied certain areas. Customer service obliged them by announcing the following over the intercom: "Sainsburys apologise for the inconvenience, there is an anti-war protest going on in aisles 6,7,8,and 9." ...www.indycymru.org.uk

Disclaimer

SchNEWS warns all readers the sting in the disclaimer can be peppered with enuff puns to make your eyes water or make you gag. Honest.

THE "AXIS OF OIL" REGIMES... VENEZUELA, IRAQ and IRAN POSE A GRAVE DANGER...

...TO THE **GOD GIVEN RIGHT OF AMERICA AND OUR ALLIES** TO DRIVE OUR CARS

weekly SchNEWS

www.schnews.org.uk

Friday 15th November 2002   Free/Donation   Issue 381

FLORENCE OF ARABIA

"Bush, Blair, Berlusconi - they don't speak for the people. We speak for the people. And we the people are going to stop this war." - Speaker at European Social Forum, Florence.

Last Saturday over half a million people marched through Florence in Europe's biggest demonstration yet against the forthcoming US invasion of the Middle East. Maybe it was a million as some reports have said, but SchNEWS ran out of fingers and toes to count on after four hours of seeing people stream along the well-reclaimed city bypass that was the only road in town big enough for the protest.

The march took place during the European Social Forum meeting in Florence and was always going to be a big march, with communists and anarchists, unions and peace groups, and social forums from across Italy taking part. But it was more than that. It was another example of the growing, often unreported movement against Bush and Blair's war plans that is sweeping the US and Europe.

While Britain was represented by everything from Essex Students to Dundee Trades Council, the march was largely Italian, young and unaligned. Local residents clapped and cheered, hanging out anti-war banners. The conference before the march saw meetings in aircraft hangers overflowing with people – 60,000 turned up for the Forum instead of the expected 20,000 - wanting to discuss anti-capitalism and the coming war. At one meeting of 2,000 people, a Vietnam war veteran told the crowd, "We didn't start protesting about the Vietnam war until it had been going on for years. This movement is much bigger, and you can stop them too". During the conference, a local Caterpillar factory that makes vehicles used to crush Palestinian homes was occupied and its contents rearranged. Demos, discussions and direct action are all part of the growing global movement against this war and the crazy system that is making it happen.

OIL JUNKIES

In order to regain control of Iraq's oilfields, the US is willing to let the Iraqi people pay a very high price. According to a new report by British health professionals, a war against Iraq could kill half a million people, mostly civilians. 260,000 are likely to die in the conflict and its immediate aftermath, with a further 200,000 dying later from famine and disease – the US will target bombs on water systems and other infrastructure to cripple the country and will ensure these deaths. In the report's worst case scenario, nuclear weapons are fired on Iraq in response to a chemical or biological attack on Kuwait or Israel, leaving a massive 3.9 million people dead.

CRAP ARRESTS OF THE WEEK
For praying!
Veteran peace activist Lindis Percy totted up yet another arrest at the beginning of this month. Lindis was peacefully praying at a Quaker meeting outside Fylingdales airbase (soon to be part of the Americas Star Wars programme) when the MOD cops swooped in and arrested her for breaching her bail condition of not going within 50 yards of the base. www.caab.org.uk
* The peace camp at Fylingdales is facing eviction and they need more support!! 01947896481

But all that's just for starters. US Deputy Secretary of Defense Paul Wolfowitz has said that a US-imposed regime in Iraq would "cast a very large shadow, starting with Syria and Iran, but across the whole Arab world". Iran is a country with a population larger than that of the UK and was described by Bush as part of the "Axis of Evil", perhaps making it the next country to be made safe for "US vital interests". The brutal Israeli occupation of Palestine could become the norm for the rest of the Arab world as a foreign power imposes its will by military force. The people of the Middle East are about to pay a very high price for capitalism's addiction to oil.

The diverse, growing movement against war knows all this. A new generation of activists in the rich countries of Europe and North America who want to live in a sustainable and just world are challenging their own governments and finding friends and allies in the

Pic: Jeff Brewster
A renaissance of the European Anti-capitalist movement takes place in Florence at the ESF

SchNEWS poser of the week

How come Neo-Labour has got enough money to bomb Iraq, but can't afford to pay striking firefighters a decent wage?

* The Brighton Firefighters support group is meeting Wednesday 20th at St. George's Community Centre (Crypt of St. George's Church), St. George's Road, Kemptown 7.45pm to discuss what steps they can take to support the strike.
* For more on the strike www.30kfirepay2.co.uk www.labournet.net

Florence of Arabia cont...

countries attacked in their name. There have been over 400 major demonstration in the US against an attack on Iraq. This was described as "a burgeoning national anti-war movement," by the Washington Post, "with protesting by people who have never protested before". Many US and European activists, often Jewish, have gone to Palestine, risking their lives in order to provide Palestinian families with some protection from Israeli attacks. In Florence, groups discussed blockading US airbases across Europe, jamming airbase radar systems with balloons and tinfoil, taking direct action to stop the supplies necessary for war. As one protester told SchNEWS, "If Bush and Blair think this movement is going to write letters, march politely and then go home, they're in for a fright."
* To read about the report on Iraq deaths www.newscientist.com/news/news.jsp?id=ns99993043
* Recommended reading 'War Plan Iraq' by Milan Rai (Verso 2002)

162

SchNEWS in brief

Help! SchNEWS needs people to help with the mailout on Friday afternoons for a couple of hours. And with desk top publishing on Thursday evenings. There will be a DTP training evening Thursday 28th, give the office a call if yer interested in either. ** **Aspire** have opened a **new social centre in Leeds** and promise a week packed with workshops, film shows, food and other groovy stuff. Buckingham House, Otley Road, Leeds. Also a free shop where you bring anything that you don't want and take things you do. ** **Woodside Caravan Park**, the travellers who brought their own site, have managed to delay eviction. They have lodged an appeal and are safe until then (although the appeal date has yet to be set). www.f-f-t.demon.co.uk/fft/WOODSIDE.HTM If you want to be on their Red-Alert list ring 01206 523 528 ** **Undercurrents BeyONd TV 3rd Annual Video Activist Festival**. 23rd Nov. noon- 9pm, Swansea Environment Centre, Pier Street, Swansea. www.undercurrents.org/beyondtv/ ** **Mad Pride** have a benefit night Tuesday 19th, Bull And Gate, 389 Kentish Town Road, London NW5. 7.30 pm. £5 on the door with performers and comedians 020 7388 8679 ** Good SchNEWS

– **McDonald is closing lots of its restaurants!** Many of these are in the Middle East, where a boycott of US goods and services is having an impact. A total of 175 restaurants in 10 countries are closing, and McD shares worth £31 two years ago are now worth only £10! ** **Anti-Capitalist Social Night**, Nov 19th, 9pm upstairs at the Princess Louise, 208-209 High Holborn, London. 07944 586416 www.temporary.org.uk ** On November 7, over 2500 people in Chicago marched in protest of the annual meeting of the **Trans-Atlantic Business Dialogue (TABD)**. TABD is yet another 'government in bed with big business' think tank and is made up of the 100 most powerful captains of industry from the EU and America. Their mission is to "remove obstacles to trade" between the EU and US, including such nuisances as the restrictions on marketing GM products. According to US officials, up to 80% of TABD's recommendations have been turned into official policy. www.schnews.org.uk/archive/news284.htm. ** **Women Speak Out Gathering next weekend (22-24)**. A gathering of women activists from all kinds of movements and backgrounds to meet and exchange experiences, views and ideas. MERCi Centre, 22a Beswick Street, Manchester. Children are welcome

and there's even crash space. £10 donation requested for the weekend including vegan food. 0161 227 8086/07753 606723 www.bellow.org.uk ** **Sweatshops, Globalisation and International Solidarity** Sat 23rd Nov. Conference to bring together campaigners and campaigns from the anti-sweatshop movement. 12-6pm, School of Oriental and African Studies, London. £5. 07904 431 959 www.nosweat.org.uk ** **Say no to US training of terrorists**!! The US Army School of the Americas has been training Latin American soldiers in counter-insurgency (read: torture, oppression, and genocide) since 1946. **Protest against the School of the Americas** Sat 16th from 1-4pm at the US Embassy, Grosvenor Square, London. ** Week of action against **Newchurch Guinea Pigs** (who breed them for vivisection) 18th-24th Nov. www.guineapigs.org.uk or 01902-564734 ** The new **Sussex Anti-Corruption Alliance** want groups and individuals to get involved www.sac-a.human-rights.org ** **"Riding the Dragon"**, a new book highlighting the abuses that **Shell oil company** have committed, was published on Tuesday accompanied by protests outside some of Shell's worst refineries. The book and other facts about Shell can be seen at www.shellfacts.com

MAPUCHE

Since the late 90s the Indigenous Mapuche people, whose ancestral lands have been occupied by the states of Chile and Argentina since 1885, have been occupying land and engaging in other forms of nonviolent direct action to defend their communities. More recently they have been involved in campaigning and land occupations to defend the environment from forestry companies and large dams. These actions have sparked a violent response from the state at levels that would make General Pinochet proud! Hundreds of Mapuches have been arrested under State Security and Anti-terrorism laws. Two community leaders have been murdered, and last week 17-year old activist Edmundo Alex Lemun Saavedra was shot in the head when police attacked a non-violent land occupation of the Mininco forest. He later died in hospital. www.mapuche-nation.org or www.chile.indymedia.org (in spanish)

Of course you lose points when you hit the babies or the Red Cross stations

kevans

War Briefs

Groups in a number of places including Brighton, Leicester and Bristol are planning **Stop the City, Stop the War** demonstrations if war is declared on Iraq. Check out the full listings on the Party and Protest section of our website and if we don't have your event listed, let us know what your plans are. ** The Stop the War group at the **School of Oriental and African Studies** have launched a new website: www.soasstopwar.org ** **Disobedience Anti-war Benefit** –with Citizen Fish, P.A.I.N. and Subsister, plus DJ's, Food & Stalls. 23rd Nov. 7pm, Chats Palace, 42-44 Brooksby's Walk, Homerton, E9. £5/£3.50 www.disobedience.org.uk ** Discussion on war coverage and the risks faced by journalists. In memory of BBC journalist **Mylvaganam Nimalarajan** who was killed two years ago reporting from the war torn Sri Lanka. NUJ, 308 Grays Inn Road, London WC1. 25th Nov, 6pm. www.rsf.org ** **NATO war-mingers** will meet in Prague, Czech Republic (21st-22nd Nov) to discuss, among other things, the so-called "War on Terrorism" and the expansion of NATO into Eastern Europe. Actions are being planned against the Summit. Border actions are also planned in the likely event that protesters are stopped from entering the country. Latest info: www.antinato.cz

CORPORATE CORPSE

Neo-Labour promised to get tough on criminals this week - but if you happen to be a company director who kills one of your workers, you're in luck! This so-called 'justice for all' doesn't include you. Five years ago, the Labour Government promised that it would do something about corporate crime. Unsurprisingly, victims and their families are still waiting. Chris Jones, father of Simon who was killed at work 4 ½ half years ago, told SchNEWS, "This is the same old Blairite crap: go for soft targets and easy results. Graffiti artists haven't killed or injured anybody. Yes, paedophiles are nasty, but corporate cowboys killed Simon at work, and at least 1500 people since him. Neo-Labour has done nothing about it. The Home Office is fast becoming the political wing of the CBI. Apart from ratting on their promise to bring in the corporate killing bill, they are also trying to sneak in the removal of compulsory inquests into work-related deaths, and have specifically excluded victims of health and safety crimes from the much-hyped 'Victims' Charter'. The cover-up goes on."

So remember - tough on chewing gum and spray paint, but not on corporate crime.

Centre for Corporate Accountability 020 7490 4494 www.corporateaccountability.org www.simonjones.org.uk

Positive SchNEWS

Another node of international resistance has sprung up in **Caracas, Venezuela**, with the opening of the Libertarian Social Studies Centre. The centre – which runs along the lines of promoting self-organisation, anarchy, and solidarity free from party politics – has opened a vast library and hopes to buy a printing press for some pamphleteering. But it needs donations (in US$$) for rent and resources! centrosociallibertario@yahoo.com www.nodo50.org/ellibertario/ellibertario

Inside SchNEWS

Robert "Seth" Hayes, a former member of the Black Panther Party and in prison for the past 30 years, has been moved from the hospital ward where he was receiving treatment for Hepatitis C and Diabetes and has been transferred to the general prison. He is suffering from dizziness, weakness, headaches, and loss of feeling in his extremities. The prison has cut off all monitoring of his medical status, claiming that it is no longer needed. They have also refused to purchase personal blood sugar testing units for Seth or any of the 40-50 other diabetics in the prison. Please write to Dr. Lester Wright, Chief Medical Officer, Department of Correctional Services, Albany, NY, 12226, USA, to demand Seth be given adequate medical care. Letters of support to: Robert "Seth" Hayes #74A-2280, Clinton Correctional Facility, Box 2001, Dannemora, New York, 12929, USA. Full details: www.wildgreens.ca/110402-3.htm

...and finally...

Security services in Germany who'd been secretly tapping the phones of 50 people got caught out recently after the people whose phones they were evesdropping on got charged for the privilege! One confused customer complained to the phone company about a mysterious phone number on his bill that he was supposed to have made calls to. But when he called the number he was told by a message that he did not have authorisation! Oops! The security services admitted there had been some error and said it was caused by a software glitch. Any geeks out there know how to cause the same "problem" in Britain?

Disclaimer

SchNEWS warns Florence not to mess around with Dougal or else Zebedee will go boing!

Tony, Tony there's a fire in the Commons!!

Don't worry, I'll piss on it like I've pissed on the firefighters

SchNEWS

weekly

www.schnews.org.uk

Friday 22nd November 2002　　**Free/Donation**　　**Issue 382**

FIREBRANDED

As SchNEWS went to press the Fire Brigade Union were planning an eight day strike over Neo Labour's refusal to pay them a decent wage. Because some people in authority are lining up to condemn the firefighters, SchNEWS has come up with a new Are You Worth It? Quiz and asked three leading figures just how much they think they're worth...

"I do not think we impress the public if we set too low a value on our own worth... If we believe our work here is important we should not shrink from putting proper value on it." Who said this? Step forward leader of the House, Robin Cook, voting with other MPs for an inflation busting 42% pay rise last year.

Bank of England governor Sir Eddie George, who over the weekend said that a "high settlement (for the firefighters)…would be very damaging indeed", earns just under £257,000 a year and can look forward to an annual pension of £167,000.

Sir George Bain, chairman of the so-called 'independent' inquiry into firefighter pay, became principal of London Business School in 1989 and secured himself "one of the most lucrative remuneration packages in the whole of academia", according to the New Statesman. He's also vice-chancellor of Queens University of Belfast, director of Blackwell Publishers, the Economist Group, Canada Life and Bombardier Aerospace Shorts Brothers.

SchNEWS knows what these people are really worth, but we do wonder if any of them went on strike, would anybody notice?

Meanwhile, greedy, selfish firefighters want £30,000 and according to the government are putting all our lives at risk by going on strike. Which is a bit rich coming from a government that can't wait to start bombing Iraq, a war which, according to a new report by British health professionals, could lead to the death of half a million people, the majority of them civilians.

The new pay deal offers pay increases with serious strings attached – what Neo Labour likes to dress up as modernisation, but what everyone else calls job cuts, penny pinching and creeping privatisation. Already Fire Stations are being built by and leased back from private companies, while fire appliances and even fire tunics and fire boots are maintained and owned by outside companies.

As a nation we are very rich - the UK is the fourth wealthiest industrial nation. But when people ask for the wealth to be distributed a bit more fairly, we are told we can't afford it. But we can, of course, afford to bomb Iraq at a cost of billions. And we can apparently afford to let big business fiddle their taxes.

> ## Don't attack Iraq, Freedom for Palestine - demonstration in Brighton
>
> Saturday 23rd, 12pm at Preston Park. Anti-war speakers before a nice stroll down to the Seafront. Info: 01273 685946 www.safp.org.uk (More stewards are needed – get in touch.)

CRAP ARRESTS OF THE WEEK
For stealing your own car!
A Brighton man was pulled over in his car on a routine police check, arrested with his two passengers, and held for 11 hours for "suspicion of theft" - of his own car which was taxed and insured. When he tried to get his car back he was told by Worthing cops that he'd have to wait. Meanwhile at the police compound, cars are only kept for a week and when he didn't show up, his car was crushed!

In 1997, a report by accountants Deloitte & Touche put the figure for legal tax avoidance at £85 billion! Minutes of an Inland Revenue meeting revealed the agency was soft on multinational tax returns for fear of driving investment away from the UK.

As one Fire Brigade Union (FBU) official said, "They are not serious about modernisation. They are serious about cutting costs and about breaking the fire brigades union for daring to ask for more. This dispute is highly political because the New Labour government are scared that the scandal of low pay in the public and other sectors will be exposed and the floodgates will open. The government want to break the FBU as a lesson to all public sector workers."

Perhaps Andrew Smith, Neo-Labour's Secretary of State for Work Till You Drop, spelt it out fairly clearly when he said, "The biggest challenge of the new decade is to encourage people to work longer." For less pay and for longer hours no doubt - unless of course you're an MP or company director, then of course we all know that's different 'because you're worth it.'

Firebranded cont...

Support the firefighters: Donate to their hardship funds, take them tea and cake on the picket lines, or just tell them you support what they are doing. Get a striker to come and talk at your workplace or group. And keep an eye out for support groups around the country. In Brighton there will be a stall outside the Open Market, London Road, 10am till 12 noon this Saturday – come and find out how to get involved. www.30kfirepay2.co.uk/ www.labournet.net

Pay the Fire Fighters, not the Fire Starters: Join the anti-war protests at the Confederation of British Industry AGM this Sunday (24th) 3.30pm at the GMEX, Manchester City Centre. Rolling protests continue till late Monday. Guests at this year's event include Gordon Brown MP; Paul O'Neill; the US Treasury Secretary; Lord Browne , boss of BP, and Tony Blair MP, plus the bosses of the arms companies and private firms after our public services. ANSWERmanchester@ aol.com

"... and when I got me hose out she just said 'keep it pumpin'..." Striking firefighters stoke a fire in the rain outside Crawley Fire Station, 21st January
Pic: Alec Smart

FIRE STRIHES: What's it all about?

Let's start with the nuts and bolts:

At the moment a full-time firefighter under 19 earns £16,941 a year. After 5 years service they get £21,531. After 15 years service they can look forward to £22,491. A fire control operator starts on £15,825 and can expect £20,577 after 15 years. Compare these with the pay of a police constable outside London, who starts on £17,733 and gets £32,721 after 14 years.

This is where the Fire Brigade Union's demand for £30K comes from, not because they want to be paid like coppers, but from the average pay of the so-called "Associate Professional and Technical" category of workers, to which they are supposed to belong. Contrary to Government propaganda, demanding more than £20K is not greedy, and there are not 40 applicants fighting for every firefighter's job. One nurse wrote to the FBU's official strike bulletin: "Firefighter's defense of their profession and fight for decent pay and conditions is the only way that the fire service will be prevented from sliding into the mess that teaching and nursing are now in."

Pay-rises of 16 - 42% have been negotiated in other public sector areas in recent years. The £650 million estimated to finance the FBU's pay demand gets spent at the drop of a hat when it comes to bailing out failing privatised polluters such as British Energy. The

vehemence with which the Government has refused to consider the FBU's pay claim unmasks its resolve to break one of the few highly unionised workforces left after Thatcher. The plainest expression of this intent is the repeated threat to ban strikes.

And they may well be worried enough to ban them. All over the country there was huge support for the strike action. Pickets were overwhelmed with donations of food, money and kids' toys. Many tube stations were closed as workers refused to work on grounds of health and safety. One haulier in South Humberside drove to his local picket, parked up and said he would refuse to work while they were on strike. Despite the Union leadership's best efforts to play down the political nature of the strikers' action, it provided a focal point for many people's hatred of Labour and disillusionment with traditional politics. At ground-level the message was clear: an effigy of Blair was hung on the picket in Brighton.

The government is trying to link any deal on pay to acceptance of a "modernisation" programme embodied in the infamous "Bain Report". This hastily scribbled document proposes a series of cuts and flexibility measures that will weaken firefighter's ability to defend themselves against their employers:

*Firefighters are to be trained as paramedics, a move emphatically opposed by the Paramedic's Association.

SICK PAY

With all the hassle these pesky fire fighters are giving our Neo-Labour boys, it's a wonder that they don't just privatise them. Surely there's nothing like bringing a private contractor in to stop all this nonsense about essential workers demanding decent pay. A company that has years of experience in driving down wages in the public sector and has been doing extremely well out of Neo Labour's drive to privatise and 'modernise' the public sector is Sodexho, a French multinational private service provider. The company has its fingers in lots of pies - defence, schools and colleges, asylum detention centres and prisons.

Sodexho is a perfect example of the private sector's drive to suppress wages in order to cut costs, win contracts and ultimately line their own pockets. The company has come under fire from labour groups and government bodies in nearly every country it operates

in, having been involved in labour disputes and court actions from Australia to the US. Now it's UK workers who are biting back.

Hospital service workers at Glasgow Royal Infirmary were the first to decide that they were worth more than the miserable £4.15 an hour Sodexho were forking out for their services. In August, around 300 staff won increased pay and conditions despite Sodexho's attempts to draft in scabs from Liverpool to break the picket lines.

Service staff at Liverpool Royal Infirmary, also on Sodexho's generous £4.15 an hour, followed Glasgow's success. They took strike action last Friday, during which a Sodexho manager on £70,000 a year showed his solidarity by helping to give out tea to patients (presumably not at £4.15 hour). Negotiations are underway, but threat of further action still looms over Sodexho.

The porters, cleaners and caterers of Glasgow and Liverpool may not be in the business of saving lives. But their success has shown that col-

lective action by workers getting shat on by the privatisation of essential services in 'New Britain' has still got teeth. As Caroline Leckie, UNISON's branch secretary said, "We won because we organised. We set our own agenda, we did not work to management's agenda." More on Sodexho disputes - www.labournet.net/default.asp#sodexho

Excellent articles on privatisation - www.monbiot.com

The number of Firefighters working the night shift is to be reduced, which is when most deaths occur.

*The disputes mechanism is to be reformed so the union will not be able to embark on any dispute without the management first agreeing on the form the dispute is to take. The ban on overtime is to be rescinded and there will be a blurring of the distinctions between full-time and retained firefighters: in effect they'll all become retained.

*Emergency Fire Control Rooms will be amalgamated with those of other Emergency Services and farmed out to Call-Centres. Section 19 of the 1947 Fire Services Act, which ensures that local communities are consulted about the closure of fire-stations, will be repealed. The Report envisages job-losses due to 'natural wastage', a point clarified by the Deputy Prime-Minister, when he said that the next wave of retiring firefighters simply would not be replaced.

It all looks and smells very much like the usual localisation and compartmentalisation, in preparation for privatisation, seen elsewhere. They tried privatising the fire-service in Northern Ireland last year. The attempt was scuppered, but it's unlikely to be the last. Northern Ireland is the traditional testing ground for projects like this.

So far there have been five official strike actions, one of 24 hours, three of 48 hours and eight one-day actions. Six strike actions have been cancelled, including three planned eight-day strikes. The FBU has been eager to demonstrate its reasonability, preferring to continue negotiations with the employers via the

conciliation service ACAS rather than pursue open conflict. This is perhaps not surprising, given the press campaign against them, but it is strategically suspect. On the other hand, open conflict seems exactly what the government wants. In December a deal, involving a 16% pay rise, had been struck hours before the planned eight-day strike was due to start. In an extraordinary turn of events, the Deputy Prime-Minister instructed the Employers not to accept the deal, thus ensuring the strike went ahead. At the time of writing (April) it seems that little progress has been made through the time and energy consuming recourse to negotiations via ACAS. The government still insists on any pay deal (and talk is now of a maximal rise of 16% by November) being directly linked to implementation of proposals in the Bain report. So far this has been rejected by the FBU membership.

After a pledge not to strike during the war on Iraq, which disappointed anti-war activists, given that the FBU has consistently taken an anti-war stance and been prominent on anti-war demonstrations, preparations are now afoot for further industrial action. You can support any further strikes by joining or forming Strike Support Groups to collect money for the FBU hardship fund or produce counter-propaganda. Raise the issue of safety at work during a firefighter strike in your work-place and try to spread the economic damage. If the firefighter's strike starts affecting other areas of the economy, they have a real chance of winning. We all do.

SCHOOL OF THE ASSASSINS

"I'll get you over the fence for a dollar" - breaking into Fort Benning, Nov 16th. Pic: Greg Roberts

"The order was to take everyone: parents, grandparents, kids, wives, everyone. It was very rare that anyone survived after being taken by my battalion. At first the children were abandoned in the park or the marketplace. But then General Alvarez Martinez said 'These seeds will eventually bear fruit'. So we had to eliminate the children as well." – School of the Americas (SOA) graduate who was once a member of Battalion 3-16, a secret death squad in Honduras. Gen. Alvarez Martinez was also trained at the SOA.

"If any government sponsors the outlaws and killers of innocents, they have become outlaws and murderers themselves." - George Bush on the day he began bombing Afghanistan.

This past weekend, nearly 10,000 people marched to shut down the US's number one terrorist training camp, the School of the Americas. Located in Fort Benning, Georgia, the US-Army-operated SOA has been around for the last 56 years, training Latin American paramilitaries whose victims total tens of thousands. As of January 2001, the SOA officially closed its doors and reopened almost immediately as the Western Hemisphere Institute for Security Co-operation, or WHISC - an attempt by school and military officials to confuse public criticism and distance the school from its violent past. Nice try, guys, but did you really think we were that thick? The name may have changed, but the underlying purpose of the school remains the same - to control the economic and political systems of Latin America by aiding and influencing Latin American militaries. Or put another way, to make Central and South America "safe" for US interests by supporting the rape, torture, and genocide of so-called dissidents.

Since 1946, the School of the Americas has trained over 60,000 Latin American soldiers and policemen. Among its graduates are many of South and Central America's most notorious torturers, mass murderers, dictators and state terrorists. In 1996, the Pentagon was forced to release SOA training manuals which included top tips on the use of torture, blackmail and execution. As hundreds of pages of documentation compiled by the pressure group SOA Watch shows, groups trained by the SOA have ripped Latin America apart. Here are just a few highlights from some of the SOA's former students:

**In Chile, SOA graduates ran both Augusto Pinochet's secret police and his three principal concentration camps.

**Former SOA student Colonel Byron Lima Estrada ran the D-2 military intelligence agency in Guatemala with the help of two other SOA graduates. Throughout the 1980's, D-2 coordinated an "anti-insurgency" campaign which obliterated 448 Mayan Indian villages and murdered thousands of innocent people..

**The list of atrocities commited during El Salvador's civil war is long and bloody, but none is more horrifying than the massacre in El Mazote, where in 1981, members of the Atlacatl Battalion murdered more than 900 villagers including women, children and the elderly. At least nine of the Atlacatl Battalion were former SOA graduates. In 1993, the United Nations Truth Commission on El Salvador named the army officers who had committed the worst atrocities of the civil war. Two-thirds of those named had been trained at the School of the Americas.

And the list goes on and on... As one Brazilian human rights group said, "The mark of the School of the Americas is engraved in the minds and bodies and in the histories of the families of the tortured, killed, and disappeared."

Meanwhile, protesters who dare to speak out against their government's support and orchestration of such acts are promptly arrested and jailed. Last week's demo in Georgia saw the arrest of 90 protesters, including a 12-year-old who we're quite sure posed a grave threat to the State. One man was arrested when he refused to submit to a police metal detector scan and bag search. Later, in a court hearing to determine the legality of searching protesters, police officers testified that they had never experienced a single act of violence or even the threat of violence in the past 13 years of protests against the SOA. They justified the searches, however, by saying they felt that hostility had been growing with the increase in numbers of anarchists and "bare breasted women". Bare-breasted women being decidedly more dangerous than military death squads trained and armed to the teeth by the US government, of course. For more info on the SOA's dirty dealings, check out the excellent website www.soaw.org Protest info at: http://indymedia.org/front.php3?article_id=217835

One of the 90 arrested breaking into Fort Benning. Nov 16th Pic: Greg Roberts

Press photographers gather around a papier-mache tank left by protestors near riot police outside the NATO Summit, Prague, Czech Rep. Nov 22nd Pic: Alec Smart

NO GLO-BALONEY

Last Friday, Italian police raided the homes of members of the Italian social movement No Global. 20 were arrested, denied access to lawyers, and held in solitary confinement, while another 22 have been placed under house arrest. The arrest warrants declared No Global "a subversive association" with intentions to "conspire against the Italian State" – proof of the intensification of the Berlusconi government's attempts to suppress the vibrant Italian social movement.

This comes after the success of the European Social Forum in Florence, attended by 40,000 delegates, with nearly 1 million people taking to the streets for Europe's largest ever anti-war demonstration (see last weeks SchNEWS). The harmony of the week-long Social Forum and the demonstration was the polar opposite of the 'terror' and 'violence' that Berlusconi and his media mouthpieces claimed the event would bring. So 'repressione' it is and even though the powers-that-be can't find anything horribly criminal to charge No Global with, they've decided to hit them with "political conspiracy" and "subversive propaganda." Protests have been called in solidarity with those arrested and over the weekend 30,000 people took to the streets of Rome and thousands more marched in Naples, Genoa, Florence and Milan. www.resist.org.uk

IN THE VANGUARD

While Blair is threatening Iraq with war if they don't grant access to weapons inspecters and has warned Britain to be on high alert for terrorist attacks, last Friday two people broke through totally non-existent security and spent thirty unhindered minutes inspecting one of Britain's illegal weapons of mass-destruction – a Trident nuclear submarine. They were eventually arrested after several attempts to set off faulty fire alarms to let security know they were there! The HMS Vanguard is one of four subs set to be refitted at Devonport Royal Navy dockyard in Plymouth, joining the 12 already there. More info phone 0845-458-8366 or see www.tridentploughshares.org.

* On 14th Dec there's plans for a **mass weapons inspection of US airforce base Fairford** in Gloucestershire, at the same time as US stealth bombers are due to arrive at the base. Transport is being organised from Bristol.

Info: http://bristol.indymedia.org

* Next **Sussex Action for Peace** meeting is Tuesday 26th, 7.30pm the Brighthelm Centre, North Street, Brighton. To join a discussion of **anti-war activities in Brighton** go to http://groups.yahoo.com/group/brightonagainstwar

STOP LAUDA AIR!

Pic: Sydney Indymedia

"I'm just not cut out for this type of work" - WTO delegate, Sydney Nov 22nd

DANGEROUS WARHEAD

WAR

It Just Ain't Cricket

Sydney residents unsure about the World Trade Organisation (WTO) meeting in their city were enlightened last Friday by the Institute For Applied Piracy, who jammed a commercial radio station for ten minutes, replacing the broadcast with a message about the dodgy dealings of the WTO. They explained to listeners how the WTO are an unelected body who represent corporate interests and promote free trade – never mind human rights, workers rights, the environment or anything else which is a 'barrier to trade'.

Meanwhile, the first meeting of the WTO since Doha focussed discussing the use of cheap AIDS drugs to bully developing countries into free trade. And outside the guarded fence, another festival of anti-capitalism kicked off. Streets were occupied in central Sydney last Thursday and even featured a padded up, all-white, Cricket Bloc.

On Friday, 2000 protesters hit the conference centre at Olympic Park where the fence was breached several times and 35 were arrested. Aboriginals re-occupied the 'tent embassy' site they created during the Olympics at Victoria Park, re-lighting the peace fire they'd started there during the Games. http://sydney.indymedia.org

* Britain has signed a trade agreement with Thailand promising to increase imports of farm produce and find new markets for Thai goods in return for supplying weapons to the Thailand military. That's good old free trade for ya.

No Purchase Necessary

With Christmas fast approaching, advertisers are stepping up their usual hype – "Buy, buy, buy! You're inadequate if you don't posses the latest gadget/colour/label/toy".

But why not take a day (or preferably the rest of your life) off from this consumer bullshit and join in on **Buy Nothing Day**. The message is simple. Shop less – live more. Spend **time** with family and friends, rather than spending **money** on them.

There's loads of events happening around the country. To find your nearest event phone 07887 608609 or see www.buynothingday.co.uk
* SchNEWS doesn't like to promote consumerism but… "The *SchNEWS of the World* book is the ideal Christmas present for the armchair activist, 300 pages rammed full of articles, cartoons, subverts, contacts and SchNEWS issues 301-350. Only £8.50 including postage from SchNEWS."

...and finally...

SchNEWS has scoured the high street to find you the most ridiculous bit of consumer crap available for the holiday season-one apple for the price of five. For 49p (the price of a whole pound of apples), Sainsbury's is offering just one ready sliced apple, with the perfect added preservative—a plastic bag. What a bargain! What's next? Pre-peeled bananas? Ready chewed food? "If you are not entirely satisfied with this product, please let Sainsbury's know on 0800 636262"

And if that's not enough to make you sick, then why not join in on mass vomiting actions planned for Buy Nothing Day? A group of anti-consumers are looking for people to join them in taking a Brazilian plant which induces vomiting. After taking the plant, the group plans to visit local consumerist meccas en masse for spectacular puking sessions. Sound appealing? If so contact them at mongrelart@yahoo.com www.fanclubbers.org

Disclaimer

SchNEWS warns all readers after a hard day fanning the flames of resistance over burning issues we always need a little hosing down. Honest.

DON'T BUY THE WAR TALK

BOOM BOOM!

weekly SchNEWS

www.schnews.org.uk

Friday 29th November 2002   Free/Donation   Issue 383

GONE TO THE DOGS

"This case is an attempt by the state to stop any demos other than those organised with the co-operation of the police - with routes, times etc. all on their terms. Anyone demonstrating now risks arrest and a charge of conspiracy." - Sue, Shoreham Protester.

In September 2000, hunt saboteur Steve Christmas was deliberately run-down by a Land Rover driven by Old Surrey and Burstow hunt supporter Martin Maynard. Steve had to be airlifted to hospital with four broken ribs, a crushed pelvis, a damaged lung and severe internal bleeding (See SchNEWS 274). The following day whilst he was fighting for his life, a group of nearly 60 protesters went to pay their respects at the local hunt kennels. Upon arriving at the kennel, the group was met by two friendly hunt supporters wielding pickaxe handles. The two men taunted the group about Steve and a scuffle broke out in which some windows were broken. Police, who had been observing the whole thing, did little to prevent a confrontation and made no arrests at the time. Instead, the powers-that-be decided to use the corruption of our legal system to bring us their very own version of justice.

Here's how it works - see if you can spot the bias. Martin Maynard, the guy who ran over and nearly killed Steve Christmas, had his charge of 'grievous bodily harm with intent' dropped, and instead paid a piddling £75 fine for not having any insurance or licence when he ran Steve down. Maynard also failed to turn up in court four times but of course was never punished for this. And to top it all off, the violent thugs who provoked the protesters at the kennels were never arrested.

Contrast this to the treatment received by anti-hunt protesters. A few weeks after the incident at the kennels, 26 of them (who had been identified from CCTV footage) had their homes raided. They were arrested for 'violent disorder', but then the story suddenly changed and 18 were charged with 'conspiracy to commit violent disorder' as there was no proof who did the damage.

After three trials lasting months, with costs running at £8,000 per day, five of those arrested have been found guilty and are due to be sentenced today at Guildford Crown Court. It is expected that they will be sent to prison for the hideous crime of breaking a few windows, even though there is no suggestion that these five are actually the ones that caused any of the damage! The Crown Prosecution Service alleges that those convicted were part of a wider conspiracy. But according to the prosecution, this so-called conspiracy happened in the few short seconds in which the group walked up the lane to the kennels. And the damning evidence the prosecution produced to prove this conspiracy? The fact that most people were wearing black hooded tops (which is what most sabs wear all the time, even down the pub!) and that the protesters weren't carrying placards (cos' that's the only way you're allowed to protest nowadays).

While the CPS were scraping the bottom of the barrel to prove their pet conspiracy theory, they presented as evidence a leaflet produced AFTER the incident happened and a t-shirt found at the home of one of the protesters which had a caricature of a fox with a shot-gun saying "I'll give you bloodsports pal".

A BREED APART

This sort of pro-hunt bias is of course nothing new, hunt supporters magically seem to have a whole set of laws to themselves. In 1991, Mark Bycroft, who is one of the main men at the Old Surrey and Burstow Hunt, was ordered to do community service after being found guilty of assaulting a hunt sab. Old Surrey and Burstow later promoted him to Huntsman. Last year, rider Joseph Wilkinson was convicted of Criminal Damage & Causing Actual Bodily Harm to a 58 year-old woman who he'd punched to the ground, busting her lip and trashing her camera in the process. His sentence? A slap on the wrist Conditional Discharge!

Justice like this had nothing at all to do with having friends in high places. In the Steve Christmas case,

---

CRAP ARRESTS OF THE WEEK
For Doing A Stall!

Two people from Dorset Animal Action were doing a stall in Bournemouth when police asked for their details. The activists had the cheek to ask if they were being nicked or issued with a summons, which led to their arrest for deception. After being strip-searched and kept at the station for 8 hours, the activists were released without charge, but not before the greedy coppers stole all the money that had been collected by the stall.

Gone to the Dogs cont...

the MP for Mid-Sussex, Nicholas lardarse Soames, who rides with another hunt, arranged a meeting with himself and the Huntsman of the Old Surrey and Burstow hunt to discuss matters with the then Home Secretary Jack Straw. Shame no one ever rang up Steve to see if HE wanted to have a chat with Straw. One of the protesters arrested over the kennel incident told SchNEWS, "It's obvious that the order to proceed with this trial came from very high up".

ARNIMATED

The animal rights movement in this country has definitely proved that it is a force to be reckoned with. The movement is unlike any other with the wide range of people and tactics involved. There is also a unity not seen in many other movements, those writing letters are not dismissed as wet-liberals and people who take direct action are not condemned as mindless yobs. This combination has enabled activists to set their sights on specific targets and in many cases win. Recent years have seen vivisection breeders such as Hillgrove and Shamrock

Farms bite the dust, a ban on the testing of cosmetics on animals, as well as the start of serious debate about fox hunting. This success, however, has come at the high cost of serious harassment, grief, and bullying from the media and the state. As surveillance expert Alan Lodge, says "Large scale news manufacturers have helped engineer an image of prevalent animal rights terrorism, whilst constructed charges worse than the actual crime have also ensured long prison sentences. The whole animal rights movement has been manoeuvred into the category of potential terrorism." This terrorism label means that animal rights activism has it's own Special Branch unit accumulating information for the Animal Rights National Index (ARNI).

The real motivation behind the prosecutions in the kennel incident is likely to have been the further intimidation of those involved in the animal rights movement. Seems the State wants to send a message out that if you support animal rights activism in any way, you are not safe. The verdict could have serious implications for anyone involved in any sort of

protest that extends beyond banner waving behind a police barrier. Full updates on the outcome of the trial at www.sahc.org.uk or www.huntsabs.org.uk

* The hunting season resumed at the beginning of this month. There are local hunt saboteur groups all over the UK who take direct action each week to save the lives of animals. Hunt Saboteurs Association - 0845 4500727

* Marsh UK, the insurance brokers for vivisecters Huntingdon Life Sciences, are spending £103,000 per week on security. Since February this year they have received 4718 emails, 324 faxes, 1198 letters and on occasions up to 400 telephone calls per hour! All of their 36 offices have been "visited" a total of 244 times. More info www.shac.net. Phone messages of condolence to Marsh on 020 7357 1000, calls may be monitored for "quality control" purposes!

* Huntingdon Life Sciences "celebrates" its 50th birthday on 1st December. www.december1.net

* A Public Enquiry about a potential primate lab in Cambridge started on Tuesday. Cambridge Against Primate Experiments: 01223 311828 www.x-cape.org.uk

President Blair speaks...

WE NEED A WAR!

A FUCKING BIG WAR!

SchNEWS in brief

It is **ten years since the battle of Twyford Down**, the beginning of the UK anti-roads movement, and there's a camp to 'Remember, Rejoice, and Resist!' 8-9 Dec, St. Catherine's Hill, Winchester. www.roadalert.org.uk ** Manchester has another **Radical Bookfair** next Saturday (7 Dec) Find out about radical activity in Manchester - stalls, workshops, and veggie food, 1-5pm, Bridge 5 Mill, 22A Beswick Street, Ancoats. www.radicalbookfair. org.uk ** Privacy International host a public meeting on the government's proposal for an **Entitlement (identity) Card**. 11 Dec, 2-4.30pm, Old Theatre, London School of Economics. www.privacyinternational.org 07960 523679 ** **Defy-ID** is "an adhoc network of groups and individuals prepared for **active resistance to increasing surveillance and the introduction** of identity or 'entitlement' cards in the UK" www.defy-id.org.uk ** **A book about the proposed Baku-Ceyhan pipeline** is now available entitled '*Some Common Concerns - Imagining BP's Azerbaijan-Georgia-Turkey Pipelines System*'. BP intends to begin construction on its proposed pipelines system in spring 2003, a system that would run from Azerbaijan in the Caspian Sea to the southern shores of Turkey via Georgia. Copies of the book for £11.50 made out to 'The Ilisu Dam Campaign', to: Baku-Ceyhan Campaign, c/o Ilisu Dam Campaign, Box 210, 266 Banbury Road, Oxford OX2 7DL. 01865 200 550 baku@gn.apc.org ** **Public meeting about the Baku-Ceyhan Pipeline**. 5 Dec. 7.30-8.30pm, London School of Economics, St Clements building, Room S75, Claremarket St., London. 01865-241097/200550.

POSITIVE SchNEWS

In the seemingly gloomy soil of Argentina, something positive is taking root. In this country, where over 6 million people now live below the poverty line and 20 percent of children suffer from malnutrition, people are re-taking control of their lives. Since the financial crisis last December, when Argentineans saw most of their savings wiped out, disillusionment with the corrupt state and greedy capitalism has led to the creation of neighbourhood assemblies and worker-controlled factories. Communities meet weekly in 'asambleas' to decide on what is vitally necessary for the community and then communicate their needs to one of the 100 worker-controlled factories.

Grissinopoli, a bread stick factory, is one example. When it was still under capitalist control, workers saw their weekly salary decline from 150 to 40 pesos in under a year. Finally in June their generous boss offered the workers 10 pesos (2 quid) and encouraged them to get lost. Fed up, they began a battle for their jobs. They took turns guarding the closed factory, making sure no equipment was removed, until the city council expropriated the factory and handed it over to the workers in October. Now the bread sticks are rolling out again.

Grissinopoli is just one factory amongst dozens of others that have seen workers taking control. Such factories are self-managed by workers' councils which means each worker has an equal say in how the factory should be run. Of course it's not easy work, as many workers in such factories are working longer hours as they balance labouring with admin tasks. But they're in control and because of this wages and productivity have risen in many factories.

With 17 factory expropriations in the Buenos Aires province in the past two years, capitalist forces have put pressure on the local government. Because of this, state repression is increasing, and just last March riot police attempted to 'reclaim' the worker-run Brukman factory but were chased off by hundreds of irate community members. www.ainfos.ca

*Days of civil disobedience are planned for the 20th and 21st of December in solidarity with the Argentinian people's social rebellion. www.ainfos.ca www.uk.indymedia.org

Umbrella of Mass Destruction: Weapon Inspectors approach Fairford December 14th

TO B-2 OR NOT TO B-2

On Saturday 14th December at 12 noon, Gloucestershire Weapons Inspectors and Bristol Stop-the-War coalition will hold a "citizens inspection" of US airforce base RAF Fairford.

This sleepy home of good old unsinkable aircraft carrier HMS Britain hosts the largest US bomber base in Europe, refurbished earlier this year at a cost of one hundred million pounds—the largest single NATO expenditure since the end of the cold war. The B-2 bombers at Fairford are thought to already be carrying the new generation of "more useable" nuclear weapons designed to attack deep bunkers and other super secret evil guy hideouts. These weapons will be fully involved in any attack on Iraq. "We want all weapons of mass destruction to be open to inspection," says Grace Trevett, one of the citizen inspectors. "The US is tearing up treaty after treaty and they act as if they have the right to do whatever they like. But rights are universal and apply equally everywhere. Iraq is prepared to allow weapons inspections, let us see if USAF Fairford can do the same."

Fairford is on the A417, 10 miles north of Swindon & 20 miles west of Oxford. Coaches are going from Brighton (details - brighton againstwar@hotmail or 01273 298 192) and Bristol (0117 9211369: james@venables.plus.com) http://bristol.indymedia.org/ and www.gwi.org.uk

* Next Wed (4), the Easton Community Centre, Bristol & i-Contact Video Network are showing the films 'Not In My Name' and 'Proud Arabs and Texas Oilmen' followed by a debate /plan of action to stop the city on the outbreak of war with Iraq. The Centre is at Kilburn Street, Easton, Bristol. Kick off is at 7.30pm and its all for free.

LEED STORY

Late last Saturday night, 100 tooled up riot cops used a battering ram to gain access to a building and randomly sprayed people with CS gas. So what provoked such a heavy police response? Er, a party in Leeds at the A-Spire squatted social centre. Once again the dance-police have been out in force, executing a pre-planned operation against unlicensed fun. Fortunately no one was injured in the panic, thanks to safety procedures put in place by the organisers, but 20 people were arrested and 4 have been charged with affray.

The A-Spire squat had been used for housing homeless people, hosting workshops, talks, film shows, a vegan café and children's area. SchNEWS reckons that Leeds Council and local police didn't like that the A-Spire crew had been providing free space, outside the confines of consumer culture.

As SchNEWS went to press on Thursday, it became apparent just how far Leeds Council and police will go to protect their new yuppy-friendly image. On Thursday afternoon, police apparently stormed two squatted buildings connected to the long-running Leeds housing co-op, Cornerstone. When alarmed activists arrived on the scene, they found both buildings boarded up and many of the squatters missing. It still remains unclear exactly what happened and or how many people have been nicked, but there's one thing for sure—Leeds police are on an arsehole roll!

*** A group of party goers who were attacked by riot police at a rave in the Cumberland Basin, Bristol**, back in July are looking to sue the police. They want witnesses of the night's events to come forward and write a statement of what they saw. If you can help email disruptive@dangerous-minds.com. The attack seems prompted by the massive rave that took place on Steart beach over the Jubilee Weekend (SchNEWS 363). The cops came under a lot of flack for not stopping the Steart beach party and afterwards promised to do better next time. To see the letter from the cops www.guilfin.net/reports/?id=rwINET1494

WAR BRIEFS

CND are taking the Labour Government to the International Criminal Court over their plans to attack Iraq. The CND are being represented by the law firm Matrix Chambers, who just happen to be the firm that Cherie Blair, the Prime Minister's wife, works for! 020 7700 2393 www.cnduk.org ** **Benefit gig**, Tuesday 3rd to raise funds to pay **for the CND court case**. With Mark Thomas, Jeremy Hardy, Ahmid Dhjihi and Michael Moore. Bloomsbury Theatre, London W1. Call 020 7388 8822 for tickets. ** **Warzone Whitehall, a nonviolent die-in against war and sanctions on Iraq** next Monday (2), 10.30am, Whitehall Place, London SW1. Prop-making, nonviolent direct action workshop & teach-in, the day before (1 Dec) 11am-5pm, Kingsley Hall, Powis Road, London E3. Accommodation available Sunday night. 0845 4582564. www.j-n-v.org/warzone.htm. ** **Witnesses are needed for arrests in London during the Halloween anti-war demo**. People are facing ridiculous charges of Violent Disorder for the privilege of getting shoved around by the police! Any information contact Moss and Co. Solicitors on 020-8986-8336 ** **Norwich Critical Mass** this Saturday (30), meet midday outside the Forum (the new library). All non-motor wheels, pedestrians, and sauce-pans needed. "Stop the City, Stop the War" is the theme.

...and finally...

Two people on a demo in Germany got whacked on the head by police recently. Er, not exactly major news, except the two injured people were actually undercover cops! The two had been monitoring a rally of 3000 people protesting against the demolition of a trailer site in Hamburg called 'Bambule' (an old fashioned German word for riot!) when violence broke out. Apparently, the undercover coppers tend to communicate their real identity to the riot police by using a secret code word - but in the chaos, no one took notice of this and the plainclothes ended up experiencing the blunt end of the justice system just like everyone else! The local police say that the incident is in no way "evidence of more widespread aggression within the police force", but the undercover police officers are still taking legal action over their injuries. But SchNEWS reckons that since riot police NEVER harm peaceful protesters, it only follows that the undercover cops must have been violent anarchist thugs who were really asking for it!

Disclaimer

SchNEWS warns all readers if you don't believe Santa Claus exists here's something for yer granny's stocking or that anarchist who hasn't got everything... As a Xmas offer we're flogging from our grotto the new SchNEWS Of The World – issues 301-350 for £5!! Past books are also goin' cheap... SchNEWSround issues 51-100 - nearly sold out - £5; SchNEWS annual issues 101-150 - going for £3!! Survival Handbook issues 151-200 - also at £3; SchQUALL issues 201-250 - almost sold out - £7; Yearbook 2001 issues 251-300 – bargain £5. Add £1.50 p&p for each book, cheques to Justice? Honest!

Subscribe!

Keep SchNEWS FREE! Send 1st Class stamps (e.g. 10 for next 9 issues) or donations (payable to Justice?) Ask for "Originals" if you can make copies. Post *free* to all prisoners. SchNEWS, c/o on-the-fiddle, P.O. Box 2600, Brighton, East Sussex, BN2 0EF.
Tel/Autofax +44 (0)1273 685913 *Email* **schnews@brighton.co.uk** *Download a* **PDF** *of this issue or subscribe at* **www.schnews.org.uk**

HENRY KISSINGER IS

I'll be back

HUMAN RIGHTS TERMINATOR

9-11 WAS NOTHING

weekly SchNEWS

www.schnews.org.uk

Friday 6th December 2002   Free/Donation   Issue 384

KISSINGER OF DEATH

Next Tuesday is International Human Rights Day - 54 years since the signing of the United Nations Universal Declaration of Human Rights, which amongst other things declared, 'All human beings are born free and equal in dignity and rights.'

Apparently the British government decided to get in on the celebrations a bit early this year by releasing a 23-page dossier on Iraqi human rights abuses, with foreign secretary, Jack Straw, telling the world, "It is important that people understand the comprehensive evil which is Saddam Hussein."

SchNEWS has no problem with spelling out the fact that Saddam is a torturing evil scumbag, but as Richard Bunting of Amnesty International pointed out, "Iraq's human rights record is appalling, but we have been saying this for years. The British and US are being selective, conveniently ignoring other countries and using this record to drive forward foreign and military goals."

Even the Iraqi dissident that Neo-Labour dragged out to support the dossier said he was "opposed to a war that may cause the Iraqi people a great loss of life and infrastructure." Hussain al-Shahristani, a former nuclear scientist, was tortured and jailed for 11 years for refusing to work on Saddam's secret nuclear programme, and is now head of the Iraqi Refugee Aid Council. "When I was in jail," he added, "I was held with British-made handcuffs. In the cells next door, I could hear the screams of people who were having holes drilled into their bones. Those drills were made in Britain…The dossier about human rights abuses is correct. Each of the

events took place. But I am critical of the silence of Britain and other European countries for over two decades about these abuses."

That's because when it comes to human rights abuses, governments seem to have selective amnesia about just who are the world's bad guys.

Before Iraq invaded Kuwait, the UK government supported President Saddam and British companies helped arm him. After the gassing of the Kurds at Halabja, British ministers and officials tried to blame the chemical attack on Iran. Human Rights Watch said that when it collected evidence of Saddam's abuses at Halabja and elsewhere in the Kurdish area of Iraq, the Foreign Office ignored it.

Or what about Turkey, who've been busy repressing the Kurdish people without anyone so much as batting an eyelid. Arbitrary arrest, detention, torture, disappearances, extra-judicial killings, the banning of political opposition and harassment of human rights groups are just some of the treats in store for you if you're Kurdish. Add to that the fact that Kurdish language, names, music, culture, and clothing are outlawed. Conservative

estimates reckon that in the past 15 years, Turkish Security Forces have destroyed 4000 Kurdish villages - leaving 30,000 dead and 3 million driven from their homes

So Kurds fighting Iraq are good, but Kurds fighting against Turkey are bad because Turkey is a member of NATO and an important ally of the United States thanks to its strategically placed air bases.

A Right Carry On

And now the American public can rest easy knowing that human rights champion Henry Kissinger is to head an 'independent' commission to investigate the attacks on America on September 11th. Who better to investigate 9/11 than Kissinger, the man behind untold amounts of state-sponsored terrorism and wanted

SURROUND RAF FAIRFORD!

A national demonstration and weapons inspection on Saturday 14th December. US stealth bombers are being deployed at RAF Fairford in Gloucestershire on their way to carpet bomb Iraq. We want these weapons of mass destruction removed. Transport from across the country. More info: http://bristol.indymedia.org
* Brighton coach leaves St Peters Church at 8.30am Tickets £6 from The Druids Pub, Ditchling Rise, or from the Sussex Action for Peace stall, Gardner St, Saturday 2-4pm. 01273 298192 www.safp.org.uk

Kissenger of Death cont...

across the world as a war criminal! A proven liar has been assigned the task of finding the truth. Brilliant!

As war criminals go, Kissinger is in the premier league. During the Vietnam War he was co-architect with Nixon in the secret bombing campaign of Cambodia, which is estimated to have claimed the lives of hundreds of thousands of civilians.

In 1971, Pakistani General Yahya Khan, armed with U.S. weaponry, overthrew a democratically elected government in Bangladesh — an action that led to a massive civilian bloodbath. Kissinger blocked U.S. condemnation of Khan and instead noted the General's "delicacy and tact."

www.uhc-collective.org.uk

In the early 1970s, Kissinger masterminded the CIA's $8 million campaign to overthrow the democratically elected government of Salvador Allende in Chile. When Allende won power, all US aid was cut and Kissinger announced, "The issues are much too important for the Chilean voters to be left to decide for themselves." So in came the murderous military dictatorship of Augusto Pinochet. On June 8, 1976, at the height of Pinochet's repression, Kissinger had a meeting with the dictator, telling him, "We are sympathetic to what you are trying to do here."

In 1975, President Gerald Ford and Kissinger offered advance approval of Indonesia's brutal invasion of East Timor, where tens of thousands of East Timorese were killed.

In 1976, as the Argentinan military junta was beginning its so-called "dirty war" against supposed subversives – between 9,000 and 30,000 people would be "disappeared" by the military over the next seven years – Argentina's foreign minister met with Kissinger and received what he believed was encouragement for his government's violent efforts. A few years later Kissinger travelled to Buenos Aires as the guest of dictator General Jorge Rafael Videla and praised the junta for having done, "an outstanding job in wiping out terrorist forces."

As journalist David Corn points out, "For many in the world, Kissinger is a symbol of U.S. arrogance and the misuse of American might. In power, he cared more for U.S. credibility and geostrategic advantage than for human rights and open government."

As the declaration goes 'All human beings are born free and equal', it just seems that some are a lot more free and a lot more equal than others.

* Check out all yer favourite war criminals www.icai-online.org
* There are lots of actions planned on Tuesday to support refugees, including a demonstration outside the Crown Prosecution Service organised by the Justice In the Yarl's Wood Trial Campaign, 5-6pm, 50 Ludgate Hill, London. EC4M 7EX (more info 07786 517379 ginn_emma@hotmail.com). Human Rights are Human Rights — Public meeting, Room 3c, University of London Union, Malet Street, W1 7.30pm. Speakers include Civil rights lawyer Louise Christian, and Emma Ginn, Campaign for Justice In the Yarl's Wood Trial (info@defend-asylum.org). For other events, check out SchNEWS Party and Protest guide on our website.

GREEDY BASTARDS!

18 years after one of the worst chemical leaks in history, the people of Bhopal are still waiting for justice in the wake of the Union Carbide disaster. Proving how little the powers that be actually care about people's suffering, Dow Chemicals (who now own Union Carbide) have told the people of Bhopal that there'll be no compensation or clean-up because it would piss off shareholders and fellow Multinationals.

On the 25th of November, a group of survivors of Union Carbide and supporters of the Campaign for Justice in Bhopal tried to clean up some of the toxic waste that's still poisoning their land and water supplies. Police waded in and 100 were arrested.

Neither the government nor Dow have done anything to protect the health of the people living round the factory site. More than 20,000 have now died as a direct result of the disastrous pesticide leak at the Union Carbide factory on December 3rd 1984. And a further 150 000 have been left chronically ill. Unsurprisingly, Dow hasn't paid a cent towards the victims' often massive medical bills.

Though every single legal investigation has found Union Carbide guilty of criminal negligence, both Union Carbide and Dow have consistently denied these findings. "We understand the anger and hurt," said Dow Spokesperson Bob Questra. "But Dow does not and cannot acknowledge responsibility. Our responsibility is to our shareholders. If we accepted responsibility we would be required to expend many billions of dollars on cleanup and compensation – much worse, the public could then point to Dow as a precedent in other big cases. We are unable to set this precedent for ourselves and the industry, much as we would like to see the issue resolved in a humane and satisfying way."

Shareholders are delighted. One said, "Bhopal is a recurrent problem that's clogging our value chain and ultimately keeping the share price from expressing its full potential. This has cleared the way." www.bhopal.net

SchNEWS in brief

Stingy Brighton Council want to **evict a group of Irish Travellers** from a derelict site at Preston Barracks. The site's been abandoned for years, but the Council has suddenly decided they need it for "development". Planning permission couldn't go through before the end of 2003 at the earliest and the travellers say they only want to stay 'til January anyway. Nevertheless, the Council are considering sending in their heavies to evict the site. Why not ring the council and give your support to the travellers. Pat Foster 01273-290000 or Heather James 01273-291142 ** An **Italian priest** from a small town near Naples was last week sacked because, according to his superiors, his behaviour is 'scandalous to the faithful'. His crimes were to speak at a **Gay Pride march** and join anti-capitalist protesters at the **Genoa G8** summit. The priest's faithful local parishioners are furious at the decision and are planning the biggest march in the town's recent history to demand he's reinstated. ** This Sat (7) **March with the Firefighters**. Noon, Cleopatra's needle, Embankment, London. www.fp4f.com ** Also this weekend, **Youth & Student CND National Gathering** with workshops, talks, and video screenings. LARC, 62 Fieldgate St, Whitechapel, London. Contact in advance if you need accommodation 020 7607 3616 info@youthstudentcnd.org.uk ** **'How UK Foreign Investment Creates Asylum Seekers,'** seminar and launch of new Ilisu Dam Campaign Project. This Sat (8) 1-6pm, at the Kurdish Community Centre, 11 Portland Gardens, London N4. 0787 6771576 rochelle.harris@ukonline.co.uk ** Brighton Council will decide on the controversial **Brighton Station development**, which includes another Sainsbury's store and posh hotels. Noon, 11th Dec, Hove Town Hall. 01273 681166 www.buddbrighton.org ** Xmas Benefit night for the **Simon Jones Memorial Campaign** and Mosaic Mixed and Black Parentage Family Group, Dec 12th, 11pm-3am, Concorde 2, Madeira Drive, Brighton. ** **If you didn't vote at the last election**, feel good about it and check out www.vetothevote.com for more about our so-called democracy. ** Sub-Cultural Radikal Arts Productions presents **Wreck n' Roll Cirkus,** Friday 13th, loadsa musik and subversion. 9.30pm- 6am, The Imperial Gardens, 199 Camberwell New Road, London. £7 b4 11pm, £10 after. 077731334958 ** **Workers Left Unity - Iran** meeting in solidarity with the growing protest movement and in support of Iranian students, journalists, writers and workers. 13th Dec, 6pm. NUJ Building 308 Grays Inn Road, London WC1web@etehadchap.com ** **West Papua Solidarity** Fri 20th 'The Wick'25 Whitepost Rd, Hackney Wick (Bus 276) after 8pm £3/2- Disruptive Element + support

There, sir - does your back feel better now?

Die-In at Whitehall, Dec 2nd. Pic: Guy Smallman

WAR BRIEFS

A coalition of Canadian peace groups is sending an international team of volunteer weapons inspectors to the US this winter. **"Rooting Out Evil"** are to send inspectors to the US and want unhindered access to all sites, including presidential compounds. A spokesperson said, "On the basis of Bush's guidelines, it is clear that the current U.S. administration poses a great threat to global security." See www.rootingoutevil.org ** Two day **'training' event in Oxford** this weekend (7-8) in preparation for next weekends weapons inspection at Fairford airbase. 01865 794 504 greening_paul@hotmail.com ** It is **twenty years since 30,000 women demonstrated against** the US's nuclear cruise missiles at **Greenham Common** and this is being celebrated at Women-with Hill Women's Peace Camp next Thursday (12), Embrace the Base: 10 am - 4 pm. The next day, Blockade the Base: Non-violent direct action. Info: 01943 468593 flossiemintballs@aol.com ** Last Monday 250 people staged a **'die in' in Whitehall**. Part of the road was blocked for 5 hours in protest against the war. 35 people were arrested for obstruction of the highway. www.viwuk.freeserve.co.uk ** Make a pledge to engage in civil disobedience if war starts at www.j-n-v.org ** **'The Fire this Time,'** a CD by Grant Wakefield which charts the history of the West's manipulation of the political landscape in the Middle East with background tunes from the Aphex and Orbital, is out now. www.firethistime.org ** Stop the War have just released **'Peace Not War'** benefit CD compilation including tracks from Public Enemy, Fun-da-mental, Massive Attack, Billy Bragg and even Crass. Available in most record shops www.peace-not-war.org

Rising Tide at the office of ERM, Dec 2nd

Inside SchNEWS

The five animal rights activists who were facing jail sentences for "conspiracy to hold a protest" at the Old Surrey and Burstow Hunt Kennels (see last week's SchNEWS) have all escaped prison sentences. Instead, thanks to the judge reading last week's SchNEWS of course, they were sentenced to do community service of between 200 and 240 hours, plus court costs.

In a further blow for the Hunt, a protester had his conviction for Harassment overturned. The judge ruled that the charge was an abuse of the Protection from Harassment Act (originally introduced to prevent stalking of women). He cited a case in the High Court where it was ruled that the Act should not be used to prevent political protest. www.shoreham-protester.org.uk

"Erm..."

On Monday morning, protestors from Rising Tide, who campaign for climate change justice, performed an environmental and social impact assessment of the London office of Environmental Resource Management (ERM), with some barricading themselves in the directors office and hanging out a banner 'Oil Makes War.' ERM has been carrying out research work for oil giant BP on the proposed 1,770-km pipeline from Baku in Azerbaijan through Georgia to the port of Ceyhan in Turkey. ERM's role is to greenwash the whole project—it plays a crucial role in convincing public funders to give financial backing to the scheme. www.ermconcerns.com

Meanwhile, last week in Tbilisi, the Georgian capital, a group of people paid a friendly visit to the office of the Georgian International Oil Company, one of BP's partners in the pipeline project. The protest came in response to the Georgian Government's decision to issue permission for construction of the pipeline by November 30th. The decision violates Georgian environmental legislation, as it allows the pipeline to pass through protected areas and water sanctuary zones in the sensitive Borjomi Gorge. The decision, the Government says, was made to meet the project timeline and thus fulfil BP's requirements.

Rising Tide network 01865 241097, www.risingtide.org.uk.

...and finally...

Some passionate Sydney activists puckered up for a mass game of "Spin the Bottle" outside the New South Wales State Parliament last month and managed to tally up a smouldering 154 kisses between them. Apart from giving themselves severely chapped lips, they were protesting against the confiscation of the Spin The Bottle Bloc's six-foot papier mache bottle at the anti- World Trade Organisation demos which took place in Sydney last month.

The confiscation of the bottle was "justified" by the Sydney police because they believed protestors were planning a violent confrontation, as proved by the Spin the Bottle Bloc's own communication, which read, "We invite you to join us for the most militant game of spin the bottle ever attempted - turning up the heat until every kiss becomes a molotov." The police, who obviously don't know much about the power of love or the classic teenage party game, have refused to return the bottle, though they obviously won't have much use for it themselves http://sydney.indymedia.org

DISCONNECTED

Workers in Ozarow Poland have been rioting against the closure of their telephone cable factory. They rejected the measly payoff they were offered, and instead started a 219 day occupation of the factory which ended abruptly two weeks ago when several buses of security guards violently evicted the protesters. There's been mass solidarity with the workers and small groups of anarchists from around Poland have joined them in helping with blockades around the factory and organising various ambushes on trucks leaving the site.

As one Polish anarchist said, "As soon as we started harassing security guards in a more organised way, they started living in a state of permanent siege, hiding inside the factory behind barricades they built to be protected from us. All day and night black bloc, workers, and small group of local hooligans attacked them. Lots of workers were amazed by our way of fighting." This pressure has triggered new negotiations, but across Poland the number of strikes are growing because of worsening economic conditions.

Subscribe!
Keep SchNEWS FREE! Send 1st Class stamps (e.g. 10 for next 9 issues) or donations (payable to Justice?) Ask for "Originals" if you can make copies. Post *free* to all prisoners. SchNEWS, c/o on-the-fiddle, P.O. Box 2600, Brighton, East Sussex, BN2 0EF.
Tel/Autofax +44 (0)1273 685913 *Email* schnews@brighton.co.uk *Download a PDF of this issue or subscribe at* www.schnews.org.uk

SchNEWS

www.schnews.org.uk

NO MOTORWAY AT STONEHENGE

Friday 13th December 2002   **Free/Donation**   **Issue 385**

WIDE-BOYS

As protesters braved the cold last weekend to set up camp at St Catherine's Hill, Twyford Down, to celebrate the 10th anniversary of the beginning of the road protest movement, the government were finalising their own plans to celebrate with the biggest road building programme in a decade. So as well as reminiscing about the good ol' times, the camp had future plans to chew over. As one protester told SchNEWS, "This government is just going back to the old model of predict-and-provide, which will see more of our countryside being trashed to make way for 'economically necessary' roads and airports"

When the Labour Government first came to power, fat controller John (two jags) Prescott blubbered "I will have failed ...if in five years there are not many more people using public transport and far fewer journeys by car. It is a tall order but I want you to hold me to it." Well Fat Boy, you've drowned in your own exhaust fumes. The new chiefs at the Department of Transport have decided that they like concrete and this week gave the green light to £5.5 billion of new transport schemes. £2 billion of which is going towards major road construction and widening schemes.

But the joke will soon be back on them, as the failure of previous road widening schemes has shown. As Professor David Begg, Chair of the government's Commission for Integrated Transport pointed out, "On the M25, when it went from three to four lanes, within one year traffic increased by one third, negating the benefits." Considering that the number of vehicles on our roads has already increased by 7% since 1997, this new roads programme is exactly the opposite of what's needed to stop

total gridlock. But that doesn't appear to bother Neo Labour, whose mates at the Confederation of British Industry have given them more than a gentle push to do something about congestion, which they believe is costing the country £20 billion a year, money which instead should be lining shareholders' pockets.

NO U-TURN

"This is a binge of road building with virtually nothing safe from the bulldozer. The Government is trying to build its way out of congestion but it won't work. All that it will do is lead to bigger, wider traffic jams. It seems that the Government aims to keep the UK the most car-dependent country in Europe." Stephen Joseph, Transport 2000

So how come roads are once again on top of the agenda? Well in 1997-8 the Government conducted a review of transport policy. One of the results of this review was to set in motion 23 Multi-Modal Studies. These studies were designed to examine some of the key transport problems and look at a full range of solutions for the next 30 years, rather than just the road schemes previously suggested. The outcome of the studies have been varied, with most suggesting mixed packages of new roads, new/reopened railway lines, and improvements to local transport. Unfortunately, the end result of many of the studies has been that the roads get built first, with public transport improvements following well behind, if ever. This is because main roads (being an 'investment') get allocated funds from central government coffers. On the other hand, local transport improvements, such as buses and trams, are paid for by often cash-strapped local councils.

And the railways (SchNEWS doesn't need to remind its readers here how well they've been performing since privatisation) only get a small amount of 'subsidy', so can't even afford to do the work they've already promised, let alone think about doing any extra improvements in the future.

So instead of more public transport, we can instead look forward to the widening or upgrading of more than a dozen motorways and trunk roads. One of the most destructive schemes given the green light is the widening of A303/A30 which runs down to the south-west ploughing through the Wiltshire Area of Outstanding National Beauty. Although the wide boys did steer clear of building the road above ground past Stonehenge, they forgot to promise to do anything about widening the rail line in this area from one to two lines, which would have helped to reduce congestion loads.

And if you think it sounds good when the government says "The World Heritage Site at Stonehenge will be enhanced and protected by putting the existing road in a bored tunnel", think again. The short tunnel they're proposing is dismissed by campaigners from the Save Stonehenge Campaign, who said, "The British government is

The hardy folk at the Bilston Glen protest camp during snow

The Government has shown a dramatic turna-round in its attitude toward road schemes. When Labour came to power in 1997 it promised a new direction on roads. It cancelled 42 road schemes inherited from the Conservative government and put other trunk schemes on hold while the alternatives could be assessed through Multi-Modal and Roads-Based Studies. The Transport White Paper in 1998 was emphatic about the need to protect environmentally important sites from road con-struction. Since then the Government has shifted ground in the face of opposition to sustainable transport from motoring groups and some newspapers.

In July 2000 £30 billion of road-building was announced as part of the Ten Year Transport Plan. Spread over a decade, this would pay for 360 miles of motorway and trunk road widening and over 100 trunk and local by-passes, with more money for local roads. In December that year the Government gave the green light to nearly all the road schemes put forward by local authorities through local transport plans, including 'litmus test' schemes that would be highly damaging at Salisbury, Weymouth, Barnstable in Devon, Camelford in Corn-wall, Carlisle, Rugby and Glossop.

Here are but a few of the planned schemes and op-position to them...

SCOTLAND
A701 upgrade project between the Edinburgh bypass and Penicuik.
Contrary to Scottish Office planning guidance on reducing the need for travel the A701 is to be "realigned" to triple its capacity. Midlothian Council has failed to conduct any meaningful strategic assessment of alternative options that could address transport problems, this will be built under the PFI (Private Finance Initia-tive) and the council will pay a private company in "shadow tolls", which means the more cars use the road, the more they get paid, there-fore there is no incentive to reduce traffic. This scheme will cost at least £10,000,000 per mile. The road will lead to more industrialisation and will destroy a local woodland, part of which is an SSSI. The woods contain many mature trees and a medieval bridge and tower. There is a protest camp up and running at Bilston Glen, visitors are welcome. Take the A701 (number 37/37a) towards Penicuik & you'll come to the village of Bilston (8 miles south of Edinburgh). Just as you come into the village there is a metal gated footpath (opposite the large VW garage), go through this & down the path till you come to the bridge, & you'll see us. Site mobile: 07986632429 bilston.glen@dhmail.net

No-alignment action group: www.spokes.org.uk/naag/

NORTH ENGLAND
A57/A628 Mottram and Tintwistle Bypass
The proposal threatens a unique landscape that has been established over centuries. The area threatened encroaches on the Peak Park and includes the beautiful Longdendale Valley. Traditional pastureland; a woodland nature reserve (Swallows Wood), and open moorland are all under threat, as is ultimately the whole of the Northern Peak Park.
www.stopmottrambypass.tripod.com/now/start.html
A69 Haydon Bridge Bypass
There is a proposal to re-route the A69 Trunk Road around the southern edge of the town at a cost of £18 million. The route of the bypass passes through mainly agricultural grassland, and it will have a negative impact on protected species in Gees Wood and the South Tyne River. It will also have a major impact on the local land-scape.
Lancaster Western Bypass
The road threatens a wide swathe of beautiful coun-tryside, including the Lune Estuary with its Sites of Special Scientific Interest (SSSIs), two branches of the Lancaster Canal, the Lancashire Coastal way, Freeman's Wood - and several other County Biological Sites - 8 farms and at least 20 public footpaths and country lanes.
www.stopthelancasterbypass.fsnet.co.uk

Wide-Boys cont...

pretending that its main concern is to do Stonehenge a favour. It isn't. The aim of this scheme is to build a new four-lane highway. Stonehenge is in the way. So the government is doing the cheapest thing it possibly can to make it politically acceptable to build a new highway through the World Herit-age Site. It's pretending to go out of its way to protect Stonehenge, which has been there for 5000 years, by spending an extra £30 million pounds. But it has £5.5 billion to spend on transport. And it

spent £800 million pounds on London's Millennium Dome."
* To check out if there's a new shiny road planned in your area and how you can get involved in stopping it, go to www.roadalert.org.uk
* Countries clamouring to become part of the European Union are already adopting western Europe's unsustainable transport policies, ac-cording to a report by the European Environment Agency. Read it at http://reports.eea.eu.int/environmental_is-

sue_report_2002_24
* Last month the South East Regional Assembly gave their approval to a series of new and widened roads to form the 'South Coast Superhighway', cutting through some of the proposed South Downs National Park. Sound good? www.scar-uk.fsnet.co.uk
* For top tips on wrecking road building check out www.eco-action.org/rr/
* Give yourself a Twyford Down history lesson www.schnews.org.uk/sotw/twyford-down%2B10.htm

THE MIDLANDS

Tunstall Northern Bypass
Under discussion for 25 years, work is due to start in January 2004. It will affect Heritage Valley, part of the Sustrans Cycle network, and the largest colony of Water Voles in Staffordshire. www.actionnet-northstaffs.co.uk

Stourbridge, Wolverhampton and Southern Dudley Bypasses
The Anti Bypass Campaign is a self-funded, non-governmental organisation made up of people from Stourbridge and the surrounding area. It aims aiming to represent the concerns of many local people and conservation groups whose remit is in or adjacent to the Borough of Dudley, and areas that are likely to be affected by the proposed road. www.antibypasscampaign.pwp.blueyonder.co.uk

LONDON

M11 Link Road
Site of the infamous Claremont Road evictions, the M11 Link Road has run into problems. A section of the road may have to be expanded to three lanes and there may be the reintroduction of the second traffic lane on the slip road coming off the Redbridge Roundabout. So much for solving traffic problems - all it has done is to increase traffic!

SOUTH ENGLAND

SCAR (South Coast Against Roadbuilding)
South Coast Against Roadbuilding was formed in 1994, as an umbrella group to local groups fighting the threat of more road building. Many of the groups support non-violent direct action and were at Twyford Down, Newbury and the A30. www.scar-uk.fsnet.co.uk

A21 South Pembury to Hastings
The existing A21 corridor passes through a very sensitive area in environmental terms with landscape, cultural heritage and ecological issues being particularly important. There is a consultation underway to widen the road to a dual carriageway. The A21 Lamberhurst Bypass is also to be built, and work will start in May 2003. It will cause temporary and permanent loss of habitat for protected species (bats, dormice, reptiles and great crested newts) and the loss of 265 metres of native hedgerow plus a loss of 3450 square metres of land south of the existing A21 not previously affected, and the partial loss of a recently planted tree belt. The bypass may make flooding worse as it will act as a dam to any floodwaters.

The section from Tonbridge to Pembury is proposed to cut into the Castle Hill scheduled ancient monument and cause the loss of semi-natural ancient woodland. There has been no archaeological investigation of Castle Hill. It is probably pre-Roman and is likely to be a Bronze Age settlement. There is evidence to suggest that the area was used in Arthurian times as a military settlement. The height of the road will be increased here, making it noisier.

A27 Arundel bypass
Arundel got a bypass in 1970, but now they want another one! A 4 km stretch of dual carriageway at a cost of £25 million. The proposed bypass would be highly intrusive where it crosses the River Arun and surrounding water meadows, which are noted as a historical landscape in the Local Plan.

It would also damage ancient woodland (Binsted Woods), Tortington Common, Scotland Barn and many Roman remains.

Titnore Woods protest

A24 Action Group
The newly formed action group called the 'A24 Alliance' is the latest in the ever-lengthening number of local groups formed to fight the threat of road building. In this case, local residents have become seriously concerned by the massive road building plans for the A24 from Worthing to Capel (nr Dorking).

Hastings Bypass
The highly controversial Hastings Bypasses is a new £240 million, 21 km scheme around Hastings and Bexhill in East Sussex. The roads will damage three Sites of Special Scientific Interest (SSSI); the Pevensey Levels wetlands, Combe Haven, and the Marline Valley Woods. A huge swathe of the High Weald Area of Outstanding Natural Beauty, including the Upper Brede Valley, will also be damaged. www.hastingsbypass.org.uk

Protect Our Woodland! (POW!)
Formed by a group of Worthing residents concerned by the threat of a housing development damaging a local unique woodland, Titnore Woods, POW! has captured the mood of environmentalists up and down the country. Ancient woodland - some over 10,000 years old with origins in the last ice age - is being lost at an alarming rate. Whether through new housing developments or road building, this wanton destruction of what has been dubbed 'Britain's rain forest' must stop. www.worthinga27.freeserve.co.uk

Priory Park Preservation Society
The fight to save Priory Park is far from over. Many groups are still involved and oppose Southend Borough Council (SBC) pushing the F5 road scheme through. Now we are planning a massive public show of opposition, to prove once again that we are not the noisy minority. SBC would like to see the issue quietly fade away, but we won't let it! www.ppps.org.uk

Stonehenge A303
In December 2002 a 2.1km tunnel for the A303 at Stonehenge was proposed. Few support it, except English Heritage. About 16 known archaeological sites along the line of the road would be damaged or destroyed by the proposals. These include a round barrow in the side of King Barrow Hill, and the long barrow adjacent to the proposed western portal. Further damage may well be caused by proposals for a dual-carriageway split-level junction at Longbarrow Roundabout. The Stonehenge scheme is only part of a wider plan to create a continuous 4-lane dual carriageway from London to the South West via Exeter. An A303 Inquiry is expected towards the end of this year. More info see: www.savestonehenge.org.uk

BNDR Opposition Committee
The BNDR, or Bridgwater Northern Distributor Road, is a proposed scheme for a 2.5km road and 900 houses. The road threatens numerous wildlife habitats including badgers, water voles and great crested newts. It has not as yet been subjected to an Environmental Impact Assessment. www.bndro.ukf.net

Road Alert is a multimedia direct action forum helping to co-ordinate a grassroots activist reaction to road-building schemes. The website gives access to streaming media, chatroom, forums and constantly updated news, press releases and contacts. www.roadalert.org.uk

Cut-Throat Politik

The topsy-turvey world of Venezuela continues. Bosses and investors are on "general strike" while the masses take action in support of the leftist government of Hugo Chavez! As Western television stations show footage of many (rich) Venezuelans out on the streets in opposition to Chavez, different stories are coming from poorer quarters. On Monday night, groups of ordinary Venezuelans took over all the main TV stations in Caracas in support of the president and the country remains in turmoil.

The US has made no secret of the fact that it would like to see a regime change in Venezuela since the CIA-backed coup in April (SchNEWS 345). This instantly failed when it became apparent that no-one but the US would recognise the new leadership and Chavez was returned to power.

As in Iraq, the motivation for US interference is oil - Venezuela is the fifth largest oil exporter in the world and its main customer is the USA.

* In London, two days of action are planned in solidarity with the first anniversary of the Argentinean popular rebellion when the Argentinean people kicked out the government (SchNEWS 350) **Night of Rage**, 20th December followed by **Day of Disobedience** chaotic mass proletarian shopping action on Oxford Street on the 21st" Dress as Santa, steal from the rich & give presents to the kids. "Just nick it." www.wombles.org.uk

* The film **"Voces Argentinas"** was shot on the streets of Buenos Aires and shows how it felt to be Argentine as the country plunged quickly from the first world to the third. **Screenings**: 13th, Use Your Loaf, 227 Deptford High Street, London SE8. 7pm. 18th, Argentine Film Night & talk about the uprising, plus food & bar. 7.30pm, Union Tavern, Camberwell New Rd, London SE5. 18th, Junk TV Christmas party - Free showing, DJs, bar, cakes, more films. Sanctuary Cafe Cella, Brunswick St East, Hove, 8pm. 22nd, **Film Afternoon for Argentina** - The Other Cinema, Rupert St, London W1, from 1pm

* 21st is **McGo-Slow As Fuck! Day** - McDonalds workers are being encouraged to work slowly in solidarity with the Argentinean popular rebellion http://mwr.org.uk

SchNEWS in brief

The **SchNEWS of the World** book is now available at the Punker Bunker (under Immediate clothes shop), Sydney Street, Brighton and in City Bookshop, Western Road, Hove. ** Doh! Last week **SchNEWS** fell for a spoof Dow Chemicals announcement that it basically didn't give a shit about the Bhopal gas leak in India which has killed 20,000 people and left thousands more ill. "Our responsibility is to our shareholders." etc. etc. We should have realised that a corporation would never be so honest! ** Tune in to **Radio 4A** in the Brighton area this weekend on 107.8FM or worldwide at www.piratetv.net ** **Injustice,** the film about black deaths in custody, Monday 16th, Brunei Gallery, 10 Thornhaugh Street, London, WC1H. 7pm. The police will even be there to take part in a Q&A session after the film! 020 8709 9777 www.injusticefilm.co.uk ** Don't forget the **Housmans 2003 Peace Diary** – now in its 50th year of printing. Listing nearly 2000 peace, human rights, and environmental organisations, covering 150 countries. To order one, send £7.95 (incl. P&P to any address in the world) to Housmans Bookshop, 5 Caledonian Road, Kings Cross, London N1 9DX 020 7837 4473 www.apoogee.com/Housmans ** **Sustainable Christmas** evening social, Saturday 14th 7.30-10pm. Phoenix Community Centre, Brighton. 07811 443038 alexp@cogs.susx.ac.uk ** Actions continue at the factory in **Ozarow, Poland** to stop it being closed (SchNEWS 384). With temperatures at minus 20, sacked workers have been pouring water on the roads, turning them to ice and making it impossible for trucks to take out any equipment! www.fko.prv.pl ** The **Advisory Service for Squatters** now has a new local rate phone number. 0845 644 5814, 2-6pm Monday to Friday. ** The **Academy of Motion Picture Arts and Sciences** (the hot shots who hand out Oscar awards) has refused to allow a Palestinian-made film to enter its foreign film category because it does not accept Palestine as a 'nation'. Tell the Academy what you think of their decision email: ampas@oscars.org ** Tuesday 17th **Cardiff Anarchist Network** hold a public meeting to discuss new forms of direct action. Cathays Community Centre, Cathays Terrace, Cardiff, 8pm. bolshybo@yahoo.co.uk ** **Thames Valley Anarchos** hope to establish a local network of activists in the region. First meeting this Sunday (15th) at the Herschel Arms Pub, Herschel Street, Slough, 7pm. ** **SCHWOOPS!** Two weeks ago, we printed a story about a raid at **Cornerstone Housing** Co-op in Leeds. The info was only a few hours old and we got a bit muddled. The facts: at 8:45am on Nov. 28th, Cornerstone houses were raided by Lincolnshire cops. The door was smashed in and after an hour or so of fruitless searching, the police arrested everyone who had slept in the houses that night and anyone who came home during the search (13 people in all) for burglary!

Insainsbury's

Neo Labour Brighton Council has approved the controversial development of the old Brighton Station goods yard site. The scheme includes just what Brighton needs more of – two posh Hotels and a Sainsbury's supermarket providing crappy low paid jobs. The only reason that this scheme is going ahead is because Sainsbury's are prepared to bribe the council with "infrastructure improvements" (i.e. roads) which will increase traffic in an already congested area. The new Sainsbury's will be nearly twice the size of its current store in London Road, and despite the council planning department saying, "There is no quantitative need for additional food retail in the area", they decided to give it the go-ahead anyway.

So a supermarket, some hotels, crap housing, no playing fields - SchNEWS just doesn't understand why Brighton Council, showing SUCH vision, failed in its bid to become city of culture!

* BUDD, who have been opposing the development, are now trying to have the development called in to a Public Enquiry. If they fail, work on the new site will begin in May. 01273 681166 www.buddbrighton.org

* Check out Corporate Watch's 'What's Wrong with Supermakets' Send £1 + 41p SAE to 16b Cherwell Rd., Oxford, OX4 1BG www.corporatewatch.org.uk/profiles/food_supermarkets/supermarkets

THOUGHT CRIMINALS

"It's clear that not only those who materially took part in the devastation should be prosecuted, but also those who facilitated the acts or gave strength to their purpose. These people should be prosecuted even if they didn't conduct any material act." – Italian judge, Elena D'Alosio.

Yep, you guessed it, Berlusconi's government have gone from bad to worse with reasons to arrest activists: two weeks ago it was for "subversive association" (SchNEWS 382) and now a new wave of arrests have occurred for "mental participation" in the Genoa demonstrations.

On the morning of 4th December, investigations against 23 people were started by magistrates and 45 houses were raided. The accusations range from devastation and depredation (crimes punishable with 8-15 years imprisonment) to possession of illegal weapons to, SchNEWS' favourite, "mental participation" and "psychological support" in the Genoa actions. The judge, D'Alosio, ordered preventative arrests for 9 of the 23 under investigation, four are under house arrest, six are obliged to remain at home and the remaining four have to present themselves at the police station. Interestingly, all of these arrests have been ordered one and a half years after the relevant events.

'Thoughtcrime' is now a punishable offence in Berlusconi's and Big Business' Italy as some of the No Global activists under investigation but not in custody are suspected of having offered psychological support to violent demonstrations. The judge has said that those who must respond to the charges of 'devastation' are not just those who participated physically but those who encouraged the crime and whose mere presence in demonstrations provides moral support to the more violent demonstrators. In the wise words of D'Alosio "The behaviour of those who were on the scene of the riots, together with the most violent ones, gave strength to these people by their very presence. Their acts were not crimes in themselves, but aided the criminal intentions of the others with their moral support."

So basically Italian activists can now be legally nicked for being at a demo that turns violent or being part of an anti-capitalist collective. And even though the judge has admitted that such acts are not "fundamentally criminal" the activists are still under investigation.

The whole legal circus has seen arrests and detentions in over twenty Italian towns and this G8-related drive for justice coincides with an interesting case: magistrates are attempting to close the case against the carabinieri accused of shooting Carlo Giuliani during the G8 protests. It seems likely the carabinieri, Placanica, will be acquitted as Giuliani's killing was 'legitimate self-defence.' So the murderers run free while the thinkers get nicked.

Inside SchNEWS

American Earth Liberation prisoner Jeff "Free" Luers, sentenced to 22 years (longer than most rapists and murderers get) for setting fire to three cars, is to appeal against his conviction and sentence. Write to Hardy Myers, the Oregon State Attorney, calling for a lesser sentence. Sample letter at: www.spiritoffreedom.org.uk under the Urgent Updates section.

* Chain Reaction's "Unshackling Captive Minds" is an anarchist zine produced by current and former Texas prisoners. Issue 9 is just out and is available free to prisoners and $2 for others. CR Collective, P.O. Box 501, Whiteface, USA TX 79379-0501. Texarchist1@wmconnect.com.

BOMBING FOR PEACE IS LIKE SHAGGING FOR VIRGINITY

UH-UH-UH-AM I A VIRGIN YET?

WAR BRIEFS

Members of **Voices in the Wilderness** in the US have been fined a total of $50,000 for having the cheek to send medicine to Iraq without a permit. Since 1996, members have broken sanctions with over fifty delegations to Iraq, travelling on humanitarian, fact-finding, and rebuilding missions, and refusing to see the people of Iraq as enemies. The group aim to collect money for the fine – then use it to buy more medicine to send to Iraq! Don't they understand that if they had sent a bomb they would have got a pat on the back?? www.nonviolence.org/vitw/ ** **Disobedience** hold a Day School to discuss ways of uniting different London-based groups opposed to the war. Sat 18th Jan: 10am-6pm, London Action Resource Centre, 62 Fieldgate Street, London E1 www.disobedience.org.uk ** Anti-war meeting followed by some peaceful protest and **civil disobedience in Brighton,** Saturday 21st, meet noon at Brighton Unemployed Centre, 6 Tilbury Place, just off Carlton Hill. ** Benefit in aid of **Hastings CND & Medical Aid for Palestine** this Sunday (15th) 2.30pm onwards at The Carlisle Pub, Hastings. ** The **United States are about to sell weapons to the Algerian government,** one American official said Washington "has much to learn from Algeria on ways to fight terrorism." According to Amnesty International around 4,000 people have "disappeared" in Algeria since 1993 after being arrested by the security forces.

...and finally...

If you're going to go on a consumer spending spree this Christmas, then it wouldn't be such a bad idea to make sure that some capitalist scum-bag is picking up the tab.

Which is just what a group calling themselves the Guinea Pig Avengers managed to do. When the group stumbled across the credit card details of two vivisectors associated with the Newchurch Guinea Pig farm, they decided to make this the best Christmas ever, running up bills of £15,000 - not bad for an afternoon's work!

Disclaimer

SchNEWS warns all readers driven up the wall to enjoy this detour to major improvements ahead. Honest.

Subscribe!

Keep SchNEWS FREE! Send 1st Class stamps (e.g. 10 for next 9 issues) or donations (payable to Justice?) Ask for "Originals" if you can make copies. Post *free* to all prisoners. SchNEWS, c/o on-the-fiddle, P.O. Box 2600, Brighton, East Sussex, BN2 0EF.
Tel/Autofax +44 (0)1273 685913 *Email* schnews@brighton.co.uk *Download a* **PDF** *of this issue or subscribe at* **www.schnews.org.uk**

WAKE UP! WAKE UP! IT'S YER CHRISTMAS   "Look what Santa got me!"

weekly **SchNEWS**
www.schnews.org.uk

Winter Solstice 2002   Free/Donation   Issue 386

CHOM'PIN AT THE BIT

Noam Chomsky first gained academic acclaim in the 60s and 70s with his theories about how people learn language. He then studied the workings of the US government in all their gory detail, producing an avalanche of books, ranging from US foreign policy and imperialism to the brainwashing role of the corporate media. Chomsky is now known as one of America's leading voices of dissent. SchNEWS went to interview him on his recent trip to London, but we didn't know what to expect. Condescending academic? Rabble-rousing revolutionary? What we found was neither of these, but simply an intelligent, honest man with a lot of knowledge about the rhetoric and motives fuelling Bush's America. It was like talking to your grandfather who just happens to have a dead-on critique of the American war machine. So here's a partial transcript of the interview that took place between Chomsky, SchNEWS, Comedian Mark Thomas (who set the whole thing up) and a collection of other British trouble makers.

Mark Thomas: *If we can start with US foreign policy in relation to Iraq and the War on Terror, what do you think is going on at the moment?*

Noam Chomsky: First of all I think we ought to be very cautious about using the phrase 'War on Terror'. There can't be a War on Terror. It's a logical impossibility. The US is one of the leading terrorist states in the world. The guys who are in charge right now were all condemned for terrorism by the World Court. They would have been condemned by the U.N. Security Council except they vetoed the resolution, with Britain abstaining of course. These guys can't be conducting a war on terror. It's just out of the question. They declared a war on terror 20 years ago and we know what they did. They destroyed Central America. They killed a million and a half people in southern Africa. We can go on through the list. So there's no 'War on Terror'.

There was a terrorist act, September 11th, very unusual, a real historic event, the first time in history that the west received the kind of attack that it carries out routinely in the rest of the world. September 11th did change policy undoubtedly, not just for the US, but across the board. Every government in the world saw it as an opportunity to intensify their own repression and atrocities, from Russia and Chechnya, to the West imposing more discipline on their populations.

This had big effects - for example take Iraq. Prior to September 11th, there was a longstanding concern of the US toward Iraq - that is it has the second largest oil reserves in the world. So one way or another the US was going to do something to get it, that's clear. September 11th gave the pretext. There's a change in the rhetoric concerning Iraq after September 11th – 'We now have an excuse to go ahead with what we're planning.'

It kinda stayed like that up to September of this year when Iraq suddenly shifted... to 'An imminent threat to our existence.' Condoleeza Rice [US National Security Advisor] came out with her warning that the next evidence of a nuclear weapon would be a mushroom cloud over New York. There was a big media campaign with political figures – we

needed to destroy Saddam this winter or we'd all be dead. You've got to kind of admire the intellectual classes not to notice that the only people in the world who are afraid of Saddam Hussien are Americans. Everybody hates him and Iraqis are undoubtedly afraid of him, but outside of Iraq and the United States, no one's afraid of him. Not Kuwait, not Iran, not Israel, not Europe. They hate him, but they're not afraid of him.

In the United States people are very much afraid, there's no question about it. The support you see in US polls for the war is very thin, but it's based on fear. It's an old story in the United States. When my kids were in elementary school 40 years ago they were taught to hide under desks in case of an atom bomb attack. I'm not kidding. The country is always in fear of everything. Crime for example: Crime in the United States is roughly comparable with other industrial societies, towards the high end of the spectrum. On the other hand, fear of crime is way beyond other industrial societies...

It's very consciously engendered. These guys now in office, remember they're almost entirely from the 1980s. They've been through it already and they know exactly how to play the game. Right through the 1980s they periodically had campaigns to terrify the population...

To create fear is not that hard, but this time the timing was so obviously for the Congressional campaign that even political commentators got the message. The presidential campaign is going to be starting in the middle of next year. They've got to have a victory under their belt. And on to the next adventure. Otherwise, the population's going to pay attention to what's happening to them, which is a big assault, a major assault on the population, just as in the 1980s. They're replaying the record almost exactly. First thing they did in the 1980s, in 1981, was drive the country into a big deficit. This time they did it with a tax cut for the rich and the biggest increase in federal spending in 20 years.

This happens to be an unusually corrupt administration, kind of like an Enron administration, so there's a tremendous amount of profit going into the hands of an unusually corrupt group of gangsters. You can't really have all this stuff on the front pages, so you have to push it off the front pages. You have to keep people from thinking about it. And there's only one way that anybody ever figured out to frighten people and they're good at it.

So there's domestic political factors that have to do with timing. September 11th gave the pretext and there's a long term, serious interest [in Iraq]. So they've gotta go to war... my speculation would be that they would like to have it over with before the presidential campaign.

The problem is that when you're in a war, you don't know what's going to happen. The chances are it'll be a pushover, it ought to be, there's no Iraqi army, the country will probably collapse in two minutes, but you can't be sure of that. If you take the CIA warnings seriously, they're pretty straight about it. They're saying that if there's a war, Iraq may respond with terrorist acts...

US adventurism is just driving countries into developing weapons of mass destruction as a deterrent - they don't have any other deterrent. Conventional forces don't work obviously, there's no external deterrent. The only way anyone can defend themselves is with terror and weapons of mass destruction. So it's plausible to assume that they're doing it. I suppose that's the basis for the CIA analysis and I suppose the British intelligence are saying the same thing.

But you don't want to have that happen in the middle of a presidential campaign... There is the problem about what to do with the effects of the war, but that's easy. You count on journalists and intellectuals not to talk about it. How many people are talking about Afghanistan? Afghanistan's back where it was, run by warlords and gangsters and who's writing about it? Almost nobody. If it goes back to what it was no one cares, everyone's forgotten about it.

If Iraq turns into people slaughtering each other, I could write the articles right now. 'Backward people, we tried to save them but they want to murder each other because they're dirty Arabs.' By then, I presume, I'm just guessing, they [the US] will be onto the next war, which will probably be either Syria or Iran.

The fact is that war with Iran is probably underway. It's known that about 12% of the Israeli airforce is in south eastern Turkey. They're there because they're preparing for the war against Iran. They don't care about Iraq. Iraq they figure's a pushover, but Iran has always been a problem for Israel. It's the one country in the region that they can't handle and they've been after the US to take it on for years. According to one report, the Israeli airforce is now flying at the Iranian border for intelligence, provocation and so on. And it's not a small airforce. It's bigger than the British airforce, bigger than any NATO power other than the US. So it's probably underway. There are claims that there are efforts to stir up Asseri separatism, which makes some sense. It's what the Russians tried to do in 1946, and that would separate Iran, or what's left of Iran, from the Caspian oil producing centres. Then you could partition it. That will probably be underway at the time and then there'll be a story about how Iran's going to kill us tomorrow, so we need to get rid of them today. At least that's been the pattern.

Campaign Against Arms Trade: *How far do you see the vast military production machine that is America requiring war as an advertisement for their equipment?*

Chomsky: You have to remember that what's called military industry is just hi-tech industry. The military is a kind of cover for the state sector in the economy. At MIT [Massachusetts Institute of Technology] where I am, everybody knows this except the economists. Everybody else knows it because it pays their salaries. The money comes into places like MIT under military contract to produce the next generation of the hi-tech economy. If you take a look at what's called the new economy - computers, internet - it comes straight out of places like MIT under federal contracts for research and development under the cover of military production. Then it gets handed to IBM when you can sell something.

At MIT the surrounding area used to have small electronics firms. Now it has small biotech firms. The reason is that the next cutting edge of the economy is going to be biology based. So funding from the government for biology based research is vastly increasing. If you want to have a small start-up company that will make you a huge amount of money when somebody buys it someday, you do it in genetic engineering, biotechnology and so on. This goes right through history. It's usually a dynamic state sector that gets economies going.

One of the reasons the US wants to control the oil is because profits flow back, and they flow in a lot of ways. Its not just oil profits, it's also military sales. The biggest purchaser of US arms and probably British arms is either Saudi Arabia or United Arab Emirates, one of the rich oil producers. They take most of the arms and that's profits for hi-tech industry in

Chomp'in at the Bit cont...

the Unites States. The money goes right back to the US treasury and treasury securities. In various ways, this helps prop up primarily the US and British economies.

I don't know if you've looked at the records, but in 1958 when Iraq broke the Anglo-American condominium on oil production, Britain went totally crazy. The British at that time were still very reliant on Kuwaiti profits. Britain needed the petrodollars for supporting the British economy and it looked as if what happened in Iraq might spread to Kuwait. So at that point Britain and the US decided to grant Kuwait nominal autonomy, up to then it was just a colony. They said you can run your own post office, pretend you have a flag, that sort of thing. The British said that if anything goes wrong with this we will ruthlessly intervene to ensure maintaining control and the US agreed to the same thing in Saudi Arabia and the Emirates.

CAAT: *There's also the suggestion that it's a way of America controlling Europe and the Pacific rim.*

Chomsky: Absolutely. The smarter guys like George Kenneth were pointing out that control over the energy resources of the middle east gives the US what he called 'veto power' over other countries. He was thinking particularly of Japan. Now the Japanese know this perfectly well so they've been working very hard to try to gain independent access to oil, that's one of the reasons they've tried hard, and succeeded to an extent, to establish relations with Indonesia and Iran and others, to get out of the West-controlled system.

Actually one of the purposes of the [post World War II] Marshall Plan, this great benevolent plan, was to shift Europe and Japan from coal to oil. Europe and Japan both had indigenous coal resources but they switched to oil in order to give the US control. About £2bn out of the £13bn Marshall Plan dollars went straight to the oil companies to help convert Europe and Japan to oil based economies. For power, it's enormously significant to control the resources and oil's expected to be the main resource for the next couple of generations.

The National Intelligence Council, which is a collection of various intelligence agencies, published a projection in 2000 called 'Global Trends 2015.' They make the interesting prediction that terrorism is going to increase as a result of globalisation. They really say it straight. They say that what they call globalisation is going to lead to a widening economic divide, just the opposite of what economic theory predicts, but they're realists, and so they say that it's going to lead to increased disorder, tension and hostility and violence, a lot of it directed against the United States.

They also predict that Persian Gulf oil will be increasingly important for world energy and industrial systems but that the US won't rely on it. But it's got to control it. Controlling the oil resources is more of an issue than access. Because control equals power.

MT: *How do you think the current anti-war movement that's building up compares with Vietnam? What do you think we can achieve as people involved in direct action and protest? Do you think there's a possibility of preventing a war from occurring?*

NC: I think that's really hard because the timing is really short. You can make it costly, which is important. Even if it doesn't stop, it's important for the war to be costly to try to stop the next one.

Compared with the Vietnam War movement, this movement is just incomparably ahead now. People talk about the Vietnam War movement, but they forget or don't know what it was actually like. The war in Vietnam started in 1962, publicly, with a public attack on South Vietnam – air force, chemical warfare, concentration camps, the whole business. No protest... the protest that did build up four or five years later was mostly about the bombing of the North, which was terrible but was a sideshow. The main attack was against South Vietnam and there was never any serious protest against that.

This time there's protest before the war has even got started. I can't think of an example in the entire history of Europe, including the

United States, when there was ever protest of any substantial level *before* a war. Here you've got massive protest before war's even started. It's a tremendous tribute to changes in popular culture that have taken place in Western countries in the last 30 or 40 years. It's just phenomenal.

SchNEWS: *It sometimes seems that as soon as protest breaks out of quite narrow confines, a march every six months maybe, you get attacked. People protesting against the war recently in Brighton were pepper sprayed and batoned for just sitting down in a street.*

Chomsky: The more protest there is the more tightening there's going to be, that's routine. When the Vietnam War protests really began to build up, so did the repression. I was very close to a long jail sentence myself and it was stopped by the Tet Offensive. After the Tet Offensive, the establishment turned against the war and they called off the trials. Right now a lot of people could end up in Guantanamo Bay and people are aware of it.

If there's protest in a country then there's going to be repression. Can they get away with it? - it depends a lot on the reaction. In the early 50s in the US, there was what was called Macarthyism and the only reason it succeeded was that there was no resistance to it. When they tried the same thing in the 60s it instantly collapsed because people simply laughed at it so they couldn't do it. Even a dictatorship can't do everything it wants. It's got to have some degree of popular support. And in a more democratic country, there's a very fragile power system. There's nothing secret about this, it's history. The question in all of these things is how much popular resistance there's going to be.

* This is an edited version. If you want to see the whole video, contact Undercurrents 01865 203661, underc@gn.apc.org.

* For more Chomsky stuff (there's loads of it) visit www.zmag.org/chomsky/index.cfm or get some of his books from AK Press: www.akuk.com, 0131-5555615 for a catalogue.

WAKE UP! WAKE UP! IT'S YER OILY RAG!!

weekly SchNEWS
www.schnews.org.uk

MAN...
I GET THESE
ESSENTIAL OILS
FROM IRAQ

DUBYA'S
OILS & EXOTIC POTIONS

Friday 10th January 2003   **Free/Donation**   **Issue 387**

OIL DRUMS OF WAR

Britons woke up to a planned terrorist attack on their shores this week. But any chemical attack using ricin produced in a north London flat is nothing compared to what's in store for the people of Iraq, with a leaked UN report saying that up to 500,000 Iraqi people could suffer serious injuries during the first phase of a terrorist attack.

That's state terrorism brought to you by America and Britain — so they can get their hands on Iraqi oil. Foreign secretary Jack Straw said as much on Monday when he told 150 British ambassadors at a meeting in London that one of the key priorities of British foreign policy was "to bolster the security of British and global energy supplies". It's just an amazing coincidence that Iraq has the second biggest known oil reserves in the world.

The US burns a quarter of all the oil consumed and is world champion at producing the greenhouse gases that are causing global warming. A study sponsored by the US Council on Foreign Relations says that "the American people continue to demand plentiful and cheap energy without sacrifice or inconvenience". Seeing as the world's oil reserves will begin to seriously decline within 5 to 10 years it's not surprising US Vice President Dick Cheney calls Iraq "the great prize".

In the National Security Strategy, a document in which each American administration outlines its approach to defending the country, Bush laid out his aggressive military and foreign policy, embracing pre-emptive attacks against perceived enemies. It speaks in blunt terms of ignoring international opinion if it suits U.S. interests and lays out a plan for permanent U.S. military and economic domination of every region on the globe – which will come from the $379 billion it's budgeting on the military.

The Strategy sounds very similar to a report issued in September 2000 by a bunch of conservative business leaders called the Project for the New American Century. This stated "At no time in history has the international security order been as conducive to American interests and ideals…The challenge of this coming century is to preserve and enhance this *American peace.*" Written way before September 11th, the authors of the Project report included Paul Wolfowitz, now deputy defence secretary, John Bolton, undersecretary of state, Stephen Cambone, head of the Pentagon's Office of Program, Analysis and Evaluation, and Eliot Cohen and Devon Cross, members of the Defence Policy Board, which advises Secretary Of Defence Donald Rumsfeld.

The Project clearly identified Iran, Iraq and North Korea as primary short-term targets, well before 'elected' President Bush dubbed them as the Axis of Evil. It says U.S. forces will be required to perform "constabulary duties" - acting as policeman of the world - and says that such actions "demand American political leadership rather than that of the United Nations." To meet those responsibilities, and to ensure that no country dares to challenge the United States, the report ad-

vocates a much larger military presence spread over more of the globe, in addition to the roughly 130 nations in which U.S. troops are already deployed. It wants permanent military bases in the Middle East, in Southeast Europe, in Latin America and in Southeast Asia.

Spin-U-Like

While the 'weapons of mass destruction' façade has well and truly fallen off the oil war in Iraq, last year's oil war in Afghanistan was far better dressed up as something else, allowing the good work to go ahead…

The latest US ambassador to Afghanistan - a senior executive of US oil company Unocal - along with the current Afghani president Hamid Karzai (once employed by a Unocal subsidiary) – are oiling the wheels for a lucrative pipeline to carry oil and gas across the country from the Caspian sea. And who's building this pipeline? Er… Unocal.

As the BBC reported on September 18, 2001: "Niaz Niak, a former Pakistani foreign minister, was told

Oil Drums of War cont...

by senior American officials in mid-July 2001 (pre 9-11) that military action against Afghanistan would go ahead by the middle of October. It was Naik's view that Washington would not drop its war against Afghanistan even if bin Laden were to be surrendered immediately by the Taliban." As journalist John Pilger puts it "One of the reasons the Americans attacked Afghanistan was not to liberate women but to liberate the pipeline deal."

Pilger continues, "This is the hidden agenda of the "war on terrorism" - a term that is no more than a euphemism for the Bush administration's ex-ploitation of the September 11 attacks and America's accelerating imperial ambitions. In the past 14 months, on the pretext of "fighting terror", US military bases have been established at the gateways to the greatest oil and gas fields on earth, especially in Central Asia, which is also coveted as a 'great prize.'"

Meanwhile Donald Kagan, who served as co-chairman of the 2000 New American Century Project, embraces the idea that the United States should establish permanent military bases in a post-war Iraq. "We will probably need a major concentration of forces in the Middle East over a long period of time. That will come at a price, but think of the price of not having it. When we have economic problems, it's been caused by disruptions in our oil supply. If we have a force in Iraq, there will be no disruption in oil supplies."

* For the past 10 years one of the world's dirtiest wars has been fought out in Algeria, between "Islamists" and "security forces", in which almost 200,000 people - mostly civilians - have been killed. Groups such as Human Rights Watch have accused the Algerian Government of "arbitrary arrest, disappearances and torture" and even America has been critical of the country's human rights record. That criticism changed after September 11th, thanks to Algeria support for Americas so called 'war on terror' and as a thank you they got promises of increased military aid. US Assistant Secretary of State William Burns, during a visit to Algiers, even went as far to say "Washington has much to learn from Algeria on ways to fight terrorism." Incidentally, Algeria is the second biggest natural gas exporter in the world and ranks fourteenth in oil reserves.

* To read more about the Project for the New American Century report visit: www.accessatlanta.com/ajc/opinion/bookman/2002/092902.html
* To see the leaked UN report www.casi.org.uk

www.mahjoob.com

War Briefs

With even Neo Labour becoming shaky about the war, now's the time to step up the protests. There will be a meeting about taking direct action against the war in London this Saturday (11) after the **Stop the War Conference.** It's being hosted by our good selves 6.30pm in the Cock Tavern, on the corner of Phoenix Road and Eversholt Street, London, five minutes from Euston Station. ** **Two Scottish train drivers** yesterday refused to move a freight train carrying ammunition destined for the Glen Douglas base on Scotland's west coast, Europe's largest weapons store. Railway managers had to cancel the Ministry of Defence service after the crewmen, described as "conscientious objectors" by a supporter, said they opposed Tony Blair's threat to attack Iraq. **

There will be another weapons inspection at **USAF Fairford** in Gloucestershire on 26th January. Fairford has just had a £100 million refit so it can house the "new" smaller bunker busting nuclear weapons firing B-2 bombers. Assemble in Fairford village 12 noon www.gwi.org.uk ** Get along to **Northwood** in London on the 18-19th January the command post for British rapid deployment forces. Northwood would play a key role in directing British forces in any attack on Iraq and officers from the base spent much of December in Qatar participating in a US wargame preparing for the invasion of Iraq . The weekend of action – Operation Internal Look (OIL) - coincides with the anniversary of the 1991 Gulf bombing and will include a tour of the base, a mass blockade, a mass breaching of the Official Secrets Act, non-violence training and autonomous affinity group actions. To find out more call 0845 458 2564 www.voicesuk.org ** Fancy going to Iraq as part of the **'Human Shield Convoy'**? It's leaving 25th January from London. www.uksociety.org 07799 650 791 donations and help needed.** Just before Christmas three people from **London Catholic Worker** were arrested and charged with criminal damage after pouring red paint from baby bottles (symbolising blood) on the two main gate signs at Northwood ** **15 anti-war protestors were arrested** by US military police at the US airforce base in **Mildenhall** on Sunday after cutting through the fence and getting onto the site. They were later released without charge.

To find out about planned protests if war starts visit... www.schnews.org.uk/pap/ ifwarbreaksout.htm

Let Them Eat Soup

'Inhuman', 'cruel', 'downright evil' .. and that's only what MPs have said about Blair and Blunket's latest assault on the human rights of Asylum Seekers which came into force on the 8th January.

Thousands of Asylum Seekers, including pregnant women and people with disabilities and special needs, will be forced to sleep rough under the draconian section 55 of the **Nationality, Immigration and Asylum Act (NIAA).**

This section states that if a refugee does not apply for Asylum immediately on arrival at the port of entry they will receive no support, no accommodation, no food... ever.

Statistically, 65% of Asylum Seekers (around a hundred a day) do not present themselves to immigration officials on arrival... for obvious reasons.

Many don't know who they can trust, typically being abused, often tortured, victims of 'the authorities'. Many are totally traumatised both by what they are fleeing (genocide for example) and the possibility of being put straight back on the next plane 'home'. Others do not speak a word of English.

Quite apart from the fact - as upheld in International Law - that many refugees are forced to travel clandestinely to avoid punishment by the regime they are fleeing.

But who cares about International Law, or Human Rights or the recently agreed EU minimum standards of support for Asylum Seekers? Not Tony and Dave.

Nor Peter Lilley (remember him, he was the 'right-wing' one) who introduced similar measures back in 1996. Appalled by the sight of homeless, starving refugees, often inadequately dressed and begging on the streets, charities and support groups set up soup kitchens and emergency shelters. Lilley's policy was successfully challenged in the high court under the 1948 National Assistance Act and stopped.

But Neo-Labour have already thought of that - their new Act specifically debars refugee agencies from going to court and trying the same thing!

Nevertheless Liberty intend to press ahead with a Human Rights case against section 55, stating that the policy is "incompatible with our fundamental human right not to be subject to cruel, inhuman and degrading treatment".

0207 654 7700
www.refugee-action.org.
To check out the act visit:
www.asylumsupport.info

Better Profits

The Baku-Ceyhan pipeline is a BP led project to channel Caspian oil and gas reserves to western markets. It is key for BP's growth, and for the strategic interests of the US who wish to secure non-OPEC oil supplies. Oil coming from the pipeline will also end up fuelling the key US Air Force base in Incirlik, Turkey. The pipeline would create a 1,750km militarised corridor through Azerbaijan, Georgia and Turkey. Under the BP-Turkey host government agreement the consortium running the pipelines will have no liability whatsoever in the event of a spill or any other form of damage. What's more BP expects the pipeline to be largely financed by tax-payers money!

To find out more come to a teach-in Saturday 25th January, 10am - 5pm, London Action Resource Centre, 62 Fieldgate St, London, E1 contact info@risingtide.org.uk or tel 01865 241 097. www.baku-ceyhan.org.uk

RIP PETE   This issue is dedicated to Pete Shaughnessy who died last weekend. Pete was one of the main instigators behind Reclaim Bedlam and Mad Pride. He helped out with SchNEWS and Worthing's Porkbolter. His funeral takes place at 9.30am on Christmas Eve, at St Thomas Moore Church, near the library in Lordship Lane, East Dulwich.

THERE'S CLEARLY BEEN A MATERIAL BREACH!

SchNEWS in brief

Cops in Genoa are in trouble after admitting fabricating evidence against protestors including planting petrol bombs during investigations into the policing of the G8 summit last July. Italian media have been publishing transcripts of the inquiry. 77 officers are under investigation for alleged brutality and three police chiefs have been moved to other jobs ** Brighton's premier pirate station **Radio 4A** is on air again this weekend (9pm Friday till midnight Sunday) on a new frequency 101.4FM. For listing and audio-streams visit www.radio4a.org.uk ** Activist Allen O'Keefe couldn't believe his ears when magistrates in Newbury ordered him to pay £750 compensation for cutting a **tiny piece of fence** at Aldermaston during the Trident Ploughshares disarmament camp there in May 2001. Courts have so far imposed fines and compensation orders totalling £52,000 on protestors but hardly anyone has paid up! 0845 4588366 www.tridentploughshares.org ** Check out a new **Legal issues website** for UK political activists (especially animal rights and environmentalists). www.freebeagles.org offers info on your rights re police tactics and intimidation. ** The **Radical Dairy social centre** is one year old next weekend and is celebrating with a birthday party next Friday 17th from 8pm onwards. There's music and food – and it will be probably be the last party as they've been served with eviction papers. They're at 47 Kynaston Road, Stoke Newington, London N16 ** There's a meeting for people interested in restarting the campaign in the UK for the release of **Mumia Abu Jamal** after 21 years on Death Row. It's next Wednesday (15) 7-9pm. Somerstown Coffee House, 60 Chalton Street (off Euston Road) London NW1. mumiauk@yahoo.co.uk ** Yet again unaccountable, unelected representatives from the corporate world of industry and media moguls will mingle with political leaders and decide the future of the planet and its people at Davos, Switzerland. International demonstrations against the **World Economic Forum** take place 25 – 28 January. www.antiwef.org ** Meanwhile in Brazil at the same time the **World Social Forum** meets to look at alternatives www.worldsocialforum.org Extensive reporting on www.zmag.org ** At least 15 000 people turned up for the **Asian Social Forum** in Hyderbad, India at the beginning of this year under the banner "another world is possible." www.wsfindia.org ** There's a call out for anarchists and anti-authoritarians to get involved in the **European Social Foum.** Read about it at www.squall.co.uk. Get along to the next meeting this Wednesday (15) 6:30 pm at the University of London Union Student Union Building, Malet Street, London www.mobilise.org.uk ** **Injustice the film about deaths in police custody** is being shown in Hackney on Jan 18th, along with live music at a squatted venue (ex-community centre) on White Post Lane, just round the corner from Hackney Wick Station. 07770 432 439. The film is also now available for people to buy www.injusticefilm.co.uk.

Drop Us A Pipe-line

After years of human rights abuse in Turkey it looks like the EU are finally taking notice. By doing exactly the same! On December the 11th last year 7 activists were arrested in London and detained for five days before being charged under the 2000 terrorism act, not for doing anything, but with "membership and fundraising for a prescribed organisation". The protesters were supporting the DHKP (Turkish Peoples Revolutionary Front) led 'deathfast' in protest of human rights abuses in Turkish prisons.

So, as we suspected, people are already being arrested under the banner of 'terrorism', not for doing anything, but for what they believe. According to Terry Harkin of the Irish solidarity group the IRSP "This is another example of how this war on terror is being used to tighten the control of America over the world". He also points out that "there is a direct correlation between Tony Blair's meeting with the Turkish premier and George Bush's pressure on Britain". Strange how we should be doing Turkey's dirty work right at the time we need their air bases!

There will be a picket outside Bow Street Magistrates Court on January 13th at 10am organised by People Against terrorism Act. For info call beth 07810 397268

...and finally...

Jumping on the 'terror' bandwagon, an enterprising London firm is offering specially designed gas masks for use by tube-travellers in the event of a chemical attack – a snip at just £188. Ozonelink also plan to offer the British public "chemihoods" and "polytection suits" in the near future.

Disclaimer

SchNEWS warns all readers when Bush talks about essential oils he ain't talking about aroma therapy. Honest.

WAKE UP! WAKE UP! WAR IS TERROR!

IT MUST BE MATING SEASON AGAIN

USAF FAIRFORD KEEP OUT

Weekly SchNEWS

www.schnews.org.uk

Friday 17th January 2003   Free/Donation   Issue 388

DIRECT ACTION STATIONS

"If you go to one demonstration and then go home, that's something, but the people in power can live with that. What they can't live with is sustained pressure that keeps building, organisations that keep doing things, people that keep learning lessons from the last time and doing it better the next time." - *Noam Chomsky*

Last Saturday around 50 people attended a meeting about taking direct action against the war. Hosted by SchNEWS it followed the Stop the War Coalition conference and there was general agreement that while large marches are important they are not enough and that direct action must form a major part of our activities if we are to be successful in stopping this war. People talked about a whole host of activities from disrupting cabinet ministers meetings, getting into American bases to becoming human shields in Iraq to try and protect essential services like water and sewage plants. One of those places where it was felt we could really make our presence felt was at RAF Fairford in Gloucestershire.

Fairford has just had a brand spanking new £100 million pound refit so it can house the new bunker busting nuclear weapons firing B-2 bombers. This is the only airbase in Europe that these bombers can take off from to murder Iraqi civilians and so will play a crucial military role in the bombing and invasion of Iraq. Already two citizens weapons inspections have taken place with some people managing to break into the base briefly – so could Fairford become the next Greenham Common?

FIGHT FAIRFORD

In 1981 Ann Pettitt organised a march from Cardiff to Greenham Common to protest against the siting of 96 cruise missiles at the US-controlled airbase and decided to stay. Within a few months the women's peace camp became a focus for hundreds of thousands of peace activists across Britain. One mass demonstration there in December 1982 attracted 30,000 women. They repeatedly made a mockery of the high security by cutting through fences and stopping the movement of the missiles, and Greenham inspired similar actions took place up and down the country.

This year, on Sunday January 26th Ann Pettitt and many of the Greenham women will be joining Gloucestershire Weapons Inspectors for another mass citizens weapons inspection at Fairford. "There are remarkable parallels between then and now and that's what caught my imagination," says Ann "Contemplating the use of weapons of mass destruction in a war that's supposed to be about eliminating such weapons is absurd... In 1981 we were told that theatre nuclear weapons, cruise missiles, at Greenham would make the world safer but we felt they edged us nearer to crossing the nuclear threshold. It took years to pull back from the threshold back then and yet we now find ourselves, once more, on the brink."

As that wise old owl Jo Makepeace said at the meeting "Marches every few months, however big, will not in themselves worry the warmongers - they are a start, not an end in themselves. We need to step things up, both locally and nationally. We need to turn people's anger into action by involving tens of thousands of people in blockading city centres, shutting military airbases, stopping 'normal' government activity and, well, you get the picture."

BATTLE PLAN

If war breaks out – check the SchNEWS website to find out what's happening in your area.

* Les Gibbons, wearing a shirt displaying the words "Dissent without civil disobedience is consent" pleaded guilty in court this week to "high quality intrusion" (whatever that means!).

Les a former British marine, had attempted to blockade the gates to Portsmouth naval base on the day the Ark Royal left for the Gulf.

* Five citizens weapons inspectors from Cambridge Students Against the War entered RAF Feltwell last week to confirm reports that the base forms part of a US Weapons of Mass Destruction development programme. They were eventually nicked but released without charge. www.camsaw.org.uk

* Get along to **RAF Northwood in London** this weekend for some direct action against the war. Northwood will play a key role in directing British forces in any attack on Iraq. Operation Internal Look (OIL)– coincides with the anniversary of the 1991 Gulf bombing and will include a tour of the base, a mass blockade, mass breaching of the Official Secrets Act, non-violence training and autonomous affinity group actions. To find out more 0845 458 2564. www.northwood.cjb.net. Transport from Brighton: 9am at St Peters Church.

* Join the regular **Menwith Women's Peace Camp** this

Direct Action Stations cont...

weekend 01943-468593 e-mail helenmenwith@yahoo.co.uk to arrange lifts from Harrogate. And don't forget the regular demonstrations every Tuesday 7-9pm. 01943 466405 www.caab.org.uk

* **Susex Action for Peace** meeting this Tuesday 7.30pm, at the Brighthelm Centre, North Road, Brighton.
* **January 26th** is the day before Hans Blix reports to the UN Security Council. To mark the day thousands of citizens weapons inspectors are expected at Fairford. Meet noon in the village 07768 418960 www.gwi.org.uk
* **Fancy going to Iraq** as part of the Human Shield Convoy? It's leaving 25th January from London. 07799 650 791 www.uksociety.org
* A **women's peace camp** has been set up outside Shannon Airport, County Clare, Ireland to protest at it being used as a refueling point for the US military. More info, email: shannonpeacecamp@hotmail.com
* February 1st: **Peace march/pedal for peace** 2pm outside Bath Abbey.
* February 8th: **Mass die-in** 1pm Bournemouth Square. Dress in military uniform or white protective suits and gas masks. 07743 537043 www.alternative answer.co.uk/stopwar.htm
* February 8th, 1pm, **anti-war gathering** in Montague Place, Worthing. worthingagainstwar@yahoo.co.uk
* People from **Faslane peace camp** blockaded British Aerospace in Edinburgh for 4 ½ hours and on Wednesday one of them locked onto the gates at Glen Douglas Europe's largest weapons store for a few hours. Earlier in the day people used a car to block the gates to try and stop the Gulf-bound aircraft carrier Ark Royal loading munitions. Last week two train drivers refused to drive a freight train destined for there.

The peace camp have organised 'make love not war' actions from 14-18 February. This includes action against Labour Party war conference in Glasgow on the 15th. Tel 01436 820901 faslanepeacecamp@hotmail.com
* February 15th **Massive demo against the war** Assemble 12 noon at Embankment, London 020 7053 2155 www.stopwar.org.uk
* Sign the **pledge of resistance** to the "war on terrorism" 0207 607 2302 www.j-n-v.org
* There's a **new direct action anti war email group** http://groups.yahoo.com/group/directactionagainstwar
* Recommended reading **'Greenham Women are Everywhere'** by Alice Cook, Gwyn Kirk, Pluto Press.

LICENCE TO KILLJOY

If you're planning a few celebratory late night drinks when the new Licensing Bill comes into effect just be careful you and your mates don't burst into song cos you might end up with six months in the nick and a £20 000 fine - the maximum penalty for performing "unlicensed live music".

The Licensing Bill, deregulates pub opening times but brings in draconian measures to clamp down on live music. Any music performed live in public will require a license to be obtained two weeks in advance by the proprietor of the venue. It's not only pubs and clubs that will be affected - also covered are buskers and a bunch of obvious threats to family values: carol singers, Morris men, bell-ringers and someone singing at a wedding. This is supposedly to tackle "anti-social behaviour" in the form of "noise", but is another crack down on civil liberties. The license won't be easy to get and will require approval from the police, environmental health (i.e. noise abatement) and local residents. Most complaints are about noise OUTSIDE pubs and clubs but rather than tackle the problem, the government are targeting musicians as an easy soft target.

But guess what? A suggestion that satellite TV (eg. MTV) being broadcast in public places should be similarly licensable was instantly thrown out with Kim Howells stating that such a move would be "resisted robustly by the Industry." That's alright then.
* Meeting regarding action against the Public Entertainment Licence this Friday (17) 8pm @ Charles Dickens, Worthing 01903 522787 dickensclub@aol.com
* 27 Jan Demo against License Bill Reforms 1pm Parliament Square, London.
* Join the guerilla music action cell seferner@macmail.com.
* To read the Bill see www.parliament.the-stationery-office.co.uk/pa/pabills.htm

Inside SchNEWS

Aliane Ahmed - who has been on remand for over a year on charges of arson relating to the fire at the Yarls Wood detention centre - has had his charges dropped, and his supporters hope he will soon be released from prison. Two men however are still on remand for charges relating to the incident, one Klodjian Gaba would appreciate letters of support or visits, Klodjian Gaba EM9676 - HMP Wormwood Scrubs, PO Box 757, Du Cane Road, Acton, London, W12 0AE.

MON-SATAN

If you worry about things like world hunger, habitat destruction or declining wildlife - chill out its all being sorted out by everyone's favourite agribiz multinational Monsanto.

On Wednesday a report published by the Royal Society said GM crops could be good for the environment! And guess who funded this research? Like a hyperactive superhero, one day they're solving world hunger by forcing their transgenic products on desperate African countries, and the next Monsanto are worried about starving wildlife. Their "scientific" experiment had two different management systems for conventional and GM crops, with the system for GM crops being impractical on a commercial basis. With these results they claimed GM crops were better for birds. But considering the two systems were different and the trial only ran for half a year the results are meaningless.

Friends of the Earth campaigner Pete Riley said "Sugar beet farmers were sold the idea of GM crops in the mid 1990s on the basis of that they were good for weed control. The techniques proposed are likely to be more costly and more trouble, it is hard to see what the appeal would be for the majority of farmers." Friends of the Earth: 02074901555 www.foe.co.uk
* The Nelson family from North Dakota, America are currently fighting Monsanto through the courts after their corn cross-pollinated with GM RoundupReady thereby making it Monsanto property. This is similar to the case of Percy Schmeiser (see SchNEWS 346) a farmer from Canada who was fined £150,000 after his canola crops became contaminated by neighbours GM crops. www.percyschmeiser.com

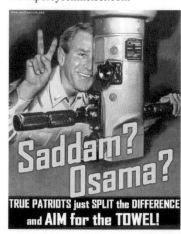
Saddam? Osama?
TRUE PATRIOTS just SPLIT the DIFFERENCE and AIM for the TOWEL!

A Badly Kept Secret

A weekend of actions at RAF Northwood, Britain's military HQ

Saturday 18th January
Mass Breach of the Official Secrets Act.

Northwood is where much of the planning for the UK's military adventures happens, and its location is so 'sensitive' that it's not marked on street maps. Over 150 took part in 'Operation Official Look', treasonously pointing cameras, telescopes and giant binoculars at the secret site. Coming along for the ride was George W Bush, and the 'back half of his pantomime horse' Tony Blair (see pic below) www.j-n-v.org

Get off yer horse and milk it

Peeping Toms against the war - spying on the secret activity at Northwood, Britain's military HQ. Pic: www.guilfin.net

Sunday 19th January

Northwood Base, the Permanent Joint Headquarters of the British Armed Forces was blockaded for eight hours on Sunday 19th January by up to 400 protestors. At 9.15am six peace activists locked themselves together at the main gates of the base with steel tubes covered with giant purple pants, and the slogan "War is Pants". They were finally cut out of the lock-ons after several hours.

There were over 70 arrests during the blockade. The main bulk of the anti-war protestors marched from Northwood tube station towards the base with a samba band and a bicycle powered sound system. Police initially tried to funnel them into a fenced off area on the pavement opposite the main gate, but the crowd staged sit downs as soon as this became apparent. The police eventually allowed them right up to the main gates. There was music and speeches for several hours as people blockaded the gates. The police gave a deadline of 3pm before they would use force and make arrests, but after discussion people decided to remain and risk arrest. Supporters cheered on the blockaders for a couple of hours as around 150 police made arrests, carrying people away and using cutting equip-

ment to remove additional lock ons. The area was cleared by around 5.15pm. Earlier in the afternoon the secondary side gate was also blockaded by four women who locked themselves together in pairs. In contrast with the main gate lock-ons they were arrested and put into police vans while still locked together.

http://uk.indymedia.org/archive/features/2003/01/2003-01.html

See www.j-n-v.org

SchNEWS in brief

The Manchester office of **Environmental Resource Management** (ERM) was occupied for over four hours this week as part of a campaign against their involvement in the green washing of the **Baku-Tbilisi-Ceyhan** oil pipeline (last weeks SchNEWS). The protesters got to talk to ERM's Director and BP's Regional Affairs Director for the Pipeline project who agreed to a meeting. Manchester Earth First! 0161-226 6814, www.risingtide.org.uk ** **Space Invaders a Festival of Arts and Resistance** will appear somewhere in Brighton from the 23rd. It aims to inspire and excite with arts, live music, film, and space for direct action and campaigning workshops. 01273 672186 or speakerpeople@hotmail.com ** The threat of **identity cards** hasn't gone away, the government are consulting the public on the issue. **Privacy International** have set up two local rate numbers, and they will pass your opinions to the government. If you're against the ID Card call 0845 330 7246, or if you're in favour 0845 330 7245. Read about the issues at www.stand.org.uk ** **The Aspire collective in Leeds** whose house was raided and illegally evicted in November are looking to pursue complaints and claims of damage against the police If you were there and want to join in, contact info@a-spire.org.uk. www.a-spire.org.uk. ** **Earth First! Winter Moot** takes place in Nottingham 7-9 Feb. Discussions on how EF! operates - actions, tactics, gatherings, communication, and strategy. Open to anyone who identifies with the EF! Network. 07763 552627 efmoot03@hotmail.com ** On Monday **Greenpeace** activists strolled past lax security at **Sizewell B nuclear powerstation** and occupied one of the sensitive control rooms. www.greenpeace.org.uk

OIL SEE YOU IN HELL

Last week, police stations throughout Caracas, Venezuela's capital, had their sub machine guns and other weapons confiscated. Complaining of the dawn raids, the police chief told Caracas' Union radio, "This leaves us at a tremendous disadvantage against criminals... It's outrageous." Hugo Chavez the President of Venezuela took over control of the Caracas Metropolitan Police from Caracas mayor Alfredo Pena of the opposition last November. Following reports of continued police violence against pro-Chavez protestors and poor folk, Chavez ordered that their weapons be taken last week too.

After six weeks of big business strikes, Venezuela is starting to feel the pinch as the battle continues between the elected socialist president Hugo Chavez and the right-wing opposition. On top of this the state oil company Petroleos de Venezuela, nationalised since the 1970s, is actually run by managers closely linked to the multinationals and the former governing party Acción Democrática. On December 4th these managers declared their support for the big business strike and were joined by the captains of Venezuelan oil tankers who dropped anchor and refused to move. Owners of fleets of road tankers also shut down and the result was the spectacle of a major oil-producing country paralysed through lack of petrol. The military were sent in to keep the oil refineries running, ship captains were dismissed and the navy took control. Fines were imposed on striking road hauliers and the top management of Petroleos de Venezuela was dismissed. Chavez also used the military to set up 'popular markets' to distribute cheap food in lower-class areas of the cities.

In a coup led by the opposition and assisted by the US last April (SchNEWS 345) 20 people were shot dead and as yet no-one has been tried for the deaths. The opposition hope that by destabilising the economy the US will step in again. As always the media propaganda wars are making it incredibly difficult for anyone to know exactly who or what to believe.

Chavez's government has a centralised socialist structure, while the main opposition group wants more links with big business and multinational corporations, aka the 'free' market. Both parties represent elitist capitalist or communist groups that haven't been able to attain social justice and freedom in any other country yet. Despite his dictatorial militant handling of opposition, Chavez does win points for some of his reforms. Since coming to power in 1999 he has been shouting about participatory democracy, trying to use popular assemblies, social movements and continuous referendums. He also set up the provision of free healthcare and education up to university level and positively restructured the courts and legal system.

Venezuela is the fifth largest oil producing country in the world yet 80% of its population live in poverty. Chavez sought to redress the balance by imposing a 30% tax paid on oil exports and by changing the law so that the government would have to have a 51% stake in all oil ventures. His government also passed a land reform bill which makes it possible for the government to seize land that has been unproductive for two years and redistribute it to the poor and landless.

More information see: www.squall.co.uk, www.nodo50.org/ellibertario

...and finally...

Colombian Guerrillas who have been fighting for 40 years for a socialist state have been spared from a planned devastating air-strike - Operation Bikini. The government was gonna bombard them with a different kind of bombshell - pocket sized photos of busty bikini-clad women. Despite 30% of the rebels being female, the Latin American temptresses were supposed to seduce the rebels to defection as they stretched provocatively next to slogans such as "DESERT! and "Obtain Benefits". Colombian models refused to be drafted in to pose for the photos so the army instead got the images from an internet porn site. The war torn nations first female Defence Minister supported the feminist protests and said she was cancelling the campaign.

Disclaimer

SchNEWS warns all readers to stay at home and build a weapon of mass destruction before the neighbours do. Honest.

DEJA VU

By January the US led invasion and occupation of Iraq which had been planned for months (having been on the agenda for years) was in the advanced stage, and all it needed was some sort of excuse. UN Resolution 1441, brought in in November was duly going through the motions of presenting the facade of an international diplomatic process, while its fait accompli end game was inevitably a green light for war. 1441 was a guilty-until-proven-innocent demand that Iraq disclose the weapons it was assumed to have, and if it didn't come clean it was war. We now know (see 'What Weapons?' at the back of this book if you're unsure) - as Bush, Rumsfeld and co. did all along - that this pretext for war was a fabrication.

While getting public approval for the war was treated as a bonus not a necessity by the 'coalition', there was still pressure on UN weapons inspections chief Hans Blix to deliver that 'smoking gun' soundbite which could be used to bring public opinion around to the war. It never came, as they knew it wouldn't, and the US just conveniently used the delays caused by the weapons inspections process to fine tune the war plan and work out which countries to use for airbases.

This was the background of a global day of actions called for the 18th of January, the 12th anniversary of the first gulf war.

(right) Weapons inspections at Volkel being obstructed by Americans - sounds rather like what happened to the UN inspectors in Iraq

Shannon Airport - Ireland

A week after a permanent peace camp was established there, around two thousand converged on Shannon Airport on January 18th - where at that stage already 7,000 troops a week were passing through to the gulf. This comes after 150 protesters had previously torn down the fence and a Hercules plane sprayed with anti-war messages. The event began with a march out of the town of Shannon, and being called by the SWP, was supposed to just involve marching and listening to speeches. But some had other ideas and a group climbed onto the roof of an airport building to make some noise and drop banners, and a portable sound system was wheeled in making the speeches difficult to hear. Later another group broke past police at a gate to enter airport warehouses, getting out without arrest. More info: http://struggle.ws/wsm/shannon.html www.shannonpeacecamp.org

Volkel Military Base

About one hundred civil inspectors gained access to the grounds of Volkel military air base in the southeast of the Netherlands. Some inspection teams somehow had their own keys to enter gates at the base, while other cut through and entered in small groups. Most were arrested, but released later throughout the day. Investigations by several groups revealed that there were in fact weapons of mass destruction stored there under US supervision. (see Trainstopping in this book)

Washington DC

There were massive anti-war demonstrations across the world on January 18th in over 38 countries from Turkey to Japan to Antarctica. In the US the focus was on two large marches in **Washington DC** with 300,000 people, and **San Francisco** with 200,000. Cities all across the 'global north' saw marches in tens of thousands, with 30 cit-

...I have written several lengthy poems concerning my feelings about this war which I'd like to share with you...

NO BLOOD NOR OIL!

A packet of frozen peace - Antarctica

ies in **Canada** coming out and a similar story around Europe.
*In **Spain** 30,000 marched on the **Torrejón military base near Madrid** on Jan. 19;
* in **Florence, Italy**, 5,000 formed a human chain around the US consulate,
* **US airbase Camp Ederle in Italy** was targeted for direct action, while 90 were arrested after carrying out a 'weapons inspection' at US airbase **Volkel in Holland**,
* 20,000 marched in **Paris**, 10,000 in **Marseille** and **Brussels**,
* 2,000 gathered at the US military headquarters in **Heidelberg, Germany**.
* In **Moscow** and **St Petersburg** marches were held at the US Embassies.
Crowds gathered all over **Central and South America**, including a march led by the Mothers of the Plaza del Mayo to the U.S. Embassy in **Buenos Aires, Argentina** on January 16th, plus another in **Mexico City**, and on the US-Mexico border.

don't BUY their WAR

"The de facto role of the US armed forces will be to keep the world safe for our economy and open to our cultural assault. To those ends, we will do a fair amount of killings."
Major Ralph Peters, US Military

Middle East, Asia

In most of the **Middle East** protesters faced an army of heavily armed riot police, but still... tens of thousands appeared in **Damascus, Syria**, 1,000 in **Cairo**, as well as large demos in **Beirut; Amman, Jordan; Bahrain**, and **Baghdad**. In **Palestine** thousands came out in the West Bank cities of **Tulkarm** and **Jenin**, plus other spots in the **West Bank** and **Gaza Strip**.
* In **Turkey** 2,000 staged protests in **Ankara**, as the US's top general arrived in the country to push for rights to use Turkish airbases in the possible war, in a country where 80% are against the war. Protests were also held in **Istanbul**.
* It kicked off in **Pakistan** – with protesters in **Lahore** being fended off by soldiers and police as they tried to march to the U.S. Embassy. In **Rawalpindi**, protesters – including many children with their parents and teachers - attempted a human chain stretching to **Islamabad**, 10 kilometres (6.5 miles) away. Marches also happened in **Karachi** and elsewhere.
* There were a series of demonstra-

tions in the **Philippines** protesting the war on Iraq and also the attempt by the U.S. to reoccupy Philippine military bases.
* 5,000 marched in **Tokyo,** many carrying toy guns filled with flowers.
* In **Hong Kong,** a rally marched through the financial district to visit the U.S. and British consulates.

San Francisco

(left) **Japan**: Etsumi Tairahori (69) is on hunger strike against the looming war with Iraq. She is staying at a nine-day protest camp outside the entrace to the US Comsulate in Urasoe, Okinawa, Japan. Etsumi has been having a sit-in at this site every Friday for the past 18 months in protest against the US military presence in Okinawa, ever since a US Air Force sergeant raped a local woman.

weekly SchNEWS
www.schnews.org.uk

Give me your tired, your poor, your huddled masses yearning to breathe free... Except that one in the turban!

Friday 24th January 2003   **Free/Donation**   **Issue 389**

INS AND OUT

"The idea that terrorism is a third world import carried in by non-white people has become the widely accepted excuse for increasingly repressive border policies throughout the global north... A border panic has been carefully constructed so that the 'terrorists' are always seen as existing 'outside' of 'our society'."
- Nandita Sharma, Green Pepper magazine, Autumn 2002

"No borders, no nations, fuck deportations."
- Marchers outside San Francisco Immigration and Naturalization Service, 18th Jan 2003

Fresh from registering his postal vote at San Francisco's British Consulate last Saturday, SchNEWS' man in California was surprised to be swept aside by 2,000 masked-up young Americans who proceeded to trash the front of the building. Intrigued by shouts of *"Tony Blair is an embarrassment to British people everywhere,"* and unable to answer queries of, *"has Britain become a colony of the United States?"* our boy followed the mob - a breakaway faction from the 200,000 strong anti-war rally - downtown where they proceeded to graffiti and smash the offices of the Immigration and Naturalization Service (INS). It turns out the INS is the US's latest tool in the 'fight against terror'...

The role of the INS is to deport people back to countries where they often face persecution and death – the US answer to Britain's Immigration Service, who you may recall suffocated Jamaican mother Joy Gardner in 1993 in her Tottenham home while trying to deport her.

Anyway, a new addition to the INS is the National Security Entry-Exit Registration System (NSEERS), a 'special registration' scheme, conceived by Bush's ultra-conservative Attorney General, John Ashcroft, and hastily added to Ashcroft's repressive post September 11th Patriot Act. It means thousands of men must report to the INS for questioning, photographing and fingerprinting. Classed as legal non-citizens and temporary foreign visitors, the chosen "non-immigrants" hail from Iran, Iraq, Syria, Libya, Sudan, Afghanistan, Algeria, Bahrain, Eritrea, Lebanon, Morocco, North Korea, Oman, Qatar, Somalia, Tunisia, United Arab Emirates, and Yemen – a good cross section of the world's population then.

Many are required to hand over credit card and bank details, names of relatives, what mosque they attend, charities they donate to and so on. If during 'special registration' your records or your answers aren't up to scratch, or if you're late for registration because you didn't hear about it, or if you have minor visa problems – even caused by incompetence at the INS *"...you may be considered to be out of status and subject to arrest, detention, fines and/or removal from the United States. Any future application for immigration may be adversely impacted,"* says the INS 'call up'. And it goes on *"...if you leave the United States, you must appear in person before an INS inspecting officer at one of the designated ports and leave the United States from that port on the same day."*

Stating the obvious, a spokesperson for the Muslim Public Affairs Council in Los Angeles has said "I don't think the terrorists will go and register." However over 15,000 men have registered, with many discovering that not even US citizenship gets them out being required to 'register.'

Dissenters have likened the scheme to the internment of the Japanese in the US during World War II. Babak Satoodeh, President of the American Iranian Alliance (AIA), in an interview with the Digital Freedom Network said 'special registrations' are creating and solidifying negative public opinion concerning people from the Middle East, South Asia, and Muslims in general. "People react to how this government makes decisions," he said.

Already around 500-700 have been detained, and immigration officials admit that anyone with a slight visa irregularity is subject to arrest, regardless of personal histories. Detainees' lawyers have challenged the US government to

"Say No To The Daily Mail's War on Refugees and Immigrants" - Demonstrate at the Daily Mail offices on Monday 27th Jan at 5:30pm, Associated Newspapers Building, 2 Derry St, Kensington, London W8. lizperetz@aol.com

Ins and Outs cont...

produce any evidence of criminal behaviour among their clients, let alone link them to international terrorist groups.

Next up for registration is any man over 16 from Pakistan, Saudi Arabia, Bangladesh, Egypt, Indonesia, Kuwait, and Jordan.

"I came here because I thought there was freedom," Ahmed, from Yemen told Washington DC Indymedia. *"It doesn't look so free now."* A middle-aged Somalian man added, *"I know the US is scared, but do they think that anyone meaning damage will come in?"*

"Turkey has had terrorists but Turkey is not on their list," said one Lebanese businessman. *"Why? Because the US needs their airbases to continue their no-fly zone."*

Shackle It All About

Back in Britain, the much maligned **Anti Terrorism, Crime and Security Act 2001** (see SchNEWS 331) has been taking to the streets. The Act gives the government the power to lock up any foreigner they reckon is a terrorist, without a trial. So far 13 people have had that privilege. In a statement to Amnesty International some of the detainees said: "Our lives and our families' lives have been destroyed and we see no hope in sight." One of those held is a Palestinian father of five who was granted refugee status as a torture victim and diagnosed as suffering from severe post-traumatic stress disorder. This week he went on hunger strike to protest being held 13 months without charge.

Under the Terrorism Act 2000 (see SchNEWS 268), around 200 people have been arrested, many under the catch-all Section 57 which reads: "A person commits an offence if he possesses an article in circumstances which give rise to a reasonable

suspicion that his possession is for a purpose connected with the commission, preparation, or instigation of an act of terrorism."

Journalist Faisal Bodi points out, "For all the hysterical headlines warning of a bin Laden in our backyard, the reality is a picture of political repression of Muslims that is starting to resemble the experience of Northern Ireland's Catholics throughout the Troubles." Remember the old Prevention Of Terrorism Act - targetted at the IRA? 5,000 mainly Irish were arrested, but less than 7% were charged let alone convicted.

*To read the full transcript of the excellent Indymedia article we used, visit: http://dc.indymedia.org/front.php3?article_id=46183&group=webcast

*For more about the Patriot Act: http://zmag.org/ZMag/Articles/dec01kaminski.htm

*Get hold of the Autumn 2002 "borders" issue of greenpepper mag: CIA office, Overtoom 301, 1054 HW, Amsterdam, Netherlands http://squat.net/cia/gp/greenpepper.htm

*Another good site on US government repression: http://www.zmag.org/repression_watch.htm

Greenpeace blocks the Marchwood Military Port in Southampton stopping shipments of military equipment to the Gulf. Jan 27th. Pic: David Sims/Greenpeace.

At the UN Headquarters, New York, as chief arms inspector Hans Blix addresses the UN Security Council, 300 demonstrate outside. Police were heavy handed and arrested 17. www.commondreams.org

Positive SchNEWS

In the past 100 years we have lost 97% of our vegetable varieties in the U.K. alone. Just 3 corporations control a quarter of the world's entire seed market – the same corporations that are trying to force us all to eat their genetically modified greens.

So what can you do about it? Get along to Seedy Sunday on 2 Feb and take part in a community seed swap happening at the Old Market, Upper Market Street, Hove. Along with talks on everything from saving your own seeds to genetics, there will be a mini farmers market, community allotment groups, tool sharpening, composting, café, creche and more. 11am-5pm, £1, children Free. 01273 622671 seedysunday2003@yahoo.co.uk

* There's a Seedy Saturday community seed swap happening on 8th Feb at the Octagon Cafe, Inkerman Street, Llanelli, Wales 11am- 3pm. seedysaturdayllanelli@hotmail.com

* Recommended reading 'Fatal Harvest – The Tragedy of Industrial Agriculture' edited by Andrew Kimbrell (Island Press 2002) Essays from 40 leading environmentalists taking an unprecedented look at America's destructive farming practices and offering positive solutions in support of a new vision of farming. Stunning photography! www.FatalHarvest.org

No Morales

Since last Monday (13ᵗʰ) many parts of Bolivia have been brought to a standstill as people have taken to the streets and blockaded major highways as part of a mobilisation against the government. The demands of the wide range of protesters are vast but include defending their rights to oil, gas, and coca, the return of privatised industries to the people, the fair redistribution of land, and the rejection of Bolivia joining the FTAA (Free Trade Area of the Americas). The government has responded to the situation with extreme aggression and clashes between protesters and police have left at least 5 people dead and an estimated 800 people arrested. Business leaders this week complained that the blockades had so far cost them at least $7.6 million and urged the government to do all they could to ensure that the export economy doesn't suffer.

Last June, the popular socialist party 'Movement toward Socialism' (MAS) came second in the Bolivian elections and it's leader, Evo Morales, came close to becoming the country's President. After the elections, MAS decided to take its fight against the destruction of coca plants and the neo-liberal policies of the government from the streets into the corridors of power. But by early December, when the Bolivian National Congress approved the entrance of U.S. troops into Bolivia to destroy coca crops as part of the US's 'War Against Drugs,' the MAS decided they'd had enough of banging their heads against a brick wall and began to mobilise for the mass street protests which now cripple the country.

The growing of coca is part of Bolivian indigenous culture. The leaves are used by local farmers for tea, chewing and medicinal purposes. But the USA was so unimpressed with Evo Morales' support for the coca farmers that they tried to intervene in last year's elections by warning people that if they voted for him it would endanger future US aid to the country. http://bolivia.indymedia.org (in Spanish) www.narconews.com/Issue27/article586.html ** 'Desire for Change: Women on the Frontline of Global Resistance' is a new book of interviews, stories and first hand accounts of women involved in various campaigns, projects, and direct actions all over the world. To order a copy email: pgabolivia@yahoo.co.uk or call 0207 3779088.

Green Washout

It seems the £20m BP spent on its fashionable green image (SchNEWS 276) was a total waste. In late 2000, BP jumped aboard the gravytrain of ethical investing by publicly acknowledging the dangers of global warming in the misguided hope they would avoid being the target of environmental protests. BP plastered its website with transparent concern for social issues, but since then its shameful working practices don't live up to its laughable rebranding as caring and progressive.

Even though the £20mil is peanuts compared to the billions BP spends yearly on fossil fuel exploration, it was still a waste of money as BP just can't *quite* seem to back up their eco-friendly, pro-worker image with action. Alaskan authorities have only just started looking at introducing regulations after a well at BP's Prudhoe Bay site exploded, causing an oil spill and maiming native Alaskan worker Don Shugak for life. BP later admitted to opening the well "without adequate safeguards."

Three months later an accident at the same site killed welder Rodney Rost. Despite their worker-friendly propaganda, BP actively fought against tightening safety procedures after the accident, saying "a rule to protect workers wasn't necessary".

On Tuesday, Hendersons Global Investments was first in the queue of 'socially responsible investors' to dump £millions worth of shares because of their activities in Alaska. On the same day, ISIS Fund Management made BP squirm by asking the board if "Problems are repeated worldwide, not just in Alaska? And has health and safety been compromised by aggressive high production targets and cost cutting?" Union rep Robert Brian suffered years of harassment for criticising BP's health and safety procedures but when he publicly announced that the well explosion was avoidable, BP harassed him so aggressively that he has filed a complaint against them with the US Dept of Labour. Now that's what we call a caring, progressive company!

War Briefs

There were massive anti-war demonstrations across the world on Saturday from Turkey to Pakistan to Japan to Antarctica! The biggest were in Washington DC, with 300,000 people, and in San Francisco with 200,000. In the UK, 2000 people travelled to Dublin and on to Shannon airport to protest the military use of the airport and to oppose the war. A permanent peace camp has now been set up outside the airport www.shannonpeacecamp.org

Also on Saturday, 70 people were nicked blockading the Northwood Military HQ. Five protestors locked arms into a giant pair of purple Y-fronts decorated with a "War is pants" slogan. ** **The Minister for War, Geoff Hoon, will be at Lambeth Town Hall, Acre Lane / Brixton Hill SW2 (Brixton tube) on Monday (27) at 6pm and would love to meet you all! ** **'No War for Oil** Tuesday 4th Feb. Call for protests at UK petrol stations—support the day of action with leafleting, vigils, street theatre, and other nonviolent direct action. If you organise a protest send details to info@risingtide.org.uk and to the action page of the Target Oil Coalition website www.targetoil.com www.risingtide.org.uk ** **'Beyond TV'** are putting together a new cd rom on direct action against war with video pieces, photos, rants, music, artwork or any inspiring, relevant material. The cds will be copied and distributed freely around the world so get involved! www.beyondtv.org ibanez_nauta@yahoo.com ** **Corporate Watch** newsletter issue 11/12 is out & packed with info on corporations that profit from war. £1 plus 43p SAE to Corporate Watch, 16b Cherwell Street, Oxford OX4 1BG ** Get down to a **Mass Weapons Inspection at RAF Fairford** on 26th Jan - info@gwi.org.uk Several coaches organised, see http://www.schnews.org.uk/pap/guide.html

ITALIAN ANARCHISTS IN PEACEFUL DEMO SHOCKER

Sat 25th January: (above) A group of 4,000 mostly from anarchist and autonomist groups visit the military installations in La Spezia, near Genoa. Despite police ruffling feathers outside one Army Barrack on the route, things were kept peaceful befitting the anti-war message. (Wot - no black block kicking off?) At the end of the demo, Food Not Bombs served food and there was a concert at a local social centre. (ainfos)

RIP

Kathleen Jannaway has died peacefully in her sleep. She was co-founder of Movement for Compassionate Living, author of the inspiring book, 'Abundant Living in the Coming Age of the Tree', an early vegan pioneer, and former secretary of the Vegan Society (UK). The Movement for Compassionate Living promotes simple living and self-reliance as a remedy against the exploitation of humans, animals and the Earth. More about Kathleen's message can be seen at www.mclveganway.org.uk/

* There will be a tree planting ceremony on Saturday 8th for 'Mad Pride' **Pete Shaunghnessy** at Moulsecoomb Forest Garden and Wildlife Project, Brighton at 11.30 am. Everyone who knew Pete is welcome - email info@forestgarden.fsnet.co.uk for directions or call the SchNEWS office.

SchNEWS in brief

Critical Mass bike ride this Sunday (26) meet 2pm Hunter Square, by the Tron Kirk, Royal Mile, Edinburgh. www.mutualaid.org **
Reclaim The Future II next Sat (1 Feb) in London with workshops, cabaret, comedy, political cinema & café from 3pm. Kids space in the afternoon, Party till late. £2 in afternoon, £5/3 after 7pm, help still needed: reclaimthefuture2003@yahoo.co.uk or 07931 560 569. Check uk.indymedia.org from noon on the day for details of venue.**
Mayday 2003 workshop Sunday 8th Feb 2pm. Calthorpe Arms, 252 Grays Inn Rd, London WC1X. **
Following a visit from **SHAC East Midlands** and hundreds of phone calls, faxes and emails, White Rose have withdrawn their services to Huntingdon Life Sciences. White Rose are a specialist incineration company who dispose of hazardous waste and until yesterday the bodies of animals murdered at HLS! Who's the only place willing to dispose of the evidence now? Cambridge Pet Crematorium! Contact the crematorium at freepost CB947, Royston, Herts SG8 7BR. Tel: 01763 208 295, Fax: 01763 208 885 mail@cpc-net.co.uk 2. ** **'The Summit'** a film which looks behind last year's **Earth Summit in Johannesburg**, and **'Zapatista'** a film which gives a first hand account of the Zapatista struggles in Mexico, are two new videos now available at **Cultureshop**. www.cultureshop.org ** If you fancy a laugh get a copy of **'Now That's What I Call Marxist'** nowmarxist@yahoo.co.uk **
Space Invaders: Festival of Arts and Resistance at the old TA building (next to B&Q), Lewes Road, Brighton (23/1-2/2) 'A non-stop celebration of underground DIY culture.' Get involved 07952512533 speakerpeople@hotmail.com. Timetable at www.partyvibe.com/brighton23

Inside SchNEWS

Dave Blenkinsop, an animal rights activist who is currently serving 4 ½ years, was sentenced to another 5½ this week for planting incendiary devices under lorries belonging to an abattoir. His sentences are to run consecutively so he is now serving a ten year prison sentence. He'd appreciate letters of support Dave Blenkinsop, EM7899, HMP Bullingdon, Patrick Haugh Road, Arncott, Bicester, Oxfordshire, OX6 0PZ

...and finally...

Ever thought, "Shit, I wish I'd been at that riot, taking back control of the city of London and pelting the riot cops with eggs and rotten fruit?" Well today is your lucky day! The newly formed London Riot Re-enactment Society is offering folks the chance to take part in the many famous riots of London, past and present. From the Peasant Revolt of 1381, to the Gin Riots of 1743, to the more up-to-date riots of Brixton (1981, 1996, 2000), the poll tax (1990), and of course J18 in 1999, the society will re-enact them all.

One of the advantages of riot re-enactment is that while trying to be as historically accurate as possible, you can decide which parts of the riot to keep in and which to skip out. For example, while re-enacting the riot of November 30th 1999, members of the society can decide to set fire to the police van but skip the part where everyone had to stand around for hours surrounded by riot cops without a toilet! The Society hopes that after a bit of practice, members will be able to form a Rapid Re-enactment Force which re-enacts riots immediately after they've happened (or even AS they happen), causing things to spiral out of control! To join send an email to: anathematician@yahoo.co.uk or visit http://c8.com/anathematician/

Disclaimer

SchNEWS warns all readers when you're having a bit of ins and out don't get the prayer rug pulled out from underneath you. Honest.

weekly SchNEWS

www.schnews.org.uk

Daily Mail SPECIAL

QUEEN: "ASYLUM SEEKER ATE MY CORGI"

Friday 31st January 2003   **Free/Donation**   **Issue 390**

HEARTBREAK HOTEL

This past Monday, Holocaust Memorial Day was observed across the world, with many British papers running large articles solemnly commemorating one of the worst tragedies in human history. And just to prove how massively they'd missed the point, many of these same papers *also* used their Holocaust Memorial Day issues to run articles that are becoming nauseatingly familiar—articles whipping up fear and hatred against asylum seekers, in some cases running on the same page as Holocaust Memorial articles without a hint of irony. As Nick Griffin, leader of the notoriously right-wing British National Party (BNP) commented earlier this month, the British press is helping to spread the BNP's anti-immigrant message. 'One could today be forgiven for thinking that the editors of five of Britain's national daily papers - the *Daily Star, The Times, Daily Mail, Daily Express* and *Daily Telegraph* - had suddenly become BNP converts,' said Griffin.

The Daily Mail is one of the worst offenders. On Monday, a group of people from all over Britain converged on the London office of the Daily Mail to try and put a stop to its racist hate-mongering. In the press release calling for the demo, the various groups organising the action stated their case, "Nearly every day there is an article in the Daily Mail attacking asylum seekers - often on the front page with an inflammatory headline such as "Stop the Asylum Invasion". Always portraying migrants and refugees as scroungers trying to take advantage

and as a threat to the 'British way of life'. As one refugee said after seeing a Daily Mail headline entitled 'A Door We Can't Close' – "It makes me feel like vermin.""

The racist articles run in the Daily Mail and other British papers contribute to scenes like the one that took place this past Sunday in Saltdean, one of Brighton's closest neighbours. Recently, one of Saltdean's hotels, The Grand Ocean Hotel, was named as a possible site for the emergency accommodation of asylum-seekers. Acting out of fear and misinformation, 250 local residents turned up to protest the use of the Grand Ocean for housing newly arrived immigrants. Many carried placards with slogans such as, "House prices will fall" and "Homes for our elderly not for phoney asylum-seekers." One anti-immigrant protestor was even dressed up as Osama bin Laden, to drive home the absurd myth that asylum-seekers and terrorists are one and the same. Another local resident, one of a small number who actually came out in support of asylum seekers, reported, "The BNP were there, there was verbal violence even towards our daughter and her friend, people said they'd like to shoot the asylum seekers all of whom would obviously be terrorists."

On Monday, the Brighton daily rag, the Argus (who incidentally ran sympathetic coverage of the anti-immigrant protest right next to their Holocaust Memorial article) printed a particularly spot-on letter from a local resident. "Whether or not refugees are housed in Saltdean,

the fear and anger the proposal has produced is worrying," the resident writes. "Do these people from Saltdean hate and fear me? Would they spit at me or wouldn't they notice me because I am white and speak with an English accent? Many of my family were slaughtered by the Nazis for being Russian Jews. The Nazis whipped up the sort of hysteria about Jews now being whipped up about refugees. Remember that when you lambaste people who flee here looking for sanctuary."

**Keep an eye on SchNEWS for further updates on the Saltdean situation.

For more news on asylum seekers and refugees across Britain, check out **The Campaign Against Racism and Fascism: http://www.carf.demon.co.uk/ , **Barbed Wire Britain**: http://www.barbedwirebritain.org.uk/ and **The National Coalition of Anti-Deportation Campaigns**: http://www.ncadc.org.uk/

Chapel of Love

There were 100,000 people and a mind boggling 1,714 events. They were crammed into a Catholic University, football stadiums, a gymnasium, five marquees and some dockside warehouses. Described by some as the "People's UN," this was the **World Social Forum** (WSF) which happened in **Porto Alegre**, Brazil last week.

Since the very first WSF three years ago, the event has become, according to Noam Chomsky, "unparallelled in world history."

So what is the WSF? Conceived as a direct alternative to the corporate knees up globalisation ball known as the World Economic Forum, the WSF is a week of workshops, discussions, and brainstorming for social change without profiteering and neoliberalism—and it runs at exactly the same time every year as the World Economic Forum.

In addition to WSF workshops, several "parallel conferences" sprang up around the city, including an anarchist convention and a youth camp in a nearby park where about 10,000 people pitched camp, including representatives of Indymedia from around the world.

The choice of Porto Alegre is symbolic too. For 15 years the city's governing Worker's Party - which now rules Brazil through the leftwing President Lula - has been deciding the budget through a process of popular participation, redistributing wealth, reducing poverty and eliminating corruption as a result.

One SchNEWS hack sorting through the myraid of events and opinions said that three issues seemed to stand out: Palestine, opposition to the war on Iraq, and the Latin American issue of the proposed Free Trade Area of the Americas, which Bolivian Indian leader Evo Morales described as a charter for "transnational pirates."

This year, Brazalian President Lula went to both the World Social Forum in Porto Alegre AND the World Economic Forum in Davos. Many weren't happy with that – the leader of Lula's Worker's Party, José Genoino, received a pie in the face as a protest.

As the Confectioners without Borders who delivered the pie-ing said in their communique, "The wave that carries Lula's Worker´s Party to electoral success is not, in any form, the same wave that supports the movement against capitalist globalization. Our movement is without leaders or representatives. No one can speak in our name. If someone in Davos 'represents' the movement, it is ourselves, the thousands that occupy the roads of Geneva in protest against the reunion of bankers, businessman, and governments that the Worker´s Party legitimates. The hope for change that we carry cannot one more time be co-opted and frustrated by politicians and political parties that wish to promote themselves at our expense. This time we are going to do things differently." www.portoalegre2003.org/publique/

RAF AMERICA

On Wednesday, the Defence Select Commitee agreed to the use of Menwith Hill and RAF Fylingdales in North Yorkshire for U.S. Ballistic Missile Defence systems otherwise known as the 'Son of Star Wars' (see SchNEWS 307). Fylingdales will house an early warning system and Menwith Hill will process the data. A public discussion paper on upgrading the facilities at these two sites was released in December, but even then it was clear that the decision to use the bases had already been made. Minister of War Geoff Hoon has come under severe attack from peace campaigners and even from his own backbenchers for the speed at which he has handed the bases over to America. His decision was of course in no way swayed by the promise of lucrative new contracts for UK arms dealers. In order to ease concerns, Hoon stressed there would be no change to the appearance of Fylingdales or its power output and that the upgrade would be paid for by the US – phew, so we can all sleep easily after all!

There are ongoing peace camps at Menwith Hill and Fylingdales. For more information contact Yorkshire CND on 01274 730795 or cndyorks@gn.apc.org www.cndyorks.gn.apc.org For more info on the 'Son of Star Wars' see SchNEWS 307.

DON'T ATTACK IRAQ!
On the 15th of Feb, London will see Britain's biggest ever anti-war demo. There are 3 starting points: 12 noon @ Embankment or 12.30pm @ Gower Street. Or for cyclists, a 'Wheels against the War' critical mass, 12 noon under Waterloo Bridge. The march ends at Hyde Park. There will also be a mass sit-down at Picadilly Circus, meet 5pm Green Park. Transport to London is being organised from across the country - www.stopwar.org.uk. Tickets on coaches from Brighton can be bought from Community Base, Queens Road £7/£4.

War Briefs

It was another busy weekend last weekend for anti-war demonstrations around the world. On Saturday there were protests in Genoa, Istanbul, Greece and closer to home Norwich was brought to a standstill, as well as protests in Edinburgh and Colchester. ** On Saturday over 200 protesters marched on **RAF St Athans, in Wales** and demanded to search for weapons of mass destruction www.icwi.org (pics below) ** Over 1,500 people took part in a demonstration last Sunday at **RAF Fairford in Gloucestershire** and 50 people managed to get into the base (see pic) www.gwi.org.uk ** On Monday the **Greenpeace ship Rainbow Warrior**, along with other boats, entered Marchwood Military port in Southampton and blocked the departure of UK

On the de-fence at Fairford Airbase, January 26th

Weapons inspectors visit RAF St Athans,Wales (above & below) 25th January Pics: www.icwi.org

military supply vessels heading for Iraq. www.greenpeace.org.uk ** On Tuesday **Trident Ploughshares** activists locked themselves to the gates of Rolls Royce in Derby and prevented workers getting to work. The factory produces nuclear fuel components for trident submarines. 0845 4588366 www.tridentploughshares.org ** On Wednesday a peace activist was arrested at **Shannon airport, Ireland** after she was found causing damage to an American military plane parked there. Although she didn't manage to disarm the plane, she did manage to cause 500,000 Euros worth of damage. There is now a permanent peace camp outside Shannon Airport. Contact 061-365871 www.shannonpeacecamp.org ** **Cambridge peace march,** Sat 1st,12 noon, Market Square ** Demonstration at USAF Lakenheath, Suffolk, used by US jets to bomb Iraq in the past and currently housing nuclear weapons, 12 noon Monday 3rd, Gate 1, USAF Lakenheath - Just off the A1065. Non-violence workshop the day before. 01508 550 446, www.lakenheathaction.org ** **Sussex Action for Peace** meeting, 4th Feb, 7.30pm, Brighthelm Centre Tel: 01273 706820 www.safp.org.uk **

Worthing against War demo next Saturday 8th 1pm in Montague Place. worthingagainstwar@yahoo.co.uk ** **Hands off Iraq**, a morning of speakers, discussion, videos, banner making and children's activities. Sat 8 Feb, Brighthelm Centre, North Road, Brighton 9.30am–1pm. ** **The D10 affinity group**, who helped organise the weekend of action at **Northwood** earlier this month, are producing a free news sheet on nonviolent action against the war for distribution at the big march in London on the 15th February. If you want to help distribute them on the day contact d10northwood@gmx.net.

"Whoops there seems to be a hole in the fence officer" Fairford Airbase, Jan 26th. Pic: Simon Chapman

MURDER BY DEGREE

As Bush blunders on with his "War on Terrorism", the US courts are busying themselves handing out draconian sentences to scores of Human Rights activists who dare to oppose the training of terrorists on their own soil. The Western Hemisphere Institute for Security Co-operation (see SchNEWS 382), formerly the School of the Americas, has spent the last 57 years spewing out 60,000 paramilitary graduates with honours in coercion and repression, ready for export to Latin America. SOA graduates include some of the region's most notorious dictators, like Norriega, Galtieri and Suarez.

This isn't just for fun. The school is an integral part of US foreign policy--influencing Latin American politics and economics in order to protect US interests by aiding and influencing South American militaries.

Last November 10,000 activists gathered peacefully at the school in Fort Benning to demand its closure. 43 were nicked for the hideous crime of 'repeated line-crossing' and have been sentenced this week with up to 6 months in federal jail, with a $2000 fine to boot! Many of these dangerous criminals were nuns.

One activist managed to get the last word. Addressing Judge Mallon Faircloth after getting 3 months, Eloy Garcia said, "Thank you Judge. These harsh sentences will only make our movement, our opposition to this unjust war which is shared by millions across the globe, even stronger." www. soaw.org/new/

* Last weekend a group of 150 Colombian paramilitaries assassinated 4 Kuna indigenous leaders in an attack on a remote mountain community in Paya. Doing the dirty work for the US-backed (often trained) Colombian military, the paramilitaries systematically terrorise rural populations and 'silence' any opposition. www.zNet.org; www.lasolidarity.org;

SchNEWS in brief

The Brighton Station site plans are on hold! This week the Government Office for the South-East ordered that no work could start until requests for a Public Inquiry were considered. It's time to keep up the pressure and save the Station site from rampant development! www.buddbrighton.org. ** Things go from bad to worse for vivisectors Huntingdon Life Sciences. Two of their key directors recently resigned and were replaced by a paper-merchant who promptly resigned a couple of weeks later. HLS has also lost the services of Cambridge Pet Crematorium who were disposing of dead animals for them. www.shac.net ** Yesterday protesters invaded the Papua New Guinea High Commission in London. Papua New Guinea are ordering the OPM (Free Papua Movement) to return to West Papua and have threatened to forcibly return all West Papuans living in the Vanimo refugee camp. Those deported to West Papua face torture and death at the hands of the murderous Indonesian military. www.fPcN-global.org ** Since 1998, there have been 4,000,000 people killed in the Congo, largely over resources for the West. However the BBC have ignored this genocide. Picket the BBC, Bush House (Africa Service), The Strand, London, 5 Feb. -7.30pm. Organised by Stop All Imperialist Wars Against Africa And Africans, 020-82651731/020-89680113. ** A 'Save Live Music!' group has been established to oppose the Government's proposed Licensing

POSITIVE SchNEWS

The government has just announced they have £10 million in grants for households and communities to develop their own renewable energy projects. Free info service availabe from the Centre for Alternative Technology (CAT), for individuals and groups who would like advice about participating in the renewable revolution. 01654-705950 www.cat.org.uk

Bill (see SchNEWS 388). Join the discussion list by sending a blank email to savelivemusic-subscrib e@yahoogroups.com. ** Imbolc Pagan Cabaret this Sat (1st), 7pm at the Ray Tindle Centre, North Laines, £4. ** Green Architecture Day 2003, learn about self-building, renewable and waste-material buildings. 1 Feb 9.30am-5.30pm, Friends Meeting House, Ship Street, South Laines, Brighton. ** The Cowley Club, a co-operative social centre run by volunteers in Brighton, has finally opened! The bar is open in the evenings from 7-11pm as a private members' club. During the day, the club will be open to the public as a cafe and bookshop starting from Feb 11th. It's located at 12 London Road, opposite Somerfield. Wednesday night video showings will start Feb 5th at 8pm. All members and their guests are welcome. ** On Tuesday 28th, Dartmoor National Park Authority lost an appeal in the highcourt which could have removed the temporary planning permission won for Steward Community Woodland. The judge said that the "...DNPA could not see the wood for the trees." This give the sustainable living project at least 4 1/2 years.www.stewardwood.org 01647 440233

...and finally...

More Crapita! CAPITA, the "outsourcing specialists" (running public services as a private business), who've been dubbed crapita after cocking up everything they touch from housing benefit to passports, have now taken over the running of TV licensing in Bristol. They sent out tens of thousands of leaflets to homes inviting punters to call a hotline. Only problem is that they printed the phone number of a tyre wholesaler, who then received over 500 TV licensing enquiries a day. The tyre company may now sue Crapita for loss of earnings.

(Stolen from Bristol's local newsheet, The Bristolian - www.bristol ian.freeservers.com)

Disclaimer
SchNEWS warns all Mail readers to beware of premature immigration. Honest.

TAKE ME TO YOUR LEADER | THAT'S ME

YOU'RE KIDDING

weekly SchNEWS

www.schnews.org.uk

Friday 7th February 2003   Free/Donation   Issue 391

WASTE OF SPACE

"Just as by the year 1500 it was clear that the European experience of power would be it's domination of the global seas, it does not take much to see that the American experience of power will rest on the domination of space" - The Future of War: Power, Technology and World Dominance in the 21st Century by George and Meredith Friedman.

On Saturday NASA- the American space agency- provided the people of Texas with a spectacular firework display, as the space shuttle Columbia burst into flames and disintegrated on re-entering the atmosphere. All 7 astronauts on board were killed and America became a grief struck nation again. SchNEWS hopes they show the same remorse when thousands of Iraqis are killed by American bombs.

The space shuttle Columbia is one of the shuttles that are used like taxis by the Kennedy Space Centre to ferry equipment and people out to the International Space Station, but on their way the astronauts on board also carry out their own 'scientific research'. Columbia's last crew included Israeli Air Force pilot Ilan Ramon, whose mission was to test a multi-spectral camera that probes the effect of sandstorms on climate change. The all-weather camera is also key technology for military spy satellites and unmanned drones searching for targets obscured by dust, smoke and clouds - sounds like that could come in useful in the looming Iraqi war! The other international astronaut onboard was Kalpana Chowla, an Indian born civilian engineer. It is probably a bit more than a coincidence that both Israel and India are trying to establish

their own space programmes, which will concentrate on, you guessed it - military purposes. It's no wonder that Columbia's ultimate mission was interpreted as a threat across parts of the Middle East and South Asia.

In recent years space shuttles have been used for everything from repairing the Hubble Telescope to studying the effects of weightlessness on tiny insects to deploying global positioning satellites that provide signals for most of today's precision-guided "smart" bombs. In recent years Congress has cut NASA's funding and they've had to rely on the Pentagon for funding. With the arrival of Bush and Dick-face Cheney at the Whitehouse this has meant many Shuttle missions have military objectives, thinly disguised as 'scientific research'. Many people believe that through a combination of financial cuts and mismanagement (the space shuttles have now been 92% privatised and are now run by aerospace giants Boeing and Lockheed Martin) the Columbia disaster was an accident waiting to happen. Over the summer a retired 36-year veteran of NASA called on President Bush to enact a temporary moratorium on all space shuttle flights, but his pleas were ignored and now 7 astronauts are dead.

Start Wars

Not content with being the world's only superpower, the USA wants to extend its military might to achieve what it so bashfully calls "Full Spectrum Dominance", which will mean backing up it's dominance on earth by building up it's weapons in space. The US is currently working on technology which is of course only for 'defensive purposes' but which still makes a ridiculous

farce of their hunt for weapons of mass destruction in Iraq.

Without the help of Darth Vader they're developing the so-called "Star Wars" programme - a series of lasers that will form a protective shield, to shoot missiles out of the sky before they ever reach American soil.

This is accompanied by development of a "Nuclear Space Initiative", which would see rockets powered by nuclear generators - this is necessary to power long distance exploration into deepest space and more significantly to provide the enormous power needed to keep their mega laser battle stations orbiting above the Earth. For America the Columbia shuttle disaster has come at a bad time just when it was looking to greatly broaden its program to use nuclear power in space on rockets launched from Kennedy Space station which has a 10% failure rate. There's already been two nuclear rocket explosions over the US and after being showered with plutonium residents of Florida were warned to stay away from the rocket's debris which should have been easy to spot cos' it glowed in the dark! If the much larger Columbia had been carrying plutonium Bush might well have lost himself a few thousand of his Texas voters.

Waste of Space cont...
Locked

So just why is the US so hell-bent on developing a Star Wars programme? Perhaps it has something to do with the people behind the unelected Muppet. People like Bruce Jackson, vice-president of Lockheed Martin, the largest weapons manufacturer and a major contractor in US space military work who claimed "I wrote the Republican Party's foreign policy platform." No doubt Lockheed Martin are doing very well out of the threat of war on Iraq. He claims he hasn't pressed for development of Star Wars "That would be an implicit conflict of interest with my day job." So who did advocate it? Stephen Hadley, a military adviser to Bush Snr, and is a lawyer who represents, er Lockheed Martin. He claims that "Space is going to be important. It has a great feature in the military." And no doubt important for swelling Lockheed Martin's bank balance and those associated with it, like Lynn Cheney, the wife of US vice-President Dick Cheney, who is a board member of…Lockheed Martin.

The rest of the world is not too impressed with America's war mongering. Last November 160 Nations passed a United Nations resolution called "Prevention Of An Arms Race In Outer Space", with only the US, Israel and Micronesia abstaining.

This re-affirmed the 1967 Outer Space Treaty, international law that sets aside outer space for peaceful uses. Canada is pressing for all weapons in outer space to be outlawed (currently only weapons of mass destruction are banned) –because they fear another arms race will start. "If one state actively pursues the weaponization of space we can be sure others will follow" commented Marc Vidricaire, Canadian representative to the UN.

The USA is to start that arms race with the development of a space air force. The US Air Force Space Command in its Almanac 2000 stated "The future of the Air Force is space… Globally dominant – The future Air Force will be better able to monitor and shape world events..." Scary stuff. It might not be too long before space terrorism becomes a reality.

*In typical Tony Blair style Britain is doing it's bit to help America retain it's world dominance by allowing two of our military bases- Menwith Hill and Fylingdales- to be used to aid their Star Wars programme. There are ongoing protests at both of these bases. Info Yorkshire CND 01274 730795 www.cndyorks.gn.apc.org.

*Foil the Base - Mass action against war and Star Wars at Menwith Hill - 22 March. Info foilthebase@yahoo.co.uk

*More information on the nuclear space race at www.space4peace.org

Shannon you Crazy Diamond

Last week Mary Kelly, *(pic above)* **was arrested for breaking into a hangar and trashing a US military plane with a hatchet, causing 300,000 Euros worth of damage.** And this week five members of the Catholic Worker Movement were arrested for cutting through fences at Shannon airport to pour human blood onto the

runway and building a shrine dedicated to Iraqi children killed by twelve years of US and British military action.

Contrary to the Irish Constitution and international law, the Irish Government continues to allow Shannon Airport to be used by US forces on their way to US bases in Kuwait and Qatar. The Shannon Peace Camp has temporarily been disbanded "as the camp was more of a news story than the war on Iraq and the use of Shannon Airport." Mary Kelly is being held at Limerick prison and is due to appear in court this Wednesday 5th Feb. The other five are at Shannon and Ennis police stations. And just so there can be no misunderstanding as to where his sympathies lie, Bertie Ahern, the Irish Taoiseach, has now ordered 150 armed troops to provide '24-hour security' at the airport. www.shannonpeacecamp.org

ELECTRICKERY

Thousands of poor people getting evicted from their homes. Water and electricity supplies cut-off. Live ammunition fired at the protesting poor. Welcome to the new South Africa! Thousands of poor people in ghettos all over the country are getting a brutal taste of neo-liberalism as the ANC government continues to open up its economy to 'market forces'. This has seen public services being handed over to western multinationals that cut jobs and raise water prices. One multinational Suez Lyonnaise is now the owner of South Africa's water utilities – it hiked water rates for the urban poor. The ANC government once promised cheap water, electricity, housing, health care and education. But they have broken their promises and sold off their country to western multinationals who are upping prices and laying off workers.

But South Africa's poor have erupted like a burst water pipe. Organisations such as the Anti-Privatisation Forum and the Anti-Evictions Campaign have sprung up in defence of the basic human right to water, warmth and shelter. In April last year 87 people from Soweto, including pensioners and children, were arrested on charges of public violence, malicious damage and assault, they had gone to the ANC Mayor of Johannesburg's house to show what it was like to have your water and electricity cut off. His bodyguard didn't reckon it was funny and shot at them with live bullets. The activists reacted, as one does when shot at, and they got nicked.

The trial of the 'Kensington 87' was delayed, following international protests, till 22 January where the mayor's bodyguard was unable to explain how two protestors were wounded by his bullets if he only fired warning shots into the air. The verdict is expected in March.

In Cape Town hundreds of residents, led by the Mandela Park Anti-Eviction Campaign, recently marched to the local ANC councillor to put forward their demands that promises of free electricity become a reality. They reckon 20 units is far too little electricity to last a month - the unemployed, pensioners, disabled people cannot afford to buy electricity beyond what's provided so they have to go without light and energy for cooking and heating. Pissed off residents are demanding that electricity cut-offs be abolished. But the AEC isn't just pleading with fat politicians- it's fighting for free education for poor students and it has led a good deal of direct action demonstrations against evictions and cut-offs The AEC protects families from being evicted by staging sit-ins and demonstrations to turn away the armed guards who come to evict families. If the 'orrible guards are determined to take the property away then AEC activists often decide make the house 'unlivable' - they smash it up so no-one else can live there! See southafrica.indymedia.org, antieviction.org.za

Positive SchNEWS

Pedal power puts polluters through their paces at the unpredictable 7th Pedal Power Convention. - DIY pedal and wind generators, pedal powered music and other contraptions to make the mind boggle, there is also a free junk pile of motors, meters, and other useful contraption-making stuff to be taken from or added to. Come along to learn about low- impact living in a comfortable atmosphere. Its on Sunday 16th Feb and starts at 12 noon till 6pm at RISC centre 35-39 London St, Reading, RG1 4PS. Please book if you're bringing stuff to display on 01344 482266 www.c-realevents.co.uk

(left) Monday, 3rd February: Six people lock-on at the entrance of RAF Lakenheath blockading the entrance to the base for an hour. They were all arrested, but at the same time six other weapons inspectors got into the base to look for weapons of mass destruction. Lakenheath is the largest US Air Force-operated base in England, and the most important tactical nuclear bombing base in Europe. www.lakenheathaction.org

HOMEBOYS

"The day after the election we will physically take over the Blair's empty flats regardless of the legal situation. We don't intend to waste time on legal niceties when families with young kids have nowhere to live." - *Sid Street, Bristolian Election Campaign Manager.*

In a town where most folks have been pushed to the outskirts thanks to rocketing house prices, the Blairs decided to buy two luxury flats last November. Empty since then, the flats are fingers up to anyone in housing need. The Blairs now have three homes, Downing Street, Chequers for the weekends, and a house in County Durham - they really NEED all of them. Honest.

John Prescott told the House of Commons this week that councils should be able to take control of empty properties by force if they've been empty for too long. So watch out you Blairs! Sadly it's unlikely the council will ever get their acts together enough to enforce it. At the moment there are 2,348 houses in Brighton and Hove and a staggering 70,000 properties in London and the south east which have been empty for at least six months (most have been empty for years). Prescott also announced that he'd cut the discount for buying an ex-council property from £38,000 to £16,000 in March. So there'll probably be a rush to buy up the remaining houses before the sale ends, er, nice one. Hurry now! Sale ends soon! Everything must go! In the last 20 years £13 billion has been re-directed from council housing into central government coffers. Neo-Labour have done this by cutting funding to most local councils all over the country, preventing councils from buying or building new houses and from repairing and improving existing ones.

Those of you familiar with Brighton will know about the (in)Sainsbury's development near Brighton station. The hugely unpopular superstore was finally given the nod this week despite opposition from local residents and small businesses, campaign group BUDD and the popular community squat at Harvest Forestry. Instead of building hundreds of affordable new homes, the council chose to suck Sainsburys proverbial cock and grant them permission to build a spanking new superstore, even though they've already got one ten minutes' walk down the road. Pissed off with all this sort of nonsense, UNISON and Brighton and Hove tenants joined people from all over the country the other week in a national Defend Council Housing rally of Westminster. Steve Foster from UNISON told SchNEWS, "The right to housing is fundamental. Our objective is to stop the unnecessary and expensive sell-off of the Council's remaining stock, and restore some of the public investment in Council Housing that has been lost in recent years." Defend Council Housing: 020 7987 9989 www.defendcouncilhousing.org

---

Worldwide protests against the war next Saturday (15). Three meet up points 12 noon @ Embankment, 12.30pm Gower St, 12 noon under Waterloo Bridge for cyclists. Sit down protest after the demo at Piccadilly Circus, meet 5pm Green Park. Transport from around the country 020 7053 2153 www.stopwar.org.uk Tickets for Brighton coaches available from Community Base, Queens Road. Help give out SchNEWS on the day. Pick up bundles on Friday afternoon at the Cowley Club, London Road, or if you see us struggling under thousands of bits of paper please give us a hand.

* **Scottish Coalition for Justice not War** will visit the Labour Party Conference in Glasgow. 15th Feb, 10am at Glasgow Green to surround the SECC for a 'Jericho Rumpus' at 1.30pm followed by a rally at 2.30pm info, transport and maps from www.banthebomb.org.uk

---

Those pranksters at Greenpeace project a peace message on the Sydney Opera House, February 13th.

...and finally...

Over the past few years many cycle lanes have sprung up making life easier for cyclists. Except that many of these cycle lanes are poorly thought out, go nowhere or are just plain stupid and a waste of money. And Brighton is no exception, one cyclist fed up with the Council's poor record has set up his own website, featuring the shortest cycle lane at less than the length of a bike! The website has a host of weird and downright dangerous cycle lanes. "Scary Cycle Lanes of Brighton" shows some life threatening lanes, like those that run down the middle of the road between two lanes of traffic travelling in opposite directions. There are also lanes with metals posts, bollards or trees right in the middle of them and a sign telling cyclists to dismount at a cycle crossing. Check out weirdcyclelanes.co.uk/

Disclaimer
SchNEWS warns all Aliens Lost in Space you must be completely warped to Klingon to the idea there's any intelligent life on Earth. Honest.

GIVE OR TAKE A FEW MILLION
FEBRUARY 15th 2003

Hyde Park, London. Pic: Simon Chapman

February 15th 2003 was the biggest worldwide day of mass demonstration in history. We will never know how many anti-war actions and events happened that day - estimates get bandied about which are always subject to the usual loaded estimations. Rounding the whole lot off to the nearest million it comes out at 20 millon. Countries with pro-war regimes drew the biggest crowds - demonstrating a clear separation between states and peoples. The list featured here of anti-war rallies in the US for instance (shortened to spare tedium) counters the image of an American public gung-ho for war - and the same goes for other 'coalition' countries like Britain, Spain and Australia. It is claimed that people in every country except China participated in this international day.

Crowd Estimates

This list has been built from a range of online sources, many of which were regional Indymedia websites, and cross checked where possible. Of course these numbers - accurate or not - don't illustrate the diversity of people who came together for these demonstrations, nor the range of events which happened on the day. In fact this article is just places and numbers - without comments - and an exercise in statistics it may be, but none-the-less a record of an incredible day which speaks for itself.

Rio de Janeiro

Melbourne

Antarctica
Amundsen-Scott Station 5

Argentina
Buenos Aires 50,000

Australia
Adelaide 100,000
Bellingen, NSW 3,000
Brisbane 100-150,000

Byron Bay, NSW 3,000
Canberra 10-15,000
Darwin 2,000
Hobart 15,000
Launceston, TAS 3,000
Lismore, NSW 7,000
Mackay, QLD 1,500
Melbourne 200-250,000
Newcastle 20,000

Perth 20-30,000
Rockhampton, QLD 600
Sydney 250-500,000

Austria
Vienna 20-30,000

Bangladesh
Dhaka 2,000

Bosnia
Mostar 400

Belgium
Brussels 100,000

Brazil
Recife 1,200
Rio de Janeiro 15,000
Salvador 1,500
Sao Paulo 30,000

Bulgaria
Sofia 2,000

Canada
Calgary 5,000
Edmonton 10,000
Montreal 100-150,000
Quebec City 3,000
Toronto 80-100,000

Vancouver 30,000
Winnipeg 5-10,000

Chile
Santiago 500

Croatia
Zagreb 10,000

Cuba
Havana 5,000

Cyprus
UK Airbase Dhekelia 800

Santiago

Prague

Paris

Douai 2,000
La Roche Sur Yon
2-2,500
La Rochelle 3,000
Le Mans 8,000
Limoges 4,000
Lorient 4,000
Lyon 20,000
Marseille 20,000
Montpelier
15-20,000
Nantes 6,000
Nice 15,000
Nimes 5-6,000
Paris 300,000
Pau 3-4,000
Perpignan
5-10,000
Rennes 5-6,000
Rouen 1,000
Saint Naraire 4,000
Strasbourg 7,000
Thonon 2,000
Toulon 6,000

Toulouse 15,000
Tours 4,000
Valence 5,000
Vannes 2,000

Czech Republic
Prague 1,000

Denmark
Copenhagen 35,000
Viborg 300

Dominican Rep.
Santo Domingo 500

East Timor
Dili 100 at US Embassy

Egypt
Cairo 2,000

France
Some of the 70 towns:
Aix En Provence 7,000
Albi 4-5,000
Avignon 2-5,000
Bordeaux 11-15,000
Bourg En Bresse 1,000
Brest 4-5,000
Chalon Sur Saone 2,000
Clermont-Ferrand 4,500
Dijon 4-5,000

Cairo

Athens - protesters decorate a fighter plane

Greece
Athens 200,000
Thessaloniki 40,000+
Demonstrations also
took place in Patras,
Volos, Giannena,
Kavala, Aleksandroupoli,
Orestiada, Komotini,
Irakleio, Rethimno,
Rodes, Mitilini and more.

Ecuador
Quito 500

El Salvador
San Salvador 2,500

Finland
Helsinki 15,000
Tampere 2,000
Turku 5,000

Germany
BERLIN 500,000+
Stuttgart 50,000

Honduras
Tegucigalpa - demonstra-
tion at US Embassy

Hong Kong
City Centre 1,000

Hungary
Budapest 20-30,000

Iceland
Reykjavik 4,000

India
Calcutta 10,000
New Delhi ?

(Left) Oh dear - police fire
tear gas as things kick off
near US Embassy in Athens

Berlin

peace action 2.15

世界の人々とともに、イラク攻撃を止めよう！
2.15 ピースアクション in 東京
日時：2003年2月15日（土）開会 PM6:30～
場所：渋谷・宮下公園

Indonesia
Jakarta 70,000+ (Feb 8th)
150 visit British Embassy

Israel
Tel Aviv 1,500

Iraq
Baghdad 100,000+

Ireland
Dublin 100,000+
Belfast 10,000

Italy
Girona 30,000
Monza 5,000
ROME 2,500,000+
Turin 1,500
1,000 at US airbase Camp Ederle
Also marches in Perugia, Bologna, Genoa, Naples
Florence human chain of 5,000

Japan
Atsugi 120
Osaka 1,000
Tokyo 25,000

Jordan
Amman 3,000

Kazakhstan
Almaty 50

Malta
Blata l-Bajda 1,000

Mexico
Mexico City 50,000

Netherlands
Amsterdam 80,000
plus anti-war actions in Rotterdam, Nijmegen and Leiden.
90 arrested at Volkel US airbase

New Zealand
Auckland 10,000
Christchurch 3,000
Dunedin 1,500
Wellington 7,000
Whanganui 70

Norway
Bergen 15,000
Oslo 60,000
Stavanger 5,000
Trondheim 11-20,000

Mexico City

Palestine
Gaza 15,000

Pakistan
Lahore 2,000 plus demos in Karachi, Rawalpindi, Islamabad and 20 other cities

Peru
Lima 300

Philippines
Manila 6-10,000

Beirut

Lebanon
Beirut 10,000

Luxembourg
Luxembourg 15-20,000

Malaysia
Kuala Lumpur 3,000

Ramallah Palestine

Rachel Corrie in Rafah, Gaza, Palestine (below)

Rome

Madrid

Spain
Algeciras 15,000
Andalusia 20,000+
BARCELONA
1,200,000+
Bilbao 100,000

Cadiz 100,000
Ferrol 15,000+
Girona 30,000
Granada 150,000
Huesca 5,000+
Irunea 20,000
Lugo 12,000
MADRID 2,000,000
Malaga 50,000
Oviedo 200,000
Las Palmas 100,000
San Sebastian 15-20,000
Santa Cruz de Tenerife
85,000
Santander 35,000
Seville 250,000
Valencia 300-500,000

Rawalpindi Pakistan

Singapore
2 - both were arrested
Slovenia
Ljubljana 4-6,000
Maribor 500
South Africa
Capetown 5-12,000
Durban 3,000
Johannesburg 10,000
South Korea
Seoul 10,000

Sweden
Goteborg 30,000
Malmo 5,000
Stockholm 80,000
Switzerland
Berne 40,000
Chur 600
St. Gallen 3,000
Syria
Damascus 200,000
Thailand
Bangkok 3,000
Pattani 10,000
Tunisia
Sfax 3,000
Turkey
Ankara ?
Istanbul 5,000
Ukraine
Kiev 2,000

Puerto Rico
San Jose 900
Reunion
Reunion 6,000
Russia
Moscow 1,000

Poland
Warsaw 8-10,000
Poznan 3-400
Gdansk 100
Wroclaw 500
Rzeszow ?
Portugal
Lisbon 80-100,000

Istanbul

Damascus

United Kingdom

Belfast 30,000
Glasgow 60,000+
LONDON 1,500,000+
Shetland Islands 600

BUTCHER SHARON! YOU ARE THE GREATEST TERRORIST!

WE DEMAND JUSTICE FOR PALESTINE

The World Says No to War

NYC FEB 15

NOON SATURDAY
FIRST AVENUE @ 49th ST.

AMSTERDAM
BARCELONA
CAPE TOWN
DAO PAULO
BANGKOK
SAN JUAN
TORONTO
ISTANBUL
LONDON
MANILA
JAKARTA
WARSAW
ATHENS
BERLIN
PARIS
CAIRO
TOKYO
ROME
and more

United States

Anchorage, AK 300
Asheville, NC 2,000
Austin, TX 10-20,000
Chicago, IL 7,000
Cleveland, OH 1,200
Columbus, OH 1,000
Colorado Springs, CO 3-4,000
Concord, NH 6-800
Corvallis, OR 1,000+
Dallas, TX 3-5,000
Detroit, MI 10,000
Eugene, OR 4,000
Flagstaff, AZ 1-2,000
Honolulu, HA 300+
Houston, TX 3-5,000
Lansing, MI 2-3,000
Las Vegas, NV 830+
Lawrence, KS 2,500
Madison, WI 3,000
Los Angeles 75-125,000
Milwaukee, WI 5,000
Minneapolis, MN 10,000
Missoula, MT 2-5,000
Montpelier, VT 1,200
New Orleans, LA 1,000
NEW YORK, 500,000+
Olympia, WA 3,000
Orange County, CA 800
Philadelphia, PA 10,000+

Los Angeles

Phoenix, AZ 5,000
Raleigh, NC 7,000
Sacramento, CA 10,000
St. Louis, MO 3,000
Salem, OR 1,000-1,400
San Diego, CA 10,000
San Francisco 150-250,000
San Jose, CA 5,000+
Santa Barbara, CA 5,400
Santa Cruz, CA 8-10,000
Santa Fe, NM 6-10,000
Santa Monica, CA 7,000
Sarasota, FL 2,500
Seattle, WA 55,000
Tallahassee, FL 4-600
Wausau, WI 1,500-2,000

Uruguay

Montevideo 50,000
Salto 1,500

Venezuela

Caracas 5,000

Sorry mate there's only yuppie bars in this part of London

And SchNEWS Estimates That...

Rounding it off to the nearest zero we calculate that:
* 1,000 American flags were burnt worldwide
* 200Ha of forests were used making the wooden stakes for banners
* There were 4,500 speeches which were listened to by 1.5% of the crowds.
* 5,000 politicians made anti-war speeches but are in fact pro-war and only said it to get votes.
* 245,037 Trotskyite newspapers were sold.
* 38% of marchers were against the war, but couldn't face reading the news and didn't actually know anything about it.
* 8,750,000 people claimed they would never vote for the current government again but probably will.
* Tony Blair has aged approximately 15 years in the past six months.
* To calculate the actual number at a march we have arrived at this formula...

$$\text{Total} = \frac{\text{Overly optimistic estimate from Indymedia posting}}{\text{Police Estimate}} \times \text{Socialist Paper Estimate}$$

As a Labour MP with a large Asian constituency, I need to be seen to be against innocent Iraqis dying in a war. Er unless it's got UN backing. Or if my job was at risk.

WAKE UP! IT'S YER PEACE MONGERING

weekly **SchNEWS**

www.schnews.org.uk

Friday 14th February 2003   Free/Donation   Issue 392

IRAQ AND RUIN

"Why of course the people don't want war…But after all it is the leaders of the country who determine the policy, and it's always a simple matter to drag the people along, whether it is a democracy or a fascist dictatorship …Voice or no voice, the people can always be brought to the bidding of the leaders. That is easy. All you have to do is tell them they're being attacked, and denounce the pacifists for lack of patriotism and exposing the country to danger." - *Hermann Goering, Nuremberg, 1946*

"The bewildered herd is a problem. We've got to prevent their rage and trampling. We've got to distract them. They should be watching the Superbowl or sitcoms or violent movies. Every once in a while you call on them to chant meaningless slogans like "Support our troops." You've got to keep them pretty scared, because unless they're properly scared and frightened of all kinds of devils that are going to destroy them from outside or inside or somewhere, they may start to think, which is very dangerous, because they're not competent to think. Therefore it's important to distract them and marginalize them." - *Noam Chomsky*

Saturday promises to be the biggest day of global action against war in world history, with demonstrations in seventy countries and hundreds of cities from Kuala Lumpur in Malaysia to Ramallah in Palestine to Tel Aviv in Israel, from Seoul in South Korea to the USA, in all the countries of Europe and in many of South America and Africa.

While the unelected Bush administration talks of "endless war" and "full spectrum

dominance", the American public gorges itself on gaffer tape and tinned prunes in case of terrorist attack or armageddon. On Tuesday, the people of Britain woke up to the appearance of tanks and armed patrols around Heathrow airport. Terrorist threat or theatre? Helping to thwart terrorists or introducing fear so that we may all eventually agree to a war on Iraq? Walter Lippman, the Pulitzer Prize winning American journalist, argued that what he called a "revolution in the art of democracy," could be used to "manufacture consent" – the skilful use of propaganda and the manipulation of facts in order to get the public to agree to things they would otherwise have opposed. As well as telling outright lies, such as the Gulf of Tonkin Incident, when the US lied about an attack on a US warship as an excuse to launch the Vietnam War, governments also try to manipulate the debate so that it takes place entirely on their terms. Hence President Blair always talking about the present situation as if it is caused entirely by Saddam Hussein's failure

to disarm (despite the fact that the US and UK governments have tolerated exactly this same situation for years) in an attempt to draw attention away from what has really changed – the political motives of the current US administration.

SLAUGHTER-HOUSE 5

Switch on the news and hear about more terrorists being arrested. But who are they? In December, five Turks and a Briton were charged under the Terrorism Act 2000 for supporting the Turkish Revolutionary People's Liberation Party-Front, or DHKP-C. They were nicked because DHKP-C has been banned by the UK government and the six arrestees were supposedly "facilitating the retention or control of terrorist property." Guns? Bombs? Er, no, the people arrested were simply in possession of magazines, videos and posters that supported the DHKP-C. At a pre-trial hearing, the judge ordered all the defendants to surrender their passports and banned them from selling or distributing copies of "Vatan," a radical Turkish-based magazine that has the bare faced cheek to criticise that bastion of human rights, Turkey.

One of On those nicked was Rory O'Driscoll, who had recently joined other people in a visit to Turkish hunger strikers protesting about prison conditions. His house was then raided and he was held for two weeks at Paddington Green police station where *every hour* someone would open up the hatch to his cell and ask if he was 'alright' (a friendly way to deny

---

Need a rest after marching? Why not pay the US Embassy a visit in Grosvenor Sq near Hyde Park? Or join a mass sit-down in Piccadilly - meet at 5pm in Green Park.
3rd February - Fairford Airbase 'Mass Weapons Inspection'. Noon, Fairford Town Centre, Gloucestershire. www.safp.org.uk www.gwi.org.uk
22nd March - Fairford again! Noon at the junction of High St/Park St, Fairford. www.gwi.org.uk and Menwith Hill 'Foil the Base' www.now-peace.org.uk.
For more info on action against the war check out: www.schnews.org.uk/stopwar/

Iraq and Ruin cont...

a prisoner of sleep, don't you reckon?). If found guilty of the 'crime' of possessing magazines and supporting Turkish hunger strikers, Rory could face up to 10 years in prison.

Meanwhile, under the Anti-Terrorism, Crime and Security Act, thirteen people have been arrested and held without charge for 14 months without being told what they have done and with no way of knowing if and when they face trial or release. One of these, a Palestinian father of five, has been transferred to Broadmoor and is suffering from mental health problems.

But wait a second... aren't Bush and Blair the real terrorists here? Just recently the Pentagon announced that it intended to shatter Iraq "physically, emotionally and psychologically" by raining down 800 cruise missiles in two days on the Iraqi people. Military strategist Harlan Ullman told American television: "There will not be a safe place in Baghdad. The sheer size of this has never been seen before, never been contemplated before." The strategy is known as "Shock and Awe" and Ullman is apparently its proud inventor. He said: "You have this simultaneous effect, rather like the nuclear weapons at Hiroshima, not taking days or weeks but minutes."

What will his "Hiroshima effect" actually do to a population of whom almost half are children under the age of 14? The answer comes in a "confidential" UN document, which says that "as many as 500,000 people could require treatment as a result of direct and indirect injuries".

A Bush-Blair attack will destroy "a functioning primary health care system" and deny clean water to 39 per cent of the population. There is "likely [to be] an outbreak of diseases in epidemic if not pandemic proportions".

The logic is brilliant. To save the Iraqi people from a murderous dictator (who we put there in the first place) we must first kill them with sanctions and then with bombs. To stamp out terrorism we must attack countries and kill innocent people, which will produce more terrorists. And to protect our civil liberties and freedoms we must, of course, take them away.

SchNEWS wants regime change in Iraq, but regime change must also happen here. Who voted to leave the running of the world to this motley crew of self-interested oil-fuelled egomaniacs? Saying no to this war *alone* is asking for trouble. We must say no to its leaders as well. As Novelist Kurt Vonnegut so aptly put it "(America) has been taken over by means of the sleaziest, low-comedy *coup d'etat* imaginable."

Recommended reading: John Pilger - *The New Rulers of the World* (Verso 2002). Noam Chomsky & Edward S. Herman *Manufacturing Consent - The Political Economy of the Mass Media* (Pantheon Books).

For an indepth analysis of world events see www.zmag.org

War Briefs

Army reservists who've been receiving their call-up papers during the last few weeks **have been refusing to go in record numbers**. So far one in three have either applied for exemption or have just ignored their call-up papers. ** Last Saturday **25,000 people took to the streets of Munich, Germany** to demonstrate against the NATO security meeting being held there. Predictably, the police raided the convergence centre, arresting 22 people and only releasing them after the protests had ended. All over Germany, several thousand people took part in antiwar demonstrations. www.indymedia.org ** Having achieved their objective of drawing attention to the unconstitutional use of **Shannon airport** for US war preparations, the victorious **Shannon Peace Camp** has now been dismantled and in a major victory for them, the US aircraft which used the base have now been moved to Germany. Unfortunately, the protestors arrested for damaging US military equipment are still being held in Limerick prison www.shannonpeacecamp.org ** **Over 30 people stormed Labour Party HQ** on Tyneside last Friday, barricading themselves in the lobby to demand that the Labour Party stop its terrorist war against the people of Iraq. ** Over 300 people marched through **Worthing** town centre last Saturday to protest against the prospect of war against Iraq. There will be a **Worthing Against War** meeting at The Downview pub in Tarring Road at 7.45pm on 4 March and an anti-war day on Sat 29th March worthingagainstthewar@yahoo.co.uk ** **Stop Europe's biggest ever death fair!** One of the world's biggest ever trade fairs for guns, bombs, military planes, small arms, mines and tanks will take place in London from 9th-12th September. There's a week long festival of action, protest and resistance planned 0781 7652 029 www.dsei.org ** To find about actions going on around the country join the **Direct Action Against the War** discussion group at http://groups.yahoo.com/group/directactionagainstwar/

BASE INSTINCT

There are regular demos at many of the military bases throughout the UK:

Menwith Hill, in North Yorkshire, is the largest electronic monitoring station in the world. Run by the US National Security Agency (NSA) & operating as a US sovereign territory (!!), Menwith Hill spies on emails, phone calls, and all sorts of communications throughout Europe and the Middle East with its vast array of satellites. It even won an award for its heroic eavesdropping in the last Gulf War! Menwith is also a key base for America's pet project of long-term military aggression – 'Star Wars'. There are regular demos, and on 23rd March there's a planned demonstration to 'Foil the Base' (disrupt the satellite signal receivers by using tin foil). There has to be as much foil in the air as possible, so bring foil kites, foil balloons, foil puppets- use your imagination. Info: Yorkshire CND 01274 730795 or cndyorks@gn.apc.org

Fairford, in Gloucestershire, is the biggest bomber base in Europe and can now house the U.S B2 Stealth bombers. These lovely friendly planes can release mini nuclear weapons, dubbed 'more usable' by the trigger-happy MoD. The U.S wants to use British soil to house these weapons of mass destruction, placing the UK in the frontline of the US war for oil. A peace camp is being set up outside Fairford military base from the 23rd February. Info: jill@gwi.org.uk.

Faslane Peace Camp, near Glasgow. Now 20 years old, Faslane naval base is home to the UK's trident nuclear submarine fleet. Even if you can't stay for very long, moral support and supplies are always appreciated. Contact: 01436 820901

PANTS AWAY!

All over the world people are protesting by taking their war briefs off. From New South Wales in Australia to Sussex to Florida to New York's Central park (where a group of women used their bodies to spell the words 'No Bush') protesters are getting together, getting naked and rolling around in snow, sand and grass to get their message across. www.theage.com

* **Chickenhawk** is the term used to describe a warmonger who has carefully avoided direct involvement in conflict themselves. Chief Chickenhawk is Bush himself who managed to not turn up for National Guard duty during the Vietnam War and since then has never been able to account for his absenteeism - we're fairly certain it had nothing to do with being a conscientious objector. In that same war, Dick Cheney also "had other priorities" than serving and Rush Limbaugh (a notorious right wing radio presenter) was excused on account of his anal cysts. For a full list of Chickenhawks: www.nhgazette.com/chickenhawks.htm

THE COST OF WAR

It's estimated that even a short war in Iraq could cost the taxpayer £3.2 billion (and the US $33bn), and that's not taking into account the money that will be needed for long term security. This is good news for the UK arms industry, but not so good for those crying out for more state funding. Here are some suggestions from SchNEWS on how the money could be better spent:
* £180 million to give the fire fighters the pay rise they deserve
* £65 million to take on 35,000 extra nurses
* £2.6 billion to give pensioners a £10 a week rise.
* And you'd still have enough spare change to buy up the Daily Mail and re-launch it as an anarchist daily!!

Alternatively we could send the whole population of Iraq on holiday to Brighton's Grand Hotel for a week while the 'special friends' bomb the fuck out of their country.

We could save the Brighton West Pier from falling into the sea and turn it into a jail for all politicians!

Or, we could blow the whole lot on getting Harrogate Railway FC and the rest of the clubs in the Northern Counties league into the Premiership.

Subscribe!

* **If war makes you sick, why not phone in sick if the bombs start to drop?** "Sorry boss I turned on the radio, heard about all the death and destruction and felt physically sick - it's just gotten worse all day.". This will leave you free to take part in a little civil disobedience later in the day - after your miraculous recovery of course.

***Australian PM John Howard has come up with a novel way to combat terrorism** - by spending ten million quid on junk mail! Every Australian household has been sent a Government Terrorism Kit, courtesy of Howard, consisting of that well known domestic terrorism deflector, a fridge magnet, plus a booklet filled with handy tips for avoiding disaster. Our personal favourite was 'keeping on the look out for people with a lifestyle that doesn't add up.' Mayor of Brisbane, Jim Soorley, has condemned Howard's propaganda exploits as scare-mongering and is urging anyone of an anti-war persuasion to send the packages right back where they came from. More info about the Return to Sender campaign at www.sydney.indymedia.org

BODY LANGUAGE

On the 17th of February, up to fifty human shield volunteers will fly to Jordan. From there, they'll travel by bus to Baghdad to meet up with the convoy of human shield volunteers who left London last month. The Human Shield movement aims to put loads of Western peace activists in Iraq around the large civilian areas in the hope of preventing bombing. Human Shield groups are now starting in Spain, Slovenia, Italy, Australia and the US. As one volunteer said, "I don't want to die. I love life. But every life is precious, and we need to recognise that a war that will kill innocent Iraqis must be opposed … I am going to Iraq to try to stop this war, and so to preserve life". If you don't want to be a shield but want to help, make out a cheque for "Human Shield Action" and send it to 90 Mercers Road, London, N19 4PR. If you'd like to sponsor a shield directly, call Uzma on 07764 603106. www.humanshields.org

SchNEWS in brief

Brighton's premier pirate radio station **Radio4A** is on air and internet this weekend with live coverage of Saturday's protest, music and allsorts. Tune in from Friday night to Sunday night 101.4 FM. www.radio4a.org.uk ** Get along to the **Sale of the Century Tour**, 17th February – 1st March, part of the World Development Movement's ongoing campaign against the General Agreement on Trade in Services (GATS- see SchNEWS 286) To find out if the tour's happening in your area call 020 72747630 www.wdm.org.uk ** **The Cowley Club café and radical bookshop is now open in Brighton!** Come in and have a cuppa whilst browsing your favourite anarchist weekly (SchNEWS of course!). The Club café and bookshop are located at 12 London Road, opposite Somerfield's, and are open Tues-Sat 12noon-4pm. The café and bookshop are co-operatively owned and run by unpaid volunteers, so new volunteers are always needed. If you have any time to spare, come in and speak to someone about helping out ** SchWOOPS! In last week's positive SchNEWS column we wrote about the Pedal Power Convention this Sunday (16th) but put the wrong web address. It's really www.c-realevents.demon.co.uk.

...and finally...

Wankers Against The War

We've all heard of groups like Doctors For Peace, Lawyers Against The War and even Businesses For Peace but here at SchNEWS Towers a new group we came across made us laugh out loud. Masturbators For Peace is a new anti war posse that is causing a stir with slogans like "I cum in peace", "Touch your sack, not Iraq" and "War is silly - Whack your willy". As they say on their website, "There's no greater antidote for war than love. However, any real love must start from within. You can't love others without loving yourself first. And of course masturbation is the greatest expression of self-love. So its natural that we, the citizens of the world, are joining together to masturbate for peace." Mind you this could be a load of old toss, so check it out for yourself at http://www.masturbateforpeace.com

Keep SchNEWS FREE! Send 1st Class stamps (e.g. 10 for next 9 issues) or donations (payable to Justice?) Ask for "Originals" if you can make copies. Post *free* to all prisoners. SchNEWS, c/o on-the-fiddle, P.O. Box 2600, Brighton, East Sussex, BN2 0EF.
Tel/Autofax +44 (0)1273 685913 *Email* schnews@brighton.co.uk *Download a PDF* of this issue or subscribe at www.schnews.org.uk

WAKE UP! WAKE UP! MAKE YOUR BED NOT WAR!

weekly SchNEWS

www.schnews.org.uk

THE ANTI-WAR MOVEMENT NEEDS YOU!

Friday 21st February 2003   Free/Donation   Issue 393

PEACE SOUP

Weapons of Mass Dissent

"The fracturing of the Western alliance over Iraq and the huge anti-war demonstrations around the world this weekend are reminders that there may still be two superpowers on the planet: the United States and world public opinion."
- *New York Times, February 2003.*

The biggest anti-war movement the world has ever seen has only a few weeks left to stop the first world war of the 21st century. Bush and his corporate backers are intent on re-carving the map of the Middle East to ensure US dominance over world oil supplies for decades ahead. If they get their way, the peoples of the Middle East, from Palestine to Kurdistan, will face more war, more poverty, and more repression so that the unsustainable gas-guzzling of countries like the United States and Britain can continue for a few more years.

But Britain is the weak link in the attack plans. Tony Blair is acting like Bush's shiny-suited lawyer, desperately digging up pseudo-legal and very pseudo-moral justifications for an invasion of Iraq. But unfortunately for US interests, Blair has very little support in Britain for his actions and if he is toppled it would be a major blow to Bush. While Blair represents the corporations, the millions who took to the streets of cities across the world last week represent the majority of world opinion. In Britain, the majority of people oppose Blair's war, and oppose it actively - the London march was the biggest in British history and actions and protests are taking place across the country.

But marches on their own are not enough. We need to do more. In the words of one of Saturday's speakers, we need to "turn up the heat". Civil disobedience on a vast scale, involving thousands of new activists in direct action, is the only reasonable response to Blair's war plans. We need to target high profile government events, the Labour Party's Swansea conference on the 28th of February for instance, and stop them from taking place. Government ministers should be harassed wherever they go. We need to be ready to stage mass walk-outs and stay-aways from work, blockade city centres if war starts, and culminate our actions in the already-planned massive occupation of Whitehall. We need to make sure that the police don't have a veto on what sort of protests we are going to carry out. In short, we need to stop business as usual for the government of this country until it is forced to listen to the people and dump the warmongers.

The anti-war movement is incredibly united around the need for action - there is little room for Judean People's Front style bickering - and people are determined to be listened to. A typical example of the new unity that is taking root in the anti-war movement is Brighton-based group Sussex Action for Peace. The group includes direct action veterans, left wing activists, local union organisers and dozens of individuals from all sorts of backgrounds. Meetings are large and practical, organising everything from stalls to banner drops in shopping centres to non-violent direct action training sessions to crèches. People understand that we are not going to affect this war if we stand around slagging off each other's diverse tactics. They understand that direct action goes hand in hand with leafleting the high street - that the people breaking into air bases and the people putting posters through letterboxes are in this together.

Groups like Sussex Action for Peace exist up and down the country, so if the bombs start to drop, phone in sick and join in the mass civil disobedience planned across the country. To find out what's happening in your area see www.schnews.org.uk/stopwar/

Statutes of Liberty?

All demonstrations in Manhattan have been banned since September 11th, and unsurprisingly, a New York judge made no exception for the February 15th anti-war march planned in the city, citing supposed "security" fears. Still, half a million people turned out to voice their opinion on Bush and his quest to rule the world. The cops allowed a rally, but then helpfully closed off

Peace Soup cont...

streets so that people couldn't get to it. At one point, 200 baton-wielding police attacked a group of 100 protestors. The provocation? Not staying on the pavement. The police claim there were only 50 arrests, but other sources, including the National Lawyers Guild, reckon that as many as 400 people were handcuffed and locked in freezing buses all day before being released without charge. Lawyers were not allowed access to their clients for up to 12 hours, during which police interrogated arrestees and asked them about their political affiliations. Congratulations Mr. Bush, Saddam would have been proud!

And yet despite all this, many New Yorkers still managed to make the most of the day, including our personal favourites, GLAMericans for Peace, who held signs bearing such only-in-America slogans as "Makeup Not War", "Baby, I AM the Bomb", and "War in Iraq is Wack". SchNEWS now reckons that Americans may actually have a sense of humour after all after reading about one sign addressed to Mr. Bush and painted with the message, "Eat Another Pretzel, Asshole." www.nyc.indymedia.org

War Briefs

If you think you were cold at London's anti-war march... this Valentine's Day, 150 people braved temperatures of -35°c in Ottawa, Canada at a 5 hour mass sit-down outside the Ottawa War department. ** **Fairford airbase** in Gloustershire is the biggest bomber base in Europe and can house US Stealth bombers which will drop depleted uranium bombs on Iraq. On Monday, a peace camp set up outside the base. They need tat, food and more people; it's at Kempsford, just south of the base. This Sunday (23rd) there's a 'No Basis for War, No Bases for War' action against the base. Meet noon in Fairford village. Camp Mobiles 07905 131020 or 07947 614941 www.gwi.org.uk ** **WAR Against War** meeting for folks who live or work in West London to discuss local action against the war. Mon 24th 7.30pm, West 12 Bar (Basement), 74 Askew Road, London W12. ** Special meeting of **Worthing Against War**, Tues 25th, 7.45pm, upstairs at The Downview, West Worthing. ** Weds 26th **'Question Time'** style debate on the War. 7-9pm at the Brighthelm Centre, North Rd, Brighton ** Also on 26th, **Sussex Action for Peace get involved benefit night**. £3. Bands and DJ's, 9pm-2am at the Hanbury Ballroom, Brighton. ** The war-mongering 'Christian' **Tony Blair is due to attend the enthronement of the new Archbishop of Canterbury,** Thurs 27th, 3pm, Canterbury Cathedral. An anti-war demo is planned, meet 1.30pm, The Burgate, Canterbury. mobilisekent@hotmail.com 07950 610257. ** Fri 28th is the **Labour Party Welsh Conference**. An anti-war demo is planned. Meet 12 noon at the Guildhall, Swansea. www.geocities.com/swansea-coalition/ ** **ARROW Resistance Gathering** to organise non-violent direct action against war, 1st March, 10.30am-5pm, 62 Fieldgate Street, London E1. www.j-n-v.org ** And finally... In North Carolina, the owner of a restaurant has renamed his French fries **"freedom fries"** in protest over France's disgusting anti-war policy towards Iraq. "It's our way of showing our patriotic pride," says the owner.

I CAN'T BOLIVIA IT'S A RIOT

Bolivia is in the grip of a massive urban uprising after high school students and the working class of La Paz and El Alto erupted in the streets on February the 12th. In the capital city of La Paz, high school students attacked the Presidential Palace with stones as crowds burned the headquarters of the major neo-liberal parties, a private television station, and various government buildings. In El Alto, rioters burned and looted the water company and the power company and later on occupied the Coke and Pepsi bottling plants. All of this happened after the military opened fired on a group of police who were marching to the Presidential Palace to protest tax increases that would reduce their already low wages. The unpopular tax increases were an attempt by the repressive de Lozado regime to follow IMF directives to reduce the government deficit. But tax increases

are just the tip of the iceberg. Coca is also on de Lozado's black list, but Coca growers and indigenous Indians have been blockading roads since January to protest against the criminalisation of coca growing and the unequal distribution of land. The de Lozado regime has also provoked opposition because of its support for the neo-liberal Free Trade Area of the Americas and its complicity in the US's dirty War on Drugs.

Finally, on February the 12th, the people of Bolivia had had enough. After a day of riots, most of the working class neighbourhoods in El Alto and La Paz had blockaded their areas and groups of several hundred were meeting in the carnage of their streets to discuss tactics. Unfortunately, military tanks, tear gas and snipers quickly dispersed a 10 000-strong demonstration held in La Paz the following day. By early afternoon, eight were dead and ten wounded. But the anger still rages

in the streets as protestors continue to blockade roads, chanting the anti-de Lozado slogan 'Gringo go home' (as the President reputedly has the annoying tendency of talking with a North American accent when speaking Spanish)

Parallels have been drawn with Argentina's social rebellion, but in Bolivia the rebellion is (unfortunately) under the control of the political party MAS (Movement Towards Socialism.) But perhaps it is too soon to express cynicism. The MAS, together with the peasants' trade unions, has formed the Joint Chiefs of the People to spearhead the rebellion and has called for a mass blockade in the rural areas. Under this unbearable pressure, de Lozado has withdrawn the tax increases and dissolved his entire cabine but the rebellious Bolivians aren't through with him yet. www.zmag.org/lam/boliviawatch.htm

NU-CLEAR WAY OUT

Reports commissioned by Greenpeace over a year ago reveal that a terrorist attack on a nuclear power station in the UK could release 25 times as much radiation as was released by the Chernobyl disaster. The reports, which conclude Britain's nuclear plants are "almost totally ill-prepared" for an airborne terrorist attack, also estimate that such an attack could kill between 1.1- 3.6 million people. So what do you think Greenpeace and the UK government want to do with this information? Sit on it, of course. Both Greenpeace and Neo Labour have actively sought to suppress any publishing of the findings, supposedly because of their "seriously alarming nature".

So while the government babbles on about a possible ricin attack or deploys tanks to Heathrow, there might actually be something much worse round the corner that no one is bothering to tell you about...

Maybe this has to do with Tony Blair's love of nuclear power. He had recently proposed to build six new nuclear power stations, but luckily for us, other ministers stood up to him and rejected the plan. But like a spoilt brat who didn't get his way, he is now insisting that if he can't have what he wants, green energy backers can't either. Blair is now insisting that a newly proposed target of producing 20% of Britain's power from renewable energy sources by 2020 also be scrapped!

* Greenpeace is mounting a legal challenge to the £650m bail out package the Government gave British Energy (who run the old Magnox nuclear power stations). If the suit is successful, British Energy would go bankrupt and perhaps have to shut all of their power stations. www.greenpeace.org.uk

PRAWNOGRAPHY

Next time you tuck into your prawn and mayo sandwich, spare a thought for the other fish that never made it to your stomach. For every 1kg of prawns caught, 10-20kg of 'bycatch' is caught. These are then discarded overboard dead or dying. 150,000 sea turtles are killed by prawn trawlers every year. Prawn trawling is also thought to be the greatest threat to seahorses. This luxury product and other factory fishing methods are destroying the world's fisheries, undermining the sustainable use of the oceans. www.ejfoundation.org/trawling.html

February 23rd: Around 10,000 march on the US air base in Rhein-Main, Germany with 2,000 blockading entrances to the base.

Positive SchNEWS

If the revolution is gonna be televised then make sure you're the one with the videocam and get yerself down to the Indymedia camcorder guerillas' weekend. Featuring screenings of radical underground films and workshops by the filmmakers giving practical and technical inspiration to activists. 7th-9th March mainly at Glasgow Film Theatre, with a party to celebrate the launch of Indymedia Scotland on the Saturday. For the workshops (£10/ £20) and party (£3/£5), book with the Glasgow Media Access Centre, Camcorder Guerillas, 34 Albion St, Glasgow. 0141 553 2620. For the screenings ring 0141 332 8128.

Inside SchNEWS

A protester from Shannon airport was this week found guilty of spray painting a US airplane which was at the base last September. The punishment was a 1,000 euro fine and a six month suspended prison sentence. The protester is appealing—donations to the appeal fund would be greatly appreciated: Cheques payable to Eoin Dubsky, Whitewalls, Ballymoney, Gorey, Co. Wexford, Ireland.

* Five catholic workers who were arrested doing a ploughshares action at Shannon airport at the beginning of the month are still on remand. Letters of support can be sent to them c/o Br. Anthony, Glenstal Abbey, Murroe, Co. Limerick. http://slack.redbrick.dcu.ie

Trainstoppers turn Embassystoppers: Activist spectacularly occupy the British Embassy in Torino, Italy , February 22nd (see 'Trainstopping' article).

NOT A LAME CLAIM

The government is in breach of the European Convention on Human Rights - and that's official.

Mr Justice Collins pulled no punches when he handed down a ruling in the High Court recently on the draconian Section 55 of the 2002 Asylum Bill. He said there was "a real risk" of death or injury for refugees who, under Section 55, are refused support because they didn't apply for asylum the minute they arrived in the UK. He went on to state that Section 55 violates asylum seekers' human rights.

The test case was brought on behalf of 6 asylum seekers but there are 150 more just like it in the pipeline! Justice Collins ordered that previous decisions made by the Home Office in respect to the 6 "must be quashed and re-considered" and that they should be given emergency support.

Keir Starmer QC, representing the asylum seekers, told the court how one Iraqi man had been forced to spend nights in a telephone box due to Section 55. Starmer em-

phasized that the hardships victims of this brutal new legislation are forced to endure - no money, no food, no home - substantially lower their ability to effectively pursue their asylum applications due to rapid physical and mental deterioration.

Liza Schuster, an expert on asylum from LSE commented: "What does the government expect people to do - patiently starve to death?" Er, yes.

Even though today's ruling means that the Home Office now has a duty to ensure people who apply for asylum are not left without food or shelter, Blunkett ain't having it. He was outside immediately after the hearing ended, telling the Press: "We will be appealing against this decision, with the Attorney General taking the appeal on behalf of the government."

* **Don't let the lunatics take over Asylum!** Find out what you can do at 0121 554 6947 www.ncadc.org.uk

* Monday 24th there will be another **pre-trial hearing** for those accused of taking part in the disturbance at **Yarl's Wood detention centre**. Meet 9am Harrow Crown Court. 07867-690332. lizscott@fish.co.uk

* **Stop the War on Asylum Seekers Public Meeting**. Hanover Room, Brighthelm Centre, North Road, Brighton. 3rd March, 7.30pm

* There's **leafleting of Saltdean** this Sunday in defence of refugees who may be housed there soon (see SchNEWS 390). Meet 12 noon at the Saltdean Tavern (next to the Lido).

DRUGS AND THUGS

"The Pharmaceuticals lobby is running the show in Washington," said a development activist at talks in Geneva last Monday, where unelected President Bush, apparently under the influence of drugs (companies), blocked a World Trade Organisation ruling that would have allowed developing countries access to drugs at affordable prices.

After the long battle between drugs companies and the South African government last year, it was decided that governments of poorer countries could ignore international patent laws in order to prevent further deaths from curable diseases (SchNEWS 290 & 328). The drug companies see this as a massive threat to their profits and with a little help from their friends in high places they're trying to stop the deal going through.

www.who.int/hiv/aboutdept/en/

...and finally...

All Coked up

A South African businessman has accused World Cup organisers of assault after he was thrown out of Saturday's match between Australia and India – for drinking a can of Coca-Cola!

The World Cup organising committee, in an effort to protect the interests of official sponsors like Pepsi, has placed arch-rivals Coca Cola on the list of items that are banned at all World Cup matches.

"Within minutes of opening our cans, we were accosted by security officials and told to stop drinking," said Arthur Williamson, the hassled Coke drinker. "They also demanded that we surrender any remaining unopened Cokes in our possession." When he refused, he and his family were chucked out! Nothing like the "Real thing", eh?!

Disclaimer
SchNEWS warns all politicians flirting with danger, Make Out, Not War. Honest!

February 25th: Mass anti-war demo in Prague, Czech Republic.

Trainstopping

"Scegli di difendere l'art.11,
Scegli una stazione utile,
Scegli la pace."

TrainSTOPping

Occupa le stazioni perché la guerra non può essere strumento di offesa alla libertà degli altri popoli e mezzo di risoluzione delle controversie internazionali.

(above) Why don't we do it on the track... Pisa Train Station

In the months leading up to the war, the US military were busy moving thousands of troops and huge convoys of war hardware from bases in Europe to ports ready for shipping to the middle east. This saw a direct action response around Europe, with tactics such as breaking into army bases and 'trainstopping', similar to what had been going on for years to stop the movement of trains carrying nuclear waste across northern Europe (see SchNEWS 299).

The Italian Mob

In Italy, Defence Minister Martino illegally guaranteed the use of public infrastructure for US transport without the necessary approval of the parliament. The antiwar movement has responded with "trainstopping". Since 21st February, hundreds of protestors have tried to block at least 26 convoys on their way to the Camp Darby US military base near Pisa.

On 22nd February, despite intimidation and threats, direct action against the trains spread to other towns: in Grisignano di Zocco; in Campo di Marte (Padua) where a train was blocked for hours. A train was blocked in Verona for half an hour until police got violent. Meanwhile hundreds caused train blockades in Brescia, Bologna and Fornovo (near Parma), until being dispersed by police. In Pisa there were two demos, the first in the morning at the military air-

Going off the rails at Brescia

port, the second in the afternoon with 600 people from the station to the centre of the city. The next day the trains were kept stationary due to the 'public disorder situation'.

Since 23rd February railways staff have been redefined as "military personnel." But while the train workers do not get much support from their labour union, the dock workers' union has announced that they will not load military equipment on the ships. The British consulate was occupied in Torino, and other actions are expected also in Ferrara, where police attacked a crowd of 1,000 people, as well as in Udine. At Magdalena Isle near Sardinia, another 1,000 trainstoppers were roughly cleared out by police.

For more see http://italy.indymedia.org

Weapons Of Mass Obstruction: Belgium

From January onwards, as the war built up, military equipment from US troops based in Germany was being shipped through ports in Belgium to the middle east on a massive scale. The Belgian government had been making so-called "hard statements" against the war, but at the end of the day was complicit by letting it's transport infrastructure be used by the US war machine.

Halfway through January, actions to stop military transports in Belgium took off when 3 Stop USA activists chained themselves on a sluice in Antwerp Harbour. A month later, a boat blockade took place by Greenpeace. "No War" was painted onto *The Catherine*, a US Army ship.

On 16th February, 11 peace activists managed to stop a train with US military equipment near Antwerp harbour. This train was part of US military transportation towards the Persian Gulf and Turkey, coming from Germany and shipping out of Antwerp. The train was stopped when people covered the signal with a cloth and used red lights to signal the driver to halt. With the engine stationary, two people chained themselves to it, while others locked themselves onto the wagons and the military equipment. Eventually all 11 were removed and arrested after 3 hours.

Stopping the train-stopping - March 1st, Melsele

A massive trainstopping action was called on 1st-2nd March, hoping to block 18 US military consignments from Germany. A 24-hour action with sports, dancing, and more was planned for on and around the railtracks in Melsele - but on the day disaster struck: At the meeting point in a village hall, just as the action was about to take off, police surrounded and entered the building to 'preventively' arrest all 150 people inside. The whole lot of them were then held for 12 hours and deported to Ghent. The reason given for deportation was to prevent the arrestees being able to do another trainstopping action immediately after release.

Dancing on the ruins of multinational corporations - Antwerp port, February 16th

Crashing The War Party: Netherlands

The good volk of Holland inspect Volkel Airbase

Citizens Inspections

Volkel 18th January: About one hundred civil inspectors gain access to the grounds of Volkel military air base in the southeast of the Netherlands. The perimeter fence was cut in several places at once, while other inspection teams somehow used their own keys to enter several gates at the base.!. Most inspectors were arrested, but released later in the day. Accord-

ing to previous investigations by several peace groups, there are weapons of mass destruction stored at Volkel under US supervision.

The dam bursts open and the protesters gush through

Actions against military transportation in Ostend

On the 8th February, about 35 peace activists held a noisy demo at the entrance of Ostend Airport against its use as a transit node for military transportation by Kalitta, Gemini and The Air Mobility Command.

On 26th March the trade entrance that is used for delivering airplane fuel got blocked, while action was taken against AviaPartner, a company doing logistic support for the transporters. Afterwards the planestoppers decided to enter the actual airport to demonstrate at the AviaPartner desk.

On 5th April, 70 took to the fence but were stopped when their ladders were stolen by police. Four still got in, despite police aggression, later to be arrested. A sympathy demo gathered at the police station, and later one of the released activists disrupted a cultural event in town by speaking about the military transports on stage.

Two days later a spectacular action happened when a few Re-
sist! activists got into the airport and ran about on the runway for a diversion, while others scaled the control tower of Ostend airport where they hung out a banner reading "No war for oil, Resist!"
(pic right)

On 20th April, while 50 marched towards the airport, several again climbed over the fence at the back of the airport but were spotted and arrested. Later a larger group attempted to enter the airport, and about 10 got past riot police but were eventually arrested. Two activists were hurt by police, one had to be taken to hospital.

Montzen Belgian-German border 17th April: (above) equipment of the 1st Armored Brigade, a pantser division of the US Army based in Germany, gets trainstopped for a few hours. The banner says 'Belgium stays accomplice' - a reference to the hypocrisy of Belgium being anti-war, yet being a major port for US arms transporting.

Venlo 11th April: Onkruit, a Dutch anti-militarist group, succesfully blocked a US military transport near Venlo. Activists chained themselves on the rails and the military cargo, heading for the port of Rotterdam, had to return to Germany. The track signal was put on red, while people ran on the tracks and forced the train to stop by locking onto the track.

Think Global, Act Volkel

Volkel 9th February: At the NATO airbase in Volkel, a Dutch woman armed with a sledgehammer smashed three satellite dishes, in protest against the war, and the existence of nuclear weapons housed at the airbase. Barbara Smedema served two months imprisonment for this, and upon her release she was surprised by her sister with the gift of a new sledgehammer.

Thanks to Joeri - see also Indymedia Netherlands, Belgium & West Vlaanderen

شهداء العراق

'to the victims of war'

FROM THE GROUND UP

A diary from inside Baghdad at the onset of war

From the day she arrived in Baghdad to the day she was finally ordered to leave, British activist Jo Wilding operated as an independent human rights observer as war engulfed the Iraqi capital. What follows is an edited selection of the frontline communiques she sent back to the UK.

16-Feb Though it's dark for most of our 960km journey from Jordan to Baghdad, there are trucks and tankers on the road without lights. Literally without them, not just without them switched on. Others have no brakes - or none to speak of - and simply have to sound their horns constantly to warn whatever is in their path. There aren't any spares, but life has to go on. Likewise the streetlights are not on until the outskirts of Baghdad. If you look closely, there are no lights: only poles.

Baghdad, though, seems surprisingly solid. All the talk of cruise missiles, uranium bunker-busters, carpet bombing and the rest made the whole city precarious in my mind, but Saturday is a gloriously sunny day and people are going about their business. We talk to a few people about the risk of bombing. There are shelters but no one wants to go in them after the coalition bombed a civilian shelter last time, burning or boiling over four hundred people who were trapped inside. Inside a building is a bad place to be. Somewhere wide open is the best bet, they say, a field, a park or the riverside.

18-Feb A gang of lads asked my name, then dissolved in giggles, slapping each other's shoulders when I told them mine and asked theirs. Overcoming their shyness, they ask where I was from, how old I was, what I thought of Baghdad, and we danced down the street together to the clatter of drums and hand clapping.

It was an anti-war march, organised by the students at the Non-Aligned Students and Youth Organisation (NASYO) conference.

I marched with a group of young Iraqi women, clapping their hands and chanting.

People talk when they know no one else can hear. The feeling is that they would prefer genuine democracy, greater freedom, but if the choice is Saddam or the USA, they will take Saddam. They do not believe, even when they speak freely, that the US and UK will be "liberating" them.

21-Feb British and US citizens have been advised to leave Iraq. Radio Five Live rang at midnight to ask for a comment on the "unrest". .... "The what?"

Our friend Ghazwan was upset because it's the clearest indication that an attack is imminent; more imminent than usual, that is. As Odai told me, they've been about to be attacked for about as long as he can remember. He was 11 in the first gulf war.

The food ration has been distributed for April and May already. In the next few days the 40,000 ration shops will be receiving the distribution for June and July. In the last war the food warehouses were destroyed. If they're hit this time the plan is that they'll be empty, and that people will have a stockpile for as long as possible.

Some people talk about going out to the country when the war starts, where the bombing may well be less intense. Others say they will stay and defend their city. What I haven't heard anyone say, even in private, is that they're looking forward to their "liberation" by the US. Ghazwan refers to Bush and Blair as a single entity – Mr Blush. "Blush is pushing for war despite the objections of his people," he says.

23-Feb Today I went out on one of the human shield buses to a Baghdad power station where some of the international activists are going to be staying, attempting to protect it from attack.

All the way from Abu Nawas Street to the power station people were waving, cheering, giving thumbs up and peace signs. The media often suggest that demonstrations in Iraq are arranged by the government, and perhaps some are, but there was no compulsion today to pay any attention to the red double decker buses painted with peace messages. People were genuinely glad to see buses full of foreign peace activists and to know people cared enough to be there.

There are peace campaigners here from Jordan, Turkey, Syria, Palestine, Congo, Chad, Nigeria, Sudan, South Africa, Mauritius, Japan, China, India, Argentina, Greece, Russia, Estonia, the Balkans, the Czech Republic, Germany, France, Britain, Ireland, Canada, the US, Australia: bring me an atlas and I'll try to find you a country that's not represented.

Not all internationals are human shields – there is a range of organisations out here – Balkan Sobranie, Voices in the Wilderness, the Christian Peacemaker Team, to name but a few, as well as independent activists like me.

25-Feb Last night I sat down to dinner with Saddam Hussein. Remarkable, I know, and what's more, he propositioned me. He said that he had always dreamed he would "make love relationship with a Christian girl". I quickly disabused him of the notion and we carried on as before. He's studying French literature at the University of Baghdad and his father named him after the then vice president 27 years ago.

Saddam was translating for us in a meeting with the National Union of Iraqi Students (NUIS), who are now "responsible for you". You have to have an organisation which is responsible for you in Iraq, and if you want to film anything you have to be accompanied by a representative of that organisation, so we had to get their approval for our plans.

We drove out to a man-made lake. On mounds, between the lake and the engineering college opposite, an anti-aircraft gun and a radar emplacement have the look of museum pieces. Khaki men fiddle about with them while passers-by ignore them as everyday sights. As we drove up to the toll booth Saddam's brother Ra'id mutters: "Don't speak English now."

The brothers joke a lot about what might be coming, as do many people - a satirical gallows humour that testifies to the spirit which has brought the Iraqi people still warm and welcoming after over twelve years of sanctions.

Their house is stocked with food, water and guns. Each house is 'an independent state' equipped with all necessities, but one family friend showed them the shopping list of provisions to be got in for the war, and the list included coffins.

13- March Small sandbag dens are sprouting out of the pavements, by way of some protection against shrapnel and flying debris. It's better than a poke in the eye with a sharp bit of metal, so to speak, but it's not much. People have taped "X"s on their windows to prevent them shattering. Sandbags and sticky tape against Stealth Bombers, Cruise Missiles, MOABs, uranium Bunker Busters!

Meanwhile, yesterday the bulk of the remaining UN and embassy staff left Iraq.

17-March The shops are all emptying of stock, piling it into sacks and taking it somewhere safer. Even Husam now warns us there's a war coming. A few days ago he swore blind there wasn't going to be an attack. It was only when we told him the UN were leaving in convoy, along with most of the embassy staff, that he rubbed his chin, frowned, and remarked that that was a bad sign. Undoubtedly there are those in this country who want war to begin, in the way you long for a thunderstorm on an unbearably humid day.

18-March There was a big puddle in the doorway into the classroom at Qataiba boys' school in Saddam City, the poorest part of Baghdad. A woman in black drags a rag across it by way of a mop, but makes little impact. The principal's office is as battered as the rest, deprived of maintenance after over twelve years of sanctions. Around half of the city's five million strong population live around here. It's a Shi'a district, touted as the most likely starting point for civil unrest after bombing starts. People tell you not to go there, even now: "It's dangerous."

"We will not fight for Saddam Hussein, but we will fight for our land," says one man. "I will accept any Arab as president but I will not accept a foreigner. If the Americans come, they will be very strong at first, but after some time they will see resistance. We will fight them. It doesn't matter about sects, Shi'a, Sunni, Kurd, Christian. I am Kurd. We will all fight together, not for the government. For our land." It was the first time I'd seen anyone vent frustration so openly here.

"We need to change the government, but I don't want America invasion. This not bring freedom. I can't talk here, because of security," ….words muttered amid the clamour of the classroom.

20-March I hardly know whether it was real. In my head I know that bombing started around 5:30am. I know because I heard low thundering booms that drew me out onto the balcony, where I could feel the pulsation through the air and see distant flashes and the occasional moving light of a Cruise missile.

I know because I saw the feral dogs that live on the riverside running down the middle of the emptied road, trying to escape the noise, which was in stereo. I know because the phone's been ringing all day with journalists asking what's happening.

The war has started.

This morning the manager of our hotel was arrested, seized by two men in uniforms and dragged, screaming and struggling in obvious panic, to a vehicle, apparently because some ignorant journalists were filming the bombing from the roof of the hotel, even though they're all supposed to be staying in the Palestine Hotel across the road. They wouldn't tell us where they were taking him and we couldn't do a thing to help him. We hardly expected to see him back, but within the hour he was escorted through the door. The edifice isn't crumbling just yet.

24-March "We are farmers. We are farmers." The woman kept repeating it through her rage and grief and incomprehension while the orderlies mopped the blood from the floor.

We had gone to the Al Kindi hospital to see people hurt when a bomb hit their house.

The doctor was called to the emergency room and told us to come with him. A family had just arrived. They had left their home in Baghdad and gone to their family's farm on the outskirts for safety. There were sitting eating when a missile struck the house.

The uncle who owned the house had a head wound and a laceration to his arm but was relatively lucid and able to explain that family members were still buried in the rubble. One of the young men got married one week ago. "The bride missing. We don't know where."

The mother held one child after another. Her eight-year-old daughter was killed.

A tiny wide-eyed boy in pyjamas cried and clapped his bandaged hands, calling out "Mama" whenever he was left alone. Safe in the lap of an aunt, he drifted off into his own world, touching his fingertip to the still-damp blood on his sleeve, looking intently at it, putting the finger to his tongue, his face chequered with cuts. In the corridor, a doctor shook with anger, as he demanded, "Where is the UN?"

25-March It's hard now to tell the bombings from the storm: both beat at the windows and thunder through the city, but after a missile explodes, flocks of birds fill the sky, disturbed by the shock waves. After a gust, they are replaced by a deluge of rubbish, drifting in the smog of sand and dust and smoke which has turned the air a dirty orange so thick it blots out the sun.

We have found out that three people died yesterday in the bombed farmhouse at Dialla, including the young wife, Nahda, eight year old Zahra, and her aunt, Hana. They were buried this morning.

Neighbours said the bomb hit at 4pm yesterday. The plane had been circling overhead for a while. It fired three rockets, one of which demolished the entire upper storey of the house. It looked as if it had only ever been a bungalow until, clambering through the hallway, we came to the stairs, leading up to nothing.

There was nothing which could explain the attack: nothing which even looked like a target that the pilot might have been aiming for. It made no sense.

26-March The Iraqi's call it orange weather: some say it is on their side. It's not even five o'clock and the sun won't set till nearly seven but it's dark outside. It stinks as well, of smoke and oil and I don't know what else. The darkness and the grime and the fierce cold wind lend an unnecessary sense of apocalypse to the flooded craters, broken trees, gaping windows and wrecked houses where the bombs have hit. At nine o clock this morning a group of caravans was hit with cluster bombs, according to the doctors. A tiny boy lay in terrible pain in the hospital, a tube draining blood from his chest, pierced by shrapnel. I'm not sure whether he knew yet, or could understand, that his mother was killed instantly and his five sisters and two brothers were not yet found.

27-March This morning the sky had cleared: a mixed blessing. It was good to be able to see through the daylight again but it seemed likely to mark the end of our period of grace, such as it was, when the weather was holding up the onslaught.

In Al Shaab market Mohammed Al Zubaidi told us he had a shop. It was the second one from the left as you look at the remains of the building which the bomb hit. His assistant, Faris El Bawi, was crushed in the blast and his body incinerated along with his eleven year old son Saif who was helping him, because school was closed for the war.

Husham Hussein was about 200 metres away. He said a lot of people were injured in the flats above the shops. The shops were all open and the market was busy. He thought 25 people were killed. Someone else said 45-50 people had gone to hospital. No one could think of a military target nearby.

We were invited in for tea and biscuits in Adamiya, where a rocket demolished five homes on Monday lunchtime. Because people are not going to work or school, they were mostly at home in the middle of Monday and six died. No one saw a plane or heard anything till the explosion: they speculate that it might have been fired from the sea.

The missile landed vertically on number 13, killing the grandmother, Khowla Sherkhli, the father, Ahmed Munier, and the daughter, Maha Waleed.

Home isn't safe, the farms are not safe, the market isn't safe. Nowhere is safe.

28-March Last night's bombs were so immense I could see the flashes from inside a room with the curtains drawn and my eyes closed. The building swayed like a treehouse in the wind, rocking long after the sound had died away. The voice of the prayer call was singing out as if from a machine activated by the sudden shaking of the minaret.

The communications' towers were hit last night and today there are no phones. I don't know how Zaid is, or Asmaa and Israa and Mimi and Omar, or Majid and Raid or Ibrahim. They are probably less than a mile away, but it may as well be a million.

As foreigners we're not even allowed to cross the road without a minder now. Six peace activists were kicked out this morning. A good friend was expelled yesterday to Syria as a "security risk".

I blew bubbles over the edge of the second floor inside balcony of my hotel, and watched as grown men jumped and laughed trying to catch or pop them. And all the while the bass thudding of bombs carried on around us. Playfulness in the face of war feels like profound defiance.

29-March A missile hit the middle of the street outside the Omar Al Faroukh mosque on Palestine Street at about 4:15 this afternoon, just as people were leaving after prayers. Ahmed was walking out behind his friend Umar when he heard an explosion and saw his friend fall. Umar is a student at Rafidain College. He had fragments of shrapnel about 3cm long removed from his liver and abdomen. His grandfather demands that Bush and Blair be charged and brought to court.

Another missile hit, close by, three minutes later. Akael Zuhair was standing in front of his house opposite the mosque. I'm not sure if it was the first or second missile that hurt him, but he's in a dangerous state in hospital. He's 20.

He began to regain consciousness while we were there, thrashing his limbs about while his family and friends tried to hold him still and comfort him. His mum's tears overflowed. "I am his mother," she whispered. Nothing else. I held her without a word.

His dad heard the explosion in the street. "Help us," he said, "because we are attacked in homes and streets and markets. We are not something to be squeezed. We thank people in all the world, but especially in America and England. More than a million people in England say no to war. There is not a problem between people. There is a problem with governments."

Again, no one could guess what the intended target was. All of the friends and family we took statements from said there was nothing military in the area.

The doctors at the hospital were doing a lot of tasks normally associated with nursing staff. Khalida, the chief nurse who never sleeps, said the international standard ratio is four nurses per doctor. Here it's the other way round: there's one nurse for every four doctors. All this as well as the bombing of another market yesterday, Al Shu'la. Dr Tariq said there were over 50 deaths and lots of injuries.

There are too many civilian casualties, too far from military targets, for all of these to be mistakes. Either they're hitting civilians on purpose, to whip up fear in the hope of spurring rebellion, or their weapons are not as precise as they say, in which case they're not suitable for use in an urban environment.

I'm being expelled from Iraq. It looked, for a while, as if we were going to have to leave this morning, but we scored another two days. Coming from the Foreign Ministry, there's not really any arguing with that. There's no shame in it either, being booted out by this government, but it hurts, it aches. I can't say goodbye to anyone because there are no phones and we can't go anywhere without a minder and permission from the foreign ministry.

The bombs have been more frequent today, and closer, than any other day.

30-March I started crying this morning. I thought I was leaving at 8am in a convoy for Jordan and I said goodbye to the staff in the Andalus Hotel.

It got worse when I said goodbye to the young soldiers on the street outside, who share their tea with us and tell jokes in mime. "Ma'assalama," I said, and added, as a reflex, "Good luck." And then I couldn't bear the thought of them having to face those overwhelmingly powerful tanks, guns and ammunition, when all they had was an aging rifle and a hard hat to protect them.

Then when all the bags were in the car, there was a mix-up and the rest of the convoy left without me and I wasn't leaving after all, and leaving was the last thing in the world I wanted to do, but by then my defences had lapsed and the crater of sorrow inside me had filled to the top and it overflowed with the tears of Akael's mother for her boy, Nahda's husband for his new wife, and all the intolerable, uncontainable sadness in this place.

The bombing is a constant background noise today, a rhythm in stereo with no visible source. Ali is playing a game on the computer involving tanks firing missiles at things in a city. Wasn't that a bit too close for comfort, I asked, or was it simulator practice in case he needed those skills in the coming weeks. He thought that was funny.

It will probably be a while before any of my friends in Iraq are able to read this, but when you do, this is what I wanted to say. I hope you make it safely through this war and I hope you find your freedom, from the bullying of the US/UK and the Iraqi government.

Your courage, dignity, kindness and humour inspire me. Ma'assalama.

Jo Wilding left Baghdad on a later convoy and returned to the UK.

Thanks to Squall for this edit of Jo's diaries. www.squall.co.uk

The full diary entries can be read at www.bristolfoe.org.uk/ wildfire

WAKE UP! WAKE UP! IT'S YER ALL-SEEING

weekly SchNEWS
www.schnews.org.uk

Friday 28th February 2003   Free/Donation   Issue 394

We've bombed 'em back to the stone age so we're sending 'em rock cakes

AFGHANI-SHAM

In the week that George W. presents his 'vision' for a post-war Iraq, a vision that he has already refused to contribute to financially, SchNEWS reckons it's appropriate to look at Afghanistan one year on. Just how has bombing and killing civilians improved the situation for the Afghan people?

The Wanted posters that litter the country, dropped by US planes, give us a clue. America's most wanted are Osama bin Laden, former Taliban leader Mullah Omar, and former Prime Minister and hardline Pashtun warlord Gulbuddin Hekmatyar. Little change there then. Hekmatyar continues to rally support among the Pashtun communities, probably due to the oversight that neglected to allow them proper representation in the Transitional Government headed up by US puppet Hamid Karzai. Karzai's credibility plummets as he turns to the US for his own security, and his power has yet to extend beyond Kabul. Someone obviously forgot to read the bit in Security Council Resolution 1378 stating that both the transitional and the pursuant democratic governments should be 'broad-based, multi-ethnic, and fully representative of all Afghan people.'

With their usual 'go for the symptom if you can't get the cause' way of looking at things, the US have been bombing the Pashtun communities in the South and East of the country. If the man's too slippery, go for the people who may, just possibly, one day in the future, support him. In January, US, Norwegian and Danish fighter planes conducted a massive bombing raid close to Spin Boldak, a refugee village near the Pakistan border that houses 65,000

men, women and children, reportedly killing hundreds of civilians. Accurate numbers were not available as the area was sealed off by troops and access denied even to the Red Cross. This is in direct contravention of UN Resolution 1379 - which underlines the importance of 'full, safe and unhindered access of humanitarian personnel and goods, and the delivery of humanitarian assistance to all children affected by armed conflict.' Earlier this month, 17 civilians, mostly women and children were killed in bombing raids designed to wipe out a handful of rebel fighters in the Baghran district to the South.

ORE OF BABYLON

US forces continue to use outlawed weapons in these attacks, such as uranium bombs and the innocuously named Daisy Cutter, a bomb the size of a VW beetle which incinerates everything within a 600 metre radius and whose shock waves can be felt miles away. Findings by the Uranium Medical Research Centre (UMRC) point out that uranium poisoning is already causing severe health problems throughout Afghanistan "The UMRC field team was shocked by the breadth of public health impacts coincident with the bombing. Without exception, at every bombsite investigated, people are ill.." Yet again the US shows its middle finger

---

BRIGHTON STOP THE WAR PROTEST

Saturday 1st March, meet 1pm War Memorial for moving protest with street theatre and samba bands 07815 983022
www.safp.org.uk

---

to resolution number 1379 that calls upon all parties to respect conditions of 'Prohibition or Restriction' on the use of weapons which have 'Indiscriminate Effects.'

And to add insult to mass destruction, George W. 'forgot' to include any humanitarian and reconstruction funds in his 2003 budget. Yet another unfortunate oversight hurriedly rescued by Congress who managed to rustle up $300 million for the cause. How many times did Bush pledge not to walk away from the Afghan people? $300million might seem like a lot, but it constitutes a small proportion of the $4billion total pledged at the Tokyo donor's conference to help rebuild Afghanistan. Compared to the $3 billion that Israel receives in US foreign aid every year, $300m figure suddenly loses its impact.

Israel has been given $240 billion since 1973, much of it used for the purchase and manufacture of weapons, plus additional funds, not counted as foreign aid, for special projects such as $180 million for the development and manufacture of the Arrow missile project. Weapons now make up 50% of Israel's manufactured exports. Contrary to the norm, Israel is not required to use this injection of funds to buy American goods, in fact Ameri-

@NTI-COPYRIGHT - INFORMATION FOR ACTION   Published in Brighton

Afghani-Sham cont...

can defence contractors are often forced to buy Israeli goods, and it has the power to block the sale of US military equipment to Middle Eastern countries. In common with other states that have earned the "rogue nation" label, Israel has the capacity to manufacture nuclear, biological and chemical weapons and maintains a stockpile of nuclear weapons, yet has not signed the Non-Proliferation Treaty and refuses to allow any independent inspection of its facilities.

Israel are now demanding an additional $3-4 billion for the next 3 to 5 years to help them cope with the continuing Palestinian uprising and the consequences of a US war in Iraq. Perhaps George W. should see someone about his blurred 'vision' before he makes more of a spectacle of himself.

More info: Uranium contamination - www.URMC.net; Daisy Cutters - www.robearly.com/911/DaisyCutter.html; Israeli foreign aid - www.csmonitor.com

It's a Fairford Cop, Guv

Last Sunday around 500 people met for a day of direct action at Fairford, a US military base in Gloucestershire. Fairford is the biggest bomber base in Europe and houses US stealth bombers that will drop depleted uranium bombs on Iraq. After gathering at the main entrance of the base, someone announced that they were weapons inspectors and wanted to inspect the base. A peace activist told SchNEWS, "We tied ropes to the top of the front gate and started pulling on them and shaking the gate. To everyone's surprise, including the cops, it collapsed on one side and swung open after a few minutes. There was a pause while everyone on the outside watched the horrified expressions on the faces of the police on the other side and then everyone rushed in." While being part of a huge crowd on the streets is an important show of dissent, "direct action allows us to slow down or stop the war machine" as one protestor told SchNEWS, "The best thing was that it was cool to see different types of people working together and not letting each other get beaten up by the police and fighting back." www.gwi.org.uk

* Since last Friday Italian protesters have been stopping and delaying US army "trains of death" (weapons, vehicles and personnel) http://italy.indymedia.org/ (See 'Trainstopping')

* Belgian cops took several hours freeing/arresting 11 Activists who chained themselves to transport trains heading to the port in Antwerp where military equipment is on its way to Turkey and the Gulf. (See 'Trainstopping'.)

* Rolls Royce, Derby producers of nuclear fuel components for Trident missiles was closed for a day last week after activists chained themselves to the gates 0796 003003

* 5 scientists in Antarctica made a banner and held a demo against the war on Iraq, which goes to show how global the anti-war movement has become!

BAe Glascoed Inspected

'Civilian weapons inspectors' visited the BAE Systems munitions factory in Glascoed, Wales on March 1st. Using a rope-ladder seven inspectors entered the premises, and got up to some interesting hi-jinks: two managed to penetrate to the centre of the site before locking-on to doors. One managed to avoid detection for an hour, running around the complex which makes weaponry such as bullets and depleted uranium bombs. After being evicted, holes were cut in the fence and the inspection continued - until the security got aggressive and an inspector was arrested. But back at Abergavenny police station BAE decided not to press charges – they don't want the bad publicity. The lesson is – these companies are scared to prosecute because they know they have something to hide. This protest was part of a campaign by Campaign Against Arms Trade, which is planning to protest at 40 BAE sites throughout the year. 020 7281 0297 www.caat.org.uk

KISS MY ESSO

The looming war in Iraq has nothing to do with oil. Or so Bush Jnr sponsored by the oil industry would try to have us believe. But, according to City analysts Deutsche Bank, the oil corporation Esso exert a "huge political weight" over Bush and "may find itself in pole position in a changed-regime Iraq."

Making this link Greenpeace shut down 119 Esso petrol stations on Monday by locking petrol pumps together and removing handles from electricity switches. Esso's head office was also shut down when a container blocked the entrance. Greenpeace have published a report showing how oil is fuelling the drive to war and the role Esso has played.

More info: Greenpeace UK: 020 7865 8255 www.greenpeace.org.uk

There'll be more action against the War-Oil-Climate Change cabal with a Kyoto March - 2 Years after Bush dumped the Kyoto agreement. It leaves on 20th March 7am from the Esso HQ in Leatherhead for a 20 mile walk to the US Embassy. But you can meet it at a Rally at the Imperial War Museum, 3.30pm and an End of the World Party, 5.30pm at the US Embassy, Grosvenor Square, London. 020 88553327 www.campaignagainstclimatechange .net

Tony Blair's Best Pals, BP

will be welcomed to their Annual General Meeting by a Carnival Against Oil Wars and Climate Chaos on the 24th April at the Royal Festival Hall, South Bank, London. London @risingtide.org.uk www.burningplanet.net

* Air pollution in the UK kills 10 times more people than road accidents every year. 24,000 deaths are caused by "peak" air pollution episodes. Another 4,000 lung cancer deaths a year are caused by air pollution, and an increase in heart diseases. National Society for Clean Air 01273-878770 www.nsca.org.uk

* March 17th – 22nd: **Towards Car-Free Cities III**, Prague, Czech Republic. A conference "promoting alternatives to car dependence and car culture." If you want to go see www.carbusters.org/conference

* This week the Government unveiled its Energy White Paper, which has produced a lot of hot air even before it's chucked on the fire. The Government announced it wants to

Greenpeace blockade the entrance to Esso's UK headquarters in Surrey. 24th February. Pic: Greenpeace/Cobbing

cut emissions of carbon dioxide by 60% by 2050. But they haven't said how this would be achieved and the target of producing 20% of energy from renewable sources energy by 2020 is now an "aspiration"! And while claiming no more nuclear power stations will be built in the near future they haven't ruled it out as a long term option.

Positive SchNEWS

The award winning community organisation the Arts Factory have submitted a planning application to develop a wind farm close to their Rhondda base. The eight turbine wind farm will generate enough electricity to meet the needs of over 6000 households (20% in the Rhondda) and over 3300 local people have signed a petition in support of the project.

The Power Factory will provide a long term income to the Arts Factory, providing jobs for at least 20 people, not just greasing the turbines, but jobs providing desperately needed services in the community, such as nursery, community and youth workers.

There will be a series of road shows at community events in Rhondda to promote the project.

More info: The Arts Factory - 01443 757954 www.artsfactory.co.uk

Fleshing out the arguments against war, Santiago, Chile, March 1st.

SchNEWS in brief

Nestlé, the company who tell mums in the third world that powered milk formula is better for kids than breast milk, have scrapped plans to sponsor a new teenage book prize after seven leading writers said that they "do not wish to be associated" with Nestlés prize "in any way". Info on the worlds longest consumer boycott - Baby Milk Action 01223 464420 www.babymilkaction.org ** The trial of the 13 asylum seekers facing charges relating to the fire at **Yarlswood Detention Centre** in February last year, starts 23rd April. Most of the defendants have been released on bail but are denied the right to work and benefits. The Justice for Yarlswood Campaign are trying to raise funds to get them to the trial in Bedford and provide them with accommodation (otherwise they will be put up in Wormwood Scrubs!).Cheques payable to 'Stop Arbitrary Detentions At Yarl's Wood', marked 'Defendants' Trial Support' on the back. Campaign For Justice In The Yarl's Wood Trial, PO Box 304, Bedford, MK42 9WX 07786-517379, ginn_emma@hotmail.com ** Home secretary **David Blunkett** whose asylum policies are leaving people in the UK destitute, while his government threatens to bomb countries and create more refugees is visiting the Marriot Hotel, College Green, Bristol, next Thurs (6th). A demo has been organised meet 6.30pm ** Last week Spanish cops raided the offices of **Egunkaria**, the only exclusively Basque newspaper, and arrested its editor and nine senior staff under anti-terror laws. The Judge claimed the paper had links to the Basque separatist organisation ETA and imprisoned five and fined the others at least £8,000 www.euskalinfo.org.uk ** If you're interested in organising another **MayDay** event this year there's a meeting this Sunday (2nd) 11am onwards (lunch provided) @LARC, 62 Fieldgate Street, London E1 (Whitechapel tube)londonmayday@yahoo.co.uk www.ourmayday.org.uk

www.takver.com

Kids teaching us a lesson - Books Not Bombs, Melbourne, March 5th.

Books Not Bombs

Tens of thousands of schoolkids bunked off school for the day in a nation-wide anti-war protest across Australia on March 5th.

In Melbourne, 5,000 rallied outside the State Library in a carnival atmosphere before marching to Parliament House. Many of the students were present in school uniform with home made banners and placards opposing war. 10,000 marched in Sydney – which saw three arrests and reports of police harassment of some arab schoolboys on a train after the demo - giving them a first taste of 'democracy' as we practise it. Also around the country 7,000 bunked off in Adelaide, 2,000 wagged in Perth marching on the US Embassy, 1,000 played hooky in Canberra, 700 skived in Brisbane, 200 truanted in Albury-Wodonga and hundreds more chose peace not school in Hobart, Darwin, Launceston, Newcastle, and other regional centres. www.indymedia.org.au (See also articles later in the book about anti-war schoolkids.)

Whadda we want? - NO RAIN - When do we want it? EVERY DAY. 15,000 come out in wet weather for an anti-war march in Manchester on Saturday March the 8th. On the same day a similar event was held in Sheffield.

WAR BRIEFS

A Piece of Peace, benefit night for a peace compilation CD this Saturday, 7pm, Ray Tindle Centre, Upper Gardener Street, Brighton £4. ** **Anti-war picket of Labour party conference** this Saturday outside Floral Hall, Southport, Merseyside. 9-11am 0151 708 7764 merseyside@stopwar.org.uk ** **Cycle for Peace** this Saturday 11:30am at the gates of Abney Park cemetery, Stamford Hill, London N16 07787 523907 hstwc@hotmail.com ** Performance of the play **"Lysistrata"**, an Ancient Greek comedy of a women's "sex strike" in order to stop their menfolk from going to war. 10.30am, Parliament Square, London and 800 other readings in 42 countries. More readings are planned during the day, with a rehearsed reading at Pleasance Theatre, Caledonian Road, 7.30pm. £5 entry – proceeds to the War Child charity. www.lysistrataproject.com

** The **small peace camp outside Fylindales** in Yorkshire are looking for more people. 01274 730795 or neil@yorkshirecnd.org.uk ** **Peace camp** on the grass of the Peace Gardens near the Town Hall, **Manchester**, March 8th after the anti war demo in the City. 0161 881 0450 ros_arnold@hotmail.com ** **Stop the warmongers.** Demonstration at the Jane's Defence Weekly conference 10th March, Royal Institute of International Affairs, Chatham House, 10 St James Street, London SW1 8am, bring whistles, banners, flags, drums etc. www.disobedience.org.uk ** **Human shields** in Iraq have now taken up their positions to defend important civilian infrastructures. Donations are urgently needed send cheque/money order made out to Human Shield Action c/o Christine Strickland, 97, Retford Road, Romford, UK, RM3 9ND Info 0207 572 1125 ** **Tell Cherie Blair: No War!** email her at cheriebooth@matrixlaw.co.uk

You Asda Be Kidding

Old Kent Road already has three supermarkets, but no decent community facilities. So guess what is gonna be built? Yep, a Wal-Mart/ASDA superstore! Traffic, pollution and respiratory disease are at an all time high along this stretch of road, which also, ironically, has the lowest car ownership in London. The Ossory Road Yard has been squatted since September as a community space with children's weekends, discussion groups, workshops and an anti-war forum. They want to build a kid's adventure playground, cultivate the land and create a genuinely community-run space. They have been served an eviction notice and expect bailiffs to arrive some time in March.

Ossory Road Social Centre: 07769 791387 ossoryrd@breathe.com

To read 'Nine reasons why not to shop at Asda' see www.corporatewatch.org.uk/news/resist_asda.htm

...and finally...

You know the scenario – soldiers leaving to go off to war being interviewed by the media and saying things like "It's a job we have to do" or "We're professional people and we're going to fight for our country". Well when 26 reservists – from all walks of civilian life – were leaving for the Gulf from the Territorial Army base in Dundee the media were invited along, but this time instead of smiling for the cameras and saying it was their patriotic duty to go and fight they angrily condemned the stance taken by the Bush / Blair axis.

Gary McIntosh, a medic who had been called up, became tearful when saying goodbye to his three–year-old daughter. "How do I say 'Daddy's got to go away, I don't know when I'll be back", he said. "I don't understand why we have to go. This is about Bush wanting to finish off what his father started and us Brits are getting dragged into it because of Blair. I don't really see why I have to be parted from my family for that." All highly embarrassing for their commanding officers.

Disclaimer
SchNEWS warns all readers having visions to stop masturbating for peace. (see SchNEWS 392) Honest.

Inside SchNEWS

Paul Kelleher, the man who knocked the head off a statue of former PM Margaret Thatcher as a protest against the ills of the world's political system, has been jailed for three months. On the day of the attack Mr Kelleher arranged a babysitter for his son and bought a cricket bat. He smuggled the bat into the Guildhall under his coat, but when he hit the statue the bat "pinged off". So he picked up a metal crowd barrier and finished the job. He then waited for the cops to turn up and when he was being arrested told them he thought the statue "looked better this way". The statue (a snip at £150,000) can be repaired for £10,000, but sadly, according to the judge, "will never look the same".

There's an online petition for clemency at: www.petitiononline.com/pkvsmt/petition.html If anyone has his prison address can they tell us, so we can send him SchNEWS each week.

* **Barbara Smedema is in prison for disabling an American com**munications dish at the military airport of Volkel in the Netherlands. The damage has been estimated at 500,000 Euros. Barbara said "We do not have the illusion that we can stop the warmachine in this way but we need to show hope and confidence that the world can be different." Write to: Barbara Smedema, P.I. Ter Peel, Patersweg 4, 5977 NM Evertsoord.

* **Long time peace activist TJ Hart** has been given the maximum possible sentence for cutting a hole in the fence at RAF Fylingdales, North Yorkshire. She'll be banged up for two months, so send letters of support to her at: TJ Hart, HMP Low Newton, Brasside, Durham. DH1 3YA

OK Tony - this next question is worth 100,000 lives...

I can't ask the audience - I'll phone a special friend

WHO WANTS TO BE A MILLIONAIRE ????!

weekly SchNEWS

www.schnews.org.uk

Friday 7th March 2003   Free/Donation   Issue 395

WHO WANTS TO BE A MILLIONAIRE?

"We back democracy all the way. All the way, that is, up to the point where they disagree with us." - Former US senior State Dept. Official

"We want to be nice to people who are nice, and good to the people who are good to us." - Senior State Dept. Official (must be one of Bush's speechwriters).

The US, aided and abetted by the Coalition of Easily Bought Countries most Willing to ignore Public Opinion (that's Britain, Spain and Bulgaria), are working round the clock to weasel the five remaining 'yes' votes needed from fellow UN Security Council members to pass their second resolution.

With the Security Council split down the middle, the heat is being turned up on Mexico, Cameroon, Guinea, Angola, Chile and Pakistan, as the US steps up its Texas-style 'persuasion' techniques with economic aid carrots and big stick trade threats in order to swing the votes their way.

A leaked US National Security Agency memo urged the gathering of information as to the 'negotiating positions', 'alliances' and 'dependencies' of these countries in order to give 'US policy makers an edge in obtaining results favourable to US goals.' The leaders of the six fence-sitting member states have been bombarded with personal phone calls and visits from Bush, Cheney, Blair and their cronies, eager to impress upon them the importance of a 'yes' vote.

The US has already pledged to punish Germany for its 'treachery' by possibly withdrawing troops and military bases and ending all military and industrial co-operation with the country. From here it doesn't sound much like punishment, but such moves would cost the German economy billions of euros. There's talk in the US of punishing the French by renaming french fries Freedom Fries, while Turkey will no longer receive $15 billion in economic aid after its parliament refused to allow the use of Turkish soil as a US base for war. "We don't like the way we were pushed around by the Americans," one Turkish MP said.

Cough Up

So, which way will the six go? And what is on offer to help them decide?

Mexican president Vicente Fox, facing an election next year and aware of massive public anti-war support, has already been visited by the Spanish PM Aznar, US officials Marc Grossman and Kim Holmes, and the Godfather himself, George Bush Snr. Mexico depends on the US to buy 85% of its exports and is desperate to resuscitate agreements surrounding immigration issues. Mexican diplomats have been warned they will 'pay a very heavy price' for non-compliance with US policy on Iraq.

Cameroon and Guinea have no doubt been reminded of the bit in the African Growth and Opportunity Act, under the terms of which both countries receive US aid, that prevents them from engaging "in activities contrary to US national security or foreign policy interests." The Guinean Ambassador to the UN, however, is reported to have said, "We are not going to sell our dignity because we need money or material. Not my country."

Meanwhile, Angolan Ambassador Ismael Gaspar Martins is underplaying the significance of sudden US promises to assist his war-ravaged country: "For a long time now, we have been asking for help to rebuild our country after [27] years of [civil] war. No one is tying the request for support [to the issue of] Iraq, but it is all happening at the same time." Yes, an amazing co-incidence.

While we await the report-back from our undercover SchNEWS operative in Santiago, all we can reveal about Chile is that the country's leaders are gagging for the US Senate to give the 'go-ahead' to a free trade agreement between Chile and the US, who knows a gagging country when they see one.

And finally we come to Pakistan, which already has billions of dollars in the hole, mainly thanks to their support of the US dropping an

Fairford Peace Camp

Who Wants to be a Millionaire cont...

orgasm of bombs on Afghanistan. Pakistan is being rewarded in other ways too, such as being allowed to hold on to their nuclear arsenal without signing the non-proliferation treaty, and probably being allowed to abstain from voting on the second resolution. In the face of growing public anti-war sentiment, Pakistani PM Jamali has said that decisions about Iraq should be left to the Iraqi people and asked his parliament to instead focus on 'domestic interests'. Jamali is scheduled to visit the US later this month, during which time he has been invited to Houston to meet 'businessmen' interested in investing in Pakistan.

Still, at the end of the day, whichever way the vote goes, the US are unlikely to back down from attacking Iraq. British Home Secretary Jack Straw's justification for war is that we must all do what America says because otherwise, in the future, we'll er...have to do what America says. Not that he should worry, as White House spokesman Ari Fleischer pointed out, "The vote is desirable. It is not necessary."

PEACENICKED

** As SchNEWS goes to press we have had multiple reports that the B-52's at Fairford are being armed as we type. **

As US B-52 bombers begin arriving at the Fairford airbase in Gloucestershire, security at the base is being stepped up. USAF security police have now tried to recruit plane spotters in their fight against evil peaceniks. The base has put out a memo asking for spotters to contact them if they see any protesters in the area. But as veteran peace campaigner Lindis Percy proved, security is still very lax once you get inside the base. After scaling the fences on Monday, Lindis managed to spend two hours roaming around the base and two hours under the wing of a B-52 before being arrested for criminal damage. If you'd like to help keep the USAF Security police busy, call them on 07740 609705 or 07876 148170.

Protesters are now maintaining a 24 hr peace watch at Gate 10 of the Fairford airbase, 5 minutes away from the permanent peace camp. More people are needed to stay at the camp, which is now located behind the very welcoming pub in Kempsford village.

There's also a big demo on the 22nd March (meet noon at the junction of High St/Park St., Fairford) Camp mobiles 07905 131020 or 07947 614941 www.gwi.org.uk

* This weekend (8th & 9th) **Picnic for Peace**, meet High St/Park St., Fairford Village, noon, for a walk to Gate 10 to support the peace watch vigil.

* Transport to the demo on the 22nd is being organised from across the country: www.cynatech.co.uk/gwi//Fairford-travel.htm. Tickets for coaches from Brighton available from Community Base reception, Queens Road, and the Cowley Club, London Road £8/6

* **Lindis Percy and Anni Rainbow** are at Harrogate Magistrates' Court next Monday (10th) 10am for a five day court case after being nicked for 'aggravated trespass' at Menwith Hill spy station. Support appreciated 01943 466405 www.caab.org.uk

* **Police have begun to use Section 60 powers to stop and search protesters at Fairford**. A Section 60 gives uniformed police the power to cordon a group of people, search for supposed weapons, and confiscate items that conceal your identity (masks, balaclavas, etc.) If you are stopped under s60, ask who authorised it and what locality it covers. You DO NOT have to give the police your name and address or answer any other questions. If asked anything, it's always advisable to answer NO COMMENT to all questions. They cannot use force to take your photo. And if they do search you (which unfortunately s60 gives them the power to do), ask the officer for their name, number and station. If they don't give it to you, the search will be illegal. Full details: www.wombles.org.uk/files/section60.php

SchNEWS in brief

Next week (12th) is the start of the **Human Rights Watch** film festival at the Ritzy Cinema, Brixton, London. Films include the UK premiere of 'Women in Black', which follows a group of women as they travel to the West Bank to form a human shield around Palestinian civilians. Showings on the 15th,16th and 19th. Full listing www.hrw.org/iff or call the Ritzy on 0207 733 2229 ** **London No Borders video night** - videos about the Strasbourg No Border camp, the Publix Theatre Caravan, and video hacktivism against the Schengen Information System. At LARC, 62 Fieldgate St., London E1. Tue 18th, 7.30pm. info@londonarc.org ** **War on Want's Annual Conference**, next Sat (15) speakers include Mary Robinson and Jeremy Hardy. University of Westminster, New Cavendish, London W1. Bookings 020 762011111 www.waronwant.org ** Not content with getting away with killing 20,000 people in the world's biggest chemical disaster, **Union Carbide** (formerly Dow Chemicals) is now suing protesters who shut down their factory last year on the 18th anniversary of the disaster. The company is looking for compensation of $10,000 for the loss of two hours work. ** There are a number of **court cases coming up soon for people who've been caught at GM actions**. Defendants are asking for support AND help with any costs. The dates are 12 March at Warrington Magistrates Court, Lancashire, Info 07762 098393. 18 March at Cupar Sheriff Court in Fife, 01382 543000, and 31 March-3 April at Chester Crown Court. Info on any of these from GEN 0845 456 9327 ** Events happening for **International Women's day** this Saturday (8) include an anti-war march in London. Meet 11.30am, Parliament Square. There will also be a demo in Camden against the notorious strip club, The Spearmint Rhino. Meet outside Spearmint Rhino, 161 Tottenham Court Road (nearest Tube: Warren Street) at noon. 0207 8407113 www.eaves.ik.com In Ireland, there will be an anti-war demo at Shannon airport outside of Dublin. Meet 2:30pm. Contact: maggie_ronayne@hotmail.com. In Glasgow, there's a three day Frock On! festival chock full of feminism, anarchism, and punk rock! 078 1294 3410 www.geocities.com/frock_on/index.html

FAT GATS

Last week GATS fat-cats were gutted when their most top-secret documents got leaked and published on the web (nice one Polaris Institute). The papers instantly exposed the true nature of the EU's GATS agenda (see SchNEWS 286) for the next negotiating round: Nothing less than a global takeover of essential services (most notably water) by EU-based transnationals.

The EU - with the full co-operation of the UK government (who have repeatedly given reassurances that water would be excluded from World Trade Organisation agreements) - is targeting state and not-for-profit service provision in the developing world as its new golden goose.

The EU has sent 'requests' to 109 (mostly developing) WTO member countries demanding trade access to water, energy, transport, telecommunications and news services. In some cases, they are targeting countries where European companies have already been booted out by government or public protest.

Each of the 109 'requests' is a strictly classified document with a warning attached: "Member States are requested to ensure that this text is not made publicly available and is treated as a restricted document." The general public was never supposed to know that public services were being traded away in secret negotiations until all the deals had been cut. The deadline for compliance with the requests- sorry, agreements - is 31st March 2003. GATS-watch are organising a national day of action on 13th March. To find out what's happening in your area 0800 328 2153 gatswatch.org.uk. Read the leaked documents: www.polarisinstitute.org

War Briefs

17-23 March has been declared a **week of direct action against the war**. Starting with a national die-in on 17th (www.j-n-v.org, 0845 458 2564) and finishing with national demos at Menwith and Fairford airbases on 22nd - Check out what's going on around the country - www.schnews.org.uk/stopwar/events.htm ** **Reclaim the Bases** – Direct action at a number of military bases on the weekend of 5–6 April, www.reclaimthebases.org.uk ** On Saturday a group of **'civilian weapons inspectors' sprung a surprise visit on a BAE Systems munitions factory** in Glascoed, Wales, which produces everything from bullets to depleted uranium shells. The protest was part of a campaign by Campaign Against Arms Trade, which is planning to protest at 40 BAE sites throughout the year. 020 7281 0297 www.caat.org.uk ** **150 people were arrested near Antrewepen, Belgium** last Saturday before they had even done anything. They were arrested under a new zero tolerance policy dreamt up to prevent people blocking trains taking American weapons to the port of Antrewepen. www.indymedia.org (see 'Trainstopping' article)** **Witnesses and video evidence needed for two arrests at Brighton antiwar demos**. Did you see someone in an orange fluoro jacket getting nicked on the 14th Feb demo at about 5pm, Western Road, or the 1st March demo at 4.30pm? Contact Teresa Blades at Kelly's Solicitors 01273 608311 ** **Peace marches next Saturday** (15th): **Lewes**, meet at County Hall, 10.30am 01273 473912 ** **Leeds**, 12 noon, Leeds Town Hall Art Gallery 0773 488 2567 mickdearuk@yahoo.co.uk ** **York**, 12 noon Clifford's Tower, City Centre www.yorkagainstthewar.org.uk ** **Hertford**, 11am Railway St, hertfordantiwaraction@yahoo.com ** **Portsmouth** 2 pm outside St Mary's Church - corner of Fratton Rd & St Mary's Rd, then to the naval dockyard. 02392 818849 grassroots@loft33.freeserve.co.uk ** Foil the Base at Star Peace Camp **Fylingdales**. A169, North Yorkshire Moors, bring foil, foil balloons, etc. 01287 660067 http://come.to/somewhere-real

SCHOOL'S OUT FOREVER

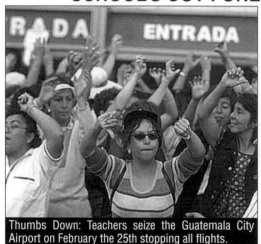

Thumbs Down: Teachers seize the Guatemala City Airport on February the 25th stopping all flights.

Guatemala's teachers have been out on strike since January 18th. Fed up with being ignored and told by the government that all 80,000 of them would be sacked if they didn't return to work, the teachers decided to turn to direct action. Government buildings (including the Ministry of Education) were occupied, major highways and border crossings were brought to a halt by Reclaim the Streets style protests, with the additional tactics of blockades of burning tyres, busses, trees and building material. The teachers are demanding more pay and more money for the education system.

In late Februry the Guatemala City Airport was paralyzed by protesting teachers, with all flights from the US being cancelled for days. As this went on shipping ports were also closed, and teachers seized a pumping station at Guatemala's only pipeline, stopping the French owned pipeline from pumping it's usual 25,000 barrels a day up to the United States of gas-guzzling vehicles.

The proportion of the budget that the Guatemalan government spends on education is tiny compared to most countries in Latin America. Even those serial misers, the International Monetary Fund, have told the government to increase its budgets for education and health! www.prensalibre.com (Spanish)

* Thousands of children in the UK bunked off school to join student protests against the war on Wednesday. Over a hundred children gathered outside Downing Street, whilst similar protests happened all over the world. One said, "Tony Blair obviously does not think. Iraqi children are too young to be bombed, so how can we be too young to protest?"

Police "Intelligence"

On Wednesday, a big pile of steaming horse manure was dumped on the steps of Neo-Labour's party offices in London to symbolise the US/UK 2nd resolution for the Iraq war. As one protester said, 'I'll be surprised if anybody notices, as it always smells of shit around the Labour Party'. Next, the cheeky muck spreaders poured fake blood over the steps of the QE2 Conference Centre, where there was a meeting of the Defence Equipment Services Organisation, (those nasty people who promote arms sales abroad).

Two people were arrested for criminal damage, but the paranoid police (who didn't get the joke) were only interested to know if the 'blood' was toxic! And as if any more proof were needed that the police can't tell their arse from their elbow... SchNEWS has learned of a man who, by sending a packet of rice to Jack Straw, managed to cause a major terror scare in the Foreign Secretary's office. The office had to be closed for three hours until special police intelligence was brought in to work out the difference between a grain of rice and the nerve toxin, ricin!

...and finally...

The popular comic "Dandy" was recently cleared from the shelves at Birmingham International Airport because it posed a menacing terrorist threat! The most recent issue of the magazine was deemed unacceptable because of a free toy gun that was being given away on the cover. The plastic toy, which punches out a clenched fist, was attached to thousands of copies of that week's issue, leading the airport's expert security personnel to fear it might be used to hijack a plane. A spokesman for the magazine's publishers said, "It might be a bit irritating if a kid fired it at your head over and over, but I don't think a terrorist would get very far if he tried to hijack a plane with a free toy from Dandy."

March 12th: Turkey sends in soldiers to defend the port in Iskenderun from protesters as the U.S. military use the port to unload munitions as it prepares to invade Iraq.

Disclaimer
SchNEWS warns all squeeze and tease politicians to grease the palm first. Honest

Bomb Stopping - just do it.

(if we did, anyone can...)

THIS IS JO

SHE'S BEEN DOING SANCTIONS BREAKING STUFF IN IRAQ

SHE'S THERE NOW * SHE WRITES A DIARY & TELLS US WHAT SHE SEES

* 23.3.03

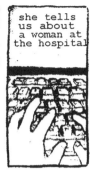

she tells us about a woman at the hospital

We are Farmers we are Farmers!

THIS IS A B52 BOMBER.

AROUND 14 FLY FROM US AIRFORCE BASE FAIRFORD. IN GLOUCESTERSHIRE. THEY TAKE CRUISE MISILES AND THE UNGUIDED DUMB BOMBS, AND CARPET BOMB IRAQ. WHERE SHE TAKES HER MUTILATED CHILD TO HOSPITAL.

ON THE TELLY THEY SHOW A CONVOY OF DUMB BOMBS BEING TAKEN FROM WELFORD ARMS STORE, TO FAIRFORD. TO GO ON THE PLANES, THAT GO TO IRAQ.

SO WE MAKE A PLAN...

WE BUMP INTO A GROUP OF FRIENDS AT THE FAIRFORD RALLY

WHO HAVE THE SAME IDEA. NOW WE ARE 10.

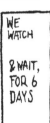

WE WATCH

& WAIT, FOR 6 DAYS

AHHHA. BRING IT ON! BRING IT ON!

BRRING

THEY'RE HERE. 8 LORRIES 3 OUTRIDERS MOTORBIKES..

CAN I GO TO THE LOO ?

THEY DON'T TAKE THE ROUTE WE EXPECT. WE HAVE TO IMPROVISE

WE REACH THE JUNCTION JUST AS THEY'RE PASSING

AMBUKA DRIVES..

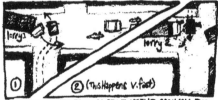

lorry 1

lorry 2

① ② (This Happens v. fast)

STRAIGHT INTO THE MIDDLE OF THE CONVOY. BUT THE ROAD'S TOO WIDE TO BLOCK WITH THE CAR AS WE PLANNED

I CAN'T FIND THE KEY! IT'S FALLEN OUT!

TRYING TO

THEY'RE AT THE FRONT

NO, THEY'RE AT THE BACK

THE OTHER LOT LAY DOWN AT THE BACK TO STOP THE CONVOY REVERSING, WHICH CONFUSES THE COPS...

CHAINED TOGETHER INSIDE

NAT NEARLY MANAGES TO USE A BIKE D'LOCK TO ATTATCH HERSELF TO THE CAR DOOR.

BEING DRAGGED OFF BY THE POLICE

ROAD IN ABOUT 6 MINS.

THE COPS SEARCH THE CAR, SNAP THE SIM CARD & STEAL THE KEYS

THEY THREATEN TO ARREST US. TAKE OUR DETAILS AND THEN - JUST WALK AWAY

PRETTY, ISN'T IT?

& SO DO WE...

WHICH WAS SURPRISING -

THEY DIDN'T NICK US BECAUSE THEY DON'T WANT PEOPLE TO KNOW IT'S POSSIBLE TO STOP THESE LORRIES. THE CURRENT LEVELS OF BOMBING CAN'T CONTINUE WITHOUT THEM. WITH MORE OF US WE COULD HAVE STOPPED THE CONVOY.

TO BE CONTINUED...

Cartoon strip: Snook

thanks www.bristle.org.uk

New Delhi March 9th

SOUTHERN DISCOMFORT

March 9th: American and British forces are massing in the Middle East, and war is looking inevitable. For the first time, protests outside Europe, North America and Australasia are beginning to outnumber those in the 'West'.

The anti-war build-up intensifies in the countries of the Middle East – many of which are already watching Iraqis stream over their borders to escape the impending war, seeking safety alongside Palestinians in the refugee camps.

Here are some of the larger and more dramatic anti-war demonstrations from late February onwards:

* On February 24th around 100,000 marched in the **Moroccan** capital of **Rabat**, then on March 9th 160,000 marched in the streets of **Casablanca**. Demonstrators were attacked by police, leaving many injured, 60 arrested and nine of the organisers in detention.

* In **Rawalpindi, Pakistan**, some 200,000 people came out on March 9th - about four times as many as the previous week in **Karachi**.

* 50,000 people demonstrated in **New Delhi, India**.

* In **Egypt**, around this time, the government shifted from repressing protests to trying to co-opt them. When protests were organised there at the end of 2002 the organisers had been arrested and tortured. Yet on March 2nd, a rally organised by opposition parties drew more than 100,000. Then on March 5th, the President's National Democratic Party called a protest and 500,000 people came out. Ashraf Al Bayoumi, a founding member of the Popular Committee to Oppose US Aggression in Iraq, predicted that the Egyptian government could channel public anger into carefully controlled forums "for a little while" but that things were very volatile and "one scene on television could spark it all."

* The Turkish state's confrontation with its fiercely anti-war population intensified. The Pentagon continued to deploy troops in **Turkey**, in spite of a parliamentary vote on March 1st that refused to authorise it. The vote was taken as 100,000 people demonstrated outside the parliament building in **Ankara**.

* On February 28th an angry demonstration kicked off in **Bahrain** – headquarters of the US Navy's Fifth Fleet and a key ally in the region. 4,000 marched from a Shi'ite mosque to the UN Office in the capital of **Manama**, burning US flags and trampling Israeli flags on the way.

* The same day saw 7,000 march in the **Yemeni** capital of **Sanaa**.

* In **Indonesia**'s second-largest city, **Surabaya**, some 800,000 people gathered to protest on March 9th.

STOP THE WAR : STOP THE CITY!

WE ARE THE CITY   WE CAN   SHUT IT DOWN!

MEET 5.30PM : CHURCHILL SQUARE : DAY AFTER WAR IS DECLARED ON IRAQ

BRING POTS AND PANS TO BANG : LETS MAKE SOME NOISE!

PHONE FOR CONFIRMATION
01273 298192
brightonagainstwar@hotmail.com

WAKE UP! WAKE UP! IT'S YER RIFF-RAF...

Is that a weapon of mass destruction in your lunch box or are you just pleased to see me?

weekly SchNEWS

www.schnews.org.uk

Friday 14th March 2003   Free/Donation   Issue 396

RUNWAY TERROR

Last Saturday the whole of Gloucestershire and Wiltshire were put on high alert and the police were given powers for 28 days under Section 44 of the Terrorism Act 2000 to stop and search anyone – without even needing to make up an excuse to do so.

SchNEWS has learnt that in Fairford, Gloucestershire, planes carrying weapons of mass destruction are being prepared for use on civilians. People from all over the country have been heading there to try and stop this happening – these very same people who are trying to stop people being killed are being treated like terrorists!

According to Liberty, this is the first time Section 44 has been used and the first lucky recipients were… people at a Picnic for Peace at Fairford! Brandishing his big Section 60 Criminal Justice Act (1994) to look for weapons, one copper demanded to search someone's lunchbox. The bemused protestor told SchNEWS, "They opened up the sandwiches to see what was in them - no razor blades, but some rather tasty houmous and vegan pate." Funny that! No weapons of mass destruction in his sandwich, but quite a few B-52's across the razor wire in the airbase, weapons which will take part in the "Shock and Awe" tactic bombing of Bagdhad, causing massive and widespread destruction "like the nuclear weapons at Hiroshima, not taking days or weeks, but minutes."

DE-FENCE SITTING

While the police are keen to know what peaceniks at Fairford are eating this time of year, they seem less keen to act when US military personnel forcibly evict and intimidate residents of the peace camp.

On Monday afternoon US soldiers ripped down banners on the fence and started constructing an extension to the Gate 10 perimeter fence on Gloucestershire County Council Land without planning permission, forcing the peace camp to move a few feet around the corner. The police just looked on and did nothing. However the camp is getting lots of support from locals, with one camp resident, Jill Chadwick, commenting, "In a way I'm surprised at the amount of support, given my experience at Greenham Common and the vigilante attacks we experienced there."

* The Peace camp and bomber watch need more support, people, tarps,water and a chemical toilet if anyone has one. 07754064146 or 07736964653.

* An Oxford student told SchNEWS about getting into Fairford "If lazy students like me and my mates who spend most of our time getting drunk can get in, anyone can. And if lots do we can stop the planes." Last Saturday about 20 people got onto the runway.

* Disobedience are holding a series of workshops in Hackney, London this Saturday (15) in preparation for the big day of action at Fairford. Workshops will include legal advice and group self-defence. For details email: disobedience@riseup.net
** Gathering of Grannies at Fairford on Monday (17) 11am main gate. For info on women's actions: tabitha@gwi.org.uk ** Next Saturday (22nd) is the Fairford Free Festival with Rinky-Dink and Lardy-Dar Cycle Powered Sound Systems for The Party At The End Of The Runway. SchNEWS hopes that The Collateral Damage Orchestra and

Friendly Fire Quartet will also be there. This is followed by a party at the Axe & Compass Pub, Kempsford 8pm - late. Free camping in the pub garden/peace camp.

* If you've been searched on spurious grounds, unlawfully arrested, detained without reason, or even assaulted at Fairford, get in touch with Berkshire Citizens Inspection Agency. They can't offer legal advice, but are collating all incidents of harassment. berkshirecia@hotmail.com

*If you are going to demos it may be worth getting clued up about your rights if you get arrested, check out www.activistslegalproject.org.uk

* Help is needed to keep an eye on RAF Welford, near Newbury in Berkshire, one of the USAF's biggest munitions dumps in Europe. The base stores bombs for use at RAF Fairford. Contact Berkshire CIA, 0118 966 8328, or berkshirecia@hotmail.com

* An anti-war protestor in Canterbury was arrested under the Terrorism Act - for throwing an egg at Tony Blair. He was charged under Section 5 of the Public Order Act, which means the crown has to prove via witness state ments that he caused distress. He's hoping to get a statement from Tony Blair.

@NTI-COPYRIGHT - INFORMATION FOR ACTION   Produced in Brighton since 1994

WAR BRIEFS

Nine people cut their way into American airbase "RAF" Lakenheath last week, then cycled around the base to disrupt preparations for war against Iraq. ** **Celebration of Iraqi culture**, Sat 15th - music and speakers, St Columba's Church Hall, Chantry Road, Moseley, B'ham. 7.30-10pm Bring food or £2.50. ** **Remembering Anfal & Halabja public meeting**, Mon 17th Grand Committee Room, Houses of Parliament, Westminster 7pm. Kurdistan National Congress 020 7250 1315 knklondon@gn.apc.org ** 800,000 people gathered to pray for peace in Indonesia's second-largest city, **Surabaya**, last weekend. ** **The SQUALL website has new anti-war related stuff** that's worth a look. Check out human shield Jo Wilding's excellent dispatches from Bagdhad and the whole 1997 statement from New American Century, (right wing US think tank, many of whom have since become key members of the Bush administration) advocating a war on Iraq as a step towards US world domination. www.squall.co.uk ** Mon 17th starts a **week of non-violent actions** against the war. Die-ins in Southampton (02380 550159), Oxford 01865 794504, London 0845 458 2564, Birmingham sarahteve rsham@yahoo.co.uk and Hastings andreaneedham@onetel.net.uk ** Tues 18th **Hastings Against War** meeting 7.30, Electric Cinema, Old Town ** Use the media to get your anti-war message across: **'Activists' guide to exploiting the media'** from ARROW, 5 Caledonian Road, London N1 9DX £1.50 or online at www.antenna.nl/eyfa/ resources/media.htm ** On 26 Feb, protestors against war on Iraq barraged the White House and Senate offices with tens of thousands of phone, fax and e-mail messages as part of a **"virtual protest march."** New EU hacker laws could make protests like this a crime, removing all distinction between online protestors, hackers, spreaders of computer viruses and terrorists. ** **Brighton Demo against the war, meet 5.30pm, 21st Mar, Churchill Square.**

240

---

* Saturday March 22 12 noon: **National demo against USAF Fairford.** Assemble Fairford Church, Fairford, Gloucestershire. Coaches from all over the country. Info, map of Fairford, transport contacts: www.gwi.org.uk, or CND 020 7700 2393. Transport from **Brighton** – tickets from The Cowley Club, London Road. From **London:** Euston 9am £10/£5. To book a seat 07817 061183 fairfordcoachlondon@ hotmail.com.
* For those up north, there's a **Foil the Base demo**, midday March 22 - main gate of Menwith Hill, North Yorkshire. Menwith is the "brains" of the US military in Europe. Bring foil kites, balloons, puppets etc. to disrupt US Military satellite signals. www.now-peace.org.uk

WIZKIDS OF OZ

The Australian Department of Defence has decided to withdraw advertising from all student media in Australia because of an "adbust" by a student newspaper. The Defence Department had been repeatedly requesting advertising space in the magazine, who kept on saying no and got a bit tired of repeating themselves and decided to run the following ad instead:

"Why settle for an ordinary office job when you could have an extraordinary and challenging career as a pawn in the power games of politicians? Not only will you get to take orders from arrogant pricks with buzz-cuts and ego-complexes, but on special occasions you'll get the chance to repress your moral integrity and accept orders to bomb the shit out of dark-skinned, teatowel-wearing foreigners. Officer positions are open in many specialised fields from engineering and logistics through to carpet-bombing and cannon fodder. You will receive over $44,700 per annum upon completion of initial training, which should just about cover treatment for Post Traumatic Stress Disorder and Gulf War Syndrome..."

SchNEWS in brief

RADIO 4A Brighton's Shambolic Pirate Radio is back this weekend with diverse sounds, political commentary, comedy and news. 101.4 FM and webcast www.radio4a.org.uk ** Sunday 16th picket the **Ideal Homes Exhibition**, sponsored by the Daily Mail, who have recently been stepping up their campaign of hate against refugees and asylum seekers. 12-2 pm, Earls Court, London. 01273-540717 ** **SEASoN alternative National Science Week**. 12-5pm, Sunday 22nd on the Commons, Church Road, Tunbridge Wells. It's not too late to register for a stall at the event. 01892 863941 http://geocities.com/ seasonscience ** **No money for new oil** – stop UK government support for the **Baku oil pipeline**. Demo Tues 25th. Meet 11.45am, Crown Place, London EC2. 020 7566 1673 www.baku.org.uk ** **Blatant Incitement Project** - day of sharing facilitation and groupwork skills and experiences. 24th March, 10am-5pm, Hebden Bridge, West Yorkshire. Free. Vegan food £3 01524 383012 dowhatyouretol d@breakthelaw.co.uk ** The **A-Infos** website contains a massive directory of anarchist organizations around the world. www.ainfos.ca/ org/Anarchist_Organizations.html ** **'Drowned Out'** film about an Indian family resolving to stay at home and drown rather than make way for the Narmada dam. March 27th, 9.30pm, The Other Cinema, 11 Rupert Street, London W1. 020 7437 0757 £5/4 ** **SchWoops**. The screening of 'Women in Black' on Saturday is at the Pheonix Theatre, East Finchley, NOT the Ritzy, Brixton. 6.30pm www.hrw.org/iff

---

WWC Out of the Closet

Sinking to new depths of greed and corruption, the Transnational Corporations (TNCs) are now getting all wet about water. Water's running out all over the planet (last week a UN report estimated that some areas may be bone dry as early as 2025) and could soon be a more valuable commodity than oil.

Under the guise of trying to sort out the global water crisis, the 3rd triennial World Water Forum (WWF) will take place in Kyoto, Japan, March 16th-23rd. Only problem is that this international debate on the subject will be run by the World Water Council (WWC), a think-tank created in 1996 by the World Bank and some of the world's largest Transnational Water Corporations. You get the picture?

Top of the agenda, naturally, is privatising the world's water supplies - especially in the developing world. When they last met in 2000, the WWF came up with a pro-privatisation manifesto entitled "World Water Vision" which, the WWF claimed, reflected the global consensus on solutions to the water crisis. Of course it did nothing of the sort—there was of course no grassroots representation at the 2000 meeting (especially from the developing world) and the whole conference was stridently opposed by activist groups (who set up their own alternative conference). Despite its own legitimacy being deeply questioned, the WWF say the time for debate is over. This 3rd conference in Kyoto will not be about "if" but about "how" to force privatisation on unwitting or unwilling populations whose governments have been bought or coerced by the World Bank.

* To find out more about the WWF and protest plans: ASEED Japan - www.aseed.org

So just what are the alternatives to letting the TNCs privatise the world's water supplies? It's true that many public water utilities are bureaucratic dinosaurs out of touch with the people they are supposed to serve, but there are many publicly owned supplies that are accountable to the needs of the population.

One example can be found in Porto Allegre, Brazil. The local water company DMAE is publicly owned, but it is financially independent from state control and is fully financed through water bills paid by the 1.4 million inhabitants of Porto Allegre. All profits are re-invested in the water supply. The daily work of DMAE is controlled by civil society representatives, while operations and investment decisions are subject to a participatory budget process and community members directly decide the budget priorities of the water company. Through a process of public meetings, every citizen can have a say in which investments should be made first.

This participatory model has massive success – awareness about water and sewage is raised and the people's needs are prioritised. As a result, 99.5% of Porto Allegre's population now have access to clean water (the highest rate in Brazil) and DMAE's water price is one of the lowest in Brazil, while overall consumption has gone down.

In the Bangladeshi capital of Dhaka, a proposed privatisation was strongly opposed by the water workers' union. So the Dhaka Water Authority contracted out one zone to the union, while another zone was given to a private water company for a one-year trial. The union co-operative's results were so much better that the private sector's that the contract was given to the union. The union co-operative's achievements included a considerable expansion of the number of people with access to running water as well as a sizable reduction in water losses.

* Corporate Europe Observatory has prepared briefs around key issues of the global water debate: www.corporateeurope.org

Inside SchNEWS

On Tuesday, Trident Ploughshare activist Ulla Roder managed to get into a hangar at RAF Leuchars in Fife and do some serious damage to a Tornado plane that had been left unguarded. Ulla later said, "I took my hammer to the nose-cone, the cockpit, the fuselage, the wings, the tailplane and other parts of the plane which it was safe to damage. I don't see it flying again". She's currently on remand until her next court appearance on the 20th March. Write to: Ulla Roder, HMP Corton Vale, Stirling, FK9 5NY.

www.tridentploughshares.org

Positive SchNEWS

It's Fairtrade Fortnight starting this week with over four thousand events going on around the country. You can go along to tasting parties and stalls and check out coffee and chocolate produced by farmers from the majority world who aren't being ripped off for their produce. For a full listing of events at 020 7405 5942 www.fairtrade.org.uk

Marcos Veron Pic: João Ripper /www.survival-international.org

SHAMAN ON YOU

Marcos Veron, Brazilian Indian shaman and leader of the Guarani-Kaiowá tribe, was brutally killed in January. The 70-year-old was beaten to death by thugs in the pay of ranchers who had taken over his homeland, Takuára, in 1953. The Guarani-Kaiowá have been exiled from their land for the last fifty years. Many live by roadsides. Without land they can't grow their own food or hunt. In their own words, without their land they have 'nothing to live for'. The Guarani-Kaiowa tribe have been trying to get their land back recently, but to no avail. For the last few months, many have lived camped on the side of a highway, and this January, they tried to move peacefully back onto their land. The attempt sadly failed - the tribe was attacked and Marcos murdered. This month, the last of those who had accompanied Marcos were again ordered off their land by the courts. www.survivalinternational.org/marcos.htm

WELFORD WORTH A LOOK

The **Welford Peacewatch Camp**, a sister to the Fairford Camp, was set up on the 12th of March within sight of USAF Welford, north of Newbury in Berkshire which is a munitions storage facility supplying the 16 B52s based at USAF Fairford in Gloucestershire 38 miles away. From the camp convoys could be observed leaving the base daily heading up the M4 with their lethal cargo. Several actions were taken to prevent them arriving...

On the 25th of march a huge convoy of bombs destined for Iraq supported by police vans and motorbike outriders was stopped by just ten people. A crossroads was blocked with a parked car then others lay in fronts of the convoy joined together with arm tubes. A week later on April the 1st protestors blocked the motorway long enough for others to start to lock themselves to the bomb trucks. Perhaps it was an April fools joke because the driver really took the piss when he knowingly started the truck in motion with people locked on underneath. They were quickly forced to unlock or be crushed. On both occasions people were searched but nobody was arrested.

After these few practice runs campaigners were more successful on 10th April when a crew of five from Bristol blocked the A417 near Cirencester with a car, and two of the group chained themselves underneath a transport vehicle with bike locks. It took police the best part of an hour with hydraulic cutters to get them free and the convoy rolling again. The activists were arrested for obstruction and all except one later released without charge.

The last of the bombers left Fairford on Thursday 24th April so the people at the Welford Peacewatch camp decided to break camp the following night.

www.gwi.org.uk
www.fairfordpeacewatch.com

CASTLE KEEPERS

Last Friday, an English judge found that activists in Littlemoor who built a big pink castle on a field about to be sown with GM seeds were acting reasonably in order to try and prevent damage to neighbouring crops. They were acquitted of all charges against them. The magistrate noted that the activists, "acted reasonably by locking themselves onto tractors because simply standing in front of them would not have prevented the crop being sown".

** Crop Pullers from GM-Free Wales facing similar charges are in Chester Crown court 31 March – 3 April. Supporters welcome. 0845 456 9327 www.fraw.org.uk/gs ** Public meeting: The Future of Food and Farming in Wales, at the Daniel Owen Centre in Mold, nr Chester. 3 April, 7.30 pm

...and finally...

So what do you do if you're a 'concerned member of the public,' or more to the point, a paranoid reader of the Daily Hate Mail, calmly minding your own business in the public library when suddenly you see a foreign-looking student viewing pictures of 'tall buildings' on the internet? You call the police of course!!

Which is exactly what happened recently at a library in Plymouth. Embarrassingly for the concerned member of the public, the 'tall buildings' turned out to be the logo of an internet radio website. The police involved, however, still had the cheek to ask if the library service could start keeping a log of any and all internet activity by asylum seekers. The head of Plymouth Libraries, Chris Goddard, "gently but firmly" refused, citing data protection and human rights issues. Way to go Chris! But is there any way we could start keeping a log of the internet activity of bored, brain-washed Daily Mail readers with way too much time on their hands….. pretty please?

Disclaimer

SchNEWS warns all readers walking around Gloucestershire or Wiltshire not to fill their lunch-boxes with something substantial and finger licking good that the police can get their teeth into! Honest.

March 16th: With less than a week go, the war machine is nearly stopped in its tracks when Slough 4 Peace take to the streets.

SCHOOL'S OUT II

5 kids from Blatchington Mill School, Hove, were baffled when they got suspended for joining nationwide student demos against the war on Iraq last Friday. The head said they were very naughty children for disobeying teachers and leaving school without permission. But the kids (15 - 16) were under the misapprehension that recent government initiatives promoting citizenship meant taking an active interest in our so-called democracy.

Other kids have been telling SchNEWS about their walkouts, with one 14 year-old girl in Birmingham saying, "We were accused of truanting but we were standing up for our political views about the world we're growing up in." More than 1000 in Leicester took part in what one local councillor described as the "most effective anti-war demo to date". As one 16 year-old demonstrator put it, "Tony Blair has only succeeded in one thing as far as we're concerned – politicising a whole generation." Nice one!

Subscribe! _ _ _ _ _ _ _ _ _ _

Keep SchNEWS FREE! Send 1st Class stamps (e.g. 10 for next 9 issues) or donations (payable to Justice?) Ask for "Originals" if you can make copies. Post *free* to all prisoners. SchNEWS, c/o on-the-fiddle, P.O. Box 2600, Brighton, East Sussex, BN2 0EF.
Tel/Autofax +44 (0)1273 685913 *Email* schnews@brighton.co.uk *Download a PDF of this issue or subscribe at* www.schnews.org.uk

Resistance Snowballs
MARCH 15th

Another major day of protest. Mass rallies against the War on Iraq were held in over 2,000 cities around the world, the day before Bush and Blair (Oh, and not forgetting that Spanish leader Aznar) met for their 'war summit' in the isolation of a US airbase in the Azores (islands in the Atlantic off the west coast of Africa.)

Half a million out on the catwalk in Milan, Italy.

You've heard of the black block - well here come the white block - Jakarta

EUROPE: Millions marched in Spain and Italy, two countries whose governments supported the US war, including 1,000,000 in Madrid, 400,000 in Barcelona, and demos in many other Spanish cities. In Italy the biggest march was 500,000 in Milan.

In other European cities there were 100,000 in Berlin; 50,000 in Paris; 40,000 in Brussels; 5,000 in Marseille, 4,000 in Stockholm, Thessaloniki and Bucharest, plus many others...

N. AMERICA: Large numbers responded to calls from the ANSWER coalition, with anti-war events in over 100 cities; the biggies being 100,000 in Washington DC, taking up more than 20 city blocks; 100,000 in San Francisco, and 50,000 in Los Angeles.

250,000 marched in Montreal, in the largest of 40 demonstrations in Canada.

Vienna

US 'OUTPOSTS' AROUND THE WORLD GET HIT: 25,000 visited the US Embassy in Athens, 10,000 at the US Embassy in Buenos Aires, Argentina and 1,000 at the US Embassy in Moscow; while 2,000 converged on the US Navy Base at Crete, and others demonstrated at US air bases in Frankfurt, Germany and Moron de la Frontera, Spain. 10,000 marched through the Turkish port city of Iskenderum where the US Military were loading up equipment for transport to Iraq.

PLUS: 50,000 in Sao Paolo, Brazil; 10,000 in Tokyo; 2,000 in Seoul, South Korea; 1,000 in Bangkok, Thailand... Then there were thousands in Calcutta, New Delhi, Frankfurt, Dunedin and Christchurch in New Zealand, plus protests in Mexico City's main square, and in Guatemala and El Salvador.

Muslims in London organised walk-bys at the embassies of Saudi Arabia, Turkey, Syria, Egypt, Qatar and Pakistan, all countries collaborating with the United States.

Union Jacks and Star Spangled Banners have certainly become hot property since the threat of war began: more flags get torcheed, this time at the Khan Younis refugee camp, southern Gaza strip, Palestine (left).

MIDDLE EAST: 200,000 demonstrated in Sanaa, Yemen; as well as demos in Amman, Beirut, Cairo (which is heavily repressed by police) and many Palestinian cities and refugee camps.

I look forward to recruiting all the young people here into the Marxist-Leninist movement.

NO BLOOD 4 OIL!

Fair Play
Direct action at Fairford airbase

Back in September it became obvious that there was the real possibility that there was going to be a war against Iraq. I started to look around for a group to join that would work against this and found my local peace group. I found this group fascinating. For once, all in the same room, working together, was a real diverse range of ages, interests and political view- points and it seemed to work. The group wanted to pick a mixture of national and local targets for its anti-war actions. One of these targets was Fairford Airbase in Gloucestershire. In the months that followed many people learned a lot about the modern way of warfare and politics and just how far the state was willing to go to protect its interests. We also learned a lot about what worked tactically and what didn't.

There were times during the anti-war campaign when it looked like we might win, that the international players would be forced to listen to us, and bow to public opinion. We didn't win, but sadly I reckon we might get to have another go at trying. If Bush goes to war against Iran or Syria, Fairford will be used again, and we will be there again, so the lessons of what happened this time need to be learned.

Our group found out that in the last Gulf War the bombs that fell on Baghdad were dropped from planes based in Fairford. B-52 bomber planes flew for hours from the tiny Cotswold village about 20 miles west of Oxford. We also read that since then, the air base had received a multi-million pound refit to make it capable of holding B-2 stealth bombers - flat, evil-looking planes that can evade radar and carry more bombs.

Fairford seemed an obvious focus. Where else was there a chance to throw a spanner directly in the war machine? What other more appropriate symbol of our government's complicity in the war? There had

apparently been talk of stationing the special, climate-controlled hangers for the aircraft in Italy, Germany or Spain. This was ruled out, as the risk of civil resistance was too high. It seemed that British apathy was being put to the test.

So we went and joined a protest in December that was to start in Fairford village and march to the gates of the base. The local group had come up with the idea of dressing in white paper boiler suits, calling themselves the Gloucester Weapons Inspectors and demanding access to the base to inspect the weapons of mass destruction inside. The idea was to highlight the ridiculous demands being made of Iraq and to contrast them with the culture of secrecy, domination and downright hypocrisy around American military power. We also wanted to show that not all the passengers on Aircraft Carrier HMS Britain were happy with the ride we were being taken on. We all hoped that if we could get enough people to Fairford and that those people made the powers-that-be nervous enough we could have an effect on whether the UK joined the war, and that that would effect the US's design, etc, etc.

Many people in our group had not been involved in direct action before and didn't know what to expect. Before we went to the base, a peace activist who had campaigned against the last Gulf War came to speak to us. He told us how he and five others had cut the perimeter fences of the base, dodged the guards and soldiers and run onto the runway. They stopped four planes from leaving with their 'payloads'. Many of us were inspired by this story and planned to use similar tactics… We had fence-cutting tools in our bags.

It's about an hour's walk from the village church to the gates of the base. There were about 500 people, small sound systems and a huge puppet stealth bomber. We walked to the gates of the base and asked to be let in. No one was shocked when they told us to go away. Then we decided to go for a walk around the base, and around 30 people managed to cut a hole in the fence and climb in, running for the hangers, climbing on containers, generally causing chaos. At that point no planes had arrived yet, so we were just slung out of the gates by some police officers.This scene was repeated in January, although it was harder to get tools for cutting the fence past the police, who had begun to search people; we became more ingenious in our hiding places. There were a few arrests.

No this isn't Glastonbury - Fairford January 26th

It wasn't just the big demos happening at Fairford. As the anti-war movement grew people set up a peace camp at Gate 10 of the airbase, the gates closest to the planes; this camp tried to monitor activity on the base. There were nighttime raids, one of which did £50,000 of damage to groundwork vehicles. Landing lights were damaged. People tried to stop the convoys of munitions arriving from Whelford, where they were stored. Another camp was briefly set up at Whelford, only to be shut down by the police.

It wasn't just Fairford either. While this was going on there were break-ins happening at Menwith Hill in Yorkshire where a nighttime raid left tens of thousands of pounds worth of damage. In Fife, training aircraft were damaged, groups broke into RAF Mildenhall and Lakenheath in Norfolk, breaching the perimeters, stopping the runways. The Fairford actions fitted into a network of large and small groups all over the country trying to stop what was happening.

There was a feeling that if we could make the demos big enough, and they continued to be as active in their determination to not just be symbolic, we could have a real impact on the base.

After the huge turn out at the London anti-war demo on 15th February, the question was obvious: how can we get these people from the centre of London to the place where we can directly effect the war effort? If we'd had just 10,000 people willing to enter the base at Fairford (a tiny fraction of the numbers on the streets on the 15th) the impact could have thrown Labour's war plans into disarray. Governments can cope with demos that do nothing but go from A to B and then home as they did in London. But groups of people willing to risk arrest, refusing to be controlled by police or any other organisation, returning week after week – this is harder to cope with. And this is what was beginning to happen at Fairford.

So we had high hopes when we returned to the base in February. The demo was 700 people. It followed the usual pattern of village assembly and march. This time, however, when we arrived at the gates people came out of the crowd and attached ropes to the razor wire topped gates and started to pull in rhythm. The gates started to rock and shake and the hinges started to buckle. The whole crowd pulled: I saw teenagers and wrinkled old peaceniks side by side with people masked up and people with flowers in their hair. The police on the other side went from pitying amusement to running for their riot gear as the gate popped open and the crowd surged through the gate. Meanwhile, holes had been cut behind a big banner leaning against the fence and people were running through. It took nearly forty minutes for the police to contain the crowd and push them back through the gate. The lessons here are: use rope with no spring in it, attach it with carabinas high on the gates (harder for the police to reach), and don't underestimate what a crowd working together can do.

The next time we went back *en masse* was 22nd March. We knew it would be different then. For a start, we were at war and all the planes had been moved there. There had been scare stories on the news for days before about shoot-to-kill policies on the base. We had heard about the harassment of the peace camp, how American soldiers had attacked them. We had heard how the Terrorism laws had been brought into force in the area, so that anyone could be stopped and searched at anytime for no reason. There were ridiculous stories about people's packed lunches being rifled by cops and how some people were searched several times a day.

But loads more people were coming and our coaches filled up quickly. Even my dad decided that writing to his MP wasn't enough and that he would join me on the front lines. I thought, if my dad was coming that finally the mass of middle England would surely come, registering their disapproval of an illegal, un-democractic war. Unfortunately the police had the same idea.

On 22nd March there must have been 1,000 police officers at Fairford in full body armour, seven police horses, cross country motorcycles and what looked suspiciously like a helicopter with mounted machine guns. Before we even got near the site our coach was stopped and searched and we were detained by the side of the road for 20 minutes. The police seemed unsure of the law, unable to answer the questions of our legal observers as to why we were being stopped or what they were looking for. Luckily we had hidden our tools well. The London coaches, holding around 150 people, were turned back from the demo for no reason and escorted by helicopter and police convoy back to London. We saw then how far the state was going to go to protect its interests.

The heavy police presence was not like other times. It made for a depressing day. Some people put flowers into the fences, others listened to speeches under the eyes of the massed constabulary. There didn't seem to be much we could do; as we marched back again a plane flew over head emphasising the nastiness that was behind the rolls of razor wire. We knew that the B-52s would take off from there to kill people.

What we learned from Fairford is that you can catch the police unawares, as we did with the gate trick. But that in times of war they will throw their full weight into making sure they don't get caught out, and they will ignore the law, as they did when they turned back the London coaches. To have a chance, you need to think around them, work in small groups that can make choices quickly, hide your tools well in unexpected places, play on their prejudices. For example, the police have a very narrow image of what a protestor looks like and they tend to search these people more often and follow them more closely; it can be useful to have some 'typical protestors' to draw attention away from everyone else.

After the 22nd people felt that a more decentralised style of demo might have been more effective. Even if you can't get inside they hate having groups of people moving around outside their control. Also although I have focused heavily here on the more 'direct action' side of the campaign this should not be to the exclusion of the other types of participation that went on at Fairford. The crowd was always very supportive there, people did legal support for those who had been arrested and fined for their actions. People tried to talk to the American servicemen, people made noise and campaigned and talked to the press, people gathered information for others to use, people researched the various types of evil that was going on inside. People were just there. If we go into Iran or Syria, or even if the US goes alone, people will be there again.

Weapons Inspectors well kitted out with identification equipment perform an inspection, 14th December. 2002 Pic: Simon Chapman

Fairford Peace Camp

A peacewatch was set up at Fairford outside Gate 10 of the airbase on February 17th to begin monitoring military activity at the base and a permanent camp was established on March the 2nd, the day before the B52 bombers arrived to be based at Fairford for the upcoming war. The camp was packed up finally on the 3rd of May. (Follow the progress in SchNEWS 393, 395, 396)

It's Sunday morning. FAIRFORD is an inoffensive looking town in the Cotswolds which happens to be home to a large air base that sometimes houses American stealth bombers (B2s).

It's one of only 3 forward bases for them outside the USA, so it's likely that in the event of a war with Iraq planes from here will take bombs (possibly nuclear) to the Gulf.

BANG! KNOCK! KNOCK!

Fran! It's 8 o'clock, we're going

Going? (my head hurts...)

Oh yes. We're going to do an independent weapons inspection today.

For more info on this see www.cynatech.co.uk/gwill/Fairford.htm

Today the area is full of weirdly attired concerned citizens.

I'm a weapons inspector.

WAR IS BAD

We've definitely got a hangover

We walked through the town, which is tiny, to the base, which is somewhat bigger. Lots of people had brought stuff to decorate the fence with.

WAR? NOT IN OUR NAME

ARMS ARE FOR HUGGING

NEVER AGAIN

We stood around at the gate for a while, then everyone wandered off and the fence magically became more permeable...

Ooooops

Shall we take the dog for a run dear?

I think so.

Have you called for back-up?

Yeah but they're being slow

Loads of people got in + ran about. For a while it was really anarchic + beautiful.

tee hee

Then we were rounded up + chucked out. Later the police decided to arrest a couple of people in quite a violent way but on the whole it was a really lovely day. More protests are planned at Fairford. See www.gwi.org.uk

FH 10/2/03

RAFAH FRONTLINE

Since SchNEWS published Occupational Hazard last September (SchNEWS 373/4) the heat has been massively turned up on Palestinians and International Solidarity Movement (ISM) activists in the occupied territories. Whilst the western media focussed its attention on the war in Iraq, Israel took the opportunity to step up the level of violence in the West Bank and the Gaza Strip, and to clamp down on the 'problem' of international activists. This has led to an increase in attacks on ISM activists, beginning with the murder of Rachel Corrie (SchNEWS 397/8). In the following article, a British activist who was with Corrie in Rafah describes his experience as an international in Palestine and explains the changing role of the ISM.

The International Solidarity Movement was set up to provide support for non-violent direct action supporting Palestinian struggle against the illegal Israeli occupation. Since August 2001 international ISM activists have been travelling to the occupied territories to join the Palestinian people and use their privileged status as 'westerners' to act as human shields, aiming to disrupt the daily attacks on people and basic infrastructure inflicted by the Israeli Occupation Forces. The ISM is a coalition movement of people from many different political and ideological backgrounds but, significantly, it remains a Palestinian-led organisation and supports the right of the Palestinian people to resist the occupation in any way they see fit.

There is no space here to document the full extent of the conflict, or the horrors it has inflicted on the population of the occupied territories. Occasionally the western media may focus on some of the more obviously brutal aspects of the occupation: the massacre in Jenin in April 2002 (see SchNEWS Of The World 2002), or the arbitrary rocket fire into the refugee camps in northern Gaza. What goes unreported and often unwitnessed by outsiders is the day-to-day repression of the Palestinian people at the hands of the Israeli military. There is a hidden psychological and economic war being conducted against the population of the West Bank and Gaza strip. This is a war of ethnic cleansing following the oldest script of all, that of land theft and seizure of natural resources such as water. It is here that the ISM takes action: sleeping in houses threatened with demolition, either as part of collective punishment (families of suicide bombers and other resistance fighters) or

simply because the house is in the way of the proposed wall; escorting ambulances through checkpoints, or kids to school; acting as human shields for workers trying to rebuild the water systems that have been destroyed by the Israeli military.

The question often raised over ISM activities is how the principles of non-violent direct action can even begin to be applied in a war zone. The answer lies in the nature of the situation: whilst there is undoubtedly a war of sorts taking place in Palestine, it is a phenomenally lopsided conflict. The Israeli state is backed to the hilt by the US, receiving $4 billion a year in direct military aid. Its air force, in a country of just 4.5million people, is larger and more advanced than the UK's. The Palestinian people are cut off from anything but token support from fellow Arabs and the armed resistance groups hold an ageing arsenal of automatic weapons and explosives. What is happening in Palestine is more like ethnic cleansing than counter-insurgency. However, the theory behind ISM actions was that the Israeli state was more susceptible to outside pressure than other states engaged in similar brutal repression. Its establishment is proud of its claim to be the only democracy in the Middle East and is at great pains to rebut, for example, any comparison between the occupation and the old South African apartheid system.

Essentially the ISM has been using its privileged status to act as human shields, knowing that the potential media backlash against the Israeli state for killing or injuring internationals would deter the occupation forces from direct violence against them. With this approach the ISM was able to win many small victories over the occupation and provide a sense of security and solidarity for many Palestinians.

But at the time of writing this situation is changing daily, and it increasingly seems that no one in the occupied territories has 'privileged status' anymore. First came the murder on March 16th of Rachel Corrie, a US activist deliberately crushed under the blade of a bulldozer as she tried to prevent Palestinian homes from being demolished. Three weeks later Tom Hurndall, a British peace activist, was shot trying to escort children from an area where they were under fire. A week later a British cameraman was shot dead despite being clearly identified as press. None of these deaths were the result of an exchange of fire. Many

ISM Workers acting as a human shield, trying to prevent a Palestinian building being flattened by an Israeli armoured bulldozer.

ISM activists in the West Bank were arrested and deported at this time. Quite simply it seemed that the rules had been abruptly changed and the simple act of being a non-violent activist in Gaza was punishable with death. There are two possible reasons for this. It may be that as Rachel's death coincided with the outbreak of the invasion of Iraq it did not generate the media attention or international pressure that the ISM had been banking on, and, taking note of this, the IOF began a campaign to eradicate what has obviously been a thorn in their side for some time. The other more sinister possibility is that international witnesses are simply being cleared out of Rafah as a prelude to an increase in the level of oppression.

I went out to Palestine at the beginning of March this year and, on my arrival, I was asked to travel to Rafah, as numbers were needed there. Although the western media prefers to focus on more easily accessible parts of the West Bank, the effects of the war are perhaps nowhere more evident than in the city of Rafah. Unlike the West Bank, Gaza is not under occupation and its population is to some extent better armed than their counterparts in Nablus, Jenin and Tulkarem. Rafah is the southernmost city in the Gaza strip. It is cut off from northern Gaza by a checkpoint, which can be closed for days at a time. It is cut off from the sea by illegal Israeli settlements and a military exclusion zone, which runs the length of the coast. It was divided in half by the 1981 agreement between Israel and Egypt, and along this arbitrary line a wall is being constructed through the centre of the city to seal it off entirely from the outside world.

Curfew in the outlying areas is enforced by live fire. It is potentially lethal for the inhabitants to even step out of their front doors after nightfall. House demolitions are a regular occurrence, with families often given only 15 minutes to clear themselves and all their possessions from the family home before it is demolished in front of them. Resistance is inevitably met with lethal force. The Shaheed or "martyr" posters which are produced and flyposted to commemorate the deaths of all those killed in the intifada are testament to the way in which sudden violent death is a way of life in Rafah. The outskirts of the city are simply post-apocalyptic, rubble-strewn wastelands guarded

Mahoud's house - the last in the row still standing, riddled with machine gun fire - Rafah, Gaza, Palestine.

View from Abu-Mahmoud's house: a wall across Salaheddin under construction - making a militarised border with Egypt, and dividing the city of Rafah in the middle.

by machines which do not hesitate to inflict death.

Possibly the most important thing which ISMers do in Rafah is to stay in the houses most visibly threatened with demolition to make way for the wall. The family I stayed with, Mahmoud and his wife Nora, live in what was once the heart of Rafah with their three young children. Before the intifada Mahmoud was able to earn enough money working in the hotels of Tel Aviv to build a house in his hometown. That house is now pockmarked with bullet holes and stands on the edge of a rubble wasteland, which has been cleared to provide a free-fire zone for the Israeli military. Trespass in this area which once was filled with homes is forbidden and will be met with live fire.

Mahmoud's house now stands at the end of the street and is in the path of the wall's construction. It is overlooked by the vast bulk of the Salaheddin watchtower. The bullets fired at his house are intended to intimidate him into leaving. Every night without fail there is some shooting, often continuously. Mahmoud has learned to tell the difference between the sounds of different Israeli weapons and to hear which direction they are firing, a vital survival skill. Tanks and bulldozers rumble past on a regular basis. The trajectories of bullets which have passed through their home are clearly visible, the most chilling being a set of bullet holes through the kitchen at head height. The Israeli army is able to kill these people with impunity. It is difficult to imagine the stress that that knowledge puts on people. It is a psychological war of terrorisation.

Mahmoud's house is now covered with signs announcing in Hebrew (courtesy of a Jewish peace activist) and English that children and internationals live there. This has at least stopped the troops from firing directly into the house and for this one family at least has made life on the frontline a little easier. Internationals maintain a constant presence there and are often visible on the roof.

It is important to understand that most of the people of Rafah have never seen an Israeli soldier, only the watchtowers and the machines. They are confronted by a capricious and lethal enemy with no human face. The Israeli approach is random terror; the incursions into civilian areas are unannounced and terrifying in their scale.

The last night I spent in Rafah there was an incursion into the Salaheddin and Hi Salaam areas, where virtually all the internationals were staying with families. The first we knew was the sound of explosions mixed with the growl of diesel engines as tanks advanced from the border. The Israeli forces advanced into the area machine-gunning the houses, creating a 'secure' area for the bulldozers to do their work. Bullets soon began to come through the walls of the house. Myself and the other British activist in the house gathered with the family in the back room, desperately trying to put as much concrete and brick as possible between ourselves and the incoming fire.

The lights went out as one of the tanks smashed down the pylons in the street outside. We were able to crawl to the balcony and announce through a megaphone that we were international citizens and that our embassies were aware of our presence. This didn't draw any noticeable response and the tank continued to lurk under the balcony. We began to hear the sounds of a nearby house being demolished, but the tank was blocking our way and there was no way to leave the house. We waited in fear that Mahmoud's house would be next and nervously contemplated our next move. In the end there was little to do other than wait and try to calm the family down whilst preparing ourselves for a swift move if it became necessary. For whatever reason, Mahmoud's was not attacked that night (we hope because of our presence), although one of his neighbours had a substantial part of the house knocked down.

In the morning we surfaced to find the place deserted by the army, but the devastation was everywhere to be seen. Throughout the night there had been no return fire by the resistance in our area, but this hadn't stopped the Israelis from machine-gunning civilian houses, killing two and wounding many. In an unusual twist, just down the road in Hi Salaam, the resistance had succeeded in severely damaging a tank and, although by morning it had mostly been dragged away, a defiant crowd gathered around the remains and were celebrating the destruction of the machine. The fact that the disabling of one tank was the cause of such joy demonstrated to me once again how uneven this conflict is. It appears that there was no military objective for this illegal invasion of Palestinian territory; the IDF spokesman told the British Embassy that they were simply "on patrol". To me it seemed to be nothing other than deliberate terrorisation of the populace.

The role of ISM in the future looks uncertain, although there is no doubt that its work will continue in some way. Rachel Corrie's death was the start of a systematic repression of internationals within the occupied territories. Even in this repression, however, there is victory of sorts. The very fact that the Israeli state has attempted to use the recent suicide bombings by British citizens to smear the ISM, and has begun to kill ISM activists, has catapulted the movement into the headlines and once more placed the oppression of the Palestinian people at the top of the international agenda.

After the self-serving cant about the liberation of the people of Iraq, perhaps the US may be forced into at least a pretence of reining in its number one client state in the region. In Rafah, however, there is little hope that the much-vaunted 'road map', or the appointment of a business friendly prime minister, will bring peace. In fact the repression is intensifying. As one man put it to me after Rachel's death, "If they do this to an American, you cannot imagine what they will do to us."

March 16th: Israeli bulldozers roam the wasteland they have created after flattening Palestinian housing in Hi-Salaam, Gaza. On this day Rachel Corrie (below) was one of several ISM workers trying to protect a Palestinian building from being bulldozed when one of the armoured bulldozers deliberately ran over her, then withdrew without stopping.

For more info on the conflict see
www.electronicintifada.net
http://jerusalem.indymedia.org
To get involved with the ISM see
www.palsolidarity.org

RACHEL CORRIE RIP

Rachel Corrie, an American international peace observer in Palestine was deliberately killed by an Israeli bulldozer on March the 16th while trying to protect Palestinian houses in Rafah.

Rachel had been volunteering for the International Solidarity Movement (ISM), a Palestinian led organisation attempting to alleviate human rights abuses in the occupied territories. As such she was a part of an international collective, taking direct action to resist the brutality of Israel's 36 year military occupation. 600 homes have been destroyed in Rafah since the beginning of the most recent Intifada. On average, 3 Palestinians a day are killed in the occupied territories.

The ISM has been criticised for supporting and protecting those involved in Palestinian violence, such as suicide bombers. But as Rachel said in an email just before she was killed "If any of us had our lives and welfare completely strangled, lived with children in a shrinking place where we knew, from previous experience, that soldiers and tanks and bulldozers could come for us at any moment and destroy all the greenhouses that we had been cultivating for however long, and did this while some of us were being beaten and held captive - don't you think we might try and use violent means to protect whatever fragments remain ... The vast majority of people here, even if they had the economic means to escape, even if they wanted to give up resisting on their land and just leave, can't leave ... I think this qualifies as genocide."

Israel's occupation of the Gaza strip and the West Bank is totally illegal under international law (The Geneva Convention), but there is no suggestion that there's going to be any pre-emptive strikes by the US. Instead the US provides Israel with $10bn a year in aid. This compares to a measly $1.7 billion that they've set aside to help rebuild Iraq after they've totally obliterated it.

Following Rachel's death, protests took place in her honour across the world. In Palestine, these were attacked by the Israeli army.

Members of the ISM have vowed to continue their peace work in the region www.palsolidarity.org

WAKE UP! IT'S THOSE PESKY KIDS FROM

SchNEWS

weekly

www.schnews.org.uk

IT'S ANOTHER TOWN OF POOR MOTHERF*CKERS WAITING TO BE LIBERATED - TIME TO KICK ASS

Friday 28th March 2003   Free/Donation   Issue 397/398

MASS DUST-RUCTION

"This war is a campaign of humanity."
- *Donald Rumsfeld US Defence Secretary.*

"The mother held one child after another. Her eight-year-old daughter had been killed. A small girl, half naked, was cradled in one of the woman's arms, emitting tearing screams whenever she was moved -- into the X-ray room, out again, into the treatment room. Her face was ripped by shrapnel. Another child was in a bed. The doctor lifted the blankets to reveal a bloody mess of open leg. She howled and screamed as they tried to clean it, called out to Allah while her mother and aunt held her. Her head was heavily bandaged and one eye closed and swollen. 'The skull is also open,' the doctor said."
- *Jo Wilding, activist staying in Baghdad.*

So let's get this straight. America and Britain are busy helping to save the Iraqi people by blowing them up (instead of liberate read eliminate), bombing them with weapons of mass destruction because we are told Iraq has, er, weapons of mass destruction. After last Friday, Iraqis have been treated to the 'mother of all bombings' – the most momentous display of firepower in the history of warfare.

This has then been followed by 'smart bombs' so pinpoint accurate that they've hit everything from a Baghdad market to a Syrian bus carrying civilian passengers to their own planes! As Dr. Mohammad T. Al-Rasheed so aptly pointed out, "The logic of killing hundreds of thousands to get rid of one man is the logic of the megalomaniacs and the demented."

Many of the bombs being dropped on Iraq contain Depleted Uranium (DU), a radioactive by-product from nuclear reactors. So no need to worry, if the bombs don't get you then the uranium will. When a DU shell explodes, it sends out dust particles contaminated with uranium that are small enough to be inhaled - high doses kill, low levels can cause cancer. And the dust particles make no distinction between civilians and the military.

The United Nations has passed two resolutions which include depleted uranium weapons among "weapons of mass or indiscriminate destruction", and have also found them incompatible with International humanitarian or human rights law. The uranium used has a half-life of 4.5 billion years (for all you non-scientists out there, that means it takes a bloody long time to decompose) and Professor Doug Rokke, a former US Army physicist, sees it as "a form of nuclear weapon that contaminates everything and everyone."

Since the last Gulf War, leukaemia and Hodgkins disease in Iraq have increased tenfold, as has the proportion of babies born with birth defects -without heads, brains, spines and limbs. Cancer specialist Dr Jawad Al-Ali describes the dust as carrying "the seeds of our death" and estimates that in the southern Iraqi city of Basra almost half the population could develop cancer within ten years.

If the bombs and poisonous dust don't kill Iraqis, then how about the last twelve years of sanctions, the most draconian ever imposed by the United Nations (see SchNEWS 235).

CRAP ARRESTS OF THE WEEK

For dressing up as a bunny! Children in New York were distressed to see the Easter Bunny being taken away in handcuffs from outside the local K-Mart last week. The bunny was protesting about the shop replacing the traditional chocolate Easter bunny in their baskets with candy toy soldiers armed with machine guns and rifles. For her trouble, she was nicked for trespassing.

The sanctions block medicines, ambulances, food, and even pencils and crayons destined for primary schools (they might take out the graphite for use in nuclear power stations!). Denis Halliday, who was sent to Iraq as the UN Humanitarian Coordinator, described the sanctions' effects on Iraq as "nothing less than genocide." Similar words have been used by his successor, Hans Von Sponeck. Both resigned in disgust.

Before the sanctions, Iraq had the best national health service in the Arab Middle East. Now, according to UNICEF, up to six thousand children die each month as a direct result of the sanctions and not, as Blair assures us, because Saddam starves them. 32% of children under 5 are chronically malnourished and suffer and die from preventable and curable diseases due to a massive lack of medical supplies. A visiting child psychologist reported that some children no longer play games because the games remind them of dead friends they used to play with.

The sanctions have also made the catastrophic effects of depleted uranium in Iraq even worse. After the last Gulf war, southern Iraq is

Mass Dust-Ruction cont...

still littered with burnt-out tanks contaminated with the remains of a million depleted uranium shells. While in Kuwait millions were spent on environmental clean-up efforts, Iraq had only scarce funds for reconstruction, leaving radio-active waste to rot, untreated. The resultant epidemic of cancers is a catastrophe that Iraq's health care system can't cope with, thanks to sanctions which block medicines getting through and which make drugs too expensive for the vast majority of people.

But then this war was never about liberating the ordinary people of Iraq, but about oil and controlling the Middle East. As journalist Paul Routledge said, "The New World Order turns out to be the The World Ordered Around by the USA. The 21st century looks like being the century of unrelenting American imperialism. Its slogan: 'Agree with Washington – or you are dead.'"

For a different perspective on the war see:

www.indymedia.org;
www.zmag.org;
ww.aljazeerah.info

Recommend reading: John Pilger "The New Rulers of the World" (Verso 2002); Anthony

www.peaceposter.org

In the Hands of Fools - Iraq Contaminated Again

Depleted uranium (DU) is a waste product from the process of enriching uranium for the nuclear energy and weapons industry. Left around it is extremely expensive and difficult to store. Turning DU into weapons 'solves' this problem for the nuclear industry – no longer are they liable for the storage of the waste they have created. For the military this ensures an endless supply of effective, and almost free, weapons material. But using DU in weapons is nothing less than bombarding your enemy with radioactive waste.

DU was first known to be used in the 1991 Gulf War and was used again in the NATO attacks on Bosnia and Kosovo in the Nineties. Its use in Iraq in 1991 has been linked closely to Gulf War Illness in British and US veterans and a massive increase in cancers and childhood birth deformities in

Iraq. Upon impact a DU weapon penetrator can oxidise up to 70% of its mass into a chemically toxic and radioactive dust that stays in the environment and can be breathed in by humans. The half-life of DU is 4.5 billion years and it is predicted by the United Nations Environment Programme that it will contaminate the local environment and food and water supplies forever. This means that Iraqi civilians will be suffering the effects of the British and US attacks for generations to come.

It is now clear that both the US and British Governments have used depleted uranium again in the recent attack in Iraq. The amount is not yet certain, but given the much greater firepower seen in this attack than was used in the first Gulf War we can expect a much greater amount of DU to have been used. Estimates have been put at around 1,000-2,000 tonnes, and although these amounts are not confirmed, it is horrifying to compare them with official figures of 320 tonnes of DU used in the first Gulf War. Another extremely disturbing development has been the use of DU weapons in urban, densely populated areas. We know the effects from the radioactive hotspots in the Balkans.

Gulf War Illness II

One of the most hypocritical aspects of this war has been the 'support our troops' line thrown out by the Government and some sections of the media to silence criticism. By continuing to expose troops to DU the government has made it clear how much concern it has for the well being of soldiers: almost as little as it has for Iraqi lives. The British government, unlike the US, has never recognised the existence of Gulf War Illness in veterans from the 1991 attack and has never paid any compensation. There is a schizophrenia in official policy which claims to instruct troops to follow strict precautions when handling DU weapons or working in areas exposed to high levels of DU contamination, while at the same time insisting they do not present a health problem and that troops have nothing to worry about.

As the fighting in Iraq slows down, depleted uranium is an issue that, literally, will not go away. There have so far been two international days of action against depleted uranium: to find out more visit the CADU (Campaign Against Depleted Uranium) website: cadu.org.uk.

Brighton, March 21st

the O.K.café

48 HRS TO WAR
2 YEARS HOSPITAL APPOINTMENT

Winston Churchill shuffles on his perch at Parliament Square, London at dusk the day war starts.

THIS IS WAR

On Thursday March 20th people woke up knowing that this was it - the bombers had left for Iraq. It was really happening. Thousands bunked off work and school and took to the streets from Dundee to Brighton, and all points in between...

* In **Worthing** a few hundred blocked roads and occupied McDonalds.

*In Tory toy town **Saffron Walden**, once host to the Levellers rebellion, people re-discovered their roots and staged a protest in the town centre.

* **Rochester** saw protesters bring traffic on the A2 near Rochester Bridge to a standstill with a demonstration and sit down protest.

Edinburgh

To keep up to date with anti-war protests check out the SchNEWS party and protest section on our website.

We are also compiling a list of regular demos and vigils etc so please send details to stopwar@schnews.org.uk. Also check out our useful list of anti war resources and let us know of any we've missed out.

Blocking the M32 motorway, Bristol

* Thousands caused gridlock in **Bristol** all day and surged through police lines to close the M32 motorway.

* After a huge lunchtime demo in **Cardiff**, main roads in the city centre were closed for the evening, later other junctions were closed.

* In **Dublin** over 3,000 people gathered at the US embassy - who heard a speech from a Libyan child speaking about the children of the middle east, and then the crowd paid the British Embassy a visit.

* In **Cambridge** 400 people sat down in the city centre bringing traffic to a halt for six hours. The nearby Army Recruitment Centre was shut down for the day following an occupation by 35 people. Aggressive Cambridge police (one had to be restrained by a colleague) arrested 22 people, some as young as 14.

* Schoolkids in **Lancaster** shut down the city for five hours and occupied the town hall.

Scotland: In **Glasgow** there were school students strikes and walkouts, 2-300 demonstrators filled George Sq, closed the whole centre of town and blocked the motorway. In **Edinburgh**, in the 4th consecutive day of strikes and protests thousands marched from Edinburgh Castle to block Princes Street, bringing the city centre to a halt for an anti-war rally. And in towns across Scotland from **Shetland** to **Dumbarton** people took to the streets.

Many cities were closed down by thousands: Leeds, Manchester, Birmingham, Sheffield, Swansea, Barnsley, Little Nothington... the list goes on.

I'm from Chertsey Mums Against The War. We feel that Tony Blair is misinformed and that the war is ill conceived. And what ever happened to fair coverage in the BBC...

Foiling around at Menwith Hill, Foil The Base, March 22nd
Pic: pza@yahoo.co.uk

UNUSUAL BUSINESS

We all know about the 200,000 people who turned out to march through central London on Saturday the 22nd, but what we're not told about are the numerous small groups, like the 300 protesters who gathered in Bangor, Wales, to mark the end of a 24 hour rally. At the US spy base at **Menwith Hill**, North Yorkshire, a thousand people took part in a '**Foil the Base**' demonstration. Attempting to disrupt satellite signal receivers by having as much foil in the air as possible, people came dressed in glitter wigs and silver body paint while decorating police vans with tinfoil, fake blood and No War signs, then deflating the tyres for good measure. There were 11 arrests, but all but two were released without charge. One of the two, Christine Reid of CAAB, was charged with criminal damage for writing a peace message on a barrier at the main gate and adding the word War to a traffic Stop sign.

And this week the protests continued. On Monday, 7 people blocked the runway at RAF Valley, Anglesey for four hours by chaining themselves to drag nets, preventing Hawk fighter jets from taking off and training pilots for the war. More people blockaded and chained shut the main gate. Fortunately, there were no arrests. At RAF Welford in Berkshire on Tuesday, 4 activists locked themselves to a car and then to each other, successfully preventing a convoy from transporting bombs to RAF Fairford.

(left) In the early hours of Wednesday morning, on March 26th, a man climbed to the top of Hulme Bridge in central Manchester and fixed a 'No War' banner to it. He stayed up there for around 8 hours, during which time the bridge, a busy road, had to remain closed. He eventually climbed down, leaving his banner behind, and was arrested for "placing items above a carriageway and causing danger to road users." This came after a hundred closed the bridge down the previous Friday with a sit-down protest. For the latest on protests see: www.indymedia.org.uk

A few selected highlights of upcoming events and demonstrations planned for the coming weekend and onwards are: **Saturday (29) London** Various stop the city actions. Meet noon outside London School of Economics, Houghton St, off Kingsway, (Holborn tube) **Wandsworth** Stop The War will be meeting at 11.30am, Clapham South Tube Station & head for Brixton Ritzy for 1pm to join a South London protest. **Edinburgh**, 1pm, assemble Waterloo Place, **Manchester**, 1pm, meet Heywood St. Cheetham Hill or Platt Fields, Wilmslow Rd, **York**, Block & Awe disruption in city centre (blockandawe@hotmail.com), **Swansea**, noon, protest in Castle Square, **Chatham**, noon, Riverside to Rochester Castle ** **Sunday (30) - London**, 1pm, picnic in Parliament Square, **Stourbridge**, 1.30pm, Balloons not Bombs, picnic area, Mary Stevens Park ** **Monday (31) Blackpool**, 6pm, assemble opposite Winter Gardens**April 5-6 Reclaim the Bases** Lots of actions across the country. To find out where 07887-585721w ww.reclaimthebases.gzzzt.net/listing.html.

March 29 banner drop at Norwich Castle

Pic: Simon Chapman

Full spectrum resistance: all walks of life walk for life to Fairford Airbase, March 22nd.

SCARE FORCE

Fairford Airbase 22nd March: Before last Saturday, SchNEWS hacks thought that going for a peaceful walk in the Cotswolds was about as law-abiding as you could get. How wrong we were! Despite it being a day of brilliant sunshine, the long arm of the state hung a dark cloud over the national day of action at USAF Fairford in Gloucestershire.

From the minute they arrived in Fairford, the 4,000 strong crowd was surrounded by layers of riot cops on horses, men with dogs, RAF police, US security police and bog-standard military police - armed with guns, batons and other maiming weapons - plus razor wire all arranged to protect B-52 bombers being loaded with cruise missiles. Police snatch squads darted into the crowd, grabbing a few people who were wearing white overalls and arresting four people. Police evidence gatherers filmed peaceniks as they strolled down country lanes, while other coppers had a go at people for sitting on a town green and threatened them with arrest for 'deviating from the agreed march.' Some coppers even refused to let children put flowers by a fence.

Three coaches driving up from London were turned back before they even reached Fairford. A would-be peace protester explains, "The police called in 4 police forces specifically to stop us. There were about 200 officers involved. We were searched and filmed when we got to within 10 miles of Fairford. We were then escorted back to London by a helicopter, 3 police vans, and 6 motorcycles, an escort which changed in each county!" Police searched people and vehicles for "offensive weapons" under Section 60 of the Criminal Justice Act, but the only things they found worth confiscating were headscarves and body padding. Among the passengers was the 64-year old aunt of one of those killed in New York on September 11th. Over the past weeks hundreds of people have been stopped and searched in the Fairford area by police using powers under the 2000 Terrorism Act. For legal info see www.gwi.org.uk

* Sam Grafton and Joss Garman were arrested inside Fairford on Wednesday night "by a Texan with a machine gun." They're being held on remand under various conspiracy and criminal damage charges. They've been told that because deadly force has been authorised in the area, it is for their own protection that they are being held! Contact: 07773 1552657.

SMART BOMB PRE-LAUNCH BRIEFING

AH... WAIT A SECOND... I KNOW THIS ONE... UM... -DON'T TELL ME- IT'S ... UM...

MILITARY TARGET: A OR B

SCHOOL

OIL EXCHANGE

A week before war started, twenty anti-war activists disrupted trading for 2 hours at London's International Petroleum Exchange (IPE), Europe's major centre for trading in futures contracts for crude oil. They highlighted the obvious links between war in Iraq and the west's compulsive oil habit. Sandra Reid, a member of the direct action group Infernal Petroleum Experience said: "Oil courses through the veins of the capitalist system, turbocharging its destructive impacts. We are taking direct action to stick a well placed spanner in the war machine."

Despite being set upon by traders, the protesters were able to unplug telephones and computers and bring trading to a standstill. Two people managed to barricade themselves into an office for 40 minutes until they were dragged out by police.

Repeated claims by politicians that the war in Iraq has nothing to do with oil are contradicted by the desperate volley of leaflets that continue to rain down on Iraq, reminding its citizens that: "If the oil industry is destroyed, your livelihood will be RUINED!", and by Bush's desperate pleas to the Iraqi people not to set fire to their oil wells.

Earlier this month, 60 anti-war student protesters, many of them dressed in tiger suits, invaded the grounds of ESSO's UK HQ. A 12 foot wooden model of an oil tanker bearing the slogan "ESSO's Going Down" was dumped in the company pond. This followed actions in February in which activists shut down the power to pumps and locked petrol nozzles together at 119 ESSO stations across the UK. Further info from

www.stopesso.com 0870 010 9510

* A Methodist minister and two grannies dressed in mourning garb were arrested on Tuesday night during a 30-strong peace demonstration at an ESSO petrol station in Exmouth. One of the women, Mo Mooney, an ex-Wren said: "I served my country for many years and as far as I'm concerned I'm serving it now." They were bailed to return to Exmouth police station next month.

* **March to the End of the World** Saturday 29th, to mark the second anniversary of Bush's dumping of the Kyoto agreement on Climate Change. The 20 mile march starts at Esso HQ in Surrey and ends at the US Embassy in London, but you can join it along the way. Contact: www.campaignagainstclimatechange.net 020 8855-3327.

* **Behind the Propaganda – deconstructing BP**. Talk about BP's dirty tricks and human rights abuses around the world, speakers from West Papua and Colombia, 31st March, 7pm, Cowley Club, London Road, Brighton.

* On April 24th join the **Carnival Against Oil Wars & Climate Chaos** as they greet BP's annual general meeting at the Royal Festival Hall in London. 01865 241097 www.burningplanet.net

Inside SchNEWS

As so many people are being arrested for non-violent direct action and protests, it's as important as ever to write to prisoners and to support them in court. Here are a few people who'd love to hear from you…

Toby Olditch and Phillip Pritchard - caught on USAF Fairford property allegedly trying to damage war machinery: Toby - JT 5132, Phillip - JT 5131, both at HMP Gloucester, Barrack Square, Gloucester, GL1 2JN. ** **Angie Zelter** - Charged for trespassing onto a US air force base near nuclear capable F-15 Strike Eagle aircraft, contact David 01508-550446. ** **Karen Fallon** - charged with criminal damage to a hanger window at Shannon Airport - Limerick Prison c/o 210 Le Fanu Rd., Ballyfermot, Dublin 10, Ireland. ** **Barbara Smedema**--Disabled an American communications satellite at the military airport of Volkel, in the Netherlands. Contact: P.I.Ter Peel, Patersweg 4, 5977 NM Evertsoord, Netherlands. ** **Arthur Milling** and **Dr Margaret Jones** will be in court on 23 May for cutting their way into Fairford and causing £50,000 of damage to B52 support vehicles two weeks ago. Contact: media@tridentploughshares.org. ** **Other peace prisoner info**: www.peacenews.info. For Legal info check out www.gwi.org.uk/legal.htm

"It was just eat, sleep and work: getting up at 4.30am, leaving the market at 8.30pm and having something to eat before falling into bed at 10pm. It really takes it out of you, standing all day, shouting on the market floor. The only relief we got was one hour when the Stop the War demonstrators burst in… It's a bit like a toyshop which must make most of its profits at Christmas. We have to make up for lean periods when the price of oil falls, as it's doing now."

- An oil trader describes the 'busy period' at the International Petroleum Exchange just before the war. In the run up to war 'uncertainty' about how oil supplies were going to be affected pushed the price up, making huge profits for lucky oil companies. Once bombing started the city realised that oil supplies were assured for the time being, and the price fell. Still, kind of those Infernal Petroleum Experience folks to shut down the trading floor at the perfect moment, and give the overworked city boys a breather…

CANNON FODDER

When two brutal regimes clash, they always need as much human cannon fodder as possible. Saddam's policy is to keep his loyal Republican Guards close to him, to protect him from the US/UK invaders. While he puts poorly-equipped conscripts as cannon fodder to face US/UK forces in the desert, and threatens them with torture of their families should they desert the frontlines. The US has a different arm-twisting technique – to dangle offers of skills training, free college education and health care in the faces of poor Americans in order to get them to sign up to whatever crazy cowboy scheme Bush comes up with. The sad result is a disproportionate number of 'people of colour' on the US frontlines in the Gulf. During the first Gulf War, over 50 percent of front-line troops were non-white, although people of colour only make up around 10 percent of the overall population. Over 30 percent of US troops are non-white but they make up only 12 percent of officers.

When recent studies showed a dip in young African-Americans' interest in becoming patriotic cannon fodder, the Pentagon schemed up a flashy new Spanish ad campaign targeting Latino youth. But all the promises of 'adventure', and 'career' are as empty as the thing between George Bush's ears. Most recruits never get any college funding from the military

SOME OF OUR BOYS MAY NOT COME BACK...

...BUT YOU WANT GAS IN YOUR TANK DON'T YOU?

KEEP MORALE AMONGST THE TROOPS HIGH - DON'T TELL 'EM THEY ARE PAWNS FOR AN EMPIRE

and only a small amount graduate. To top it all off, the skills you learn in the military are geared towards military jobs, not civilian careers; so when you finally leave after years of blind discipline, many employers may tell you to go back to school and get some proper training.

As vice-president Dick Cheney smugly put it, "The reason to have a military is to be prepared to fight and win wars... it's not a jobs program."

So the US military can't guarantee that you'll get educated or that you'll even be alive at the end of your eight-year commitment. They can't even promise you won't be desperately ill from one of many "mystery illnesses" like those of the Vietnam and Gulf wars. What they can promise is a series of absurd conflicts, all aimed at lining the White House's pockets and often placing the soldiers in extreme health risk. Whether it's atomic testing in the 1950s , Agent Orange during the war against Vietnam or exposure to depleted uranium in Gulf War I the US military excels in using its soldiers as guinea pigs and then covering up any supposed 'side effects'. The big hush hush at the moment is the disastrous effects of Gulf War Syndrome.

Gulf War II has proved to be not too dissimilar from the first Gulf War. The US frontlines are filled with stupendous amounts of 'cannon fodder of colour.' As coalition casualties pile up, the human faces of the US military machine are revealed. The dead US Marine, Kendall Waters-Bey, comes to mind. His irate father appeared on CNN berating George Bush and saying the only reason his son had joined the Marines was to escape the streets and be able to provide for his son. Kendall's sister Nakia also hit out "This war's all about oil and money. (Bush) ought to send his own daughters over there to fight."

See www.objector.org, www.afsc.org

War briefs

If you want some interesting new **anti-war posters** check out www.uhc-collective.org.uk/ ** **Media Storm Shelter** everyday at the London Action Resource Centre (LARC) with a café and open access radio - where the war media gets torn to pieces. Broadcast across London on Resonance 104.4 FM, online at http://freeteam.nl:8000/uknowar 11am-12pm. LARC is open daily 10:00am till 10:00pm, 62 Fieldgate St E1 (Whitechapel Tube) 020 73779088. ** **'Salt in the Wound' an anti-war single** featuring Jello Biafra and Conflict is out this week. If you fancy seeing Conflict on Top of the Pops, why not get yer hands on a copy. www.peace-not-war.org ** If you get arrested at a military base, you could use the defence that you are upholding **international law.** http://osstw.lautre.net/article.php3?id_article=30

SchNEWS in brief

The Court of Appeal has upheld a High Court Ruling that **Section 55 of the Immigration and Asylum Act is illegal**. Section 55 was set to withdraw all financial support to asylum seekers who didn't immediately apply for asylum on arrival in the UK. Because of the finding, asylum seekers can now continue to look forward to a massive 70% of the dole, but this may be short-lived as David Blunkett has vowed to make changes to Section 55 in order to make it legal. www.refugeecouncil.org.uk ** While war hysteria continues, the state is continuing to further erode our rights. In the latest **Criminal Justice Bill** making it's way through Parliament are proposals to give police powers to take fingerprints and DNA from anyone who is arrested regardless of whether they're charged or not. ** **Stuff the War!** The SchNEWS mailout will bite the dust if we don't more help, if you've got a couple of hours spare on Friday afternoon to help out in the office then get in touch with us.

...and finally...

Last Thursday in San Francisco, direct action found a new form of expression when a group tired of samey-samey protesters set up Pukers4Peace – inducing vomitting in the plaza outside the Federal Building in San Francisco to show how sick the war made them feel. One barfer said, "Militarism makes me sick. Puking is the most disgusting display of emotion that is still legal." "My puddle is the longest-lasting one," proudly declared one protester, as pools of chuck had people pegging their noses for the afternoon.

The pukers were part of a protesting marathon during which a San Francisco cop told the local paper, "After 16 hours of fighting communists and anarchists, a Red Bull can help us go another 16 hours. We're here as long as they are." Lovely product placement! Don't it make you want to puke?

Disclaimer

SchNEWS warns all pigs with wings not to take any bull.Honest!

Subscribe!

Keep SchNEWS FREE! Send 1st Class stamps (e.g. 10 for next 9 issues) or donations (payable to Justice?) Ask for "Originals" if you can make copies. Post *free* to all prisoners. SchNEWS, c/o on-the-fiddle, P.O. Box 2600, Brighton, East Sussex, BN2 0EF.
Tel/Autofax +44 (0)1273 685913 *Email* schnews@brighton.co.uk *Download a* **PDF** *of this issue or subscribe at* **www.schnews.org.uk**

MINORS STRIKE

Perhaps the best thing about the global protests against the War in Iraq was the central role played by schoolchildren. Taking adult activists and headteachers alike completely by surprise, a pattern was repeated all over the world of kids forming their own groups and sorting out their own actions and protests.

It's hard to say where this wave of autonomous schoolkid militancy came from. Some reckon that its because mobile phones and the internet have given this generation of kids access to new channels of information and communication that can't be monitored or controlled by adults, allowing them more space to form their own politics and hatch their own plans. Being adults ourselves (well we're trying) SchNEWS doesn't know if that's true or not, but there are two things that are certain: first, whatever the kids were doing, they were definitely doing it for themselves. Even the cops recognised, for the most part, that the schoolkid actions were schoolkid led. Second, in the UK at least, kids have got more than a few things to teach seasoned 'revolutionaries' about 'having it on the streets'. Whilst so-called anti-war unions organised lame rallies outside workplaces, outside working hours, kids sent shockwaves through the education system with a series of illegal student walkouts. In Brighton, on the day the war started, anarchists watched in slack-jawed admiration as GCSE students smashed in the windows of HSBC bank and tore up publicly displayed US flags. Probably not what Tony's cronies had in mind when they added "citizenship" classes to the curriculum last September to combat the "political apathy" of kids today!

There was spontaneous resistance all over the country, without coordination from any one point. One group or another would spring up, and word then passed from school to school, often by email or text messaging. Some kids uploaded mouthy websites,

> *"Tony Blair doesn't think Iraqi children are too young to be bombed, so how can we be too young to protest?"* - 16 year-old anti-war protestor.

including the Cornwall-based Kres – the Cornish word for peace – which had one page titled: "Humiliation – Let's destroy the President".

Kids were already out in force on the February 15th demo in London, making a sizeable presence among the 2 million protestors. Also in February 60 teenagers and students dressed in tiger suits invaded Esso's UK HQ. And this was just the beginning.

On March 5th thousands of children walked out of classrooms nationwide to make their feelings clear. Seven sacks of dung were deposited outside Labour HQ and kids tried to storm Downing Street.

Plenty of cops managed to overcome any qualms about grappling with pint-sized activists. In Cambridge one baton-wielding child abuser had to be forcibly restrained by colleagues and three kids were arrested 'on suspicion of public order offences'.

March 19th saw the biggest ever coordinated child demos, with 10,000 kids bolting from classrooms nationwide. Many schools tried to stop them by locking the gates, forcing kids to break out. This was the first truly national protest by children since the 1970s and the media coverage was frenzied, comparing it to the May 68 riots in France which started with schoolkids and university students and almost brought down the government.

While some school heads turned a blind eye, many teachers' unions joined police in condemning this outbreak of freedom. "Treat it as normal truancy and take appropriate action" ordered the draconian secondary heads' association. Several expulsions followed across the country. Kids were given lines: "I will not walk out of school." But they did anyway.

When the US started bombing on the 20th March, school was out again. In Lancaster schoolkids shut down the city for 5 hours and occupied the town hall; in Brighton the chant of "One two three four Tony Blair is Bush's whore" rang through the streets as kids shredded the stars and stripes outside the American Express building (see SchNEWS 297/8). In Cambridge 22 people, some as young as 14, were nabbed by the nasty child-catchers. The list goes on.

On 24th March police in Bristol decided it was time to find the dangerous and manipulative adult activists behind the continuing under-age unrest, and began questioning onlookers in the city centre where kids had yet again brought traffic to a halt. But the other grown-ups present were

as baffled as the cops and the horrible truth finally dawned - the kids were doing it on their own.

But anti-war kids in the UK weren't the only ones showing the grown-ups how it's done. Here are some of the global highlights from the playground insurrections that swept the planet:

In Australia 27,000 kids joined a nation wide demonstration called 'Books Not Bombs' on 26th March. Aussie cops proved not to be very child friendly, with observers saying there was a 'clear attempt to intimidate the kids' with large numbers of mounted police and riot cops present. When one kid in Sydney got his first taste of pepper spray the kids fought back and 33 were arrested. Overall 56 kids were nicked on the day, some as young as 11. A day earlier 1,000 angry 12-14 year-olds joined Aboriginals at the entrance of the national parliament in Canberra, and then despite intimidation from 'Walk Against War Coalition' (!) another 'Books Not Bombs' took place on April the 2nd.

In Germany it kicked off at a 20,000-strong schoolkid demo in Hamburg on 24th March, when 8,000 kids (according to police) splintered off from the main march and made for the US embassy. The cops (who later claimed that they were pelted with tree branches) then waded in with batons and water cannon, splitting up the group and forcing some onto nearby train tracks and others into a kettle formation. Numerous kids were injured, 36 arrested, and 125 held by police.

In Athens on March 20th a Black Bloc of around 1,000 was joined by unruly schoolkids who helped them 'unrenovate' a recently restored posh hotel, stone the embassies of Italy, Portugal and the UK and set the Ministry of Internal Affairs ablaze with Molotov

"Come on love - you don't want to miss Top Of The Pops" March 21st, Westminster Abbey

cocktails. Sadly their plans for the US Embassy were put to a halt by such massive quantities of tear gas that an over-flying pigeon fell out of the sky stone dead!

In Spain there was a series of 'general strikes' by schoolkids and students. The fourth, on March 26th, saw student walk-outs in more than 70 towns and cities, with over 1,000,000 kids taking part in protests.

In Bahrain 400 teenagers held a sit-down outside the US embassy, burning US and UK flags.

In Seoul enterprising teenagers eager to occupy the US embassy decided their best bet was to dress up in business suits and pretend they were going in for a meeting - unfortunately the cops thought they were a bit too young and innocent looking to be bona fide fat cats and an unseemly scuffle ensued.

In Jakarta 50 children dressed in black protested outside the US embassy with placards reading 'UN useless'. In Syria 1,500 school kids demonstrated outside UNICEF on April 2nd with banners saying 'stop killing Iraqi children.'

Back in the UK a lot of schools are determined that kids should pay a heavy price for missing the point of the 'political participation' module in Citizenship class. An estimated 30–40 have been suspended or expelled, with one girl from Essex being excluded for 30 days for organising demos even though she was due to sit her GCSEs. She refused to accept her punishment and took the school to high court where the judge ruled in her favour, but not before telling her she was a 'very silly girl'!

But it's going to take more than lines and detention to put the spectre of under-age anarchism back in its box. Neo Labour's determination to go to war at any cost, and to silence or ignore all protest, has taught the next generation of activists a more valuable lesson than a decade of Citizenship classes could: that democracy's a joke, voting's pointless, and the only way to change the world is to fight for it. As one Pimlico 6th former said, "We're questioning the whole way the government works and are finding that it lies, it stinks and it's hypocritical." Apathetic? If you say so, Tony…

Hamburg riot police give the schoolkids a taste of a warzone.

Hey man - peace, Perth, West Australia, March 26th

A new generation reclaims the Old Steine, Brighton, March 20th

CLASS STRUGGGLE

Striking school children, some as young as 11 and 12, brought Brighton City Centre to a halt on Thursday March 20th in protest over the British and American invasion of Iraq. Taking to the streets with chants of "No War," "One, two, three, four, Tony Blair is Bush's whore," and other brilliantly unprintable slogans, the students blocked roads in the city centre for nearly four hours, telling perturbed motorists to "Turn off your engines, you ain't goin' nowhere." Cynical, disillusioned Brighton activists were spotted in the area, wandering in a haze of shock, awe and respect, gobsmacked by people half their age with twice as much energy and imagination. "I was just about to trade in my Palestinian scarf and trendy body jewellery for a thankless call centre job," said one old, formerly disenchanted 23-year-old in a faded Che Guevara t-shirt. "But today has convinced me that the revolution may still be possible!"

Meanwhile, one group of school kids (pursued by rabid Socialist Worker's Party paper-sellers) broke off from the main march and paid a visit to the local American Express building. The pledge of allegiance was not said, the star spangled banner was not played, but nonetheless, the American flag became the centre of attention for much of the crowd, who decided the old stars and stripes were in need of a drastic makeover. An upstanding, tax-paying, Daily Mail-reading bystander who was later quoted in the Argus, described the event as sickening and depraved, but a nearby American reckoned it was the most beautiful thing she had ever seen.

Earlier in the day, in an important lesson on free speech, teachers and heads around the city locked many young pupils into their schools, desperate to keep them from expressing an opinion. Pupils at Blatchington Mill, Cardinal Newman, Dorothy Stringer, Varndean, and Patcham were threatened with suspension, expulsion, and extra citizenship classes (to teach them the real meaning of democracy and blind obedience) if they left school to participate in protests. In some cases, pupils even faced locked gates and the harrowing spectre of future visits from local blood-thristy pro-war MPs.

But in a series of daring walk-outs and escapes, hundreds of locked-down school kids still managed to join the protests in the town centre.

SchNEWS were on the scene at Blatchington Mill when, at 11am, a brave group of around 50 students walked out of school past barely-opened iron gates and a grimly frowning head-master. (Readers may remember Blatch's open-minded head, one Mr. Neil Hunter, when he referred to pupils that had staged a spontaneous anti-war demo a few weeks ago as "mindless idiots." Since the spontaneous walk-out, six Blatch kids have been excluded and the "always wanting to show both sides of the argument" Mr. Hunter has invited the local pro-war MP, Ivor Caplin, to come and spew pro-war propaganda at the school.) After leaving Blatchington, the triumphant procession of Blatch kids met up with nearly 200 other excited and out-of-breath pupils who had just rushed out of Cardinal Newman. "We've just escaped, we've just escaped our school," they panted. "They tried to lock us in!" Teachers had tried to lock gates and chase anti-war escapees through the school grounds, but many kids still managed to find a way out. As SchNEWS rounded a corner near Cardinal Newman school, the sight that awaited was grand indeed - 20-30 blue and grey-jumpered Newman kids pouring over an exterior stone wall after teachers had blocked all other routes of exit from the school.

Eventually the whole group of anti-war pupils made it safely and soundly down to the Old Steine for a day of protest and road-blocking. Many of the kids were still around at 5:30 the same afternoon, when nearly 5,000 people (probably Brighton's biggest ever demo) converged on Churchill Square. Even in the evening, most of the chants and road sit-downs were led by school kids from all over the city. As one young protestor explained, "We did it because we wanted our voices to be heard. We were rebelling against the Government because we feel it is rebelling against us."

* Kids in Therfield school Leatherhead who bunked off to go to an anti war demo where given lines by the Headmaster "I will not walk out of school."

* Thousands of newly politicised school kids took part in anti-war demonstrations all across the UK last week. For more info from the school-uniformed frontlines in Manchester, London, and hundreds of other cities around the world, check out www.indymedia.org

KIDS SPEAK OUT

When the schoolkids came out in force on the streets against the war, right-wing hacks and headteachers alike made the same assumptions: that they were too young to understand the issues, that they must have been following the lead of *agent provocateurs*, or that they were just doing it to have a day off. In fact it wasn't just a matter of bunking off for a laugh - many were walking out of school in the knowledge that they might face expulsion or suspension for their actions.

So let's see what kids from Brighton comprehensive schools had to say about it all, their responses to some of the criticisms levelled at them, and reflections on what they learned from their involvement in the protests.

1. Anti-war protestors 'incite' or 'encourage' school walk-outs

'What's great is, we organised this ourselves!' (Yr 10 student, Varndean).

'Contrary to the opinion of many teachers, young people aren't sheep: they form their own opinions and organise their own protests' (Yr 12 student, Varndean).

2. Walk-outs and other protests put students at risk.

'Young people are considered incapable of looking after themselves, but adults have put us and the world at most risk by going to war.' (Yr 11, Falmer)

'Young protestors get called 'delinquent' while pro-war MPs who voted for a war we don't want get paid to 'represent' us!' (Yr 10, Dorothy Stringer)

3. Protesting damages young people's education

'We aren't educated in school, we're suppressed' (Yr 9, Cardinal Newman).

'It's all tests and being told off for not wearing uniform. And you pass exams, for what? To do more exams at college or get a boring job.' (Yr 11, Dorothy Stringer).

'Anxiety over students' walk-outs highlights the real purpose of schools: teaching young people to accept authority, become a passive, efficient workforce, and accept that 'democracy' just means putting a cross on a ballot paper every 5 years (if you are 'mature' enough)' (Yr 11 Falmer)

Can someone pass me a chair?
Books Not Bombs, Sydney March 26th

What next?

'We're guinea pigs for tests and new types of school and we'll have to pay for university education. They tell us what to wear and we can't even go on strike. But if lots of us refuse to do the exams or wear the uniform, Tony Blair will have to listen – or get out.' (Yr 12, Varndean College).

'This was about a war but it was also about us having no rights. If there's another war, that'll be really big because what I didn't realise was that loads of people do what I do, watch TV and stuff and think I can't do anything, but then when something big happens, you do, everyone does, and we scared the government, even if we didn't stop them, we showed what we could do and next time there'll be more, but the other fight is for our rights and that seems like a small thing, just one school in one town in England, but it should go on'. (Yr 11 Patcham)

'At the anti-war demo in Brighton people shouted 'Our Town Hall!' when it got occupied. I want to shout 'Our school!' We've got to keep protesting, occupy schools or walk out, keep shouting about exams and all the other crap until someone listens.' (Yr 11, Blatchington Mill).

Blocking traffic at Churchill Square, Brighton March 21st

THE SECOND SUPERPOWER

"There may still be two superpowers on the planet: the United States and world public opinion." - New York Times, February 2003.

What happened when the bombing started was always going to be a moment of truth for those opposing the war. The military build-up and the movement of troops and equipment from bases in Europe to the Gulf had been the target of direct action from Ireland to Turkey. An unprecedented series of mass demonstrations before the war had begun with the biggest marches for a generation in Europe, North America and Australia. As war got closer, countries in the Middle East, North Africa and Asia started to wade in with their own big rallies - many targetting US and British Embassies.

Here is a global round-up of anti-war protests from the start of the war onwards...

This report - of course only a glimpse of the full story - pays particular attention to the Middle East, Asia and North Africa, but covers the rest of the world in much less detail. Sorry, but we just can't do it all! If you're interested check out the large network of Indymedia websites www.indymedia.org

One last point: however big, mass marches alone were unlikey to, and of course didn't stop the war - symbolic gestures will only take things so far. That said, there was something unique about the scale and momentum of these protests which made them more important and exciting than the usual inconsequential a-to-b marches. Frequently in these protests the distinction between symbolic and direct action was blurred. The fact that anti-war demos were often violently repressed even by states who were opposed to the war may indicate the potential that these actions had to spill over into more generalised expressions of discontent.

Middle East/Nth Africa

A picture emerged of people in the Arab world seeing the huge international opposition to the war, and being empowered to come out onto the street *en masse* and even have a swing at some US Embassies. But to put some context on this list of marches it is worth remembering that on some of the days mentioned below it was more life threatening to be out on the streets of Sanaa, Amman or Cairo than it was to be on the perimeter fence at Fairford Airbase. Note also that some Middle Eastern countries don't even feature here, even though their populations were certainly anti-war, such as Saudi Arabia. This only goes to show the level of state oppression in these places.

The events listed are only what we could find on the web - and as such don't necessarily reflect the actual shape of what happened. Factors which influenced this research included Arab news websites mysteriously going offline during the war, and their focus changing towards events in Iraq.

War Starts the night of March 20th
March 21 Friday
Egypt: In Cairo a peaceful protest of 40,000 is brutally suppressed by police, with 500 arrested. One group of 5,000 is dispersed by the police spraying blue soapy water! In eleven other Egyptian cities large demos and strikes take place, with several hundred injured in police attacks.
Yemen: Tens of thousands march in the capital of Sanaa. 3 protesters and a policeman are killed, plus 23 injured, when police try to disperse a crowd as it approaches the US Embassy. The crowd is angry that the Yemen government is cooperating with the US's "war on terror".
Jordan: Depite a ban on pro-Iraq demonstrations, 80,000 gather in Amman, where tear gas is used to break up crowds in the predominately Palestinian neighbourhood of al-Wahdat.

March 22 Saturday
Lebanon: 1,000 march in Beirut, where protesters are repelled with water cannons as they charge the British Embassy. Other towns in Lebanon saw large anti-war demonstrations.
Palestine: 20,000 demonstrate in Gaza.

March 24 Monday
Yemen: 15,000 gather peacefully in the Yemeni port of Aden.
Sudan: Police use tear gas to break up a demonstration of hundreds of students in the capital, Khartoum.

Cairo, March 24th

Palestine: Demonstrations continue in the West Bank.
Egypt: More than 12,000 students rally on two university campuses.

March 25 Tuesday
Lebanon: More than 10,000 march in Beirut. Demonstrators try to storm the British Embassy, but are pushed back by riot police with batons, water cannons and tear gas.
Syria: An estimated 500,000 demonstrate in Damascus. Schools, universities and government institutions are closed to allow people to take part. Five are arrested when a large group try to break past roadblocks to get to the US Embassy.
Libya: In the capital of Tripoli, hundreds of thousands of demonstrators chant anti-US slogans as they march to the Iraqi embassy.
Tunisia: Some 10,000 gather in the capital of Tunis, marching 3km through the city centre under heavy police presence.

Damascus, Syria, March 25th

The Stars and Stripes burns brightly in Amman, Jordan

March 26 Wednesday

Bahrain: About 400 people, mostly teenagers and young men, hold an anti-war sit-in outside the US Embassy.

March 27 Thursday

Algeria: Several hundred thousand people around the country converge on the capital Algiers - flouting an official ban on demonstrations - and march through the main streets shouting anti-war slogans.

Yemen: 100,000 turn out in the capital Sanaa venting their anger at the "unjustified" invasion of Iraq.

Egypt: More than 10,000 rally in the northern city of Zagazig. 4,000 students gather on the campus of Cairo University, but are held back from marching to Giza Square by riot police. Professors give speeches surrounded by banners reading "Jihad is the answer" and students burn American flags. The Egyptian government threaten to violently prevent any further political unrest.

Iran: Hundreds of families of victims of the Iran-Iraq war rally in front of the UN office in Tehran. The demonstrators denounce the war and voice support for the "innocent Iraqi nation".

Lebanon: About 40,000 students march through the northern city of Tripoli. As the march is winding down several hundred trash a Kentucky Fried Chicken outlet. Students throw stones at police in response to water cannon attacks which injure 10. Some 2,000 people gather in the main square of the southern town of Jeb Jannine to watch the burning of an effigy of Bush and an Israeli flag.

Palestine: In the West Bank and Gaza Strip, Palestinians march through the streets, holding posters of Saddam and waving Iraqi and Palestinian flags, whilst stomping over Israeli and US flags placed on the ground.

Syria: In Damascus some 1,000 Syrians and Palestinians march through the main streets, while 30 women hold an anti-war sit-in at the Red Cross building.

March 28 Friday

Iran: Tens of thousands demonstrate in Tehran. Some pelt stones at the British Embassy, breaking windows and shouting for the embassy to be closed.

Yemen: 100,000 take to the streets in the capital of Sanaa.

Egypt: In the first authorised demonstration on Cairo's streets, some 15,000 march in Cairo behind a huge Iraqi flag. Riot police guard the US Embassy.

Lebanon: Protesters take to the streets for the eighth day running, with 5,000 school children and university students marching from the UN building in central Beirut to the British Embassy. In southern Lebanon, more than 7,000 women march through the Palestinian refugee camp of Bourj ash-Shamali.

Jordan: Riot police attack 2,000 people who have gathered after prayers for an attempted march on the Israeli Embassy in Amman. Police attack and tear gas a group of 10,000 anti-war protesters in the southern city of Ma'an, some of whom marched on the police station. Protesters at the Palestinian refugee camp at al-Wahdat are also attacked by police. Much of the protest centres on the Jordanian government's aiding of the invasion forces.

Palestine: In the Nasser district of Gaza City more than 20,000 march, including many from the islamic resistance movement, Hamas. In the West Bank, 5,000 + march in Nablus and burn effigies of Bush and Blair.

March 29 Saturday

Egypt: 10,000 march in Port Said.

Libya: Thousands of protesters demonstrate in several Libyan cities. Libyans fasted on Friday in solidarity with the Iraqi people and held sunset prayers at Tripoli's main square, praying for Iraq's victory over its enemies.

March 30 Sunday

Morocco: 30,000 march through Rabat, which winds up with several hundred battling riot police guarding a McDonalds.

Palestine: In the Nusseirat refugee camp south of Gaza City, 5,000 people demonstrate with Iraqi and Palestinian flags, chanting "Death to Israel and America," and "From Jenin to Baghdad, Arab leaders have let us down." In Bethlehem 200 Palestinian Christians stage an anti-war demonstration in the Church of the Nativity.

Israel: More that 20,000 Arab Israelis gather in the northern town of Sahhnin.

April 2nd - Schoolkids in Damascus, Syria

April 02 Wednesday

Yemen: Thousands march to the Iraqi Embassy in Sanaa demanding the expulsion of US and British Embassy staff.

Lebanon: In the southern city of Sidon, 10,000 Lebanese and Palestinian demonstrators voice their anger with Arab leaders for failing to act against the war.

Syria: 1,500 Syrian school children stage a sit-down outside the UNICEF offices in Damascus. Government employees observe a ten-minute work stoppage.

April 18th Saturday

Iraq: As the process of installing a US-friendly regime in Iraq begins, so too does the long journey for the Iraqi people to reclaim power and autonomy for themselves.

Over 200,000 Iraqis demonstrate in Baghdad and other cities shouting "Iraq for the Iraqis!" with many gathering after Friday prayers. A large spectrum of Baghdad society comes out, including Shias from the eastern parts of the city; Sunnis from the west and central Baghdad; clerics; members of the Baath Party; merchants, members of professional associations, and students. The largest of the demonstrations occurs when 50,000 people jam the streets of Al-Sadr City (formerly known as Saddam City) despite the presence of Kalashnikov-wielding guards.

In addition, hundreds of thousands pour out of mosques in Najuf, Karbala, Mosul and Basra to protest against the US occupation.

To follow the events in Iraq under US occupation visit Iraq Indymedia at www.almuajaha.com

263

Asia

March 20 Thursday
Philippines: The US Embassy in Manila is pelted with red paint bombs.

March 21 Friday
Pakistan: Students and teachers go on strike at Karachi University.

India: Six protesters and 12 police are injured in Calcutta when 1,000 people storm the US cultural centre. Thousands of workers took the day off work in Delhi to demand that the government oppose the war.

March 22 Saturday
Bangladesh: 15,000 in Dhaka.
India: 15,000 in Calcutta, 5,000 in New Delhi.
Indonesia: Jakarta: 2,000, Yogyakarta: 1,500.
Philippines: 10,000 farmers plus workers, students and children from poor urban communities gather outside the US embassy in Manila.

March 23 Sunday
Indonesia: Thousands take to the streets across the country to express their opposition to war. In Jakarta, 2,000 protesters stage peaceful rallies in front of a heavily guarded US Embassy in Jakarta.
Pakistan: 100,000 march in Lahore with numerous smaller protests in other cities.
Bangladesh: 3,000 are confronted by police as they march on the US Embassy in Dhaka.

March 24 Monday
Bangladesh: 1,000 students protest as riot police stop dozens of women from marching on the US Embassy.
Thailand: Around 3,000 stage a peaceful protest in front of the UN Building in Bangkok.
Afghanistan: Fearing protests could get out of hand, authorities in the eastern Afghan province of Laghman clamp down on a second day of demonstrations against the war after more than 10,000 had hit the streets of Mehtarlam the previous day.

Lahore, Pakistan March 23rd

March 25ᵗʰ Tuesday
Bangladesh: 3,000 protesters are attacked by police soon after beginning their procession from central Dhaka towards the US Embassy.

March 26 Wednesday
Pakistan: Some 2,000 march through the city of Multan. On the same day, workers in the towns of Mailsi and Hasilpur go on general strike, while 1,000 students rally in Karachi. In the north western tribal district of Bajaur bordering Afghanistan several thousand tribesmen and traders take to the streets.

Indonesian protesters burn an effigy of President Bush in front of the U.S Embassy in Jakarta Friday, March 28

South Korea: In Seoul, police arrest 30 after they scale a wall at the US Embassy and unfurl a banner reading "Stop The War". Another protester with a toy rifle and a George W. Bush mask climbs a 50-foot McDonalds sign.

Give us a hug - Seoul, South Korea March 28

March 27 Thursday
Indonesia: Protesters cause a ruckus outside McDonald's branches in Java: "We warn Indonesians to shun American products because a portion of the profits goes to Israel," said a protester outside a McDonald's in Central Java

March 28 Friday
India: 20,000 Muslims in New Delhi take to the streets, as police arrest India's chief Islamic priest for alleged incitement to take up arms. Protests also build up in Madras, Guwahati and Ranchi, and tens of thousands of students in Calcutta boycott classes to join a large rally. In Andhra Pradesh anti-war protesters force the closure of a water bottling unit owned by Coca-Cola.
Bangladesh: In Dhaka 10,000 take to the streets after weekly Friday prayers.

March 29 Saturday
Malaysia: 10,000 march in Kuala Lumpar in heavy rain.

March 30 Sunday
Indonesia: Around 1 million people demonstrate in Jakarta with 100,000 congregating outside the US Embassy.
India: 30,000 march in Calcutta.
Pakistan: 300,000 flood into the north-west city of Peshawar for an anti-war demo.
South Korea: 50,000 march in Seoul.

April 2 Wednesday
Pakistan: 25,000 demonstrators march through Quetta

- a provincial capital in southwestern Pakistan - in a protest organized by Islamic leaders.

April 3 Thursday
Indonesia: 5,000 university students demonstrate in the city of Makassar in South Sulawesi. At Cirebon in West Java some 2,500 people rally outside the city hall and torch a Bush effigy. Meanwhile another 1,000 school students take to the streets of Semarang City in Central Java.
Thailand: In the southern town of Pattani, tens of thousands of Muslims demonstrate in Thailand's largest protest against the war.

April 4 Friday
Bangladesh: In Dhaka police clamp down as thousands of people demonstrate in the streets after Friday prayers. US-owned shops are attacked, and police lines hold back hundreds from marching on the US Embassy.
Indonesia: A crowd of 10,000 people burn a mock Statue of Liberty and chant "Bush is a Terrorist" during a boisterous rally in Jakarta.
Pakistan: More than 50,000 people march through the streets of Multan.

April 6ᵗʰ Sunday
Indonesia: Thousands gather for an anti-war protest outside two McDonald's stores, demanding they cease business. In Bandung on the island of Java, around 2,000 protesters shout anti-US slogans outside a McDonald's in the city centre.

April 13ᵗʰ Sunday
Indonesia: 300 high school students hold a protest outside the US embassy in Jakarta.

Dhaka, Bangladesh, April 12

Africa
March 21 Friday
South Africa: Schoolkids lead the protests in Cape Town and are joined by factory workers. The US consulate sees a continuous picket once the war starts, with at least 50 people continually maintaining a presence.

March 24th Monday
Mauritania: 40,000 demonstrators shouting "Death to Bush, Victory for Saddam" march to the US Embassy in Nouakchott.

March 27th Thursday
South Africa: 500 schoolkids lead a mock funeral through the city of Pietermaritzburg.

March 28th Friday
Senegal: In the capital Dakar, more than 1,000 teachers and students march through the streets.

April 2nd Wednesday
Ghana: Around 10,000 people take over the streets of Accra in a five-hour anti-war demonstration that brings the government and business districts to a standstill. Breakaway groups repeatedly breach mounted and armed police lines that have cordoned off the American and British Embassies.

Melbourne

Australasia
March 21 Friday
Melbourne: With less than 3 hours notice 30,000 people converge on the city centre: a simulated air-raid siren is sounded to remind residents of the realities of war. Later, 500 pelt the US Consulate with paint bombs.

Books Not Bombs 2, Sydney April 2r

Sydney: 20,000 take to the streets in the pouring rain. The New South Wales premier has his car paint bombed.
Perth: 2,000 workers down tools and walk off construction sites in the city centre to join protest against the war. Schoolkids walk out of classes to hold a sit-in in front of the US consulate before police wade in and arrest eleven.

March 22 Saturday
Perth: 10,000 march
New Zealand: 4,000 march in Wellington. One police photographer suffers cholesterol damage when he is hit by an egg.

March 23 Sunday
Sydney: A 50,000-strong crowd march through the city.

March 24, Monday
Canberra: 15,000 anti-war protesters attempt to storm Australia's parliament, demanding the withdrawal of Australian troops fighting in Iraq. When police halt entry into the building, protesters block the entrance with a sit-down protest.

March 25 Tuesday
Canberra: Police are confronted by 1,000 angry 12-14-year-old school kids screaming in their faces at the national parliament building. Aboriginal leaders join them at the doors of parliament.

March 26, Wednesday
Books Not Bombs: Tens of thousands of schoolkids across the country participate in a national day of action which sees police turn violent and arrest over 60 kids – one as young as eleven (see **Minors Strike**).

March 29, Saturday
Melbourne: 40,000 march in the city's third major demonstration in 10 days.

April 2 Wednesday
Sydney: Despite intimidation from police, pro-war media and even a sections of the anti-war movement, school children in Sydney stage another Books Not Bombs event.

April 7 Monday
Melbourne: Anti-war protesters shut down an Australian Defence Force in the city centre, the third such Monday-morning action in as many weeks.

Athens: the US Embassy gets a friendly visit from that happy-go-lucky Greek black block. March 21st

Europe

(minus stuff from Britain cos you'll find all that all through the SchNEWS issues)

March 21 Friday

Spain: Thousands take to the streets in opposition to Prime Minister Aznar's support of the war. In Madrid police charge a crowd attempting to kick off at the US Embassy.

Slovenia: In the capital of Ljubljana, protesters gather in front of the US Embassy as soon as the bombing starts at 2pm. A presence is maintained until the main demo at 4pm. When a 1,500-strong crowd tries to storm the embassy they are driven back by riot cops.

Turkey: 250,000 demonstrate in Diyarbakir, with hundreds of thousands marching in other cities. In Istanbul, protesters are greeted by friendly cops with submachine guns & tanks. Despite such massive police presence, protesters close down the streets for a few hours.

Barcelona, March 26th

Greece: In Athens, up to 500,000 gather as up-for-it Greek Anarchists are joined by hoards of unruly schoolkids. The embassies of pro-war countries (Italy, Portugal, Britain) are pelted with stones; the Ministry of Internal Affairs is attacked with Molotov cocktails, and a branch of American Citibank is firebombed (for more details see **Minor's Strike**).

It was the third demo in three days since the war began: On the 20th about 200,000 took to the streets, and on the night of the 19th 3,000 people stayed outside the US Embassy until the morning.

In other parts of Greece: more than 11,000 people march to the US Consulate in Thessaloniki, while about 10,000 hit the British Consulate in Patras, with many throwing eggs and petrol bombs at it.

PLUS... In **Göteborg, Sweden**, over 40,000 people march through the city on Saturday, as well as 60,000 in **Stockholm** * 20,000 gather for a march in **Bern, Switzerland**. * 40,000 in **Helsinki, Finland**, 12,000 in **Koln**, 10,000 in **Berlin** and 8,000 in **Nuremburg Germany** and finally the **Danish PM** is covered with red paint, just after he gives a speech offering support for George W. Bush.

March 22 Saturday

Turkey: 15,000 march in Istanbul

March 23 Sunday

Italy: Several thousand anti-war demonstrators rally outside two US bases in Italy (see **Trainstopping**). In addition, protesters set off air-raid style sirens outside the US Naval Air Service base at Sigonella, Sicily in solidarity with the people of Baghdad.

March 24, Monday

Italy: 500,000 teachers and students march across Italian cities, with demonstrations in Rome, Milan Turin, Venice, Bologna, Naples and Palermo. Although the strike was initially planned to protest about school reform and teachers' pay disputes, the protest soon turns into an antiwar rally, with demonstrators waving rainbow flags and chanting peace slogans. Union officials say that 60 percent of the schools remained closed across the country.

Germany: An estimated 25,000 protesters join in a peace march through the streets of Leipzig, following the route used by demonstrators before the collapse of the former East Germany in 1989. A similar demonstration in Berlin marches peacefully from the Brandenburg gate to the US Embassy. In Hamburg 20,000 - including 8,000 school kids - get attacked by police with water cannons. Over 125 under-18's are arrested (see **Minors Strike**)

March 26, Wednesday

Spain: A general student strike is called as a protest against the war - the fourth of its kind - which sees 90% of school and university students walking out (see **Minors Strike**). There are marches of around 250,000 students in Madrid, 150,000 in Barcelona, 30,000 in Seville, 25,000 in Valencia, 15,000 in Bilbao, 10,000 in Tarragona and Oviedo, plus thousands in Santiago, Salamanca, Gijon, Granada and Vitoria.

Turkey: A rally is held in Dolmabahce, with a public workers protest in Ankara the following day.

March 28 Friday

Italy: 100 activists block access to a refinery of Eni's AGIP in central Italy for three hours in the morning, disrupting tanker deliveries. Protesters also burn at least 10 brand new US-made Ford cars at a dealership near Rome leaving behind a banner saying, "Sabotage the Imperialist War".

March 29, Saturday

Germany: 100,000 demonstrate in several cities including around 30,000 who form a human chain between the northern cities of Munster and Osnabrueck - a 35-mile route taken in 1648 by negotiators who ended Europe's Thirty Years War.

Ireland: 30,000 march in Dublin as a reaction to the US use of Shannon Airport as a military airbase.

Italy: Marchers in Rome hang black mourning banners from the city's bridges. At Vicenza in northeastern Italy, demonstrators throw red paint and flares at the walls of a

Athens on general strike against the war, April 2nd

U.S. military base where hundreds of paratroopers sent to northern Iraq have been based.

Greece: 15,000 turn out in Athens with protesters spattering paint on the road outside the U.S. Embassy and on the windows of a McDonald's restaurant.

France: Protests in Paris attract about 10,000.

Scotland: In Edinburgh 15,000 march from Waterloo Place.

Hungary: 2,000 people whistle and jeer as they marchpast the U.S. and British embassies in Budapest.

Poland: 2,000 march to the US Embassy in Warsaw – the biggest anti-war demo in Poland yet.

Russia: Around 6,000 people demonstrate at the U.S. Embassy in Moscow.

March 30 Sunday

Turkey: A convoy of US military trucks in the south east of Turkey is damaged after being showered with stones – the stone throwers leave before the security forces arrive. This

March 30th, Sanliurfa, southern Turkey - villagers throw eggs at US military vehicle.

was one of several similar attacks on military convoys.

April 2 Tuesday

Greece: State services, banks, transport, schools and shops are closed around the country as Greece has a general strike in protest against the war. In Athens, about 10,000 people march past the US Embassy shouting anti-war slogans while another 15,000 head towards the American consulate in Thessaloniki. Smaller protests are held in cities around Greece.

April 5 Saturday

Bulgaria: Some 2,000 held a demonstration outside the governments HQ in Sofia against Bulgaria's complicity in the war.

Germany: 2,000 went down to make some noise at the US Army HQ in Heidelberg

April 12 Saturday

Glasgow: 5,000 march.

Berlin: More than 12,000 congregate at the Brandenburg Gate.

North America

In the first two weeks of the war there are almost continuous protests in **San Francisco.** Unsuprisingly, the scale of the protests is matched by unprecedented police numbers and levels of harassment, with over 2,000 arrests, mostly for failure to disperse and highway obstruction.

The whole of San Francisco is shut down for 16 hours on Thursday March 20th. Rather than having one mass march protestors split into many different mobile groups. The mobility of the protests is particularly effective in shutting down the city - by blocking intersections, occupying buildings and performing hit and run actions on corporate targets, the cops were out-manoeuvred and overstretched all day. Many police vehicles are rendered useless by having their windows smashed and tyres slashed.

* The award for most unlikely US protest goes to a group of women who held a knit-in under the banner "Crafty Bitches, Knitting for Peace."

March 22 Saturday

250,000 people march through **New York** city centre, while in **Chicago** over 10,000 gather. There are over 800 arrests when police pen in protesters and refuse to allow protesters to return to their convergence point. They are then arrested for not leaving the area!

See www.indymedia.org for the full story...

Latin America

Would you like fries with that sir? March 26th, Quito, Ecuador

March 26th

Ecuador: Police in Quito attack students with tear gas at the US Embassy and as two branches of McDonalds get re-decorated.

March 27th

Bolivia: Riot police use tear gas and rubber bullets to try and rein in a 7,000-strong protest outside the US embassy in Bogota.

March 29th Saturday

Chile: 3,000 protest in Santiago.

March 30 Sunday

Brazil: 30,000 march in Sao Paulo

Apologies for several sections of this 'round up' being lame. It's because the whole thing started out as a brief rundown of demonstrations around the world the day the war commenced called 'World Opinion' in SchNEWS 397, which got heavily expanded. Before we knew it, it was developing into a rambling, running timeline of protests around the world from the beginning of the war onwards. A lot of work was put into researching activity in the Middle East and Asia, because it was barely covered in any media, and the war was on their doorstep. To follow up some of the massive and continual protests and direct action in both North and South America visit the regional Indymedia websites (start at www.indymedia.org), Africa is more difficult to research online.

...like war's bad cos yeah and I'm not going back to school until they stop having wars and like I hate Tony Blair yeah and no more bombs and ...

NO BLOOD 4 OIL!

A Day Out In Barcelona

The city of Barcelona was shaken on Thursday April 10th as thousands of people took to the streets in a day of protest against the killing in Iraq and the permanent war. Many businesses were closed, following a call by several unions for a 24 hour general strike. Actions continued until the late evening.

From early in the morning, groups held protest actions in front of banks and chain shops, shutting many down and convincing others to participate in the general strike. Around midday, large groups of people - many of whom gathered spontaneously - converged on the city centre from all sides. There at least 10,000 people started a loud and colourful cacerolazo demonstration, banging on pots and pans, lampposts and police cars, and setting up mobile sound systems. Protest rallies were held in front of a big bank (BBVA, which is involved in the arms business), at the stock exchange, and at the Ministry of the Economy.

Moving back to the city centre, a group of protestors shut down the Burger King "restaurant" at Plaza Catalunya and opened a popular kitchen on the street in front of it as part of the "Active Boycott" campaign. Demonstrations continued until late evening, including an anarchist demo, a shut-down protest at a petrol station, and a human mosaic. As had happened every night for a few weeks previously, the day ended with a giant cacerolazo.

All over the city, people were going for it with the pans. Each night a deafening roar filled the streets, a massive outcry against the war. Also heard was the increasingly popular demand of "Que se vayan todos!" (They all must go!), a slogan taken from Argentina's popular revolt and now shouted in Barcelona as a rejection of the right wing Popular Party government. *from www.indymedia.org.uk*

WAKE UP! WAKE UP! IT'S YER PERLEY EVIL

Weekly SchNEWS
www.schnews.org.uk

Friday 4th April 2003   **Free/Donation**   **Issue 399**

PERLES OF WISDOM

"There are a lot of people getting rich during war." - *Chuck Lewis, Centre for Public Integrity.*

"If we just let our vision of the world go forth, and we embrace it entirely, and we don't try to piece together clever diplomacy, but just wage a total war ...our children will sing great songs about us years from now." - *Richard Perle.*

Despite whimperings from Prime Sinister Blair, US corporations look set to single-handedly rebuild the health, education, transport and political systems of Iraq - with the UN and international aid agencies not getting a sniff of the £60 billion worth of contracts being dished out by the US government. As fat corporate cats lick their lips at the money to be made from building airports and modernising Iraqi telecommunications and oil wells, SchNEWS can reveal that this is indeed a war of liberation – liberating Iraq's resources from Iraqis and handing them over to caring US companies.

A spokesman for the Muslim Council of Britain, Inayat Bunglawala, warned that these contracts will stoke anti-US sentiment and cause further violent resistance in Iraq. "People will believe the US is there to loot the wealth of the Iraqi people and draw money from Iraq back to the US, benefiting US corporations."

And what do you know - the reconstruction of Iraq will be awarded to a coalition of Bush's closest cronies! Overseeing rebuilding and humanitarian relief (if Bush has his way) will be Jay Garner, a retired US general who is, incidentally, the president of an arms company! Garner, a firm supporter of the Israeli military, has spent the last few years building weapons systems now being used in

the Iraq war. How handy! And then there's Halliburton, the firm who'll get the job of putting out oil fires and making emergency repairs to Iraq's oil infrastructure, who oddly enough used to be run by US vice-president Dick Cheney. Cheney was chief executive of Halliburton until three years ago and still receives up to a million dollars a year from them. Union-busters Stevedoring Services of America have been handed the $4.8 million contract to run the port of Umm Qasr, while bidders for other contracts include Fluor, whose board includes a former director of the National Security Agency and deputy director of the CIA, and the Bechtel Group, whose boardroom boasts a former secretary of state *and* a former defence secretary!

But where is all this money coming from, one may well ask? After being bombed back to the Stone Age by the non-coalition US forces, Iraq certainly won't be able to cough up the money to pay the non-coalition US companies for its reconstruction. But here's the most beautiful part of all – it's the very people who Bush refuses to give a decent healthcare and education system to (i.e. the US taxpayer) that will line his mates' pockets. A significant chunk of the money being paid to US firms to rebuild Iraq was made available by the Iraq war bill, passed by Congress and giving Bush a $75 billion budget to wage war with taxpayers' money. Half of the money goes to blow things up, while the other half goes to make the rebuilders rich.

According to Charles Tiefer, author of a book on US government contracting, this is naked evidence that the Bush administration has used 'shortcuts' and 'exceptions'

to put billions of taxpayer dollars into the pockets of its mates. Tiefer believes "a large credibility gap looms between the administration's plausible excuses that tight deadlines and exceptional security needs compelled them to forgo the usual competutuve sageguards and the the critics' observations that it is awfully convenient for juicy plums to land in the lap of the the vice president's former company."

Diamonds & Perles

That credibility gap grew even wider last week following Richard Perle's resignation as chairman of the Defence Policy Board. Though the board does not pay its members and is technically not a government agency, it wields tremendous influence. Perle decided to leave after revelations of a fairly huge conflict of interest - he is in line to receive $600,000 from bankrupt telecommunications company Global Crossing for helping it to 'overcome Defence Department resistance' to its proposed sale to a foreign company. The person he is being paid for persuading is none other than his old pal and a man he regularly advises, Secretary of Defence Donald Rumsfeld.

In 1996 Perle helped write a study for an Israeli think tank entitled, 'A Clean Break: A New Strategy for Securing the Realm', calling for regime change in Iraq

Perles of Wisdom cont...

and a redrawing of the geopolitical map of the area. Just before the current bombing began, Perle spoke at a conference sponsored by Goldman Sachs titled, "Implications of an Imminent War: Iraq Now, North Korea Next?" At the conference, he advised business leaders about possible investment opportunities that might arise from the war.

Perle is also on the board of British firm Autonomy Corporation, a Cambridge based computer company that, surprise surprise, recently won a huge contract with America's new Department of Homeland Security, set up after September 11th to increase public monitoring and surveillance. Autonomy has developed high-tech eavesdropping software that is capable of monitoring hundreds of thousands of e-mail and phone conversations at the same time. Add to all this the fact that Perle was one of the 'brains' behind the Project for the New American Century think tank whose demands included the establishment of a global American empire with the US policy of 'total war' and 'full spectrum dominance' (See SchNEWS 387) and it's hard not to feel sick to one's stomach.

And now our beloved Perle stands to do very nicely out of the foreign policy he has campaigned so strongly for. His own pockets are sure to be lined by his role in the venture capital firm Trireme Partners, which invests in homeland security and defence projects. SchNEWS is sure that the fear of terrorism stoked by bombing other countries does a handy job at helping his investments to prosper. For daring to insinuate that Trireme's and Perle's agenda might not be strictly altruistic, journalist Seymour Hersh has himself been labelled a "terrorist" by Perle and threatened with a libel suit. Apparently not confident enough to face US courts, however, Perle plans to bring his case to the UK, where libel laws are more relaxed.

As Chuck Lewis points out, "A defence contractor class that was already well fed is now getting bloated because we have so increased the defence budget in the last couple of years…(it is) the military industrial complex that Eisenhower warned this country about 40 years ago, the former generals and the former defence security experts that serve in government then go into the private sector. They go to work for contractors and people see their names, they're impressed, it has credibility. And that's how they get their contracts. And it just is a continuation of itself. And then they tell us what weapon systems we need, and they tell us what wars we should be fighting, and it's a self-perpetuating situation. And it's been going on for years, but what we're seeing in this instance is absolutely unabashed."

* To read the full interview with Chuck Lewis www.alternet.org

* To read more about fingers in dirty pies http://cryptome.org/iraq-booty.htm

* Check out 'Corporations and War' – by Corporate Watch £1 inc postage from 16 Cherwell St Oxford OX4 1BG www.corporatewatch.org/newsletter/issue11/isue11_part1.htm

POSITIVE SchNEWS

This weekend, the **Centre for Alternative Technology** in Llanelli, North-Wales, will be turning on the first ever community managed wind turbine. At the moment, all the wind turbines in this country are owned by big energy companies, but CAT's turbine is different in that it is owned and managed by a local community. About half of the energy produced will be used to power the CAT site, while the rest will provide green energy for the local grid www.cat.org.uk 01654 705950

SchNEWS In Brief

What's happening in Palestine? This Saturday (5th) 2pm-5pm, people fresh back from Palestine talk about their experiences there. Cornerstone Community Centre, Church Rd, Hove 07776 183619 ** **Benefit night for the people of West Papua** featuring Papuan Musicians, Matt Black from Coldcut and the showing of new film 'Merdeka'. 15th April, The George IV - Brixton, London.

Freedom - how many crimes have been committed in your name?

OBJECT OF DEFECTION

As the current UK/US war on Iraq has no United Nations backing, it is an illegal invasion. Any British soldier fighting in Iraq may find themselves hauled up in front of the War Crimes Tribunal in the Hague and SchNEWS would advise all of them to down their guns and come home.

And that's exactly what two have done! The two soldiers have been sent back from the Gulf after refusing to take part in a war where innocent civilians are being killed. Under British law, you are legally entitled to an honourable discharge as a conscientious objector, but the procedure can be difficult and prolonged. Lawyers for the two servicemen believe that rather than looking at a long summer's break, the two could be looking at two years inside for showing concern about who's at the receiving end of their bullets.

If you know anyone in the Armed Forces who's struggling with their conscience, there's an organisation called At Ease who will provide free, totally confidential advice. At Ease, c/o 28 Commercial St, London E1 6LS. 020 7247 5164, atease@advisory.freeserve.co.uk www.ppu.org.uk/special/co_stuff_03.html

* See Bush's excuses for not serving in the Vietnam war: http://awolbush.com/

UNFAIR-FORD

The area surrounding Fairford airbase in Gloucestershire is now a mini-police state where, depending on your political persuasion, you are either left alone to get on with your day-to-day life or harassed continuously for your beliefs. For the past 28 days, Section 44 of the Terrorism Act has been used to stop and search people who are opposed to the US Air Force using Fairford to launch bombing raids on Iraq. In a clear case of intimidation, Section 44 has been used by the police to search people living at the local peace camp up to nine times a day. The police are physically preventing anyone who looks like they are going to stay a while (carrying rucksacks, tents, water, whatever), from going anywhere near the camp... And what legislation are they using to justify this? Er, the boys in blue don't really seem to know and usually say "common law" or "we're not telling you". The Section 44 order runs out tomorrow (Saturday) but is likely to be extended for another terror-filled 28 days.

Despite all this blatant police harassment, the peace camp is still there, so try and visit them if you can! Mail is also getting through, and they could use money and postcards, so write to people at: Peacewatch, Gate 10, USAF Fairford, Near Kempsford, Fairford, Gloucestershire GL7 4EJ. www.gwi.org.uk

Reclaim the Bases! This weekend will see loads of actions at military bases across the country. Details from 07887-585721 www.reclaimthebases.org.uk. ** On Sunday 6th, protest at Northwood, the British Military HQ. This is where the war in Iraq is being planned! Meet 11am, Pretty Corner, Sandy Lane/Watford Road (North London, nearest tube Northwood). www.thed10group.org.uk 0845 458 2564. Tickets for coaches from Brighton from the Cowley Club, London Road. ** **March on the US Embassy**, this Saturday (5). Assemble 2pm BBC Broadcasting House, Portland Place, London. 020-7538 2521 www.stopwar.org.uk ** **Peace Soup – A new Anti-War CD** featuring music and poetry by people from Brighton is out next week. Launch Cabaret Tuesday (8), Marlborough Theatre, Pavillion St, Brighton. £4/3. 01273 672354 ** **Day of direct action against army recruitment centres**. Meet this Wednesday (9) 11.30am, Burger King, Charing Cross Road, London. ** **Rant against the War**- an evening of songs and poetry to raise funds for the anti-war movement, Hobgoblin Pub, London Rd, Brighton, next Thurs (10) 7.30pm. £5/£3.50 ** **Mayday 2003: Weapons of Mass Construction**. Plans are underway for this year's May Day. A map is out now with details of targets for possible pre-emptive strikes against capitalism. Send an SAE to BM Mayday, London WC1N 3XX

www.ourmayday.org.uk ** **The Labour Party have a Freepost address**, which means they have to pay the postage on anything you send them. Please don't send bricks or heavy phone directories to: The Labour Party, FREEPOST LON 10417, London, SW1P 4UT. All the local party offices also have freepost addresses that can be found on election leaflets ** **3 US military vehicles in Italy have been firebombed**. No one has claimed responsibility yet, but SchNEWS lays odds on: Friendly fire 2-1; Anti-War Activists 4-1; Al-Qaeda 5-1; Local Hooligans 10-1. ** SchNEWS has heard rumours that one of the US Air Force's smart bombs hit the run-down **West Pier** in Brighton last Friday, leaving it a burnt out shell. What a Noble act! ** For an in-depth look at **how the US treats international weapons treaties** see "Rule of Power or Rule of Law?" at www.lcnp.org/pubs/RuleofLawPDF.pdf ** The **Working Class Movement Library** in Salford, a national collection of the history of British and Irish radical and labour movements from the 1790s to the present day, is continually collecting material and would love to receive any books, pamphlets, leaflets, videos, press cuttings, photos or newsletters from the current anti-war movement. Send them stuff at Jubilee House, 51 The Crescent, Salford M5 4WX Tel: 0161-736-3601, enquiries@wcml.org.uk

---

The World's First Ever Sponsored 'Stop & Search'

There is a weekend of independent weapons inspections and the world's first ever sponsored Stop and Search at Fairford this weekend (5-6). According to the creators of the event, "If you are in the vicinity of the base, visiting G10 Peacewatch camp or observing the bombers, you will likely be stopped by police and searched. This can easily occur several times in one day. So get your mates to sponsor you a fixed amount or an amount per search.

Once you've collected your sponsorship money send it direct to the charity of your choice. A list of charities working in Iraq can be found at http://www.casi.org.uk/info/charities.html." SchNEWS top tip to increase your tally: Be sure to mask up and wear a white boiler suit with padding! But PLEASE don't carry any bin bags filled with manure, as the poor old police would be sure to get their hands dirty searching them!

H2O-KAY

Organisers of the World Water Forum in Kyoto, which ended on March 23rd, were expecting a rubber-stamping session of their plans to put the planet's most precious resource in the hands of the corporations.

Instead they got no resolution, no agreement and no common ground thanks to the robust determination of activists who crashed their party from all over the world.

More than 200 of the regular delegates lost their appetite for workshops with tasteless titles like "How the Poor will become Customers" and signed up instead to "Water is Life" – a statement condemning plans to privatise water supplies in the developing world and stating that access to clean drinking water is a basic human right.

When World Water Council chair Michael Camdessus, ex Managing Director of the International Monetary Fund, took to the platform to champion the Global Water Grab, people jumped up waving homemade lie-detector tests.

When Camdessus advocated that corporations should start their water grab by seizing control of ground water supplies , activists spoke up from the floor, telling the forum that in Brazil, where underground water is owned by private companies, the water often ends up getting bottled for sale as mineral water while the people have to make do with polluted surface water.

Activists also brought up the riots in Bolivia in 2000 which left several dead and over 200 injured when peasant farmers took to the streets to protest water privatisation. The Bolivian privatisation had resulted in 200% hikes in water costs, with some families paying $20 a month for water out of an average wage of $100. Shocked delegates also learned that poor families in South Africa, where water supplies are privatised, routinely get their water cut off if they can't pay the bills.

Meanwhile, alternative Social Water Forums sprung up in Florence, New Delhi, New York and Brazil. The latter was the largest, attended by 400 delegates who resolved to take the case against water privatisation to the International Court of Justice. They also initiated a co-ordinated defence of water reserves in the Amazonian jungle and river systems extending into Argentina, Brazil, Bolivia, Paraguay and Uruguay.

As the bloody war in Iraq continues, writer Norman Mailer issued a water wake-up call, pointing out that control of the Tigris and Euphrates Rivers in a region where water sources are scarce could be very important for the US's intentions of future domination in the Middle East.

More info: www.blueplanetproject.net

...and finally...

Never mind that they've been sent to fight a war that's illegal and which nobody wants, and that they're more likely to be killed by the person sitting next to them than by an Iraqi soldier, American soldiers are now being told that they must pray daily for the chimp of a President who sent them there. George W, who successfully managed to snort his way out of fighting in the Vietnam War, is now asking for pledges from his soldiers to pray daily for him, his family, and his staff. The pledge comes from a pamphlet given to US marines called "A Christian Duty". Maybe somebody should send them an insert to pray that they suddenly discover a conscience and get the hell out of there. Or that a smart bomb finally finds its way to the White House. Or that Bush himself becomes the next victim of friendly fire. Hmmmm, let's see now… Dear God… www.abc.net.au/news/newsitems/s819685.htm

Disclaimer

SchNEWS warns all readers that any resemblance to reality in this issue is Perly imaginary.

"...AND WE WILL NOT WITHDRAW UNTIL WE HAVE COMPLETELY LIBERATED THE PEOPLE OF IRAQ...

...OF THEIR OIL SUPPLIES.

WAKE UP! WAKE UP! IT'S YER TREASURE CHEST

weekly **SchNEWS** 400

www.schnews.org.uk

Friday 11th April 2003   Free/Donation   Issue 400

AID 'N' A BET

"Unfortunately, Bush and Co are not through yet. This invasion and conquest will encourage them to do it again elsewhere. The real purpose of this war was to say to the rest of the world, 'Don't Mess with Texas – If You Got What We Want, We're Coming to Get It!'"
- Oscar-winning comedian Michael Moore.

Last week the White House got the green light for yet another $75 billion to be spent on the Iraqi invasion and on it's favourite new form of at-home repression, homeland security. This is on top of the $360 billion budgeted for 'defence' every year – an annual military budget that exceeds the combined annual military budgets of the next 25 top countries! The sums are mind-boggling, but to put them in some sort of perspective, the cost of a single cruise missile costs $800,000, which means that the opening blitz on Baghdad, when 320 missiles were dropped in a single day, cost the US a stupendous $256 million. Considering that the war was touted as a "humanitarian war," this has to be the biggest single expenditure of "aid" in world history.

Last year, after America finished bombing the living hell out of Afghanistan (while still never managing to get hold of Osama bin Laden), the United Nations estimated that Afghanistan would need at least $10 billion for reconstruction over the following five years. The US, which had just spent $4.5bn on bombing the country, offered a measly $300m for the first year of reconstruction and refused to make any commitment for subsequent years.

This year, George Bush managed to "forget" to produce an aid budget for Afghanistan at all until he was forced to provide another $300m by Congress. That George Dubya! Ain't he such a great liberator!

SchNEWS is overwhelmed by his boundless generosity and concern for oppressed and suffering peoples throughout the world. However, the US government's true priorities are highlighted by the amount it's willing to shell-out on a single stealth bomber—$1.26 billion—which is about the same amount as America gives in aid each year to sub-Saharan Africa.

And while the US and UK have focused their budgets and military might on Iraq, the United Nations is facing a massive shortfall in feeding the world's poorest people: In the drought-struck Horn of Africa, 11 million Ethiopians are at risk from hunger, yet only half their food needs have been pledged by richer nations. In neighbouring Eritrea, two thirds of the population face starvation, but just over 2 per cent of the $163 million asked for by the UN has been offered. Southern Africa is also in the grips of drought with 14 million

people in desperate need of food aid yet Western aid has been trickling in. In Burundi, almost one sixth of the inhabitants have been forced out of their homes by conflict and natural disasters. The country has now been officially listed as the third poorest nation on earth, but has received only 3% of its UN request.

Two and a half years ago at the Labour party conference, Prime Sinister Blair talked about Africa as "a scar on the conscience of the world, but if the world focused on it, we could heal it." Now, however, Tony's so focused on scarring Iraq with his war of conscience that any chance of helping Africa is remote at best. As journalist George Monbiot points out, "The payments and promises that have been extracted so far chart the collapse of international concern for the people of almost every nation except Iraq." Yet in the post war carve-up of Iraq, while Western companies battle for control of resources, it will be the Iraqi people's turn to be forgotten by their 'liberators', just as the people of Afghanistan have been.

Whose side were you on in the war Grandad · CNN or SKY?

@NTI-COPYRIGHT - INFORMATION FOR ACTION   Published in Brighton since 1894

'You're such easy going people! I wish all the world were just like you!!'

HOME-MADE TERROR

While the "humanitarian war" was taking place in Iraq, liberating an entire nation through massive bombing raids and civilian deaths, the IDEX arms fair was happening in the United Arab Emirates. "The Gulf region remains the ideal market in the world for military hardware," said Major-General Sultan Al-Suwaidi, head of the committee that organised the five-day event. Every permanent member of the UN Security council had big exhibitions at the fair, hoping to entice countries like Iran, Syrian Algeria, and Libya to step right up and buy their weapons of mass destruction. But Britain held pride of place by being the largest exhibitor at the show, with some 100 UK firms taking part. Organisers of the fair had, after all, announced that despite the war 'the show must go on.' Oh well, at least the next time that "our boys" follow the US into battle, they can be proud of being shot by British-made bullets.

WEAPONS OF MASS CONSTRUCTION

The tradition of Mayday has always been about the celebration of life, a way of people uniting all over the world to celebrate their power and to reclaim public spaces. A day of defiance against authority. This year's action on will see a pre-emptive strike against the real weapons of mass destruction: oil companies, the arms manufacturers, multinationals and banks.

In London on May 1st there will be a number of autonomous actions with the main meet ups at 2pm at Lock-Heed Martin - the biggest arms company in the world - Berkshire House, corner of High Holborn & Endell St, and 4pm at the headquarters of oil company Shell UK, The Strand. More info: www.ourmayday.org.uk or send an SAE to BM Mayday, London WC1N 3XX.

HAPPY 400th SchNEWS

Well done our readers for keeping us in biscuits and stamps ever since 1994. If you want to be part of the next 400 issues get in contact...

The SchNEWS office on a 'dress down' Friday

SchNEWS OF The World
Available now - 2002 annual * 300 pages * Issues 301-350 plus loadsa photos, cartoons, satire, and more * £8.50 incl. p&p - cheques payable to Justice?

SchNEWS in brief

Radio 4A is on the airwaves in Brighton this weekend 101.4 FM and internet streams at www.radio4a.org.uk ** **Atkins Education**, who'd taking on running schools in the London Borough of Southwark, have discovered that running schools ain't as profitable as they had hoped and so they've walked away after just two years. Whoopee for privitisation!! ** The **Mayday Football Tournament** is on May 4th, Clissold Park, Stoke Newington, London, they're looking for teams to enter. 07958-112870 Blackstarrebels@aol.com ** **October Books**, Southampton's co-operatively run independent book-shop, has moved to 243 Portswood Road, Southampton SO17 2NG. 023-80581030 ** **The Anarchist Press: What's it for?** Discussion Tuesday 15th at LARC, 62 Fieldgate St, London, 7.30 pm ** **Mad Pride**, which campaigns for improved civil liberties and social conditions for psychiatric patients, is launching a **'Stop the Suicides'** campaign, Friday 18th, 8pm, at Chat's Palace, 42 Brooksby's Walk, Homerton, London. £4 on the door. 07985780385 madpridelondon@hotmail.com ** **Francisco Ramirez**, president of a Colombian mine workers' union, is in Britain April 21st - May 12th and is willing to give talks to groups. Info: 020-7254-4699 solly@talk21.com ** To see how all the companies that are pushing for the commercialisation of GM crops are linked, then get hold of the **biotech family tree poster** from Corporate Watch, 16b Cherwell Street, Oxford, OX4 1BG. 01865 791391 mail@corporatewatch.org (Donations appreciated) ** The ETC Group have produced a report on **Terminator Technology & Exorcist Technology** in GM crops. www.etcgroup.org ** **Benefit night for the people of West Papua**, with Papuan Musicians, Matt Black from Coldcut, and film showing of the new film 'Merdeka'. Next Tuesday (15), The George IV, Brixton, London ** **Greg Pallast**, author of **"The Best Democracy Money Can Buy"**, will be signing books and talking at Conway Hall, Red Lion Square, London, 6pm, 23rd April. £5/£2 07077-229459 Proceeds go to the firefighters.

War Briefs

Stop the War national demonstration, Saturday 12th, in memory of those that have died in Iraq. Bring flowers, cards, wreaths etc to lay outside 10 Downing Street. Assemble 12 noon at either York Road, Waterloo or Victoria Street 020 7053 2153 www.stopwar.org.uk ** If you don't want to trudge through London on Saturday but want to listen to the same old speakers, then stay at home and listen to www.cableradio.co.uk who'll be broadcasting live from the main stage. ** For **anti-war protest in Scotland**, meet 11.30am Blythswood square, Glasgow 0131 538 0257 www.edinburghstw.org.uk ** On Monday (14) there's **a Kites for Peace at MOD Llanbedr**, nr Harlech, at 2pm. Meet Machynlleth Station, 12.30pm. Bring pictures, ribbons and flowers and a kite to fly. Flying kites is forbidden at MOD Llanbedr, so they will be flown as a symbol of opposition to the war machine. Info: 01654-702166 ** **London school students Direct Action planning meeting**: To create a network of school activists and to follow up the anti-war student walk-outs with a student strike on Mayday. Meet 19th April, 1pm on Houghton St, WC2 near Holborn and Temple tubes. schoolaction@london.com ** The next mass blockade of **Faslane Naval Base** in Scotland, the home of Britain's very own weapons of mass destruction, will be on 22nd April. More info: www.banthebomb.org/rbb. Coaches from London and elsewhere. £20/£30. To book a seat ring 07810 192905 or email faslanecoach@hotmail.com. ** **Australian Prime Minister John Howard** and other top Defence officials watched red-faced as HMAS Sydney set sail for the Gulf with a "No War" banner attached to its bow after protesters arrived on inflatables and surfboards and clambered up the hull in a daring anti-war demonstration. Two protesters were arrested, but not before they had forced the ship to a halt ** Film Premier of **'Jeremy Hardy versus The Israeli Army'**, 23-24 April at Bloomsbury Theatre, UCL, 15 Gordon Street, London, 8pm.Tickets £6.50 020-7388-8822 ** A BBC television producer, moments before he was wounded by an American fighter aircraft that killed 18 people with friendly fire, spoke to his mother on a satellite phone. Holding the phone over his head so that she could hear the sound of the American planes overhead, he said: "Listen, that's the sound of freedom." For more brilliant cover of the war see http://pilger.carlton.com/print

Summit To Shout About

The EU Summit in Athens on April the 16th was supposed to focus on European unity, with a ceremony to welcome the 10 new member states into the Union. But in the end it was about bitter divisions between pro and anti-war leaders, and about the EU's role in the rebuilding of Iraq (not that they had a say).

These 'bitter divisions' pailed into insignificance next to the divisions between the 'representatives' inside the conference and the people they were supposed to represent. While the leaders choked on their vol-au-vents, only a block away from the summit there was a full-scale street riot kicking off between 20,000 riot police and 8,000 protesters. The nearby Italian, British and French embassies were attacked, and banks and stores were trashed and burned by a black block armed with stones, Molotov cocktails and buckets of red paint. Greek police retaliated with tear gas rounds (as is their habit) and eventually arrested 30 demonstrators. A large banner reading "Killers, Imperialists" was hung over the

FRIENDLY FIRE

"The 'fog of war' obscures more than just news from the battlefield. It also provides cover for radical domestic legislation, especially ill-considered liberty-for-security swaps which have been historically popular at the onset of major conflicts." - Matt Welch, Alternet.

Nearly two years ago, while American troops was busy 'sorting out' Afghanistan, Bush and his cronies used their patented 'if you're not with us, then you're against us' rhetoric to push the USA Patriot Act 2001 through Congress. The Patriot Act became law just 7 weeks after the downing of the Twin Towers and was the most dramatic expansion of state power at the expense of civil liberties in the history of the US. It gave the state new powers to wiretap phones, confiscate the property of suspected terrorists, spy on its own citizens without judicial review, conduct secret searches, and even snoop on the reading habits of library users.

So with the US war machine pounding away once again, it's no surprise that there's a whole new round of even more repressive laws in the pipeline for Americans - this time in the form of The Domestic Security and Enhancement Act, the so-called Patriot Act II. This Act includes more than 100 new provisions aimed at taking away all the freedoms they accidentally left people with in the first Patriot Act. The Patriot Act II does quite a nice job of filling in the cracks in the first Act, adding a whole new range of oppressive measures to the state's already massive arsenal. The act allows the connection of DNA from people "suspected of wrong-doing", the ability for American citizens to have their citizenship revoked if they are deemed to have contributed material support to organisations deemed to be 'terrorist', the ability to monitor a person's internet usage without a warrant, and the expansion of the death penalty to include 15 new offences. The Patriot Act II would also allow for the creation of a vast database of consumer, personal and political information on all US citizens, called the Total Information Awareness system - 'We got all the information on you, little citizen, and you're completely unaware of it.' For further info on Patriot Act II www.alternet.org/story.html?StoryID=15541

With the euphoria of the war 'victory' setting in, the US government may have to wait for the next terrorist attack to get their new bit of dodgy legislation passed, but in the meantime the US police and the legal system are acting as if they've already got totalitarian powers.

On Monday morning, California police opened fire on a peaceful anti-war protest at the Port of Oakland where military supplies were being shipped from. 500 protesters had blockaded the port and many dockworkers had walked out in solidarity. On arrival, police gave protesters two minutes to disperse, then opened fire with wooden bullets, concussion grenades and tear gas. Several people, including six dockworkers, were injured when police began shooting at very close range. The protesters didn't manage to close the docks for long, but the incident caused dockworkers to go on strike for the day. The union official Trent Willis said, "They shot my guys. We're not going to work today. The cops had no reason to open up on them." See http://sf.indymedia.org/ for more on the California port situation.

Last October, three Roman Catholic nuns entered the N-8 Minuteman III missile silo in Colorado to protest against US war mongering. This week they have been convicted of obstructing national defence and damaging government property. The nuns are expected to receive five to eight years each for cutting two gate chains and a fence, painting six crosses on the missile silos with their own blood and symbolically tapping hammers on the railway tracks used to transport the missile.

Inside SchNEWS

Swiss anti-nuclear eco-anarchist prisoner, **Marco Camenisch** is serving 10 years in jail for blowing up power lines leading to nuclear power plants. He can read and write in French, German, Spanish and Italian. He can read English, but does not feel confident to write long letters in English. Write to: Marco Camenisch, Sennhofstrasse 17, 7000 Chur, Switzerland.

Animal rights campaigner **Sonia Hayward** has been sentenced to 15 months for her involvement in campaigns against Huntingdon Life Science. Letters of support can be sent to her Sonia Hayward, KV 5943, HMP Cookham Wood, Rochester, Kent, ME1 3LU.

Carnival Against Oil Wars and Climate Chaos

Protest outside BP's Annual General Meeting on April 24th. 10am, Royal Festival Hall, Belvedere Road, South Bank, London.
BP would like to give the impression that they are a lovely, green, sustainable corporation, while still keeping busy wrecking the environments of Colombia, West Papua, Alaska and Azerbaijan. Let them know the game's up! Expose them for the liars they are!
www.burningplanet.net
Transport going from Brighton. Tickets available for £5 from the Cowley Club, London Road.

...and finally...

War! What is it good for? Well, apart from the obvious, like arms dealers, oil companies, world dictators and George Bush's mates, it's also pretty good for toy companies. Hasbro, one of the largest toy manufacturers in the world has just marketed its latest costume for 'G.I. Joe', America's equivalent to Action Man. Joe's new get-up is none other than a stunning Gulf War II nuclear, chemical and biological suit, complete with gas mask, boots and gloves. Another topical 'action doll' that's been marketed in the U.S. recently is the National Guard 'Homeland Security Amy'. Too bad it doesn't come complete with life size wire taps, computer monitoring systems, and loads of new jails in which to put evil-doers.

Disclaimer

SchNEWS warns all readers don't toy around..We'll be back on the 25th April. Honest!

weekly SchNEWS

www.schnews.org.uk

IRAQI'S NEW REGIME

Friday 25th April 2002   Free/Donation   Issue 401

LIBERATE THIS!

"25,000 litres of anthrax. 38,000 litres of botulinum toxin. 500 tons of sarin, mustard [gas] and VX nerve agent. Several mobile biological weapons labs. An advanced nuclear weapons development program." - what George W. Bush reckoned Saddam was hiding under his moustache.

Remember why the US/UK went to war? Supposedly Iraq had a massive stockpile of weapons of mass destruction and was therefore a threat to world peace. Hans Blix and his team of UN weapons inspectors went looking for them, Saddam Hussein grudgingly cooperated, and the inspectors found… er, not a lot.

But despite the blatant lack of justification, Emperor Bush invaded Iraq anyway (he'd been told to by his dad's mates) and Iraq used its weapons to defend itself – not mustard gas or intercontinental ballistic missiles after all, but rifles and crappy old tanks against the world's foremost military superpower. Someone should have listened to former UN weapons inspector Scott Ritter who described the Iraqi army as being "in total disarray, capable of little more than manning security pickets along the Iran-Iraq border… I have visited numerous Iraqi military barracks and have seen soldiers in tattered uniforms and bare feet."

So, where DID all those supposed evil weapons of mass destruction get to? Well, your on the ball SchNEWS has managed to track down some of them at Britain's own Faslane naval base in Scotland. 166 people were nicked at the base on Tuesday when hundreds of protestors blocked the gates for hours while others jumped the fences, sparking a security alert and waving banners that read "Here Blix, we've found them."

Faslane is home to three of Britain's four Trident submarines. Each submarine carries 48 nuclear warheads, each one 8 times as powerful as the bomb dropped on Hiroshima which destroyed the city and killed 140,000 people. British Minister of War Geoff Hoon was keen to use them, threatening Iraq that if they unleased THEIR weapons of mass destruction, his country would do the same. But Saddam never did unleash anything, which is a bit strange since he never seemed one for restraint.

And now, if Bush doesn't turn up some weapons of mass destruction soon, he will be exposed as the bullying liar he truly is. Tony Blair is worried too - worried that no big bad weapons will be found, or that if they are, the Americans will be accused of planting them (surely not!). Last week, Blair said that "some sort of objective verification" of any weapons found might be a "good idea." Smart boy, Tony.

Thank-you and goodbye

Saddam's statue in Baghdad was pulled down by a US tank for the benefit of the Western corporate media, who fell all over themselves to show a crowd of happy Iraqis on the scene (Who wouldn't be happy that a scumbag tyrant had been overthrown?). But if the TV cameras had panned out just a little, you'd have seen that the square was really quite empty. Maybe it was because those who had been maimed or killed by US bombs (we'll never know how many cos' the US can't be bothered to find out) just couldn't be asked to join in welcoming their liberators.

And now the army of "liberation" is all too quickly and predictably becoming an army of occupation. "No to America, no to Saddam, no to tyranny," people chanted in Arabic on Tuesday during a religious pilgrimage organized by Shia

leaders in Iraq. In the city of Kerbala on Wednesday, hundreds of thousands of Shia protested at America's first attempt to put together a puppet government, while in Mosul thousands protested and the pro-American governor's car was torched. American soldiers killed at least 10 Iraqis and wounded dozens of others when they fired on the rally. One Iraqi demonstrator warned, "If the US prevents us having a religious leader as president, we will reject it. If al-Hawza [the Shia leadership] orders us to turn ourselves into bombs, we can make the US leave Iraq. We say, 'Thank you for getting rid of Saddam. Now goodbye.'"

Respected journalist Robert Fisk observed, "All across Baghdad you hear the same thing, from Shia Muslim clerics to Sunni businessmen, that the Americans have come only for oil, and that soon - very soon - a guerrilla resistance must start. No doubt the Americans will claim that these attacks are 'remnants' of Saddam's regime or 'criminal elements'. But that will not be the case." As Dr Wamid Omar Nadmi, a leading political scientist at Baghdad university commented "What we're faced with today is not a choice between secularism and religion. We're facing an invasion and foreign rule. We have to work together to end it."

* Read 'War Plan Iraq' by Milan Rai (Verso 2003)

'OIL 'AVE IT!'

Fancy that! Amnesty International has accused US-led forces of better "preparation to protect the oil wells than to protect hospitals, water systems or civilians." Ever since US forces rolled into central Baghdad, one of the sole public buildings untouched by looters has been the massive oil ministry, which is under round-the-clock surveillance and guarded by 50 US tanks, with sharpshooters positioned on the roof and in the windows. "They came from the other side of the world. Do you believe they're going to do much for me? They've just come for the oil," fumed Salam Mohammad Hassan, a doctor who lives near the ministry. Just next-door, the Irrigation Ministry has been torched, with US soldiers apparently unable to do anything to help.

* The US is demanding North Korea halt its nuclear weapons programme, but the US has, after a 14-year break, recently resumed production of plutonium parts for nuclear bombs. Where's Hans Blix when you need him?

PRE-EMPTIVE STRIKE

Next Thursday is May Day, when hoards of rioting anarchists try to bring the very foundations of our society crashing to the ground....or something like that. This year it's time for our very own war on terror, with pre-emptive strikes and "an attack on the real weapons of mass destruction: oil companies, the arms manufacturers, multinationals and banks." In London there will be a number of autonomous actions with main meet ups at 2pm at Lockheed Martin - the biggest arms company in the world whose F-16 and F-22 fighter jets were used extensively by the US during the war in Iraq and whose profits have shot up accordingly. Meet 2pm Berkshire House, corner of High Holborn & Endell St. There will also be a critical mass bike ride meeting 11am under Waterloo Bridge, South Bank, and a 1pm Mayday Picnic at Queen Anne's Gate. There is also a 2pm meet up at the Home Office, Birdcage Walk, SW1. Later, everyone will be meeting up at the headquarters of oil company Shell UK, on The Strand, 4pm.

* London Class War have called a picket of the Wilkinson store in Stratford, London. Wilkinson's use prison slave labour to make many of their goods, picket 11.30am-1pm at Wilko's, 78-102 The Broadway, Stratford.

* To help your day run smoothly send an SAE to BM Mayday, London WC1N 3XX www.ourmayday.org.uk

* For the incomplete history of the origins of Mayday www.midnightnotes.org/mayday

* There's a Mayday benefit this Saturday (26), music featuring Headjam, The Lams, Fusing Naked and the Serum Soundsystem. At Eton Mission Social Club, Hackney Wick, London E9. 8pm till late. £4/3

IRAte

As Tony Bliar presses the IRA to provide 'crystal clarity' as a prerequisite for restoring devolution in Northern Ireland, his own government continues to ensure that the £10 million Stevens 3 report - which details how senior-ranking British army officers and police helped Ulster Defence Association (UDA) paramilitaries commit murder - will never see the light of day.

Last Thursday, a 20-page 'summary' was all that was released of the massive 3000 page report (the result of 14 years of investigation) which centres on the murder of human rights solicitor Patrick Finucane in 1989, and details how this was just one of many killings by UDA paramilitary murder gangs acting on direct instructions from the British army's Forces research Unit (FRU), targeting 'IRA sympathisers'. In other words, the kind of state-sponsored terrorism that Bliar is so busy criticising when it happens anywhere else in the world.

The report also proves conclusively that MI5, Special branch (RUC), and the army colluded to ensure that nobody was ever investigated, let alone prosecuted for what Finucane's son, Michael, has described as "a policy of state-selected assassination". The report is known to contain the names of at least 20 army and police officers who, if the evidence ever reached the public domain, would certainly face prosecution.

One such prominent army figure is former head of the FRU, Brigadier Gordon Kerr, recently spirited away to the 'theatre of war' in the Gulf. What's more the key witness in any such prosecutions would have been the main double agent, Brian Nelson (codenamed 1033), who infiltrated the UDA whilst working for the FRU. Conveniently he 'passed away' last week just days before the Stevens 3 report was due to be released. What a strange coincidence!

Metropolitan police commissioner John Stevens (who headed the investigation detailed in the report) has openly complained of obstruction, being spied on, and betrayed by police and army colleagues. An arson attack destroyed his first report Stevens 1, in 1990.

As early as February this year, N. Ireland's Chief cop Hugh Orde predicted that the Stevens 3 report - which has cost £10 million in tax payers' money - would never be published in full due to 'intelligence issues'. With Human rights groups protesting this blatant cover up, the call is out for justice and a 'full, transparent public enquiry.' Now surely 'crystal clear' Tony Bliar can't have a problem with that? Can he?

Read all about it in the book they tried to ban: "The Committee: Political Assassinations in Northern Ireland" by Sean McPhilemy and "Ten-Thirty-Three" by Nicholas Davies.

Find out more: www.relativesforjustice.com www.irlnet.com

CAGEY DEALINGS

After a 30 month battle, the animal rights group Uncaged have overturned a court order and won the right to publish over 1000 leaked pages of details on animal experiments.

The leaked documents relate to xeno-transplantation, the use of animal organ transplants in humans. The company involved, Imutran, now part of Novartis, had claimed back in 1995 that it was on the verge of successful xenotransplants. But the documents, detailing work done at Huntingdon Life Sciences, reveal a different picture - pig hearts were transplanted into baboons, who all showed signs of organ rejection. The baboons then suffered spasms, vomiting, diarrhoea, grinding teeth and uncontrollable eye movements.

The research was sloppy, fraudulent and cruel - all with the backing of the Home Office inspectors whose job it was to regulate the experiments. At least 520 errors and omissions occurred in the research and Imutran made lots of false claims - so that they would be granted more licences by the Home Office. The Home Office then failed to prosecute for breaches in the law, instead sending letters of "admonishment" and working with Imutran to underestimate the degree of suffering caused.

Read the reports at www.xenodiaries.org

* The campaign to close Huntingdon Death Sciences continues: 0845 458 0630, www.shac.net

PEACE ACTIVIST SHOT

British peace activist Thomas Hurndall is still in a coma after an Israeli sniper shot him in the head two weeks ago as he shielded children from the line of fire in the Israeli occupied Gaza strip. Thomas is the third International Solidarity Movement (ISM) activist to be killed or seriously injured in the region over the past month. The Israeli military has so far refused to comment.

It now appears that international peace activists may be being specifically targeted by the Israeli military, but volunteers are still continuing their work in the region.

London ISM: 07817 554 814
www.palsolidarity.org

War briefs

The peace camp at Welford in Berkshire has been re-established. Bombs from Welford are regularly transported to nearby Fairford to be loaded onto B52s which are still flying missions over Iraq. Campers have vowed to stay at the camp until the B52s leave the UK. More people are always welcome. Info: 07736 964653/ 07984 290842. ** In the run-up to Mayday, Campaign Against the Arms Trade Direct Action Network is organising a series of protests in London aimed at stopping the corporations that are profiting from the war on terrorism, including a visit to BAE Systems AGM next Wednesday. Meet 30th, 9.30am at QEII Conference Centre, Tothill St, London. More info on other actions 020 7281 0297 action@caat.demon.co.uk ** Enraged by local newspaper magnate Sir Ray Tindle's decision to stop printing anti-war stories once the war began in the 100 local newspapers he owns, a group in Totnes have produced their own anti-war spoof newspaper 'Troubled Times' Copies at http://images.indymedia.org/imc/uk/the_paper.pdf or send an SAE with 44p of stamps to the SchNEWS office ** Taking Sides is a website that takes a critical look at news about the war from around the world http://takingsides.blogspot.com ** The producer of a US television mini-series called "Hitler: The Rise of Evil" has been sacked for comparing the situation in Germany which gave rise to Hitler and his evil plans to the current situation in the US. In an interview he said, "I can't think of a better time to examine this history than now."

HOME OFFENSE

Now that we've 'liberated' their country, the UK government has started to draw up plans to bribe Iraqi asylum claimants in the UK with offers of £3000 to go back to their once beautiful but now barely functioning country. A similar scheme that was put in place after they'd flattened Afghanistan unsurprisingly didn't get many takers, so instead the Home Office has now had to resort to forcibly repatriating Afghanis, despite aid agencies describing the situation in Afghanistan as far from safe. The Home Office are hoping that by declaring Iraq and Afghanistan safe, they will be able to kick out enough people and increase their chances of meeting the target of halving the number of asylum applications by September.

* On Wednesday the trial of eleven asylum seekers, accused of involvement in the fire that destroyed part of Yarlswood Detention Centre in February last year, began at Harrow Crown Court (See SchNEWS 348). The eleven face charges of Arson and Violent Disorder, the trial is likely to be totally biased as many witnesses to the events on the day have since been deported. The case is expected to last 8-12 weeks. The Campaign For Justice in the Yarlswood Trial desperately need volunteer observers to watch court proceedings each day - 07786 517379 observer_yarlswoodtrial@yahoo.co.uk

*Over Easter a camp was set up against the Baxter refugee detainee centre in the South Australian desert. The camp was forced to move 3km away though after police rode their horses over people's tents. At the new site police arrested one person for flying a kite! - Kite flying was banned under the Taliban, who obviously no longer in control of Afghanistan now run the Australian police. Armed police also stormed the camp when they mistook a camera tripod for a gun!

Detainees inside the centre, were subject to a lockdown during the weekend. http://adelaide.indymedia.org

Inside SchNEWS

Two Danish activists who threw paint at their Prime Minister in protest at their country's involvement in the war on Iraq have been remanded in custody awaiting trial. Messages of support can be sent to them- Lars and Runes at antikrig@ulydighed.dk

SchNEWS in brief

Anarchist punk band CONFLICT will release an anti-globalisation anthem 'Carlo Giuliani' on Monday (28), a call to arms in memory of the protester killed by Italian police at the G8 summit in Genoa. Order it through your local DIY record shop or from www.sisterray.co.uk ** On Workers' Memorial Day, Monday (28), there will be events around the country, www.tuc.org.uk/h_and_s/tuc-6445-f0.cfm ** Film showing of 'Evolving Minds' about psychosis, spirituality and mental health, this Saturday (26) 7pm at Cinemateque, Middle St., Brighton. Donation ** Tribute concert for friends of Pete Shaughnessy, May 4th at the Foundry, Great Eastern Street, London (Old Street tube). Pete, a legendary figure for all those involved in the world of mental health, died tragically last Christmas. Check out the new website in honour of him www.peteshaughnessy.org.uk ** Annual Cannabis march and festival, Brockwell Park, London. Saturday, 3rd May, Carnival style march from Kennington Park, meet at noon. Festival starts 1pm, £3 donation. Info: 07931 243 855 www.ccguide.org.uk/cannabisfestival.html

...and finally...

We all know that anti-French frenzy in the US of A has led some Americans to rename French Fries 'Freedom Fries,' but now there's an American online petition dedicated to "Sending back Liberty". No not THAT kind of Liberty - they mean the Statue of Liberty! The designers of the petition are claiming to want the New York landmark, which was once a gift from the French, returned to France. And what do they want to replace Lady Liberty with? Why a giant statue of Ronald Reagan, of course-"The greatest president the world has ever seen."

The website also recommends that 'patriots' chuck out any French wine and cheese they've got stored, just one of many helpful 'deFrenchyfying self-help methods'. Surely its a piss take, isn't it?

See for yourself at:
www.sendbackliberty.us

Subscribe!

Keep SchNEWS FREE! Send 1st Class stamps (e.g. 10 for next 9 issues) or donations (payable to Justice?) Ask for "Originals" if you can make copies. Post *free* to all prisoners. SchNEWS, c/o on-the-fiddle, P.O. Box 2600, Brighton, East Sussex, BN2 0EF.
Tel/Autofax +44 (0)1273 685913 Email schnews@brighton.co.uk Download a PDF of this issue or subscribe at www.schnews.org.uk

What Weapons?

EMPTY WARHEAD FOUND IN WHITE HOUSE

So the war's over, the oil fields are safely in the hands of coalition soldiers, the UN has been forced to accept the occupation, and a lot of US companies are lined up to make a fuck-load of cash reconstructing everything that the US army destroyed. George and Tony must be feeling pretty pleased with themselves. Probably the only flies in the ointment right now are the people who keep reminding them that since they occupied Iraq they haven't been able to turn up anything resembling a Weapon of Mass Destruction. Where are the buckets of anthrax that Saddam was planning to hand out to every crazed terrorist who could carry one away? Where is the nuclear weapons program that wily Iraqis had hidden under a dairy farm?

SchNEWS suspects that some readers will be saying, "of course they haven't found anything. There's nothing there. This just proves what we've been saying all along, that the whole WMD thing was just a way of scaring the shit out of the general public and giving them an excuse to go to war." But wait. Let's not be cynical. Just because there's nothing there doesn't mean they didn't *think* there was something there. Maybe they did have good reason to suspect that the Iraqi government still had huge stockpiles of WMDs.

Let's ask an expert in the field. Scott Ritter became chief weapons inspector for UNSCOM in Iraq in 1991 and served as chief of the concealment investigations team until 1998, when he resigned in protest against the US government's manipulation of the inspection process. (By the way, don't let that resignation make you think that this is some kind of anti-establishment rebel. Scott's an ex-marine who served in Operation Desert Storm, a Republican – he voted for Dubya – and, just to complete the stereotype, a 6-footer with a lantern jaw.)

MEET MISTER RITTER

At the outset of the inspections, says Ritter, the Iraqi government lied. They declared less than 50 percent of their chemical and missile stockpiles and failed to declare the existence of their biological and nuclear programs. They hid everything they could, as cleverly as they could. Ritter infamously set up an 'aggressive and intrusive inspection process' meaning he and his team spent the next seven years meticulously tracking down every bomb, every missile, every factory designed to produce chemical, biological and nuclear weaponry. They tracked the shipping of materials and cross-referenced this data against the invoices taken from manufacturers who sold them the equipment and shoved them into the faces of Iraqi officials. Video cameras and heat sensors were set up to monitor known sites and ensure they were never again used to make weapons. The foundations of buildings were lifted, facilities and missiles were catalogued and destroyed as they found them.

The Iraqis soon gave in. This Ritter guy and his people weren't messing about, and, fearing military retaliation if they hid anything, the Iraqis opted for a policy of full disclosure. Despite this revealing most of their weapons and weapon making potential, Ritter became even more suspicious, realising the Iraqis feared a US attack and would be destroying stuff that hadn't yet been found so they could pretend it had never existed. UNSCOM wasn't gonna be

fooled, so Ritter headed up a counter-concealment team and sites were subjected to forensic archaeology to discover in mind-numbing detail exactly what had been destroyed.

When he left in the summer of '98, Ritter was sure that UNSCOM had stripped Iraq of 90-95 percent of all their weapons of mass destruction, the rest of the missing material lost during the ravages of the Gulf war and in the governmental chaos caused by sanctions. Inspectors discovered and disposed of 38,500 chemical munitions, 625 tons of chemical weapons agents, 2,700 tons of precursor chemicals and 426 pieces of chemical production equipment.

Still, 10% is too great a margin of error for a hardass like Ritter and, as nerve gases like sarin have a shelf life of at maximum 5 years and biological agents turn to goo even faster, special attention was paid to the relatively stable VX nerve agents. In the Summer of 2002 Ritter boldly stated that "[the VX] research and development factory is destroyed, the product of that factory is destroyed. The weapons they loaded up have been destroyed. More importantly, the equipment procured from Europe that was going to be used for their large-scale VX nerve agent factory was identified by the special commission – still packed in its crates in 1997 – and destroyed. Is there a VX nerve agent factory in Iraq today? Not on your life." On the subject of other Weapons of Mass Destruction he commented, "It was possible as early as 1997 to determine that, from a qualitative standpoint, Iraq had been disarmed. Iraq no longer possessed any meaningful quantities of chemical or biological agents, if it possessed any at all, and the industrial means to produce these agents had either been eliminated or were subject to stringent monitoring. The same was true of Iraq's nuclear and ballistic missile capabilities. As long as monitoring inspections remained in place, Iraq presented a WMD based threat to no one" Hmmm, interesting... So presumably the US was feeling pretty relaxed about the 'Iraqi threat' by that point?

WAR GAMES

Well no. By the beginning of 1998 The UNSCOM investigators were beginning to find Washington more obstructive than Baghdad, with the US orchestrating confrontations, delaying surprise inspections until more sensitive times, creating arguments over the number of inspectors allowed on a site, and such like. It was this, more than the fact that the CIA had infiltrated UNSCOM and was using it as its own private intelligence-gathering agency, that made Ritter resign in protest. Less than six months later his worst fears were confirmed when the Pentagon effectively ordered the UNSCOM inspectors withdrawal (for their own safety) after telling them that US missile strikes were imminent. The UN Special Commission, reviewing the report on the withdrawal, concluded the crisis was "artificially created."

Interviewed on the NBC Today show in December 1998, Ritter said "The U.S. has perverted the U.N. weapons process by using it as a tool to justify military actions, falsely so. ... The U.S. was using the inspection process as a trigger for war."

More recently in September 2002 he said "The Bush administration has provided the American public with little more than rhetorically laced speculation, there has been nothing in the way of substantive fact presented that makes the case that Iraq possesses these weapons or has links to international terror, that Iraq poses a threat to the United States of America worthy of war." He added "The opportunity finally exists to bring clarity to years of speculation about the potential threat posed by Iraq's weapons of mass destruction, as well as an opportunity to resolve this ongoing crisis of international law peacefully. But President Bush refuses to take 'yes' for an answer. The Bush administration's actions lay bare the mythology that this war is being fought over any threat posed by Iraqi weapons of mass destruction."

DON'T MENTION THE WAR...

As this book goes to print, the 'War on Iraq' isn't front-page news anymore. There are still big stories about the 'Aftermath of War' – the big news at the moment is that all that 'evidence' of Weapons of Mass Destruction turned out to be bullshit and forgery. There are no weapons, and there was no evidence. So the mainstream press keeps running stories asking, 'Did Tony know? Did George know?' (Strangely, no-one has run a story asking, 'Is there anyone who didn't know?')

As far as the war itself goes, the story's over. It went like this: George and Tony decide to take out Saddam; everyone else says no; they go to war anyway; Saddam legs it; Iraq now free; The End. Now we can get back to other things – did you know that a new series of *Big Brother* has started?

But the war on Iraq isn't over. It didn't start on 20th March, and it didn't end when Saddam Hussein disappeared off the face of the planet. The US and Britain waged a 'low-intensity' war on the country, with bombing raids and cruise missiles, ever since Gulf War 1 officially finished in 1991. (Between 1997 and the beginning of 2003, Britain alone spent £1billion bombing Iraq.) During that time the UN enforced sanctions that knowingly killed hundreds of thousands of Iraqis. And Saddam's disappearing act hasn't brought an end to this violence: a few weeks ago US soldiers broke up a 'boisterous but peaceful' demo in Falluja by firing automatic weapons into the crowd, killing 15 Iraqis and wounding 75. The war's still going on.

Saddam isn't the main issue, and he never was. The main issue has always been how to keep the people of the Middle East under control, and make sure that nothing interferes with the global economy's connection to the richest supplies of oil on the planet.

> At this moment in time, there's nothing on this planet that's more important to capitalist profits than oil, except workers.

The war *is* about 'the Iraqi people's right to govern themselves', but not the way they talk about it on *Newsnight*. The Iraqi people have a long history of fighting to take control of their own lives: rebelling against occupying armies, repressive governments and the oil companies who exploit them (see *A Really Brief History of Iraq*). This is a direct threat to the stability of the capitalist house of cards, and it has to be dealt with brutally. People in the Middle East trying to govern themselves have to be stopped at all costs.

Saddam Hussein is just one of a long list of gangsters and torturers that the West has propped up to keep the region locked down. The Baath party came to power in a *coup* backed by the CIA, who encouraged them to round up, murder and imprison thousands of Iraqi radicals and revolutionaries. In the 80s Saddam was armed and funded by governments in the West

and East, who relied on him to weaken Iranian power in the region. When Iraqi deserters kicked off an uprising against Saddam's regime during Gulf War 1, the US immediately stopped the war to give him a chance to massacre the rebels, before the rebellion turned into revolution (see *Milan Rai Article*).

Saddam wasn't a reliable employee anymore, so he got the sack. But the war against the Iraqi people, and the people of the Middle East, goes on. For the time being the US/UK will have to do a lot of the dirty work themselves. It's not ideal, but they haven't had much luck hiring a new set of bastards that's strong enough to guarantee 'security and stability' in the country (for investors that is, not Iraqis). It looks like the occupying forces might be doing the dirty work in Iraq for a long time yet – unless, of course, they're forced to get out.

Oil Be Back

There's nothing new about wars over resources. The most obvious example at the moment is the war in the Congo, "possibly the most mineral rich place on earth", where soldiers from half a dozen countries are tearing the country apart "to loot Congo's rich resources and sell them" (see *The Lost World War*). But this isn't exactly what's happening in Iraq. As Milan Rai put it, the war's not being fought for 'access to oil' but for control of the production of oil, and the profits that flow from it. This isn't just to guarantee US/UK based companies a good slice of the profits, it's an attempt to prop up the capitalist system as a whole.

of recession that ended the first President Bush's political career". The conclusion? "If Iraq just exported oranges, nearly 250,000 American troops probably wouldn't be in the region". No shit, Sherlock.

Of course, it's not impossible that capitalism will find a way to cut down its oil habit, or even replace it. But don't count on that happening any time soon. The US Department of Energy and the International Energy Agency both estimate that global demand for oil will increase over the next 20 years from 77mbd to 120mbd, driven mainly by the needs of the US and 'emerging' markets in Asia. Those figures aren't based on the needs of people, by the way, but on the needs of the capitalist economy, which needs to constantly 'grow', or expand the amount of things produced and sold, in order to guarantee profits – regardless of the social, political or ecological consequences. If you're worried about climate change, you're probably better off thinking about those numbers than going over the small print in the Kyoto treaty.

As long as oil remains the lifeblood of the global economy, power will demand as much control as possible over its production and supply. And as long as that's the case, the people who are unlucky enough to live where the oil is will be at the sharp end of the capitalist system.

"We Will Fight Them"

"If the Americans come, they will be very strong at first, but after some time they will see resistance. We will fight them. It doesn't matter about sects, Shi'a, Sunni, Kurd, Christian. I am Kurd. We will all fight together, not for the government. For our land." – Man speaking to Jo Wilding in Saddam City (now Sadr City), 18th March, two days before the invasion began (see *From the Ground Up*).

"We are not loyal to Saddam. He was a dictator and a tyrant. Now he has gone, but the Americans are acting like dictators themselves." – Member of the crowd that destroyed the al-Tawhid police station, Falluja, 6th June. The US military was negotiating to set up a permanent base in the station, so local residents gathered and turned the building to rubble with mallets, axes and metal poles.

The past year was dominated by anti-war activism. Whatever you think about that, you can't help but be impressed by the size and power of what happened. Yes, there were boring meetings dominated by SWP droids. And some direct action crew will never get bored of reminding us that "marching from A to B won't change the world". But marches and meetings were only a part of it. There were also mass schoolkid strikes, illegal 'Stop the City' actions, covert and open sabotage of military property, mass invasions of military bases, successful blockades of vehicles transporting military equipment, people travelling to Iraq to act as independent human rights observers and human shields, occupations, and riots. Embassies, government property and branches of McDonalds were smashed up. The link between the war and oil didn't go unnoticed either: petrol stations got occupied, and occasionally 'dismantled', all over the place; in the UK the International Petroleum Exchange and Esso headquarters were both occupied. And whilst marching from A to B

At this moment in time, there's nothing on this planet that's more important to capitalist profits than oil, except workers. Oil is involved in the production of every other commodity: it powers factories and it powers the transportation of goods and people. As such, it figures in a lot of basic capitalist strategies for guaranteeing profits, like replacing people with machines, and moving production to wherever labour costs are cheapest. Without oil, there is no 'global free market'. Because oil is involved in the cost of everything, as the price of oil goes up or down, the price of everything else tends to rise or fall accordingly. This means that there are constant political struggles for control over the price of oil.

If you want to read about the war without all the bollocks about 'democracy' or 'terrorism', you can rely on the business press to give it to you straight. One week into the invasion, *Fortune* magazine, every capitalist's favourite glossy, couldn't help gloating about the shot-in-the-arm that was coming for the global economy. Iraq has the second largest proven oil reserves in the world, after Saudi Arabia. What's more, Iraqi oil is high quality and cheap to produce: in the US it costs about $15 dollars to produce a barrel of crude; in Iraq it costs less than $5. "Whilst rebuilding Iraq's decrepit oil industry could cost the US billions of dollars," wrote *Fortune*, "that will be more than made up for by lower oil prices in the long term... Cheaper oil will boost the entire economy, from manufacturing to farming". "For the global economy, that kind of relief couldn't come at a better time": global economic growth is dangerously slow, and the only thing keeping the US economy afloat is people letting themselves get deep into debt. If oil prices were to rise at this point, the stage would be set for "the kind definitely isn't as sexy as vandalising your Army Recruitment Centre or pulling down the fence at a US base, we can't just write off the global anti-war marches. Millions filled the streets in almost every major city in the world to warn their governments off support for the attack. Marching (well, shuffling) through London with 2 million other people might be boring (frankly there's no 'might be' about it – it is), but to be honest that march probably put the fear up Neo Labour as much as anything else that happened in the run up to war. And it let people in Iraq know that this country isn't entirely made up of heartless wankers, which is no bad thing either.

What all this added up to was a massive, and global, act of refusal – unlike anything that's been seen before. It didn't stop the war machine, but it made it much more difficult to set it in motion. Governments like Turkey, who normally march in lockstep with the US military, were forced to withdraw support for the invasion. Even Tony "who shall we kill today?" Blair was nearly forced to abandon his commitment to the war by the massive force of resistance in this country.

Now the war has become an occupation, and there's nothing that Tony and Co. would like more than for us to forget about all this as quickly as possible. You didn't stop the war, now get over it. Let the troops get on with their 'policing activities' as quietly as possible. But for Iraqi people, resistance is just beginning. It's hard to get a clear picture of what's going on in Iraq at the moment, but it's clear that most people there are under no illusions about why US troops are on the streets. In coming months they will have to fight military repression and attempts to set up a new puppet government; they will also have to deal with all kinds of dodgy fuckers who try to use the brewing anti-American feeling in the country to get a bit of power for themselves. Being against the occupation doesn't mean we have to take sides with these would-be governments against the US government, or the government that the US will try to install. It means taking sides with ordinary people, against all the groups trying to exploit and control them.

Just because we didn't manage to stop the war doesn't mean there's nothing left for us to do. If we can make the occupation unworkable, people in Iraq will have a better chance of taking back some control over their lives and their land. If the occupation doesn't work, it will also make it more difficult for the US to try this strategy elsewhere. We don't have any vested interest in what's being planned for the Iraqi oilfields. We don't have shares in Exxon Mobil or General Motors. For most of us, 'economic growth' doesn't mean anything except more work, more exploitation, more environmental devastation.

There are all kinds of possibilities for activism. At the moment there are loads of Western companies crowding around trying to get their share

of the lucrative contracts for reconstruction that the US is doling out. If possible, the US will make sure that the money for that work comes out of revenues from Iraqi oil. Most of those companies will be American, but not all of them. Some of the American companies will have offices in the UK. As soon as coalition forces can create a 'secure environment' for investment in Iraq, the oil companies will start lining up for their cut as well. A more irresponsible newssheet than SchNEWS might well suggest that all of these companies are legitimate targets for activists. Depending on how the occupation develops, it might also be possible that tactics like those used by the International Solidarity Movement in Palestine will be useful in Iraq. It will definitely be useful to develop links with activists in Iraq. When Jo Wilding was in the country at the start of war she met people who were setting up an Iraq Indymedia. Giving support to this kind of project will make it easier to get around the bullshit in the Western media about the occupation, give us a better understanding of what's going on there, and might open up possibilities for coordinated resistance. Most of all, it's important not to let the government and the press sweep the occupation under the carpet. The war isn't going away; neither are we.

Useful Sources

Midnight Oil – Midnight Notes Collective (www.midnightnotes.org)
Fortune, 31st May, "Oil: Why Prices Will Fall".
Iraq Indymedia: www.almuajaha.com

SchNEWS goes to the movies...

Free CD with SchNEWS Annual 2003
Peace de Resistance

pc linux mac [ish]
insert -> click index.htm

BeYONdTV.org VIDEO DISK

Thanks to Beyondtv.org for putting together this CD to go with the book you're now reading, containing a selection of choice video cuts from the digital direct action underground. Take a byte and feel free to copy these recipes and cook them up for your friends. There is also a copy of (almost) the entire SchNEWS website. Unfortunately, due to CD size restrictions we've not been able to include the whole site but most of it's there.

There are contributions from Indymedia, Corporate Watch, Undercurrents, Pirate TV and artwork by the UHC collective. The video clips are broadly about Anti-War action, including DIY activity to remove yourself from the Oil Economy. There's a video the Labrats made telling us how to run a Vehicle and Generator from Vegetable Oil. Other highlights include Direct Action at Fairford Airbase, the dismantling of US military satellites in Holland, the birth of the Pro-Capitalism movement in Manchester and some radical retweaking of George W.

TECHNICAL HELP: The video files are in Mpeg1 format, which should be playable in even really old computers, no matter if they're pc, linux or mac.

If you can help create a screening network for this kind of Video on CD and activist Video in general. Please contact us 0161 226 6814 and/or sign up for the imc-uk-video mailing list.

Details : http://uk.indymedia.org/video.page.php3

ni New Internationalist Publications

big bad world
cartoon molotovs in the face of corporate rule
by Polyp

AVAILABLE NOW

£5.99 from bookshops
ISBN 0 9540499 3 4
or from www.newint.org

"...as sharp and cutting as a storm of glass."
RED PEPPER

"...incisive, brilliantly ironic and a bit rithless."
JOHN PILGER

"Anti-American, unbalanced and unreasonable."
COCA-COLA COMPANY

Bulk order discounts (17+) available from NI magazine details- antheam@newint.org

SchNEWS Round

Issues 51-100: ~~Reclaim the~~ Streets... Squatters Estate Agents... 3rd Battle of Newbury... The Land Is Ours... cartoons... and loads more

SchNEWS Annual

Issues 101-150: Anarchy... Networks... Ecology... Campaigns... Information... Sabotage... Weird Shit... Comics...

SchNEWS Survival Handbook

Issues 151-200: GM crop trashings, streets get reclaimed & much more PLUS all-round how-to guides to everything DIY and direct action...

SchQUALL NEARLY SOLD OUT!! Get 'em while you can.

Issues 201-250 of SchNEWS and the best of SQUALL magazine
GM crops... June 18th... Privatisation... Seattle... DIY culture... Photos... Cartoons... Satirical grafix... Subverts...

SchNEWS & Squall Yearbook 2001

Issues 251-300 of SchNEWS and the best of SQUALL magazine: Winston Gets A Mohawk... Prague S26... Summit round-ups: Nice, Davos, Melbourne... Cartoons... Subverts... the IMF... the WTO... the WEF... the ERT... TABD... ECGs... SAPs... and the BBC... BB King... Matt Busby... Dig It... Dig It... Dig It...

SchNEWS Of The World

Issues 301-350 of SchNEWS: **The stories that shook the world including...** September 11... G8 summit in Genoa... Argentina enters meltdown... international activists help Palestinians fight Israeli occupation... the anti-war movement has round one with the Afghanistan war and many other stories global and local...

Legal Warning

Section 6 Criminal law Act 1977
As amended by the
Crmininal Justice and Public Order Act 1994

TAKE NOTICE

THAT: *we live in this house,* it is our home and *we intend to stay here.*

THAT: *at all times there is at least one person in this house*

THAT: *any entry into this house without our permission* is a **CRIMINAL OFFENCE** as any of one of us who is in physical possession is opposed to any entry without their permission.

THAT: *if you attempt to enter by violence* or by threatening violence we **WILL PROSECUTE YOU,** you may receive a sentence of up to **SIX MONTHS IMPRISONMENT** and/or a **FINE** of up to **£5,000**

THAT: *if you want us to leave* you will have to take out a summons for possession In the County Court or in the High Court, or produce to us a written statement or Certificate in terms of S. 12a Criminal Law Act 1977 (as inserted by Criminal Justice And Public Order Act 1994.

THAT: it is an offence under S. 12 a (8) Criminal Law Act 1977, (as amended), to knowingly make a false statement to obtain a written statement for the purposes of S. 12a. A person guilty of such an offence may receive a sentence of up to **SIX MONTHS** imprisonment and/or a fine of up to **£5,000.**

The Occupiers

N.B. SIGNING THIS LEGAL WARNING IS OPTIONAL.
IT IS EQUALLY VALID WHETHER IT IS SIGNED OR NOT.

Squatting is still legal, necessary and free.
Advisory Service for Squatters:
tel: 020 7359 8814 *web:* www.squat.freeserve.co.uk

Issues 351-401 Index

NB This index refers only to articles originally published in the SchNEWS issues, and the numbers given refer to issue, not page. Numbers in bold indicate front page stories.

YELLOW PAGES

Don't Just Let Your Fingers Do The Walking

The SchNEWS Yellow Pages is information for action - a list of hundreds of groups and resources to inform and inspire you to put down this book and get up and do something positive. This contacts list is a selection of the full list of over 800 entries on our website. Hopefully this categorised version is more useful than an A-Z list, but obviously a lot of the categories overlap. Many of the groups listed can put you in touch with more specific or local groups. This list is constantly updated and is never 'complete', if you want to see your group added (or your details change) please get in touch.

The categories are: Anti-War / Anarchism / Animal Rights / Anti-Capitalsim / Anti-Racism / Bookshops / Cafes & Clubs / Children & Parenting / Community Groups / Culture / Disability Rights & Action / Drugs / Economics / Education / Energy / Environment / Food & Farming / Forests & Woodlands / Gardening / Genetics / Health / Housing & Homelessness / Human Rights / Indigenous Peoples / Media / Networking Support / Prisoner Support / Refugees / Sexuality / Transport / Travellers / Women / Workers Rights.

The format of the entries are: **Name** Address. T phone number F fax number email@address www.website Description.

ANTI-WAR

Abolition 2000 (A2000 UK) 601 Holloway Rd, London, N19 4DJ. T 020 7281 4281 A2000UK@gn.apc.org www.gn.apc.org/abolition2000uk To achieve for the 21st century a global treaty to abolish nuclear weapons.

Active Resistance to the Roots of War (ARROW) 162 Hollway Road, London, N7 8DQ. T 020 7607 2302 info@justicenotvengeance.org www.j-n-v.org Nonviolent action affinity group.

Aldermaston Women's Peace Camp c/o 157 Lyndhurst Rd, Worthing, W. Sussex BN11 2DG. T 0845 4588362 / 07904 450307 awpc@gmx.co.uk www.aldermastonwpc.gn.apc.org Based around a monthly peace-camp at AWE Aldermaston - opposes Britain's nuclear weapons through campaigns and nonviolent direct action.

Campaign for the Accountability of American Bases (CAAB) 8 Park Row, Otley, West Yorkshire LS21 1HQ. T 01943 466405 / 01482 702033 F 01482 702033 anniandlindis@caab.org.uk www.caab.org.uk Working for accountability of American bases through the systems and structures available and taking direct action when these fail.

Campaign Against Arms Trade (CAAT) 11 Goodwin St, London, N4 3HQ. T 020 7281 0297 F 020 7281 4369 enquries@caat.demon.co.uk www.caat.org.uk Broad coalition of groups and individuals committed to an end to the international arms trade, together with progressive demilitarisation within arms-producing countries.

Campaign Against Depleted Uranium (CADU) Bridge 5 Mill, 22a Beswick Street, Ancoats, Manchester M4 7HR. T 0161 273 8293/8283 F 0161 273 8293 info@cadu.org.uk www.cadu.org.uk Campaigns specifically on trying to achieve a global ban on the manufacture, testing, and use of depleted uranium weapons.

Campaign for Nuclear Disamament (CND) 162 Holloway Rd, London, N7 8DQ T 020 7700 2393 F 020 7700 2357 enquiries@cnduk.org www.cnduk.org Campaigns non-violently to rid the world of nuclear weapons and other weapons of mass destruction and to create genuine security for future generations.

Campaign to Free Vanunu & for a Nuclear Free Middle East 185 New Kent Rd, London, SE1 4AG T 020 7378 9324 F as phone www.vanunu.freeserve.co.uk campaign@vanunu.freeserve.co.uk Campaign for the release of Vanunu, the Israeli nuclear whistleblower who, in 1986 was sentenced for 18 years imprisonment for revealing Israel's nuclear stockpiles.

Civil Disobedience www.civildisobedience.org.uk A resource for people who want to make their voice heard using non-violent direct action.

Conscience - The Peace Tax Campaign Archway Resource Centre, 1b Waterloo Rd, London, N19 5NJ. T 0870 777 3223 F 020 7281 6508 info@conscienceonline.org.uk www.conscienceonline.org.uk Campaigns for right of conscientious objectors to war to have the military part of their taxes spent on peacebuilding initiatives.

Direct Action Against War www.groups.yahoo.com/group/directactionagainstwar/ Email list for exchanging information about direct action against the war on Iraq in Britain.

Fairford Peace Watch www.fairfordpeacewatch.co

m Fairford is where the US Airforce launched B52 bombers from, to attack Iraq.

Faslane Peace Camp A814, Shandon, Nr Helensburgh, Dumbartonshire, G84 8NT. T 01436 820901 faslanepeacecamp@hotmail.com www.faslanepeacecamp.org.uk Live across the road from Britain's nuclear arsenal, stop nuclear convoys and generally harass the MoD.

Free Flyingdales Network www.freeflyingdalesnetwork.co.uk A small organisation that aim to stop America's "Son of Star Wars" Plans and, in particular, the use of RAF Fylingdales in North Yorkshire as part of this plan.

Gloucestershire Weapons Inspectors info@gwi.org.uk www.cynatech.demon.co.uk A group of concerned citizens who aim to eliminate weapons of mass destruction from Gloucestershire.

Gush Shalom POB 3322 Tel-Aviv 61033 Israel. info@gush-shalom.org www.gush-shalom.org Aims to influence Israeli public opinion and lead it towards peace and conciliation with the Palestinian people.

Housmans Peace Resource Project (HPRP) 5 Caledonian Rd, Kings Cross, London, N1 T 020 7278 4474 F 020 7278 0444 worldpeace@gn.apc.org Produces World Peace Database: 3500 organisations in 170 countries (includes major environmental & human rights groups) - abbreviated annual Directory appears in Housmans Peace Diary.

International Solidarity Movement (ISM) (See entry under Indigenous Peoples)

Lakenheath Action Group Forge Bungalow, The Street, Shotesham, Norwich, NR15 1YL. T 01508 550446 info@lakenheathaction.org www.lakenheathaction.org Action group who campaign against the stationing of 30 US nuclear weapons at RAF Lakenheath.

Non-Violent Resistance Network (NVRN) 162 Holloway Rd, London, N7 8DQ T 020 7607 2302 F 020 7700 2357 c/o cnd@gn.apc.org Network non-violent direct action activists in the UK and supply with information about NVDA events.

Nonviolent Action Magazine reporting nonviolent actions. (See entry under Media)

Not in our Name Project info@notinourname.net www.notinourname.net Citizens of the United States resisting the injustices done by their government, in their names.

Other Israel, The PO Box 2542, Holon 58125, Israel. AICIPP@igc.org (North America) otherisr@actcom.co.il (Rest of World) other_Israel.tripod.com Bi-monthly peace movement magazine (hardcopy), for free sample send address.

Peace Brigades International British Section (PBI) 1b Waterlow Rd, London, N19 5NJ. T 020 7281 5370 F 020 7272 9243 pbibritain@gn.apc.org www.igc.org/pbi Send teams of international observers to provide protective accompaniment to local human rights defenders who are at risk as a result of their work for social justice.

Peace Museum, The: Office: Jacob's Well, Manchester Rd., Bradford, BD1 5RW. Visitor Gallery: 10 Piece Hall Yard, Bradford Centre, BD1 1PJ T 01274 754009 F 01274 752618 peacemuseum@bradford.gov.uk www.peacemuseum.co.uk Covers peace history, non-violence, conflict resolution. Four travelling exhibitions. Educational outreach. Open 11-3 Wed and Fri or by appointment.

Peace News Radical, international, antimilitarist, quarterly magazine. (See entry under Media)

School of the Americas Watch PO Box 4566 Washington, DC 20017, USA. T +1 202 234 3440 info@soaw.org www.soaw.org SOA Watch is an independent organization that seeks to close the US Army School of the Americas which trains dodgy military regimes.

Scottish Campaign for Nuclear Disarmament (CND), 15 Barrland Street, Glasgow G41 1QH. T 0141 4231222 F 0141 4332821 scnd@banthebomb.org www.banthebomb.org Largest Peace organisation in Scotland. Campaign against Trident at Faslane, co-ordinates the Coalition for Justice Not War. Supports direct action and political action.

Stop the War Coalition PO Box 3739, London E5 8EJ. T 020 7053 2153. office@stopwar.org.uk www.stopwar.org.uk Organisation who organise big marches and ask Tony Blair not to go to war.

Sussex Action for Peace PO Box 241 Brighton BN1 3UQ. T 01273 706820 / 07815 998127 / 07789 154582 mail@safp.org.uk www.safp.org.uk Local peace activist group.

Trident Ploughshares 42-46 Bethel St, Norwich, Norfolk, NR2 1NR T 0845 4588366 F 0845 4588364 tp2000@gn.apc.org www.tridentploughshares.org Open, accountable & non-violent disarmament of the British nuclear Trident system.

Truth Justice Peace Action - Human Shields human@humanshields.org www.humanshields.org Mass direct action, in conflict zones, with the objective of protecting life by getting in the way.

Voices in the Wilderness UK 16b Cherwell St, Oxford, OX4 1BG T 0845 4582564 voices@viwuk.freeserve.co.uk www.viwuk.freeserve.co.uk Breaks sanctions by taking medical supplies to Iraq without export licences. Regular newsletter and briefings.

Wake The World www.waketheworld.org Copyright free anti-war posters that you can print off and display in windows, on walls and at protest marches

WoMenwith Womyn's Peace Camp PO Box 105, Harrogate HG3 2FE. T 01943 466825 cndyorks.gn.apc.org/mhs/index.htm Camp against the world's largest spy base. Operated by the US government and based in the Yorkshire Moors.

World Court Project UK 67 Summerheath Rd, Hailsham, Sussex BN27 3DR T 01323 844269 F 01323 844269 geowcpuk@gn.apc.org www.gn.apc.org/wcp Working to have implemented the Advisory Opinion of the International Court of Justice that nuclear weapons are illegal.

Youth & Student Campaign for Nuclear Disarmament (Y&SCND) 162 Holloway Rd, London, N7 8DQ T 0207 607 3616 F 0171 700 2357 youth_cnd@hotmail.com www.nonukes.org.uk Campaigning to trash Trident through actions, demonstrations, awareness raising & letter writing. New volunteers are welcome.

ANARCHISM

A-Infos www.ainfos.ca Regular anarchist newsfeed over the internet in various languages.

Anarchist FAQ www.anarchistfaq.org Frequently Asked Questions about anarchism. Its aim is to present what anarchism really stands for and indicate why you should become an anarchist.

Anarchist Federation c/o 84b Whitechapel High St, London, E1 7QX. T 07946 214590 anarchistfederation@bigfoot.com www.afed.org.uk *Class struggle anarchists aiming to abolish capitalism and all oppression to create a free and equal society. This is Anarchist Communism.*

Anarchist Federation (AF) Greater Manchester PO Box 127, Oldham OL4 3FE. anarchist_federation@yahoo.co.uk www.af-north.org *The local group of the AF in the Manchester area. Members in Manchester, High Peaks, Oldham and more*

Anarchist Federation (Ireland) PO Box 505, Belfast, BT12 6BQ. T 07951 079719 ireaf@yahoo.ie *Irish Anarchist Federation.*

Anarchist Teapot Mobile Kitchen (See entry under Food and Farming)

Anarchist Yellow Pages flag.blackened.net/agony/ayp/ *An international directory of anti-authoritarian groups, publications and self-managed spaces.*

Anarchist Youth Network c/o 84b Whitechapel High St, London E1 7QX. T 07814 629780 info@anarchistyouth.net www.anarchistyouth.net *The only revolutionary youth network in the UK set up independently by young people, for young people, and not as a recruiting ground for some sad leftwing political party*

Azzjoni Pozittiva (M.A.M.) manarkikum@yahoo.com azzjonipozittiva.cjb.net *Anarchist movement in Malta.*

Black Flag *Comprehensive list of UK Anarchist groups.* (See entry under Media)

Class War Federation PO Box 467, London E8 3QX. T 07931 301901 classwaruk@hotmail.com www.classwaruk.org *Exists to promote class consciousness and working class control over our day to day lives. Publish Class War paper.*

Collective for Libertarian Idea (K.S.I. - Kolektiv Za Slobodarska Ideja) slobodarska@hypocrisy.org slobodarska@yahoo.com *The first anarchist collective in Macedonia.*

Czechoslovak Anarchist Federation (CSAF) POBox 223, 111 21 Praha 1, Czech Republic. intersec@csaf.cz csaf.cz *Anarchist propaganda, street actions, publishing anarchist materials, ABC group.*

Federation Collective Rampenplan PO Box 780, 6130 At Sittard, The Netherlands T +31 46 452 4803 F +31 46 451 6460 ramp@antenna.nl www.antenna.nl/rampenplan *Federation based on basic democracy and anarchism. Includes a mobile vegetarian/vegan ecological kitchen, anarchist/environment book publisher and a video action newsgroup.*

Kate Sharpley Library Archive of Anarchist and related material. *(See entry under Media)*

Radical Routes *Mutual aid network.* (See entry under Networking Support)

Solidarity Federation (SolFed) PO Box 469, Preston PR1 8XF. T 01772 739724 solfed@solfed.org.uk www.solfed.org.uk *Anarcho-syndicalist federation of groups (contact them for your local group). Dedicated to an anti-authoritarian future based on mutual aid and individual freedom.*

ANIMAL RIGHTS

Animal Contacts Directory Veggies, 245 Gladstone Street, Nottingham NG7 6HX:T 0845 458 9595. acd@veggies.org.uk www.veggies.org.uk *The essential guide to thousands of animal welfare rights campaigns across the world available online or as a book from Veggies.*

Animal Liberation Front UK Supporters Group BM 1160, London WC1N 3XX. T 0870 1385037 F as phone info@alfsg.co.uk *Info about animal rights prisoners and defence funds plus articles/news in bi-monthly newsletter.*

Animal Liberation Press Office (See entry under Media)

Animal Rights Calendar c/o Veggies, 245 Gladstone Street, Nottingham NG7 6HX. T 0845 458 9595 Arc@veggies.org.uk www.veggies.org.uk/calender *Comprehensive, monthly diary of UK animal rights events. Also appears in ARC News*

ARCNEWS POBox 339, Wolverhampton, WV10 7BZ T 0845 458 0146 james@arcnews.co.uk www.arcnews.co.uk *Independent animal rights magazine aimed at grass-roots campaigning. Available on subscription of £10 per year or on line.*

British Union For The Abolition of Vivisection (BUAV) 16a Crane Grove, London, N7 8NN. T 020 7700 4888 F 020 7700 0196 campaigns@buav.org www.buav.org *Anti-vivisection organisation specialising in public campaigning, hard-hitting undercover investigations, political lobbying and legal/scientific expertise.*

Close Harlan UK PO Box 152, Crowborough, E. Sussex, TN6 2EP. T 07870 929384 www.freespeech.org/chuk *Demos, letter writing, phone calls and leafleting to close Harlan, the biggest supplier of animals to the vivisection industry.*

Compassion in World Farming Charles House,5A Charles Street, Petersfield, Hampshire GU32 3EH T 01730 264208/268863 F 01730 260791 compassion@ciwf.co.uk www.ciwf.co.uk *Campaigning to end the factory farming of animals and long distance transport through hard-hitting political lobbying, investigations and high profile campaigns.*

Greyhound Rescue UK jill@rigolo.f9.co.uk www.greyhoundrescue.co.uk *Donate free Internet presence to any non-profit making organisation or charity for greyhound rescue in the UK. List of local contacts.*

Hunt Saboteurs Association (H.S.A) PO Box 5254, Northampton, NN1 3ZA. T 0845 4500727 /Press office only: 0961 113084 F as phone - call first. info@huntsabs.org.uk www.huntsabs.org.uk *The H.S.A is dedicated to saving the lives of hunted animals directly, using non-violent direct action.*

National Anti-Hunt Campaign (NAHC) 27 Old Gloucester Street, London WC1N 3XX. T 01442 240 246 nahc@nahc.freeserve.co.uk *Peaceful campaigning against all hunting with hounds through petitioning, demonstrations, investigations, lobbying and civil disobedience. Info pack on request.*

National Anti-Vivisection Society 261 Goldhawk Rd, London, W12 9PE. T 020 8846 9777 F 020 8846 9712 info@navs.org.uk www.navs.org.uk *Campaigns against vivisection and on animal rights issues.*

National Federation of Badger Groups (NFBG) 2B Inworth Street, London SW11 3EP. T 020 7228 6444 F 020 7228 6555 enquiries@nfbg.org.uk www.badger.org.uk *Promote conservation & protection of badgers. Represent 85 local voluntary badger groups. Provide information & advice, membership system.*

Seriously Ill Against Vivisection (SIAV) (See entry under Disability Rights and Action)

Shoreham Protester, The c/o 7 Stoneham Rd, Hove, Sussex, BN3 5HJ T 01273 885750 F as phone shoreham-protestr@ntlworld.com www.shoreham-protester.org.uk *Fortnightly newspaper reporting local and national animal rights news, especially reports from demonstrations. Input welcomed.*

Stop Huntingdon Animal Cruelty (SHAC) 6 Boat Lane, Evesham, Worcs WR11 4BP. T 0845 4580630 info@shac.net www.shac.net *SHAC campaigns to close down the animal testing lab Huntingdon Life Sciences, and target anyone connected with them.*

Uncaged Campaigns St Matthew's House, 45 Carver St, Sheffield S1 4FT. T 0114 272 2220 F 0114 272 2225 uncaged.anti-viv@dial.pipex.com www.uncaged.co.uk *Not for profit organisation dedicated to bringing about the abolition of vivisection by democratic means.*

Vegan Prisoners Support Group (VPSG) PO Box 194, Enfield, EN1 3HD T 020 8292 8325 F as phone www.cares.demon.co.uk hvpc@vpsg.freeserve.co.uk *VPSG assists vegan animal rights prisoners either held in police custody or within the prison system.*

Vivisection Information Network (VIN) (See entry under Health)

World Animal Net 24 Barleyfields, Didcot, Oxon, OX11 0BJ. T 01235 210775 info@worldanimal.net www.worldanimal.net *The world's largest network of animal protection societies with over 1700 affiliates in more than 90 countries campaigning to improve the status and welfare of animals.*

ANTI-CAPITALISM

A SEED Europe PO Box 92066 1090 AB Amsterdam, The Netherlands. T +31 20 6682236 F +31 20 4682275 aseedeur@antenna.nl www.aseed.net *Action for Solidarity, Equality, Environment, and Diversity is a global organisation linking youth groups and individuals on all continents.*

Adbusters 1243 West 7th Av, Vancouver, BC, V6H 1B7, Canada. T 604 736 9401 F 604 737 6021 info@adbusters.org www.adbusters.org *A global network of artists, activists, writers, pranksters, educators and entrepreneurs who aim to launch the new social activist movement of the information age.*

Autonomous Centre of Edinburgh (ACE) 17 West Montgomery Place, Edinburgh, EH7 5HA T 0131 557 6242/Pager 07626 128984 ace@autonomous.org.uk www.autonomous.org.uk *Campaign base for social and ecological resistance with a view to bring about the revolutionary overthrow of capitalism.*

Bilderberg www.bilderberg.org *Research into The Power Elite's secretive Bilderberg Conferences.*

Biotic Baking Brigade c/o Whispered Media, POB 40130, San Francisco, CA 94140. USA. Bbb@asis.com www.asis.com/~bbb/ *Pie-throwing is just one tool in the large toolbox of resistance.*

Buy Nothing Day 25 Gloucester Road, Littlehampton, West Sussex, BN17 7BT. T 07887 608609 info@buynothingday.co.uk www.buynothingday.co.uk *Buy Nothing Day is a simple idea, which challenges consumer culture by asking us to switch off from shopping for a day.*

ChiapasLink *Provides a link between the Zapatista struggles in Chiapas, Mexico and in the UK.* (See entry under Indigenous Peoples)

Cuba Solidarity Campaign Red Rose Club, 129 Seven Sisters Road, London N7 7QG. T 020-7263-6452 office@cuba-solidarity.org.uk www.cuba-solidarity.org.uk *Provide material aid to Cuba, fundraising and produce a magazine called Cuba Si*

Earth First! Action Update (EF! AU) *Has list of contacts of all UK Earth First! groups.* (see entry under Media)

Ejercito Zapatista de Liberacion Nacional (EZLN) www.ezln.org *The EZLN web provides reliable information on the Zapatista uprising and serves as the mouthpiece for the Zapatistas in cyberspace.*

Fanclub mail@fanclubbers.org www.fanclubbers.org *Fusing art and activism to create culture-jams with a focus on surveillance and the excesses of consumer culture.*

Green Socialist Network c/o 15 Linford Close, Harlow, Essex CM19 4LR. T 01279 435735 F as phone. pete@petebrown.fsnet.com *Campaigning group for green and left ideas - we believe that environmental protection and issues of social justice are inseparable.*

Industrial Workers of the World *Union for all run by its members.* (See entry under Worker's Rights)

McDonalds Workers Resistance (MWR) *We work for McDonalds and fuck shit up.* (See entry under Worker's Rights)

McLibel Support Campaign 5 Caledonian Rd, London, N1 9DX T 020 787131269 F as phone mclibel@globalnet.co.uk www.mcspotlight.org

Encouraging people everywhere to see the sordid reality behind corporate propaganda, and to fight back against McWorld.

Movement Against the Monarchy (MA'M) PO Box 14672, London, E9 5UQ T 07931 301901 www.geocities.com/capitolhill/lobby/1793/index mam_london@hotmail.com *Local and national direct action against the parasitic, undemocratic Royals.*

Our Mayday BM Mayday, London WC1N 3XX. T 07786 716335 londonmayday@yahoo.co.uk www.ourmayday.org.uk *Mayday is a traditional day of struggle and has become a regular event on the anti-capitalist calendar.*

Peoples' Global Action c/o Canadian Union of Postal Workers, 377 Bank Street, Ottawa, Ontario, Canada pga@agp.org www.agp.org *A global instrument for communication and co-ordination for all those fighting against the destruction of humanity and the planet by the global market.*

Reclaim the Streets (London) PO Box 9656, London, N4 4JY T 020 7281 4621 rts@gn.apc.org www.reclaimthestreets.net *Direct-Action for global and local social-ecological revolution(s) to transcend hierarchical and authoritarian society, (capitalism included), and be home in time for tea.*

Red Star Research BCM Box 3328 London WC1N 3XX. T 07960 865601 info@red-star-research.org.uk www.red-star-research.org.uk *Information about the Labour Party's shift to the right wing of politics. Identifies the links and networks of wealth and power and helps you to uncover the connections.*

Revolutionary Communist Group (RCG) BCM Box 5909, London WC1N 3XX. T 020 7837 1688 F 020 7837 1743 rcgfrfi@easynet.co.uk www.revolutionary communist.com *Supports Cuba, the Palestinian people, and the fight against racism and against poverty pay. It publishes Fight Racism! Fight Imperialism!*

Rhythms of Resistance info@rhythmsofresistance.co.uk www.rhythmsofresistance.co.uk *Radical pink and silver samba band that uses percussion and carnival to mobilise and move people on demos/actions.*

Rock around the Blockade c/o FRFI, BCM Box 5909, London WC1N 3XX. T 020 7837 1688 boycott bacardiuk@yahoo.co.uk www.boycottbacardi.co.uk *Rock around the Blockade was founded in 1995 and is open to anyone who supports Cuba's socialist revolution.*

RTMark info@rtmark.com www.rtmark.com *RT-Mark supports the sabotage of corporate products, with no risk to the public investor.*

Subvertise! *An archive of 100s of subverts, political art, cartoons and articles.* (See entry under Culture)

Temporary Anti-Capitalist Teams c/o BCM Box 3328, London WC1N 3XX. T 07944 586416 TACT1@temporary.org.uk www.temporary.org.uk *Temporary Anti-Capitalist Teams are a powerful way to make dynamic networks of support and communication within the anti-Capitalist movement.*

The Struggle Site revolt@newmail.net http://struggle.ws *Irish web site that hosts pages for many campaigns and libertarian groups in Ireland as well as general anarchist information.*

They Rule theyrule.net *web site about how the different companies that run the world are interconnected.*

Wombles (White Overalls Movement Building Libertarian Effective Struggles) wombles@hushmail.com www.wombles.org.uk *Promote anarchism, libertarian solidarity, autonomous self-organisation and humour... To join the discussion list send a blank email to: maydaywhite-overalls-subscribe@yahoogroups.com*

World Socialist Web Site editor@wses.org www.wsws.org *Provides analysis of major world events, comments on political, cultural, historical and philosophical issues.*

Yes Men administrative@theyesmen.org www.theyesmen.org *The Yes Men are a genderless, loose-knit association of some three hundred impostors worldwide. Eg. Send spoof WTO delegates to conferences.*

ANTI-RACISM

AntiFa.net www.antifa.net *Portal to anti-fascism and anti-racism on the web. Offer secure web hosting to anti-fascists.*

Campaign Against Racism & Fascism (CARF) BM Box 8784, London, WC1X 3XX. T 020 7837 1450 F 0870 052 5899 info@carf.demon.co.uk www.carf.demon.co.uk *CARF magazine exposes racism in multicultural Britain. Details the European offensive against refugees and shows how the domestic fight against racism is shaped by international forces.*

Evil:Austria! raw@raw.at www.raw.at *Multilingual monthly newsletter providing information about the Austrian coalition government including the far right FPOe.*

Institute of Race Relations 2-6 Leeke Street , London WC1X 9HS. T 020 7278 0623 F 020 7278 0623 info@irr.org.uk www.irr.org.uk *The IRR carries our research into issues of racism, from the rise of racial violence to the plight of asylum seekers. The IRR publishes Race & Class and the European Race Bulletin.*

Minority Rights Group International 379 Brixton Rd, London, SW9 7DE T 020 7978 9498 F 020 7738 6265 minority.rights@mrgmail.org www.minorityrights.org *Work to secure rights for ethnic, religious and linguistic minorities world wide, and educating people about minority issues in order to counter racism and prejudice.*

National Assembly Against Racism (NAAR) 28 Commercial St, London, E1 6LS T/F 020 7247 9907 info@naar.org.uk www.naar.org.uk *Initiates campaigns, set agendas and raise awareness on the whole range of anti-racist issues affecting British society.*

Newham Monitoring Project (NMP) 63 Broadway, Stratford, London, E15 4BQ T 020 8555 8151 F 020 8555 8163 nmp@gn.apc.org *Local grassroots anti-racist organisation, offers independent advice and casework support for victims of racial harassment, police harassment and civil injustice.*

No Platform Anti-Fascist Network BM Box 5827, London, WC1M 3XX. noplatform@antifa.net noplatform.antifa.net *Network of anti-fascist socialists, anarchists and anti-capitalists, united by a commitment to the policy of 'no platform' for fascism.* Northern: 07970 398933; Midlands: 07940 305017; South East: c/o Brigthon ABC; London: 07960 771572.

Notes From the Borderland BM Box 4769, London, WC1N 3XX Pager: 07669-175886 larry@borderland.co.uk www.borderland.co.uk *We publish cutting edge parapolitical research into the secret state, fascists, etc - material that is too sharp for Guardian/Red Pepper.*

The Monitoring Group (TMG) 14 Featherstone Rd, Southall, Middx, UB2 5AA. T 020 8843 2333 Emergency Helpline 0800 374618 www.monitoring-group.co.uk *Agency helping victims of racial harassment, police misconduct, domestic violence and immigration detention.*

BOOKSHOPS

56a Infoshop 56 Crampton St, London, SE17. 56a@safetycat.org www.safetycat.org/56a *Books, tea, zines, info, empties, bikes, library, history, action, people.....sometimes cafes...sometimes otherthings...*

Avalon 73 Fawcett Rd, Southsea, Hants, PO4 0DB. T 02392 293673 F 02392 780444 info@avalonheadshop.co.uk *Portsmouth's only head shop. Stock Under-*

currents; distribute SchNEWS as well as information on local, national and international campaigns.

Blackcurrent Bookshop 4 Allen Rd, Abington, Northampton NN1 4NE. T 07833 17328 *Specialises in radical and independent books, comix, cards, badges, tapes and CDs.*

Broken Arrow Bookshop 13 Leigham Hall Parade, Streatham High Road, London, SW16 1DR Tel 020 8769 9777 *New and second hand books, cafe and smoking accessories.*

Cowley Club *Radical bookshop in Brighton* (see entry under Cafes and Clubs)

Freedom Book Company 73 Fawcett Rd, Southsea, Hants, PO4 0DB. T 023 92780600 F 023 92780444 www.freedombooks.co.uk info@freedombooks.co.uk *Massive range of informative drugs related books and magazines (cultivation, legality, effects etc), Undercurrents videos, radical magazines and periodicals.*

Greenleaf Bookshop 82 Colston St, Bristol BS1 5BB. *Radical bookshop in Bristol.*

Housmans Bookshop 5 Caledonian Rd, King's Cross, London, N1 9DX. T 020 7837 4473 F 020 7178 0444 shop@housmans.idps.co.uk *London's oldest radical bookshop, home to the weird & the wonderful, publisher of annual Housmans Peace Diary.*

News From Nowhere Bookshop 96 Bold Street, Liverpool, L1 4HY T 0151 708 7270 www.newsfromnowhere.org.uk *Long established, busy radical community bookshop run by a women's co-operative. Books, magazines, world music CDs and more. Open Mon-Sat 10am-5.45pm.*

October Books 243 Portswood Road, Southampton SO17 2NG. T 023-80581030 info@octoberbooks.org *Cooperatively run independent bookshop in Southampton.*

R.E.C.Y.C. 54 Upperthorpe Rd, Sheffield, S6 3EB. T 0114 263 4494 *Re-use and second hand, recycling, waste campaigns, newsletter.*

Reading International Solidarity Centre (RISC) *Shop selling fair trade products, books and teaching materials.* (See entry under Cafes)

Silvermoon Women's Bookshop at W & G Foyle, 113-119 Charing Cross Road, London WC2H 0EB silvermoon@foyles.co.uk www.foyles.co.uk/silvermoon/index.htm *Europe's largest women's bookshop selling books by and for women.*

Word Power Bookshop 43 West Nicholson St, Edinburgh, EH8 9DB. T 0131 6629112 F as phone books@word-power.co.uk www.word-power.co.uk *Scotland's radical bookshop and mail order. Organise Edinburgh Radical Book Fair in May each year.*

CAFES & CLUBS

1in12 Club 21-23 Albion St, Bradford, BD1 2LY. T 01274 734160 info@1in12.com www.1in12.go-legend.net *Members social club based on the principles of self-management.*

CASA Club 29, Hope St, Liverpool. T 0151 709 2148 dockers@gn.apc.org www.gn.apc.org/initfactory *Club run on co-operative principles, run by sacked Liverpool Dockers. Profits go toward an employment-training centre.*

Cowley Club, The 12 London Road, Brighton BN1 4JA. T 01273 696104. *A collectively run libertarian social centre - café and radical bookshop during the day and a private members bar during the evenings.*

Kebele Kulture Projekt 14 Robertson Rd, Eastville, Bristol, BS5 6JY T 0117 939 9469 : info@kebele.org www.kebele.org *Anarchist collective run drop-in and meeting centre, vegan cafe, bike workshops, anarchist library, housing co-op, exhibitions, campaign catering, political activities and more.*

Okasional Café Dept.20, 22a Beswick Street, Manchester, M4 7HS. T 0161 2266814 Okasional-café@nematode.freeserve.co.uk *Occasional squat cafes &*

reclaimed autonomous spaces in Manchester.

Reading International Solidarity Centre (RISC) 35-39 London St, Reading, RG1 4PS. T 0118 9586692/0118 9569800 F 0118 9594357 admin@risc.org.uk www.risc.org.uk *Development Education Centre with World Shop selling fair trade products, books and teaching materials, Global Café, community meeting space.*

Sumac Centre *Collectively run cafe and private members club in Nottingham.* (See entry under Community Groups)

Swansea Community Resource Centre 217 High Street, Swansea SA1 1NN. T 01792 642404 / 07974 892651 no217crc@yahoo.co.uk www.geocities.com/no217crc/ *Free space for all, including cybercafe, gallery space, stage, perma-culture garden. Free workshops, meeting space, information and other stuff.*

CHILDREN & PARENTING

Baby Milk Action 23 St. Andrew's St, Cambridge, CB2 3AX. T 01223 464420 info@babymilkaction.org www.babymilkaction.org www.ibfan.org *Aims to save lives and to end the avoidable suffering caused by inappropriate infant feeding.*

Informed Parent, The PO Box 870, Harrow, Middlesex, HA3 7UW. T 020 8861 1022 F as phone www.informedparent.co.uk *Quarterly newsletter to help parents make a decision regarding vaccination based on knowledge, not fear.*

Real Nappy Project PO Box 3704, London SE26 4RX. www.realnappy.com *Central source of information and advice on all nappy-related issues, for local authorities, health professionals, the media and individuals.*

Woodcraft Folk, The 13 Ritherdon Road, London, SW17 8QE. 13 Ritherdon Rd., London, SW17 8QE. T 020 8672 6031 info@woodcraft.org.uk www.woodcraft.org.uk *We aim to develop self-confidence in young people and aim to building a sustainable world based on equality, peace, social justice and co-operation.*

COMMUNITY GROUPS

1990 Trust, The Suite 12, Winchester House, 9 Cranmer Road, SW9 6EJ, T 020 7582 1990 F 0870 127 6657 blink1990@gn.apc.org www.blink.org.uk *A national Black (African, Asian & Caribbean) organisation to increase the capacities of the Black communities to combat racism.*

Cornerstone Housing Co-op *Have a resource centre open to local groups and individuals.* (See entry under Housing)

Diggers & Dreamers *"The Guide to Communal Living in Britain"* (See entry under Media)

Dropseven T 07949 913123 team@dropseven.co.uk www.dropseven.co.uk/ *Concerned with community led collective action and strives to develop active, sustainable solutions to community development, capacity building and regeneration.*

Haringey Solidarity Group (HSG) PO Box 2474 London N8. T 020 8374 5027 hsg@globalinternet.co.uk hsg.cupboard.org *Local working class group encouraging radical solidarity, co-operation, and mutual aid in our community, workplaces, and lives.*

London Action Resource Centre a.k.a. Fieldgate, 62 Fieldgate St, London E1. T 020 7377 9088. www.londonarc.org *Collectively run building providing space and resources for London activists.*

Living Streets 31-33 Bondway, London, SW8 1SJ. T 020 7820 1010 F 020 7820 8208 info@livingstreets .org.uk www.livingstreets.org.uk *Help people improve the safety and condition of local streets and public spaces through information and local support.*

Newham Monitoring Project (NMP) *Local grass-roots anti-racist organisation.* (See entry under Anti-Racism)

Spitalfields Market Under Threat (SMUT) T 020 7613 5897 smut@smut.org.uk www.smut.org.uk *Oppose the destruction of three-fifths of the historic old covered market to make way for yet another office development.*

Steward Wood Moretonhampstead, Newton Abbot, Devon TQ13 8SD. T 01647 440233 Mob 07050 674464 affinity@stewardwood.org www.stewardwood.org *Demonstrating positive sustainable alternatives - a vegan community based in a woodland in Dartmoor. Permaculture, renewable energy, organic growing, low impact living. Visitors welcome.*

Sumac Centre 245 Gladstone St., Nottingham, NG7 6HX. T 0845 458 9595 F phone first sumac@veggies.org.uk www.veggies.org.uk/sumac *Resource centre for local groups campaigning for human and animal rights, the environment, peace, etc.*

Swansea Community Resource Centre (See entry under Cafes)

The Resource Centre Priory House, 6 Tilbury Place, Brighton, BN2 0GY. T 01273 606160 F 01273 673663 info@resourcecentre.org.uk www.resourcecentre.org.uk *Hires out a range of equipment for meetings and fundraising events and has computers and printing facilities in the Centre*

Truth & Reconciliation Commission for Stonehenge (TRCS) 96 Church Road, Redfield, Bristol BS5 9LE. T 0117 9542273 george@greenleaf.d emon.co.uk www.greenleaf.demon.co.uk (follow Stonehenge link) *Open forum for resolution of Stonehenge conflict by discussion with all people including officials.*

CULTURE

Art, music, festivals, etc.
(for film see Media - Film, Video & TV)

Banksy www.banksy.co.uk *Political graffiti artist.*

Banner Theatre Company The Friends Institute, 220 Moseley Rd, Highgate, Birmingham, B12 0DG. T 0121 440 0460 voices@btinternet.com *Promotes political change in support of disenfranchised sections of society, through the use of documentary, multi-media cultural productions rooted in radical experiences.*

Brighton Alliance of Sound Systems (BASS) 43 Park Crescent Road, Brighton, BN2 3HE. info@bass23.org wwwbass23.org *BASS is about positive free party politics. BASS generates funds to pay for communal safety equipment and courses.*

Chumbawamba PO Box TR666, Armley, Leeds, LS12 3XJ. chumba@chumba.demon.co.uk www.chumba.com *We are a music combo, we don't do weddings and barmitvahs but we would dance at several people's funerals.*

Continental Drifts Hilton Grove Business Centre, London, E17 4QP T 020 8509 3353 F 020 8509 9531 chris@continentaldrifts.co.uk www.continenta ldrifts.co.uk *Not for profit organisation representing the finest in UK underground performing arts from "outside the mainstream".*

Fanclub mail@fanclubbers.org www.fanclubbers.org *Fusing art and activism to create culture-jams with a focus on surveillance and the excesses of consumer culture.*

Festival Eye BCM 2002, London, WC1N 3XX. T 0870 737 1011 F 0870 7371010 subscriptions@festival eye.com www.festivaleye.com *Published each May (£3 + SAE) with the most comprehensive listings of UK festivals side by side with beautiful artwork, photography and reviews.*

Festival Zone, The info@thefestivalzone.com www.thefestivalzone.com *Website listing rock festivals in Europe.*

Green Road Show Ham Mill's Yard, Bowlish, Shepton Mallet, Somerset BA4 5JH. T 01749 343953 Mobile 07831 405661 or 07778 765724 info@gree nroadshow.demon.co.uk www.greenroadshow.co.uk *Environmental education and family entertainment based in, and around, the Worlds only Wind and Solar powered Circus Top.*

Guilfin PO Box 217, Guildford, Surrey GU1 1WS. T 07957 193195 moneypenny@mi5.uk.com www.guilfin.net *The essential alternative guide to what's going on in the South East's underground scene.*

Levellers 55 Canning Street, Brighton, BN2 0EF. T 01273 608887 otf@levellers.co.uk www.levellers.co.uk *Band. Produce a magazine, sell merchandise.*

Network 23 www.network23.org *Free party network.*

New York Surveillance Camera Players *Situationist-inspired anti-surveillance camera group.* (See entry under Media)

Northern Arts Tactical Offensive, c/o Bridge 5 Mill, 22a Beswick st, Ancoats, Manchester. tacticalarts@yahoo.co.uk www.nato.uk.net *A collective effort at bringing radical political art back into the streets.*

Overload Media PO Box 41, Bristol, BS16 3ZB. offic e@overloadmedia.co.uk www.overloadmedia.co.uk *Independent, non-profit making organisation dedicated to electronic music. Many music and non music related articles and essays, and an active community forum.*

Partyvibe collective www.partyvibe.com/ freeparties.htm *Bringing together partygoers, musicians and artists. This site is dedicated to offering resources to the free party community.*

Positive Outlook Records PO Box 233 Peterborough PE4 6UB mail@positiveoutlookrecords.com www.positiveoutlookrecords.com *A youth collective of punk-rock kids, run a DIY record label, put on punk-rock shows and help causes with distribution of material through their stall.*

Raise Your Banners 641 Ecclesall Road, Sheffield, S11 8PT. T 0114 249 5185 pete@ryb.org.uk www.ryb.org.uk *Biennial festival of political song.*

Rhythms of Resistance *Radical pink and silver samba band.* (See entry under Anti-Capitalism)

SCRAP Records PO Box 2023, Brighton, BN1 1AA. di rtysquatters@hotmail.com www.dirtysquatters.com *Hardcore underground label bringing music and culture for your hot, drowning planet.*

Stonehenge Campaign c/o 99 Torriano Av, London, NW5 2RX. T 07970 378572 stonehenge@stones.com www.phreak.co.uk/ stonehenge/psb/stonecam.htm *Meet at Solstice and Equinox sunrises at Stonehenge, want more Free Festivals at Stonehenge, and free access into the Stones for all who come in peace.*

Subvertise! c/o PO Box 68, Headington, Oxford OX3 7YS. webmaster@subvertise.org www.subvertise.org *An archive of 100s of subverts, political art, cartoons and articles.*

Sw@rm swarmlist@yahoo.co.uk www.geocities.com/swarmlist *Mobile radical infospace and information for action!.*

ThePartyParty.Org www.thepartyparty.org *Promoting the positive aspect of the party, its benefits to our society and our basic human right to celebrate our lives as we are moved.*

UHC Collective PO Box 23, Bridge 5 Mill, 22A Beswick Street, Manchester M4 7HR. mail@uhc-collective.org.uk www.uhc-collective.org.uk *A political art collective producing stickers, websites, posters, banners and propaganda, for ourselves and other grassroots groups.*

Wolfs Head Press PO Box 77, Sunderland, SR1 1EB. wolfsheadpress@hotmail.com *Fanzine (Wearwolf), music (Frankenstein Sound Lab), mail art* and other stuff with a home made slant.

Zion Train (Universal Egg) PO Box 3, Whitland, Dyfed, SA34 0YU T 01994 419800 F 01994 419357 perch@wobblyweb.com www.wobblyweb.com *Dub musicians with a conscience. Check out the Wobbler newsletter on the web.*

DISABLITY RIGHTS & ACTION

Federation of Deaf People PO Box 11, Darwen, Lancs BB3 3GH. F 01254 708071 contact@fdp.org.uk www.fdp.org.uk *A voluntary organisation that campaigns for Deaf people's rights funded by donations and membership.*

Incapacity Action 104 Cornwallis Circle, Whitsable, Kent CT5 1DT. T 01227 276159 F as phone incapacityaction@onetel.net.uk *Campaign for rights to benefits, independent living/home care supprt, other resources and linking with anti-war struggle.*

Seriously Ill Against Vivisection (SIAV) PO Box 116, High Wycombe, Bucks, HP14 3WX. T 0845 4581720 info@siav.org www.siav.org *Campaigning for a ban on all vivisection. We want non-animal, scientific methods of research to establish cures for disease.*

WinVisible: Women with Visible and Invisible Disabilities Crossroads Women's Centre, 230A Kentish Town Rd, London, NW5 2AB. T 020 7482 2496 (voice and minicom) F 020 7209 4761 crossroads womenscentre@compuserve.com womenstrike8 m.server101.com *Multi-racial self-help network of women with visible and invisible disabilities. Want the caring work we do recognised and paid for.*

DRUGS

Avalon *Portsmouth's only head shop.* (See entry under Bookshops)

Chillout Collective, The c/o 28 Partington Close, Archway, London N19 3DZ. T 07956 450 267 thechilloutcollective@hotmail.com www.caffeinehit.com/clients/chill *A collective of drug and health workers, legal advisers, researchers and activists, who run chillout spaces at dance events promoting harm reduction practices.*

Drug Culture www.drugculture.net *A non profit making website to collect names and emails addresses of people who feel that cannabis should be totally de-criminalised.*

Freedom Book Company *Massive range of informative drugs related books and magazines* (See entry under Bookshops)

Green Party Drugs Group c/o 1a Waterlow Rd, London, N19 5NJ T 020 8671 5936 F phone first greenpartydrugsgroup@gn.apc.org www.greenparty.org.uk/drugs *Promote and sell ecstasy testing kits, part of core group for annual Cannabis March and Festival, info stalls & E-testing at clubs, provide speakers, change drug policy.*

Legalise Cannabis Alliance (LCA) PO Box 198, Norwich, NR2 2DH T 01603 442215 lca@lca-uk.org www.lca-uk.org *A political party dedicated to campaigning for the full legalisation and utilisation of cannabis (hemp) - standing candidates in elections.*

Release 388 Old St, London, EC1V 9LT T 020 7729 525524 F 020 7729 2599 24-hour Helpline: 020 7729 9904 Drugs In Schools Helpline: 0808 8000 800 Sex Workers & The Law Advice Line: 020 7729 9904 www.release.org.uk *24 hour drugs and legal helpline. Also produces publications, such as the bustcard and runs training programmes.*

Transform Easton Business Centre, Felix Road, Easton, Bristol, BS5 OHE. T 0117 9415810 F 0117 9415809 Mob 07980213943 www.transform-drugs.org.uk info@transform-drugs.org.uk *Campaign for a just and effective drug policy including the legalisation of all drugs.*

ECONOMICS

ATTAC London Flat 1A, Rose Court, 34 Woodside, London SW19 7AN. info@attac.org.uk attac.org.uk *ATTAC campaigns for economic reforms, in order to re-conquer space lost by democracy to the sphere of finance.*

Corporate Europe Observatory, Paulus Potterstraat 20, 1071 DA Amsterdam, The Netherlands. T +31 20 612 7023 ceo@corporateeurope.org www.corporateeurope.org *Targeting the threats to democracy, equity, social justice and the environment posed by the economic and political power of corporations and their lobby groups.*

Corporate Watch 16b Cherwell St, Oxford, OX4 1BG T 01865 791391 mail@corporatewatch.org.uk www.corporatewatch.org.uk *Research organisation investigating and exposing corporate power. Website for anti-corporate campaigners. Publishes bi-monthly newsletter (sub. £5/year).*

CorpWatch India PO Box 29344, San Francisco, CA 94129, USA. T +1 415 5616472 F +1 415 5616493 india@corpwatch.org www.corpwatchindia.org *Exposes the social and environmental impacts of corporate investment in India.*

Ecology Building Society 18 Station Rd, Cross Hills, Keighley, BD20 7EH. T 0845 674 5566 F 01535 636166 info@ecology.co.uk www.ecology.co.uk *A mutual building society dedicated to improving the environment by promoting sustainable housing and sustainable communities.*

Ethical Consumer Unit 21, 41 Old Birley St, Manchester, M15 5RF. T 0161 226 2929 F 0161 226 6277 mail@ethicalconsumer.org www.ethicalconsumer.org *Alternative consumer organisation looking at the social and environmental records of the companies behind the brand names.*

Ethical Junction 1st Floor, Dale House, 35 Dale Street, Manchester, M1 2HF. T 0161 236 3637 info@ethical-junction.org www.ethical-junction.org *Ethical Junction is a one-stop shop for ethical organisations and ethical trading.*

Fairtrade Foundation, Suite 204, 16 Baldwin's Gardens, London, EC1N 7RJ. T 020 7405 5942 F 020 7405 5943 mail@fairtrade.org.uk www.fairtrade.org.uk *Exists to ensure a better deal for marginalised and disadvantaged third world producers.*

Green Guide Publishing Ltd 271 Upper St, London, N1 2UQ. T 020 7354 2709 F 020 7226 1311 sales@greenguide.co.uk greenguide.co.uk *Covers environmental, ethical and fairtrade products and services and provides the latest news, reviews, stories and information.*

LETSlink UK 12 Southcote Road, London N19 5BJ. T 020 76077852 F 020 76097112 Mob 07966 216891 letslink@synergynet.co.uk letslinkuk.org *National Development Agency and support network for Local Exchange Trading Schemes and other forms of local currency in the UK.*

New Economics Foundation (NEF) Cinnamon House, 6-8 Cole St, London, SE1 4YH T 020 7089 2800 F 020 7407 6473 info@neweconomics.org www.neweconomics.org *NEF works to put people and the environment at the centre of economic thinking.*

Public Citizen's Global Trade Watch 1600 20th Street NW, Washington DC, 20009, USA. T +1 202 588 1000 www.tradewatch.org *Educates the American public about the enormous impact of international trade and economic globalization on jobs, the environment, health and democratic accountability.*

Rootstock 50 Whateley Road, Handsworth, Birmingham, B21 9JD. T 0870 458 1132 info@rootstock.org.uk www.rootstock.org.uk *A social investment society set up as an initiative of the Radical Routes network of co-operatives supporting co-operatives working for social change.*

Shared Interest Society Limited 25 Collingwood St, Newcastle upon Tyne, NE1 1JE T 0191 2339101 F 0191 2339110 www.shared-interest.com post@shared-interest.com *Co-operative lending society, lending money on fair terms to enable Third World producer groups to pay for labour, materials and equipment.*

UpStart Services 1 Court Ash, Yeovil, Somerset, BA20 1HG. T 0845 4581473 F 01935 431222 upstart@co-op.org users.cooptel.net/upstart *Provide help for people starting or running co-operatives and non-profit businesses, especially those with ecological or social change objectives.*

Women's Development Service No.30 Galtota Mulla, Kandy Road, Yakkala, Sri Lanka. T +94 33 27962 janawomented@lanka.com.lk *Movement of poor mothers united together to develop themselves and their families, economically, socially and culturally. An alternative banking system for elevation out of poverty.*

World Development Movement (WDM) 25 Beehive Place, London, SW9 7QR T 020 72747630 F 020 72748232 wdm@wdm.org.uk www.wdm.org.uk *Campaigns to tackle the root causes of poverty. Are currently campaigning to rewrite global trade rules to put people before profits.*

EDUCATION

Education Otherwise PO Box 7420, London N9 9SG. enquiries@education-otherwise.org www.education-otherwise.org *UK-based membership organisation which provides support and information for families whose children are being educated outside school.*

Education Workers Network PO Box 29, Southwest PDO, Manchester, M15 5HW. T 07984 675 281 ewn@ewn.org.uk www.ewn.org.uk *Network of education workers who favour collective direct action for decent education. Contact EWN for free bulletins.*

Educational Heretics Press, 113 Arundel Drive, Bramcote Hills, Nottingham, NG9 3FQ. T 0115 9257261 www.edheretics.gn.apc.org *Questions the dogmas of schooling in particular, and education in general, and to develop the logistics of the next learning system.*

Emerson College Trust Ltd Forest Row, East Sussex, RH18 5JX. T 01342 822238 F 01342 826055 bmail@emerson.org.uk www.emerson.org.uk *An international centre for adult education, especially in the areas of Biodynamic Organic Agriculture and Steiner Waldorf Teacher Training.*

Free Range Education AskFredService@aol.com www.free-range-education.co.uk *Home education site - stacked with resources, links, information, qualified legal help and an e-mail support service called Ask FREd.*

Home Education Reading Opportunities (H.E.R.O Books) 58 Portland Rd, Hove, East Sussex, BN3 5DL T 01273 775560 F 01273 389382 *Home education books via mail order. For a catalogue and list of local newsletters send a large SAE. Free Range Education book on how to home educate £13.20 inc. postage.*

Human Scale Education Fairseat Farm, Chew Stoke, Bristol BS18 8XF. Info@hse.org.uk www.hse.org.uk *Promotes smaller structures in education and a more holistic approach to learning.*

Lifecycles PO Box 77, Totnes, Devon, TQ9 5UA. T 01803 840098 people@lifecycles.info www.lifecycles.info *A pedal powered cinema and outreach collective dedicated to the pursuit of sustainability and sequins.*

Scientists for Global Responsibility (SGR) PO Box 473, Folkestone, CT20 1GS. T 07771 883696 info@sgr.org.uk www.sgr.org.uk *Promotes the ethical practice and use of science and technology.*

SELFED Collective (SelfED) PO Box 1095, Sheffield,

S2 4YR selfed@selfed.org.uk www.selfed.org.uk *For self-education ideas and practice, developing real alternatives to state-sponsored education. Courses, self-help materials, workshops, etc.*

Travellers' School Charity PO Box 2, Goodwick, Pembrokeshire, SA64 0ZQ. T 01239 891343 stigstrunk@aol.com www.travellersschool.plus.com *The Travellers' School Charity's aim is to support traveller families access opportunities, freedom and choice through education.*

Wealden Home Educators Network (wHEn) c/o 6 East Cliff Road, Tunbridge Wells, TN4 9AD. T 01732 362151 / 01892 863941 wealdenhomeeducatorsn etwork@yahoo.com www.when.omnia.co.uk *Free monthly newsletter of activities and groups, Group Email List and LEA support, enquiries welcome.*

Wild Things (Ecological Education Collective) c/o 15 The Square, Bestwwod Village, Nottm NG6 8TS. T 0845 458 4727 info@wildthings.org.uk www.wildthings.org.uk *Environmental education for primary & secondary school children through hands on projects.*

ENERGY

Campaign for Real Events info@c-realevents.demon.co.uk www.c-realevents.demon.co.uk *Providing renewable energy support for art projects and producing free DIY plans for pedal generators and other renewable energy devices.*

Centre for Alternative Technology (C.A.T) Machynlleth, Powys, SY20 9AZ. T 01654 705950 F 01654 702782 info@cat.org.uk www.cat.org.uk *Environmental centre covering renewable energy, building, sewage and water and organic growing. Displays, publications, courses, mail-order, consultancy and free information service.*

Energy Efficiency Advice Centre T 0845 7277200 www.saveenergy.co.uk *An independent, government-funded body - advice on saving money on your electricity/gas bill. Free action pack*

Energy Saving Trust 21 Dartmouth St, London, SW1H 9BP T 020 7222 0101 F 0207 6542444 info@est.co.uk www.est.co.uk *Set up by the government to stimulate energy efficiency in UK households and create a market for clean fuel vehicles.*

Gaia Energy Center Delabole, North Cornwall, PL33 9DA T 01840 213321 F 01840 213428 support@gaiaenergy.co.uk www.gaiaenergy.co.uk *Centre for the promotion of, and education about, renewable and sustainable energy and energy conservation.*

Green Builder www.greenbuilder.co.uk *Page of useful links all to do with Green Building in the UK*

Green Dragon Energy Ceredigion, Wales. T 01974 821564 dragonrg@talk21.com www.greendragonen ergy.co.uk *Electricity from Sun, Wind & Water.*

Hemp Food Industries Association *Hemp food, fibre, fuel and more.* (See entry under Farming and Food)

UK Solar Energy Society, The c/o School of Engineering, Oxford Brookes University, Headington Campus, Gipsy Lane, Oxford OX3 0BP. T 01865 484367 F 01865 484263 uk-ises@brookes.ac.uk www.thesolarline.com *A forum for all those interested in the advancement of the utilisation of the sun's energy.*

unit[e] UK Freepost (SCE9229) Chippenham SN15 1UZ. T 0845 6011410 enquiries@unit-e.co.uk www.unit-e.co.uk *Provides renewable electricity services to domestic and corporate customers.*

World Information Service on Energy PO Box 59636, 1040 LC Amsterdam, Netherlands. T +31-20-6126368 F +31-20-6892179 www.antenna.nl/wise *Information and networking centre for citizens and environmental organisations concerned about nuclear power, radioactive waste, radiation, and sustainable energy issues.*

ENVIRONMENT

A SEED Europe Action for Solidarity, Equality, Environment, and Diversity. (See entry under Anti-capitalism)

Black Environment Network (BEN) UK Office, 9 Llainwon Uchaf, Llanberis, Wales, LL55 4LL. T 01286 870715 F as phone ukoffice@ben-network.org.uk www.ben-network.co.uk *Established to promote equal opportunities, with respect to ethnic communities, in the preservation, protection and development of the environment.*

British Trust for Conservation Volunteers 36 St Mary's Street, Wallingford, Oxfordshire OX10 0EU. T 01491 821600 F 01491 839646 info@btcv.org.uk www.btcv.org.uk *Practical environmental conservation charity.*

Centre for Alternative Technology (C.A.T) (See entry under Energy)

Climate Independent Media Centre www.climate.indymedia.org *The Climate Independent Media Center provides up-to-the-minute independent and honest coverage of the climate summit, the backgrounds, the corporate lobby and the actions.*

Common Ground Gold Hill House, 21 High Street, Shaftesbury, Dorset SP7 8JE. T 01747 850820 F 01747 850821 kate.ofarrell@commonground.org.uk www.commonground.org.uk *Common Ground offers ideas, information and inspiration to help us learn about, enjoy and take more responsibility for our own localities.*

Communities Against Toxics (CATS) (See entry under Health)

Council for the Protection of Rural England (CPRE) Warwick House, 25 Buckingham Palace Rd, London, SW1W 0PP T 020 7976 6433 F 020 7976 6373 info@cpre.org.uk www.cpre.org.uk *Promotes the beauty, tranquillity and diversity of rural England by encouraging the sustainable use of land and other natural resources in town and country.*

Earth Centre Denaby Main, Doncaster, DN12 4EA T 01709 513933 F01709 512010 www.earthcentre.org.uk *Exhibition centre aimed at developing understanding of sustainable development.*

Earth First! Action Update (EF! AU) *A monthly round-up of ecological and other direct action from around Britain. Has list of contacts of all UK Earth First groups.* (See entry under Media)

Earth First! Journal *Voice of the radical environmental movement.* (See entry under Media)

Ecologist, *The Environmental magazine.* (See entry under Media)

Ecovillage Network UK (EVNUK) (See entry under Housing)

Envirolink support@envirolink.org www.envirolink.org *Links to Sustainable Business Network, Animal Rights Resource Site where to buy environmental books. Essential & extensive web directory.*

Environmental Rescue International (ERI). PO Box 894, Benin City, Nigeria. environmentalrescu e@yahoo.co.uk eri@justice.com *ERI - local and internationally focus environmental, human rights and community development organisation. Organises research, training, conferences and direct actions regularly.*

Friends of the Earth 26-28 Underwood St, London, N1 7JQ. T 020 7490 1555 F 020 7490 0881 info@foe.co.uk www.foe.co.uk *Friends of the Earth exists to inspire solutions to environmental problems, making life better for people.*

Friends of the Earth Scotland 72 Newhaven Rd, Edinburgh, EH6 5QG T 0131 554 9977 F 0131 554 8656 www.foe-scotland.org.uk *We stand for environmental justice. And we aim to make the right to a decent environment available to everyone in Scotland and around the globe.*

Greenpeace Canonbury Villas, London, N1 2PN T 020 7865 8100 Press office T 020 7865 8255 F 020 7865 8200 info@uk.greenpeace.org www.greenpeace.org *Independent non-profit global environmental campaigning organisation that uses non-violent, creative confrontation to promote solutions to environmental issues and bring about change.*

Green Socialist Network (See entry under Anti-Capitalism)

Groundwork 85-87 Cornwall St, Birmingham, B3 3BY T 0121 236 8565 F 0121 236 7356 www.Groundwork.org.uk *Environmental regeneration charity making sustainable development a reality in many of the UK's most disadvantaged communities.*

How to Build a Protest Tunnel www.discodavestu nnelguide.co.uk *Online manual on how to dig your own protest tunnel.*

Judi Bari Website www.judibari.org *Detailing the bombing of eco-activist Judi Bari and how the FBI tried to frame her for blowing herself up, the FBI later paid $4.4 million in damages.*

Low Level Radiation Campaign (See entry under Health)

Manchester Environmental Resource Centre initiative (MERCi) Bridge-5 Mill 22a Beswick Street, Ancoats, Manchester, M4 7HR T 0161 273 1736 F 0161 274 4598 merci@bridge5.org www.bridge5.org/merci.htm *Sustainable development innovator and the largest membership based environmental charity in Manchester.*

Marine Conservation Society 9 Gloucester Road, Ross-on-Wye, Herefordshire, HR9 5ZZ. T 01989 566017 F 01989 567815 www.mcsuk.org *Charity dedicated to protecting the marine environment and wildlife.*

Mines & Communities Roger Moody, c/o Partizans, 41 Thornhill Square, London, N1. T 20 7700 6189 F 20 7700 6189 info@minesandcommunities.org. www.minesandcommunities.org *Seeks to empower mining-affected communities so they can struggle successfully against damaging proposals and projects. Has links to many anti-mining campaigns.*

Multimap.Com uk8.multimap.com/map/places.cgi *A complete interactive atlas on the web!*

Nine Ladies Anti-Quarry Campaign Bramble Dene, Stanton Lees, Matlock, Derbyshire DE4 2LQ. all@ni neladies.uklinux.net www.nineladies.uklinux.net *Opposing destruction of ancient landscape at the edge of National Park, endangering standing stones.*

Peat Alert c/o CRC, 16 Sholebroke Avenue, Leeds, LS7 3HB. T 0113 262 9365 info@peatalert.org.uk www.peatalert.org.uk *Information for action against peat mining on Thorne and Hatfield Moors, South Yorkshire.*

People & Planet (P&P) *UK student action on world poverty, human rights and the environment.* (See entry under Human Rights)

People Against Rio Tinto and Subsidiaries (PARTiZANS) 41a Thornhill Square, London N1 1BE T 0207 700 6189 F same as phone partizabs@gn.apc.org www.minesandcommunities.org/Aboutus/ partizans.htm *Partizans has been campaigning since 1978 against the damage wreaked by the world's most powerful mining company.*

Pesticide Action Network UK (See entry under Health)

R.E.C.Y.C. 54 Upperthorpe Rd, Sheffield, S6 3EB. T 0114 263 4494 *Re-use and second hand, recycling, waste campaigns, newsletter.*

Rainbow Keepers PO Box 52, Kasimov, 391330, Russia. T +7 09131 41514 rk@lavrik.ryazan.ru, rk2000@mail.ru www.chat.ru/~rk2000 *Russian radical ecological movement.*

Rising Tide 16b Cherwell Street, Oxford OX1 1BG. T 01865 241097 info@risingtide.org.uk www.risingtide.org.uk *A network of independent* groups and individuals dedicated to taking local action and building a national movement against climate change.

River Ocean Research & Education (RORE) info@rore.org.uk www.rore.org.uk A charity dedicated to increasing awareness and encouraging care for our water environments - focussed in the fields of environmental education and research.

Scottish Opencast Action Group c/o 42 Woolfords, by West Calder, West Lothian, EH55 8LH soag.info@virgin.net A network of people across Scotland opposed to opencast coal mining. Mainly information exchange & help with opposing planning applications.

Sea Shepherd Conservation Society PO Box 6095, 4000 HB Tiel, Netherlands. T +31 0344 604130 F +31 344 604808 info@seashepherd.nl www.seashepherd.nl Dedicated to the protection and conservation of marine ecosystems and biodiversity. Take direct action where authorities are unwilling to enforce conservation regulations.

Surfers Against Sewage (See entry under Health)

Tourism Concern Stapleton House, 277-281 Holloway Rd, London, N7 8HN. T 020 7753 3330 F 020 7753 3331 info@tourismconcern.org.uk www.tourismconcern.org.uk Tourism Concern is an educational charity promoting awareness of the impact of tourism on people and their environment.

UK Rivers Network (UKRN) T 07092-335227 F 07092-335227 info@ukrivers.net www.ukrivers.net Community action, information and networking to improve rivers and inland waters across the UK and Ireland.

Voice of Irish Concern for the Environment 7 Upper Camden St., Dublin 2, Ireland. T +353 1 6618123 F +353 1 6618114 avoice@iol.ie www.voice.buz.org Ireland's leading independent environmental organisation with members throughout the country. We are committed to promoting positive solutions to environmentally-destructive activities.

Womens Environment Network (W.E.N) PO Box 30626 London E1 1TZ. T 020 74819004 F 020 74819144 info@wen.org.uk www.wen.org.uk A national UK charity and membership organisation educating, informing and empowering women and men who care about the environment.

FOOD & FARMING

Anarchist Teapot Mobile Kitchen, PO Box 74 Brighton BN1 4ZQ. katchoo63@yahoo.co.uk Catering collective based on volunteer labour to cook vegan, mostly organic food for events we care about. Can cook outside, inside, anywhere for up to 300 people.

Banana Link 38 Exchange Street, Norwich, NR2 1AX T 01603 765670 F 01603 761645 blink@gn.apc.org www.bananalink.org.uk Works towards environmentally, socially and economically sustainable banana production and trade through campaigns, awareness raising and lobbying.

Emerson College Trust Ltd Adult education in Biodynamic Organic Agriculture (See entry under Education)

ETC Group (Action Group on Erosion, Technology and Concentration) 478 River Avenue, Suite 200, Winnipeg, MB R3L 0C8, Canada. T 204 453 5259 F 204 284 7871 www.etcgroup.org Dedicated to the conservation and sustainable advancement of cultural and ecological diversity and human rights.

Federation of City Farms and Community Gardens The Green House, Hereford St, Bedminster, Bristol, BS3 4NA T 0117 923 1800 admin@farmgarden.org.uk www.farmgarden.org.uk Bringing together information on city farms and community gardens across the county.

Foundation for Local Food Initiatives PO Box 1234, Bristol BS99 2PG. T 0845 4589525

F 0117 9260221 mail@localfood.org.uk www.localfood.org.uk Independent not-for-profit co-operative company promoting and supporting the growth of healthy local food economies.

Hemp Food Industries Association PO Box 204, Barnet, Herts, EN4 8ZQ T 07050 600418 F 07050 600419 hemp@hemp.co.uk www.hemp.co.uk Hemp food, fibre, fuel, plastic, paper (+more) information for farmers, manufacturer's, retailers, consumers, press + you.

McLibel Support Campaign Encouraging people everywhere to see the sordid reality behind corporate propaganda, and to fight back against McWorld. (See entry under Anti-Capitalism)

National Association of Farmers' Markets South Vaults, Green Park Station, Green Park Road, Bath BA1 1JB. T 01225 787914 F 01225 460840 nafm@farmersmarkets.net www.farmersmarkets.net Promoting and supporting farmers' markets across the UK.

Permaculture Association (Britain) BCM Permaculture Association, London, WC1N 3XX. T 0845 4581805 F as phone office@permaculture.org.uk www.permaculture.org.uk Support people and projects to learn about and use permaculture in their homes, gardens, schools, business, farms and communities.

Primal Seeds 22a Beswick Street, Manchester M4 7HR. mail@primalseeds.org www.primalseeds.org Information on industrial agriculture with a focus on seeds, and its alternatives.

Single Step Co-Op 78A Penny St, Lancaster, LA1 1XN T 01524 847234 Selling wholefoods and organics in a democratic, non-hierarchical, workers' co-op stylee. Also stock non-mainstream mags and journals.

Soil Association Bristol House, 40-56 Victoria St, Bristol, BS1 6BY T 0117 929 0661 F 0117 925 2504 info@soilassociation.org www.soilassociation.org Campaigning and certification organisation for organic food and farming.

Sustain 94 White Lion Street, London N1 9PF. T 020 78371228 F 020 78371141 sustain@sustainweb.org www.sustainweb.org Sustain advocates food and agriculture policies and practices, that promote equity and enrich society and culture.

Tools For Solidarity (TFS) Unit 1B1, Edenberry Industrial Estate, 326 Crumlin Rd, Belfast, BT14 7EE T 028 9074 7473. Refurbishes unwanted hand tools and sewing machines for skilled tradespeople in Africa. Committed to the equal distribution of power and resources.

Vegan Society, The Donald Watson House, 7 Battle Rd, St. Leonards On Sea, E. Sussex, TN37 7AA T 01424 427393 F 01424 717064 www.vegansociety.com info@vegansociety.com Educational charity promoting ways of living which avoid the use of animal products - for the benefit of people, animals and the environment.

Vegetarian Society of the UK, The Parkdale, Dunham Rd, Altringham, Cheshire, WA14 4QG T 0161 925 2000 F 0161 926 9182 info@vegsoc.org www.vegsoc.org Educational Charity dedicated to the promotion of the knowledge of vegetarianism.

Veggies Catering Campaign 245 Gladstone Street, Nottingham NG7 6HX T 0845 458 9595 mobile: 0787 0861837 info@veggies.org.uk www.veggies.org.uk Event catering (all-vegan) and support for human, animal rights & environmental campaigns.

Viva! 12 Queen Square, Brighton, E. Sussex, BN1 3FD. T 01273 777688 F 01273 776755 info@viva.org.uk www.viva.org.uk Organisation campaigning to end the factory farming of animals and promote the vegetarian and vegan diets.

Wholesome Food Association 1 Barton Cottages, Dartington Hall, Totnes, Devon. TQ9 6ED.

T 01803 840427 info@wholesomefood.org.uk www.wholesomefood.org Campaigning for smaller-scale, sustainable, local food production, with low cost labelling scheme.

World Wide Opportunities On Organic Farms (WWOOF) PO Box 2675, Lewes, E. Sussex BN7 1RB. T 01273 476286 F as phone fran@wwoof.org www.wwoof.org Opportunities with vast variety of host organic farms & holdings. Accommodation and food provided in exchange for work.

FORESTS & WOODLANDS

Agroforestry Research Trust 46 Hunters Moon, Dartington, Totnes, Devon, TQ9 6JT T 01803 840776. F 01803 840776. mail@agroforestry.co.uk www.agroforestry.co.uk Charity, which researches temperate agroforestry and into all aspects of plant cropping. Produce several publications and a quarterly journal, and also sell plants and seeds

Forest Stewardship Council (FSC) Unit D, Station Building, Llanidgoes, Powys, SY18 6EB T 01686 413916 F 01686 412176 fsc-uk@fsc-uk.demon.co.uk www.fsc-uk.demon.co.uk Certifying forests managed to standards which protect people and the environment and identifying timber products from them with the FSC logo.

Rainforest Action Network 221 Pine St., Suite 500, San Francisco, CA 94104 USA rainforest@ran.org www.ran.org Working to protect tropical rainforests and the human rights of those living in and around those forests.

Reforesting Scotland 62-66 Newhaven Rd, Edinburgh, EH6 5QB. T 0131 554 4321 F 0131 554 0088 info@reforestingscotland.org www.reforestingscotlan d.n.apc.org Promote awareness of the deforestation of Scotland and to facilitate ecological restoration and community development through reforestation.

Taiga Resue Network (TRN) Box 116, Ajtte, S-962 23 Jokkmokk, Sweden. T +46 971 17039 F +46-971-55354 info@taigarescue.org www.taigarescue.org The TRN is an international network of non-governmental organisations and indigenous peoples working for the protection and sustainable use of the world's boreal forests.

Tree Council 51 Catherine Place, London, SW1E 6DY. T 020 7828 9928 F 020 7828 9060 info@treecouncil.org.uk www.treecouncil.org.uk Promoting the improvement of the environment through the care and planting of trees.

Trees For Life The Park, Findhorn Bay, Forres, Moray, IV36 3TZ. T 01309 691292 F 01309 691155 trees@findhorn.org www.treesforlife.org.uk A Scottish conservation charity dedicated to the regeneration and restoration of the Caledonian Forest in the Highlands of Scotland.

GARDENING

Association Kokopelli, Ripple Farm, Crundale, Canterbury, Kent, CT4 7EB T 01227 731815 comments @terredesemences.com www.terredesemences.com Organic seed catalogue with many unusual varieties. Also online gardening advice.

Community Composting Network 67 Alexandra Road, Sheffield, S2 3EE. T 0114 2580483 ccn@gn.apc.org www.othas.org.uk/ccn Help and support on all issues around involving your local community in managing its organic resources, through composting.

Composting Association www.compost.org.uk Information about composting and its benefits.

Forest Garden Network A.R.T., 46 Hunters Moon Dartington, Totnes, Devon, TQ9 6JT. mail@agroforestry.co.uk www.agroforestry.co.uk An informal network of people planning or already cultivating a forest garden, aiming to visit each other's gardens and share knowledge of temperate agroforestry.

Future Foods Luckleigh Cottage, Hockworthy, Wellington, Somerset TA21 0NN. T 01398 361347 F 01398 361541 enquiries@futurefoods.com www.futurefoods.com *Small independent mail order supplier specialising in rare and unusual edible plants. (Seed company only - do not supply produce.)*

Henry Doubleday Research Association Ryton Organic Gardens, Coventry CV8 3LG. T 024 7630 3517 F 024 7663 9229 enquiry@hdra.org.uk www.hdra.org.uk *Europe's largest organic membership organisation. Dedicated to researching and promoting organic gardening, food, and farming.*

Naturewise 20 The Triangle, Cromartie Rd, London, N19 3RX. T 0845 4584697 naturewise1@hotmail.com *Promotion of: sustainable land use and lifestyles in cities growing food in cities, education through permaculture courses. Permaculture consultations given.*

Permanent Publications The Sustainability Centre, East Meon, Hants GU32 1HR. T 0845 4584150 F 01730 823322 info@permaculture.co.uk www.permaculture.co.uk *Publishers and distributors of Permaculture Magazine - solutions for sustainable living and hundreds of books and videos on all aspects of sustainable living.*

Plants For a Future Blagdon Cross, Ashwater, Beaworthy, Devon EX21 5DF. T 0845 458 4719 / 01208 872963 F 01208 872963 (ring first) webmaster@pfaf.org www.pfaf.org *Research and provide information on edible, medicinal and useful plants, woodland gardening and vegan-organic horticulture.*

GENETICS

A SEED *Europe Action for Solidarity, Equality, Environment, and Diversity* (See entry under Anti-Capitalism)

Bayer Hazard bayerhazard@lycos.com www.bayerhazard.com *Find out more about Bayer and GM crops, as well as its involvement with heroin, the holocaust, withdrawn pharmaceuticals and toxic chemicals.*

Genetic Engineering Network (GEN) Archway Resource Centre, 1a Waterlow Road, London N19 5NJ. T 020 7272 1586 F as phone (call first) genetics@gn.apc.org www.geneticsaction.org.uk *Providing information for action for the grassroots campaign against genetic engineering. Has list of local contacts and field trial sites.*

Genetic Food Alert (GFA) 4 Bertram House, Ticklemore St, Totnes, Devon. TQ9 5EJ T 01803 868523 info@geneticfoodalert.org.uk www.geneticfoodalert.supanet.com *Campaigns to keep the UK wholefood trade GM-free, ban GM food & crops and meanwhile introduce full labelling and liability.*

Genewatch The Mill House, Manchester Road, Tideswell, Buxton, Derbyshire SK17 8LN. T 01298 871898 F 01298 872531 mail@genewatch.org www.genewatch.org *Questions how, why and whether the use of genetic technologies should proceed and believes that the debate over genetic engineering is long overdue.*

Human Genetics Alert 22/24 Highbury Grove, 112 Aberdeen House, London N5 2EA T 020 7704 6100 F 020 7359 8426 info@hgalert.org www.hgalert.org *We are a watch-dog group for Human Genetics, providing information to the public on the developments and policies.*

Percy Schmeiser www.percyschmeiser.com *Canadian farmer who was sued by Monsanto for having his fields contaminated by their genetically modified crops! He is fighting a legal battle against them.*

Pro-Natural Food Scotland 35 Hamilton Drive, Glasgow G12 8DW. hotlink@gmfreescotland www.gmfreescotland.net *Anti-GM food campaign for Scotland.*

Totnes Genetics Group (ToGG) PO Box 77, Totnes, Devon TQ9 5ZJ T 01803 840098 info@togg.org.uk www.togg.org.uk *A local grassroots Genetics group that publish stuff and do a spot of gardening…*

HEALTH

Bayer Hazard *Find out more about pharmaceutical giant Bayer.* (See entry under Genetics)

Black Cross Health Collective info@blackcrosscollective.org www.blackcrosscollective.org *First aid resource for radicals and activist, including advice on coping with and treating the effects of CS gas and pepper spray.*

British Anti-Vivisection Association (BAVA) PO Box 73 Chesterfield S41 0YZ. Bava@esmail.net www.eurosolve.com/charity/bava *Organisation trying to expose the uselessness and counter-productiveness of animal experimentation in regards to human health.*

Communities Against Toxics (CATS) POBox 29, Ellesmere Port, CH66 3TX T 0151 339 5473 F as phone ralph.ryder@communities-against-toxics.org.uk www.communities-against-toxics.org.uk *Campaigns against unsafe methods of waste disposal, industrial processes and polluting industries. Produces Toxcat newsletter.*

Herb Society Sulgrave Manor, Sulgrave, Banbury OX17 2SD. T 01295 768899 F 01295 768069 email@herbsociety.co.uk www.herbsociety.co.uk *The Herb Society aims to increases the understanding, use and appreciation of herbs and the benefits to health.*

International Campaign for Justice in Bhopal www.bhopal.net *International coalition fighting to get justice for the victims of the 1984 Bhopal tragedy.*

London Hazards Centre 213 Haverstock Hill, London NW3 4QP. T 020 7794 5999 F 020 7794 4702 mail@lhc.org.uk www.lhc.org.uk *Resource centre for Londoners fighting health and safety hazards in their workplace and community.*

Low Level Radiation Campaign The Knoll, Montpelier Park, Llndrindod, Powys, LD1 5LW T 01597 824771 bramhall@llrc.org www.llrc.org *Publicising the effects of radioactivity in the environment; lobbying for use of sound science in setting radiation protection standards for such exposures.*

Médecins Sans Frontières 124-132 Clerkenwell Road, London EC1R 5DJ. T 020 7713 5600 F 020 7713 5004 office@london.msf.org www.uk.msf.org *Independent humanitarian medical aid agency providing medical aid wherever needed and raising awareness of the plight of the people.*

National Gulf War Veterans and Families Association 4 Maspin Close, Kingswood, Kingston upon Hull HU8 8LU. T 01482 833812 F 01482 833816 flusem666@aol.com *Support network, proactive at looking into what veterans have been exposed to.*

National Pure Water Association 12 Dennington Lane, Wakefield WF4 3ET T 01924 254433 F 01924 242380 jane@npwa.freeserve.co.uk www.npwa.freeserve.co.uk *Campaign for safe drinking water. against the artificial fluoridation of water supplies. International contacts.*

Natural Death Centre, 6 Blackstock Mews, Blackstock Road, London N4 2BT, UK T 020 8 208 2853; F 020 8 452 6434 rhino@dial.pipex.com www.naturaldeath.org.uk *Aims to support those dying at home and their carers and to help them arrange funerals. It has as a more general aim that of helping improve 'the quality of dying'.*

Pesticide Action Network UK Eurolink Centre, 49 Effra Rd, London SW2 1BZ. T 020 7274 8895 F 020 7274 9084 admin@pan-uk.org www.pan-uk.org *A scientifically based charity concerned with the health, environmental and policy aspects of pesticide manufacture, trade and use.*

PeteShaughnessy.org.uk www.peteshaughnessy.org.uk *Tribute to a 'legendary figure' for all those involved in the world of mental health and founder of Mad Pride*

Plants For a Future *Information on medicinal plants.* (See entry under Gardening)

Surfers Against Sewage Wheal Kitty Workshops, St Agnes, Cornwall. England TR5 0RD. www.sas.org.uk *Call for full non-chemical treatment of sewage discharged into our seas.*

Vaccination Awareness Network UK (VAN UK) PO Box 6261, Derby DE1 9QN. T 0870 444 0894 F 08707 418 415 enquiries@van.org.uk www.van.org.uk *Information about vaccinations and their side effects. Support group, meetings, newsletter.*

Vivisection Information Network (VIN) PO Box 223, Camberley, Surrey, GU16 5ZU. vivisectionkills@hotmail.com (Recommended website www.vivisection-absurd.org.uk) *VIN provides information by post and email which proves vivisection is failed and enables ordinary people to prove this.*

What Doctors Don't Tell You (WDDTY) Satellite House, London SW19 4EZ. T 0870 444 9886 F 0870 444 9887 office@wddty.co.uk www.wddty.co.uk *Publishers of Newsletter giving information on alternative health treatments and challenging traditional views on health treatments.*

HOUSING & HOMELESSNESS

Advisory Service for Squatters (A.S.S) 2 St. Paul's Rd, London, N1 2QN T 0845 6445814 F 020 73595185 advice@squat.freeserve.co.uk www.squat.freeserve.co.uk *We give legal and practical advice and support to squatters and other homeless people.*

Big Issue, *The Paper sold by homeless vendors.* (See entry under Media)

Confederation of Co-operative Housing (CCH) Unit 19, 41 Old Birley Street, Manchester, M15 5RF. T 0161 232 1588 F 0161 226 7307 info@cch-uk.org www.cch-uk.org *National representative body for co-operative housing, made up of volunteer co-op members from all over the country.*

Cornerstone Housing Co-op 16 Sholebroke Avenue, Leeds, LS7 3HB T 0113 262 9365 cornerstone@gn.apc.org www.cornerstone.ukf.net *Communal housing for people engaged in working for social change. We have a resource centre open to local groups and individuals.*

Defend Council Housing P.O Box33519, London, E8 4XW T 0207 9879989 info@defendcouncilhousing.org.uk www.defendcouncilhousing.org.uk *To oppose transfer of council houses to private landlords & to campaign for more and better council housing.*

Ecovillage Network UK (EVNUK) PO Box 1410, Bristol, BS99 3JP T 0117 3730346 evnuk@gaia.org www.ecovillages.org/uk/network *Sustainable settlement project information/advice service. Our focus is on ecovillages as a way out of cash-based living.*

Empty Homes Agency (EHA) 195-197 Victoria St, London, SW1E 5NE T 020 7828 6288 F 020 7828 7006 info@emptyhomes.com www.emptyhomes.com *Highlight the disgrace of empty, wasted and under used homes and property throughout England.*

Glasgow Homelessness Network 32 Albion Street, Glasgow, G1 1LH. info@ghn.org.uk www.ghn.org.uk *Raise awareness about homelessness. Improve planning, provisions and practice for homeless people. Prevent, alleviate the impact of, and eradicate homelessness.*

Groundswell Elmfield House, 5 Stockwell Mews, London SW9 9GX. T 0207737 5500 F 020 7733 1305 info@groundswell.org.uk www.groundswell.org.uk *Supporting & promoting self help approaches to tackling homelessness and poverty. Info & advice, publications, grants, exchanges, training and networking events.*

Homeless International Queens House, 16 Queens Rd, Coventry, CV1 3DF. T 024 76632802 F 024 76632911 info@homeless-international.org www.homelss-international.org *Charity that supports community-led housing and infrastructure related development in partnership with local partner organisations in Asia, Africa and Latin America.*

Radical Routes *Network of radical housing co-ops. (See entry under Networking Support)*

UK Cohousing Network coordinator@cohousing.c o.uk www.cohousing.co.uk *CoHousing Communities are mutually beneficial neighbourhoods where individual households are clustered around a Common house with shared facilities.*

HUMAN RIGHTS

Action for Southern Africa (ACTSA) 28 Penton Street, London N1 9SA T 020 7833 3133 F 020 7837 3001 actsa@actsa.org www.actsa.org *ACTSA campaigns for peace, democracy and development in Southern Africa and is the successor organisation to the Anti-Apartheid Movement.*

Amnesty International 99-119 Rosebery Avenue, London EC1R 4RE T 020 7814 6200 F 020 7833 1510 info@amnesty.org.uk www.amnesty.org *International organisation promoting human rights. In particular, campaigning to free all prisoners of conscience; ensure fair and prompt trials for political prisoners; abolish the death penalty, torture and other cruel treatment of prisoners.*

Anti-Slavery International Thomas Clarkson House, The Stableyard, Broomgrove Yard, London SE27 9LA. T 020 7501 8920 F 020 7738 4110 antislavery@antislavery.org www.antislavery.org *Anti-Slavery is committed to eliminating slavery: debt bondage, forced labour, forced marriage, the worst forms of child labour, human trafficking and traditional slavery.*

Burma Campaign UK, Third Floor, Bickerton House, 25-27 Bickerton Rd, London, N19 5JT. T 020 7281 7377F 020 7272 3559 info@burmacampaign.org.uk www.burmacampaign.org.uk *Campaigns for human rights and democracy in Burma. We campaign to improve government and commercial policy on Burma.*

Campaign for Freedom of Information Suite 102, 16 Baldwins Gardens, London EC1N 7RJ. T 020 7831 7477 F 020 7831 7461 admin@cfoi.demon.co.uk www.cfoi.org.uk *Campaigns against unnecessary secrecy and for a Freedom of Information Act.*

Christian Aid, PO Box 100, London, SE 1 7RT. info@christian-aid.org www.christian-aid.org.uk *Funds projects in some of the world's poorest countries. It helps people to improve their own lives and to tackle the causes of poverty and injustice.*

Defy ID admin@defy-id.org.uk www.defy-id.org.uk *An adhoc network of groups and individuals prepared for active resistance to increasing surveillance and the introduction of identity or 'entitlement' cards in the UK.*

Environmental Rescue International (ERI) *Nigerian environmental, human rights and community development organisation. (See entry under Environment)*

Free Tibet Campaign *(See entry under Indigenous Peoples)*

Haiti Support Group PO Box 29623, London, E9 7XU. T 020 7525 0456 haitisupport@gn.apc.org www.gn.apc.org/haitisupport *Solidarity with the Haitian people's struggle for justice, real democracy and equitable development.*

Human Rights Watch 2nd Floor, 2-12 Pentonville Road, London N1 9HF. T 020 7713 1995, F 20 7713 1800 hrwuk@hrw.org www.hrw.org *Independent non-governmental organisation who investigate and expose human rights violations and hold abusers accountable.*

Kurdish Human Rights Project (KHRP) 162-168 Regent St, Suite 319 Linen Hall, London, W1B 5TG T 020 72872772 F 020 77344927 khrp@khrp.demon.co.uk www.khrp.org *KHRP is committed to the protection of the human rights of all persons within the Kurdish regions.*

Peace in Kurdistan (PIK) and Kurdistan Solidarity Committee (KSC) 44 Alnger Road, London NW3 3AT. T 020 7586 5892 F 020 7483 2531 knklondon@gn.apc.org *Campaigning for international recognition for the right of the Kurdish people to self-determination in collaboration with the Kurdish community in the UK and Europe.*

People & Planet (P&P) 51 Union St, Oxford, OX4 1JP. T 01865 245678 F 01865 791927 people@p eopleandplanet.org www.peopleandplanet.org *UK student action on world poverty, human rights and the environment.*

Privacy International T 07960 523679 pi@privacy.org www.privacyinternational.org *International anti-surveillance organisation. Campaigns on Big Brother issues like data tracking, ID cards, CCTV, encryption, police surveillance, corporate biometrics.*

Project Underground 1916A MLK Jr. Way, Berkeley, CA 94704, USA. T +1 510 705 8981 F +1 510 705 8983 project_underground@moles.org www.moles.org *Supporting the human rights of communities resisting mining and oil exploitation.*

Scottish Human Rights Centre (SHRC) 146 Holland St, Glasgow, G2 4NG T 0141 332 5960 F 0141 332 5309 info@scottishhumanrightscentre.org.uk www.scottishhumanrightascentre.org.uk *Aims to promote human rights in Scotland through advice/ information, research, scrutiny of legislation, monitoring international human rights treaties.*

TAPOL, The Indonesia Human Rights Campaign 111 Northwood Rd, Thornton Rd, Surrey, CR7 8HW T 020 8771 2904 F 020 8653 0322 tapol@gn.apc.org www.gn.apc.org/tapol *TAPOL - which means political prisoner in Indonesian - is an English language authority on the human rights situation in Indonesia and East Timor.*

INDIGENOUS PEOPLES

Amazon Alliance for Indigenous and Traditional Peoples of the Amazon Basin 1367 Connecticut Ave, N.W Suite 400, Washington DC 20036, USA. T 1-202-785-3334 F 1-202-785-3335 amazon@amazonalliance.org www.amazonalliance.org *Works to defend the rights, territories, and environment of indigenous and traditional peoples of the Amazon Basin.*

Bougainville Freedom Movement PO Box 134, Erskineville, NSW 2043, Australia. T +61 2 9558 2730 F +61 2 9804 7632 vikki@law.uts.edu.au www.eco-action.org/bougainville *To assist the Bougainville people in their struggle for peace and freedom. To educate the world about the Bougainville.*

Brighton & Hove Palestine Solidarity Campaign PO Box 208, Brighton BN1 4WZ info@brightonpalest inecampaign.org www.brightonpalestinecampaign.or g *Local site of the Palestine Solidarity Campaign for Brighton & Hove. Aims to support the wider struggle for justice in Palestine.*

Centre For World Indigenous Studies PMB 214, 1001 Cooper Point Rd, SW Suite 140, Olympia WA 98502-1107, USA. T +1 360 754 1990 www.cwis.org *Non-profit research and education organisation dedicated to wider understanding and appreciation of the ideas and knowledge of indigenous peoples.*

ChiapasLink PO Box 79, 82 Colston St, Bristol, BS1 5BB. chiapaslink@yahoo.com www.chiapasnews. ukgateway.net *Chiapaslink hopes to provide a link between the Zapatista struggles in Chiapas, Mexico and in the UK.*

Ejercito Zapatista de Liberacion Nacional (EZLN) *Information on the Zapatista uprising (See entry under Anti-Capitalism)*

Free Tibet Campaign 1 Rosomon Place, London, EC1R 0JY T 020 7833 9958 F 020 7833 3838 mail@freetibet.org www.freetibet.org *An independent membership organisation campaigning in support of the rights of the Tibetan people to freedom and independence.*

International Solidarity Movement (ISM) Occupied Palestinian Territories. T +972-22774602 F +972-22772018 Mobile +972-67473308 info@palsolidarity.org www.palsolidarity.org *Palestinian-led movement of Palestinians and internationals working to confront and challenge Israeli occupation forces and illegal policies using nonviolent direct-action.*

Palestine Solidarity Campaign Box BM PSA, London WC1N 3XX. T 020 7700 6192 info@palestineca mpaign.org www.palestinecampaign.org *Aim to build an effective mass campaign, organising protests, political lobbying and raising public awareness.*

Solidarity South Pacific c/o Prior House, 6 Tilbury Place, Brighton BN2 2GY. T 01273 695505 ssp@eco-action.org www.eco-action.org/ssp *Solidarity actions with Pacific tribal and eco-anarchist groups. Send an SAE for free newsletter.*

Survival International 6 Charterhouse Buildings, London, EC1M 7ET T 020 7687 8700 F 020 7687 8701 www.survival-international.org info@survival-international.org *World-wide organisation supporting tribal peoples. It stands for their right to decide their own future and helps them protect their lives, lands and human rights.*

Tibet Foundation 1 St. James's Market, London SW1Y 4SB. T 020 7930 6001 F 020 7930 6002 enquiries@tibet-foundation.org www.tibet-foundation.org *Non-political organisation working to preserve Tibetan Culture, and assist the Tibetan People across the world.*

Western Sahara Campaign T 0113 245 4786 www.arso.org *The struggle of the Sahrawi people for Self-determination - Western Sahara former Spanish colony is the last African colonised country still waiting for independence.*

JUSTICE AND THE LAW

Anti-Corruption Network PO Box 187, Chesterfield, Derbyshire, S40 2DU. T 01246 555713 F as phone. *The title says it all.*

Bindman & Partners Solicitors 275 Gray's Inn Rd, London, WC1X 8QF T 020 7833 4433 F 020 7837 9792 info@Bindmans.com www.Bindmans.com *A solicitor's firm specialising in human rights - including criminal law, protest, civil actions against the police.*

Campaign Against Criminalising Communities (CACC) c/o Haldane Society, Conway Hall, Red Lion Square, London WC1. T 020 7586 5892 knklondon@gn.apc.org www.cacc.org.uk *The supposed war on terrorism is in reality a war on dissent and holds inherent dangers for everyone's civil liberties.*

Criminal Cases Review Commission (CCRC) Alpha Tower, Suffolk St, Queensway, Birmingham, B1 1TT. T 0121 633 1800 F 0121 633 1804/1823 info@ccrc.gov.uk www.ccrc.gov.uk *An independent body responsible for investigating suspected miscarriages of criminal justice in England, Wales and Northern Ireland.*

Earthrights Solicitors Little Orchard, School Lane, Molehill Green, Takeley, Essex, CM22 6PS. T 01279 870391 F 01279 870391 pager - 07669 127601 earthrights@gn.apc.org www.earthrights.org.uk

Provide legal advice and assistance to the environment movement and landrights campaigners.

Environmental Law Foundation Suite 309, 16 Baldwins Gardens, London, EC1N 7RJ. T 020 7404 1030 F 020 7404 1032 info@elflaw.org www.elflaw.org *National charity that secures environmental justice for communities and individuals through a network of legal and technical experts.*

FreeBEAGLES beagles@protest.co.uk *www.free beagles.org*Website with legal information for UK activists, your rights and what to expect if you are misfortunate to run into trouble with the law.

Freedom To Be Yourself, The 13 C, Pioneer House, Adelaide Street, Coventry M 07788 557078 thehumanmind@yahoo.co.uk www.geocities.com/ thehumanmind *The right to be unclothed in all public places. Human skin. Body visibility. The human race: Every body!*

Index on Censorship *(See entry under Media)*

Injustice 020 7254 9701/07770 432 439 (evenings-w/ends) www.injusticefilm.co.uk *A film about the struggle for justice by the families of people that have died in police custody.*

Innocent Dept. 54, PO Box 282, Oldham OL1 3FY. innocent@uk2.net www.innocent.org.uk *We are committed to fighting miscarriages of justice in general and campaigning on behalf of specific cases.*

INQUEST 89-93 Fonthill Road, London, N4 3JH T 020 7263 1111 F 020 7561 0799 inquest@inquest.org www.inquest.org *Advice, campaigning and information for bereaved people facing Coroner's Inquests, especially those involving deaths in custody (Police, prison, detained patients).*

Irwin Mitchell Solicitors St. Peter's House, Hartshead, Sheffield, S1 2EL T 0114 276 7777/273 9011 F 0114 275 3306 www.imonline.co.uk *Produce Claiming Compensation For Police Misconduct- A Guide To Your Rights, a booklet of civil liberties when dealing with the police.*

Kellys Solicitors Premier House, 11 Marlborough House, Brighton, BN1 1UB. T 01273 608311 F 01273 674898 *Criminal defence solicitors with experience in defending protestors 24 hour helpline 0800 387463*

Legal Defence & Monitoring Group (LDMG) BM Haven, London, WC1N 3XX. T 020 8245 2930 ldmgmail@yahoo.co.uk www2.phreak.co.uk/ldmg/ index.php *Legal monitoring at demos & advice for others doing so, plus advice on police tactics, prisoners & legal stuff.*

Liberty 21 Tabard St., London, SE1 4LA. T 020 74033888 F 020 74075354 info@liberty-human-rights.org.uk www.liberty-human-rights.org.uk *Lobbies Parliament on proposed legislation and takes test case litigation to domestic and European Courts.*

Miscarriages of Justice Organisation (MOJO) 52 Outmore Road, Sheldon, Birmingham, B33 0XL. T 0121 7898433 / 07946 367447 mojonational@aol.com www.mojo.freehosting.net *Founded by Paddy Hill, one of the Birmingham 6, they fight for people who are wrongly imprisoned.*

Miscarriages of Justice UK (MOJUK) Tardis Studios, 52-56 Turnmill St., London, EC1M 5QR T 0121 554 6947 F 0870 055 4570 www.mojuk.org.uk

Public Law Project (PLP) Birkbeck College, 14 Bloomsbury Square, London WC1A 2LP T 020 72690570 F 020 72690579 admin@plp.bbk.ac.uk www.publiclawproject.org *Undertakes specialist research, training and information, advice and representation in public law to access justice for poor and disadvantaged people.*

Roger Sylvester Justice Campaign PO Box 25908, London N18 1WU. T 07931 970442 rsjc@hotmail.com www.rsjc.org.uk *Campaigns to establish how Roger, a fit and healthy 30 year old man came to a horrific and premature death after being detained by the police.*

Statewatch POBox 1516, London, N16 0EW T 020 88021882 F 020 88801727 office@statewatch.org www.statewatch.org *Statewatch monitors the state and civil liberties in the UK and Europe.*

United Families and Friends Campaign (UFFC) c/o Inquest, Ground Floor, Alexandra National House, 330 Seven Sisters Rd., London N4 2PJ. kevin@copwatcher.org *Vocal campaigning coalition of families and friends of people who have died in police custody, prison or in psychiatric care.*

Walkers Solicitors 2 Bouverie Road, Stoke Newington, London N16 0AJ. T 020 8800 8855 F 020 8800 9955 info@walkerssolicitors.co.uk *Specialist advice & representation in animal rights, political defence, etc.*

LAND RIGHTS & PLANNING

Brighton Urban Design & Development (BUDD) PO Box 108, Brighton BN1 4XN. T 01273 681166 mail@BUDDbrighton.org www.BUDDbrighton.org *BUDD aims to stimulate, encourage and initiate sustainable urban design and development through an inclusive and participatory process.*

Chapter Seven The Potato Store, Flaxdrayton Farm, South Petherton, Somerset, TA13. T 01460 249204 F 01460 249204 chapter7@tlio.demon.co.uk www.oneworld.org/tlio/chapter7 *Chapter 7 provides planning assistance to people wanting to build low-impact eco-homes, smallholders and ecovillagers. Want to change the planning system to allow for low-impact homes and more sustainable land usage.*

Land & Liberty 35 Rayleigh Avenue, Westcliff On Sea, Essex SS0 7DS. grahamburnett@blueyonder .co.uk www.landandliberty.co.uk *Earthright books, posters, teeshirts, forest gardening, permaculture design, consultancy and teaching.*

Land Is Ours, The (T.L.I.O) 16B Cherwell St, Oxford, OX4 1BG. T 07961 460171 office@tlio.demon.co.uk www.tlio.org.uk *Campaigns peacefully for access to the land, its resources and the decision making processes affecting them, for everyone - irrespective of race, age, or gender.*

Mast Sanity Unit 12, Old Boat Yard Worsley, Worsley Road, Manchester. T 08704 322 377 www.mastsanity.org *Voluntary organisation dedicated to supporting, advising and actively aiding and representing local campaigns fighting the current mobile phone mast invasion that is sweeping the country.*

Open Spaces Society (OSS) 25A Bell St, Henley-On-Thames, Oxon, RG9 2BA T 01491 573535 F 01491 57305 hq@oss.org.uk www.oss.org.uk *Exists to protect common land and public rights of way.*

Opposition To Destruction of Open Green Spaces (OTDOGS) 6 Everthorpe Rd, London, SE15 4DA T 020 8693 9412 F as phone *Advising people on how to prevent food giants building on open green spaces.*

Ramblers' Association 2nd floor Camelford House, 87-90 Albert Embankment, London SE1 7TW. T 020 7339 8500 F 020 7339 8501 ramblers@london.r amblers.org.uk www.ramblers.org.uk *Encouraging walking, protecting rights of way, defending the beauty of the countryside and campaigning for freedom to roam over uncultivated open country.*

Royal Town Planning Institute (RTPI) 41 Botolph Lane, London, EC3 8DL T 020 79299494 online@rtpi.org.uk www.rtpi.org.uk *To provide free and independent town planning advice to groups and individuals that cannot afford professional fees.*

MEDIA -
Distribution and Publishers

Active Distribution BM Active, London, WC1N 3XX jo n@activedistribution.org www.activedistribution.org *Anarchist (DIY) distribution, mailorder, wholesale, stalls etc of a non-profit, Books, Mags, Music, Badges t-shirts etc. Send SAE for a catalogue.*

AK Distribution PO Box 12766, Edinburgh, EH8 9YE. T 0131 5555165 F 0131 5555215 ak@akedin.demon.co.uk www.akuk.com www.akpress.org *Co-operative who distribute & publish a wide range of radical politics: books, mags. audio & t-shirts. Send for free mail-order catalogue.*

Anarchy: A Journal of Desire Armed C.A.L. Press, PO Box 1446, Columbia, MO 65205-1446, USA. jmcquinn@coin.org www.anarchymag.org *Anti-ideological anarchist publishing (magazines & books).*

Diggers & Dreamers BCM Edge, London, WC1N 3XX. T 07000 780536 F 0870 163 4661 info@digge rsanddreamers.org.uk www.diggersanddreamers.org .uk *"Diggers & Dreamers - the Guide to Communal Living in Britain" and books on related subjects.*

Eco-Logic Books 10-12 Picton St, Bristol, BS6 5QA. T 0117 9420165 F 0117 9420164 books@eco-logic.demon.co.uk www.eco-logicbooks.com *Publishes and sells mail order books on practical solutions to environmental problems, sustainability, permaculture, organic gardening, etc.*

Edge of Time Ltd, BCM Edge, London WC1N 3XX. T 07000 780536 F 0870 1634661 sales@edgeoftime.co.uk www.edgeoftime.co.uk *Distributes books on communal living and other items associated with cultural change.*

Enabler Publications 3 Russell House, Lym Close, Lyme Regis, Dorset, DT7 3DE. T 01297 445024 F as phone adearling@aol.com www.members.aol.com/ adearling/enabler *Books about counter culture, Travellers, protest and creative work with young people.*

Factsheet 5 PO Box 4660 Arlington, VA 22204, USA. T 703-553-2945 F 703-553-0565 twbounds@po p.mail.rcn.net www.factsheet5.org *Comprehensive quarterly guide to zines/alternative publications. Each issue packed with reviews/contact/ordering info for hundreds of independent publications.*

Freedom Press, 84b Whitechapel High St, London, E1 7QX. T 020 7247 9249 F 020 7377 9526 freedom@ecn.org www.ecn.org/freedom *Anarchist publishers and propagandists since 1886, through our periodicals, books and pamphlets, available from our bookshop or by mail order. Contact us for free sample copy of 'Freedom'.*

Godhaven Ink Rooted Media, The Cardigan Centre, 145-149 Cardigan Rd, Leeds, LS6 1LJ. T 0113 278 8617 merrick@stones.com www.godhaven.org.uk *Publishers of cheap books and zines about direct action and other counter-cultural stuff. Promoting a feeling of well-being since 1994.*

Green Books Foxhole, Dartington, Totnes, Devon, TQ9 6EB. T 01803 863260 F 01803 863843 paul@greenbooks.co.uk www.greenbooks.co.uk *Publishers of a wide range of books on politics, ecology, economics, eco-philosophy, eco-building, renewable energy and the environment.*

INK - Independent News Collective 2nd Floor, The Shiatsu Place, 97-99 Seven Sisters Road, London N7 7QP. T 020 7561 0683 ink@pro-net.co.uk www.ink.uk.com *Umbrella organisation for the alternative press. Deals with marketing and publishing, but not editorial matters.*

Kate Sharpley Library (KSL), BM Hurricane, London, WC1N 3XX. Or PMB 820, 2425 Channing Way, Berkeley CA 94704, USA. kar98@dial.pipex.com www.katesharpleylibrary.org/index.htm *Archive of Anarchist and related material, reclaiming Anarchist history to inform current struggles. Write for details of our (many!) publications.*

National Small Press Centre, The BM Bozo, London, WC1N 3XX. *Publishes small press handbook with information on thousands of small presses world-wide.*

Photon Press 37 The Meadows, Berwick-Upon-Tweed, Northumberland, TD15 1NY. photon.press@virgin.net *Publish "Light's List" of 1500 independent press*

magazines world-wide printing fiction, poetry, art, reviews etc. £2.50 inc. postage.

Pluto Press 345 Archway Rd, London, N6 5AA. T 020 8348 2724 F 020 8348 9133 pluto@plutobooks.com www.plutobooks.com *One of the UK's leading independent publishers. Committed to publishing the best in critical writing across the social sciences and humanities.*

Revolutions Per Minute BCM Box 3328, London WC1N 3XX T 07967 886257 revopermin@ukonline. co.uk www.red-star-research.org.uk/rpmframe.html *A radical publishing project, which aims to help liberate the working class. Includes books on strikes, fox-hunting and anti-racism.*

Rural Media Company, The Sullivan House, 72-80 Widemarsh St, Hereford, HR4 9HG. T 01432 344039 F 01432 270539 info@ruralmedia.co.uk www.ruralmedia.co.uk *We are a National Media Communications Charity, we cover print, web publishing, video production and multimedia production.*

Zabalaza Books Postnet Suite 116, Private Bag X42, Braamfontein, 2017, Johannesburg, South Africa. zabalaza@union.org.za www.struggle.ws/ africa/safrica/zababooks/HomePage.htm *Publishers of Anarchist writings/pamphlets on the various issues effecting the building of a free and equal non-statist society under workers self-management.*

Zed Books, 7 Cynthia St, London, N1 9JF. T 020 7837 4014 F 020 7833 3960 hosie@zedbooks.dem on.co.uk www.zedbooks.demon.co.uk *Independent workers co-op publishing annually 50+ scholarly, critical books on international issues, politics, the environment, feminism and 'the third world'*

MEDIA - Film, Video & TV

Beyond TV mick@beyondtv.org, anna@beyondtv.org www.beyondtv.org *A website hosting alternative news features - in an online database linking features to campaigns, upcoming events and current projects.*

Conscious Cinema, 110 Elmore St, London, N1 T 020 7359 2755 F as phone inbox@consciouscine ma.co.uk www.consciouscinema.co.uk *Media arts collective turned production company. Broadcast standard equipment available for commercial work and projects creating greater value than money.*

Cultureshop.Org PO Box 29683, London E2 6XH. T 07950 699562 admin@cultureshop.org www.cultureshop.org *Online distribution to allow progressive film makers to sell there work, may be extended to other forms of media soon.*

Direct Action Media Network (DAMN) Video www.tao.ca/earth/damn *Multimedia direct action news service with live direct action footage on the web.*

Exploding Cinema, The c/o 26 Fairwall House, Peckham Road, London SE5 8QW. T 020 7708 3501/ 020 7732 8058 explodingcinema@hotmail.com www.explodingcinema.org *Open Access Screenings for Short Films.*

Fifth Sun Archive, The T 07940 393671 5un@freeuk.com www.fifithsunarchive.org *The Fifth Sun Archive is a video library of social and environmental protest in the UK, established in 1994.*

Groovy Movie Picture House, The mail@grooviemovie.org www.groovymovie.org *Documenting alternative issues, lifestyles and arts using the latest in cutting edge digital technology and powered only with green energy.*

Guerillavision Box 91, Green Leaf Bookshop, 82 Colston St, Bristol BS1 5BB guerillavision@ang elfire.com *Troublemakers with other people's dv cameras.*

I-Contact Video Network c/o 76 Mina Rd, St. Werburghs, Bristol, BS2 9TX. T 0117 9400636 I-contact@videonetwork.org www.VideoNetwork.org

A non-profit making initiative set up to provide support for those using video for positive change.

New York Surveillance Camera Players [SCP-New York] POB 1115, NYC 10009-9998, USA. T 001 212 561 0106 notbored@panix.com www.notbored.org/the-scp.html *Situationist-inspired anti-surveillance camera group.*

Organic Chaos Network PO Box 234, 2300 AE Leiden, Netherlands, T +31-6-12520674 ocn@antenna.nl www.antenna.nl/organicchaos *Video action news group, part of Federation Collective Rampenplan (See entry under Anarchy).*

Reclaim the Streets -The Film T 07092 044579 reclaim_streets_film@yahoo.com www.come.to/ rtsfilm *Video clips, background info and ordering details for this essential documentary, taking a frantic look at RTS actions in the UK and abroad.*

SKA TV Suite 75 Trades Hall Carlton Vic 3053 Australia T 61 3 9663 6976 accessnews@skatv.org.au www.skatv.org.au *A grass-roots community organisation using TV and video as tools for social change; training, screenings, broadcast, distribution.*

Turn Off Your TV www.turnoffyourtv.com *Articles on issues such as the role of advertisers, corporate ownership of mass media, and the potential effects of images on children.*

TV Go Home tvgohome@tvgohome.com www.tvgohome.com *Send up of the Radio Times.*

Undercurrents alternative video news 16B Cherwell St, Oxford, OX4 1BG. 01865 203661/203662 underc@gn.apc.org www.undercurrents.org *Produce and distribute videos and CD-ROM on direct action. Organise BeyondTV video activist festival.*

Undercurrents foundation undercymru@joymail.com www.undercurrents.org *Train activists how to use video for social change.*

Video Activist Network (VAN) PO Box 40130, San Francisco, CA 94140, USA. +1 415-789-8484 info@videoactivism.org www.videoactivism.org *Informal association of activists and politically conscious artists using video to support social, economic and environmental justice campaigns.*

White Dot PO Box 2116, Hove BN3 3LR. info@whitedot.org www.whitedot.org *International campaign against television.*

MEDIA - Internet News Services

A-Infos www.ainfos.ca *Regular anarchist newsfeed over the internet in various languages.*

Alternet www.alternet.org *San Fransisco alternative media site with hard-hitting news and investigations not covered in the mainstream press, fiery columns, insights into cultural trends.*

Anarcho-Syndicalism 101 www.anarchosyndicali sm.org *A web archive of texts, articles, image and mp3 files, cultural items and outreach material (otherwise known as propaganda).*

Centre for Cooperative Research info@cooper ativeresearch.org www.cooperativeresearch.org *A shedload of articles and writings from a variety of sources (many mainstream media), and a veritable goldmine for reference material.*

GreenNet 33 Islington High Street, London N1 9LH. T 0845 055 4011 F 020 7837 5551 : info@gn.apc.org www.greennet.org.uk *GreenNet is an internet service provider that specialises in Internet services for organisations involved in Peace, The environment, Human Rights and Development.*

Indymedia www.indymedia.org *A collective of independent media organisations and hundreds of journalists offering grassroots, non-corporate coverage - links to Indymedia outlets around the world.*

Indymedia UK www.indymedia.org.uk *An evolving network of media professionals, artists, and DIY*

media activists committed to using technology to promote social and economic justice.

Lobster www.lobster-magazine.co.uk/ *The journal of parapolitics, intelligence, and State Research.*

Monbiot, George www.monbiot.com *He's got a website about the corporate take-over of everything...*

Protest.Net rabble-rouser@protest.net www.protest.net *A site to help progressive activists by providing a central place where the times and locations of protests and meetings can be posted.*

Spunk Library, The spunk@spunk.org www.spunk.org *Collects and distributes literature in electronic format, with an emphasis on anarchism and related issues.*

SQUALL Magazine POBox 8959, London, N19 5HW mail@squall.co.uk www.squall.co.uk *Regularly updated online magazine presenting radical journalism, photography and culture with content.*

[Squat!net] squat@squat.net www.squat.net *An international internet magazine with main focus on squatted houses, car sites and other free spaces.*

Straight Goods www.straightgoods.com *Canada's independent on-line source of news*

URBAN 75 contact@urban75.com www.urban75.com *Serves up non-mainstream viewpoint on a wide range of issues including environmental action, rave culture and civil rights. Plus drug information, cartoons, short stories and useless games.*

YellowTimes.org www.yellowtimes.org *Unconventional viewpoints from which to observe current events, and to encourage new thinking about the causes and effects of those events.*

MEDIA - Overseas

A4 Newsbot c/o L38 Squat Infoshop, Via Giuliotti, 8-00143 Roma, Italy. a4newsbot@paranoici.org www.tmcrew.org/laurentinokkupato/a4newsbot/ *A SchNEWS inspired quarterly A4 multi-language publication distributed on paper, e-mail, website and PDF about social, eco and anarchist issues.*

A-kontra POBox 223, 111 21 Praha 1, Czech Republic. www.a-kontra.net *Czech anarchist magazine.*

Alternative Press Review PO Box 4710, Arlington, VA 22204, USA. T +1 703-553-2945 editors@altpr.org www.altpr.org *Your Guide Beyond the Mainstream! Each issue is packed with creative ideas, fresh perspectives, insightful analysis and pointed humour.*

An Phoblacht (Republican News) 58 Parnell Square, Dublin 1. T +353 1 873 3611 F +353 1 873 3839 aprn@irlnet.com www.irlnet.com/aprn *Ireland's biggest selling political weekly newspaper has been a source of uncensored news on world affairs and the Irish struggle for national self-determination for over 25 years.*

Earth First! Journal PO Box 3023, Tucson AZ 85702-3023, USA. T +1 520.620.6900 F 413.254.0057 collective@earthfirstjournal.org www.earthfirstjou rnal.org *Voice of the radical environmental movement containing direct action reports, articles on preservation of wild places, investigative articles, and discussions on monkeywrenching.*

Green Pepper CIA Office, Overtoom 301, 1054 HW Amsterdam, The Netherlands. T +31 20 665 7743 F +31 20 692 8757 greenpep@eyfa.org www.squat.net/cia/gp *An environmental and social justice magazine focussing on a different (anti-neoliberal/activist friendly) topic every edition.*

Kontrapunkt www.kontrapunkt-online.org *Serbo-Croation on-line magazine covering all aspects of libertarian thought, and it is open for all views which are in-support of liberating all human minds and lives.*

KUD Anarhiv Metelkova ulica 6, SI-1000 Ljubljana, Slovenia. T +386 1 434 03 45/+386 1 432 33 78 F +386 1 432 33 78 anarhiv@mail.ljudmila.org www.ljudmila.org/anarhiv *A resource centre for radical social change, also publish a magazine and organize events.*

Motkraft www.motkraft.net *The internet infocenter of the Swedish libertarian left. Publish news and information about actions, lectures, etc.*

No God-No Master PO Box 300, East Brunswick, Victoria 3057, Australia. anthropia@hotmail.com www.punk.gr/nogod-nomaster *Anarchist bulletin and publication of small Pamphlets in Greek.*

Paper, The PO Box 1733, Collingwood VIC 3066, Australia. info@thepaper.org.au www.thepaper.org.au *Fortnightly free independent paper from Melbourne - available online as PDF.*

Rocky Road Environmental Magazine Anne Ruimy, Mullagh, Co. Clare, Ireland. T +353 (0)65 708 7144 editor@rockyroadmagazine.com www.rockyroad magazine.com *Publishing a bi-monthly magazine offering unbiased, investigative and science-based news, features and analyses on Irish and global environmental issues.*

Tactical Media Crew c/o Radio Onda Rossa, Via dei Volsci, 56, Roma 00185, Italy. tactical@tmcrew.org www.tmcrew.org *A collective of media and political activists from the radical autonomous/anarchist scene of Rome.*

Thrall PO Box 22-076 Christchurch, Aoteroa/New Zealand thrallnet@yahoo.com www.thrall.orcon.net.nz *Monthly anarchist magazine from NZ.*

Warhead PO Box 43, 15-662 Bialystok, Poland soja2@poczta.onet.pl *Anarchist news service for Poland.*

Z Magazine 18 Millfield Street, Woods Hole MA 02543, USA. T +1 508 5489063. sysop@zmag.org www.zmag.org *Z is an independent political magazineof critical thinking on political, cultural, social, and economic life in the United States, Z accepts no paid advertising.*

MEDIA - UK Based

Alan Lodge (Tash) T 0115 9113804 tash@gn.apc.org www.tash.gn.apc.org *Photographer (One Eye On The Road): travellers, festivals, raves, environmental direct actions and protest & police surveillance methods.*

Animal Liberation Press Office BM4400, London, WC1N 3XX. T 01623 746470 mobile: 07752 107515 F as phone *Media contact for the ALF and other radical animal rights groups. Supplies speakers for groups, rallies, etc.*

Aufheben POBox 2536, Rottingdean, Brighton, BN2 6LX aufheben@yahoo.co.uk www.geocities.com/ aufheben2/ *Not an organisation, but a magazine dedicated to the theory and practice of revolutionary class struggle.*

Bellow Box 35, 82 Colston Street, Bristol, BS1 5BB. Bellow1@bigfoot.com *Radical women's newsletter, instigated by Women Speak Out - free, available for photocopying/ distribution - hardcopy or PDF*

Big Issue, The London, SW8 2LN T 020 75263200 F 020 75263302 news@bigissue.com www.bigissue.com *UK's biggest current affairs weekly, with 1.2 million readers. Campaigning for social justice. Sold by homeless vendors who keep 70p of each issue.*

Black Flag BM Hurricane, London WC1N 3XX blackflagds@hushmail.com flag.blackened.net/blackflag *Class struggle anarchist quarterly magazine with strong international coverage, recently revamped. Contact for subs info. Comprehensive list of UK Anarchist groups.*

Class War Paper Promotes class consciousness and working class control over our day to day lives. (See entry under Anarchism)

Corner House, The, Station Rd, Sturminster Newton, Dorset DT10 1YJ. T 01258 473795 F 01258 473748

cornerhouse@gn.apc.org www.thecornerhouse .uk *Research, advocacy and solidarity work on social & environmental justice issues. Publish regular briefing papers. Free via email.*

Counter Information c/o ACE, 17 West Montgomery Place, Edinburgh, EH7 5HA T 0131 557 6242 ci@counterinfo.org.uk www.counterinfo.org.uk *Free anarchist newssheet reporting on struggles from around the world.*

Direct Action Collective PO Box 29, SW PDO, Manchester. M15 5HW. T 07984 675281 da@direct-action.org.uk www.direct-action.org.uk *DA - magazine of the anarcho-syndicalist Solidarity Federation. No political parties or dogma. Packed with positive anti-authoritarian ideas, news, comment and actions.*

Do or Die c/o Prior House, 6 Tilbury Place, Brighton, East Sussex, BN2 2GY doordtp@yahoo.co.uk www.eco-action.org/dod *Voices from the Ecological Resistance - an annual magazine crammed with reports and analysis from the world-wide ecological frontlines.*

Earth First! Action Update (EF! AU) PO Box 487 Norwich, NR2 3AL T 01603 219811 efactionupdate @bigfoot.com www.eco-action.org/efau *A monthly round-up of ecological and other direct action from around Britain. Has list of contacts of all UK Earth First! groups.*

Ecologist, The 18 Chelsea Wharf, 15 Lots Rd, London, SW10 0QJ T 020 7351 3578 F 020 7351 3617 sally@theecologist.org www.theecologist.org *Investigative journalists, leading thinkers and campaigners are constantly rethinking the basic assumptions which underlie mankind's steady march towards self-destruction.*

Freedom anarchist fortnightly 84b Whitechapel High St, London, E1 7QX. T 020 8771 8317 F as phone FreedomCopy@aol.com *Carries news and views from a growing range of activists. All contributions welcome.*

Green Anarchist Green Anarchist, BCM 1715, London WC1N 3XX. www.greenanarchist.org *UK's original and best anarcho-primitivist paper - uncensored forum for direct action news and discussion.*

Index on Censorship 33 Islington High St, London, N1 9LH. T 020 7278 2313 F 020 7278 1878 natasha@in dexoncensorship.org www.indexoncensorship.org *Publish a magazine, run a website and organise events on free expression and censorship around the world.*

Inkthief Rm 304, Maryland House, Manbey Park Road , London E15 1EY. T 020 8223 6011 / 07984 875471 contact@inkthief.org.uk *Designers committed to social and environmental justice who formed a professional design agency for socially progressive organisations.*

Morgenmuffel PO Box 74, Brighton BN1 4ZQ. *Personal anarchist zine with cartoons and rants published irregularly. Send three stamps for an issue.*

New Internationalist Tower House, Lathkill St, Market Harborough, LE16 1T 01858 438896 F 01858 461739 newint@subscription.co.uk www.newint.org *Monthly informative magazine reporting on issues of world poverty and inequality; focusing attention on the unjust relationship between the powerful and the powerless.*

Nonviolent Action (NVA) 5 Caledonian Rd, London, N1 9DY T 020 7713 nva@gn.apc.org *Magazine serving campaigners seeking positive social change through non-violent means with news of activists and activities - and a stimulus to thought and action.*

Peace News 5 Caledonian Rd, London, N1 9DY T 020 7278 3344 F 020 7278 0444 admin@peacenews.info www.peacenews.info *Radical, international, antimilitarist, quarterly magazine. For nonviolent revolution. Bringing activists and campaigners together worldwide, sharing ideas, theories, and tactics.*

Positive News 5 Bicton Enterprise Centre, Clun, Shropshire, SY7 8NF. T 01588 640022 F 01588 640033 office@positivenews.org.uk www.positivenews.org.uk *A free quarterly newspaper which publishes good news stories from around the world to do with peace, environment, health & education.*

Red Pepper 1b Waterlow Rd, London, N19 5NJ T 020 72817024 F 020 72639345 redpepper@red pepper.org.uk www.redpepper.org.uk *Green - left monthly magazine.*

Resurgence Ford House, Hartland, Bideford, Devon, EX39 6EE T 01237 441293 F 01237 441203 ed@resurgeence.org www.resurgence.org *Encompasses environmental, social, economic and cultural issues. Thought-provoking and informative, bringing articles which nourish all aspects of your life.*

Total Liberty Magazine Box EMAB, 88 Abbey Street, Derby DE22 3SQ. ain@ziplip.com mysite.freeserve.com/total_liberty1/ *Evolutionary Anarchist magazine promoting the ideas of a peaceful and evolutionary path to Anarchism. Subscription £8.00.*

YearZero (YZ) PO Box 26276, London, W3 7GQ. T 07752 358928 feedback@yearzero.org www.yearzero.org *The disobedient current affairs quarterly.*

MEDIA - UK Local News

ActionNet-North Staffs Mob 07748 883981 Webgimp@ActionNet-NorthStaffs.co.uk www.ActionNet-NorthStaffs.co.uk *Web-based resource for activists based in N. Staffordshire who are campaigning about various issues social, environmental and humanitarian.*

Bangor-Werdd http://groups.yahoo.com/group/ bangor-werdd *North Wales email discussion network of non-violent direct action protesters including peace, environment and animal rights.*

Brighton Sucks! T 07092 297412 info@brightonsucks.com brightonsucks.com/2003/ *Keeping us in touch with what sucks about Brighton.*

Bristle Box 25, 82 Colston St. Bristol, BS1 5BB. editor@bristle.org.uk www.bristle.org.uk *Quarterly magazine for Bristol activism and anarchism treating all relevant subjects from news to campaigns.*

Bristolian Box 3 Greenleaf Bookshop 82 Colston Street, Bristol BS1 5BB. localnews4us@yahoo.co.uk www.bristolian.freese rvers.com *Local newsletter for Bristol, reclaiming the city back from corporate media. Available at various outlets in Bristol and via email: bristolian-subscribe@yahoogroups.com*

Bristol Indymedia www.bristol.indymedia.org *Bristol's own IndyMedia site with news from Bristol and beyond.*

Broughton Spurtle c/o Broughton Books, 2A Broughton Place, Edinburgh.T 0131 556 0903 F 0131 557 6752 Spurtle@tpuntis.demon.co.uk www.tpuntis.demon.co.uk *Publish monthly free paper for local area - publicise work of local action groups and generally stir things up.*

BuryGreen, richb@bradgate.u-net.com www.BuryGreen.org.uk *A service and gateway to the various groups in and around Bury St Edmunds, Suffolk, dedicated to protecting and improving our environment.*

Cardiff Activists Network bozavine@yahoo.co.uk www.geocities.com/bozavine/can/index.html *For everyone interested in direct action based in Cardiff - allowing information about future actions to be advertised and planned.*

Cold Bath Times c/o Dave Hubble, 7 Ainsley Gardens, Eastleigh, Hants SO50 4NX. T 023 80611307 coldbathinfo@yahoo.co.uk *Multi-issue newsletter covering the Hampshire area plus wider issues,* generally with an environmental theme. Follows no party or organisational line.

Dan-Cymru www.groups.yahoo.com/group/dan-cymru *Direct action Cymru discussion group*

Direct Action Scotland www.groups.yahoo.com/group/directactionscotland *A discussion and information email list focusing on direct action and protest in Scotland.*

Elffinews PO Box 923, Luton, LU2 0YQ. T 01582-512184 F 01582 619218 M 07903 382228 elffinews@aol.com *Activist news letter for Luton and Dunstable. Scurrilous! A community based monthly newsletter, reporting on local activists' actions.*

Eroding Empire c/o 56a Crampton St. London. SE17 3AE. eroding@eroding.org.uk www.eroding.org.uk *Monthly listings for London area, diy, actions, centres, gigs.*

FutureManchester www.futuremanchester.org.uk *Site dedicated to sign-posting you to others working for positive change in Manchester*

Global Action Scotland www.egroups.com/invite/globalactionscotland *an email discussion group for global justice Visit the website to sign up.*

Hackney Indymedia (Link from)_ www.indymedia.org.uk *Gives an insight into the fourth poorest borough in Britain and to show how the council's and central government policy affects the local people.*

Interference FM Box 6, Green Leaf, 82 Colston St, Bristol, BS1 5BB. *Bristol's anarchist pirate radio station.*

Loombreaker, The c/o Manchester EF!, Dept.29, 22a Beswick St, Manchester, M4 7HS. T 0161 226 6814 editorial@loombreaker.org.uk www.loombreaker.org.uk *Monthly free Manchester direct action & campaigns round-up - Spreading news the mainstream media won't print.*

Norwich Anarchists PO Box 487, Norwich, NR2 3AL. T 07941 657485 www.norwich-anarchists.org.uk *Produce a community based newspaper.*

Pork-Bolter,The POBox 4144, Worthing, West Sussex, BN14 7NZ porkbolter@eco-action.org www.eco-action.org/porkbolter *Radical local newsletter with historically-vindicated pig obsession. Rages against CCTV, Big Business, councils, police etc. etc. Free with SAE.*

Radio 4A T 07980 168115 info@radio4a.org.uk www.radio4a.org.uk *Monthly pirate radio with a substantial speech output. Open access, non-profit and broadcasting live as well as creating programmes. 107.8FM in Brighton or webcast on www.piratetv.net*

Rebel Bull info@herefordanarchists.cjb.net *Newsletter for the Hereford area produced by the Hereford Anarchists.*

SchOUND OFF!, schound_off@hotmail.com *Plymouth's direct action newssheet.*

SEReN PO Box 661, Wrecsam LL11 1QU. news@serencymru.org www.serencymru.org *Non-sectarian newspaper reporting on all trade union, green, socialist, anti-war and republican news stories.*

Sheffield Mayday sheffieldmayday@ukf.net www.sheffieldmayday.ukf.net *News and information for activists in the Sheffield area, also e-mail discussion group*

Swan Net SwanNetwork@yahoogroups.com www.geocities.com/swan_net *Diary of events for Swansea.*

Think Globally Act Locally POBox 1TA, Newcastle, NE99 1TA. tapp@sandyford.techie.org.uk www.tapp.cjb.net *Newsletter that reports and informs campaigns and direct action in North East England.*

Underdog, The PO Box 35832, London E11 3WT. T 07810 288889 info@walthamstowanarchy.org.uk

www.walthamstowanarchy.org.uk *Bi-monthly newsletter published by Walthamstow Anarchist Group.*

WARCRY c/o BM Makhno, London, WC1N 3XX war1921war@yahoo.co.uk *Monthly newsletter produced by West London Anarchists & Radicals*

NETWORKING SUPPORT

Blatant Incitement Project (BLINC) Dept.29, 22a Beswick Street,Manchester M4 7HS. T 0161-226 6814 doinit@nematode.freeserve.co.uk www.eco-action.org/blinc *Empower people to organise themselves without hierarchy, for radical action towards social ecological change, by sharing skills, knowledge, and inspiration.*

Confederation of Indian Organisations 5 Westminster Bridge, London, SE1 7XW T: 0207 928 9889 F: 0207 620 4025 cio@gn.apc.org www.cio.org.uk *Working with south Asian voluntary organisations in the UK.*

Cynefin y Werin Uned 2, gwasg Dwyfor, Stad Ddiwydiannol, Penygroes, Gwynedd LL545 6DB. T 01286 882359 Pager 07669 179015 benica@gn.apc.org *All Wales network for organisations working on international peace, solidarity and social justice.*

Edinburgh CITY (Change IT Yourselves) c/o ACE, 17 West Montgomery Place, Edinburgh EH7 5HA. in fo@edinburghcity.org.uk www.edinburghcity.org.uk *A A new independent forum with no set agenda. Monthly discussion/social evening for people interested in social change.*

European Youth For Action (EYFA) Minahassastraat 1, 1090 GC Amsterdam, The Netherlands. T +31 20 665 7743 F +31 20 6928757 eyfa@eyfa.org www.eyfa.org *International network of grassroots groups and individuals working on environmental and social justice issues.*

LeftDirect www.leftdirect.co.uk *More than just a comprehensive directory of all left, radical and progressive organisations in the UK.*

Leicester Radical Alliance (LRA) c/o Dept Z, Littlethorn Books, Humberstone gate, Leicester T 07718 629 651 leicesterradical@hotmail.com http://radical.members.beeb.net *Monthly meetings and newsletetr to bring together all those who are now without a political home, disillusioned Labour supporters, and all others, who want to see radical changes in the social order.*

Networking Newsletter Project 6 Mount St, Manchester, M2 5NS T 0161 226 9321 info@networkingnewsletter.org.uk www.networkingnewsletter.org.uk *Network activists around Manchester who are working for positive change on issues of peace, development, environment, human rights, animal rights and other areas of social change.*

Radical Routes c/o Cornerstone Resource Centre, 16 Sholebroke Av, Leeds, LS7 3HB. T 0113 262 9365 cornerstone@ukf.net www.radicalroutes.org.uk *Mutual aid network of radical housing & worker co-ops and social centres. Support, advice & loans to member co-ops.*

SAMIZDAT ourangadan@hushmail.com http://samizdat.zapto.org *A discussion and news service to track the various Social Forum events being organised around the UK.*

Seeds for Change Network 96 Church Street, Lancaster, LA1 1TD. T 0845 3307853 hello@seedsforchange.org.uk www.seedsforchange.org.uk *Free training + support on campaign planning, tactics, non-hierarchical organising, consensus and facilitation plus advice on low cost computing and free software (linux).*

PRISONER SUPPORT

Anarchist Black Cross, Brighton PO Box 74, Brighton BN1 4ZQ. mail@brightonabc.org.uk www.brightonabc.org.uk *Support group for anarchists, black liberation activists, anti-fascists and others we feel an affinity with who have ended up in prison.*

Anarchist Black Cross Network c/o Austin ABC, PO Box 19733, Austin, TX 78760-9733, USA. abc-help@anarchistblackcross.org www.anarchistblackcross.org *Network of ABC organisations, has list on website of all ABC groups.*

Animal Liberation Front UK *Supporters Group Info about animal rights prisoners and defence funds.* (See entry under Animal Rights)

Campaign Against Prison Slavery The Cardigan Centre, Cardigan Road, Leeds LS6 1LJ. Againstprisonslavery@mail.com *Challenges forced prison labour and exposes the companies that exploit it.*

Campaign to Free Vanunu & for a Nuclear Free Middle East *Israeli nuclear whistleblower sentenced in 1986 to 18 years.* (See entry under Anti-War)

Earth Liberation Prisoners BM Box 2407, London, WC1N 3XX. www.spiritoffreedom.org.uk *Supports people who have been arrested and imprisoned for acts of direct action in defence of animals and the earth.*

Eddie Gilfoyle Campaign c/o Susan Caddick PO Box 1845, Stoke on Trent ST7 4EG. T 0781 501 2372 Paul.Caddick@btinternet.com *Campaigning for the release of Eddie Gilfoyle who was wrongly convivted of murder in 1993.*

Haven Distribution 27 Old Gloucester St, London, WC1N 3XX. *Supplies free educational literature to prisoners in UK and Ireland. Donations make this possible.*

International Concerned Family & Friends of Mumia Abu-Jamal www.mumia.org *Information and networking to save this journalist/activist's life.*

Justice For Mark Barnsley PO Box 381, Huddersfield, HD1 4XX MarkBarnsley@ncadc.demon.co.uk www.freemarkbarnsley.com *Campaign supporting Mark an anarchist who served 8 years in prison after getting beaten up by a group of students. He is still trying to clear his name.*

Legal Defence & Monitoring Group (LDMG) (See entry under Justice and the Law)

Mumia Must Live! BM Box 4771, London, WC1N 3XX mumia@callnet.uk.com www.callnetuk.com/home/mumia *Mumia Abu-Jamal is a political Prisoner facing death row in the USA. This is a coalition fighting to free Mumia and end the racist death penalty.*

Vegan Prisoners Support Group (VPSG) (See entry under Animal Rights)

REFUGEES

Asylum Aid 28 Commercial St, London, E1 6LS. T 020 7377 5123 F 020 7247 7789 info@asylumaid.org.uk www.asylumaid.org.uk *Provides free legal advice and representation to refugees seeking safety in the UK from persecution and campaign for fair treatment of refugees in the UK.*

Asylum Support www.asylumsupport.info *Online information focusing on all matters that concern people seeking asylum, together with a directory of hundreds of online resources relating to asylum and refugees.*

Barbed Wire Britain T 01865 558145/726804, 01993 703994, 07767 414714, 01753 852853 F 01865 558145 barbedwirebritain@yahoogroups.com www.barbedwirebritain.org.uk *Linking and helping to establish local campaigns outside places of detention, demos, lobbies, publications, working with detainees past and present*

Campaign to Close Campsfield c/o 111 Magdalen St, Oxford. T 01865 558145/557282 info@closecampsfield.org.uk www.closecampsfield.org.uk *Campaign for the closure of Campsfield House Immigration Detention Centre and for the end of detention of refugees nation-wide.*

Close Down Harmondsworth Campaign 10 Endsleigh Rd, Southall UB2 5QL. T 07960 309457 F